Most of the avid award collectors tell me they are now only interested in awards that are given on a national level. They must fit on a shelf or hang on a wall and display well. If they don't fit this description, they may not appeal to another collector when you decide to sell your collection.

A word of warning! I know how excited many collectors get to find a new item or award and pay a big price to get it, then find it much lower in price in a few months. This is particularly true with the Albee figurine awards. I have seen this happen on every Albee award to date. Have patience. Wait a few months and you will save a lot.

The National Association of Avon Clubs is no longer issuing club bottles, plates, or convention bells. There will be no new items of this type in the future in the NAAC collectibles section.

To sell or buy Avon collectibles, see page 642 for information.

I hope this information helps guide you in your Avon collecting hobby.

About Bud Hastin

Wilbur H. "Bud" Hastin was born in late April, in Butler, Missouri, a small farm town south of Kansas City, Missouri. His father was an automobile dealer and taught Bud many of the things he would need in his life.

The most important thing was to always be honest and be self-reliant. Bud grew up with a burning desire to achieve success in everything he did, and see and learn as much about this wonderful world as he could. Bud opened his first bank savings account at age nine and it continued to grow through his childhood business ventures. For years, Bud picked up every pop and beer bottle within three miles of Butler. He then moved on to his own bicycle repair shop. By the time he got to high school and at age 14 he was cutting grass, and at age 17 he was cutting 55 yards a week and making more money than most men in Butler.

After finishing high school he joined the U.S. Air Force and became a fireman. His first day on the flight line in Denver, Colorado, he witnessed a jet crash and watched two pilots burn

Bud and Sandra Hastin

to death. He knew then how precious life was and to live life to its fullest from that day on. After a year in Denver and two years on the Japanese island of Okinawa, Bud returned to Butler, Missouri, to work for his father at Hastin Glass Company. Bud spent more of his time running a used car lot and making grain trailer truck tarps for all the local truckers than he did working for his father. After 18 months of this, Wilbur, Sr., fired Wilbur, Jr. He told Bud he would be better off working for himself. They laughed years later and said it was the best thing that ever happened to Bud.

Bud went to Ft. Lauderdale, Florida, in 1963 for one year working in the auto glass business before returning to Kansas City. He went to work for an auto glass company which lasted for three months. The owners were always fighting and Bud decided he had worked for others long enough. This was to be his last job. With a young wife and two baby girls, Roxanne and Stephanie, Bud bought an old 1949 truck for $75. He put his tools in the truck (which had no heater for the cold Kansas City winters), had $50 to his name, and started down the street in Kansas City, stopping at every auto dealership asking for glass business. He knew no one but had a burning desire to succeed. He says he made more money the first day on his own than he ever made working for someone else. He knew then he would never work for anyone else again.

Bud says his career in auto glass peaked when he made $504 profit in one day. His worst day was after he had shot himself in the right kneecap while hunting with his 11-year-old nephew in Butler a week before Christmas in 1970. The very next day, it was 15 degrees and Bud had to put in 10 windshields outside in the cold. He said his leg was killing him but he always put business first. He was so busy that by the third day, he had forgotten about the pain and didn't even know he had been shot. He says that when you are busy, you don't have time to think about your problems.

By June of 1971, Bud had already published his first three books on Avon collecting and the book business was getting much bigger than the auto glass business. He decided to go full-time into the publishing business. This business exploded on Bud and up to now, with this eighteenth edition, Bud has written, photographed, researched, and published 805,000 books on Avon collecting. In 1971, when Avon collecting really started to take off, he started the Bud Hastin Avon Collector's Club. He said, "If we have a book about collecting Avon, then we need a source to buy, sell, or trade Avon on a national scale." Within one year, Bud had over 1,000 members subscribing to a monthly newsletter. He would build his club to over 6,500 members. The club name was later changed to Avon Times. Bud sold Avon Times to Dwight and Vera Young in 1982 and this club is now defunct. Bud decided in early 1971 to organize all the smaller local clubs around the country into one organization under the name National Association of Avon Collectors. This organization thrived and grew to over 200 clubs.

In 1972, at the first NAAC convention in Kansas City, Bud had created and sold the idea of a National Avon Collector's Club bottle series. The first club bottle was sold to all club members for $10.95 and the resale price rose to $250.00 over the years. Bud continued to create and produce these limited edition club bottles and club bells until 1986. Bud served as founder and chairman of the board of the NAAC until he retired in 1986.

Back in 1970, Bud thought if Avon and others could sell bottles, why couldn't he? He then started out with a series of cologne-filled bird and animal bottles under the name Collector's Art™. This is when he started doing business in Japan making fine detailed hand-painted, limited edition porcelain bottles. He then branched out his Collector's Art™ line to include whiskey bottles. All of these series were filled and distributed by McCormick Distilling Company in Western, Missouri, under Bud's personal whiskey label, Collector's Art™. The bottle business ran out of steam in 1985 for Bud but not before over 100 different collector bottles were created and distributed in all 50 states. Collector's Art™ bottles have been selling recently on the internet on e-bay.com in the $40 to $60 price range. Bud Hastin's father was responsible for getting him interested in the bottle hobby when someone gave him some fancy cut glass bottles and Bud liked them so much that he started collecting.

In 1972, Bud took his first trip out of the U.S., since he came back from Okinawa in 1960. From 1972 to 2007, Bud has traveled to over 200 different foreign countries. It is this love of travel that has taught Bud about every corner of this planet and all the differences of the people. Traveling is Bud's personal hobby and he hopes to travel to at least 250 countries before he can't go anymore. Bud also wrote a book, *Travel by Eurail to 24 Countries of Europe*. He sold this book in 1990 to a European publisher.

Bud likes to keep up on world events. He left his home of Kansas City in 1979 and moved to Ft. Lauderdale, Florida. In 1981 he moved to Las Vegas, Nevada, and returned to Ft. Lauderdale in 1988 where he and his wife, Sandra Hitchcock Hastin, now reside.

Besides publishing, Bud invented a showerhead water saver valve in 1975 and sold it all over the world wherever there was a shortage of water. In 1979, Bud produced a full-length motion picture, *Scream for Vengeance*, which was sold and distributed worldwide but never in U.S. theaters. It was sold in the U.S. in video stores.

In 1991, Bud bought an old waterfront home in Ft. Lauderdale. He designed most of it and contracted it himself and tore most of the old house down. Nine months later it was done and won first place for the best new designed and landscaped home in the beach area of northeast Ft. Lauderdale. Bud said he always wanted to be a contractor and wanted to see if he could do it. "I knew I was working hard 16 hour days, 7 days a week, but never expected to win an award for my first house." He lives in the only area of Ft. Lauderdale where you can water ski in your backyard. He says it reminds him of the 15 years he spent going to the Lake of the Ozarks when he lived in Missouri. Bud's major regret is his father, who died of cancer in 1990, never got a chance to see him build his house (his father was also a builder). Bud has always believed that hard work brings good benefits no matter what it is you do in life. There is no success without effort. "I believe you can do anything you want in life if you have the desire to do it and the willingness to do what is necessary to achieve that success."

Bud's lifelong idol is Ray Kroc, the founder of McDonald's. Mr. Kroc was 55 years old when he changed careers and started McDonald's as a poor man. Before he died he had built one of the most successful companies in the world and one of the biggest personal fortunes for himself. Bud says, "If Ray Kroc can do it, so can we, at whatever we want in life."

Since 1969 Bud has sold over 805,000 copies of his Avon collector's book. This book is the twentieth book on Avon collecting by Bud Hastin. The first, sold in 1969, was the *Avon Collector's Guide, Vol. 1*, followed by the 1970 *Avon Collector's Guide Vol. II, The Avon Collector's Encyclopedia*, the 1971 *Avon Collector's Guide for Beginners*, the 1972 *Avon Collector's Encyclopedia*, the 1972 *Avon Beginner's Guide*, the 1974 *Avon Collector's Encyclopedia*, and the *Avon Collector's Encyclopedia* special hardbound edition for collectors. Only 1,000 were printed and each was signed by Bud.

There were 500 hardbound copies of the 1976 *Avon Collector's Encyclopedia* and 350 special hardbound collectors' editions each of the 1979, 1982 – 1983, 1984, and 1987 encyclopedias, the 1991 *Avon Price Guide*, 1993 (13th Edition), 1995 (14th Edition), 1998 (15th Edition), 2001(16th Edition), and 2004 (17th Edition) encyclopedias. A total of 805,000 books sold. All books on Avon, beginning with this eighteenth edition, are owned and published by Collector Books, Paducah, Kentucky. In 2007 Bud sold his copyright to Schroeder Publishing, Inc. Not fully ready to let it go but wanting to turn over some of the long hours of photography and design, Bud has stayed on board to advise and help out when needed.

Sandra Hitchcock Hastin has been at Bud's side since they met in 1988. She has traveled to over 176 foreign countries with Bud. Sandra has a degree in business as well as a B. S. degree in organizational management, and graduated Magna Cum Laude. They have lived in Ft. Lauderdale, Florida, since 1988.

BUD HASTIN'S

Avon

#1 BEST-SELLER

EIGHTEENTH EDITION

COLLECTOR'S ENCYCLOPEDIA™

Avon and California Perfume Company products—1886 to present

Thousands of Avon & California
Perfume Company products.
Latest market prices & Avon
representative awards.

db

COLLECTOR BOOKS
A Division of Schroeder Publishing Co., Inc.

The Official Avon Collector's Price Guide

On the front cover, top left: Cape Cod wine decanter, 1977 – 1980. CMV, $28.00 MB.
Center: Christmas plate, 2003. CMV, $20.00 MB.
Top right: California Perfume Company, Natoma Rose perfume, 1914 – 1921. CMV, $300.00 BO. $425.00 MB.
Right center: Porcelain figurine, Images of Hollywood, Scarlett O'Hara, 1983 – 1984. CMV, $45.00 MB.
Bottom row, left to right: Theodore Roosevelt men's decanter, 1975 – 1976. CMV, $10.00 MB; California Perfume Company, American Ideal face powder, 1922. CMV, $50.00 CO. $75.00 MB; Mrs. Albee figurine award, 1997. CMV, $100.00 MB; Firefighter's men's stein, 1989. CMV, $55.00 MB.

On the back cover, top left: Little Bo Peep, Story Time Doll Collection, 1996. CMV, $30.00 MB.
Top center: Jeep Renegade men's decanter, Transportation Series, 1981 – 1982. CMV, $10.00 MB.
Top right: Cape Cod candy dish, 1987. CMV, $20.00 MB.
Center right: Gabriel nativity figurine, 1992. CMV, $65.00 MB.
Bottom: American Fashion Thimbles, 1982 – 1986. CMV, $12.00 each, MB. Display rack, 1983. CMV, $13.00 MB.

Bud Hastin is in no way responsible for buying, selling, or trading Avon bottles at the prices quoted in this book. It is published only as a guide and prices vary from state to state as much as 95%. Most prices quoted are top prices in mint condition and it is not uncommon for prices to be quoted differently, usually being lower. Bud Hastin does not buy or sell Avon bottles. The current market values (CMV) in this book should be used only as a guide.

Bud Hastin's Avon Collector's Encyclopedia™ is recognized by Avon collectors, Avon representatives, and insurance companies as the official appraisal guide and only complete Avon collector's guide in print.

Bud Hastin, the National Association of Avon Collector's Clubs, and Collector Books are not affiliated with Avon Products, Inc. Avon is a registered trademark of Avon Products, Inc.

Cover design: Beth Summers
Book design: Lisa Henderson
Cover photography: Charles R. Lynch

COLLECTOR BOOKS
P.O. Box 3009
Paducah, Kentucky 42002-3009

www.collectorbooks.com

Copyright © 2008 Schroeder Publishing Co., Inc.

The current values in this book should be used only as a guide. They are not intended to set prices, which vary from one section of the country to another. Auction prices, as well as dealer prices, vary greatly and are affected by condition as well as demand. Neither the author nor the publisher assumes responsibility for any losses that might be incurred as a result of consulting this guide.

Searching for a Publisher?

We are always looking for people knowledgeable within their fields. If you feel that there is a real need for a book on your collectible subject and have a large comprehensive collection, contact Collector Books.

Proudly printed and bound in the
United States of America

3 9957 00141 2176

Contents

Acknowledgments

Nobody can undertake a job this size without input from others in the field. A special thanks goes to not only the people listed below, but all the people who have contributed to this book over the last 35 years. We invite your comments and any errors you may find.

Traci and Eric Kent, Utah — furnished Avon catalogs for research
Barry Typhin, Plantation, Florida — furnished Avon catalogs for research
Dwight and Vera Young, Pleasant Hill, Missouri — supplied color photos throughout the book
Rusty Mills, Littlestown, Pennsylvania — supplied CPC information and color photos throughout the book
Jeff Holcomb, Ft. Lauderdale, Florida — furnished Avon catalogs for research
Bud and Sandra Hastin, Ft. Lauderdale, Florida — remained on board for this edition as advisors
Charles R. Lynch, Collector Books, Paducah, Kentucky — traveled to Kansas City, Missouri, to photograph pieces from a large Avon collection

A special thanks goes to Avon Products Inc., for all the literature they have printed since 1886, from which most all the dates and prices came from since Bud Hastin's first book on Avon collecting in 1969.
If you have a large collection of Avon products and could contribute color photographs for our next edition, please contact Collector Books at the address below.

Bud Hastin
P.O. Box 11004, Ft. Lauderdale, FL 33339
Please send a self-addressed, stamped envelope (SASE) for reply.
954-566-0691
e-mail: budhastin@hotmail.com

Collector Books
P.O. Box 3009, Paducah, KY 42002-3009
270-898-6211
e-mail: editor@collectorbooks.com

Dos and Don'ts in Avon Collecting

Certain Avon items are not included in this book. Avon collecting has changed so much since 1967, when collectors first started saving Avon decanters. Many Avon items and even complete categories of items that were once very popular cannot be *given* away today.

If it's a household kitchen or decorator item and not marked "Avon," it is not a true Avon collectible. The product must be marked "Avon." We have removed all Christmas tree ornaments and hanging ornaments that do not have the Avon name or logo or the year or date on each item. Collect only ornaments that can be identified as Avon.

Avon plates are still very popular, but most collectors only want porcelain or ceramic plates. Pewter plates are not as desirable to most collectors.

Candles are popular in glass and ceramics. Wax candles must have "Avon" on them, but not many are included in this edition as there is little interest in them. Taper candles are not marked "Avon" and will not stand and display on their own; therefore, all taper candles have been removed from this book. We have included candles made by Avon that are now collectible.

Soaps of all kinds in the Avon line are very popular. Soaps must not be damaged in any way. If they are, we suggest not buying them. All soaps must be in new, mint boxed condition.

We have taken inflation into consideration when pricing many of the older men's and women's decanters, candles, and plates. The new products now issued by Avon are much higher in original issue cost. They cost more than similar, much older items we had priced in past books. We feel if you will pay the price to get a new item from your Avon representative that is plentiful, you should be willing to pay the same price for older and much harder to find Avon collectibles in mint condition.

Avon representative awards and gifts are still very popular with many collectors. We have removed many items from the Avon Representative Awards section. Many paper items, purses and bags, clothing, scarves, and award plaques that are not national level awards, as well as trophies, have been removed. All awards should be marked "Avon" on the award or possess an Avon trademark.

We have weeded out many items in each category and left many in. If an item is not included, it's because it's becoming less popular over the years. If you have any of these items and they are not pictured in this book, just use a item in this book that is similar to get a price for the current value.

The Avon hobby as a whole covers a tremendous volume of material. There is far too much to collect for the average person to work on all categories. The No.1 rule in Avon collecting: Set a goal for your hobby and collect only what you want to collect. You rule the hobby, it doesn't rule you. Decide what part of the overall hobby appeals to you, set your goal, and work hard toward that goal. Ask yourself some questions. How much room do I have? How much can I spend each month? What do I enjoy most about Avon collecting? Base your goal on the answers.

Here are Bud's personal views on collecting. Avon collecting is one of the few hobbies that you will probably never find all items. That's what collecting is all about, the challenge to find something you don't have. The thrill is finding a high priced Avon or California Perfume Company bottle in a flea market or garage sale for a low price. You see very few of the same Avon collections and this always makes the challenge greater — to find the one that your friend may have. Avon collecting is one of the biggest hobbies in the U.S. I wonder how many old and rare CPC or old Avon bottles or old sets are lying around in someone's attic or cellar just waiting to be discovered by some informed collector! Garage sales are the gold fields and it is almost as big a thrill to find a $200 CPC as it was for the treasure hunters of old to find gold. Avon collecting is for all ages, both young and old. It's a hobby for the entire family.

New Products 1984 to Present

How They Are Priced and What Is Truly Collectible
Avon collecting has matured and is in for some adjustment and a little regulation. Avon Products has expanded its product lines to include many products that do not seem to fit into an Avon collection. They are making a number of household products, decorator items, and etc., that are not marked "Avon" and do not have an Avon trademark or labels. We suggest that this type of product be purchased for the purpose it was intended and not as a collectible. If we include everything in the book that Avon is mass producing, this book would be 1,000 pages thick and most of it with little or no value as a collectible.

I, along with many others I have talked to in the last couple of years, agree that unless it is marked "Avon" on the product, it doesn't belong in an Avon collection. It probably will never have any real value. We have also found little or no interest in cosmetic fragrance lines newer than 1975. This applies both to men's and women's products. For this reason we have not included fragrance lines 1975 or newer. The only products in these lines to collect are soaps, sets, and awards after 1975. These products are produced in the millions of pieces. *There may never be a resale market for this type of product in our lifetime.*

We want Avon collecting to be as exciting as possible, but for the prices to be fair to all concerned.

What's Hot and What's Not in Avon Collecting
For the absolute best advice on Avon collecting, nothing can beat something old that is in new condition, especially the California Perfume Company products. California Perfume Company was the original Avon Products' name from the late 1800s to 1939, when the name was changed to Avon Products, Inc., which it remains today. Almost anything in mint condition with the CPC label will sell quickly and will usually bring a good price. It's like any other collectible, the older the better. Cape Cod, Mrs. Albee porcelain doll awards, decanters, figurines (both men's and women's), steins, soaps, Avon representative awards, old fragrance lines (both men's and women's), Perfection products, miscellaneous bottles 1935 or older — these are the collectibles that are hot if they are older and in mint condition.

What Not to Collect for Future Resale
We have not included items that are mass produced in the millions of pieces and may never have a value for resale. We have chosen the older items for each category that are truly rare or harder to find and valuable for a collection. Many new items may not be included in this book in the future as collectors just do not want them.

In Bud Hastin's opinion, items to collect are: Avon jewelry, all tubes, tin cans, miscellaneous bottles, stuffed animals, non-porcelain head dolls, and any plastic bottle unless it is part of a set or a children's toy (unless it is listed in this book). This goes for American, Canadian, and foreign products. All fragrance lines from 1975 to present should be avoided as there is little or no resale market for them. Any Avon item may be collectible after a period of 30 to 50 years; in other words, when it becomes an antique.

Collect only what you truly enjoy. If you decide to collect any of the things I have listed as not collectible, please understand that there is not much of a resale market for them. Otherwise when you are done with them, you might want to dispose of them. Happy collecting.

Helpful Hints and Abbreviations Used in This Book

To best understand this book and its contents, please read this section carefully before starting through the book. All items from 1929 to 1984 will give the first year and the last year that the items were sold by the Avon Company. Dates will read, for instance, 1930 – 1936. This means the item was introduced sometime in 1930 and was discontinued for the last time in 1936. Dates like 1970 – 1971 mean the item sold in both years, but very possibly sold for less than one year. An item dated for three years like 1958 – 1960 means it sold in all three years, but could have only been on the market for a period of about two years total time. All items dated 1886 to 1928 mean the first and last year sold. All dates from 1929 to 1983 with only one year given means the item was sold during that one year only, and usually for a very short period. These items are usually considered a short-issue and hard to find. Items from 1984 and later give only the issue date. The following abbreviations are used in this book:

OSP — Original Selling Price. This is the price Avon sells an item for when new.

CMV — Current Market Value, the value that collectors are willing to pay for that particular item. Most items priced in this book are priced first by item only (BO, bottle only) and then by item in box, "MB." Items in the original box need not be full. The collector's price is for an empty bottle. If it is current and full, and in the box, then you can expect to pay full retail price or the special selling price for which Avon sells this item. Only after Avon stops selling the item and demand for that item rises will it be considered a collector's item, and the value may start to increase.

BO — Bottle Only, mint, no box.

MB — mint and boxed, in perfect condition.

CO — Container Only (or in the Candles section, Candle Only).

TO — Tube Only.

All Avon tube prices in this book are for full mint condition tubes. If a toothpaste tube or other type of tube has been used then it would not be mint. Tubes and soaps are the only items in this book that have to be full to be in mint condition. Most all other items are priced empty unless otherwise stated. In most cases all older items will bring as much empty as they would full.

This book has been compiled largely from original CPC and Avon catalogs. Many original California Perfume Company catalogs are pictured in this book. The CPC catalogs were used from the years 1896 to 1929. From 1916 to 1929 the CPC sales catalogs had black leather type covers, and from 1916 to 1923 they were hardbound. From 1924 to 1929 the same size books were softcover. January 1929 saw the introduction of Avon Products, with the Avon name first appearing on a number of CPC products.

The CPC sales catalogs from 1896 to 1906 were smaller booklet types with soft covers measuring 6⅝" x 4¾". The 1915 book is dated and measures 4" x 7⅛". From 1930 through 1935 the sales catalogs had CPC/Avon Products in them in a 6¾" x 10" dark blue softcover book. From 1936 through 1957 the sales catalogs were the same size, only with green covers.

An entire set of Avon sales catalogs from 1930 to the present was used to compile the *Avon Collector's Encyclopedia*. *Avon Sales Outlook* catalogs and *Avon Calling* catalogs from 1905 to 1993 were also used. Special Christmas sales catalogs from 1934 to present were also used, showing many special sets sold only at Christmas time each year.

Grading Condition of Avon

People have asked me what a bottle is worth without a label. If it's an old bottle where the label is the main thing that identifies the bottle and it is missing, then it's worth whatever you can get, which is usually not too much. If it is a new figural bottle, then it will usually take a few dollars off the price.

Mint condition — new condition as originally sold, with all labels bright and correct, complete with cap and/or stopper. Items need not be full or boxed, but will bring a higher price in most cases if they are in the box. All items in the book are priced empty in mint condition, with the right cap and all labels. Bottles with no cap or label are of little or no value.

If any Avon is damaged in any way, I would not buy it. Collect only mint Avon and throw away the less than mint items. If anything is too badly damaged, don't buy it or sell it!

CPC bottles may have the same shape, but different labels. Be sure to check labels and boxes to get the right dates on your bottles.

All items are dated in this book from actual old Avon catalogs. They did not change the CPC bottles for many years in the early days. The first CPC catalog was printed in 1896.

Garage sales and flea markets are the best places to buy Avon bottles locally. To sell Avon, don't waste your time with garage sales or local ads in your hometown paper. See page 642 for the best places to buy and sell.

Don't Pay Too Much: Pricing CMV ("Current Market Value")

All pricing in this book for CMV has been set by several qualified Avon bottle dealers and collectors across the United States. The prices reflected are what the item brings in its respective area. While many items have increased in value, some have been lowered. We are trying to reflect the approximate collector's value, or, what a collector might pay for the item in mint condition. All items are priced empty unless otherwise stated. There are several reasons for pricing all items empty. Aftershave bottles are known to explode in sunlight or heat. Full bottles sitting on glass shelves increase the chance of the shelves breaking. After a few years, the contents become spoiled or unsafe to skin and dangerous in the hands of children. I feel if you buy the item new, use the contents and you will still have the pretty bottles. On the pricing of new Avon products dated 1980 to 2008, the CMV is usually at or below the special Avon selling price. Remember, the price paid to the Avon representative is not a collector's price, but a new product price. You are paying for the contents. After you use the product, the price usually goes down and it becomes used and a collectible. It takes some time for the item to become scarce on the collector's market before you see a true collector's price established. It could take up to 20 – 30 years or more for an item to increase in value over the original selling price from Avon.

Boxes – Boxes were made to protect the container, keeping it clean and brilliant. Boxes advertise the product and instruct the user. Boxes tell a story. When you say original condition, that was with a box. Boxes (especially men's) were usually thrown away immediately. A good clean, crisp box will help make the item bring a premium price to many collectors. Grading and condition become even more important for an item with a CMV over $25.00. Example: 1966 – 1967 Tall Pony Post. The box is probably the hardest to find of the modern figural. This box should have a premium price of $10.00.

Box prices – All containers are priced empty but in mint new condition. For 1960s, deduct $3 each, no box. For 1970s, deduct $2 each, no box. For 1980s and 1990s, deduct $1 to $2 each, no box.

As Avon boxes ages 30 to 40 years or more, they become more valuable. Mint boxes are very important.

Warning: All Avon must be marked "Avon" on the item. Most collectors do not want any Avon that is not marked "Avon" on the product. Keep this in mind when buying and selling.

Avon Sets – Many sets have a premium value because they display so well. They are packaged in unusual ways and are much harder to find with perfect boxes and superior contents. I agree with the statement: Poor box, poor set; subtract 50% to 75% of listed value if you have a box in poor condition.

A mint box is at least twice as hard to obtain as the mint bottle that came in it. As good as Avon is in packing, if you order 10 like items, chances are only four will have truly mint boxes and containers. That is, you will get a creased or crushed box, or a corner of a label not securely glued.

Several people ask about insurance on bottle collections. Bottle insurance is available through your homeowner's policy. Check with your local agent.

Bottles will differ in color shades due to various dates in manufacture. It is difficult to get exactly the same color each time. Unless a bottle comes out in a completely different color, it will be of the same value.

The silver metal salt and pepper shakers with Avon patent dates 1926 – 1928 are not Avon Products, Inc. items. The Avon name was not used until 1929. The name Avon has been used by several companies and still is. Only the name Avon Products Incorporated is copyrighted.

For new collectors and to refresh seasoned collectors, we have found collecting, like other investments, has rules to follow for the best results:

- If you don't like an item, don't buy it no matter how much of a bargain it seems to be. The only good investments are those that are enjoyed.
- The old goes up in value, or at least retains its resale value. New items take longer to increase in value and stay around longer. Buy it when you see it. Avon doesn't stay put; some don't have very long shelf lives.
- If you don't know your dealers, be sure you know your Avon.

- It is acceptable to haggle — it cannot hurt to ask if there is a lower price. Often in a booth or flea market there will be a better price available; don't be timid.
- Start small and learn the market. Browse, study this book, and learn all you can before you start buying.
- Measure your space — don't be the collector who buys a lot of items only to bring them home with no place to put them.
- Don't change your item in any way — don't paint it, wash it in water, add lettering, remove labels, etc.; this may destroy the value.

The above rules are good ones to keep in mind. The advice I've found most helpful is to have *fun* while collecting, whether it be at a flea market, garage sale, Avon collector's show and sale, or Avon collector's convention.

"Avon Calling"

The phrase "Avon Calling" rings round the world as the signature of a firm devoted to the manufacture and sales of high quality cosmetic and toiletry items for all members of the family. "Avon Calling" is a registered trademark of Avon products.

From its start in 1886 as the California Perfume Company, Avon has grown steadily, expanding its operation throughout the world. Avon's growth from a one-room laboratory in downtown New York to the current worldwide network of manufacturing laboratories and distribution branches is a success story based on quality. Avon is the world's largest manufacturer and distributor of cosmetics, fragrances, and costume jewelry. Its products are sold by more than 1,600,000 active representatives to customers in the home in the United States and other countries. Avon products are sold in almost every country in the world.

National Association of Avon Collectors

Bud Hastin founded the National Association of Avon Collector's Clubs in 1971 and served as chairman of its board of directors until 1986. The NAAC is not a club, but an organization that helps promote Avon collecting worldwide. The NAAC is run by an elected board of directors. The NAAC is ready to help anyone start a new Avon collector's club in your area. For information on starting a new Avon collector's club, write to NAAC, P.O. Box 7006, Kansas City, MO 64113. All NAAC material will be sent to you. A national convention is held each year along with a national Avon bottle show, in a different section of the U.S. The NAAC is a non-profit organization. See the NAAC section of this book for NAAC club bottles. Please send a SASE when writing for information.

A History of the California Perfume Company

–Now called Avon Products Incorporated. Written by the Founder, D. H. McConnell, Sr., in 1903.

To give you a sketch or history of the birth and growth of the California Perfume Company is, in a measure, like writing an autobiography. Our lives have become so identical and so interwoven that it seems almost impossible to separate us, even in history. I will ask you, therefore, to pardon whatever personal reference I may make of myself in describing to you how the California Perfume Company has become the largest of its kind, not only in the United States, but I believe, in the entire world. In 1878, when but a mere lad, I left my father's farm located near Oswego City, New York. Here I spent my boyhood days, and through hard work and proper training developed a good, strong, hardy, rugged constitution. When I started out in the world "to make my fortune," I had this positive advantage over many who were less favored. My first experience in the business world was as a book agent. I took this up during my school vacation, and developed quite a faculty for talking, which I have since learned is quite essential, and has stood me well in hand many times. My success in canvassing was such as to invite me into the same field the following year, and after two years hard work in the canvass, I was promoted from local canvasser to that of general traveling agent. As general agent I traveled in nearly every state east of the Rocky Mountains; this gave me valuable knowledge regarding the country. And my experience, both as canvasser and as general agent, gave me a good insight into human nature.

It is uninteresting to you to follow me through the different work from Chicago to New York and from New York to Atlanta, Georgia, and back to Chicago, and finally back to New York. During all these years I represented in different ways the same publishing company with which I originally started as a canvasser: canvassing, appointing, and drilling agents; starting and drilling general agents; and corresponding with both after they once entered the field. My work as a canvasser and on the road taught me not to enter right into the everyday work of the canvasser and advise and encourage, so as to obtain the best results. If I learned to be anything, I learned to be practical. The book business was not congenial to me, although I was, in every sense, successful in it, but there were many things that were not pleasant.

On my return from Chicago, I purchased the entire business from my employer and managed it myself for some time. During this time the one thing I learned successfully was how to sell goods to the customer. My ambition was to manufacture a line of goods that would be consumed, used up, and to sell it through canvassing agents, direct from the factory to the consumer. The starting of the perfume business was the result of most careful and thorough investigation, guided by the experience of several years successful operation in the book business. That is, in selling goods direct to the consumer or purchaser. I learned during this time that the proper and most advantageous way of selling goods was to be able to submit the goods themselves to the people. In investigating this matter nearly every line of business was gone over, and it seemed to me, then, as it has since been proved, that the perfume business in its different branches afforded the very best possible opportunity to build up a permanent and well established trade. Having once decided that the perfume business was the business, the question naturally presented itself, "By what name are these perfumes to be known: by what name is this company to be called?" The gentleman who took me from the farm as a boy became in the past years, not only my employer but my personal friend, and after buying him out he moved to California, and while there wrote me glowing accounts of the country, and to him belongs the idea of the name California, as associated with this business. I started the perfume business in a space scarcely larger than an ordinary kitchen pantry. At first I manufactured but five odors: Violet, White Rose, Heliotrope, Lily of the Valley, and Hyacinth. I did much experimental work in making these odors, and the selling price to the first batch of perfumes I made did not cover one-half the actual cost of the goods, but experience is a great teacher, and I applied myself to the task of making perfumes with the same vim and energy that I had in selling books and after a short time, I fancied that I could produce as fine an odor as some of the old and tried perfumes. At least my perfumes pleased my customers; they were the natural perfumes of the flower, made in the most natural way and by the process employed by the large French perfumers.

I soon found it necessary to increase the odors, and to add to the line other articles for the toilet. Among those first put out were: Shampoo Cream, Witch Hazel Cream, Almond Cream Balm, and Tooth Paste, which afterwards was made into the Tooth Tablet, Toilet Waters, etc. As the business increased the laboratory, of necessity, had to grow, so that at the end of two years I was occupying one entire floor in this building for manufacturing purposes alone.

It is perhaps unfair to note the progress of one side of the business without carrying with it the natural development on the other.

My ambition was to manufacture a line of goods superior to any other, to be moneyed value into the goods themselves, and just enough money in the package to make them respectable, and as stated above, take these goods through canvassing agents direct from the laboratory to the consumer.

While in the book business I had in my employ as general traveling agent, a Mrs. P.F.E. Albee, of Winchester, New Hampshire. Mrs. Albee was one of the most successful general agents.

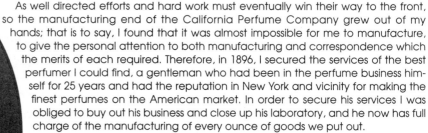

I had in the book work, and it was in her hands I placed the first sample case, or outfit, in the perfume business. Mrs. Albee was the only general agent employed for the first six months of the business. During that time she secured a number of good workers, some of whom are with us today. It is, therefore, only befitting that we give her the honorary title of Mother of the California Perfume Company, for the system that we now use for distributing our goods is the system that was put in practical operation by Mrs. Albee.

As the business grew, through the work of our agents, we were forced from time to time to increase our laboratory space, and in 1895 we built our own laboratory in Suffern, New York, 32 miles out on the main line of the Erie Railroad. This building has been enlarged and remodeled three different times, until today we have a building 120 feet long, main building 50 feet wide, and the wing 30 feet, all three stories and basement giving us four working floors, each floor having 4,800 square feet of floor space, or a total floor capacity of 17,200 feet. This building is equipped with the best possible machinery, the latest devices for bottling goods and so on, until I feel we can truthfully say that there is not a plant of our kind in the country so large and so well fitted for our business, as the laboratory of the California Perfume Company.

Mrs. P.F.E. Albee
First CPC-Avon sales lady

As well directed efforts and hard work must eventually win their way to the front, so the manufacturing end of the California Perfume Company grew out of my hands; that is to say, I found that it was almost impossible for me to manufacture, to give the personal attention to both manufacturing and correspondence which the merits of each required. Therefore, in 1896, I secured the services of the best perfumer I could find, a gentleman who had been in the perfume business himself for 25 years and had the reputation in New York and vicinity for making the finest perfumes on the American market. In order to secure his services I was obliged to buy out his business and close up his laboratory, and he now has full charge of the manufacturing of every ounce of goods we put out.

My object in locating the laboratory at Suffern was that as Suffern is my home I can give much more personal attention and supervision to the affairs of the laboratory than if it was located in New York. So that every day in the year, unless I am out on one of my trips visiting agents and general agents, I am at the laboratory every morning, and spend an hour with our chemist, going over his work and seeing that every ounce of goods, every package in every department is made and put up in the best possible shape.

Contrast, if you please, the appearance of our office today with that of when Mrs. Albee first started out with the California Perfume Company's goods. Then, I had one stenographer, and I myself filled the position of correspondent, cashier, bookkeeper, shipping clerk, office boy, and manufacturing chemist. Today we have on our weekly payroll over 125 employees. Mrs. Albee for the first six months was the only general agent on the road. Today we have 48 general agents traveling over this country and selecting and drilling agents for this work. The first six months we had perhaps 100 agents in the field; today we have over 10,000 good, honest, industrious and energetic depot managers. All of you have your own customers, so that it is difficult to accurately estimate today the vast number of families that are using our goods. If each of you has 100 customers, or sell goods to only one different family, we are supporting goods to at least one million families in the United States. This will give you an idea of the magnitude of our business. The growth of the California Perfume Company only emphasizes what energy and fair dealing with everyone can accomplish. We propose first to be fair to our customers — your customers — by giving them the very best goods that can be made for the money. We propose to be fair and just, even liberal, with you who form the bone and sinew of our business.

(Avon representatives, in the early days of the California Perfume Company, were called agents or depot managers.)

David Hall McConnell

Founder, CPC – Avon Products

David Hall McConnell, manufacturer, was born in Oswego, New York, on July 18, 1858, son of James and Isabel (Hall) McConnell, who came from Calvin County, Ireland, in 1845 and settled in Oswego, where James McConnell became a farmer and brick manufacturer. Brought up on a farm, David Hall McConnell attended a district school and the Oswego State Normal School and was planning to become a mathematics teacher, but instead entered business life in 1879 as a salesman for a New York book selling agency. In 1880 he joined the Union Publishing Co. of Chicago and three years later was placed in charge of the southern territory, making his home in Atlanta, Georgia. He decided that if books could be sold house-to-house, perfumes could also. Out of this conception grew his California Perfume Company. At first he manufactured his own perfumes at home and went out during the day selling them along with books until the enterprise grew and he had to discontinue his book selling and establish a perfume laboratory in Suffern, New York. Other toiletries and cosmetics were soon added to his line of products which he sold under the name of CPC, standing for California Perfume Co. Later the company also began to manufacture flavoring extracts and other household articles sold under the brand name, Perfection. From the onset McConnell effected distribution of his products through housewives and other women who could devote only a portion of their time to the work. The years brought steadily increasing success and at the time of his death his sales force had grown to over 30,000 agents and the volume of sales was measured in the millions. The California Perfume Co. was incorporated in January 1916, and through subsequent changes in name it became Allied Products, Inc., and later Avon Allied Products, Inc., with the following subsidiaries: Avon Products, Inc., distributors of Avon cosmetics and toiletries, the trade name Avon having been adopted in 1929 because of the similarity of the landscape surrounding the laboratories in Suffern, New York, to that of Avon, England; Perfection Household Products; Avon Products of Canada, Ltd., incorporated in 1924, being an outgrowth of the California Perfume Company of Canada, Ltd., which was started in 1906; Hinz Ambrosia, Inc., and Technical Laboratories, Inc. McConnell was president, chairman of the board, and principal owner of Avon Allied Products, Inc., and its affiliated companies until his death. He was also treasurer of G.W. Carnrick and Co., manufacturers of pharmaceutical supplies in Newark, New Jersey, and a director of the Holly Hill Fruit Products, Inc., a large orange grove and canning enterprise of Davenport, Florida. He was one of the founders of the Suffern National Bank, of which he became vice president in 1901, president in 1922, and chairman of the board in 1927. He was again elected chairman of the board, and president in 1933 and continued in one or the other office until his death. For varying periods he was superintendent of schools in Suffern; president of the Suffern Board of Education; and treasurer of the Rockland County Republican committee. During the First World War he was chairman of the Rockland County selective service board. A Presbyterian in religion, he was instrumental in starting and played a major part in building the Suffern Presbyterian Church and for many years was superintendent of its Sunday school. He was a Mason and a member of the Union League Club of New York City, the Ormond Beach Club of Florida, the Arcola, New York Country Club, and Houvenkoph Country Club of Suffern, New York. Fishing, golf, and horseback riding were his recreations. He was married in Chicago, March 31, 1885, to Lucy Emma, daughter of Ward Hays of Le Porte, Indiana, and had three children: Edna Bertha, who married William Van Allen Clark; Doris Hall, who married Edward Hall Faile; and David Hall McConnell, Jr. His death occurred in Suffern, New York, January 20, 1937.

Early Days

The company's name suggests a likely California beginning, but it has no such meaning; the manufacturing, shipping, and office work in the beginning was done at 126 Chambers St., New York City. The name followed a suggestion made by a friend of Mr. McConnell's who had just visited California and returned to New York greatly enthused over the gorgeous flowers he had seen there. Since only perfumes were being sold, he suggested that the name of the company be "The California Perfume Company."

A Large Line

By 1915 Avon had a large line. Its products were well and favorably known among its customers but were not known to the public at large. No advertising was done. The customers told their friends about these splendid products and the CPC Representatives' Service. From the beginning all products were sold under the CPC trademark. All were offered to customers by representatives (the products have never been sold through stores) and, always, the products were unconditionally guaranteed. This was most unusual in the early days.

The Panama Pacific Exposition

The company was invited to exhibit at the Panama Pacific Exposition in San Francisco in 1914 – 1915. This was a World's Fair, and prizes were given for the best articles exhibited in various classifications. The entire line of perfumes, toilet articles, and household products was entered in competition with like products from all over the world, and Avon was awarded the gold medal, both for the quality of its products, and the beauty of its packages. This gold medal appeared on all packages until it was replaced by the seal that is recognized and followed throughout the world as a consumer's guide to the highest quality of merchandise — The Good Housekeeping Seal of Approval.

New Names — New Packages

Through the years, Avon's chemists were following every avenue of research, improving products wherever possible, and discovering new ones that in every way measured up to the standards of the first one. Manufacturing methods were improved to the point that every product was the sum of perfection as to blending and handling. Then in 1929, the chemists suggested an entirely new line of cosmetics. They had it ready, the managers agreed, and the Avon line was presented to representatives and customers. The household line was named "Perfection" and given its own trademark.

Good Housekeeping Seal of Approval

In 1931, the first group of Avon cosmetics were approved by Good Housekeeping, and from that time on, other groups were sent, tested, approved, and the Seal added to their packages. By 1936, Avon's 50th Anniversary year, Good Housekeeping completed their tests and approved all Avon and Perfection products which came within their scope. All products added since that time bear the Seal of Approval.

A New Policy — National Advertising

Steadily increasing business over a period of years without any advertising was a remarkable record, but with the celebration of a Golden Jubilee policy was changed and the company began to advertise. All during 1936 and 1937, advertisements appeared in *Good Housekeeping*. They told the public that Avon products were unconditionally guaranteed and that representatives give the Avon service. They told readers how convenient shopping the "Avon Way" was for them.

The 1900 California Perfume Factory in Oswego, New York.

Late 1800s
David McConnell starts the California Perfume Company, at the age of 28, in a room in downtown Manhattan. He and his wife, Lucy, create and manufacture the first products. It is sold by the first representative, Mrs. P.F.E. Albee, who recruits others to sell at the same time.

1894
Mr. McConnell expands to four floors in the Manhattan building.

1896
The first catalog is issued on November 2. (Text only, no pictures).

1897
The first laboratory is built, a three-story wooden structure in Suffern.

1902
10,000 representatives are now selling the company's products.

1903
The first branch is opened in Kansas City, Missouri.

1905
The first *Outlook* is published, with news and selling tips for representatives.

1906
The first company advertisement appears. The product: Roses perfume. The magazine: *Good Housekeeping*.

1912
Over 5,000,000 products are sold during this year.

1914
A Canadian office is opened in Montreal.

1915
The company wins the Panama Pacific International Exposition gold medal for quality and packaging.

1920
Sales reach the $1,000,000 mark.

1928
A line of new products, called "Avon" is introduced. It includes a toothbrush, cleaner, and talc.

1932
Three-week selling campaigns begin in August. Up to this time, representatives have been asked to send in orders every month. As a result of the change, sales increase by over 70% during America's bleak Depression years. The first specials also appear, with products sold at less than regular prices.

1935
The company sponsors a national radio program, called *Friends*, a twice weekly show of music and chatter.

1936
An important step is taken to reach customers in urban and suburban areas. Site of this experiment is the Midwest, where several cities, Kansas City, Wichita, and Oklahoma City, are divided into territories. Each territory is to be covered by a representative with a manager in charge. Later, after the war, this is to become the universal Avon sales structure.

1937
The home office moves to 30 Rockefeller Plaza in New York City. David McConnell dies at age 79.

1939
On October 6, the California Perfume Company changes its name to Avon Products, Inc.

1942 – 1945
The company joins the war effort, with over 50% of the Suffern plant converted to production for the armed forces. Among the items manufactured are insect repellent, pharmaceuticals, paratrooper kits, and gas mask canisters.

1949
Avon now has 2,500 employees, 1,175 shareholders, 65,000 representatives, and $25 million in sales. The company has facilities in New York City, Suffern, Kansas City, Middletown, Chicago, and Pasadena.

1951
The Atlanta distribution branch opens.

1952
The Newark distribution branch opens.

1954
On TV advertising, the "Ding-Dong, Avon Calling" bell is heard for the first time. Avon goes international with its entry into Puerto Rico and Venezuela.

1955
Sales brochures are introduced to support campaign selling.

1956
The Morton Grove shipping facilities open.

1959
Monrovia shipping and warehousing facilities open.

1960
The Rye branch opens.

1964
On April 2, the New York Stock Exchange starts trading Avon stock. The "advance call-back" brochure selling plan is adopted, with representatives leaving mini-brochures at customers' homes, then returning for the orders.

1965
The Springdale laboratory distribution facilities open. A new research and development laboratory is completed in Suffern.

1968
Two week selling is introduced in the U.S. The first car decanter appears, launching the most successful decanter series.

1970
The Glenview distribution branch opens.

1971
Jewelry is first introduced in the U.S.

1972 – 2007
Avon moves into new world headquarters in New York City. Sales top the 3 billion dollar mark. Sales continue to climb worldwide. Avon continues to open new operations around the world each year.

Trademarks

Trademarks of Quality, 1890s to present

It is interesting to see the changes that have been made over the years in the Avon trademark. As you may know, in the early days the Company was called the California Perfume Company. The founder, Mr. D. H. McConnell, selected this name for his flourishing perfume business because he had heard so many glowing accounts of the great beauty and abundance of flowers in the state of California. This name, however, was changed in the early 1930s to Avon . . .a name that today is known and respected in all parts of the world.

These labels and trademarks are given as reference only. Some dates may vary. Some early CPC products also have Chicago on the label. This label is very rare.

1888-1904

1904-1911

1911-1930

1929

1930-1936

1936-53

1940's

1953

1976

1978. . .

AVON
1991

Avon Collectibles seal.
This seal appears on Avon collectibles from the 1980s.

Avon Collectibles seal.
This gold seal appears on Avon collectible figurines, ornaments, plates, nativity pieces, steins, and other items from the 2000s.

If any collectors have other information about trademarks not shown here, or know definite dates these seals were used, please contact Collector Books.

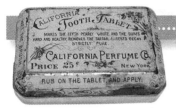

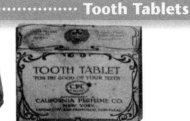

1892 – 1900.
Blue and white painted metal lid. Clear glass bottom has embossed "California Tooth Tablet, Most Perfect Dentifrice." OSP, 25¢. CMV, $110.00 tablet only, mint. $140.00 MB.

1901 – 1921.
Painted metal top with clear glass bottom embossed with "Calif. Tooth Tablet" in glass. Two different boxes. 1906 to 1921 lid is painted just under New York with Food and Drug Act 1906. OSP, 25¢. CMV, $75.00 each, tablet only, mint. $110.00 each, MB.

1921 – 1923.
Aluminum lid and clear glass bottom. OSP, 25¢. CMV, $60.00 mint.

1923 – 1924.
Aluminum lid with white glass bottom. OSP, 36¢. CMV, $55.00 mint. Same lid (different bottom) as 1921 tablet. Add $30.00 each MB.

1934 – 1936.
Aluminum lid on white glass bottom. OSP, 36¢. CMV, $60.00 tablet only, mint. $90.00 MB.

1936 – 1939.
Aluminum lid on white glass bottom. Avon Tulip "A" on lid. OSP, 36¢. CMV, $55.00 tablet only, mint. $80.00 MB.

Lavender Fragrance Jars, 1914 – 1923.
Three different sizes. *Left:* 5½" high, 3" wide. *Center:* 5⅞" high, 3" wide base. *Right:* 7" high, 3⁹⁄₁₆" wide base. OSP, $2.50 each. CMV, $90.00 each. One on far right is first issue. Add $40.00 each MB.

American Beauty Fragrance Jar Liquid, 1921.
4 oz. cork stopper, brown label. OSP, 96¢. CMV, $100.00 BO. $125.00 MB.

American Beauty Fragrance Jar Cubes, 1923.
4 oz. can. OSP, 48¢, Front and back views shown. CMV, $55.00 mint.

American Beauty Fragrance Jar, 1923 – 1933.
Clear glass jar and lid. Red ribbon around neck. OSP, $2.95. CMV, $75.00.

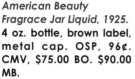

Fragrance Jar Liquid, 1934 – 1936.
6 oz. bottle, aluminum cap. Silver and blue label. OSP, $1.75. CMV, $45.00 BO, mint. $50.00 MB.

American Beauty Fragrance Jar, 1934 – 1943.
6 oz. glass jar and stopper. Red tassel around neck. OSP, $2.75. CMV, $20.00, jar only mint, with tassel. $30.00 MB.

American Beauty Fragrace Jar Liquid, 1925.
4 oz. bottle, brown label, metal cap. OSP, 96¢. CMV, $75.00 BO. $90.00 MB.

Fragrance Jar Liquid, 1936 – 1954.
6 oz. bottle, green cap and label. OSP, $1.39. CMV, $20.00 BO. $25.00 MB as shown.

American Beauty Fragrance Jar Cubes, 1943 – 1949.
3 oz. jar. OSP, 85¢. CMV, $25.00 jar only. $35.00 MB.

Fragrance Jar, 1946.
Made of pink ceramic, white flower on pink lid. Very short issue. Does not say "Avon" on it. Also came with white, blue, and green flowers on lid and white flowers on white lid. OSP, $2.75. CMV, $40.00 jar only, mint. $70.00 MB.

Rose Fragrance Jar Test, 1948.
Dark amber glass. Was not sold. Test bottle at factory. CMV, $100.00.

Rose Fragrance Jar, 1948 – 1957.
6 oz. First issue came out with clear rose shaped glass stopper. 1949 issue had frosted rose glass stopper. Both had red silk neck ribbon. OSP, $3.50. CMV, $20.00 BO, clear stopper, $15.00 with stopper. Add $20.00 each, MB.

Rose Fragrance Jar Set, 1948 – 1957.
Box contains one 6 oz. fragrance jar liquid, one 3 oz. fragrance jar cubes, and one 8 oz. empty fragrance jar. CMV, $100.00 set MB.

Fragrance Jar Liquid, 1955 – 1957.
7 oz. white cap, gray label. OSP, $1.39. CMV, $15.00 BO. $20.00 MB.

American Ideal

Sachet, 1908.
Glass bottle with metal cap. Two-piece gold label. OSP, 50¢. CMV, $110.00 BO, mint. $135.00 MB.

Perfume Introductory Size, 1910.
Glass stopper in round screw-on wood box, gold label. OSP, 75¢. CMV, $120.00 BO. $225.00 MB.

Perfume, 1910 – 1911.
Wood case with dark velvet lining holds 1 oz. glass stopper bottle with green and gold label with lady's face. Neck ribbon matches inside of box. OSP, $2.00. CMV, $150.00 BO, mint. $210.00 MB.

Sachet, 1910 – 1911.
Box holds bottle with ribbed sides. Brass cap and lady's face on green and gold label. OSP, 50¢. CMV, $100.00 BO, mint. $135.00 MB.

Box C Set, 1910 – 1911.
Flip-top box holds glass stopper perfume and powder sachet. OSP, 50¢. CMV, $325.00 MB.

Perfume, 1908.
Glass stopper bottle came in 1 and 2 oz. sizes. Velvet lined wood box. Neck ribbon on bottle, gold front and neck labels. OSP, $2.00 and $3.75. CMV, $150.00 each, BO. $200.00 each, MB.

Perfume, 1912 – 1915.
1 or 2 oz. size bottle, glass stopper. Lady's face on paper label in green box. OSP, $2.50 and $4.75. CMV, $125.00 each, BO, mint. $175.00 MB.

American Ideal Set, 1912 – 1916.
Large fancy box with green lining holds talcum powder, powder sachet, 1 oz. glass stopper perfume, and bar of toilet soap in pink soap can. OSP, $4.00. CMV, $500.00 MB.

Perfumes, 1913 only.
Introductory size, octagonal shaped glass stopper bottles fit in wood boxes with screw-on wood lids, and paper labels with ladies' faces. OSP, 75¢, Both came with neck ribbons. CMV, $120.00 each, BO, mint. $225.00 MB.

Talcum, 1912 – 1915.
Pink can with gold top. OSP, 35¢. CMV, $110.00 can only. $140.00 MB.

Toilet Soap, 1912 – 1918.
Pink and gold metal can holds one bar of soap wrapped in same design as can. OSP, 50¢. CMV, $60.00 can only. With wrapped soap, $110.00 mint.

Perfume, Introductory Sizes, 1913.
Two different size glass stopper bottles with different size labels. CMV, $120.00 each, mint.

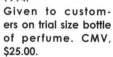

Introduction Letter, 1914.
Given to customers on trial size bottle of perfume. CMV, $25.00.

Powder Sachet, 1912 – 1915.
Large size sachet bottle with brass cap and lady on paper label. OSP, $1.00. CMV, $75.00 BO, mint. $100.00 MB.

Perfumes.
Shown for the different sizes of bottles and glass stoppers. CMV, same as bottles listed with the same labels.

Face Powder, 1915.
Green and gold box. OSP, 75¢. CMV, $65.00 powder box only, mint. $80.00 MB.

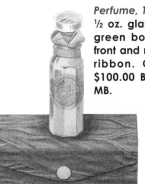

Perfume, 1917.
½ oz. glass stopper bottle, green box, gold label on front and neck. Green neck ribbon. OSP, 75¢, CMV, $100.00 BO, mint. $135.00 MB.

Perfume, 1919.
1 oz. with frosted flower embossed glass stopper. Green label. OSP, $2.40. CMV, $125.00 BO. $150.00 MB.

Perfume, 1916.
Introductory size glass stopper bottle with green neck ribbon and pink paper label with lady's face, in green box. OSP, 60¢, CMV, $120.00 BO, mint. $190.00 MB.

Powder Sachet, 1917.
Two-piece label on front. Rare with this label. Metal cap. CMV, $85.00 BO, mint. $115.00 MB.

American Ideal Set, 1919.
Green silk lined box holds 1 oz. glass stopper perfume, powder sachet, bottle of talcum powder, and toilet soap. All have green labels. OSP, $5.50. CMV, $550.00 MB.

Talcum Powder, 1917.
3½ oz. glass jar, gold metal lid and gold label. OSP, 75¢. CMV, $90.00 BO. $125.00 MB.

Perfume, 1919.
1 or 2 oz. glass bottle with glass stopper, green and gold label, green box, and green neck ribbon. OSP, $2.40 and $4.65. CMV, $125.00 BO. $160.00 MB.

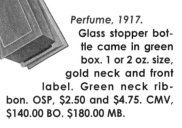

Perfume, 1917.
Glass stopper bottle came in green box. 1 or 2 oz. size, gold neck and front label. Green neck ribbon. OSP, $2.50 and $4.75. CMV, $140.00 BO. $180.00 MB.

Powder Sachet, 1919.
Glass bottle with brass cap, green label. OSP, $1.20. CMV, $80.00 BO. $110.00 MB.

Toilet Soap, 1920.
White box, green label. OSP, 48¢. CMV, $75.00 MB.

Face Powder, 1923.
Green and gold box with green and gold label. OSP, 96¢. CMV, $50.00 powder box only, mint. $65.00 MB.

Compact, 1920.
Contains face powder or rouge. Brass container with mirror on lid. OSP, 59¢. CMV, $60.00 compact only, mint. $75.00 MB.

Powder Sachet, 1923.
Glass bottle, brass cap, green label. OSP, $1.20. CMV, $100.00 BO, mint. $125.00 MB.

Threesome, 1923.
Green box contains 2 oz. toilet water, bottle of sachet, and glass bottle of talc. Green and gold label. OSP, $3.95. CMV, $375.00 MB.

Double Compact, 1921.
Contains face powder and rouge. Made of solid brass. OSP, $1.17. CMV, $70.00 compact only, mint. $85.00 MB.

Talcum, 1923 – 1928.
3½ oz. glass jar, brass cap, gold and green label. OSP, 72¢. CMV, $90.00 BO, mint. $125.00 MB.

Cream Deluxe, 1923.
White glass jar with CPC on metal lid. Gold and green label. OSP, 96¢. CMV, $40.00 jar only, mint. $60.00 MB.

Face Powder, 1922.
Green box holds green and gold paper container. OSP, 96¢. CMV, $50.00 jar only. $75.00 MB.

Perfume, 1923.
Introductory size bottle. Glass bottle and stopper. Green label and neck ribbon. Green box. OSP, 75¢. CMV, $110.00 BO, mint. $135.00 MB.

Soap, 1923.
One bar toilet soap in white paper with gold label. OSP, 48¢. CMV, $60.00 mint.

Toilet Water, 1923.
2 and 4 oz. glass stopper bottle with green front and neck label and neck ribbon. Green box. OSP, $1.50 and $2.85. CMV, $115.00 BO, mint. $150.00 MB.

Perfume, 1925 – 1933.
Flaconette embossed with brass cap over long dabber glass stopper. OSP, $1.10. CMV, $90.00 BO. $115.00 MB.

Foursome Set, 1925 – 1927.
Green box holds 1 oz. bottle with glass stopper of perfume, glass bottle of talcum, green box of face powder, and white jar of vanishing cream. OSP, $6.50. CMV, $425.00 MB.

Lipstick 1929.
"CPC" on green metal tube. OSP, $1.00. CMV, $40.00 tube only. $65.00 MB.

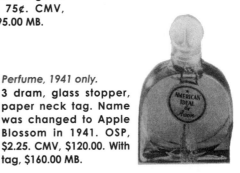

Perfume, 1925 – 1927.
1 oz. bottle with wide flat glass stopper. Green neck ribbon and gold and green label. OSP, $2.40. CMV, $125.00 BO, mint. $150.00 MB.

Talcum, 1928 – 1936.
Frosted glass bottle with brass lid, gold and green label. OSP, 75¢. CMV, $70.00 BO. $95.00 MB.

Perfume, 1941 only.
3 dram, glass stopper, paper neck tag. Name was changed to Apple Blossom in 1941. OSP, $2.25. CMV, $120.00. With tag, $160.00 MB.

Face Powder, 1925.
Green and gold box. OSP, 96¢. CMV, $50.00 jar only, mint. $65.00 MB.

Toilet Soap, 1925.
Green box holds two bars. OSP, 96¢. CMV, $90.00 MB.

American Ideal Perfume, 1929 – 1933.
1 oz. glass stopper bottle in green satin lined box. Paper label on top of bottle. OSP, $2.20. CMV, $110.00 BO, mint. $150.00 MB.

Perfume 1941.
⅛ oz. clear glass bottle, gold cap. Gold and blue label. OSP, 75¢. CMV, $35.00 BO. $55.00 MB.

Ariel ··

*Bath Salts,
1929 – 1930.*
10 oz. clear glass with chrome cap, silver and blue label. CMV, $60.00 BO. $75.00 MB.

Face Powder, 1930 – 1936.
Silver and blue round box and special issue 1935 red Christmas box. OSP, 78¢. CMV, $8.00 CO, mint. $16.00 MB as shown in Christmas box. $11.00 in regular issue box on left.

Threesome, 1932 – 1933.
Blue and silver compact, blue and silver Avon face powder, and flaconette with brass cap. In silver and blue box. OSP, $3.12. CMV, $145.00 MB.

Perfume Flaconette, 1930.
Brass cap over glass stopper embossed bottle. OSP, 84¢. CMV, $90.00 BO, mint. $115.00 MB.

Toilet Water, 1930 – 1935.
2 oz. glass stopper bottle, small label on top of bottle. Came in silver and blue box. OSP, $1.75. CMV, $110.00 BO. $135.00 MB.

Powder Sachet, 1932 – 1936.
1¼ oz. ribbed glass. Dark blue cap. OSP, 78¢. CMV, $28.00 BO. $33.00 MB.

Perfume, 1930.
1 oz. glass stopper bottle with small silver label. Silver box. OSP, $2.50. CMV, $100.00 BO. $150.00 MB.

Sachet, 1930– 1932.
Metal cap, silver and blue label. OSP, 78¢. CMV, $60.00 BO, mint. $75.00 MB.

Perfume, "Ribbed," 1933 – 1936.
½ oz. ribbed glass bottle with black octagonal cap and gold label. Came in Gold Box Set (see Gold Box Sets section). CMV, $45.00 mint.

Perfume, 1930.
1 oz. glass stopper bottle, large silver and blue label. Came in silver box. OSP, $2.50. CMV, $105.00 BO, mint. $135.00 MB.

Set No. 2, 1931 – 1933.
Silver and blue box holds silver and blue fan compact and silver box of Ariel face powder. OSP, $2.50. CMV, $75.00 MB.

Bath Salts Sample, 1933 – 1936. Small ribbed glass bottle with dark blue or black octagonal shaped cap. Silver label. CMV, $65.00 mint.

Perfume, 1933 – 1936. Small six-sided octagonal shaped bottle with black octagonal cap. Came in Little Folks set and Handkerchief set. Silver label. CMV, $45.00 mint.

Bath Salts, 1933 – 1936. 8½ oz., ribbed glass, navy blue cap, silver and blue label. OSP, 63¢. CMV, $40.00 BO, mint. $60.00 MB.

Daphne

Perfume, 1916 – 1918. 1 and 2 oz. bottles shown with frosted glass stoppers. Also came in ½ oz. size. Each came in green box. OSP, $1.00, $1.90, and $3.50. CMV, $120.00 BO. $145.00 MB.

Face Powder Vanity Compact, 1917. Green box, came in white, pink, and brunette tints. OSP, 75¢. CMV, $50.00 MB. Same box also came in Daphne Rouge. Same CMV. $35.00 compact only, mint.

Daphne Set, 1918 – 1922. Green box holds perfume in 1 oz. glass stopper bottle, green box of face powder, and green box of rouge. OSP, $3.50. CMV, $275.00 MB.

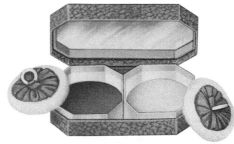

Double Vanity Compact, 1917. Contained face powder and rouge. Green compact with mirror on lid. OSP, $1.00. CMV, $45.00 compact only, mint. $70.00 MB.

Vanity Compact, 1917. Face powder came in white, pink, and brunette. Green compact with mirror on lid. OSP, 50¢. CMV, $45.00 compact only, mint. $55.00 MB.

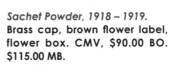

Sachet Powder, 1918 – 1919. Brass cap, brown flower label, flower box. CMV, $90.00 BO. $115.00 MB.

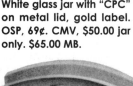

Lipstick, 1919 – 1922. Metal case. "Daphne" on case. OSP, 50¢. CMV, $55.00 lipstick only, mint. $70.00 MB.

Rolling Massage Cream, 1923. White glass jar with "CPC" on metal lid, gold label. OSP, 69¢. CMV, $50.00 jar only. $65.00 MB.

Talcum Powder, 1923 – 1929. 4 oz. green can, brass cap. OSP, 48¢. CMV, $65.00 CO. $80.00, MB.

Powder Sachet, 1920. Brass cap and gold label. OSP, 96¢. CMV, $80.00 BO, mint. $110.00 MB.

Cerate, 1923. White glass jar with "CPC" on metal lid, gold label. Small and large size jars. OSP, 72¢ and $1.35. CMV, $50.00 jar only, $65.00 MB.

Threesome Set, 1923. Green box contains 2 oz. toilet water, bottle of sachet, and can of talc. OSP, $3.20. CMV, $360.00 MB.

Powder Sachet, 1922. Brass cap, green and gold square label. Very rare. OSP, 96¢. CMV, $90.00 BO, mint. $115.00 MB.

Toilet Water, 1923. Green box holds 2 or 4 oz. bottle with frosted glass stopper, gold front and neck label, and green neck ribbon. OSP, $1.20 and $2.25. CMV, $105.00 BO. $135.00 MB. Came with two different glass stoppers set in cork and outer box. CMV for both boxes, $140.00 MB.

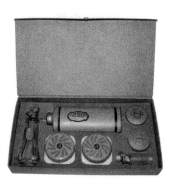

Perfume, 1922. ¼ oz. vial given to customers for each $5.00 order in March 1922. CMV, $140.00 BO, mint. $175.00 MB.

Duplex Compact, 1923 – 1925. Green compact and puffs, mirror on lid. OSP, 98¢. CMV, $55.00. $70.00 MB.

Septette Gift Box, 1924 – 1929. Green box holds jar of Derma Cream, jar of Cerate, green box of face powder, rouge compact, can of talcum, 1 oz. bottle of toilet water, and flaconette of perfume. All in Daphne fragrance. OSP, $2.95. CMV, $550.00 MB.

Glycerine Soap, 1925.
Green box and wrapping with gold labels. Two bars of soap. OSP, 72¢. CMV, $90.00 MB.

Bath Salts, 1925.
Ribbed glass jar with brass lid, gold label. OSP, 98¢. CMV, $50.00 BO. $70.00 MB.

Perfume, 1925 – 1930.
Clear glass, brass cap, box is brown, yellow, and green. Came in Jack and Jill Jungle Jinks Set (see CPC sets). CMV, $60.00 MB.

Lipstick, 1925 – 1929.
2⅛" metal lipstick has embossed name and "CPC" on side. OSP, 39¢. CMV, $35.00 lipstick only, mint. $55.00 MB.

Eyebrow Pencil, 1925 – 1929.
Metal tube in box. CMV, $30.00 pencil only, mint. $60.00 MB.

Cerate, 1925 – 1929.
½" thick white glass jar, green lid. Came in Septette Gift Box. CMV, $40.00 mint. Also came in large size jar.

Cerate, 1926.
½" thick white glass jar, solid green lid reads "Daphne CPC Cerate" on top. Also came in Derma Cream. Came in Septette Gift Box Set. CMV, $35.00 each, mint.

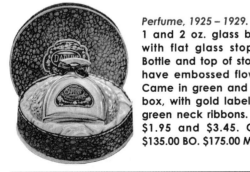

Perfume, 1925 – 1929.
1 and 2 oz. glass bottle with flat glass stopper. Bottle and top of stopper have embossed flowers. Came in green and gold box, with gold label and green neck ribbons. OSP, $1.95 and $3.45. CMV, $135.00 BO. $175.00 MB.

Derma Cream, 1925 – 1929.
½" thick white glass jar, green lid. Came in Septette Gift Box. CMV, $40.00 mint.

Creams, 1926.
Large and small size glass jars with gold and green labels and green lids. Came in Derma Cream and Rolling Massage Cream. Came in large size jars only. OSP, 72¢. CMV, $45.00 each, jar only. $60.00 each, MB.

Creams, 1928 – 1929.
Square white glass jars with ribbed sides and "CPC" on aluminum lids and gold labels. Came in Cerate, Derma Cream, and Rolling Massage Cream. OSP, 75¢ each. CMV, $40.00 each, jar only. $55.00 each, MB.

Talcum, 1935.
Silver can in Christmas box. OSP, 20¢. CMV, $20.00 CO. $40.00 MB.

Talcum, 1937 only, 51st Anniversary.
Special box was given to Avon customers with any purchase. CMV, $35.00 MB as shown.

Talcum, 1931 – 1936.
Silver and blue can with blue cap. OSP, 35¢. CMV, $20.00. $30.00 MB. Same can in gold color. CMV, $35.00. Silver and blue can in large, 1 lb. family size. OSP, $1.00. CMV, $30.00 CO. $40.00 MB.

Talcum, 1935 – 1936.
Silver can in two special boxes. "49 Years" box on left (1935) and "50th Year Celebration" box on right (1936). OSP, 20¢ each. CMV mint and boxed only, in either box, $50.00 each. Also came in gold can in 50th year box. CMV, $60.00 MB.

Talcum, 52nd Anniversary, 1938 only.
Turquoise and white can in special box sold for 10¢ during 52nd anniversary campaign. CMV, $35.00 in box shown.

Talcum, 1933 – 1936.
Metal can, came in sets only. CMV, $35.00 mint.

Talcum, 1936 – 1943, then 1946 – 1950.
14½ oz. turquoise and white can, turquoise cap. OSP, $1.19. CMV, $20.00 CO. $25.00 MB.

Talcum, 1936 – 1943, then 1946 – 1950.
2¾ oz. turquoise and white can, turquoise cap. OSP, 37¢. CMV, $8.00 CO. $10.00 MB.

Talcum, Maypole Box, 1940 only.
Yellow box with dancing girls around Maypole holds regular issue 2¾ oz. talcum can. Sold in May 1940 for 10¢ with regular order from Avon lady. CMV, $35.00 MB as shown.

Talcum Christmas Package, 1940 – 1941.
Outer sleeve fits over short issue blue Christmas box with white Christmas tree. Holds large size 14½ oz. metal talc, turquoise and white can. Can only sold 1936 – 1950. OSP, 89¢. CMV, $45.00 MB as shown.

Talcum Christmas Box, 1943.
Pale blue and pink outer box issued only at Christmas 1943 with cardboard large size talc with top and bottom cover caps. OSP, 98¢. $30.00 talc only, mint. CMV, $40.00 MB as shown.

Talcum, 1943 – 1946.
Turquoise and white paper box. No top cover, bottom cover, cap only. Family size. OSP, $1.19. CMV, $30.00 MB.

Talcum, 1944 – 1946.
Turquoise and white paper container, plastic cap. OSP, 39¢. CMV, $20.00 mint.

Mission Garden

Toilet Water, 1922 – 1925.
2 and 4 oz. glass bottle with frosted glass stopper. Gold label on front and neck. OSP, $2.25 and $4.35. CMV, $135.00 BO. $175.00 MB.

Sachet Powder, 1922 – 1925.
Glass bottle with brass cap and gold label. OSP, $1.75. CMV, $90.00 BO. $120.00 MB.

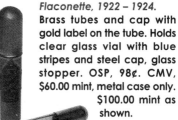

Flaconette, 1922 – 1924.
Brass tubes and cap with gold label on the tube. Holds clear glass vial with blue stripes and steel cap, glass stopper. OSP, 98¢. CMV, $60.00 mint, metal case only. $100.00 mint as shown.

Double Compact, 1922 – 1925.
Contains face powder and rouge. Made of solid brass. OSP, $1.45. CMV, $45.00 CO. $60.00 MB.

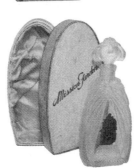

Perfume, 1922 – 1925.
1½ oz. Bohemian glass bottle with frosted sides and frosted glass stopper. Satin lined tan box. OSP, $4.95. CMV, $150.00 BO, mint. $200.00 MB.

Flaconette, 1922 – 1924.
Glass tube of perfume in brass case. Sold at Easter time. OSP, 98¢. CMV, $85.00 tube in case only, mint. $110.00 MB.

Talc Set, 1923.
Two cans of talc in a gift set given to CPC employees. Red and gold silk lined box. CMV, $235.00 MB.

Perfume, 1925 – 1926.
Flaconette, gold box, embossed glass bottle with glass stopper. Brass cap over stopper. OSP, $1.20. CMV, $95.00 BO. $115.00 MB.

Perfume, 1925.
1 oz. glass bottle, flat embossed glass stopper. Satin lined gold box. OSP, $2.85. CMV, $110.00 BO. $145.00 MB. Also came in 2 oz. size, $150.00 MB.

Talc, 1925.
4 oz. red and gold can, brass cap. CMV, $90.00 mint.

Compact, 1925.
"Mission Garden CPC" on edge of compact. Embossed brass case in single or double compact. OSP, 98¢ and $1.48. CMV, $50.00 compact only, mint. $65.00 each, MB.

Threesome Set, 1925.
Satin lined gold box holds 1 oz. perfume, talc, and gold compact. OSP, $7.00. CMV, $360.00 MB.

Narcissus

Perfume, 1925.
1 oz. glass bottle with frosted embossed glass stopper. Bottle in blue and gold box, blue label and neck ribbon. OSP, $2.19. CMV, $120.00 BO, mint. $180.00 MB.

Perfume, Flaconette, 1925 – 1929.
Embossed bottle with glass stopper with long glass dabber under brass cap. OSP, 84¢. CMV, $95.00 BO, mint. $115.00 MB.

Perfume, 1929 – 1930.
1 oz. glass stopper bottle. Came in silver, blue, and gold box. Blue label on top of bottle. OSP, $2.20. CMV, $110.00 BO. $185.00 MB.

Perfume, 1931 – 1934.
1 oz. glass stopper bottle came in silver and blue box, label on top of bottle. Same as 1929 perfume, only box is changed. OSP, $2.25. CMV, $115.00 BO. $150.00 MB.

Natoma/Natoma Rose

Massage Cream, 1911.
First issue, glass jar, cork lid stopper. Side, neck, and lid labels. OSP, 75¢. CMV, $165.00, $200.00 MB.

Talcum Powder, 1912 – 1915.
3½ oz. metal can. Label and cap a little different from 1915 issue. Different caps as shown. OSP, 25¢. CMV, $300.00 CO, mint. $360.00 MB as shown.

Natoma Rose Perfume, 1914 – 1915.
½ oz. glass stopper bottle with front and neck label. Green ribbon, green snap shut box. OSP, 40¢. CMV, $150.00 BO. $190.00 MB.

Rolling Massage Cream, 1912.
Green front label, white label on back side. Aluminum lid. Label does not say Natoma, only Indian Head and CPC. 5 oz. white glass jar. Rare. CMV, $170.00 mint.

Leather Table Cover, 1913.
Full size sheepskin leather cover with Natoma Indian head or male Indian head in center. Laid out like a baseball field. Given to reps for meeting sales goals. CMV, $425.00.

"The Art of Massage" booklet, 1913.
Ten-page booklet on giving a massage with Natoma Massage Cream. CMV, $40.00.

Sample, 1914 – 1918.
1 oz. bottle with atomizer. Green Natoma labels. Back label says bottle is a free sample. Rare. CMV, $210.00 mint.

Talcum, 1916 – 1921.
Three different, 4 oz. green can with pink roses, brass cap. One has green sifter cap, one has brass cap, and one has flowers painted on top of can and brass cap. OSP, 25¢. CMV, $200.00 each, can only, mint. $250.00 each, MB.

Perfume, 1914 – 1921.
Green box, holds 1, 2, or 4 oz. size glass stopper bottle with green front and neck label with green neck ribbon. OSP, $1.40, $2.75 and $5.25. CMV, $300.00 BO. $425.00 MB.

Talcum Powder, 1915.
Left: 2" tall, brass top. Came in 1915 Juvenile Set only. CMV, $300.00 mint. Also came in 3½ oz. regular size on right. OSP, 33¢. CMV, $300.00 mint.

Perfume, 1916.
½ oz. glass stopper bottle, green ribbon on neck, green neck and front label. Green box. OSP, 40¢. CMV, $150.00 BO, mint. $185.00 MB.

Perfume, 1914 – 1921.
1 oz., clear glass, glass stopper, green label. OSP, $1.40. CMV, $150.00 BO, mint. $195.00 MB.

Rose Perfume, 1915 – 1918.
1 oz. bottle, glass stopper, front and neck label. OSP, 60¢. CMV, $150.00 BO, mint. $195.00 MB.

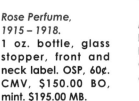

Rolling Massage Cream, 1918 – 1922.
Metal screw-on lid, green paper label. OSP, 75¢. CMV, $165.00 jar only. $195.00 MB.

Rolling Massage Cream, 1914 – 1917.
Glass stopper jar with front and neck label. OSP, 50¢. CMV, $175.00 jar only, mint. $215.00 MB.

Perfume, 1915 – 1918.
1 oz. glass stopper bottle, green front and neck label. Green neck ribbon, green felt box. OSP, 40¢. CMV, $150.00 BO, mint. $190.00 MB.

Rolling Massage Cream, 1918 – 1922.
Same as above jar, different lid. OSP, 75¢. CMV, $165.00 jar only. $195.00 MB.

Talcum Powder, 1914.
4 oz. blue can. 1914 – 1917 can had brass sifter cap with grooved edge. CMV, $70.00 can only. $90.00 MB.
1917 – 1929 can came with removable brass cap. OSP, 33¢. CMV, $45.00 can only, mint. $70.00 MB. Both came with "The Story of Italian Talc" in box. Two different labels on can. With the top section of can all gold, rare, CMV, $110.00 mint.

Talcum Powder Sample, 1914.
Small blue sample can, gold cap. Front of box in English and back side in French. CMV, $85.00 CO, mint. $105.00 MB.

Perfume, 1915 – 1922.
Fancy embossed box holds glass stopper bottle with front and neck label. Came in 1, 2, and 4 oz. sizes. OSP, $1.10, $2.10, and $4.00. CMV, $140.00 BO, mint. $185.00 MB.

Trailing Arbutus Toilet Water, 1915.
2 oz. clear glass bottle with blue and gold front and neck label. Metal crown stopper set in cork. OSP, 35¢. CMV, $140.00 BO, mint. $175.00 MB.

Sachet, 1915 – 1918.
Brass cap, flowered label, clear glass, two different labels. OSP, 60¢. CMV, $90.00 each, BO, mint. $115.00 MB.

Talcum Powder, 1920 – 1929. 16 oz. blue can, brass cap. OSP, 89¢. CMV, $70.00 CO, mint. $85.00 MB.

Brillantine, 1923. A hair dressing with Trailing Arbutus perfume scent. Glass bottle with frosted glass stopper. Also came with cork stopper. Blue front and neck labels. OSP, 39¢. CMV, $125.00 BO, mint. $160.00 MB.

Gift Box "T," 1915 – 1922. Red, green, and pink box contains talcum can, powder sachet, and 4 oz. toilet water. OSP, $1.25. CMV, $425.00.

Perfume, 1923. 2 oz. glass stopper bottle. Basket design on front and neck labels. OSP, $2.10. CMV, $125.00 BO, mint. $155.00 MB.

Threesome, 1923. Blue box contains 2 oz. bottle of toilet water, 4 oz. can of talcum, and bottle of sachet powder. OSP, $1.85. CMV, $375.00 MB.

Talcum Refill Can, 1918. 1 lb. metal can with brass finish. Front paper label. CMV, $85.00 mint.

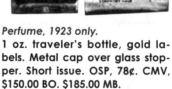

Bath Powder, 1920 – 1929. Blue, 1 lb. can with brass cap. This label says only "Trailing Arbutus Bath Powder." OSP, 89¢. CMV, $80.00 can only, mint. $95.00 MB.

Perfume, 1923 only. 1 oz. traveler's bottle, gold labels. Metal cap over glass stopper. Short issue. OSP, 78¢. CMV, $150.00 BO. $185.00 MB.

Perfume, 1923. ½ oz. bottle with crown glass stopper set in cork. Front and neck label. OSP, 59¢.

**Cold Cream Can,
1925 – 1930.**
Came in Jack and Jill Jungle Jinks Set (see CPC sets), gold can with blue and pink lid. Box is brown, yellow, and green. Also came in plain brown CPC box. CMV, $40.00 MB.

Cold Cream Sample, 1925.
Small sample tube in box marked "sample." Came with CPC instruction sheet. CMV, $40.00 tube only, mint. $65.00 MB.

Perfume, 1925.
1 and 2 oz. sizes. Ribbed bottle with glass stopper. Came in blue box. Front and neck label. OSP, $1.17 and $2.10. CMV, $115.00 BO. $145.00 MB.

*Powder Sachet,
1925 – 1929.*
Brass cap and blue and green label with pink flowers. Rare label is all pink with black border. (Same CMV.) OSP, 72¢. CMV, $90.00 BO, mint. $115.00 MB.

Face Powder, 1925.
Blue box. OSP 33¢. CMV, $40.00 powder box only, mint. $55.00 MB.

*Vegetable Oil Soap,
1925 – 1929.*
Blue box holds three embossed soap bars. OSP, 39¢. CMV, $110.00 MB.

*Vegetable Oil Soap Sample,
1925.*
Small, 2" x 1⅛" size sample bar. CMV, $55.00 mint.

Toilet Water, 1925.
2 and 4 oz. sizes. Ribbed bottle with metal and cork cap. OSP, 59¢ and $1.08. CMV, $80.00 BO. $105.00 MB.

Bath Powder, 1925 – 1929.
4¾ oz. blue can and cap. OSP, 35¢. CMV, $65.00 can only, mint. $85.00 MB.

Creams,
1925 – 1927.
Large and small round white glass jars with CPC on blue lids. Came in Cold Cream and Vanishing Cream. OSP, 33¢ and 59¢. CMV, $45.00 each, jar only. $65.00 each, MB.

Cold Cream Tube,
1925.
Came in large and small sizes. Blue tubes. OSP, 23¢ and 45¢. CMV, $35.00 tube only, mint. $50.00 MB.

Perfume, 1928 – 1929.
Came in 1 and 2 oz. glass stopper bottle with blue label. Blue box. OSP, $1.20 and $2.10. CMV, $120.00 BO, mint. $160.00 MB.

Sextette Box, 1925 – 1929.
Box only, showing label in center of box. CMV, $40.00 box only, mint.

Perfume Flacon, 1926.
Frosted ribbed glass with long glass stopper under CPC embossed brass cap. Front paper label. OSP, 59¢. CMV, $90.00 BO, mint with brass cap and label. $110.00 MB.

Rouge, 1928 – 1929,
Blue box. OSP, 40¢. CMV, $30.00 rouge only, mint. $35.00 MB.

Sextette Gift Box, 1925 – 1927.
Blue box holds two bars of Vegetable Oil Soap, Cold Cream jar, Vanishing Cream jar, box of Face Powder, and can of Talcum Powder. All are trimmed in blue and have Trailing Arbutus labels. OSP, $1.60. CMV, $385.00 MB.

Creams, 1928 – 1929.
Large and small white glass jars of Cold Cream and Vanishing Cream. "CPC" on blue or plain aluminum metal lids. OSP, 33¢ and 59¢. CMV, $45.00 jar only, mint. $60.00 each, MB.

Sextette Set, 1928 – 1929.
Large blue box holds white glass jars of cold cream and vanishing cream (both have blue lids), blue can of talcum powder, blue box of face powder, and two bars of vegetable oil soap. OSP, $1.59. CMV, $425.00 MB.

Perfume, 1940 – 1942.
3/8 oz. bottle, gold octagonal cap, gold speckled box. OSP, $1.50. CMV, $50.00 BO, mint. $85.00 MB.

Face Powder, 1928 – 1929.
Blue and pink box. OSP, 35¢. CMV, $35.00 powder box only, mint. $45.00 MB. Same design as Rouge.

Toilet Water, 1933 – 1934.
2 oz. ribbed glass, black cap. Silver label. OSP, 75¢. CMV, $50.00 BO, mint. $65.00 MB.

Perfume, 1941 – 1945.
1/8 oz. bottle, white paper label, brass cap. OSP, $1.00. CMV, $25.00 BO, mint. $40.00 MB.

Perfume, 1930.
1/2 oz. bottle with frosted glass stopper, silver label. CMV, $95.00 mint.

Trailing Arbutus Perfume, 1933 – 1936.
Small six-sided octagonal bottle and black cap, came in Little Folks Set and Handkerchief Set. Silver label. Came with CPC or CPC Avon Products, Inc. division label. CMV, $35.00 mint.

Vernafleur

Perfume Extract, 1923.
¼ oz. glass bottle with glass stopper. Neck label and ribbon. OSP, 48¢. CMV, $80.00 BO, mint. $100.00 MB.

Tissue Creme, 1924 – 1926.
White glass jar with ribs on sides. "CPC" on metal lid. Large and small size jars. OSP, 48¢ and 89¢. CMV, $40.00 each, jar only, mint. $50.00 each, MB.

Vernatalc, 1923 – 1926.
4 oz. can of talcum powder, gray. OSP, 30¢. CMV, $60.00 can only, mint. $75.00 MB.

Toilet Water, 1923 –1924.
2 or 4 oz. glass bottle with metal and cork shaker cap. OSP, 74¢ and $1.35. CMV, $90.00 each, BO, mint. $110.00 each, MB.

Nutri Creme, 1924 – 1926.
Large and small white glass jar with ribs on sides. "CPC" on metal lid. OSP, 48¢ and 89¢. CMV, $40.00 each, jar only, mint. $50.00 each, MB.

Samples, 1923.
Four different small glass vials with cork stoppers. One is 1½", one is 2" high, and the fat one is 1¾" high. "Not for sale" on labels. CMV, $75.00 each, mint.

Perfume, 1924 – 1926.
Gray box holds 1 oz. ribbed glass bottle with frosted glass stopper. Front and neck label. Green ribbon on neck. 1 oz. size, OSP, $1.44. 2 oz. size, OSP, $2.70. CMV, $110.00 each, BO, mint. $135.00 each, MB.

Adherent Powder, 1923.
Gray metal can. OSP, 48¢. CMV, $35.00 can only, mint. $45.00 MB.

Threesome Gift Box, 1924 – 1926.
Gray box holds 2 oz. bottle of Vernafleur Toilet Water, jar of Vanishing Cream, and can of Face Powder. OSP, $2.10. CMV, $240.00 MB.

Toilet Soap, 1925 – 1928.
Gray box and wrapping holds three bars. OSP, 69¢. CMV, $110.00 MB.

Nutri-Creme Sample, 1925.
Multicolored tube, says on back side "not for sale, sample." CMV, $35.00 TO. $50.00 MB.

Perfume Flacon, 1925.
Brass cap over glass stopper with long glass dabber. OSP, 69¢. CMV, $75.00 BO. $100.00 MB.

Face Powder Sample, 1927.
1½" small paper box used as sample. CMV, $50.00 mint.

Toilet Water, 1925 – 1926.
2 or 4 oz. ribbed glass bottle with metal and cork cap. OSP, 74¢ and $1.35. CMV, $85.00 each, BO. $105.00 each, MB.

Face Powder, 1927 – 1930.
Blue, yellow, and black metal can. OSP, 48¢. CMV, $15.00 can only, mint. $40.00 MB. This was also called Vernafleur Adherent Powder.

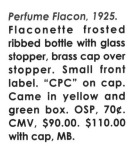

Perfume Flacon, 1925.
Flaconette frosted ribbed bottle with glass stopper, brass cap over stopper. Small front label. "CPC" on cap. Came in yellow and green box. OSP, 70¢. CMV, $90.00. $110.00 with cap, MB.

Bath Salts, 1927 – 1929.
Clear glass, brass cap. Sent to representatives to give to each customer that ordered $2.00 worth of merchandise. Representative had to attain $45.00 in customer sales on January 1927 order. Offer expired Jan. 31, 1927. (Not a sample). Rare. CMV, $150.00 BO, mint. $185.00 MB as shown with paper.

Tissue Cream, 1928.
Small and large size white glass jar with ribbed sides. Came with or without "CPC" on aluminum lid. OSP, 50¢ and 90¢. CMV, $40.00 jar only, mint. $55.00 MB.

Toilet Water, 1928.
4 oz., ribbed glass, CPC brass crown top, front and neck label. OSP, $1.35. CMV, $90.00 BO, mint. $115.00 MB.

Atomizer Perfume, 1928.
2 oz., 5¾" tall. Green frosted bottle with gold plated top. Came in Vernafleur perfume. Is not marked Avon or CPC. OSP, $2.50. CMV, $80.00 BO, mint. $110.00 MB.

Vernatalc, 1928.
4 oz. multicolored can, brass cap. OSP, $1.15. CMV, $75.00 can only, mint. $95.00 MB.

Perfume, 1928.
1 oz. ribbed clear glass bottle, frosted glass stopper, front label, neck ribbon. OSP, $1.17. CMV, $110.00 BO, mint. $140.00 MB.

Face Powder Sample, 1928.
Adherent Powder sample. Came several in a box. OSP, 48¢ per box of samples. CMV, $25.00 per box.

Perfume, 1928.
1 oz. glass stopper bottle, blue, yellow, and black box. OSP, $1.45. CMV, $110.00 BO, mint. $150.00 MB.

Compact, 1928.
Silver compact with "Vernafleur" on lid. Single and double compact. OSP, $1.00 and $1.50. CMV, $40.00 compact only, mint. $55.00 MB.

Toilet Soap, 1928 – 1931.
Box holds three bars of soap in blue paper. OSP, 75¢. CMV, $90.00 MB.

Bath Salts, 1928 – 1930. 10 oz. glass bottle with brass lid, ribbed glass sides. OSP, 75¢. CMV, $70.00 jar only, mint. $85.00 MB.

Bath Set, 1929. Black and gold box holds bottle of Vernafleur Bath Salts, Dusting Powder in gold and black striped can, and one bar of Vegetable Oil Soap. OSP, $3.50. CMV, $275.00 MB.

Bath Salts, 1931 – 1935. 8½ oz., ribbed glass, navy blue cap, silver and blue label. OSP, 63¢. CMV, $40.00 BO, mint. $60.00 MB.

Atomizer Gift Set, 1933. Blue box with green and red holly leaves holds 1 oz. bottle of Vernafleur perfume with small silver label and 1 oz. red glass bottle with spray atomizer. OSP, $2.86. CMV, $190.00 MB.

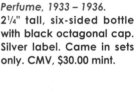

Perfume, 1933 – 1936. 2¼" tall, six-sided bottle with black octagonal cap. Silver label. Came in sets only. CMV, $30.00 mint.

Quintette Set, 1929. Blue, black, and gold box holds Vernafleur Tissue Cream and Nutri-Cream, Face Powder, Talc, and flaconette of perfume. OSP, $2.25. CMV, $375.00 MB.

Toilet Soap, 1931 – 1936. Lavender in color, in white wrapper. Box of three bars. OSP, 75¢. CMV, $60.00 MB.

Toilet Soap, 1936 – 1939. Turquoise and white box and wrapping holds three violet colored bars. OSP, 77¢. CMV, $60.00 MB.

Christmas Cheer, 1929. Red, white and blue boxes of Vernafleur Sachet Powder. Came in sets of four boxes. OSP, $1.20. CMV, $50.00 each box.

Perfume, 1931 – 1933. 1 oz. bottle with plastic sealed cork stopper, silver and blue label. Silver box. CMV, $70.00 BO, mint. $100.00 MB.

Bath Salts, 1946. 9 oz. jar, turquoise lid. Short issue. Special blue and white label. OSP, 63¢. CMV, $40.00 jar only. $65.00 MB.

Violet ··

See CPC Jars for other Violet products.

Almond Meal, 1893.
8 oz. glass jar with metal lid. OSP, 50¢. CMV, $135.00 jar only, mint. $185.00 MB.

Almond Meal, 1908.
8 oz. glass jar with metal lid. OSP, 50¢. CMV, $115.00 jar only, mint. $150.00 MB. 1910 issue same, only Eureka trademark in place of CP at top of label.

Talcum Powder, 1912.
Blue paper sides, metal shaker top and metal bottom. Eureka trademark label. CMV, $85.00 mint.

Perfume, 1896.
New York label. Eureka trademark. Round glass stopper. Colored flower box. CMV, $175.00 BO. $210.00 MB.

Talcum Powder, 1908.
3½ oz. glass jar with metal cap has two variations of labels. OSP, 25¢. CMV, $110.00 jar only, mint. $145.00 MB.

Almond Meal, 1907.
8 oz. clear glass, metal shaker top. OSP, 50¢. CMV, $135.00 jar only, mint. $175.00 MB.

Nutri-Creme, 1912.
Small and large size white glass jars with aluminum lids. OSP, 50¢ and 90¢. CMV, $45.00 each, jar only, mint. $55.00 each, MB.

Water, 1908.
8 oz. glass bottle, glass stopper. Eureka trademark label in color. Neck ribbon. CMV, $180.00.

Nutri-Creme, 1910.
White glass jar, aluminum lid. Paper label all around jar. Bottom pat. Dec. 9, 1890. OSP, 50¢. CMV, $55.00 jar only, mint. $65.00 MB.

Almond Meal, 1912.
Glass jar with metal shaker lid. Came in 3½ oz. and 3¾ oz. sizes. Two different labels. OSP, 50¢. CMV, $110.00 jar only. $150.00 MB.

Toilet Water, 1915. 2 oz. bottle, metal crown stopper in cork, front and neck label. OSP, 35¢. CMV, $100.00 BO, mint. $135.00 MB.

Gift Set H, 1915. Green, white, and purple box contains bottle of talcum, 1 oz. perfume bottle with cork stopper and atomizer, and powder sachet. OSP, $1.35. CMV, $450.00 MB.

Talcum, 1923. 3⅓ oz. violet and green colored can, brass cap. OSP, 23¢. CMV, $75.00 CO, mint. $95.00 MB.

Nutri-Creme, 1923. Large and small white glass jars with CPC on metal lid. OSP, 49¢ and 89¢. CMV, $45.00 each, CO. $55.00 MB.

Toilet Water, 1915. ¼ oz. clear glass, cork stopper. Came only in 1915 Juvenile Set (see CPC sets). Rare. CMV, $125.00 mint.

Talcum Powder, 1915. 3½ oz. glass jar, OSP, 25¢. CMV, $95.00 BO. $130.00 MB.

Perfume, 1915. Front and neck label, glass crown stopper in cork. OSP, 50¢. CMV, $175.00 mint.

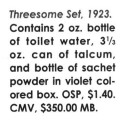

Almond Meal, 1923. 4 oz. sifter top metal can. Two different labels. OSP, 48¢. CMV, $60.00 CO. $75.00 MB.

Perfume, 1915. 1 oz. size, cork stopper. Used with spray atomizer. Came in 1915 Gift Set H only. CMV, $100.00 mint.

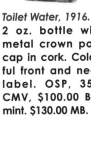

Toilet Water, 1916. 2 oz. bottle with metal crown pour cap in cork. Colorful front and neck label. OSP, 35¢. CMV, $100.00 BO, mint. $130.00 MB.

Threesome Set, 1923. Contains 2 oz. bottle of toilet water, 3⅓ oz. can of talcum, and bottle of sachet powder in violet colored box. OSP, $1.40. CMV, $350.00 MB.

Baby Items

Baby Powder, 1898. Metal can. Eureka trademark on label. OSP, 25¢. CMV, $120.00 CO, mint. $145.00 MB.

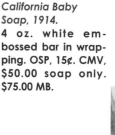

California Baby Soap, 1914. 4 oz. white embossed bar in wrapping. OSP, 15¢. CMV, $50.00 soap only. $75.00 MB.

Baby Set, 1910. Box with kids playing on lid holds 1905 baby powder can, 2 oz. bottle of Violet toilet water, and box of baby soap. OSP, 75¢. CMV, $375.00 MB.

Baby Set, 1916. Baby Set box holds can of baby powder as pictured above, bar of baby soap, and 2 oz. bottle of Violet toilet water. OSP, 75¢. CMV, $365.00 MB.

California Baby Soap, 1902. Box with one bar. OSP, 15¢. CMV, $85.00 mint.

Baby Powder, 1905. Metal can, lift-off cap. 1906 cap has sifter top, "CP" in center of trademark. 1910 can has similar sifter cap, and Eureka trademark in place of "CP." CMV, $115.00 CO. $140.00 MB.

Baby Powder, 1912 – 1916. Blue and pink can. OSP, 25¢. CMV, $110.00 CO, mint. $135.00 MB.

Baby Set, 1923. Yellow box contains 2 oz. bottle of toilet water, bar of baby soap, and can of baby powder. OSP, 99¢. CMV, $125.00 toilet water only, mint. $350.00 MB.

Baby Powder, 1923.
4 oz. yellow can. OSP,
29¢. CMV, $80.00 CO.
$95.00 MB.

Baby Set, 1925.
Yellow box holds 4 oz.
bottle of Supreme Olive
Oil, 4 oz. yellow can of
baby powder, yellow
box of boric acid, and 5
oz. yellow cake of gen-
uine imported Castile
soap. OSP, $1.78. CMV,
$350.00 MB.

Supreme Olive Oil
for Babies, 1925.
4 oz. bottle with yel-
low label and cork
stopper. Came in
1925 Baby Set only.
CMV, $100.00 mint.

Boric Acid for Baby, 1925.
Yellow box with soldiers
on top. OSP, 33¢. CMV,
$50.00.

Castile Soap for Babies,
1925.
5 oz. cake wrapped in
yellow paper. Came
in Baby Set only. CMV,
$75.00 mint.

Bay Rum

Also see Avon Bay Rum section. All bottles priced mint.

Superior Bay Rum,
1892 – 1897.
4 oz. and 8 oz., cork
stoppers. "126 Cham-
bers St." on label,
where CPC started.
Very rare. CMV, $200.00
BO, 4 oz. $240.00 MB,
4 oz. $250.00 BO, 8 oz.
$300.00 MB, 8 oz.

Superior Bay Rum,
1898 – 1900.
4 oz. clear glass square bottle. Glass
stopper, colored label. OSP, 40¢.
CMV, $240.00 BO. $285.00 MB.

Superior Bay Rum, 1898.
4 oz. bottle, "126 Cham-
bers St., New York" ad-
dress on label. Chrome
crown stopper in cork.
CMV, $175.00 mint.

Superior Bay Rum,
1901 – 1904.
4 oz. glass stopper bottle.
OSP, 40¢. CMV, $150.00. Also
came in 8 and 16 oz. sizes
with glass stoppers. OSP, 75¢
and $1.25. CMV, $150.00
each, BO. $200.00 each, MB.

1905.
4 oz. glass stopper.
CMV, $140.00 mint.

1912.
16 oz., clear glass,
cork stopper. Rare.
CMV, $150.00 BO.
$175.00 MB.

1915.
4 oz. bottle with crown
metal and cork stop-
per. OSP, 25¢. CMV,
$125.00 BO, mint.
$150.00 MB.

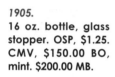

1905.
16 oz. bottle, glass
stopper. OSP, $1.25.
CMV, $150.00 BO,
mint. $200.00 MB.

1912.
4 oz. glass stop-
per bottle. Also
came in 8 and 16
oz. size glass stop-
per bottles. OSP,
40¢. CMV, $140.00
each, BO, mint.
$165.00 MB.

1915.
4 oz. bottle, glass stop-
per. CPC logo label.
CMV, $125.00 mint.

1908.
4 oz. glass stopper bottle. OSP,
40¢. CMV, $140.00 BO. $175.00
MB. Also came in 8 and 16 oz.
sizes shown below.

1920.
4 oz. clear glass
bottle, glass stopper.
CMV, $110.00 BO,
mint. $145.00 MB.

1908.
4 oz., 8 oz., and 1 pint (16 oz.)
glass stopper bottles. OSP, 40¢
each. CMV, $170.00 BO, 8 oz.
$200.00 MB, 8 oz. CMV, $200.00
BO, 16 oz. $225.00 MB, 16 oz.

1921.
4 oz., front and
neck label, cork
stopper. OSP, 47¢.
CMV, $125.00 BO.
$175.00 MB.

1923.
4 oz. bottle, metal shaker cap in cork. OSP, 47¢. CMV, $85.00 BO. $95.00 MB. Also came in 8 oz. OSP, 84¢. 32 oz., $2.40. CMV, $95.00 each, BO. $110.00 each, MB.

1927 – 1929.
16 oz., metal cap. OSP, $1.44. CMV, $95.00 BO. $110.00 MB.

1930 – 1936.
4 oz. ribbed glass bottle with black cap and green label. OSP, 50¢. CMV, $35.00 BO. $45.00 MB. Also came in 16 oz. size, OSP, 89¢. CMV, $50.00 BO. $60.00 MB.

1927 – 1929.
4 oz., metal and cork CPC embossed stopper. Front and neck label. Also came in 8 oz. and 16 oz. sizes with cork stopper. OSP, 50¢. CMV, $100.00 BO. 4, 8, and 16 oz. sizes, $120.00 each, BO. Add $25.00 for box, mint.

1930 – 1936.
8 oz. clear glass bottle, black cap, green and black label. OSP, 89¢. CMV, $40.00 BO, mint. $50.00 MB.

1936.
4 oz. bottle sold 1930 – 1936. Yellow label, black cap. Shown with red and green Christmas box. *Good HouseKeeping* on label. CMV, $40.00 BO. $65.00 MB as shown.

Bottles

Witch Hazel,
1900 – 1905.
4 and 8 oz. bottles came with sprinkler top. OSP, 25¢ and 45¢. CMV, $100.00. Pint bottle came with glass stopper. OSP, 75¢. CMV, $150.00 BO, mint. $200.00 MB.

Lait Virginal, 1900.
2 oz., cork stopper. OSP, 60¢. CMV, $115.00 BO. $150.00 MB.

California Nail Bleach, 1900.
1 oz., Eureka trademark, New York label. Glass stopper. CMV, $135.00 BO, mint.

Eau de Quinine Hair Tonic, 1902.
Glass stopper in cork. Eureka trademark on neck label. OSP, 65¢. CMV, $125.00 BO. $150.00 MB.

Eau de Quinine, 1906.
6 oz. glass bottle with metal crown and cork cap. OSP, 65¢. CMV, $100.00 BO. $145.00 MB.

Eau de Quinine Hair Tonic, 1908.
Glass bottle has cork stopper with metal cap. Front and neck label. Label has Eureka CP trademark. OSP, 65¢. CMV, $125.00 BO. $150.00 MB.

Tooth Wash, 1902 – 1905.
Glass bottle has cork stopper with metal crown top. Eureka trademark on neck label. OSP, 25¢. CMV, $115.00 BO, mint. $140.00 MB.

Witch Hazel, 1908.
16 oz., glass stopper. OSP, 75¢. CMV, $150.00 BO, mint. $200.00 MB.

Face Lotion, 1908.
Glass bottle with cork stopper. OSP, $1.00. CMV, $110.00, BO. $145.00 MB.

Face Lotion, 1903.
Glass bottle, cork stopper, front and neck label. OSP, $1.00. CMV, $110.00 BO. $145.00 MB.

Witch Hazel, 1905.
16 oz., glass stopper. OSP, 75¢. CMV, $150.00 BO, mint. $200.00 MB.

Witch Hazel, 1908.
Came in 4, 8, and 16 oz. bottles with glass stoppers. Eureka trademark on label. OSP, 25¢, 45¢, and 75¢. CMV, $150.00 BO, mint. $200.00 MB.

Lait Virginal, 1908.
2 oz. ribbed glass bottle has ribbed glass stopper set in cork. OSP, 65¢. CMV, $150.00 BO, mint. $185.00 MB.

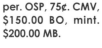

Liquid Rouge, 1908. Eureka trademark on label and "CP" in center of early label instead of Eureka. OSP, 25¢. CMV, $100.00 BO. $125.00 MB.

Nail Bleach, 1912. 1 oz., cork stopper. OSP, 25¢. CMV, $100.00 BO. $120.00 MB.

Liquid Shampoo, 1914. 6 oz. glass bottle with metal cap. OSP, 35¢. CMV, $95.00 BO. $120.00 MB.

Witch Hazel, 1910. 16 oz., clear glass, glass stopper. OSP, 75¢. CMV, $150.00 BO. $175.00 MB.

Face Lotion, 1912. 6 oz. clear glass bottle, cork stopper. Front and neck label. Came in white and pink shades. OSP, $1.00. CMV, $100.00 BO. $125.00 MB.

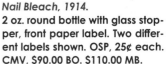

Lait Virginal, 1910. 2 oz., metal crown in cork stopper. Also came in 4 and 8 oz. sizes. Front and neck labels. OSP, 65¢, $1.25, and $2.00. CMV, $100.00 BO, mint. $125.00 MB.

Nail Bleach, 1912. 2 oz. clear glass round bottle, cork stopper, front and neck label. OSP, 25¢. CMV, $95.00 BO. $110.00 MB.

Nail Bleach, 1914. 2 oz. round bottle with glass stopper, front paper label. Two different labels shown. OSP, 25¢ each. CMV, $90.00 BO. $110.00 MB.

Witch Hazel, 1910. 8 oz. size glass stopper. CMV, $125.00 mint.

Witch Hazel, 1913. Rare 16 oz. jug, clear glass, cork stopper. 7" high. OSP, 75¢. CMV, $140.00 mint as shown.

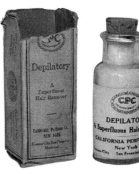

Depilatory, 1914. 1 oz. bottle with cork stopper. OSP, 50¢. CMV, $100.00. $120.00 MB.

Benzoin Lotion, 1915.
2 oz. size, metal crown stopper in cork. Flowered label. OSP, 75¢. Also came in 4 oz. size, OSP, $1.50. CMV, $100.00 each, BO, mint. $125.00 each, MB.

Eyebrow Pencil, 1915.
Wood box holds metal pencil. Has CPC label and tax stamp. CMV, $50.00 mint as shown.

Nail Bleach, 1916.
2 oz., glass stopper, square bottle. Rare. OSP, 25¢. CMV, $125.00 BO. $150.00 MB.

Witch Hazel, 1915.
4 oz. glass bottle with cork stopper. OSP, 25¢. CMV, $90.00. Also came in 8 and 16 oz. sizes with glass stoppers. OSP, 45¢ and 75¢. CMV $125.00 each, BO, mint. $145.00 each, MB.

Liquid Rouge, 1916.
Glass bottle, cork stopper. OSP, 25¢. CMV, $80.00 BO. $100.00 MB.

Lotus Cream, 1917.
12 oz. bottle has glass stopper. OSP, $1.23. CMV, $160.00. 4 oz. bottle has cork stopper. Both have front and neck labels. Also came in 1 quart, ½ gallon, and 1 gallon sizes. OSP, 48¢. CMV, $120.00. Add $25.00 MB each.

Tooth Wash, 1915.
Glass bottle with metal and cork cap. Back side of bottle is embossed "California Tooth Wash." OSP, 25¢. CMV, $25.00 BO, embossed. $110.00 with mint label. $140.00 MB.

Lotus Cream Sample, 1917.
Blue and white box holds ½ oz. sample bottle with cork stopper. Blue label. CMV, $65.00 BO, mint. $80.00 MB.

Face Lotion, 1918.
6 oz. glass bottle has cork stopper, green front and neck labels. Came with small sponge tied to neck. OSP, $1.00. CMV, $80.00 BO. $100.00 MB.

Tooth Wash, 1921.
2 oz. glass bottle, brass and cork stopper. OSP, 25¢. CMV, $100.00 BO. $135.00 MB.

Face Lotion, 1923.
6 oz. glass bottle, blue label, cork stopper. OSP, 97¢. CMV, $80.00 BO. $100.00 MB.

Liquid Face Powder, 1920.
6 oz. clear glass, cork stopper, green front and neck labels. OSP, 97¢. CMV, $80.00 BO, mint. $100.00 MB.

Benzoin Lotion, 1923.
2 oz. bottle with metal and cork stopper. OSP, 59¢. CMV, $75.00 BO. $100.00 MB.

Witch Hazel, 1923.
16 oz., cork stopper. CMV, $85.00 BO, mint.

Witch Hazel, 1920.
16 oz., clear glass, cork stopper. Front label. Rare. OSP, 75¢. CMV, $135.00 BO, mint. $160.00 MB. Also came in 8 oz. size with metal crown and cork stopper. OSP, 45¢. CMV, $100.00 BO, mint. $125.00 MB.

Liquid Shampoo, 1923.
6 oz. front and neck labels. Metal shaker cap in cork. OSP, 48¢. CMV, $90.00 BO. $120.00 MB.

Eau de Quinine, 1923.
6 oz. glass bottle, metal shaker cap in cork. OSP, 69¢. CMV, $90.00 BO. $110.00 MB.

Witch Hazel, 1923.
4 oz. bottle with cork stopper, green front and neck label. OSP, 39¢. CMV, $75.00. Also came in 8, 16, and 32 oz. sizes. OSP, 69¢, $1.20, and $2.25. CMV, $75.00 each, BO, mint. Add $25.00 each, MB.

Cutrane, 1924.
Glass bottle with cork stopper with camel hair brush on stopper. Gold and black label. OSP, 30¢. CMV, $70.00 BO, mint. $85.00 MB.

Rose Water, Glycerine and Benzoin Sample, 1924.
Glass bottle, cork stopper. CMV, $60.00 BO, mint. $75.00 MB.

Tooth Wash, 1923.
2 oz. glass bottle, metal and cork cap. Front and neck labels. OSP, 33¢. CMV, $85.00 BO. $110.00 MB.

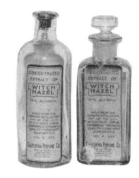

Witch Hazel, 1924.
Both bottles are 8 oz. size, same label. Left has cork stopper and right has glass stopper. CMV, $85.00 cork stopper, round bottle. $110.00 for glass stopper, square bottle.

Rose Water, Glycerine and Benzoin, 1924 – 1925.
6 oz. bottle with cork stopper. Front and neck labels. This was a very short issue bottle. OSP, 60¢. CMV, $100.00 BO. $125.00 MB.

Rose Water, Glycerine and Benzoin, 1923.
6 oz. clear glass bottle. Glass stopper set in cork. Printed front and neck label. OSP, 60¢. CMV, $100.00 BO. $125.00 MB.

Witch Hazel, 1925.
4 oz. bottle with cork stopper, green label on front and neck. OSP, 39¢. CMV, $75.00 each, BO, mint. Add $25.00 each, MB.

Witch Hazel, 1924.
4 oz. clear glass bottle, cork stopper. Front and neck label, three different labels, two shown. OSP, 39¢. CMV, $75.00 BO, mint. $90.00 MB.

Rose Water, Glycerine and Benzoin Sample, 1925.
Small sample bottle on first introduction of this product in January 1925. Rare. CMV, $75.00 BO. $85.00 MB.

Nulodor, 1927 – 1929.
Bottle has clear stopper, front and neck labels. Rare. OSP, 35¢. CMV, $120.00 BO, mint.

Rose Water, Glycerine and Benzoin, 1929 only.
4 oz. clear glass ribbed bottle with black cap. Bottle came from Avon with small sample, pink label marked "not for resale." Bottle with this label rare. CMV, $100.00 BO, mint.

Benzoin Lotion, 1925.
2 oz. ribbed glass bottle with metal and cork stopper, blue and gold label. OSP, 59¢. CMV, $75.00 BO. $95.00 MB.

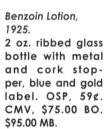

Lotus Cream, 1925.
4 oz. ribbed bottle with cork stopper, front and neck labels. OSP, 48¢. CMV, $85.00 BO, mint. $100.00 MB.

Gertrude Recordon's Peach Lotion, 1929 only.
Clear glass. Box states "This merchandise sent free for demonstration purposes or personal use. It must not be sold." CMV, $85.00 BO. $100.00 MB.

Brilliantine, 1930 only.
2 oz. bottle with frosted glass stopper in cork. Silver label. OSP, 50¢. CMV, $75.00 BO, mint. $95.00 MB.

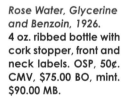

Rose Water, Glycerine and Benzoin, 1926.
4 oz. ribbed bottle with cork stopper, front and neck labels. OSP, 50¢. CMV, $75.00 BO, mint. $90.00 MB.

Cuticle Softener, 1929 – 1930.
½ oz. bottle with brown label and cork stopper with glass dabber. Also came in Boudoir Set. OSP, 35¢. CMV, $70.00 BO. $85.00 MB.

Deodorant, 1930 only.
2 oz. bottle with corked frosted glass stopper. OSP, 50¢. CMV, $80.00 BO. $100.00 MB.

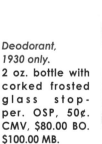

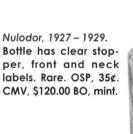

Witch Hazel, 1930.
4 oz. ribbed glass bottle, black cap, green label. Rare. CMV, $80.00 BO. $90.00 MB.

Rose Water, Glycerine and Benzoin, 1930.
4 oz. ribbed glass, black screw-on cap, color label. CMV, $75.00 BO.

Hair Tonic Eau de Quinine, 1931 – 1936. Ribbed glass bottle with black cap and silver label. OSP, 90¢. CMV, $40.00 BO. $45.00 MB. Also came in 16 oz. size. OSP, $1.75. CMV, $50.00 BO, mint. $60.00 MB.

Jars

Lavender Salts, 1890s.
Teal green glass, octagonal shaped bottle. Round glass stopper. Rare. OSP, 35¢. CMV, $275.00 jar only. $320.00 MB.

Shampoo Cream, 1896.
4 oz. glass jar. Picture of man washing his hair on lid. Rare. OSP, 35¢. CMV, $135.00 jar only. $165.00 MB.

Rose Pomade, 1900. Eureka trademark. Same in CPC sets. White glass, top and side paper labels. CMV, $65.00 mint.

Lavender Salts, 1890s.
Emerald green glass, glass stopper with screw-on metal top. Rare. OSP, 35¢. CMV, $275.00 jar only. $320.00 MB.

Shampoo Cream, 1900 – 1906.
4 oz. white glass jar, metal lid. OSP, 35¢. CMV, $100.00 jar only. $135.00 MB.

California Shampoo Cream, 1900.
Both 4 oz. glass jars, metal lids are different sizes. One plain, one with man washing his hair and "CPC." Both have plain paper flower design front labels. CMV, $100.00 for plain lid. $125.00 with man's head lid.

Cold Cream, 1896.
White glass jar with metal lid. Eureka trademark on label. OSP, 25¢. CMV, $90.00 jar only, mint. $110.00 MB.

Lavender Salts. 1901 – 1905. Emerald green glass bottle with green glass stopper, leather liner. OSP, 35¢. CMV, $200.00 jar only, mint. $240.00 MB.

California Cold Cream, 1908. 2 oz. white glass jar with metal lid. OSP, 25¢. CMV, $80.00 jar only, mint. $95.00 MB.

Massage Cream, 1912. Glass jar with glass stopper. OSP, 75¢. CMV, $150.00 jar only, mint. $185.00 MB.

Shampoo Cream, 1908. 4 oz. white glass jar with metal lid. OSP, 35¢. CMV, $75.00 jar only. $100.00 MB.

Tooth Powder, 1908. White glass bottle with metal cap. OSP, 25¢. CMV, $110.00 BO, mint. $135.00 MB.

Lavender Salts, 1908. Green glass bottle and stopper with rubber base. OSP, 35¢. CMV, $160.00 BO, mint. $195.00 MB.

Lavender Salts, 1912. Glass stopper bottle. OSP, 35¢. CMV, $110.00 BO. $145.00 MB.

Bandoline, 1908. 2 oz. glass bottle, cork stopper. OSP, 25¢. CMV, $90.00 BO. $110.00 MB.

Rouge, 1908. Rouge powder can. Eureka trademark on label and "CP" in center of early label instead of Eureka. OSP, 25¢. CMV, $50.00 CO. $70.00 MB.

Lavender Salts, 1910. Emerald green glass. Same label only one bottle is ⅛" bigger than the other. Green glass stoppers set in rubber. OSP, 35¢. CMV, $200.00 each, BO, mint. $245.00 each, MB.

Lavender Salts, 1915.
Glass stopper bottle.
OSP, 35¢. CMV, $115.00
BO, mint. $150.00 MB.

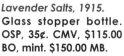

Shampoo Cream, 1912.
4 oz. white glass jar,
metal lid, with or with-
out "CPC" on lid. Early
issue 1912 has Eureka
trademark on box
— 1915 one does not.
OSP, 35¢. CMV, $80.00
jar only. $95.00 MB
for Eureka trademark,
$10.00 less without it.

Bandoline, 1915.
Glass bottle with
cork stopper. OSP,
25¢. CMV, $75.00 jar
only, mint. $90.00
MB.

Shampoo Cream
Sample, 1915.
Small 1" size aluminum
round bottom container.
Rare. CMV, $50.00 mint.

Cold Creams,
1915 – 1922.
Large and small
white glass jars with
"CPC" on metal lids.
OSP, 25¢ and 45¢.
CMV, $60.00 each,
jar only, mint. $80.00
each, MB.

Rose Pomade, 1914.
White glass, top and
side paper labels.
CMV, $65.00 mint.

Rouge, 1916.
OSP, 25¢. CMV, $45.00
CO. $60.00 MB.

Massage Cream,
1916.
Glass jar, glass
stopper, green
ribbon on neck.
OSP, 50¢. CMV,
$125.00 jar only,
mint. $145.00 MB.

CPC Cold Cream, 1915 – 1919.
Large white glass jar with metal lid. OSP,
45¢. CMV, $60.00 jar only. $75.00 MB.

Cold Cream, 1920 – 1922.
Large milk glass jar with
metal lid. Very rare. OSP,
63¢. $100.00 jar only.
$130.00 MB.

Dermol Massage Cream,
1920 – 1923.
Glass jar with metal screw-on lid. OSP, 96¢. CMV $75.00 jar only, mint. $90.00 MB.

Dermol Massage Cream, 1923.
1 lb. white glass jar. Aluminum lid, colored front label. Very rare. 4¼" high. CMV, $100.00 jar only, mint. Shown next to 1915 regular size jar Cold Cream, for size comparison.

Violet Nutri-Creme, 1926.
White glass jar with flowered label. OSP, 89¢. CMV, $50.00 jar only. $60.00 MB.

Bandoline Hair Dressing,
1923 – 1930.
2 oz. yellow label and cork stopper, clear glass jar. OSP, 24¢. CMV, $60.00 jar only, mint. $75.00 MB.

Lavender Salts, 1923.
Glass stopper bottles, front and neck label. OSP, 49¢ each. CMV, $110.00 each, jar only, mint. $135.00 each, MB.

Bandoline Hair Dressing, 1923 – 1930.
4 oz. glass bottle, cork stopper, front and neck labels. OSP, 45¢. CMV, $65.00 jar only. $80.00 MB.

Bandoline, 1930 – 1935.
Frosted glass or clear glass bottle with blue wrapped cork stopper. OSP, 37¢. CMV, $60.00 jar only. $70.00 MB.

Dermol Massage Cream, 1923.
White glass jar with ribbed sides. "CPC" on metal lid. OSP, 96¢. CMV, $50.00 jar only. $60.00 MB.

Cold Cream, 1926.
White glass jar with CPC on aluminum lid. OSP, 63¢. CMV, $50.00, jar only, mint. $65.00 MB.

Bandoline Hair Dressing,
1923 – 1930.
Tall, 4 oz. clear glass with cork stopper. Must come with neck label to be mint. OSP, 45¢. CMV, $75.00 BO, mint. $90.00 MB.

Lemonol Cleansing Cream, 1926 – 1930.
Frosted glass jar with brass lid. OSP, 50¢. CMV, $65.00 jar only, mint. $75.00 MB.

Perfumes

1896 to 1914 Perfumes

The following list of perfumes were sold by CPC from 1896 to 1914. Use this list to identify miscellaneous perfumes. The regular line of CPC floral extracts consists of 30 odors, in the following range of prices and sizes:

Roses	Heliotrope	
Lily of the Valley	Carnation	Ylang Ylang
White Rose	Bouquet Marie	Jack Rose
Violet	New Mown Hay	Tube Rose
White Lilac	Marie Stewart	Treffle
Sweet Pea	Rose Geranium	California Bouquet
Hyacinth	Stephanotis	

1 ounce bottle	$ .60
2 ounce bottle	$1.10
4 ounce bottle	$2.00
½ pint bottle	$3.75
1 pint bottle	$7.00

| Crab Apple Blossom | Frangipanni | Jockey Club |
| Trailing Arbutus | May Blossom | White Heliotrope |

1 ounce bottle	$ .75
2 ounce bottle	$1.40
4 ounce bottle	$2.75
½ pint bottle	$5.25
1 pint bottle	$10.00

| Lou Lillie | Golf Club | |
| Musk | Venetian Carnation | Golf Violet |

1 ounce bottle	$ .50
2 ounce bottle	$ .90
4 ounce bottle	$1.75
½ pint bottle	$3.25
1 pint bottle	$6.00

1915 to 1921 Perfumes

The very extensive CPC line from 1915 to 1921 gives a wide range of selection, and among the 23 different odors there is sure to be one or more to satisfy the most fastidious and exacting.

The prices are based according to the cost of production and the value of the goods offered. All perfumes come in attractive bottles, in beautiful lithographed boxes, as illustrated in this section.

Concentrated Floral Odors, Triple Extracts

Violet	Hyacinth	
White Rose	California Bouquet	
Carnation	Roses	Rose Geranium
Heliotrope	New Mown Hay	Jack Rose
Lily of the Valley	Sweet Pea	
White Lilac	Treffle	

1 ounce bottle	$ .50
2 ounce bottle	$ .90
4 ounce bottle	$1.75
½ pint bottle	$3.25
1 pint bottle	$6.00

Quadruple Extracts

| Crab Apple Blossom | Jockey Club | |
| Trailing Arbutus | Honeysuckle | White Heliotrope |

1 ounce bottle	$ .60
2 ounce bottle	$1.10
4 ounce bottle	$2.00
½ pint bottle	$3.75
1 pint bottle	$7.00

Extra Concentrated Odors

| Natoma Rose | Golf Violet |
| Venetian Carnation | Musk |

1 ounce bottle	$ .75
2 ounce bottle	$1.40
4 ounce bottle	$2.75
½ pint bottle	$5.25
1 pint bottle	$10.00

Extract Rose Geranium Perfume, 1896.
1 oz. glass stopper, paper label. OSP, 40¢. CMV, $200.00 BO, mint.

White Rose Perfume, 1896.
1 oz. glass stopper. Bottom part of label is missing on bottle shown. OSP, 40¢. CMV, $150.00 BO. $200.00 MB.

Hyacinth Perfume, 1899 – 1904.
1 oz., glass stopper. CMV, $150.00 BO, mint.

Perfume, 1896.
1 oz. octagonal shaped bottle, front and neck labels with Eureka trademark. Came in Atomizer Perfume Set with cork stopper. Came in all 1896 fragrances. CMV, $165.00 BO, mint.

French Perfume, Roses, 1897.
¼ oz. bottle, cork stopper. CMV, $160.00 mint.

Musk Perfume, 1900.
1 oz., glass stopper. Came in all 1896 fragrances. Rare with San Francisco label. CMV, $125.00 BO, mint. $150.00 MB.

Extract Perfumes, 1896 – 1904.
2 oz., round glass stopper. "New York, Chicago, San Francisco" on label. Came in all 1908 fragrances. OSP, 90¢ to $1.40. CMV, $150.00 BO. $200.00 MB.

Sweet Pea Perfume, 1899 – 1904.
1 oz., cork stopper. CMV, $150.00 BO, mint.

Little Folks Perfume, 1900 – 1906.
2" high. Came in 1896 and 1906 Little Folks Sets only, in Rose, White Rose, Heliotrope, Violet, or Carnation. Cork stopper. CMV, $75.00 each BO, mint.

French Perfume 1896 – 1906.
½ oz. bottle with glass stopper. Eureka trademark in center of label. Came in Le Perfume des Roses, Peau d'Espagne, or L'Odeur de Violette. OSP, 55¢. CMV, $150.00 BO. $200.00 MB.

White Rose Perfume, 1899 – 1904.
1 oz., cork stopper (missing). CMV, $150.00 BO, mint.

White Rose Perfume, 1900 – 1906.
1 oz., round glass stopper, long neck. Square round shoulder bottle. CMV, $150.00 BO, mint.

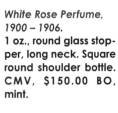

Carnation Perfume, 1900. 1 oz., glass stopper. Plain paper label. CMV, $150.00.

Traveler's Perfume, 1900 – 1923. Right, ½ oz. size. Metal cap over glass stopper. Gold label. Bottle is octagonally shaped. Came in all fragrances of 1896 – 1908. Red flowered box. OSP, 50¢. CMV, $125.00 BO, mint. $150.00 MB. Also came in 1 oz. size on left. Rare. CMV, $150.00 BO. $175.00 MB.

Christmas Perfume, 1905. 2 oz., glass stopper. OSP, 75¢. CMV, $150.00 BO. $200.00 MB.

French Perfumes, 1900. Trial size, ¼ oz. on left, 2 oz. size on right. Cork stoppers. CMV, $125.00 trial size, BO. $175.00 BO, 2 oz. size, mint. Add $30.00 MB.

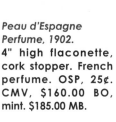

White Lilac Perfume, 1900 – 1906. 1 oz., glass stopper, long neck. Square round shoulder bottle. CMV, $150.00 BO, mint.

Violet Perfume, 1905. 1 oz., glass stopper. CMV, $150.00 BO, mint. $200.00 MB.

Violet Perfume, 1900. Eureka trademark. Neck ribbon. Neck label is plain. CMV, $165.00 BO, mint.

Peau d'Espagne Perfume, 1902. 4" high flaconette, cork stopper. French perfume. OSP, 25¢. CMV, $160.00 BO, mint. $185.00 MB.

White Lilac Perfume, 1905. 1 oz., glass stopper. CMV, $150.00 BO, mint. $200.00 MB.

White Rose Perfume, 1905. 1 oz., with round glass stopper. Eureka trademark on label. CMV, $150.00 BO, mint. $200.00 MB.

Rose Perfume Sample, 1900. ½ oz., cork stopper. Came in all fragrances of 1900. CMV, $125.00 mint.

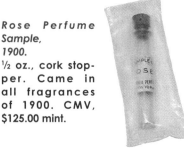

Perfume, "Floral Extracts," 1902 – 1906. 1 oz. glass stopper bottle with Eureka CP trademark on label. Came in all 1908 fragrances. OSP, 50¢. CMV, $150.00 BO. $200.00 MB. Also came in 2, 4, 8, and 16 oz. bottles. (CMV same as 1 oz. size.)

French Perfume, 1905.
Glass stopper bottle, came in ½, 1, 2, and 4 oz. sizes in these fragrances: Le Perfume des Roses, L'Odeur de Violette, and Peau d'Espagne. OSP, 25¢ to $3.75. CMV, $165.00 BO. $215.00 MB.

Treffle Perfume, 1905.
1 oz., with glass stopper. Eureka trademark on label. CMV, $150.00 BO, mint. $200.00 MB.

Perfume Christmas Box, 1905.
Embossed paper box, satin lined. Holds 8 oz. glass stopper bottle with neck ribbon. OSP, $3.50. CMV, $200.00 BO. $275.00 MB.

Extract Perfume, 1905.
1 oz., glass stopper, white paper label. Came in all fragrances of 1896. OSP, 50¢. CMV, $175.00 BO, mint. $215.00 MB.

Perfume Christmas Box, 1905.
Fancy flowered box holds 4 oz. glass stopper bottle. Front and neck labels. OSP, $1.50. CMV, $175.00 BO. $225.00 MB.

Perfume Christmas Box, 1905.
Embossed paper box, satin lined. Holds 4 oz. glass stopper bottle with neck ribbon. OSP, $2.00. CMV, $175.00 BO. $250.00 MB.

Crab Apple Blossom, 1905.
1 oz. clear glass bottle, glass stopper, label has CPC Eureka trademark. Came in all 1908 fragrances. Bottle came with different shaped stopper also. OSP, 50¢ – 75¢. CMV, $150.00 BO. $200.00 MB.

Perfumes, 1905.
8 oz. glass stopper bottle. Came in California Bouquet (shown), Violet, White Rose, Carnation, Heliotrope, Lily of the Valley, White Lilac, Hyacinth, Roses, New Mown Hay, Sweet Pea, Treffle, Rose Geranium, or Jack Rose. Front paper label and neck label. OSP, $3.25 each. CMV, $175.00 each, BO. $225.00 each, MB.

Sweet Pea Perfume, 1906.
1 oz., cork stopper. Plain paper label. CMV, $150.00.

Perfumes, 1906.
1 oz. round bottle, came in Atomizer Perfume Set with cork stopper. Came in all fragrances of 1908. CMV, $110.00 each, BO, mint.

Atomizer Perfume, 1908.
1 oz., six-sided bottle with cork stopper. Green neck and front labels. Came in all fragrances of 1908. Came only in CPC Atomizer Sets. Used with Spray Atomizer. OSP, 50¢. CMV, $100.00 mint.

Perfume, 1906.
1 oz., gold front and neck labels. Came in all 1908 perfumes. CMV, $150.00 BO. $200.00 MB.

Christmas Box No. 5 Perfume, 1906.
White leather covered box holds 3 oz. glass stopper perfume. OSP, $1.50. CMV, $175.00 BO, mint. $225.00 MB.

Heliotrope Perfume, 1908.
1 oz., glass stopper. Special Christmas box. OSP, 70¢. CMV, $225.00 MB.

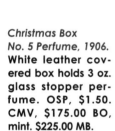

Perfume, 1906 – 1918.
4 oz. glass stopper bottle, gold embossed front and neck label. Came in all perfumes of the period. (See list p. 58). OSP, $2.75. CMV, $150.00 BO. $200.00 MB.

Crab Apple Blossom Perfume, 1908.
1 oz., glass stopper. Special Christmas box. OSP, 70¢. CMV, $225.00 MB.

Jockey Club Perfume, 1908.
Green front and neck labels and green neck ribbon. OSP, 50¢. CMV, $100.00 BO, mint. $130.00 MB.

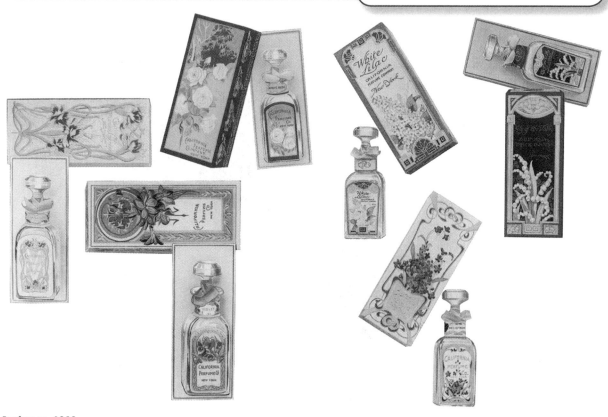

Perfumes, 1908.
1 oz., glass stopper bottles. Came in California Bouquet, Carnation, Heliotrope, Hyacinth, Lily of the Valley, New Mown Hay, Rose Geranium, Sweet Pea, Treffle, Violet, White Lilac, and White Rose. OSP, 50¢ each. CMV, $150.00 BO. $195.00 MB.

Perfumes, 1908.
1 oz., glass stoppers. Eureka trademark on label. In gray flowered box. Came in all fragrances of 1908. Each fragrance came with different flower on label. Crab Apple Blossom, Heliotrope, and White Lilac are shown. OSP, 50¢ to 75¢. CMV, $150.00 each, BO. $200.00 each, MB.

Perfume, 1908.
1 oz., glass stopper, gold label. Eureka trademark on label. Came in all fragrances of 1908. Also came with several different glass stoppers. CMV, $150.00 BO, mint. $180.00 MB.

Perfume, 1914 – 1918.
4 oz., came in all fragrances. CMV, $150.00 BO. $200.00 MB.

Crab Apple Blossom Perfume, 1910.
1 oz., glass stopper, front and neck labels. "CPC" on label. CMV, $110.00 BO, mint. $135.00 MB.

Little Folks Perfume, 1910.
2" high, cork stopper. Came in Little Folks Set only, from 1910 to 1915. CMV, $75.00 BO, mint.

Cut Glass Perfume, 1915 – 1920.
2 oz. bottle with cut glass stopper. Two different labels in embossed gold. White leatherette box. Came in Trailing Arbutus and Crab Apple Blossom. OSP, $2.25 each. CMV, $225.00 each, BO. $265.00 each, MB. Octagonal label on bottom is 1911 issue (Same CMV).

French Perfumes, 1910.
Bottle at left is 1 oz., center is ¼ oz. trial size, right is ½ oz. size. Each has glass stopper. Came in L'Odeur de Violette, Le Perfume des Roses, and Peau d'Espagne. Also came in 2 and 4 oz sizes. OSP, 25¢, 55¢, $1.00, $1.90, and $3.75. CMV, ½ oz. size to 4 oz., $150.00 each, BO. ¼ oz. size, $125.00 BO. $175.00 MB.

Little Folks Perfume, 1915.
Small gem size bottle with front label and ribbon on neck. Cork stopper. Came in 1915 Little Folks Set only. Came in Carnation, Violet, White Rose, or Heliotrope. CMV, $75.00 each BO, mint.

Perfumes,
1915 – 1919.
2 oz. on left and 1 oz. on right, different labels and diamond cut shaped glass stoppers. CMV, $125.00 each, BO, mint.

French Perfumes, 1915.
¼ oz. glass bottle, cork stopper. Came in Le Perfume des Roses, L'Odeur de Violette, or Peau d'Espagne. OSP, 25¢. CMV, $125.00 BO, mint. $150.00 MB.

Perfume, 1915.
½ oz. bottle with glass and cork stopper. Came in Gift Box No. 2, 1915. CMV, $125.00 BO. $150.00 MB.

Extra Concentrated Perfumes, 1915.
1 oz., front and neck labels. Came in Golf Violet, Musk, Crab Apple Blossom, Natoma Rose, or Venetian Carnation. OSP, 75¢. CMV, $135.00 BO. $175.00 MB.

French Perfumes, 1916.
Two different embossed glass bottles with cork stoppers. Trial size ¼ oz. on right, 2 oz. on left. OSP, 25¢ each. CMV, $150.00 each, BO, mint. $185.00 MB.

Perfume, 1915.
1 oz. clear glass bottle with glass stopper. Came in all 1915 fragrances. OSP, 75¢. CMV, $150.00 BO, mint. $175.00 MB.

Perfumes, 1915.
1 oz., glass stopper. CMV, $125.00 BO, mint.

Perfume, 1916.
Three different glass stoppers shown. 1 and 2 oz. sizes. OSP, 50¢ each. CMV, $135.00 each, BO, mint. $175.00 each, MB.

Perfumes, 1915.
½ oz. bottles with glass stoppers set in cork. Front and neck labels. Came in Violet, White Rose, Carnation, White Lilac, Heliotrope, or Lily of the Valley. OSP, 25¢ each. CMV, $110.00 each, BO. $135.00 each, MB.

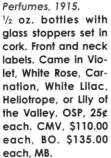

French Perfumes, 1916.
Two different embossed glass bottles with cork stoppers. Trial size ¼ oz. on right, 2 oz. on left. OSP, 25¢ each. CMV, $150.00 each, BO, mint. $185.00 MB.

Perfume, 1918.
½ oz. bottle, crown glass stopper. Came in Gift Box No. 3, 1918. Came in all fragrances of 1917 – 1918 period. CMV, $110.00 BO, mint.

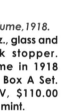

Perfume, 1916.
2 oz., glass stopper, either faceted or round. Front and neck labels. Came in all fragrances of 1915. OSP, $1.10. CMV, $150.00 BO. $200.00 MB.

Perfume, 1918.
½ oz., glass and cork stopper. Came in 1918 Gift Box A Set. CMV, $110.00 BO, mint.

Perfume, 1919.
½ oz. glass crown-shaped stopper set in cork. Came in all 1919 fragrances. OSP, 75¢. CMV, $100.00 BO, mint. $125.00 MB.

Traveler's Perfume, 1917.
1 oz. octagonal shaped bottle with glass stopper and screw-on nickel lid. OSP, 90¢. CMV, $135.00 BO, mint. $160.00 MB.

White Rose Perfume, 1918.
2 oz., rare, cork stopper. Front and neck labels with neck ribbon. OSP, $1.00. CMV, $125.00 BO, mint.

Perfume Sample Set, 1920s.
Black carrying case with California Perfume Company on front. Came with four (3 dram) glass bottles. Each has off-green label. Fragrances were American Ideal, Trailing Arbutus, Roses, and Vernafleur. CMV, $70.00 each, BO. $325.00 set.

Perfume, 1918.
½ oz. bottle with crown glass stopper set in cork. Front and neck labels. Came in all fragrances of 1918. OSP, 50¢. CMV, $100.00 BO, mint. $125.00 MB.

Perfume and Atomizer, 1918.
1 oz. bottle with atomizer came in black box. Bottle has cork stopper and green front and neck labels. Came in all fragrances of 1918, including American Ideal and Daphne. OSP, $1.50. CMV, $100.00 BO, mint. $150.00 MB, with atomizer.

CPC Perfume Sample Set, 1922.
Black carrying case with "California Perfume Co." on front. Came with four glass flaconettes with gold caps that fit into gold case. CMV, $350.00 MB. $75.00 each flaconette.

Perfume, 1923.
1 oz. glass stopper bottle, ribbed. Came in Carnation, Crab Apple Blossom, Heliotrope, Lily of the Valley, Violet, and White Rose. Front and neck labels. OSP, $1.17. CMV, $135.00 BO. $160.00 MB.

Perfume Flaconette, 1923.
Octagonal shaped bottle with long glass stopper, neck label. Came with and without brass cap with "CPC" on cap. Came in Daphne, Crab Apple Blossom, Vernafleur, Trailing Arbutus, White Rose, Carnation, Violet, White Lilac, Heliotrope, Rose, Lily of the Valley, or Mission Garden. OSP, 49¢. CMV, $75.00 with brass cap. Without cap, $65.00. $90.00 MB.

Perfume Sample Set, 1923.
Black box holds four glass stopper perfume samples. Box has "California Perfume Co." on front. Bottles are 3 dram size. Each has neck labels. Labels read Daphne, Vernafleur, American Ideal, Trailing Arbutus, or Roses. CMV, $65.00 each bottle. $300.00 set MB.

Perfume Flaconette, 1925.
Flaconette embossed glass bottle with glass stopper. Brass cap over stopper, with the name of fragrance on it. Came in Mission Garden, American Ideal, Narcissus, Daphne, or Jardin d'Amour. OSP, $1.10. CMV, $65.00 BO, mint with brass cap. $80.00 MB.

Little Folks Perfume, 1925 – 1932.
½ oz. bottle with brass screw-on cap. Came in 1925 Little Folks Set only. Came in Violet, Carnation, Heliotrope, White Lilac, Daphne, Vernafleur, or Trailing Arbutus. CMV, $65.00 each, mint.

Perfumes, 1923.
½ oz. bottles with crown glass stoppers set in cork. Front and neck labels. Came in Crab Apple Blossom, White Rose, Trailing Arbutus, Rose Carnation, Heliotrope, Violet, White Lilac, or Lily of the Valley. Came in red boxes. Two different bottles as shown. OSP, 59¢ each. CMV, $110.00 each, BO. $135.00 each, MB.

Perfumes, 1923.
1 or 2 oz. bottle in same shape and design with glass stopper. Front and neck labels with gold basket design. Beige box. Came in Carnation, Rose, Heliotrope, Violet, White Lilac, Lily of the Valley, Crab Apple Blossom, Trailing Arbutus, or White Rose. OSP, $1.17 and $2.10. CMV, $135.00 BO. $170.00 MB. Also came in 4 oz. size.

Perfume Flaconette, 1926.
Frosted ribbed glass bottle with long glass stopper. Small paper labels on front. Came with brass cap with "CPC" on cap. Came in Crab Apple Blossom, Daphne, Trailing Arbutus, Vernafleur, American Ideal, Carnation, Heliotrope, White Rose, Violet, or Lily of the Valley. OSP, 59¢. CMV with brass cap, $75.00. $60.00 BO. $95.00 MB.

Perfume Spray Atomizers, 1928.
One is green opaque over clear glass and one is green painted over clear, gold plated top. CMV, $90.00 each.

White Rose Perfume, 1930.
Silver and blue box holds 2 oz. bottle with flat glass stopper, pink neck ribbon, and red paper rose label. Rare. CMV, $115.00 BO, mint. $150.00 MB.

Perfume Sample Set, 1931.
Four 3 dram ribbed and frosted glass bottles with clear ribbed stoppers. Black carrying case. Came in Daphne, Trailing Arbutus, Vernafleur, American Ideal, Crab Apple Blossom, Carnation, Heliotrope, White Rose, Violet, or Lily of the Valley. CMV set, $315.00 mint. Came with card on proper way to demonstrate perfumes. Add $10.00 for card.
Not shown: Perfume Sample Set, 1931.
Same CPC black case and bottles as above, only has very rare silver and blue labels on bottles. CMV, $400.00 set, mint.

Trial Size Perfumes.
To show different size glass stoppers, bottles, and labels.

Perfume Flaconette, 1930 – 1935.
Embossed clear glass stopper, brass cap over glass stopper. "Avon"on cap. Came in all perfume fragrances of 1930 – 1935. OSP, $1.10. CMV, $65.00 each, BO, mint. $80.00 MB.

Toilet Waters

Eau de Cologne for the Toilet, 1896.
2 oz. ribbed glass bottle. Front and neck labels with Eureka trademark. Glass stopper in cork. OSP, 35¢. CMV, $175.00 BO, mint. $210.00 MB.

1896.
2 oz. ribbed glass bottle, glass stopper in cork. Front and neck labels have Eureka trademark. Came in California Sweet Cologne, Violet Water, White Rose, Lavender Water, or Florida Water. OSP, 35¢. CMV, $175.00 BO. $210.00 MB.

Triple Extract Toilet Water, 1896.
4 oz. and 8 oz. size glass stopper, labels has Eureka trademark. Came in Violet Water, White Rose, Lavender Water, Florida Water, Eau de Cologne, or California Sweet Cologne. OSP, 65¢ each. CMV, $150.00 BO, mint. $200.00 MB.

Violet Water, 1900.
2 oz. bottle, glass stopper. OSP, 35¢. CMV, $175.00 BO, mint. $210.00 MB.

Florida Water, 1905.
1½ oz., glass crown and cork stopper. OSP, 35¢. CMV, $175.00 BO, mint. $200.00 MB.

Lavender Water, 1910.
2 oz. glass stopper bottle with Eureka trademark on labels. Also came in Violet, White Rose, Florida Water, California Sweet Cologne, or Eau de Cologne. Also came in 4 and 8 oz. and 1 pint sizes with glass stoppers. OSP, 35¢. CMV, $150.00 BO, mint. $190.00 MB.

1906.
2 oz. clear ribbed glass bottle and glass corked stopper. "Pure Food Act 1906" on labels. Came in Violet Water, White Rose, Lavender Water, Florida Water, California Sweet Cologne, or Eau de Cologne. OSP, 35¢. CMV, $175.00 BO, mint. $210.00 MB.

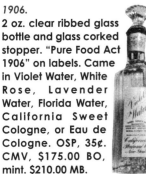

White Rose Water, 1910.
4 oz. clear glass stopper. Eureka trademark on labels. OSP, 35¢. CMV, $150.00 BO, mint. $190.00 MB.

1910.
8 oz. bottle with glass stopper. Front and neck labels. Came in all fragrances of 1916 toilet waters. OSP, $1.25. CMV, $175.00 BO, mint. $225.00 MB.

1908.
2, 4, 8, and 16 oz. sizes. Glass stopper bottle. Came in Violet, White Rose, Lavender, Florida, California Sweet Cologne, or Eau de Cologne. Bottle shown is 2 oz. size. OSP, 35¢, 65¢, $1.25, and $2.00. CMV, $150.00 each, BO, $200.00 MB.

1910.
2 oz. bottle with metal pour cap in cork, 1916 up. Came in California Sweet Cologne, Lait Virginal, Eau de Cologne, Trailing Arbutus, White Rose, Violet, White Lilac, Lavender Water, Florida Water, Crab Apple Blossom, or Carnation. Front and neck labels in two styles. OSP, 35¢. CMV, $115.00 BO, mint. $140.00 MB. Also came with brass crown and cork stopper in 1910.

1910 – 1919.
2 oz. size with metal crown cork stoppers. Came in either of two labels shown in Carnation, Florida Water, Trailing Arbutus, White Lilac, White Rose, Violet, Lavender Water, Eau de Cologne, or California Sweet Cologne. OSP, 35¢ each. CMV, $115.00 each, BO, $140.00 MB.

1916.
4 oz. bottle with metal and cork stopper. Came in red and gold box. Came in California Sweet Cologne, Carnation, Eau de Cologne, Florida Water, Lavender Water, Trailing Arbutus, Violet, White Lilac, White Rose, or Crab Apple Blossom. OSP, 65¢. CMV, $120.00 BO. $150.00 MB.

Lilac Vegetal, 1925 – 1930.
2 oz. ribbed glass bottle with metal stopper in cork. Pink front and neck labels. OSP, $1.08. CMV, $80.00 BO. $100.00 MB.

1922 – 1925.
Came in 2, 4, or 8 oz. sizes in Violet, Vernafleur, Lavender, White Lilac, Lily of the Valley, Carnation, White Rose, Trailing Arbutus, Crab Apple Blossom, or Eau de Cologne. 2 and 4 oz. size same as pictured. Front and neck labels. Metal crown stopper in cork. OSP, 59¢, $1.08, and $1.95. CMV, $90.00 BO. $115.00 MB.

1923 – 1929.
2 or 4 oz. metal crown cork stopper, ribbed bottle, front and neck labels. Came in Lily of the Valley, Violet, White Rose, Carnation, or Crab Apple Blossom. OSP, 59¢. CMV, $80.00 each BO, mint. $125.00 MB.

Lilac Vegetal, 1928 – 1929.
2 oz. ribbed glass bottle with crown metal top in cork. Pink front and neck labels. This bottle with CPC on front labels came in Humidor Shaving Set only. (See CPC Men's Sets section). CMV, $80.00 BO. $100.00 MB.

Baby Toilet Water, 1923.
2 and 4 oz. size bottles. Red soldier on front labels, blue neck labels. Brass and cork stopper. OSP, 48¢ and 89¢. CMV, $125.00 BO. $145.00 MB.

Powders

Sachet Powder, 1890s.
Small envelope of powder. "CPC Eastern Agency — 7 Summer St., Bradford, Mass." on envelope. Rare. CMV, $50.00 mint.

Sweet Sixteen Face Powder, 1898 – 1906.
Paper box with outer box which is different from the 1905 box. OSP, 25¢ each. CMV, $65.00 CO, 1898. $110.00 MB, 1898. CMV, $60.00 CO, 1906. $100.00 MB, 1906.

Hygiene Face Powder, 1906.
Leatherette box trimmed in gold. OSP, 50¢. CMV, $90.00 mint.

Sachet Powder Envelope, 1910.
Paper packet of sachet in Violet, White Rose, or Heliotrope. OSP, 25¢. CMV, $50.00 mint.

California Nail Powder, 1912.
Two different labels, came with either paper lift-off top or metal sifter top. OSP, 25¢ each. CMV, $45.00 each, mint.

Rose Talcum Powder Antiseptic, 1907 – 1908.
Metal can with brass sifter cap. OSP, 25¢ each. CMV, $100.00 each, CO, mint. $120.00 each, MB.

Sweet Sixteen Face Powder, 1914.
Paper box with outer box. OSP, 25¢. CMV, $55.00 CO. $75.00 MB.

California Bath Powder, 1910.
Gold, white, and green can. Came with sifter cap or take-off cap. OSP, 25¢. CMV, $65.00 CO. $85.00 MB.

Tooth Powder, 1911 – 1912.
Metal can. OSP, 25¢. CMV, $70.00 CO, mint. $85.00 MB.

Hygiene Face Powder, 1915.
Green paper box. OSP, 50¢. CMV, $60.00 mint.

Shaving Powder, 1915.
2 oz. metal can. OSP, 25¢. CMV, $70.00 CO, mint. $85.00 MB.

Depilatory, 1916.
Metal can of of hair remover. Came with brass lift-off cap. OSP, 50¢. CMV, $75.00 CO, mint. $90.00 MB.

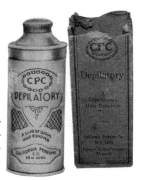

Smoker's Tooth Powder, 1918.
2³⁄₄ oz. bottle with metal and cork stopper also comes with metal crown stopper. OSP, 50¢. CMV, $105.00 BO. $130.00 MB.

Hygiene Face Powder, 1918.
Green, gold, and red powder box. OSP, 50¢. CMV, $125.00 mint.

Tooth Powder, 1915 only.
Small metal can came in 1915 Juvenile Set. (See CPC Sets). CMV, $75.00 CO, mint.

California Nail Powder, 1916.
Two different labels, came with either paper lift-off top or metal sifter top. OSP, 25¢ each. CMV, $45.00 each, mint.

Elite Powder, 1918 – 1922.
Glass jar with aluminum lid. OSP, 25¢. CMV, $80.00 CO, mint. $100.00 MB. Brown glass jar, $150.00.

White Lilac Talcum, 1919.
4 oz. blue metal can, blue sifter cap. OSP, 24¢. CMV, $75.00 CO, mint. $90.00 MB.

White Lilac Talcum, 1917.
4 oz. paper box, purple in color. OSP, 25¢. CMV, $70.00 CO, mint. $90.00 MB.

American Ideal Card, 1915.
Small white card. CMV, $10.00.

White Lilac Talcum, 1917.
Two sizes, both 4 oz. Two different metal shaker tops. Both lavender paper sides. CMV, $75.00 each, CO. $90.00 MB.

Elite Foot Powder, 1919.
Round container, paper sides. Sold for 25¢ each after WWI from the Army and Navy kits. Rare. CMV, $85.00 CO. $100.00 MB.

Powder Can Refill, 1920.
1 lb. gold tone can. Came in several fragrances as a refill. CMV, $75.00 mint.

Elite Powder, 1923.
Blue metal can with sifter cap. Came with two different sifter caps and two variations in labels. Same CMV, OSP, 24¢. $35.00 CO, mint. $50.00 MB.

Elite Powder, 1920.
Glass jar with aluminum lid. Rare. OSP, 25¢. CMV, $75.00 CO, mint. $100.00 MB.

California Rose Talcum, 1921.
3½ oz. glass jar with brass cap. OSP, 33¢. CMV, $85.00 jar only. $105.00 MB.

White Lilac Talcum, 1920.
4 oz. blue metal can with brass take-off cap. Box came with paper, "The Story of Italian Talc." OSP, 24¢. CMV, $75.00 CO, mint. $90.00 MB as shown.

Radiant Nail Powder, 1923.
Blue and pink can. Two different labels. OSP, 24¢ each. CMV, $65.00 each, CO, mint. $80.00 MB.

California Rose Talcum, 1923.
4 oz. pink can with brass cap. OSP, 33¢. CMV, $90.00 CO. $110.00 MB.

Smoker's Tooth Powder, 1920.
2¾ oz., metal and cork stopper. OSP, 50¢. CMV, $105.00 BO. $130.00 MB.

Elite Powder, 1923.
1 lb. blue can with English and French labels. Two different brass caps and narrow or wide blue band around top. OSP, 89¢. CMV, $85.00 each, CO. $95.00 MB.

Radiant Nail Powder, 1924 – 1929.
Small gold and black can. Came in 1924 Manicure Set. (See Manicure Sets). CMV, $35.00.

Cuti Creme or Nail Cream, 1924 – 1929. Small gold and black can. Came in 1924 Manicure Set. CMV, $15.00 CO. $30.00 MB.

Nail White, 1924 – 1929. Small gold and black can. Came in 1924 Manicure Set. CMV, $15.00 CO. $30.00 MB.

Pyrox Tooth Powder, 1925. Blue metal can. OSP, 24¢. CMV, $60.00 CO, mint. $75.00 MB.

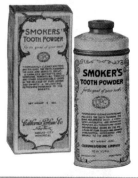

Smoker's Tooth Powder, 1925 – 1933. 4 oz. cream colored can. Labels in French and English. OSP, 50¢. CMV, $60.00 CO, mint. $80.00 MB.

Body Powder, 1928 – 1929. Yellow, black, and maroon metal can. "CPC New York, Montreal" on bottom. Came in Trailing Arbutus, Daphne, or Baby Powder. OSP, $1.19. CMV, $50.00 CO, mint. $65.00 MB.

Powder Sachets

All CPC powder sachets must be in new mint condition for CMV.

Sachet Powder, 1890s. Eureka trademark on label. Maroon box contains powder in Violet, White Rose, or Heliotrope. OSP, 25¢. CMV, $75.00 per box, mint.

Sachet Powder, 1890s. Heliotrope, Violet, or White Rose sachet in box. Metal cap. OSP, 25¢. CMV, $90.00 BO, mint. $110.00 MB.

Powder Sachet, 1890s – 1912. Silver or gold cap on glass bottle with front label. Came in Lilac, Rose, White Rose, Violet, or Heliotrope. Each one has different label. OSP, 25¢. CMV, $90.00 BO, mint. $110.00 MB.

Powder Sachet, 1890s – 1912. Clear glass, gold cap, front labels. Came in French odors of Le Parfume de Roses, L'Odeur de Violette, or Peau d'Espagne. OSP, 25¢. CMV, $90.00 BO, mint. $110.00 MB.

Powder Sachet, 1905.
Round glass bottle, aluminum lid. Came in Violet, Lilac, Rose, White Rose, or Heliotrope. Came in sets only. CMV, $100.00 BO, mint.

Face Powder Leaves, 1916.
Small book of 72 sheets of scented paper. Came in Rose, White, or Rachel. OSP, 20¢. CMV, $50.00 mint.

Sachet Powder, Boxed, 1908.
In Violet, White Rose, or Heliotrope. Box holds matching envelope. OSP, 25¢. CMV, $75.00 MB.

Heliotrope Powder Sachet, 1919.
Clear glass bottle, gold cap, yellow label with lavender flowers and green leaves. Came in Carnation, Heliotrope, White Rose, Violet, or White Lilac. Rare. CMV, $110.00 BO. $125.00 MB.

Powder Sachets, 1915.
Gold caps, paper labels on glass bottles. Came in Carnation, White Rose, Violet, White Lilac, or Heliotrope. Two different boxes as shown. OSP, 25¢ each. CMV, $65.00 each, BO, mint. $85.00 each, MB.

Powder Sachets, 1922 – 1925.
Large and small bottles with brass caps. Came in Carnation, Heliotrope, Violet, White Rose, or Trailing Arbutus. OSP, 49¢ and 72¢. CMV, $100.00 each, BO. $115.00 each, MB.

Sample Cases

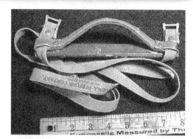

1890s.
Small wood case, 6½" x 12½". Red felt lining. List of CPC products inside of lid. CMV, $100.00 mint.

Early 1900s.
Plain wood box with brass handle. Case was used by CPC reps to sell products. CMV, $125.00 mint with CPC price list.

Early 1900s.
Plain wood box with leather handle. Red felt lining, printed paper price list inside lid. CMV, $95.00 mint with list.

School Book Straps, 1915 – 1929.
Yellow straps and leather handle. Says "California Perfume Co. New York City." Given to school kids to carry books. Rare. CMV, $75.00.

Sales Case, 1920.
Black case with red velvet lining. "California Perfume Co." on chrome handle. Used by reps to show products. Case measures 14½" long, 8" wide, 3½" high. CMV, $100.00 mint.

1915.
Straw basketweave case and leather handle and trim. Measures 11" x 17". The large CPC black catalogs fit inside perfectly. A CPC label is inside lid stating all contents that came in sample case. CMV, $100.00 with CPC label.

Sets

Warning! Grading condition is paramount on sets. Value can vary up to 90% on condition.

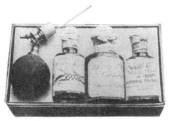

Atomizer Set, 1896 – 1906.
Box holds atomizer and three 1 oz. bottles with cork stoppers. Two bottles are round and center bottle is octagonal shaped. Each has front and neck labels. Came in all fragrances. OSP, $1.35. CMV, $550.00 MB, complete set.

Perfume Set No. 5, 1905.
Holly Christmas Box holds two 1 oz. glass stopper bottles. OSP, $1.00. CMV, $350.00.

Atomizer Set, 1906.
Box holds three 1 oz. bottles of perfume with cork stoppers and atomizer. Came in all fragrances of 1908. OSP, $1.50. CMV, $425.00 MB.

Atomizer Set, 1900 – 1906.
Box holds atomizer and two 1 oz. bottles with cork stoppers. Came in all fragrances. OSP, $1.35. CMV, $425.00 MB, complete set.

Perfume Set No. 2, 1905.
Lithographed box holds two crown shaped bottles with glass stoppers in cork. Front and neck labels. OSP, 50¢. CMV, $350.00 MB.

Christmas Box Set No. 4, 1906.
Box holds Hygiene Face Powder, Savona soap, and glass stopper perfume. Box is 6¾" square. OSP, $1.00. CMV, $325.00 MB.

Christmas Set No. 4, 1905.
Fancy box holds 1 oz. bottle with glass stopper, round bottle of powder sachet with screw-on cap, and one wrapped bar of Savona Bouquet soap. OSP, $1.00. CMV, $450.00 MB.

Christmas Box Set No. 3, 1906.
Roses on box, two perfumes, glass stoppers. Gold labels. Box is 5¼" x 4¾" inches. OSP, 65¢. CMV, $335.00 MB.

Christmas Box Set No. 2, 1906.
Babies on box, two glass stopper perfumes. Gold labels. OSP, 50¢. CMV, $335.00 MB.

Holly Set, 1910.
Holly design box holds two half-ounce bottles with glass and cork stoppers. Gold front and neck labels. Choice of Violet, White Rose, White Lilac, Carnation, Heliotrope, or Lily of the Valley perfume. OSP, 50¢. CMV, $325.00 MB.

Manicure Set, 1912.
Gray box contains buffer, scissors, file, Nail Bleach, Nail Powder, and Rose Pomade. OSP, $3.00. CMV, $265.00 MB.

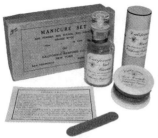

Manicure Set, 1906 – 1912.
Box holds bottle of Nail Bleach with glass stopper (CMV, $100.00), jar of Rose Pomade (CMV, $70.00), and paper container of Nail Powder (CMV, $50.00). OSP, 25¢ each; 65¢ complete set. CMV, $275.00 complete set.

Holly Set, 1912.
Holly design box holds two half-ounce glass and cork stopper bottles. OSP, 50¢. CMV, $300.00 MB.

Gift Box E, 1913 – 1914.
1 oz. bottle of perfume, a box of hygiene powder, and one cake of Savona toilet soap. CMV, $325.00 MB.

Atomizer Box Set, 1908.
Three 1 oz. bottles with cork stoppers and atomizer. Came in all fragrances of 1915. Green box. Each bottle has green front and neck labels. OSP, $1.50. CMV, $375.00 MB, complete set.

Box A Set, 1909.
Holly green, red, and gold box holds two half-ounce perfumes with glass stoppers. OSP, 50¢. CMV, $325.00 MB.

Memories That Linger Set, 1913.
Three glass stopper perfumes in book shaped box. Box is 8" x 5½". Holds Violet, White Rose, and Carnation perfumes. OSP, $2.00. CMV, $450.00 MB.

Juvenile Set, 1915 only.
Box holds miniature size cans of Natoma Talcum Powder and Tooth Powder, a small bottle of Violet Water with cork stopper, and a small cake of Savona Bouquet Soap. Each item is about 2" high. OSP, 50¢. CMV, $450.00 MB.

Gift Box No. 2, 1915. Yellow and purple box holds half-ounce perfume and powder sachet. Choice of Carnation, Heliotrope, White Lilac, Violet, or White Rose. OSP, 50¢ per set. CMV, $275.00 MB per set.

Gift Box No. 3, 1918. Box holds two half-ounce bottles of perfume. Crown glass stopper set in cork. Came in all fragrances of 1917 – 1918 period. CMV, $300.00 MB.

California Ideal Hair Treatment Set, 1915.
Box holds 4 oz. glass stopper bottle of Bay Rum, white jar of shampoo cream, and 6 oz. Eau de Quinine. All products in set came in separate boxes. Included pamphlet on the three products. OSP, $1.35. CMV, $500.00 MB as shown.

Gift Box A, 1915.
Green and red holly box. Two half-ounce glass stopper perfumes in choice of Violet, White Rose, Carnation, White Lilac, Heliotrope, and Lily of the Valley. OSP, 50¢. CMV, $300.00 MB.

Manicure Set, 1920.
CPC box holds Rose Pomade jar, 1 oz. bottle of Nail Bleach (cork stopper), and can of Radiant Nail Powder. OSP, 65¢. CMV, $250.00 MB.

Gift Box No. 2, 1915.
Box holds half-ounce perfume with glass and cork stopper and powder sachet in Carnation, White Lilac, Heliotrope, Violet, or White Rose. OSP, 50¢. CMV, $275.00 MB.

Manicure Set, 1916.
Box holds glass stopper bottle of Nail Bleach, jar of Rose Pomade, and paper container of Nail Powder. OSP, 65¢. CMV, $250.00 complete set.

Holly Pattern Box A, 1921.
Set has two half-ounce glass and cork stopper perfume bottles. Came in Carnation, Lily of the Valley, Violet, White Rose, White Lilac, or Heliotrope. OSP, 50¢. CMV, $300.00 set MB.

Gift Box No. 2, 1922. Half-ounce bottle of perfume and bottle of sachet. Came in Violet, White Rose, Carnation, Heliotrope, or White Lilac. OSP, 97¢. CMV, $250.00 MB.

Jack and Jill Jungle Jinks Set, 1925 – 1930. Brown decorated box holds one can Superite Trailing Arbutus Talcum, one bottle of Daphne Perfume, one cake of Apple Blossom soap, one can of Trailing Arbutus Cold Cream, one tube of Sen-Den-Tal Cream, and one imported juvenile size toothbrush. OSP, $1.50. CMV, $75.00 metal box only, mint. $335.00 MB.

Manicure Set, 1923. White box holds can of Radiant Nail Powder, bottle of Nail Bleach with glass stopper, orange wood stick, and jar of Rose Pomade. OSP, 72¢. CMV, $250.00 MB.

Dressing Table Vanity Set, 1926 – 1930. Orange and gold two-section box has brass lipstick, eyebrow pencil, and rouge compact in top half of box. Bottom half is full of Jardin d'Amour or Ariel face powder. OSP, $2.25. CMV, $150.00 MB.

Manicure Set Box, 1924 – 1930. Gold and black striped metal can. CMV, $25.00 metal box only, mint.

"Lovely Hands" Booklet, 1924 – 1930. Came in Manicure Set shown. CMV, $10.00 booklet only, mint.

Gertrude Recordon's Introductory Facial Treatment Set, 1928 – 1929. Box holds white jars of Gertrude Recordon's Cleansing Cream and Skin Food. CMV each jar, $60.00. Two bottles with cork stoppers of Peach Lotion and Astringent. CMV each bottle, $60.00 and roll of facial tissues. CMV, $300.00 set mint, MB.

Manicure Set, 1924 – 1928. Gold and black striped metal can holds gold and black can of Radiant Nail Powder, one can each of Nail White and Cuticreme, and bottle of Cutrain with cork stopper. OSP, $1.20. CMV, $165.00 MB.

CPC Atomizer Set, 1929. Black box with green liner and gold tone lid holds green glass lift-off lid jar, and a 2 oz. green glass spray atomizer bottle. Both have gold tone tops. Does not say CPC on it or box. CMV, $150.00 MB.

Gertrude Recordon's
Facial Treatment Set, 1929 only.
4 oz. bottle of Astringent with cork stopper, $85.00. 4 oz. bottle of Peach Lotion with cork stopper, $85.00. Ribbed white glass jar with "CPC" on metal lid, each in Cleansing Cream and Skin Food. OSP, $4.00 for set. CMV, $60.00 each jar. CMV, $350.00 complete set, MB.

Not shown:
Boudoir Manicure Set, 1929 – 1930.
Same set as 1924 Manicure Set with name changed and has bottle of Cuticle Softener or Cuticle Remover, and small can of Nail Cream, Nail White, and Radiant Nail Powder. All in same design. Set came with "Lovely Hands" booklet. OSP, $1.20. CMV, $175.00 MB.

Little Folks Sets

Little Folks Set, 1903.
Blue flowers and farmhouse on inside lid. Boy in 1700 style clothes in blue coat holding

white flowers on outside lid. Four gem sized perfumes: Violet, Rose, Carnation, and Heliotrope. Very rare. Light blue box. CMV, $400.00.

Little Folks Set, 1904.
Small red border box and four small cork stopper perfumes. Sleeping boy with red hat on lid. Sleeping girl in bed on inside lid. CMV, $400.00 mint.

Little Folks Set II, 1903.
Same as 1903 set, only boy on top of lid is different, and inside lid is different. CMV, $400.00.

Little Folks Set, 1905.
Boy and girl with dog inside lid of box. Four gem sized perfume bottles of Violet, Carnation, White Rose, and Heliotrope. Bottles had cork stoppers and ribbons on necks. Flowers on labels. Box size is 5½" x 3¼". OSP, 40¢. CMV, $75.00 each bottle. $400.00 for set, mint.

Little Folks Set, 1906.
Four small bottles of Violet, Carnation, White Rose or Rose, and Heliotrope perfumes. Birds and kids on lid and edge of box. OSP, 40¢. CMV, $350.00 MB.

Little Folks Set, 1908.
Four gem sized bottles of perfume: Violet, Carnation, Rose, and Heliotrope. Cork stoppers. Same bottles and labels as 1905 Little Folks Set. OSP, 50¢. CMV, $75.00 each bottle. $350.00 for set, mint.

Little Folks Set, 1910. Same box as 1908 set, same bottles and labels as 1912 set. OSP, 50¢. CMV, $350.00 MB.

Little Folks Set, 1912. Same box as 1906 set, only different labels. Birds and kids on lid. OSP, 40¢. CMV, $350.00 MB.

Little Folks Set, 1913. This set has four small bottles: Heliotrope, Carnation, and two bottles of Violet or White Rose perfume. Cork stoppers have paper covers with green ribbons. Box has girl picking flowers on the top and inside of lid. CMV, $400.00 MB.

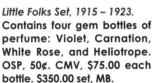

Little Folks Set, 1915 – 1923. Contains four gem bottles of perfume: Violet, Carnation, White Rose, and Heliotrope. OSP, 50¢. CMV, $75.00 each bottle. $350.00 set, MB.

Little Folks Set, 1923 – 1932. Blue box contains four gem sized bottles of floral perfumes in Daphne, Vernafleur, Trailing Arbutus, Carnation, Violet, Heliotrope, or White Lilac. All have brass caps. OSP, 69¢. CMV, $65.00 each bottle. $300.00 for set, mint.

Little Folks Set, 1923 – 1932. Outer sleeve and closed box.

Little Folks Set, 1932 only. Same box as 1923 – 1932 Little Folks Set. Holds four octagonal shaped bottles. Silver labels, black caps. Came in Ariel, Bolero, Gardenia, and Trailing Arbutus. OSP, 90¢. CMV, $275.00 set, MB.

Little Folks Set, 1932 – 1936. Four small bottles, choice of Ariel, Vernafleur, Gardenia, Bolero, 391, or Trailing Arbutus perfumes with black caps and silver labels. OSP, 90¢. CMV, $200.00 MB. $225.00 MB with outer turquoise box as shown.

Little Folks Set, 1937 – 1939. Fancy box has four bottles of perfume in Gardenia, Cotillion, Narcissus, and Trailing Arbutus. 2 dram size. OSP, 94¢. CMV, $20.00 each bottle. $165.00 MB.

Men's Sets

Shaving Set Box, 1914. Black cardboard box. CPC label inside lid. Contents list on lid. CMV, $20.00 box only.

Army and Navy Kit, 1918. Heavy cardboard box holds two bars of peroxide toilet soap, styptic pencil, Elite Foot Powder, Cream Shaving Stick, and Dental Cream. OSP, $1.25. CMV, $275.00 MB.

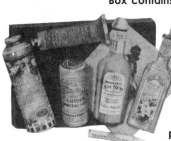

Gentlemen's Shaving Set, 1919. Box contains blue can of White Lilac talcum, green tube of Menthol Witch Hazel Cream, can of Cream Shaving Stick, 4 oz. Bay Rum with cork stopper, styptic pencil, 2 oz. bottle of White Lilac toilet water, and 50 sheet shaving pad. OSP, $2.25. CMV, $450.00 MB.

Gentlemen's Shaving Set, 1915. Box holds glass bottle of Violet talcum powder, can of Cream Shaving Stick, tube of Menthol Witch Hazel Cream, styptic pencil, 4 oz. glass stopper bottle of Bay Rum, 2 oz. White Lilac toilet water, and 50 sheet shaving pad. OSP, $1.50. CMV, $460.00 MB.

Gentlemen's Shaving Set, 1923. Box contains Bayberry Shaving Cream tube, White Lilac Talcum, White Lilac toilet water, styptic pencil, Bay Rum, Menthol Witch Hazel Cream, and shaving pad. OSP, $1.95. CMV, $375.00 MB.

Gentlemen's Shaving Set, 1917. Brown box holds Cream Shaving Stick, Menthol Witch Hazel Cream tube, 50 sheet shaving pad, 2 oz. bottle of White Lilac toilet water, styptic pencil, 4 oz. bottle of genuine Bay Rum with glass stopper, and box of White Lilac Talcum or jar of Violet Talcum. OSP, $1.50. CMV, $450.00 MB, complete set.

Humidor Shaving Set, 1925 – 1928. Woodgrain box trimmed in gold and black holds 2 oz. bottle of Lilac Vegetal, 4 oz. bottle of Bay Rum, blue can of White Lilac Talcum, Trailing Arbutus Cold Cream, tube of Menthol Witch Hazel Cream, Bayberry Shaving Cream tube, and styptic pencil. OSP, $1.95. CMV, $360.00 MB.

Humidor Shaving Set Box, 1925 – 1929. Maroon and gold metal box only. Measures 9¼" wide x 5¾" x 3" deep. Bottom says "Metal Packaging Corp. of New York." CMV, $40.00 box only, mint.

Humidor Shaving Set, 1928 – 1929.
Gold and black metal box holds 4 oz. bottle of Bay Rum, 2 oz. bottle of Lilac Vegetal, styptic pencil, green tube of Menthol Witch Hazel Cream, green tube of Bayberry Shaving Cream, and can of either White Lilac Talcum or Avon Talc for Men. OSP, $2.25. CMV, $350.00 complete set, MB.

Humidor Shaving Set, 1930 – 1932.
Gold and black metal box holds 4 oz. ribbed bottle of Bay Rum, 2 oz. bottle of Lilac Vegetal with crown cork stopper, styptic pencil, green tubes of Menthol Witch Hazel Cream and Bayberry Shaving Cream, and a green can of Talc for Men. OSP, $2.50. CMV, $300.00 MB.

Humidor Shaving Set Box, 1928 – 1933.
Metal gold striped box. Measures 9¼" wide x 5¾" x 3" deep. Does not say CPC on box. Picture of ship on lid. CMV, $40.00 box only, mint.

Humidor Shaving Set, 1930 – 1933.
Gold and black metal box holds 4 oz. ribbed glass Bay Rum, 2 oz. ribbed glass Lilac Vegetal (black cap), styptic pencil, green tubes of Bayberry Shaving Cream, and a green can of Talc for Men. OSP, $2.50. CMV, $265.00 MB.

Women's Fragrance Lines

What's Hot and What's Not in Women's Fragrance Lines

We suggest you do not collect any women's fragrance lines 1975 or newer as there is little to no collector demand. Only soaps, sets, and Avon representative awards are collectible. All fragrance line awards will be found in the Avon Representative Awards section of this book. Mass production and over supply means there may be no resale demand to collectors for fragrance lines in the future. Some children's fragrance lines might be added because of the cuteness of the product and some collectors' interest in this type of product. We suggest you buy the newer fragrance products, use them, and dispose of them. They may never have any future value. The older fragrance lines are very collectible. The older the better for resale, just like any collectible. All fragrance line products 1975 or newer are not included because they are of no value to most collectors. The following fragrance lines have been removed from this book as of 1987 and no new fragrance lines will be added after 1987:

Ariane	Mineral Spring	Sweet Honesty
Avonshire Blue	Odyssey	Tasha
Candid	Patchwork	Tempo
Come Summer	Private World	Tender Blossoms
Country Breeze	Queen's Gold	Timeless
Delicate Daisies	Raining Violets	Toccara
Emprise	Sea Garden	Tracy
Foxfire	Sportif	Unspoken
Lemon Velvet	Sun Blossom	Zany

Apple Blossom

Complexion Soap, 1925.
Yellow and pink wrapping on three bars of soap. CMV, $85.00 MB.

Colonial Set, 1941 – 1942.
Satin lined box holds Apple Blossom Perfume with gold cap and blue feather box of face powder. CMV, $80.00 MB. Also came with perfume on right side of box.

Beauty Dust, 1941 – 1948.
6 oz. blue and white paper box. CMV, $15.00 for Beauty Dust only, mint. $20.00 MB.

Blue Bird Set with Lipstick, 1941.
Satin lined box holds Apple Blossom Body Powder, blue feather box of face powder, and turquoise and gold lipstick. CMV, $80.00 MB.

Toilet Water, 1941 – 1942.
2 oz., pink, white, and blue. CMV, $30.00 BO. $40.00 MB.

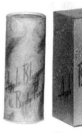

Body Powder, 1941 – 1944.
Blue feather design, flat sifter top container in special issue box as shown. CMV, $22.50 CO, mint. $25.00 MB as shown.

Blue Bird Set with Perfume, 1941.
Blue satin lined box holds Apple Blossom Per-fume, Apple Blossom Body Powder, and blue feather box of face powder. CMV, $90.00 MB.

Perfume, 1941 – 1943.
Box holds ⅛ oz. bottle with gold cap and label. CMV, $27.50 BO, mint. $40.00 MB as shown.

Cologne, 1941 – 1943.
6 oz. bubble sided bottle with pink cap. CMV, $45.00 BO. $60.00 MB.

Perfume, 1941 – 1942.
⅛ oz., gold cap. This bottle has two dif-ferent gold labels and round or flat top caps. CMV, $27.50 BO. $45.00 MB.

Beauty Dust, 1941 – 1948.
6 oz., blue and white feather design paper container. CMV, $18.00 mint. The feather plume outer box shown was issued Christ-mas, 1942 only. Add $7.00 for this box.

Mother's Day Beauty Dust, 1942 – 1943.
Special issue blue, pink, and white lace design box. Holds feather design Apple Blossom beauty dust. Sold around Mother's Day only in this special box. CMV, $30.00 MB as shown.

Beauty Dust, 1943 – 1945.
Blue and white feather design paper box. CMV, $35.00 CO, mint. $40.00 MB. Outer box pictured is 1943 Christmas issue only, rare. CMV, $45.00 MB as shown.

Petal of Beauty Set, 1943 – 1944.
Blue flowered box, pink satin lining, holds 6 oz. Apple Blossom cologne, and pink cap and blue feathered Apple Blossom Beauty Dust. CMV, $100.00 MB.

Flowertime Set, 1943.
Green satin lined box with flower carts on lid. Holds 6 oz. Apple Blossom cologne and Apple Blossom Body Powder. CMV, $90.00 MB.

Beauty Dust, 1946.
Special short issue box holds regular issue beauty dust. CMV, $25.00 MB as shown.

Attention

Body Powder, 1941 – 1943.
Pink box, flat sifter top on paper container. CMV, $20.00 CO, mint. $25.00 MB.

Sachet, 1942.
Special first issue blue box as shown. 1¼ oz. bottle, turquoise cap. CMV, $20.00 MB as shown.

Scentiments Set, 1943 only.
2 oz. clear bottle of toilet water, gold foil label, white cap or gold cap. White and pink or pink and blue satin sachet pillows. CMV, $75.00 MB.

Toilet Water, 1942 only.
Special issue Christmas box holds 2 oz. Attention toilet water with purple cap and label. CMV, $30.00 BO. $45.00 MB as shown.

Sachet Christmas Box, 1942.
1¼ oz. bottle with turquoise cap, sold 1942 – 1948. Regular issue box shown in Powder Sachets section. The box pictured here was a special issue for Christmas. CMV, $12.00 BO, mint. $18.00 MB as shown.

Sachet 57th Anniversary Box, 1943.
Special issue purple and pink box with flowers. Holds regular issue Attention powder sachet. Sold for 25¢, to celebrate Avon's 57th Anniversary. CMV, $20.00 MB as shown.

Bath Salts, 1943 – 1944, then 1946 – 1948.
Tulip "A" box holds 9 oz. or 8½ oz. glass jar with turquoise lid. CMV, $15.00 BO, mint. $25.00 MB.

Pink Ribbon Set, 1943 – 1945.
Blue and pink box holds blue and pink can of Attention body powder and paper box of Attention Bath Salts. OSP, $1.61. CMV, $75.00 for set in box.

Flowertime Set, 1943 – 1945.
Box holds 6 oz. Attention cologne and Attention body powder. OSP, $1.65. 1943 set had green satin lined box with flower carts on lid. CMV, $90.00 MB. 1944 set in plain box with flower design on lid, CMV, $90.00 MB. 1945 set in white box with boy and girl in 1700 style dress under a tree, CMV, $90.00.

Body Powder, 1943 – 1945.
Blue and pink cardboard container. Came in Pink Ribbon Set only. CMV, $30.00.

Bath Salts, 1943 – 1945.
9 oz. blue and pink cardboard container. Came in Pink Ribbon Set only. CMV, $30.00.

Toilet Water, 1943 – 1946.
2 oz. bottle came with gold ribbed cap or plastic cap. CMV, $25.00 BO, mint. $35.00 MB.

Body Powder, 1943 – 1947.
Blue and white cardboard with feather design. CMV, $20.00 CO, mint. $25.00 MB.

Flowertime Set, 1944.
Box with flowers on lid holds 6 oz. Attention cologne and Attention body powder. CMV, $85.00 MB.

Scentiments Set, 1945 only.
Box holds 6 oz. Attention cologne and two satin sachet pillows. OSP, $2.50. CMV, $90.00 MB.

Cologne, 1943 – 1947.
6 oz. bubble sided bottle with pink tall or short cap. CMV, $50.00 BO. $65.00 MB.

Avon Cologne

Avon Cologne, 1941. 6 oz. flat sided bottle. Soon after Avon Cologne was introduced, the name was changed to Orchard Blossoms Cologne. CMV, $50.00 BO. $65.00 MB.

Avon Cologne Representative Gift, 1943. 6 oz. clear bottle, maroon and gold label, blue cap. Bottom label reads "This is a gift to our representatives and must not be offered for sale." Came in blue and pink box, pink ribbon on box and bottle. 57th Anniversary Campaign card. CMV, $100.00 BO, mint. $150.00 MB as shown.

Avonshire Blue

Also see page 433 in Women's Decanters and Collectibles section.

Avonshire Blue Products, 1971 – 1974. Wedgwood blue and white over clear glass.

Cologne Decanter. 6 oz. Comes in Field Flowers, Brocade, Elusive, or Charisma. CMV, $8.00 BO. $10.00 MB.

Perfume Candle. Holds Patchwork, Sonnet, Moonwind, Bird of Paradise, Charisma, Wassail, Roses Roses, Bayberry, or Frankincense and Myrrh. CMV, $8.00 CO. $10.00 MB.

Bath Oil Decanter. 6 oz. Holds Skin So Soft, Field Flowers, or Bird of Paradise. CMV, $8.00 BO. $10.00 MB.

Soap Set. Three bars, 2 oz. each, blue soap. CMV, $10.00 MB.

Soap Dish and Soap, 1972. 6" long blue dish trimmed in white with white bar of soap. Came with oval soap or round soap. CMV, $10.00 oval. $23.00 round soap MB.

Baby Products

Baby products 1975 or newer are not collectible except soaps and sets.

CPC Baby Book, 1915. CMV, $30.00 mint.

Lanolin Baby Soap, 1946 – 1950. Pink box holds two wrapped bars. CMV, $20.00 each bar. $45.00 MB.

Baby Talc, 1951 – 1955.
Blue and white box and can. CMV, $13.00 CO. $18.00 in box.

Lanolin Baby Soap, 1951 – 1955.
Blue and white box and wrapping, holds two bars. CMV, $25.00 in box.

Baby Lotion, 1951 – 1955.
4 oz. white plastic bottle, blue cap. CMV, $8.00 BO. $12.00 MB.

Baby Powder, 1954 – 1956.
2 oz. pink can and cap, paper label around can. Came in Little Lamb Set (see Women's Sets of the 1950s). Rare. CMV, $25.00.

Baby Powder, 1954 – 1956.
2 oz., blue, white, and pink can, pink cap. Came in Little Lamb Set (see Women's Sets of the 1950s). CMV, $20.00.

Baby Oil, 1955 – 1960.
8 oz. bottle with indented sides, white cap. OSP, 79¢. CMV, $15.00.

Baby Soap, 1955 – 1961.
Blue and white box holds Castile with Lanolin white cake baby soap. OSP, 29¢. CMV, $12.00 MB. Also came with "Castile with Lanolin" on box and printed on soap horizontally. Same CMV.

Baby Lotion, 1955 – 1957.
8 oz. bottle with indented sides, white cap. OSP, 89¢. CMV, $12.50 BO. $15.00 MB.

Baby and Me Set, 1957 – 1958.
Clear glass bottle of baby lotion, white cap, and Cotillion toilet water, gold cap, pink paper around neck. Box is white, blue, and pink. CMV, $45.00 MB.

Baby Cream, 1961 – 1964.
2 oz. blue and white tube. CMV, $4.00.

Baby Soap, 1961 – 1964.
Blue and white wrapper. OSP, 39¢. CMV, $8.00.

Tot 'N' Tyke Baby Shampoo, 1959 – 1964.
6 oz. white plastic bottle, blue cap. CMV, $6.00 BO. $7.00 MB.

Baby Lotion, 1958 – 1964.
6 oz. white plastic bottle, blue cap. CMV, $5.00.

Baby Oil, 1960 – 1964.
6 oz. white plastic bottle, blue cap. CMV, $6.00.

Baby Powder, 1955 – 1964.
9 oz. blue and white can. OSP, 59¢. CMV, $10.00.

Sweetest One Baby Set, 1962 – 1964.
Pink and white box holds one bar Baby Soap, Baby Powder, and Baby Lotion or Baby Oil. Bar of soap had blue ends with white center or white ends with blue center. CMV, $40.00 MB.

Tot 'N' Tyke Baby Shampoo, 1959 – 1964.
Special issue box as shown. CMV, $12.00 MB as shown.

Baby Soap, 1962 – 1964.
White ends and blue center line. CMV, $8.00 mint.

Baby Lotion Samples, 1964 – 1968.
White foil with pink and blue design. Came 10 to a box. CMV, $6.00 box or 50¢ per sample.

Tree Tots Set, 1966.
Box holds white plastic hairbrush, 3 oz. plastic tube of Non-Tear Shampoo gel, 3 oz. baby soap with lanolin, and 6 oz. Nursery Fresh Room Spray. CMV, $20.00 MB.

Baby Powder, 1964 – 1968.
9 oz. white plastic bottle, blue cap. CMV, $5.00.

Baby Oil, 1964 – 1966.
6 oz. white plastic bottle with blue cap. CMV, $6.00.

Baby Lotion, 1964 – 1968.
6 oz. white plastic bottle with blue cap. CMV, $5.00.

Baby Shampoo, 1964 – 1968.
6 oz. white plastic bottle with blue cap. CMV, $5.00.

Baby Soap, 1964 – 1968.
Blue and white wrapper, white cake of baby soap. CMV, $7.00.

Baby Cream, 1964 – 1968.
2 oz. blue and white tube with blue cap. CMV, $3.00.

Baby Products, 1968 – 1975.

Shampoo, 1969 – 1974.
Blue, white, and pink, 6 oz. plastic bottle. CMV, $1.00.

Baby Powder, 1969 – 1972.
9 oz., blue, white, and pink plastic bottle. CMV, $2.00.

Baby Cream, 1969 – 1975.
2 oz. tube, blue, pink, and white. CMV, $1.00.

Nursery Fresh Room Spray, 1968 – 1979.
6 oz., blue, white, and pink can. CMV, $1.50. Also came with upside-down label. CMV, $8.00.

Baby Soap, 1969 – 1975.
3 oz. bar wrapped in blue, pink, and white paper. CMV, $2.00.

Baby Lotion, 1969 – 1975.
6 oz., blue, white, and pink plastic bottle. CMV, $1.00.

Ballad

Perfume, 1939 – 1945.
3 dram glass stopper bottle with gold neck cord and gold label at base of bottle. Front of box lays down. See Perfumes section for 1 dram Ballad perfume. CMV, $90.00 BO. $130.00 MB. Very rare.

Award Perfume, 1945.
Avon label on bottom, Ballad label across top, glass stopper. CMV, $375.00 MB. Rare.

Perfume, 1945 – 1953.
Gold and white box holds 3 dram glass stopper bottle with gold neck cord and gold label at base of bottle. CMV, $90.00 BO. $130.00 MB. Rare.

Perfume, 1945 only.
3 dram, clear glass with gold neck cord and label. Gray, white, and gold box. CMV, $90.00 BO. $135.00 MB. Rare.

Bird of Paradise

Bath Brush and Soap, 1970 – 1971.
Blue box holds blue plastic bath brush and blue soap. CMV, $8.00 MB.
Bath Oil Emollient, 1969 – 1975.
6 oz., gold cap and neck tag. CMV, $1.00.
Cologne, 1969 – 1972.
4 oz., gold cap and neck tag. CMV, $2.00.
Beauty Dust, 1969 – 1974.
6 oz. turquoise and gold paper box. CMV, $3.00 CO. $5.00 MB.
Cologne Mist, 1970 – 1976.
3 oz. blue plastic coated bottle with gold cap and neck tag. CMV, $1.00.
Cream Sachet, 1969 – 1975.
⅔ oz., blue glass with gold lid. CMV, 50¢.
Soap Set, 1970 – 1976.
Three bars blue soap, 3 oz. each, in blue and turquoise box. First issue, no flower on soap. 1972 soap had flower. CMV, $4.00 MB, no flowers. $6.00 MB.

Cologne Fluff, 1969 – 1972.
3 oz. blue plastic coated bottle with gold top. Blue and gold neck tag. CMV, 50¢.

Perfume Rollette, 1970 – 1976.
⅓ oz. bottle with gold cap, turquoise and green box. CMV, $1.00 MB.

Perfume Glace Ring, 1970 – 1972.
Gold ring with turquoise top. Perfume glace inside. CMV, $7.00.

Cologne, 1970 – 1972.
½ oz. bottle with gold cap. CMV, $2.00 MB.

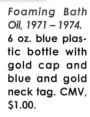

Foaming Bath Oil, 1971 – 1974.
6 oz. blue plastic bottle with gold cap and blue and gold neck tag. CMV, $1.00.

Perfumed Talc, 1971 – 1978.
Two different labels. Left and center have same label but top is turquoise on one and dark blue on the other. One on right has dark blue label and top. Each is 3¼ oz. CMV, 50¢ each. Also came with upside down label. CMV, $4.00.

Perfumed Powder Mist, 1971 – 1977.
7 oz. blue and gold can, gold cap. CMV, 50¢.

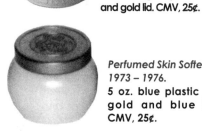

Perfumed Skin Softener, 1971 – 1973.
5 oz. blue glass jar with blue and gold lid. CMV, 25¢.

Perfumed Skin Softener, 1973 – 1976.
5 oz. blue plastic jar, gold and blue lid. CMV, 25¢.

Scented Hair Spray, 1971 – 1972.
7 oz. blue can and lid. CMV, $3.00.

Soap, 1975.
3 oz. blue bar with blue wrapper and floral center. CMV, $1.00 mint.

Bird of Paradise Soap, 1975 – 1978.
3 oz. blue bar with blue wrapper. CMV, $1.00 mint.

Blue Lotus

After Bath Freshener, 1967 – 1972.
6 oz. glass bottle with blue cap. CMV, $2.00.
Cream Sachet, 1968 – 1972.
⅔ oz., blue frosted glass with blue cap. CMV, $1.00.
Not shown: Foaming Bath Oil, 1970 – 1973.
6 oz. plastic bottle with blue cap. CMV, 50¢.
Cream Lotion, 1969 – 1972.
5 oz. plastic bottle with blue cap. CMV, 50¢.
Demi Stick, 1969 – 1973.
³⁄₁₆ oz., white plastic with blue and green center. CMV, $1.00.
Perfumed Soap, 1967 – 1971.
3 oz., blue, white, and purple wrapper. OSP, 75¢. CMV, $2.00.
Perfumed Talc, 1967 – 1971.
3½ oz. cardboard container with plastic shaker top. OSP, $1.10. CMV, $2.00.

Bright Night

Perfume, 1954 – 1959. Gold and white box holds ½ oz. glass stopper bottle with white label on gold neck cord. CMV, $75.00 BO. $120.00 MB. Also came with 1 dram perfume in felt wrapper on top of lid. Add $15.00 for 1 dram perfume with ribbon around box.

Melody Set, 1955 – 1956. Gold and white box holds 1 dram perfume, cream sachet, 4 oz. cologne, and beauty dust. CMV, $85.00.

Golden Beauty, 1957. Gold base box lined with gold acetate with gold plastic lid, holds beauty dust, 4 oz. cologne, cream sachet, and 1 dram perfume. CMV, $85.00.

Cologne, 1954 – 1961. 4 oz., gold speckled cap with gold neck cord and white paper label. CMV, $14.00 BO, mint. $20.00 MB.

Toilet Water, 1955 – 1961. 2 oz. gold speckled cap with white paper label on gold neck cord. CMV, $14.00 BO. $20.00 MB.

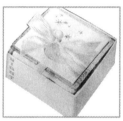

Beauty Dust, 1957 – 1958. White cardboard box trimmed in gold. Issued for Christmas with ⅝ oz. dram Snowflake perfume bottle with white ribbon and cap. CMV, $30.00 MB.

Cream Sachet, 1954 – 1961. White glass jar with stars on white lid. CMV, $6.00 CO. $8.00 MB.

Beauty Dust, 1956. Issued for Christmas 1956 with long neck perfume bottle with white cap and ribbon. CMV, $30.00 MB.

Not shown: Beauty Dust, 1954 – 1959. Same powder box as above, without perfume. CMV, $18.00 mint.

Powder Sachet, 1955 – 1961. ⁹⁄₁₀ oz., 1¼, or 1½ oz. white glass jar with stars on white lid. Front paper label. CMV, $8.00 BO. $12.00 MB. 1½ oz., rare. CMV, $16.00 BO. $20.00 MB.

Magic Hours Set, 1956. Gold and white box holds 2 oz. toilet water and white cologne stick. CMV, $45.00.

Beauty Dust, 1959 – 1961.
White plastic box with gold stars on lid. CMV, $8.00 BO. $12.00 MB.

Gems, 1957.
Gold and white flip-open box holds 2 oz. toilet water in top and cream sachet in pull-out drawer in bottom. CMV, $45.00 mint.

Cologne Mist, 1958 – 1961.
3 oz. white plastic coated over clear glass. Gold speckled cap, gold neck cord with white paper label. Came with two different caps. CMV, $8.00 BO. $10.00 MB.

Golden Glamor Set, 1958.
Gold and white box holds cologne mist, 1 dram perfume, cream sachet, and beauty dust. CMV, $95.00 MB.

Bristol Blue

Cologne, 1975.
5 oz. translucent blue glass filled with Moonwind, Sonnet, or Imperial Garden cologne. CMV, $4.00 BO. $5.00 MB.

Bath Oil, 1975 – 1976.
5 oz. blue opaline glass decanter with plastic inner bottle that holds Skin So Soft bath oil. CMV, $4.00 BO. $5.00 MB.

Soap Dish and Soap, 1975 – 1976.
Translucent blue opaline glass dish with Moonwind, Sonnet, or Imperial Garden soap. CMV, $10.00 MB.

Brocade

Perfume Glace, 1967 – 1972.
Gold case. CMV, $6.00 CO. $7.00 MB.

Left: Cologne, 1967 – 1972.
4 oz., frosted ribbed glass with brown and white cap. CMV, $2.00 MB.

Center: Cologne Mist, 1967 – 1972.
3 oz., ribbed frosted glass with brown and white cap. Some lids have design only and some say "Brocade" on top. CMV, $2.00 MB.

Right: Cologne Mist Refill, 1967 – 1972.
3 oz. brown plastic coated bottle, white cap. CMV, $2.00 MB.

Deluxe Gift Set, 1967.
Brown and white box with white lining holds beauty dust, perfume rollette, and cream sachet. CMV, $35.00 MB.

Perfume Rollette, 1967 – 1972.
Left: **Brown frosted glass, gold cap with 4A design. Ribs horizontal. OSP, $3.00. CMV, $3.00.**
Inside left: **Same as above, only no 4A design. CMV, $3.00.**
Inside right: **Brown carnival glass, gold cap. Vertical ribs. CMV, $8.00.**
Right: **Brown frosted glass, brown and white paper band on cap. Ribs horizontal. CMV, $5.00.**

Soap, 1968.
Brown and white wrapper. Came in Perfume Pair only. CMV, $4.00 mint.

Perfume Oil, 1967 – 1969.
½ oz., frosted brown glass with gold cap. CMV, $5.00 MB.

Perfumed Skin Softener, 1968 only.
Manufactured during glass strike. 5 oz., round smooth brown glass, label painted on top. CMV, $15.00 mint.

Perfumed Powder Mist, 1967 – 1974.
7 oz. brown and white painted can with gold cap. CMV, 50¢. Some came with 7 oz. weight listed on center label, xome at bottom of can in front. Center label, CMV, $3.00.

Cologne Silk, 1968 – 1970.
3 oz. frosted bottle with gold cap. CMV, $2.00 BO. $4.50 MB.

Perfumed Skin Softener, 1968 – 1969.
5 oz., ribbed sides, brown glass, label printed on top. CMV, $3.00 MB.

Beauty Dust, 1967 – 1971.
Brown ribbed plastic, patterned lid. CMV, $6.00 CO. $9.00 MB.

Brocade Foaming Bath Oil, 1968 – 1972.
6 oz. plastic bottle with gold cap. CMV, $1.00.

Cream Sachet, 1967 – 1968.
⅔ oz., brown ribbed glass, label on top. CMV, $2.00 MB.

Cream Sachet, 1968 – 1975.
⅔ oz., brown ribbed glass, designed cap. CMV, 50¢.

Talc, 1968. 2¾ oz. metal talc, brown, white, and gold. Sold only in Perfume Pair set. CMV, $2.00.

Perfumed Talc, 1969 – 1972. 3½ oz. brown and white cardboard. CMV, $1.00.

Scented Hair Spray, 1969 – 1972. 7 oz. brown and white can. CMV, $1.00.

Perfumed Skin Softener, 1969 – 1972. 5 oz., ribbed sides, brown glass, designed top. CMV, $2.00 BO. $3.00 MB.

Cologne, 1970 – 1971. Ribbed clear glass with gold cap. CMV, $2.00 MB.

Manager's Demo Kit, 1969. Box holds round talc and cologne mist. CMV, $27.50 MB.

Beauty Dust, 1971 – 1975. Pattern printed cardboard, non-refillable. CMV, $4.00 MB. Also came with upside down lettering. CMV, $6.00.

Buttons 'n' Bows

Beauty Dust, 1960 – 1963. Pink and white cardboard box with clear plastic lid. CMV, $16.00.

Button Button Set, 1961 – 1962. Pink and white box holds 2 oz. cologne and beauty dust. CMV, $40.00 MB.

Nail Polish, 1961 – 1963. Pink and white box holds nail polish with white cap. CMV, $6.00 BO. $8.00 MB.

Cream Sachet, 1960 – 1963. Pink glass jar with white and pink lid. CMV, $9.00 BO. $12.00 MB.

Left: Cologne, 1960 – 1963. 2 oz. clear glass, white cap, pink lettering, came with pink ribbon bow around neck. CMV, $9.00 BO. $12.00 MB.
Right: Cologne Mist, 1960 – 1963. 2½ oz., pink plastic with white cap. Bottom is 2 shades of pink. CMV, $9.00. $12.00 MB.

Lipstick, 1961 – 1963. Pink and white box holds pink and white striped lipstick. CMV, $4.00 TO. $7.00 MB.

Soap, 1961 – 1963.
Pink box and soap. Some buttons have thread through holes. CMV, $25.00 MB, no threads, $27.50 with threads. Two boxes are shown. Each box holds two bars. Boxes are the same.

Cute as a Button Set, 1961 – 1963.
Pink and white box holds Buttons 'N' Bows nail polish with white cap and pink and white lipstick. CMV, $17.00 MB.

Roll-on Deodorant, 1962 – 1963.
1¾ oz., white and pink painted label on clear glass, pink cap. CMV, $8.00 BO. $12.00 MB.

Pretty Choice Set, 1962 – 1963.
2 oz. frosted plastic bottle of cream lotion, white cap. Cologne, clear glass, white cap, light pink ribbon on neck. Choice of cream lotion or bubble bath. CMV, $30.00 MB.

Left: Cream Lotion, 1962 – 1963.
4 oz. pink plastic bottle with white cap, CMV, $6.00 BO. $10.00 MB.

Right: Bubble Bath, 1962 – 1963.
4 oz., pink plastic, white cap, pink lettering. CMV, $6.00 BO. $10.00 MB. Cream lotion and bubble bath both came in solid pink plastic and clear frosted plastic bottle. Pink has pink letters. Frosted has white letters.

Sachet, 1961 – 1963.
Gold metal base holds pink painted over milk glass jar with white lid with lady's face. Came in Topaze, Cotillion, Somewhere, To a Wild Rose, Persian Wood, and Here's My Heart. CMV, $7.00 BO. $11.00 MB.

Brooch, 1965.
Gold brooch with pink and white lady's face. Came in Cameo Set only. CMV, $9.00 brooch only. $15.00 MB.

Cameo Set, 1965.
White, gold, and green box holds Cameo compact, lipstick, and brooch. CMV, $30.00.

Lipstick, 1965 – 1966.
White lipstick with gold base and lady's face on top. CMV, $2.00 tube only. $3.00 MB.

Compact, 1965 – 1966.
White plastic with gold edge and pink lady's face on top. CMV, $6.00 compact only. $8.00 MB.

Soap, 1966.
Blue and white box holds four white Cameo soaps. CMV, $20.00 MB.

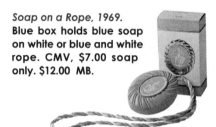

Soap on a Rope, 1969.
Blue box holds blue soap on white or blue and white rope. CMV, $7.00 soap only. $12.00 MB.

Cameo Set, 1973 – 1974.
Reddish brown plastic with white Cameo beauty dust, 6 oz. Came in Sonnet, Moonwind, Hana Gasa, Charisma, Unforgettable, Rapture, Somewhere, Cotillion, Here's My Heart, Topaze, Occur!, and To a Wild Rose. CMV, $4.00.
Brush and Comb Set. CMV, $3.00.
Mirror. CMV, $2.00.

Charisma

Tray, 1968 – 1970.
Left: Dark red plastic with gold trim. 11" diameter. This one used as introduction. CMV, $8.00 MB.
Right: Lighter red plastic with gold rim. 10" diameter. CMV, $3.00 tray only. $5.00 MB.

Beauty Dust, 1968 – 1976.
6 oz. red plastic powder box trimmed in gold. CMV, $3.00 CO. $6.00 MB.

Cologne Mist, 1968 – 1976.
3 oz., red plastic coated, trimmed in gold. CMV, $1.00.

Cologne, 1969 – 1972.
4 oz., red glass, some are silver tip (rare) with red plastic cap trimmed in gold. CMV, $3.00.

Cream Sachet, 1968 – 1976.
⅔ oz. red glass jar with red and gold lid. CMV, 50¢.

Perfume Rollette, 1968 – 1976.
⅓ oz., red glass trimmed in gold. CMV, $1.00.

Cologne, 1969 – 1972.
½ oz., red glass, gold cap. CMV, $2.00.

Cologne Silk, 1969.
3 oz., frosted glass, red cap. CMV, $3.00 MB.

Perfumed Powder Mist, 1969 – 1970.
7 oz. red and gold can, gold top, has paper label. Also came boxed. CMV, $3.00.

Perfumed Talc, 1970 – 1976.
3½ oz. red cardboard. CMV, 50¢.

Soap, 1970 – 1976.
Red box holds three bars. CMV, $6.00 MB.

Scented Hair Spray, 1970 – 1972.
7 oz. red can. CMV, $3.00.

Cologne Silk, 1970 – 1971.
3 oz., clear glass, red cap. CMV, $2.00 MB.

Perfumed Powder Mist, 1971 – 1976.
7 oz. red and gold can, gold top, painted label. No longer boxed. CMV, $1.00.

Soap, 1975.
Three pink soaps in special Christmas 1975 design box. CMV, $8.00 MB.

Cotillion

All white caps on 1961 – 1974 Cotillion bottles will turn dark gray when exposed to sunlight. The gray or faded caps are not considered to be in mint condition.

Perfume, 1934.
¼ oz. metal cap. First Cotillion bottle issued in honor of Mr. McConnell's birthday. CMV, $55.00 BO. $75.00 MB.

Tulip Perfume Christmas Box, 1935.
Red and green Christmas box holds ¼ oz. glass stopper perfume with gold label. This bottle was sold from 1934 to 1939. With this box, Christmas 1935 only. CMV, $90.00 MB as shown.

Perfume, 1935 only.
¼ oz., gold cap, green and yellow label and box. For 77th birthday of D. H. McConnell. CMV, $60.00 BO. $80.00 MB.

Perfume, 1936 only.
2 dram, gold ribbed cap. Sold for 20¢ from July 7 to 27, 1936 only, with purchase of other Avon. In honor of Mr. McConnell's 78th birthday. CMV, $60.00 BO. $80.00 MB.

53rd Anniversary Talcum, 1939 only.
Special 53rd anniversary box to first introduce Cotillion talcum. May 23 to June 12, 1939. 2¾ oz. turquoise and white can. This can was sold 1939 – 1943, then 1946 – 1950. CMV, $10.00 CO. In special 53rd box, $25.00.

Perfume, 1937.
2 dram, gold cap. CMV, $50.00 BO. $70.00 MB.

Enchantment Set, 1938 – 1939.
White box with satin lining holds Cotillion 2 dram glass stopper perfume, 2 oz. toilet water and powder sachet. CMV, $150.00 MB.

Sachet, 1937 – 1938.
1¼ oz. ribbed glass bottle with turquoise cap. CMV, $18.00 BO, mint. $24.00 MB.

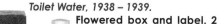

Toilet Water, 1938 – 1939.
Flowered box and label. 2 oz. bottle, white plastic cap. Sold for 20¢ with purchase of other Avon, May 2 – 22, 1939. "CPC" on box and back side of label. CMV, $37.50 BO, mint. $52.50 MB.

Face Powder, 1939 – 1942.
Gold and turquoise powder box. CMV, $8.00 CO. $10.00 MB. Add $3.00 for CPC label.

Sachet, 1937.
Red and green box sold around Christmas only, for 25¢. "CPC" on box and bottle. CMV, $18.00 BO, mint. $25.00 MB.

Talcum, 1938 – 1950.
2¾ oz. turquoise can. Box marked 2¾ oz. size. Can sold 1938 – 1943, then 1946 – 1950. CMV, $10.00 CO. $15.00 MB, mint.

Sachet, 1939 – 1944.
1¼ oz., turquoise cap, clear glass, paper label. CMV, $12.00 BO. $16.00 MB.

Sachet, 1937.
Blue and white box special issue. CMV, $25.00 MB. Bottle only, ribbed glass, turquoise cap, sold 1937 – 1938. CMV, $18.00 BO, mint.

Perfume, 1939 only.
2 dram, ribbed cap with "A" on cap. Sold for one campaign only for 20¢ with purchase of other Avon. CMV, $55.00 BO. $75.00 MB.

Sachet Special Issue Box, 1939.
Special issue box is blue with lace design. Holds regular issue powder sachet. CMV, $20.00 MB as shown.

Perfume,
1940 only.
2 dram, ribbed gold cap with "A" on top. Also came with plain gold cap. Sold for 20¢ with purchase of other Avon. CMV, $55.00 BO. $75.00 MB.

Classic Set, 1940 – 1941.
Satin lined box with people dancing on lid held 2 oz. toilet water and gold box of talc. CMV, $67.50 MB.

Talcum, 1942 – 1946.
2¾ oz. turquoise and white all paper box. War time. Paper top fits over top of box, shaker top. CMV, $20.00 without top in mint. CMV, $25.00 mint.

Talcum, 1940 – 1943
Then 1946 – 1950.
14½ oz. metal can, turquoise and white. CMV $20.00, add $5.00 for CPC label.

Talcum, 1941 only.
Blue box with fan. 2¾ oz. can. Sold to reps for 10¢ to use as a demonstrator. CMV, $30.00 MB as shown.

Talcum Christmas Box, 1943.
Pale blue and pink outer box issued only at Christmas 1943 with cardboard large size talc. CMV, $35.00 MB as shown.

Talcum Christmas Box, 1940 – 1941.
Special issue blue and white Christmas box held regular issue metal can of talcum in large size. Rare. CMV, $30.00 MB as shown.

Talcum, 1943 – 1946.
14½ oz. paper box used during war. Rare. CMV, $35.00.

Enchantment Set, 1940 – 1943.
Silk lined gold and green box held powder sachet, 2 oz. toilet water, and 1 dram perfume with gold cap. CMV, $95.00 MB.

Sachet Box, 1941 only.
Special issue box to Avon ladies only, for 20¢. Held regular issue Cotillion sachet, 1939 – 1944. CMV, $20.00 MB as shown.

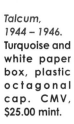

Talcum, 1944 – 1946.
Turquoise and white paper box, plastic octagonal cap. CMV, $25.00 mint.

Sachet, 1944 – 1945. 1¼ oz. paper box, pink plastic flowers on lid. CMV, $18.00 BO, mint. $20.00 MB.

Cologne, 1946 – 1950. 6 oz. pink cap. CMV, $50.00 BO. $65.00 MB.

Cotillion Duet/ Cotillion Garland Set, 1946. Pink round box held toilet water and pink painted powder sachet. This set was introduced as Cotillion Duet then changed to Cotillion Garland for Christmas 1946. CMV, $80.00 MB.

Perfume, 1945. 3 dram bottle. Inset box with feather design. CMV, $90.00 MB.

Body Powder, 1946 – 1950. 4½ oz., light pink cardboard. Blue metal sifter top. CMV, $15.00, CO. $20.00 MB. Came in sets, 5 oz. size with pink and white plastic sifter top. Same CMV.

Classic Set, 1946 – 1947. Pink flowered box held 6 oz. cologne and body powder. CMV, $95.00.

Perfume, 1945 – 1947. 3 dram glass stopper bottle with gold neck tag. Came in blue, pink, and white box as shown. CMV, $100.00 BO, mint. $125.00 MB.

Sachet, 1946 – 1947. 1¼ oz., pink glass and cap with painted label. Rare. Sold only in Cotillion Garland Set. Same set in 1947 was called Cotillion Duet. CMV, $20.00 jar only. $22.00 MB.

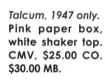

Talcum, 1947 only. Pink paper box, white shaker top. CMV, $25.00 CO. $30.00 MB.

Toilet Water, 1946 – 1949. 2 oz., pink, gold, or white cap. OSP, $1.19. CMV, $25.00 BO, mint. $35.00 MB.

Sachet, 1946 – 1949. 1¼ oz., clear glass, pink cap, paper label. CMV, $16.00 jar only. $18.00 MB.

Duet Set, 1947 – 1948. Pink box holds 2 oz. toilet water with gold cap and powder sachet. OSP, $2.75. CMV, $70.00 MB.

Swirl Perfume, 1948 – 1950.
3 dram glass stopper, swirl glass design, gold neck tag. Purple and white flowered box. CMV, $75.00 BO, mint. $100.00 MB.

Toilet Water, 1949 – 1950.
2 oz., pink cap. OSP, $1.25. CMV, $22.50 BO. $25.00 MB. Cologne water in same design bottle and label. 2 oz. size, pink cap. Same OSP and CMV.

Always Sweet Set, 1950.
Pink and white box holds straw handbag with green and yellow ribbon and pink flower. Holds bottle of cream lotion with blue cap, talc, and ⅝ dram perfume. CMV, $95.00 MB.

Your Charms Set, 1949.
White, blue, and pink box, with or without ribbon band around lid, came with gold heart and arrow charm on lid. Box contained pink and blue paper box of Cotillion talc, 2 oz. Avon hand lotion, pink and blue label with blue cap, and ⅝ dram Cotillion perfume with blue cap. Set came with and without perfume. CMV, $65.00 with perfume. $50.00 without perfume.

The Cotillion Set, 1950 – 1952.
Pink and white box with green lining holds cream lotion and cologne. CMV, $60.00 MB.

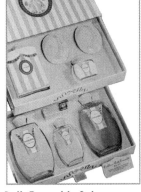

Bath Ensemble Set, 1950 – 1952.
Pink and white drawer box holds two drawers with talc, powder sachet, and two bars of pink soap in top drawer. Bottom drawer holds cream lotion, toilet water, bath oil, and 1 dram perfume. OSP, $8.25. CMV, $175.00 MB.

Hairribbons Set, 1948 – 1949.
Pink and white box held bottle of Avon hand lotion, talcum, and ⅝ dram bottle of Cotillion perfume. This box also came with hand lotion and Cotillion talcum from 1949 Your Charms Set. Set came with or without perfume. OSP, $1.59. CMV, $65.00 with perfume. $50.00 without perfume.

Garland Set, 1950.
Pink, white, and green box held talc and 2 oz. toilet water. CMV, $52.50.

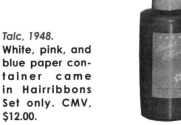

Talc, 1948.
White, pink, and blue paper container came in Hairribbons Set only. CMV, $12.00.

Hand Lotion, 1949.
2 oz. clear glass bottle with pink and blue label, blue cap. Came in Your Charms and Hairribbons sets. CMV, $15.00.

Talc, 1950 only.
2 oz. white cardboard, pink top and bottom. Came in Always Sweet Set only. CMV, $15.00.

Powder Sachet, 1950 – 1953. 1¼ oz., pink cap and pink and white label. CMV, $15.00, jar only. $20.00 MB.

Bath Oil 1950 – 1953. 6 oz., pink and white label and pink cap. Pink and white box. CMV, $18.00 BO. $22.00 MB.

Body Powder, 1950 – 1953. 5 oz. pink and white paper box, sifter top with metal lid and bottom. CMV, $17.00 powder only. $20.00 MB.

Soap, 1950 – 1953. Pink and white box holds pink bars. CMV, $37.50 MB.

Cream Lotion, 1950 – 1953. 6 oz. pink and white label, pink cap and pink and white box. CMV, $18.00 BO. $22.00 MB.

Perfume, 1950. ⅛ oz., pink cap. Very rare. CMV, $70.00 BO. $85.00 MB.

Beauty Dust, 1950 – 1953. Pink and white container. CMV, $20.00 CO, mint. $25.00 MB.

Cologne, 1950 – 1953. 4 oz. bottle with pink cap and label. CMV, $18.00 BO. $22.00 MB.

Perfume, 1951 – 1952. 3 dram glass stopper swirl glass bottle. White, pink, and blue flower design around neck with neck tag. Pink and white box. CMV, $100.00 BO, with tag and flower design mint. $125.00 MB.

Toilet Water, 1950 – 1953. 2 oz., pink cap, pink and white label and white box. Box came solid and with open window so label shows through. CMV, $18.00 BO. $22.00 MB.

Talc, 1950 – 1953. Pink and white can with pink cap. CMV, $12.00 CO. $15.00 MB.

Cream Sachet, 1951 – 1953. White glass jar with pink and white lid. CMV, $15.00.

Enchantment Set, 1951.
Pink, white, and green box held toilet water and cream sachet. OSP, $2.50. CMV, $60.00 MB.

Fantasy Set, 1952.
Pink and white body powder with cream sachet on top under clear plastic lid. CMV, $40.00 MB.

Beauty Dust, 1953 – 1959.
Pink paper sides with pink and white tin top. CMV, $12.00 CO. $16.00 MB.

Jolly Surprise Set, 1951 – 1952.
Pink and white box held powder sachet and 1 dram perfume in pink net lining. CMV, $42.00 set.

Valentine Sachet, 1952.
1 1/4 oz., white cap. CMV, $18.00 BO, mint. CMV, $25.00 MB.

Powder Sachet, 1953 – 1956.
9/10 oz. or 1 1/4 oz. clear glass, pink cap, and pink painted label, white lettering (rare). CMV, $8.00 BO. $12.00 MB. White lettering, $18.00.

Talc, 1951.
2 oz., blue, white, and pink paper container. Came in 1951 Always Sweet Set. CMV, $12.00.

Sachet Valentine Box, 1952.
1 1/4 oz., pink cap. Came in gold, pink, and white Valentine box. Rare in this box. CMV, $25.00 MB as shown.

Always Sweet Set, 1951.
White, blue, and pink box with girl's hat on lid, held straw handbag containing talc, 5/8 dram perfume, and cream lotion with blue cap. CMV, $95.00 MB.

Talc, 1953 – 1954.
4 oz. clear glass bottle with pink cap and pink or white (rare) painted label. 1955 was called "Talcum" in painted label, pink and white box. CMV, $10.00 BO. $15.00 each, MB.

Soap, 1953 – 1961.
Pink and white box held three pink or white bars. Box came as sleeve top with round edge white soaps. 1953 – 1956 CMV, $35.00 MB. 1956 – 1961 came as sleeve top box with three flat edge pink soaps. CMV, $32.50 MB.

Toilet Water, 1953 – 1961.
2 oz., gold cap, pink band around neck, pink or white painted label. CMV, $10.00 BO, mint. $15.00 MB.

Duet Set, 1953 – 1955.
Pink and white flowered box with pink satin lining held 4 oz. cologne and talc. CMV, $42.00 MB.

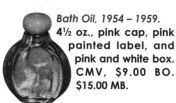

Bath Oil, 1954 – 1959.
4½ oz., pink cap, pink painted label, and pink and white box. CMV, $9.00 BO. $15.00 MB.

Cologne, 1953 – 1961.
4 oz., gold cap, pink band around neck, and pink or white painted label. CMV, $10.00 BO, mint. $15.00 MB.

Enchantment Set, 1953 – 1956.
Pink and white box held powder sachet and 1 dram perfume. CMV, $37.00 MB.

Cream Lotion, 1954 – 1961.
4¼ oz., pink cap and pink painted label, and pink and white box. CMV, $8.00 BO. $12.00 MB.

Cream Sachet, 1953 – 1957.
Pink lid, white glass bottom. CMV, $8.00 jar only. $10.00 MB.

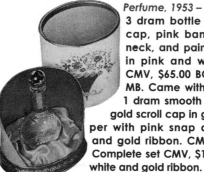

Perfume, 1953 – 1958.
3 dram bottle with gold cap, pink band around neck, and painted label, in pink and white box. CMV, $65.00 BO. $100.00 MB. Came with perfume, 1 dram smooth glass with gold scroll cap in gold wrapper with pink snap and white and gold ribbon. CMV, $12.00. Complete set CMV, $115.00 with white and gold ribbon.

Deluxe Set, 1953 – 1955.
Pink and white box flips open in center. Held 1 dram perfume, 4 oz. cologne, powder sachet, and talcum. Same set also came with lift-off lid. CMV, $60.00 MB.

Garland Set. 1954 – 1955.
Pink and white box holds 4½ oz. bath oil and cream lotion. CMV, $37.50 MB.

Perfumed Talc, 1956 – 1961.
White can with pink cap and design. Also came in just talc. CMV, $8.00 MB.

Talc, 1956 – 1958. 3 oz., frosted glass with pink lid and paper label, pink and white box. CMV, $9.00 BO. $14.00 MB.

Bath Oil, 1955 – 1956. 2 oz. clear glass bottle with pink cap and pink and white label. Came in That's for Me Set only. See Women's Sets of the 1950s. CMV, $15.00.

Powder Sachet, 1957 – 1961. Pink paint over clear glass, pink cap. Rare issue, came with no painted label. Plain pink all over. CMV, $14.00 jar only. $18.00 MB.

Bath Bouquet Set, 1956 only. Pink and white box held 2 oz. cologne, 2 oz. bath oil, and one bar of soap. CMV, $55.00 MB.

Cologne, 1956 only. 2 oz., white cap. Came in Bath Bouquet Set only. CMV, $20.00 mint.

Cream Sachet, 1957 – 1961. Pink lid, pink glass bottom. OSP, $1.50. CMV, $7.00 jar only. $9.00 MB.

Carol Set, 1956. Pink and white box held cream sachet with white glass bottom and talc. CMV, $35.00 MB.

Bath Oil, 1956 only. 2 oz., white cap. Came in Bath Bouquet Set only. CMV, $20.00 mint.

Powder Sachet, 1957 – 1961. 1¼ oz. or 9/10 oz., pink cap and pink bottom with painted label. Came light or dark pink bottom and either white or pink painted lettering. CMV, $9.00 jar only. $13.00 MB.

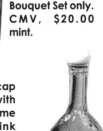

Cologne, 1957 only. 3 dram, white cap. Came in Fragrance Rainbow Set only (see Women's Sets of the 1950s). CMV, $8.00 BO. $10.00 with neck bow.

Princess Set, 1956. Pink, white, and gold box holds beauty dust and 4 oz. cologne. CMV, $40.00 MB.

Sachet Christmas Box, 1957. 9/10 oz., pink painted glass, pink cap. Bottle sold from 1957 to 1961. Pink, green, and blue triangle box sold in 1957 only. CMV, $15.00 MB as shown.

The Cotillion Set, 1957. Pink and white box holds beauty dust, cream sachet, with white glass bottom and 4 oz. cologne. CMV, $45.00.

Cologne Mist, 1958 only. Rare, 3 oz. pink plastic bottle. CMV, $42.50 BO. $52.50 MB.

Perfumed Bath Oil, 1959 – 1961. 8 oz., pink plastic, pink cap. CMV, $5.00.

Cologne Mist, 1959 – 1961. 3 oz., pink plastic coated bottle with white cap and paper label. CMV, $12.00 BO. $17.00 MB.

Body Powder, 1958 – 1959. 3 oz., frosted glass with pink lid and paper label and pink and white box. CMV, $11.00 BO. $15.00 MB.

Treasures Set, 1957. Gold, white, and pink box holds 3 oz. bottles of bath oil and cologne with gold caps and one pink bar of soap. CMV, $75.00 MB.

Cologne, 1957 only. 1 oz., pink cap. Came in Beautiful Journey Set (see Women's Sets of the 1950s). CMV, $15.00.

Bouquet Set, 1958. Pink and white box holds cologne mist and pink glass cream sachet. CMV, $65.00 MB.

Cologne, 1960 only. 4 oz., clear glass, gold cap, pink paper band around neck with pink painted label. Pink and gold box. CMV, $22.00 MB.

Cologne Mist, 1958 – 1959. 3 oz., pink plastic coated bottle. CMV, $16.00 BO. $20.00 MB.

Beauty Dust, 1959 – 1961. Pink plastic bottom, white plastic top with gold center. CMV, $6.00 CO. $12.00 MB.

Spray Perfume, 1960 – 1961. Rose, white, and gold box holds rose and gold metal spray container. CMV, $10.00 BO. $16.00 MB.

Soap, 1961 – 1967.
Gold and white box held three bars with gold centers. CMV, $22.50 MB.

Cologne Mist, 1961 – 1974.
3 oz., white plastic coated bottle with white cap. CMV, $1.00. Same bottle with yellow plastic coated bottom. CMV, $7.00 BO. $10.00 MB. 1975 – 1976 issue has white cap, pink top, and pink painted label. CMV, $1.00.

Cologne, 1961 – 1971.
2 oz., frosted glass with white cap. CMV, $1.00 BO. $2.00 MB.

Cream Sachet, 1961 – 1975.
⅔ oz., frosted glass with pink and white lid, gold or silver lettering. CMV, 25¢.

Perfumed Bath Oil, 1961 – 1966.
6 oz., pink plastic bottle, white cap. CMV, $1.00.

Cologne, 1961 – 1963.
4 oz., frosted glass with white cap. CMV, $1.00 BO. $2.00 MB.

Powder Sachet, 1961 – 1967.
⁹⁄₁₀ oz., frosted glass with pink and white cap. CMV, $6.00 MB.

Left: Beauty Dust, 1961 – 1970.
White frosted plastic bottom with clear plastic lid. CMV, $3.00 jar only. $5.00 MB. Some with yellow plastic bottoms. CMV, $6.00 jar only. $8.00 MB.

Center: Perfumed Talc, 1961 – 1974.
2¾ oz., bright pink can with white cap. CMV, $1.00.

Right: Perfumed Skin Softener, 1964 – 1973.
5 oz., pink glass jar with gold and white or silver lid. CMV, 50¢ gold, $1.00 silver. Regular issue came pink painted over clear glass. CMV, 50¢. Some came pink painted over white milk glass. CMV, $5.00.

Not shown: Perfumed Skin Softener, 1973 – 1975.
5 oz., pink plastic with white and gold cap. CMV, 50¢.

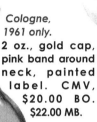

Cologne, 1961 only.
2 oz., gold cap, pink band around neck, painted label. CMV, $20.00 BO. $22.00 MB.

Cream Lotion, 1961 – 1968. 4 oz., pink plastic, white cap. CMV, $3.00.

Debut Set, 1961 – 1962. White and gold box held beauty dust, cream sachet, and cologne mist, in satin lined, flip-open compartment. CMV, $35.00.

Debutante Set, 1963. Pink, white, and gold box holds cologne mist and beauty dust. Came in two different inner boxes. CMV, $20.00 MB.

Body Powder, 1961 – 1964. 4 oz., pink plastic, white cap. CMV, $6.00 jar only. $8.00 MB.

Bath Oil, 1962. 6 oz., pink and white plastic bottle. Came in Bath Bouquet Set only (See Women's Sets of the 1960s). CMV, $1.00.

Perfumed Oil, 1964 – 1969. ½ oz., frosted glass with white cap. CMV, $5.00 BO. $7.00 MB.

Spray Perfume, 1961 – 1963. 2 dram, pink and white metal with gold band. CMV, $8.00 BO. $10.00 MB.

Beauty Dust, 1962 – 1963. Gold and white paper box with clear plastic lid with 4A design on lid. Came in 1962 – 1963 Fragrance Magic Set only (See Women's Sets of the 1960s). CMV, $17.00 mint.

Perfume Mist, 1964 – 1968. 2 dram, pink and white metal with gold band. CMV, $6.00 CO. $7.00 MB.

With Someone Like You Set, 1961 – 1962. Pink and white box held 2 oz. cologne and cream sachet. CMV, $22.00.

Perfumed Oil for the Bath, 1963 – 1964. ½ oz., frosted glass with white cap. CMV, $7.00 BO. $9.00 MB.

Duo Set, 1964.
White, pink, and gold box held powder sachet and 1 dram perfume. CMV, $22.50 MB.

Foaming Bath Oil, 1966 – 1974.
6 oz., pink plastic bottle, white cap. CMV, $1.00 MB.

Scented Hair Spray, 1966 – 1970.
7 oz. pink can. CMV, $3.00.

Perfumed Powder Mist, 1966 – 1972.
Left: 7 oz. (1966 – 1970), pink can has paper label and pink cap and came in white box lined in pink. CMV, $2.00.

Right: 7 oz. (1970 – 1971), pink can, pink cap. Label was painted. Not boxed. CMV, $1.00.

Cologne, 1969 – 1972.
½ oz., white cap, clear glass. CMV, $1.00 BO. $2.00 MB.

Perfumed Talc, 1974 – 1977.
3½ oz., pink and gold cardboard. CMV, $1.00.

Perfume Demi Stick, 1975 – 1978.
3/16 oz., white with pink and gold. CMV, 50¢.

Cream Sachet, 1975 – 1978.
⅔ oz. clear glass with gold and pink cap. CMV, 50¢.

Country Garden

Foaming Bath Oil, 1971 – 1973.
4" high, 6 oz. white glass bottle, white cap, green ribbon on neck. Came in Bird of Paradise, Elusive, or Charisma. OSP, $5.50. CMV, $5.00 MB.

Soap Dish and Soap, 1971 – 1972.
4" long white soap dish with 3 oz. bar of soap. OSP, $4.50. CMV, $6.00 MB.

Beauty Dust, 1971 – 1972.
4½" high, 5 oz. white glass jar with white lid and green ribbon. Came in Bird of Paradise, Elusive, or Charisma. OSP, $6.00. CMV, $6.00 MB.

Powder Sachet, 1971 – 1973.
3" high, 1¼ oz. white glass jar with white lid and green ribbon. Came in Bird of Paradise, Elusive, or Charisma. OSP, $4.50. CMV, $4.00 MB.

Country Kitchen

Moisturized Hand Lotion, 1981.
10 oz., glass, with pump dispenser. OSP, $9.50. CMV, $3.00 MB.

Ceramic Salt and Pepper Shakers, 1981.
Made in Brazil. 4" high. OSP, $12.00. CMV, $6.00 MB set.

Courtship

Perfume, 1937 only.
2 dram, gold cap. Sold for 20¢ with other purchase during Founder's Campaign, July 6 – 26, 1937. CMV, $40.00 BO, mint. $60.00 MB.

Perfume, 1938 only.
2 dram bottle, gold cap. CMV, $40.00 BO, mint. $60.00 MB.

Perfume, 1940 – 1944.
Box holds ⅛ oz. bottle, gold cap and label. CMV, $25.00 BO, mint. $35.00 MB as shown.

Crimson Carnation

Perfume, 1946 – 1947.
Blue and white box holds 3 dram bottle with white cap. CMV, $60.00 BO. $100.00 MB.

Toilet Water, 1946 – 1948.
2 oz., gold or plastic cap. CMV, $40.00 BO. $55.00 MB.

Crystalique

Beauty Dust, 1966.
All glass powder dish. CMV, $10.00 CO. $14.00 MB.

Cologne, 1966 – 1970.
4 oz., 5½" high glass bottle with matching plastic cap, gold trim. Came in Unforgettable, Rapture, Occur!, Somewhere, Topaze, Cotillion, Here's My Heart, or To a Wild Rose. CMV, $5.00 MB.

Beauty Dust, 1972.
Clear crystal plastic powder box and lid with gold base. CMV, $5.00 CO. $7.00 MB.

Beauty Dust, 1972.
Clear glass, came with choice of powder: Moonwind, Charisma, Régence, Elusive, Rapture, Occur!, Somewhere, Topaze, Cotillion, Unforgettable, or Here's My Heart, with matching puffs. CMV, $10.00 CO. $13.00 MB.

Beauty Dust, 1979 – 1980.
Clear glass, holds all beauty dust refills (Sold empty). CMV, $5.00 MB.

Daisies Won't Tell

Beauty Dust, 1956.
Yellow, white, and blue paper box. Short issue. CMV, $20.00 CO, mint. $25.00 MB. Also came with blue sided container.

Cream Lotion, 1956 – 1957.
Yellow and white box holds 2 oz. bottle with rib around center and white flower cap, painted label. CMV $10.00 BO. $12.00 MB.

Cologne with Atomizer, 1956.
Yellow, white, and pink box holds 2 oz. bottle with rib around middle, and white and gold spray atomizer. Short issue. CMV, $15.00 BO. $20.00 MB.

Bubble Bath, 1956 – 1958.
4 oz. bottle with rib around center. Painted label, white flower cap. CMV, $8.00 BO. $10.00 MB.

Wee Two Set, 1956.
Blue, white, and yellow box has two tubes with yellow caps of hand cream and cream shampoo. CMV, $18.00.

Little Charmer Set, 1956.
Black and white plastic basket with flowers on top. Holds 2 oz. cologne, gold pomade, and tube of hand cream. CMV, $65.00 MB.

Playmate Set, 1956.
Daisies carrying case holds 2 oz. cologne, cream lotion, and gold or black pomade with plastic doll with movable arms and satin and net dress. Eyes open and shut. Doll has red hair. CMV, $90.00 MB.

Daisy Petals Set, 1957.
Yellow and white box with pink hearts holds 2 oz. cologne and lime yellow pomade lipstick in corner of box. CMV, $25.00 MB.

Daisies Won't Tell Set, 1956.
Daisy box holds 2 oz. cologne and bubble bath with center rib on each, and can of 3¼ oz. talc. CMV, $20.00 talc can only. $60.00 MB with outer sleeve.

My Dolly Set, 1957.
White, yellow, and green box holds 2 oz. cream lotion and cologne, pink or yellow pomade, and plastic doll with movable arms, brown hair, blue hat, and yellow dress trimmed in pink satin. CMV, $90.00 MB.

Daisies Won't Tell Set, 1957.
Box holds 2 oz. each in bubble bath, cream lotion, and cologne. White and yellow daisy caps. Came with outer sleeve. Also came with talc can in place of cream lotion. CMV, $60.00 MB.

Blossoms Set, 1956.
Daisy box holds 2 oz. cologne with blue ribbon and gold pomade. CMV, $5.00 gold pomade BO. $27.50 MB.

Daisy Bouquet Set, 1957.
Blue, white, and yellow box holds 2 oz. cologne, beauty dust, and lime yellow pomade. CMV, $5.00 CO, yellow pomade. $45.00 MB.

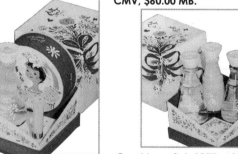

One I Love Set, 1957 only.
Floral box contains 2 oz. cologne, cream lotion, and bubble bath. White flower caps with yellow centers. Any sets you find with pink caps are taken off Cotillion bottles and not considered a mint set. CMV, $50.00 MB.

Miss Daisy Set, 1956.
Daisy box holds 2 oz. cologne and beauty dust. Top of bottle sticks through top of box. CMV, $40.00.

Dainty Hands Set, 1957. Pink, white, and yellow box holds two tubes with pink hearts and yellow caps of hand cream. CMV, $18.00 MB.

Beauty Dust, 1958. Blue and white box holds blue and white paper powder box with white daisy on top. CMV, $18.00 beauty dust only, mint. $23.00 MB.

Cologne, 1957 – 1958. 2 oz., with rib around center. Came in One I Love Set and Daisies Won't Tell Set. CMV, $12.00.

Hearts 'N' Daisies, 1958. Blue and white box holds 2 oz. cologne and pink pomade lipstick. CMV, $22.00 MB.

Spray Cologne, 1958 – 1960. Pink plastic coated bottle with white cap. CMV, $10.00 BO. $12.00 MB.

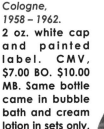

Cologne, 1958 – 1962. 2 oz. white cap and painted label. CMV, $7.00 BO. $10.00 MB. Same bottle came in bubble bath and cream lotion in sets only. Same CMV.

Spray Cologne, 1957 only. 1½ oz. blue plastic coated bottle with white and painted label. CMV, $13.00 BO. $15.00 MB.

Beauty Dust, 1958. Blue, white, and yellow paper powder box with girl on lid. CMV, $20.00 CO. $25.00 MB.

Daisy Dust, 1958 – 1961. 2 oz. white plastic bottle and cap. OSP, $1.19. CMV, $10.00 BO. $12.00 MB.

Daisy Cream Lotion, 1958 – 1961. 4 oz. white plastic bottle and cap. Two different labels. Newer one has large letters and painted address at bottom. Older one has smaller letters and embossed address at bottom. OSP, $1.19. CMV, $10.00 BO. $12.00 MB.

Daisy Bubble Bath, 1958 – 1961. 4 oz. white plastic bottle and cap. OSP, $1.19. CMV, $10.00 BO. $12.00 MB.

Fairy Touch, 1958. Blue and white box holds two blue and white tubes with yellow caps of hand cream. CMV, $16.00 MB.

Hand Cream, 1958 – 1961. Blue and white box holds blue and white tube with flat or tall yellow cap. CMV, $6.00 MB.

Daisy Pomade, 1958 – 1959. Blue and white flowered holder holds pink daisy pomade. Also came in lime green color. CMV, $2.00 pomade only. $12.50 in holder.

Field Daisies Set, 1958. Blue and white flowered box holds 2 oz. bottles of cologne, cream lotion with red ribbon, and bubble bath. CMV, $50.00 MB.

Daisy Darling Set, 1958. Blue box with daisies and red ribbon holds spray cologne and beauty dust. CMV, $42.50 MB.

Love Me – Love Me Not, 1959. Blue, white, and green box holds spray cologne and cream sachet in pink glass. CMV, $30.00.

Daisy Shampoo, 1959 – 1961. 4 oz. white plastic bottle and cap. CMV, $10.00 BO. $12.00 MB.

Cream Sachet, 1959 – 1961. Pink glass jar with floral metal lid. CMV, $11.00 jar only. $13.00 MB.

Daisy Soap on a Rope, 1959 – 1962. Blue, white, and pink flowered box holds white Daisy soap with yellow center on a blue rope. CMV, $20.00 MB.

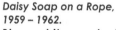

Daisy Bouquet Set, 1959 – 1960. Blue and white flowered box holds 4 oz. cream lotion and bubble bath, and 2 oz. dust. CMV, $37.50 MB.

Daisy Treasures Set, 1959. Pink box with yellow slide-open cover. Light blue ribbon on daisy flower. Holds three bottles of nail polish with white caps and nail file. CMV, $60.00 MB.

Daisy Fluff-On, 1959 – 1960. Blue paper powder box with Daisy puff and clear plastic lid. CMV, $12.00 powder only. $16.00 MB.

Daisy Pink Nail Polish, 1960. Blue and white box holds nail polish with white cap. CMV, $6.00 BO, mint. $8.00 MB.

Not Shown: First Waltz Nail Polish, 1960. Blue and white box holds nail polish with white cap. CMV, $6.00 BO, mint. $8.00 MB.

Daisy Pomade Lipstick, 1960 – 1961. Blue and white box holds pink and gold pomade in shades of First Waltz or Daisy Pomade. CMV, $6.00 MB.

Cologne Mist, 1962 – 1964.
2 oz. white plastic coated bottle with white cap and blue painted label. CMV, $7.00 BO. $9.00 MB.

Daisy Pink Set, 1960.
Box holds pink nail polish with white cap and pink metal pomade in box. CMV, $20.00 MB.

Pretty Beginner Set, 1961.
Blue, white, and yellow box holds 2 oz. cologne and choice of soap, dust, cream lotion, shampoo, or bubble bath. CMV, $25.00. $35.00 MB, with soap.

*Cream Lotion,
1962 – 1964.*
4 oz. white plastic bottle and cap. Blue painted label. CMV, $6.00 BO. $8.00 MB.

*First Waltz
Lipstick, 1960.*
Blue flowered box holds pink lipstick. CMV, $6.00 MB.

*Daisy Pomade Lipstick,
1962 – 1964.*
Pink box holds pink lipstick with gold base. CMV, $4.00 MB.

Gay Daisies Set, 1960.
Blue, white, and pink box holds soap on a blue rope and choice of bubble bath, daisy dust, cream lotion, or shampoo. CMV, $35.00 MB.

*First Recital Set,
1962 – 1964.*
Pink and blue fold-over box holds Daisy soap on a rope and choice of cream lotion, bubble bath, or Daisy Dust. CMV, $35.00 MB.

*Hand Cream,
1962 – 1964.*
Pink tube with white flower cap. In pink and blue box. CMV, $5.00 TO. $7.00 MB.

First Waltz Set, 1960.
Blue and white box holds First Waltz nail polish and pink pomade. CMV, $20.00 MB.

Bubble Bath, 1962 – 1964.
4 oz. white plastic bottle and cap with blue painted label. CMV, $8.00 MB.

Daisy Dust, 1962 – 1964.
2 oz. white plastic bottle and cap with blue painted label. CMV, $8.00 MB.

Cologne, 1962 – 1964.
2 oz. glass bottle, white cap and painted label. CMV, $6.00 BO. $9.00 MB.

Cream Sachet, 1963 – 1964.
Pink glass jar with white plastic lid. CMV, $9.00 jar only. $11.00 MB.

Pick a Daisy Set, 1963 – 1964.
Pink and blue box holds soap on a rope and cream sachet. CMV, $32.50 MB.

Daisy Chain Gift Set, 1963 – 1964.
Pink and white box holds 2 oz. cologne and pink tube of hand cream. CMV, $22.00 MB.

Daisy Soap on a Rope, 1963 – 1964.
Pink, white, and yellow box holds white soap with yellow center on a white rope. CMV, $20.00 MB.

Delft Blue

Delft Blue, 1972 – 1974.
White milk glass with blue flowers.

Skin So Soft Softener.
5 oz. CMV, $5.00 BO. $6.00 MB.

Foaming Bath Oil.
5 oz., holds Patchwork, Moonwind, or Sonnet. CMV, $6.00 BO. $7.00 MB.

Pitcher and Bowl.
5 oz. CMV, $7.00 BO and bowl. $10.00 MB.

Soap Dish and
Skin So Soft Soap.
3 oz. CMV, $6.00 MB.

Elégante

Elégante fragrance line features some of the most beautiful packaging Avon ever made. It is very popular and very hard to find. A set in mint condition is something to be proud to add to your collection.

Perfume, 1956 – 1959.
Red and silver box holds ½ oz. bottle with silver cap and neck tag with red ribbon. CMV, $75.00 BO with neck tag and ribbon. $125.00 MB.

Left: Beauty Dust, 1956 – 1959.
Red paper sides with tin top and bottom. Silver letters on lid. CMV, $15.00 CO. $20.00 MB.

Right: Cologne, 1956 – 1959.
Red and silver box holds 4 oz. bottle with silver cap and neck tag and red ribbon. CMV, $20.00 BO with neck tag and ribbon. $40.00 MB.

Powder Sachet,
1957 – 1959.
⁹/₁₀ oz. bottle with silver cap. CMV, $12.00 BO. $17.00 MB.

Snow Dreams Set,
1957.
White box with red ribbon holds 2 oz. toilet water, cream sachet, and 1 dram perfume, in red wrapper. CMV, $75.00 MB.

Cream Sachet,
1956 – 1959.
²/₃ oz. jar with silver cap. CMV, $8.00 BO. $13.00 MB.

Toilet Water,
1957 – 1959.
Red and silver box holds 2 oz. bottle with silver cap and neck tag and red ribbon. CMV, $20.00 BO with tag and ribbon. $40.00 MB.

Sparkling Burgundy Set,
1957.
Round neck and silver box with red satin lining. Holds 4 oz. cologne, cream sachet, 1 dram perfume, and beauty dust. CMV, $115.00 MB.

Beauty Dust, 1969 – 1974.
Pink plastic with gold or silver trim. CMV, $3.00 CO. $5.00 MB.
Samples, 1969 – 1974.
Ten samples to a box. CMV, 50¢.
Rollette, 1969 – 1975.
⅓ oz., frosted glass. CMV, 75¢.
Perfumed Demi Stick, 1970 – 1973.
Paper center, white cap. CMV, $1.00.
Cologne, 1969 – 1975.
½ oz., pink frosted glass. CMV, $1.00.
Cream Sachet, 1969 – 1975.
Pink frosted glass. OSP, $3.00. CMV, 50¢.
Perfumed Skin Softener, 1970 – 1972.
Pink frosted glass. Lid came with gold or silver trim. CMV, $1.00.
Tray, 1970 – 1971.
Pink plastic, gold trim. CMV, $4.00 tray only. $6.00 MB.

Left to right:
Scented
Hair Spray,
1970 – 1972.
7 oz. pink can and cap with gold letters. CMV, $3.00.
Perfumed Powder Mist,
1971 – 1974.
7 oz., pink painted label. CMV, 50¢.
Perfumed Powder Mist, 1970 – 1971.
7 oz., pink paper label. CMV, $2.00.
Perfumed Talc, 1971 – 1974.
3½ oz. pink paper container. CMV, 50¢.
Cologne Mist, 1969 – 1974.
3 oz. pink plastic coated bottle. CMV, 50¢.
Foaming Bath Oil, 1970 – 1972.
6 oz., pink plastic with pink cap. CMV, 50¢.
Front: Perfumed Soap, 1970 – 1974.
Three pink bars in pink box. CMV, $5.00 MB.

Left: Elusive Cologne Mist, 1969 – 1974.
Pink painted bottle with pink and gold cap. Paint doesn't go to bottom.
Right: Later issue pink plastic coated bottle, pink and gold cap. CMV, 50¢ plastic coated. $1.00 painted.

Field Flowers Cologne Sample, 1970 – 1978.
Clear glass, white cap. CMV, 25¢.

English Provincial ·······················

English Provincial, 1972 – 1974.
White milk glass with blue and pink flowers and aqua blue lid with flowers. Came in Charisma or Bird of Paradise.
Left: Foaming Bath Oil.
8 oz. CMV, $1.00 BO. $2.00 MB.
Inside Left: Cologne.
5 oz. CMV, $1.00 BO. $2.00 MB.
Inside Right: Powder Sachet.
1¼ oz. CMV, $1.00 BO. $2.00 MB.
Right: Soap Dish and Soap.
1¼ oz. CMV, $4.00 soap only. $5.00 MB.

Field Flowers Products.
Cologne Mist, 1971 – 1976.
3 oz., green plastic coated over glass, yellow cap. CMV, $1.00.
Cologne Gelée, 1971 – 1972.
3 oz., green ribbed glass and orange cap. CMV, $1.00.
Perfumed Skin Softener, 1971 – 1973.
5 oz., green glass, bright or pale blue cap. CMV, $1.00.
Cream Sachet, 1971 – 1975.
⅔ oz., green ribbed glass with purple cap. CMV, 50¢.
Perfumed Powder Mist, 1971 – 1976.
7 oz., green, white, and pink can. CMV, 50¢. Also came with upside down label. CMV, $4.00.
Soap Set, 1971 – 1976.
Flowered box holds yellow, pink, and green flower bars. CMV, $7.00 MB.
Scented Hair Spray, 1971 – 1972.
7 oz., pink and green can with green cap. CMV, $3.00.
Cologne Ice, 1976.
1 oz. tube. CMV, $1.00.

Field Flowers ·····························

Perfumed Talc, 1970 – 1973.
3½ oz., green paper label. CMV, $1.00. 1973 – 1977 perfumed talc had pink label. CMV, 50¢.

Demi Stick, 1970 – 1978.
Green paper band, white cap. CMV, 50¢.

Fragrance Samples, 1970 – 1977.
Ten samples in a box. CMV, 50¢.

Field Flowers Bath Brush and Soap, 1971 – 1972.
Pink brush, approx. 16" long, and 5 oz. flower embossed pink soap. CMV, $4.00 MB.

Flower Talk

Flower Talk, 1972 – 1973.
White with orange, blue, yellow, green, and purple designs.
Perfumed Talc.
3½ oz. OSP, $1.50. CMV, $1.00.
Cologne Mist.
3 oz. OSP, $5.00. CMV, $1.00.
Fragrance Rollette.
⅓ oz. OSP, $1.75. CMV, $1.00.
Fragrance DemiStik.
⁹⁄₁₀ oz. OSP, $1.50. CMV, 50¢.
Sample.
CMV, 25¢.
Cream Sachet.
⅔ oz. OSP, $2.50. CMV, $1.00.

Flowertime

Talc, 1949 – 1953.
5 oz. bottle with brass shaker top. CMV, $15.00 BO. $20.00 MB.

Toilet Water, 1949 – 1953.
2 oz., pink cap. CMV, $10.00 BO. $15.00 MB.

Flowertime Set, 1949 – 1952.
Turquoise and gold box with satin lining holds 4 oz. cologne and talc. CMV, $60.00 MB.

Powder Sachet, 1949 – 1950.
1¼ oz. bottle has flat or indented pink cap. CMV, $10.00 BO. $15.00 MB.

Doubly Yours Set, 1949.
White and blue swing-open box holds 2 oz. bottles of cologne with pink caps in Cotillion and Flowertime. CMV, $65.00 MB.

Powder Sachet, 1950 – 1953.
1½ oz. with indented pink cap. CMV, $10.00 BO. $15.00 MB.

Cologne, 1949 – 1953.
4 oz. pink cap. CMV, $10.00 BO. $15.00 MB. Same bottle came in 2 oz. size in sets only. CMV, $10.00.

Flower Cluster Set, 1949.
Blue and gold box contains box of face powder, gold lipstick, and 1 dram perfume. OSP, $3.00. CMV, $50.00 MB.

Flowers in the Wind Set, 1950 – 1952.
Blue and silver flip-open box with pink satin lining holds cologne talc, powder sachet, and 1 dram perfume. CMV, $95.00 MB.

Valentine Gift Sachet, 1952.
In special red and white gift box. Came in Flowertime, Golden Promise, Quaintance, or Cotillion. CMV, $10.00 BO, mint. $15.00 MB as shown.

Forever Spring

Beauty Dust, 1951 – 1956.
Green and white can. CMV, $20.00 CO. $25.00 MB.

Perfume, 1951 – 1952.
1 dram, ribbed glass, gold cap. Came in green felt folder. CMV, $10.00 BO. $15.00 in sleeve.

Representative Gift Set, 1951.
CMV, $85.00 MB.

Cologne, 1951 – 1956.
4 oz. with yellow tulip cap and green painted label. Came in green box. CMV, $15.00 mint, BO. $20.00 MB.

Toilet Water, 1951 – 1956.
2 oz., yellow tulip cap and green painted label. Came in green box. CMV, $15.00 BO, mint. $20.00 MB.

Spring Corsage Set, 1951 – 1952.
Green box with clear plastic lid and bouquet of flowers holds 4 oz. cologne and 1 dram perfume. CMV, $55.00 MB.

Perfume, 1951 – 1956.
Yellow and green box with blue and green ribbon holds 3 dram glass stoppered bottle, blue ribbon on neck and neck tag. CMV, $85.00 BO, with tag and ribbon mint. $110.00 MB.

Cream Sachet, 1951 – 1956.
Green box holds white glass jar with green lid. CMV $7.00 jar only, mint. $12.00 MB.

Body Powder, 1951 – 1956. Green and white paper container. CMV, $15.00.

Spring Creation Set, 1953. Green box with net lining holds cream sachet and 1 dram perfume. CMV, $40.00 MB.

Powder Box Cologne, 1956. $\frac{1}{16}$ oz. bottle came in special beauty dust box set only. Came tied to silk ribbon. CMV, $5.00 BO, mint. $10.00 mint with ribbon.

Spring Melody Set, 1952 – 1953. Body powder and cream sachet sitting on top under clear plastic lid. CMV, $40.00 MB.

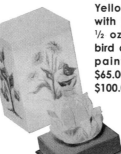

Powder Sachet, 1953 – 1956. 1¼ oz. bottle with yellow cap and green painted label. Came in green box. CMV, $10.00 BO. $15.00 MB.

Cream Sachet, 1956 – 1959. Yellow glass bottom and cap with flowers. CMV, $8.00 CO. $11.00 MB.

Gift Perfume, 1956 – 1959. Yellow and white box with purple base holds ½ oz. bottle with blue bird on yellow cap and painted label. CMV, $65.00 BO, with bird mint. $100.00 MB.

Spring Song Set, 1953. Blue and green box holds 4 oz. cologne and 1 dram perfume. CMV, $45.00 MB.

Powder Sachet, 1956 – 1959. $\frac{9}{10}$ oz., yellow glass and cap. CMV, $9.00 CO. $12.00 MB.

Beauty Dust, 1956 – 1959. Yellow and white paper box with tin top and bottom. CMV, $16.00 CO. $20.00 MB.

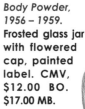

Body Powder, 1956 – 1959. Frosted glass jar with flowered cap, painted label. CMV, $12.00 BO. $17.00 MB.

Forever Spring Set, 1953. Green and white box with green net lining holds body powder, cream sachet, and 1 dram perfume in green felt sleeve. OSP, $3.95. CMV, $55.00 MB.
Not shown: Forever Spring Set, 1952. Same as above, only did not have 1 dram perfume. CMV, $45.00 MB.

Cologne, 1956 – 1959. 4 oz. bottle with blue bird on yellow cap, painted label, yellow and white flowered box. CMV, $15.00 BO, with bird. $20.00 MB.

Cream Lotion, 1956 – 1959. 4 oz. green painted over clear glass bottle with yellow cap. CMV, $18.00 BO, mint. $25.00 MB.

Spring Goddess Set, 1957. Yellow and white box holds beauty dust, cream sachet, and 4 oz. cologne. CMV, $55.00 MB.

Spring Mood Set, 1956. Yellow and white box holds body powder and 4 oz. cream lotion in green glass. CMV, $40.00 MB.

Cream Lotion, 1956 – 1959. 4 oz. clear glass with yellow cap, painted label. No bird on cap. Came in yellow and white box. CMV, $12.00 BO, mint. $14.00 MB.

Springtime Set, 1956. Yellow and white box holds beauty dust and 4 oz. cologne. CMV, $55.00 MB.

Toilet Water, 1956 – 1959. 2 oz., yellow cap with tiny blue bird, painted label. Came in yellow and white flowered box. CMV, $15.00 BO, with bird mint. $20.00 MB.

Perfumed Talc, 1957 – 1959. 2¾ oz. yellow and white can, yellow cap. CMV, $10.00 CO. $12.00 MB.

Merry Merry Spring Set, 1956. Yellow, white, and blue box holds 2 oz. toilet water and cream sachet. CMV, $37.50 MB.

April Airs Set, 1956 – 1957. Yellow and white box with blue ribbon top holds body powder and cream sachet. CMV, $45.00 MB.

Gardenia

Perfume, 1940 – 1942.
Gold speckled box holds ³⁄₈ oz. bottle with gold octagonal cap. CMV, $40.00 BO, mint. $80.00 MB.

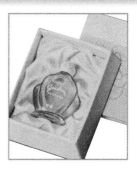

*Perfume, "Ribbed,"
1933 – 1936.*
½ oz., ribbed glass with black octagonal cap. Came in Gold Box Set. (See Gold Box Sets section). CMV, $45.00 mint.

*Perfume, "Octagonal,"
1933 – 1936.*
Six-sided bottle and black octagonal cap. Came in Little Folks Set and Handkerchief Set. CMV, $45.00 mint.

Perfume, 1948 – 1952.
³⁄₈ oz. or 3 dram bottle with flowered cap, paper or painted label. Came in satin lined box with clear plastic lid. CMV, $40.00 BO, mint. $80.00 MB.

Garden of Love

*Powder Sachet,
1940 – 1946.*
1¼ oz. bottle with black or turquoise metal cap. CMV, $15.00 BO. $20.00 MB.

Perfume, 1940 – 1944.
Orange lid, gold base box holds 3 dram glass stoppered bottle with gold neck tag. Rare. CMV, $100.00 BO, mint $130.00 MB.

Sachet, 1944 – 1945.
1¼ oz. pink paper sachet. Came with pink plastic flower on lid. CMV, $18.00 CO, mint. $23.00 MB.

*Powder Sachet,
1946 – 1948.*
1¼ oz., turquoise ribbed plastic cap and flowered label. CMV, $17.00 BO. $22.00 MB.

Swirl Perfume, 1948 only.
3 dram glass stoppered bottle is swirl glass design with gold neck tag. Purple and white flowered box. CMV, $80.00 BO, mint with neck tag. $120.00 MB.

Golden Promise

*Beauty Dust,
1947 – 1956.*
Standard issue gold and white can. CMV, $20.00 CO, mint. $25.00 MB.

Body Powder, Christmas Demo, 1947.
Regular issue talc in gold box given to Avon ladies in special Merry Christmas demo box. CMV, $30.00 MB, with outer box shown.

2-Piece Set, 1947 – 1949.
Gold and white box holds 4 oz. cologne and body powder. CMV, $65.00 MB.

*Beauty Dust,
1947 – 1951.*
Smaller than regular issue. Came in sets only. CMV, $20.00 mint.

*Cologne,
1947 – 1956.*
4 oz., painted label, gold cap. CMV, $20.00 BO. $25.00 MB.

*Body Powder,
1947 – 1956.*
Gold and white shaker top can. CMV, $16.00 CO, mint. $20.00 MB.

Sachet, 1948.
Special gold box, 62nd Anniversary issue. 1¼ oz. ribbed gold plastic cap or threaded brass cap. CMV, $22.00 MB as shown.

3-Piece Set, 1947 – 1949.
Gold and white box holds 1 dram perfume, 4 oz. cologne, and beauty dust. OSP, $4.95. CMV, $85.00 MB.

Perfume, 1947 – 1950.
Gold and white flip-open box holds ½ oz. bottle with gold cap and painted label. OSP, $5.00. CMV, $75.00 BO, mint. $175.00 MB.

Perfume Gift, 1947.
Clear bottle, gold cap. Label is gold with red lettering, says "Golden Promise Perfume with Best Wishes of Avon Products Inc., Pasadena, Cal." Came in gold box with same statement. CMV, $50.00 BO, mint. $75.00 MB.

Golden Duet Set, 1949.
Small gold purse holds Lipstick and gold metal case with ½ dram bottle of perfume inside. CMV, $35.00 CO, mint. $40.00 MB.

Perfume, 1949 only.
¼ oz. glass bottle fits in gold metal case. Came in Golden Duet and Evening Charm sets. CMV, $25.00.

Deluxe Set, 1952 – 1954.
Gold box with clear plastic lid and gold satin lining holds 4 oz. cologne, powder sachet, 1 dram perfume, and body powder. Gold ribbon around box. CMV, $100.00 MB.

Perfume, 1950 – 1954.
Gold and white box holds 3 dram glass stoppered bottle with gold base label and neck cord. CMV, $100.00 bottle with label and cord, mint. $125.00 MB.

Powder Sachet, 1952 – 1956.
1¼ oz., yellow plastic cap. CMV, $9.00 BO. $12.00 MB.

Perfume, 1954 – 1956.
Gold and white box holds ½ oz. bottle with flat glass stopper and gold and white label. CMV, $90.00 BO, mint. $125.00 MB.

Toilet Water, 1953 – 1956.
2 oz., gold cap and painted label. CMV, $20.00 BO. $24.00 MB.

Golden Promise Set, 1950 – 1951.
Gold box with clear plastic cover and gold tie-down ribbon holds 4 oz. cologne and beauty dust. CMV, $65.00 MB.

Cream Sachet, 1953 – 1956.
White glass, square base with yellow flowered top. CMV, $9.00 BO. $13.00 MB.

Sachet, 1948.
Special gold box, 62nd anniversary issue. 1¼ oz., threaded brass cap. OSP, $1.19. CMV, $22.00 MB as shown.

Powder Sachet, 1951 – 1952.
1¼ oz., gold cap. CMV, $9.00 BO. $12.00 MB.

Golden Jewel Set, 1953 – 1954.
White and gold box with gold jewel on front. Holds 2 oz. toilet water and 1 dram perfume. Toilet water cap fits through top of box. CMV, $40.00 MB.

Hana Gasa

Fragrance Samples, 1970 – 1974.
Ten in a box. CMV, 50¢ box.
Cologne Sample, 1970 – 1974.
Sample bottle, white cap. CMV, 25¢.
Cologne, 1970 – 1975.
½ oz., clear glass, yellow cap. CMV, $1.00 MB.
Perfume Rollette, 1970 – 1974.
Yellow painted glass, yellow cap. CMV, $1.00.
Cream Sachet, 1970 – 1975.
⅔ oz., yellow painted over milk glass with yellow lid. CMV, 50¢.
Beauty Dust, 1970 – 1976.
6 oz., yellow plastic. CMV, $5.00 MB.

Hair Spray, 1971.
7 oz. yellow can, CMV, $3.00.
Perfume Powder Mist, 1971 – 1974.
7 oz. yellow can. CMV, $1.00.
Perfumed Talc, 1971 – 1974.
3½ oz., yellow cardboard. CMV, $1.00.
Cologne Mist, 1970 – 1976.
3 oz., yellow plastic coated glass, yellow cap. CMV, $1.00.
Soap, 1971 – 1975.
Three yellow bars in pink and yellow box. CMV, $5.00 MB.

Happy Hours

All Happy Hours items are rare and hard to find.

Set, 1948 – 1949.
Pink and blue box holds talc, cologne, and perfume. CMV, $112.00 MB.

Talc, 1948 – 1949.
2¾ oz., metal shaker cap. Sold in sets only. CMV, $20.00 BO, mint.

Cologne, 1948 – 1949.
1 oz., plastic cap. Came in sets only. CMV, $20.00 BO, mint.

Memento Set, 1948 – 1949.
Blue and pink box holds cologne and perfume. CMV, $95.00 MB.

Perfume, 1948 – 1949.
3 dram bottle, pink cap. Rare. Came in sets only. CMV, $50.00 BO, mint.

Star Bouquet Set, 1948 – 1949.
Green and pink box holds talc and cologne. CMV, $75.00 MB.

Hawaiian White Ginger

After Bath Freshener, 1965 – 1967.
5 oz. bottle with white painted label and cap. Also came with and without gold 4A design. CMV, $6.00 MB.

Cream Sachets, 1968 – 1972.
Both ⅔ oz. green frosted jars with flowered caps. Short jar 1967, same as Lily of the Valley jar. CMV, $2.00. Tall green jar, 1969. CMV, $1.00.

Cologne Mist, 1972 – 1976.
2 oz. clear glass bottle with clear plastic cap with inner cap of green, red, and white. CMV, 75¢.

Bath Freshener, 1967 – 1972.
6 oz. glass bottle with white cap. CMV, $2.00.

Floral Duet Set, 1972 – 1973.
Came with rollette and bar of soap. CMV, $5.00 MB. Soap, 1970 – 1978.
3 oz. single bar soap (same as shown in set). CMV, $1.00.

Rollette, 1972 – 1974.
⅓ oz. clear bottle, white cap with colored band. CMV, 50¢.

Cream Sachet, 1973 – 1978.
⅔ oz. glass jar, white, green, and red cap. This had three different lid labels. Early one — no zip code. ⅔ oz. — zip but no numbers and doesn't have weight on lid. Later ones have zip and numbers, but no weight on lid. CMV, 50¢.

Talc, 1968 only.
2¾ oz. green and white talc, sold in perfume pair only. CMV, $2.00 CO.

Demi Stick, 1970 – 1978.
⁹⁄₁₀ oz., green, red, and white, white cap. CMV, 50¢.

Cologne Mist, 1971 – 1972.
2 oz. light green glass bottle with white cap. CMV, $1.00 MB.

Not shown: Fragrance Kwickettes, 1969 – 1975. Box holds 14 packets. CMV, $1.00 box.

Talc, 1968 – 1973.
3½ oz. multicolored cardboard, gold letter label. CMV, $1.00. 1974 – 1977 talc came with pink letter label. CMV, 50¢.

Beauty Dust, 1972.
Multicolored cardboard. CMV, $4.00 CO, mint. $5.00 MB.

Hello Sunshine

Hello Sunshine Products, 1979 – 1980.
Cologne.
2½ oz., clear glass, yellow cap. Yellow and pink decal on glass. OSP, $3.50. CMV, $1.00.
Hand Cream.
White, yellow, and pink. 1½ oz. tube. Green cap. OSP, $2.00. CMV, 50¢.
Fun Shine Nail Tint.
½ oz., clear glass, pink cap. OSP, $2.00. CMV, 75¢ MB.
Lip Balm.
Three different colors as shown. OSP, 99¢ each. CMV, 50¢ each.
Solid Perfume.
½ oz., plastic compact holds solid perfume. OSP, $3.50. CMV, 50¢.

Her Prettiness

Enchanted Cologne Mist, 1969 – 1972.
Brown tree base holds 3 oz. cologne mist in green bubble top and green bird spray button. CMV, $7.00 MB.

Secret Tower Rollette, 1969 – 1972.
Red cap on bottle. CMV, $3.00 MB.

Brush and Comb Set, 1969 – 1972.
Pink box with yellow comb and brush. CMV, $5.00.

Magic Mushroom Cream Sachet, 1969 – 1972.
Green, pink, and blue plastic. CMV, $4.00.

Pretty Me Doll, 1969 – 1971.
5 oz. plastic bottle with gold hair, cap, and pink neck ribbon. Holds powdered bubble bath. 6½" high. CMV, $8.00 MB.

Bunny Fluff Puff, 1969 – 1972.
3½ oz., white plastic rabbit with pink fluff tail. Holds talc. CMV, $5.00.

Ladybug Fragrance Glace, 1969 – 1972.
Red, black, and green plastic bug. CMV, $4.00 MB.

Not shown: Bunny Fluff Puff, 1976.
Reissued. Same as above except holds Pink and Pretty Talc. CMV, $4.00. Also has "R" on bottom for reissue. Also reissued in 1979 (yellow rabbit). See Children's Decanters and Toys section.

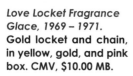

Love Locket Fragrance Glace, 1969 – 1971.
Gold locket and chain, in yellow, gold, and pink box. CMV, $10.00 MB.

Flower Belle Cologne Mist, 1969 – 1972.
Blue top with yellow base, holds 2 oz. cologne mist. CMV, $4.00.

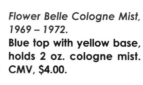

Art Reproduction Print, 1969 – 1970.
14" x 18", pink, green, and white, was free with purchase of any Her Prettiness products. Came in cardboard tube with Her Prettiness sticker and a poem "Her Prettiness Serves Ten in The Garden." CMV, $4.00, print alone. $8.00, three pieces.

Cologne Sample, 1969 – 1972.
⅛ oz., clear glass white cap. Painted label. Came in envelope. CMV, $1.00 mint in envelope.

Lip Kisses, 1970 – 1971.
Lip Pomade, tubes blue and white, pink and white, and orange and white, in cherry, chocolate, or peppermint. Mirror on back side of cap. CMV, $2.00 each, MB.

Royal Fountain Creme Sachet, 1970.
Blue base with silver and gold fountain top. Contains creme sachet. CMV, $5.00 MB.

Perfumed Talc, 1970 – 1971.
3½ oz., flowered box. CMV, $2.00.

Here's My Heart

Perfume, 1946 – 1948.
½ oz. glass stoppered bottle with painted label and pink neck ribbons. Bottle is tied to pink satin heart shaped base and box. CMV, $75.00 BO, with ribbon mint. $100.00 MB.

Perfume Sample, 1950.
With gold lid. CMV, $30.00.

Sweethearts Set, 1958.
Blue and white heart shaped box with white satin lining and white rose on lid. Holds cologne mist and plastic powder sachet or lotion sachet. CMV, $50.00 MB.

Lotion Sachet, 1957 – 1958.
1 oz. blue plastic coated bottle with hearts on gold cap, painted label. CMV, $5.00 BO. $10.00 MB.

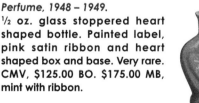

Perfume, 1948 – 1949.
½ oz. glass stoppered heart shaped bottle. Painted label, pink satin ribbon and heart shaped box and base. Very rare. CMV, $125.00 BO. $175.00 MB, mint with ribbon.

Cologne Mist, 1957 – 1958.
3 oz. blue plastic coated bottle with indented heart, two hearts on gold cap. Plain lid. CMV, $18.00 BO, mint. $23.00 MB.

Cream Lotion, 1958 – 1968.
4 oz. bottle with painted label and white beaded cap. CMV, $2.00 MB.

Powder Sachet Christmas Box, 1959.
Blue box with gold butterflies sold Christmas only 1959, with choice of powder sachet in Here's My Heart, Persian Wood, Nearness, Cotillion (pink painted), Bright Night, or To a Wild Rose. CMV, $15.00 each, MB as shown.

Cologne Mist, 1958 – 1976.
3 oz. blue plastic coated bottle with white beaded cap and painted label. Blue and white box. CMV, $1.00.

Toilet Water, 1959 – 1962.
2 oz. painted label and white beaded cap. Came in blue and white box. CMV, $2.00 BO. $5.00 MB.

Beauty Dust, 1958 – 1970.
White plastic powder box with beaded edge. Some with yellow lid and white handle. CMV, $10.00 MB, yellow and white. CMV, $5.00 MB, white issue.

Perfumed Talc, 1958 – 1962.
2¾ oz. blue and white can, white beaded cap. CMV, $1.00 CO. $3.00 MB.

Lotion Sachet, 1958.
½ oz. clear glass fan shaped bottle with blue cap. Came in Here's My Heart and Persian Wood. Came in Wishing Coin Trio Set only (see Women's Sets of the 1950s). CMV, $4.00 BO. $8.00 each, MB.

Here's My Heart Soap, 1959 – 1964.
Blue and white box, holds two white heart shaped bars. CMV, $25.00 MB.

Powder Sachet, 1958 – 1960.
Blue and white plastic squeeze bottle with white beaded cap. CMV, $10.00 MB.

Spray Perfume, 1958 – 1963.
Blue, white, and gold box holds blue tin container with gold cap with hearts on top. CMV, $12.00 MB.

Lotion Sachet, 1958 – 1961.
1 oz. blue plastic coated bottle with white beaded cap and painted label. Blue and white box. CMV, $5.00 MB.

Cream Sachet, 1959 – 1975.
⅔ oz., white beaded cap. Came blue painted over clear glass or blue paint over white milk glass. CMV $1.00.

Heart O'Mine Set, 1959.
Blue and white box with blue heart on lid with white rose and blue satin lining. Holds cologne mist, cream sachet, beauty dust, and spray perfume. CMV $50.00 MB.

Cologne, 1960 – 1963.
4 oz. bottle with white beaded cap and painted label. Came in blue and white box. CMV, $2.00 BO. $5.00 MB.

Sentimental Heart Set, 1961.
Blue box with blue satin lining holds cologne mist and beauty dust. CMV, $32.50 MB.

Soap, 1960 – 1965.
Blue and white box holds two white heart shaped soaps. CMV, $25.00 MB.

Perfumed Bath Oil, 1960 – 1966.
6 oz., blue plastic, white beaded cap. CMV, $2.00 MB.

Body Powder 1961 – 1963.
4 oz. blue plastic bottle with white beaded cap, painted label. CMV, $5.00 BO. $8.00 MB.

Perfumed Talc, 1962 – 1972.
2¾ oz. blue and white can with white cap. CMV, $1.00.

Romantic Mood Set, 1960.
Blue and white box with blue satin lining holds cologne mist, cream sachet, and beauty dust. CMV, $40.00 MB.

Cologne Special Issue, 1961.
Blue and white box (short issue) holds 4 oz. cologne. CMV $16.00 MB as shown.

New Remembrance Set, 1963.
Blue and white box holds cologne mist and beauty dust. CMV, $35.00 MB.

Cologne, 1961 – 1968.
2 oz., white beaded cap and painted label, blue and white box. First Introduced in red and white rose box. CMV, $3.00 in blue box. $8.00 in rose box.

Perfume Oil for the Bath, 1963.
½ oz., painted label and white beaded cap. Came in blue and white box. Hard to find. CMV, $3.00 BO. $5.00 MB.
Cologne, 1970 – 1971.
½ oz., painted label, white beaded cap, blue and white box. CMV, $1.00 BO. $2.00 MB.

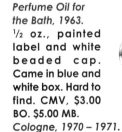

Two Hearts Gift Set, 1961.
Blue and white box holds 2 oz. cologne and cream sachet. CMV, $30.00 MB.

Powder Sachet, 1960 – 1966.
⁹⁄₁₀ oz., blue glass, white beaded plastic cap. CMV, $8.00 MB.

Perfume Mist, 1964 – 1968. 2 dram, blue and white metal with gold band. CMV, $5.00 MB.

Perfumed Skin Softener, 1964 – 1973. 5 oz., painted over milk glass or clear glass jar with gold and white lid. CMV, $1.00.

Perfumed Cream Rollette, 1963 – 1965. 1/3 oz., 4A embossed bottle with gold cap. CMV, $3.00 MB.

Scented Hair Spray, 1966 – 1970. 7 oz. blue and white can, 4A on cap. CMV, $3.00.

Heart Felt Set, 1964. Blue and white box holds 2 oz. cologne and cream sachet. CMV, $25.00 MB.

Perfume Oil, 1964 – 1968. 1/2 oz. painted label and white beaded cap. Came in blue and white box. CMV, $8.00 MB.

Foaming Bath Oil, 1966 – 1968. 6 oz., blue plastic, white beaded cap. CMV, $2.00 MB.

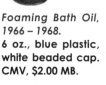

Here's My Heart Perfume Rollette, 1967 – 1968. 1/3 oz. ribbed glass, smooth gold cap. CMV, $3.00 MB.

Hearts in Bloom Set, 1964. Blue and white box holds cologne mist, cream sachet, and cream lotion. CMV, $40.00 MB.

Perfumed Soap, 1965 – 1966. 3 oz. white soap in blue and white wrapper. CMV, $3.00.

Soap, 1966 – 1967. Blue and white box holds three heart shaped bars. CMV, $25.00 MB.

Demi Stick, 1975 – 1978. 9/10 oz., blue and white, white cap. CMV, $1.00 MB.

Cream Sachet, 1976 – 1977. 2/3 oz., clear glass, gold, blue, and white lid. CMV, $1.00 MB.

Honeysuckle

After Bath Freshener, 1967 – 1972.
8 oz. bottle with orange cap and center band label. CMV, $1.00 MB.
Perfumed Talc, 1967 – 1977.
3 1/2 oz., yellow and white paper container. CMV, $1.50.
Soap, 1968 – 1969.
Six-sided box holds three yellow bars. CMV, $9.00 MB.
Perfumed Demi Stick, 1970 – 1974.
9/10 oz., yellow, green, and white. Yellow cap. CMV, $1.00 MB.
Perfumed Soap, 1967 – 1978.
3 oz. bar in yellow and orange wrapper. CMV, $3.00.
Cream Sachet, 1967 – 1975.
2/3 oz., yellow frosted glass with orange lid. CMV, $1.00 MB.
Not shown: Cologne Mist, 1971 – 1972.
2 oz. yellow glass bottle, yellow cap. CMV, $1.00 MB.

Floral Duet Set, 1972 – 1973. Box came with rollette and bar of soap. CMV, $5.00 MB.

Imperial Garden

Cologne Mist, 1973 – 1977.
3 oz., white with orange flowers and gold stems. Two different designs as pictured. CMV, $2.00 each, MB.

Ceramic Test Vase, 1973.
Test vase from factory, never sold by Avon. Has gold band around top of cap and bottom is glazed over Avon. Blue and green flowers on front different from regular issue. CMV, $25.00.

Perfumed Talc, 1974 – 1976.
3½ oz., white, gold, and orange, cardboard. CMV, 50¢.

Ceramic Vase, 1973 – 1975.
Came with short neck and tall cap, or long neck and short caps. White with orange flowers and gold stems. 18 oz. ceramic vase, holds bath crystals. 7" high. CMV, $20.00 MB.
Cologne Mist, 1973 – 1977.
3 oz. CMV, $1.00 MB.
Cream Sachet, 1973 – 1977.
⅔ oz. CMV, $1.00 MB.
Rollette, 1973 – 1977.
⅓ oz. CMV, $1.00 MB.
Sample Bottle Cologne, 1973 – 1977.
CMV, $1.00 MB.

Perfumed Soap, 1974 – 1976.
Three, 3 oz. cakes of white soap. Came in white and orange box. CMV, $9.00 MB.
Perfumed Powder Mist, 1974 – 1977.
7 oz. orange painted can, white lid. CMV, 50¢.
Perfumed Skin Softener, 1974 – 1976.
5 oz., orange plastic, white and gold cap. CMV, 50¢.
Coasters, 1973.
Four in set, white plastic, orange design. CMV, $25.00 MB, set.

Beauty Dust, 1974 only.
6 oz., white plastic with orange and gold. CMV, $7.00 MB.

Jardin d'Amour

See Powder Sachets section for additional Jardin d'Amour bottles.

Sachet, 1926 – 1930.
Brass cap, silver and blue label. Rare. CMV, $85.00 mint.

Perfume, 1926 – 1933.
Orange box with gold base for 1 oz. glass stoppered bottle. Black label at neck. CMV, $85.00 BO. $135.00 MB.

Talc, 1926 – 1936.
Frosted glass with brass shaker top. Front paper label. CMV, $60.00 BO, mint. $75.00 MB.

Sachet, 1932 – 1936.
1¼ oz. ribbed glass jar, black cap. CMV, $25.00 BO, mint. $30.00 MB.

Vanity Compact, 1926 – 1932.
Silver compact. CMV, $35.00 compact only, mint. $45.00 MB.

Perfume, 1929 – 1933.
2 oz. glass stoppered bottle. Orange box. Label on top of bottle. CMV, $85.00 BO, mint. $135.00 MB.

Face Powder, 1928.
Ardent face powder paper box available in flesh, white, peach, or Rachael. $65.00 MB.

Perfume, 1930s.
1 oz. clear glass bottle with frosted glass stopper. Silver and blue CPC label. Very rare. CMV, $150.00 mint.

Perfume Set, 1954 only.
Blue and gold bucket with gold tie-down cord. Holds 1½ oz. bottle with gold label, clear plastic cap with blue stone in gold set. Bottom of bucket holds 1 dram perfume. Came in blue, white, and gold laydown box. CMV, 1 dram perfume, $15.00. 1½ oz. bottle only, $50.00 mint. 1½ oz. bottle in bucket mint. $175.00. $200.00 MB, complete.

Jasmine/Royal Jasmine

Jasmine Soap, 1934 – 1936.
Beige and gold box holds three bars. CMV, $50.00 MB.

Royal Jasmine Soap, 1936 – 1945.
Turquoise and gold box holds three embossed bars. CMV, $47.50 MB.

Jasmine Bath Salts, 1936 – 1944.
9 oz. glass jar, turquoise lid. CMV, $20.00 BO, mint. $25.00 MB.

Jasmine Soap Set, 1939 only.
Gold striped box holds three bars. "Avon" on back of soap. CMV, $60.00 MB.

Bath Ensemble Set, 1940 – 1943.
Blue flowered flip-open box holds Jasmine bath salts, Jasmine 2 oz. toilet water, two bars of Jasmine soap, and can of dusting powder. CMV, $150.00 MB.

Fantasy in Jasmine Set, 1945 only.
Black box with pink flowers holds Jasmine bath salts and two Jasmine soaps. CMV, $77.50 MB.

Jasmine Powder Sachet, 1946 – 1950.
1¼ oz. bottle with black cap and label. Came in black box. CMV, $15.00 BO. $20.00 MB.

Fantasy in Jasmine Set, 1940.
Blue box with flowers holds 9 oz. Jasmine bath salts and two bars of soap or two powder sachets, boxed. CMV, $100.00 MB.

Fantasy in Jasmine, 1946 – 1947.
Black box with pink flowers holds two bars of Jasmine soap and 9 oz. bottle of Jasmine bath salts. CMV, $75.00 MB. Set also came with two bottles in boxes of 1¼ oz. Jasmine sachet in place of soaps. CMV, $100.00 MB with boxed sachets.

Jasmine Dusting Powder, 1947 – 1950.
13 oz. black and gold tin can with pink flowers on lid. CMV, $25.00 CO. $30.00 MB.

Fantasy in Jasmine Set, 1942 – 1944.
Green box holds two bars of Jasmine soap and 9 oz. Jasmine bath salts with turquoise lid. CMV, $75.00 MB.

Jasmine Toilet Water, 1946 – 1948.
2 oz., gold cap, also came in turquoise box. CMV, $30.00 BO. $40.00 MB.

Jasmine Bath Salts, 1945 – 1952.
9 oz., clear glass with black cap and label. Label came with either a large or small pink flower on front. Came in black box. CMV, $30.00 BO. $40.00 MB.

Jasmine Soap Set, 1946 – 1953.
Black flowered box holds three bars. CMV, $45.00 MB.

Jasmine Soap Set, 1948 – 1949.
Christmas only. Black flowered box holds three white bars. CMV, $45.00 MB.

Fantasy in Jasmine Set, 1948.
Black box with pink flowers holds two bars of Jasmine soap and 2 oz. Jasmine toilet water. CMV, $75.00 MB.

Royal Jasmine Set, 1954 – 1957.
Yellow and white flowered box holds 8 oz. Royal Jasmine bath salts and bar of Royal Jasmine soap. CMV, $40.00 MB.

Jasmine After Bath Freshener, 1964 – 1968.
8 oz. glass bottle with yellow cap and painted label. Yellow flowered box. CMV, $2.00 BO. $3.00 MB.
Perfumed Soap, 1964 – 1967.
3 oz. bar in yellow flowered wrapping. CMV, $2.00.
Cream Sachet, 1967 – 1972.
2/3 oz. yellow frosted glass with gold and white lid. CMV. 50¢.
Perfumed Talc 1964 – 1968.
3½ oz. yellow flowered paper container with plastic shaker top. CMV, $2.00.

Jasmine Powder Sachet, 1949.
1½ oz. clear glass bottle, black cap and label. CMV, $20.00 BO. $25.00 MB.

Royal Jasmine Soap Set, 1954 – 1959.
Box holds three bars, with round or flat edges. Box lid lifts off. CMV, $28.00 MB.
Not shown: Royal Jasmine Soap Set, 1959 – 1966.
Same box, only lid flips back and not off. The soap has flat edges. CMV, $27.00 MB.

Jasmine Toilet Water, 1949.
2 oz. black cap and label. CMV, $35.00 BO. $40.00 MB.

Fantasy in Jasmine Set, 1956 – 1957.
White box with flowers holds two bars Royal Jasmine soap and 2 oz. Royal Jasmine bath oil with white cap and black label. CMV, $25.00, 2 oz. bath oil, BO. $45.00 MB.

Jasmine Gift Soap Set, 1966 – 1967.
Floral box contains three yellow Jasmine soaps. CMV, $25.00 MB.

Royal Jasmine Bath Salts, 1954 – 1957.
Yellow and white flowered box holds 8 oz. bottle with yellow cap. CMV, $20.00 BO. $25.00 MB.

Royal Jasmine Bath Oil, 1957 – 1959.
Yellow, white, and green box holds 8 oz. bottle with yellow cap and flowered label. CMV, $20.00 BO. $25.00 MB.

Lavender

Toilet Water, 1934 – 1937.
4 oz. ribbed bottle with blue or gold cap. Lavender label, box shown, was used from 1934 to 1936. CMV, $45.00 BO, mint. $55.00 MB.

Soap Set, 1935 only.
Box holds three bars of soap. CMV, $75.00 MB.

Lavender Set, 1939.
Yellow box with lavender, green, and pink flowers holds 4 oz. toilet water, two cakes of soap, and two sachet cakes with plain lavender paper ribbons. CMV, $125.00 MB.

Ensemble Set, 1934 – 1938.
Lavender box holds 4 oz. toilet water, two bars of soap, and package of Lavender Blossoms. CMV, $50.00 MB, Lavender Blossoms only. $125.00 MB, set.

Ensemble Set, 1938 only.
Flip-open box holds 4 oz. toilet water with same label as 1934 toilet water, two bars of soap, and two sachet cakes. CMV, $45.00 BO. $100.00 MB.

Ensemble Set, 1940 – 1943.
Flowered box with satin lining holds 4 oz. toilet water, two bars of soap, and two sachet cakes. CMV, $100.00 MB.

Toilet Water, 1934 – 1937.
4 oz., ribbed glass, gold cap, pink and lavender box. Box shown dates 1936 – 1937. CMV, $45.00 BO. $55.00 MB.

Toilet Water, 1938 – 1943.
4 oz., lavender cap. CMV, $35.00 BO. $40.00 MB. CPC on box, 1938 – 1939, add $5.00.

Blossoms, 1935 – 1938.
Lavender and pink box holds package of Lavender Blossoms. CMV, $40.00 MB.

Ensemble, 1938 – 1940.
Flip-open box with cardboard liner holds 4 oz. toilet water, two bars of soap wrapped in lavender paper, and two sachet cakes with lavender bands around them. CMV, $100.00 MB.

Toilet Water,
1946 – 1948.
4 oz. bottle
with pink cap.
CMV, $35.00
BO. $40.00 MB.

Ensemble Set, 1941 only.
Box holds two sachet cakes,
bottle of toilet water, and two
bars of soap. CMV, $100.00
MB set.

Sachets, 1945 – 1946.
Beige box holds two foil wrapped cakes of
sachet. Plain band. CMV, $30.00 MB.

Lavender Soap Set,
1946 only.
Box holds three bars of soap.
CMV, $60.00 MB.

Sachet, 1944 – 1945.
Beige box holds two lavender
wrapped cakes of sachet. One
set is wrapped in clear cellophane with a flowered band. The
other set is wrapped in lavender
flowered paper, no band. Some
boxes have label printed on box.
CMV, $25.00 MB.

Ensemble Set, 1945 – 1946.
Box is blue, pink, and white with silver
bottom. Holds 4 oz. toilet water, two
bars of soap, and two sachet cakes.
CMV, $100.00 MB.

Toilet Water,
1945 – 1946.
4 oz. bottle with
lavender cap.
CMV, $40.00 BO.
$45.00 MB.

Ensemble Set, 1946.
Blue, pink, and
green flowered
box with satin lin-
ing holds two bars
of soap, 4 oz. bottle
of toilet water, and
two flower wrapped
cakes of sachet.
CMV, $100.00 MB.

Sachet Cakes,
1946 – 1948.
Box holds two flower de-
sign wrapped cakes of
sachet. CMV, $30.00 MB.

Ensemble Set,
1946 – 1948.
Blue and pink flowered
flip-open box holds 4
oz. bottle of toilet water
with pink cap, two
pink bars of soap, and
two paper wrapped
cakes of sachet. CMV,
$100.00 MB.

Soap Set, 1946.
Pink box holds three embossed
bars. OSP, 85¢. CMV, $60.00 MB.

Powder Sachets, 1961 – 1968.
⁹/₁₀ oz., pink and white label and neck band, glass and plastic stopper. Box on right is 1965, box in center is regular issue. CMV one with 4A design in place of size, $4.00 BO. $7.00 MB. CMV, ⁹/₁₀ oz., $15.00 BO. $20.00 MB.

Lavender Bouquet Sachet Pillows, 1977 – 1978.
Pink box holds six satin lavender filled sachet pillows. Came with pink ribbon around them. CMV, $4.00.

Lilac

Toilet Water, 1940.
2 oz., gold ribbed cap with "A" on top, gold label. Blue box. Has "Avon Products Inc." label. CMV, $35.00 BO, mint. $40.00 MB. Same bottle sold 1934 to 1939, only bottom of label says "Toilet Water" and does not say Avon Products. CPC on back side of label. Same CMV as above.

Soap, 1966.
Lavender box holds three-piece lavender soap in cellophane wrapper. CMV, $17.00 MB.

Soap, 1968 – 1977.
Box holds three lavender bars. CMV, $10.00 MB.

After Bath Freshener, 1964 – 1968.
8 oz. glass bottle with pink cap and pink or white painted label. Pink box. CMV. $2.00.
Perfumed Talc, 1964 – 1976.
3½ oz. pink paper container with plastic shaker top. CMV, $1.00.
Perfumed Demi Stick, 1970 – 1976.
⁹/₁₀ oz., lavender label with white cap and bottom. CMV. 50¢.
Perfumed Demi Stick, 1968 – 1970.
⁹/₁₀ oz., lavender label, cap, and bottom. CMV, $1.00.
Perfumed Soap, 1964 – 1967.
One bar in pink flowered wrapping. CMV, $3.00 MB.
Cream Sachet, 1967 – 1975.
⅔ oz., purple frosted glass with gold and white lid. CMV, 50¢.
Cream Sachet, 1975 – 1976.
⅔ oz., clear glass, white cap with lilacs on top. CMV, 50¢.

Lily of the Valley

Toilet Water, 1934 – 1940. 2 oz., gold ribbed cap, "A" on top. Gold front label. CMV, $35.00 BO. $40.00 MB.

After Bath Freshener, 1964 – 1968. 8 oz. glass bottle with green cap, painted label in green or white letters, green box. CMV, $2.00 MB.
Perfumed Talc, 1964 – 1970. 3½ oz. green paper container with plastic shaker top. CMV, $1.50.
Perfumed Soap, 1964 – 1967. 3 oz. bar with green and white flowered wrapping. CMV, $3.00 MB.

Toilet Water, 1946 – 1949. Green box holds 2 oz. bottle with gold cap and label. CMV, $30.00 BO. $40.00 MB.

Soap, 1966 – 1968. Green box holds two green cakes. CMV, $25.00 MB.

Perfume, 1948 – 1952. 3 dram bottle with flower cap. Came in satin lined box with clear plastic lid. CMV, $40.00 BO. $80.00 MB.

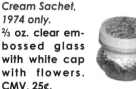

Cream Sachet, 1974 only. ⅔ oz. clear embossed glass with white cap with flowers. CMV, 25¢.

Left: Cologne Ice Stick, 1979 – 1980. Yellow and green plastic. CMV, 50¢.
Center: Perfumed Talc, 1979 – 1980. 3½ oz. cardboard sides, plastic bottom and top. CMV, 25¢.
Right: Chateau of Flowers Book, 1979 – 1980. Green hardback book, story of Lily of the Valley. Book does not say "Avon" on it. Must be in Avon box cover as shown. CMV, $2.00 MB.

Toilet Water, 1949 – 1952. 2 oz., white cap. CMV, $35.00 BO. $45.00 MB.

Perfume Demi Stick, 1974 – 1976. ⁹⁄₁₀ oz., white with flowers. CMV, $1.00.

Perfume, 1952 – 1954. 3 dram, white cap, white satin lined box. CMV, $40.00 BO. $85.00 MB. Also came in Gardenia.

Cream Sachet, 1975 – 1976. ⅔ oz., clear ribbed glass with white cap with flowers. CMV, 25¢.

Little Blossom

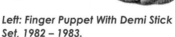

Scented Picture Frame, 1981 – 1982.
Pink plastic frame, 4½" x 4½", has scented fabric picture of Little Blossom. CMV, $6.00 MB.
Whisper Soft Cologne, 1981 – 1982.
1½ oz., clear glass, painted decor, pink cap. CMV, $2.00 MB.
Cheerful Lip Tint, 1981 – 1982.
White flowered tube, pink cap. CMV, $1.00 mint, no box.
Cheeky Rose Blush, 1981 – 1982.
Pink and white plastic jar. CMV, $1.00 MB.

Left: Finger Puppet With Demi Stick Set, 1982 – 1983.
Box holds small finger puppet and blue, white, and pink demi stick. CMV, $4.00 MB.
Right: Light Switch Cover.
Box holds blue and green light switch plate with pink flowers. CMV, $4.00 MB.

Bubble Bath Packets, 1983.
Flowered box holds ten packets. CMV, $1.00 MB.

Lip and Nail Tint, 1982 – 1983.
Lip tint on left, pink cap, no box. OSP, $2.00. Nail tint in ½ oz. plastic bottle, white cap, boxed. CMV, $1.00 each.

Little Blossom and Friends, 1983 – 1984.
Shaker Talc with Puff Sets.
2 oz. talc and small hand puff. Choice of Little Blossom Pink, Daisy Dreamer Yellow, or Scamper Lily Orange. OSP, $5.00 set. CMV $4.00 each set.
Mini Dolls.
2¼" high soft plastic, choice of Little Blossom, Daisy Dreamer, or Scamper Lily. OSP, $5.00, each. CMV $2.00 each.
Dab O' Cologne.
5/11 oz. rollette, choice of Little Blossom in Whisper Soft, Daisy Dreamer in Secret Wishes, or Scamper Lily in Sparkle Bright. OSP, $4.00 each. CMV $2.00 each.
Hand Cream.
1½ oz., Daisy Dreamer, lemon scent. Little Blossom, strawberry scent. Scamper Lily, orange scent. OSP, $2.00 each. CMV 50¢ each.

Lucy Hays

Perfume, 1936 only.
2 dram, gold cap. Sold for 20¢ with other purchase to celebrate Mr. and Mrs. McConnell's 51st wedding anniversary. Hays was Mrs. McConnell's maiden name. Sold March 3 to 23, 1936 only. CMV, $65.00 BO, mint. $85.00 MB.

Lullabye

Baby Talc, 1946 – 1950.
5 oz. pink paper container with pink and white plastic top and bottom. CMV, $30.00 talc only, mint. $35.00 MB.

Baby Oil, 1946 – 1950.
6 oz. clear glass bottle, back side flat. Pink cap and painted label. CMV, $40.00 BO. $50.00 MB.

Baby Cream, 1946 – 1950.
White milk glass jar with pink lid and label. CMV, $25.00 jar only. $30.00 MB.

Baby Soap, 1946 – 1950.
Plastic wrapper with pink painted bow and flowers on wrapper. CMV, $25.00 mint.

Baby Set, 1946 – 1950.
Pink box holds baby oil, baby soap, baby cream, and baby talc. CMV, $150.00 MB.

Baby Set, 1951 – 1955.
Blue, pink, and white box holds baby lotion, baby talc, and lanolin baby soap. CMV, $75.00 MB.

Lullabye Set, 1955 – 1956.
Blue and pink box holds baby oil and baby powder. CMV, $45.00 MB.

Baby Set, 1964 – 1966.
Pink and blue box holds two bars of baby soap and choice of Tot 'N' Tyke baby oil, baby lotion, or baby shampoo. CMV, $27.50 MB.

Luscious

Perfume Award, 1950.
Gold and purple box holds 3 dram bottle with ribbed glass stopper. Stopper different from regular issue. Given when Luscious was first issued. CMV, $100.00 BO. $150.00 MB.

Perfume, 1950.
1 dram clear bottle with gold cap and label. Came in brown felt wrapper. CMV, $12.00 BO. $18.00 in wrapper.

Perfume, 1950 – 1955.
1 dram, painted label with smooth gold cap. Came in felt wrapper. CMV $10.00 BO, mint. $15.00 in wrapper.

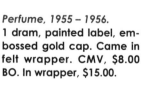

Perfume, 1950.
3 dram glass stoppered bottle, came with painted label or with gold neck tag label. CMV, $85.00 BO, mint with tag. $125.00 MB.

Perfume, 1955 – 1956.
1 dram, painted label, embossed gold cap. Came in felt wrapper. CMV, $8.00 BO. In wrapper, $15.00.

Marionette

Perfume.
1940 – 1944.
1 dram bottle, plastic cap. CMV, $25.00 BO. $30.00 MB.

Perfume, 1938.
¼ oz., gold ribbed cap with "A." CPC on label. Sold in honor of Mr. McConnell's birthday. CMV, $40.00 BO. $50.00 MB.

Sachet, 1938 – 1946.
1¼ oz., with turquoise plain metal cap or ribbed turquoise plastic cap. Shown with regular issue box. CMV, $15.00 BO. $20.00 MB.

Sachet, Special Issue Box, 1940 only.
Short issue blue and pink box holds regular issue powder sachet in 1¼ oz. size. Sold for 20¢ with regular order. CMV, $30.00 MB in this box only.

Sachet, 1938 only.
1¼ oz. ribbed glass bottle with turquoise plain metal cap or ribbed plastic turquoise cap. CMV, $25.00 BO. $30.00 MB.

Toilet Water, 1939 – 1940.
2 oz., plastic cap, long front label. CMV, $35.00 BO. $45.00 MB.

Toilet Water, 1940 – 1946.
2 oz., gold ribbed cap and gold label. Also came with plastic cap. CMV, $30.00 BO, mint. $35.00 MB.

Merriment

Jolly Surprise, 1955.
Pink and blue flip-open box holds choice of 4 oz. bottle of Merriment cologne or bubble bath, both with pink caps. OSP, $1.75 cologne, $1.50 bubble bath. CMV, $40.00 each, BO. $55.00 each, MB.

Miss Lollypop

Cologne Boot, 1967 – 1969.
2 oz. glass boot with gold cap and red tassel. Red and white box. CMV, $8.00 MB.

Cream Sachet, 1967 – 1970.
⅔ oz. dark or light yellow glass jar with white kitten on red, white, and pink cap. Kitten's eyes are blue or black, head also turns on some. CMV, $5.00 MB. Also came with white base. CMV, $7.00 MB.

Cologne Mist, 1967 – 1970.
3 oz., pink plastic coated bottom with red band, white hat with red and yellow ribbon. CMV, $6.00 MB.

Soap and Sponge, 1967 – 1970.
Pink soap and 9" long sponge. Pink and white box. CMV, $12.00 MB.

Lip Pops, 1967 – 1969.
Girl's face on handle. Pink lemonade, cherry, raspberry, peppermint, and cola flavors. CMV, $4.00 MB.

Powderette, 1967 – 1968.
3½ oz. container of perfumed talc. Red plume on top is long handled puff. CMV, $10.00 MB.

Powder Mitt, 1968 – 1970.
Yellow, orange, and white plastic mitt filled with powder. Pink and white box. CMV, $5.00 MB.

Rollette, 1968 – 1969.
Pink, yellow, and white cap. ⅓ oz. CMV, $3.00 MB.

Perfumed Talc, 1968 – 1970.
3½ oz. paper container with plastic shaker top. CMV, $5.00 MB.

Hand Cream, 1968.
2 oz. white plastic tube, black boots and purse, yellow cap. CMV, $3.00.

Lip Pop, 1967.
First issue, pink and white dots, mirror top, came in box with face on back. CMV, $5.00 MB.
Lip Pop, 1968.
Two pink and white dot lip pops, no mirror top. CMV, $5.00 MB.

Hand Cream, 1968.
2 oz. white plastic tube, white boots and purse, yellow cap. CMV, $3.00.

Ice Cream Puff, 1968 – 1970.
3½ oz., yellow plastic bottom with pink fluff. Holds talc. CMV, $4.00 BO. $6.00 MB.

Double Dip Bubble Bath, 1968 – 1970.
5 oz. orange and white plastic bottle, red cap. CMV, $4.00 BO. $5.00 MB.

Pretty Me Set, 1968.
Box with white plastic tray holds perfume rollette and lip pop in choice of peppermint, pink lemonade, cherry, raspberry, or cola. CMV, $12.00 MB.

Pretty Touch, 1969.
Yellow, pink, green, and orange plastic light switch plate. OSP, 29¢ with purchase of Miss Lollypop items. Hard to find. Sold during only one campaign. CMV, $9.00 MB.

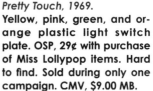 

Moonwind

Moonwind Fragrance, 1971 – 1978.
All are blue trimmed in silver.
Cologne Mist, 1971 – 1975.
3 oz., blue with silver painted top. CMV, $1.00.
Cologne Mist, 1975 – 1980.
Blue with flat top, $2^{7}/_{10}$ oz. CMV, 50¢.
Perfume Rollette, 1971 – 1976.
$1/3$ oz. CMV, 50¢.
Beauty Dust, 1971– 1976.
6 oz. CMV, $3.00 CO. $6.00 MB.
Perfumed Powder Mist, 1972 – 1977.
7 oz., silver or blue caps. CMV, 50¢. Some have upside down painted label. CMV, $8.00.
Perfumed Skin Softener, 1972 – 1973.
5 oz., blue glass. CMV, 50¢.
Cream Sachet, 1971 – 1975.
$2/3$ oz. CMV, 50¢.
Perfumed Soaps, 1972 – 1973.
Three blue bars, in blue box. CMV, $7.00 MB.
Not shown: Foaming Bath Oil, 1972.
6 oz. CMV, $1.00.

Cologne and Bath Oil, 1973.
4 oz. clear glass bottles, gold caps. Came in Treasure Chest Set only (See Women's Sets of the 1970s). CMV, $4.00 each.

Perfumed Soap, 1975 – 1978.
Three cakes of blue soap. Blue and silver lid slides over gold box. CMV, $10.00 MB.

Nearness

Cologne, 1955 – 1961.
4 oz. bottle with blue cap and see-through label on back side. Came in blue and gold box. CMV, $10.00 BO. $15.00 MB.

Perfume, 1955 – 1959.
Blue satin draw bag holds clam shell with pearl and ½ oz. bottle with blue cap and see-through label on back side. CMV, $50.00 BO, mint. $100.00 in bag.

Perfume, 1955 – 1959.
1 dram, clear smooth glass, gold scroll cap. Came in blue felt wrapper. CMV, $8.00 mint.

Cream Sachet,
1955 – 1961.
Blue glass bottom, blue metal cap. CMV, $5.00 BO. $8.00 MB.

Beauty Dust, 1956 – 1959.
Blue cardboard container with tin bottom. CMV, $15.00 CO, mint. $20.00 MB. CMV, $22.00 for special 1956 Christmas issue box as shown, MB.

Body Powder,
1956 – 1958.
Frosted glass bottle with blue cap and label. Blue and gold box. CMV, $10.00 BO. $13.00 MB.

Two Pearls Set,
1956 – 1957.
Blue and gold box with two pearls on lid holds body powder and cream sachet. CMV, $40.00 MB.

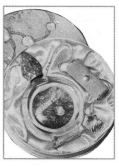

Always Near Set, 1956.
Blue seashell box with pink satin lining holds 2 oz. toilet water, 1 dram perfume, and gold seashell necklace with pearl. CMV, $75.00 MB.

Powder Sachet,
1956 – 1961.
1¼ oz. blue glass bottle with blue cap and label. CMV, $7.00 BO. $10.00 MB. Also came in ⁹⁄₁₀ oz. size. Same CMV.

Toilet Water,
1956 – 1961.
2 oz. bottle with blue cap and see-through label on back side. Came in blue and gold box. CMV, $10.00 BO. $15.00 MB.

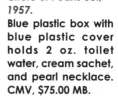

Gift Perfume Combo Set,
1956.
½ oz. perfume on the clam shell in blue satin bag. Came with 1 dram perfume in blue felt wrapper in white box and outer sleeve. CMV, $130.00 MB.

Seashell Necklace,
1956 only.
Gold finished pendant with pearl on fine chain. Came only in Always Near Set. CMV, $25.00.

Circle of Pearls Set,
1957.
Blue plastic box with blue plastic cover holds 2 oz. toilet water, cream sachet, and pearl necklace. CMV, $75.00 MB.

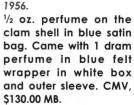

Nearness Charm, 1957.
Blue box holds toilet water and can of talc. CMV, $40.00 MB.

Cologne, 1957 only.
½ oz., clear glass. Sold in Gems in Crystal set only (See Women's Sets of the 1950s). Came with two different caps. Available in four fragrances. CMV, $7.00.

Cologne Mist, 1957 – 1959.
3 oz. blue plastic coated bottle with blue cap and blue and gold box. CMV, $15.00 BO, mint. $20.00 MB.

Perfumed Talc, 1957 – 1961.
Blue can and cap. CMV, $5.00 CO. $7.00 MB.

Sea Mist Set, 1958.
Blue and gold box with net lining holds cologne mist and cream sachet. CMV, $60.00 MB.

Beauty Dust, 1959 – 1961.
Plastic pearl color lid with lavender rim and turquoise bottom. General issue. CMV, $10.00 CO. $15.00 MB. Rare issue came with all lavender matching rim and bottom. CMV, $13.00 CO, mint. $18.00 MB.

Cologne Mist, 1959 – 1961.
3 oz. blue plastic coated bottle with pearl on pearl colored cap. Cap will turn gray in sunlight and will not be considered mint. Blue and gold box. CMV, $15.00 BO, mint. $20.00 MB.

Occur!

Cologne Mist, 1963 – 1976.
3 oz. black plastic coated bottle with gold cap and painted label. Came in black and gold box. Older issue was gold bottom under plastic coating. Came with and without "3 oz." on front of bottle. CMV, $2.00.

Powder Sachet, 1963 – 1967.
⁹/₁₀ oz., black glass and cap, painted label. CMV, $3.00 BO. $5.00 MB.

Cream Sachet, 1963 – 1975.
⅔ oz., black glass and cap. Two caps: one says "Occur!," one says "Occur! Cream Sachet." CMV, 50¢.

Beauty Dust, 1963 – 1970.
Black plastic box with gold handle on black lid. CMV, $3.00 CO. $5.00 MB.

Perfume Oil for the Bath, 1963.
Black and gold box holds ½ oz. bottle with gold cap and painted label. CMV, $8.00 MB.

Cologne Mist, 1963 – 1966.
2 oz., frosted glass with black cap and gold painted label. Came in black and gold box. CMV, $4.00 BO. $6.00 MB. Also came with 4A embossed bottle with black neck label and gold plastic cap. CMV, $3.00 BO.

Fragrance Fortune Set, 1964 – 1965.
Black and gold box holds 2 oz. cologne and 1/2 oz. perfume oil. CMV, $30.00 MB.

Perfumed Skin Softener, 1964 – 1972.
5 oz., black painted over white milk glass or clear glass jar with black and gold lid. CMV, $1.00. Also came in white milk glass painted black or solid black glass. CMV, $3.00 each.

Perfumed Cream Rollette, 1963 – 1965.
1/3 oz. 4A embossed bottle with gold cap. CMV, $2.00 MB.

Elegance Set, 1964.
Black and gold box holds 4 oz. cream lotion, perfumed talc, and 2 oz. cologne. CMV, $35.00 MB.

Perfumed Talc, 1964 – 1974.
2 3/4 oz. black can with black cap and gold painted label. CMV, $1.00.

Perfumed Bath Oil, 1964 – 1965.
6 oz. black plastic bottle with gold cap and painted label. Black and gold box. CMV, $2.00 BO. $4.00 MB.

Perfume Mist, 1963 – 1968.
Gold box holds 2 dram black and gold metal case with white cap. CMV, $3.00 MB.

Cream Lotion, 1964 – 1968.
4 oz., gold cap and painted label. Came in black and gold box. CMV, $2.00 BO. $4.00 MB.
Cologne, 1970 – 1971.
1/2 oz., gold cap and painted letters. Came in black and gold box. CMV, $1.00 BO. $2.00 MB.

Sophisticate Set, 1963 – 1964.
3 oz. cologne mist, perfume cream rollette, and beauty dust. Black and gold box. CMV, $35.00 MB.

Perfume Oil, 1964 – 1969.
1/2 oz., gold cap and painted label. Came in black and gold box. CMV, $4.00 BO. $6.00 MB.
Cologne, 1964 – 1971.
2 oz. bottle with gold cap and painted label. Came in black and gold box. CMV, $1.00 BO. $2.00 MB.

Soap Set, 1965 – 1967.
Black and gold box holds three yellow bars. CMV, $15.00 MB.

Perfumed Soap, 1965 – 1968.
Black wrapped soap. CMV, $2.00.

Perfume Rollette, 1965 – 1969. ⅓ oz., gray ribbed carnival glass, gold cap. CMV, $3.00 MB.

Deluxe Set, 1965. Black and gold box holds beauty dust, perfumed skin softener, and cologne mist. CMV, $35.00.

Cream Sachet, 1976 – 1978. ⅔ oz., clear glass with black and gold lid. CMV, 50¢.

Scented Hair Spray, 1966 – 1970. 7 oz. black can with black cap. CMV, $3.00 MB.

Foaming Bath Oil, 1966 – 1974. 6 oz. black plastic bottle with gold cap and painted label. Came in black and gold box. CMV, $2.00 MB.

Beauty Dust, 1971 – 1975. 6 oz. black cardboard, non-refillable. CMV, $5.00 MB.

Orchard Blossoms

Cologne, 1941 – 1945. 6 oz. bubble sided bottle. Short front label has tree with flowers on it. Pink cap. CMV, $30.00 BO. $40.00 MB.

Petal of Beauty Set, 1943 – 1944. Blue box with pink satin lining holds 6 oz. cologne and blue feather design beauty dust or Apple Blossom beauty dust. CMV, $100.00 MB.

Cologne, 1945 – 1946. 6 oz. bubble sided bottle, long blue and white front label, pink cap. CMV, $35.00 BO. $45.00 MB.

Petal of Beauty Set, 1945 – 1946. Blue and white box holds 6 oz. cologne and beauty dust in blue and white box. CMV, $100.00 MB.

Patterns

Not shown: Tray, 1969 – 1970. 10" black plastic tray with gold edge. When held to light shows purple, red, and gray (these are transparent). There is an opaque black one that is rare. CMV, $5.00 red, gray, and purple, MB. Reissued in 1975 in black (no light comes through). CMV, $8.00.

Powder Shadow Compact, 1969 – 1970. Black and white plastic. CMV, $1.00.

Lipstick, 1969 – 1970. Cream Sachet, 1969 – 1974. Cologne Mist, 1969 – 1972. Perfume Rollette, 1969 – 1974. Perfume Glace Ring, 1969 – 1970. Gold ring with black set. CMV, $6.00 MB. All others CMV, $1.00 each.

Pennsylvania Dutch

Pennsylvania Dutch Decanters, 1973 – 1976. Yellow painted over clear glass with orange fruit and yellow caps. All items CMV, $2.00 MB.

Hand and Body Lotion, 1973 – 1976. 10 oz., came in Patchwork or Sonnet only.

Cologne Decanter, 1973 – 1974. (Salt or pepper shaker). Holds Moonwind, Patchwork, or Sonnet. 4 oz.

Foaming Bath Oil, 1973 – 1976. 6 oz.

Powder Sachet Shaker, 1973 – 1975. 1¼ oz.

Perfumed Skin Softener, 1973 – 1976. 5 oz.

Persian Wood

Mist, 1956 – 1959. 3 oz., red plastic coated glass, raised gold cap with 4A on top. Came in red and gold box. CMV, $6.00 BO. $8.00 MB.

Mist, 1957 – 1959. 3 oz., red plastic coated glass, smooth gold cap. Came in red and gold box. CMV, $6.00 BO. $8.00 MB.

Persian Wood Beauty Dust, 1957 – 1960. Red glass bottom with red and gold tin lid. Lid also came in cardboard just like tin lid shown. Same CMV. CMV, $12.00 CO, mint. $17.00 MB.

Perfumed Talc, 1958 – 1962. Red and gold box holds red can with a white or red plastic cap. CMV, $3.00 MB.

Cream Sachets, 1959 – 1976. *Left to right:* ⅔ oz., red bottom with smooth gold lid. CMV, $6.00 MB. Gold embossed cap with straight sides. CMV, 50¢. Came with red paint over clear or milk glass. Gold embossed cap with curved sides. CMV, $4.00 MB.

Powder Sachet, 1957 – 1966. 1¼ oz. red plastic squeeze bottle, gold cap, red and gold box. CMV, $4.00 BO. $7.00 MB.

Spray Perfume, 1957 – 1963. 2 dram, red metal with gold cap, red and gold box. CMV, $7.00 MB.

Lotion Sachet, 1957 – 1961. Red plastic coated, gold cap. Came in red and gold box. CMV, $4.00 BO. $7.00 MB.

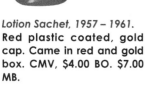

Fancy Set, 1957 – 1958. Red and gold box with red lining holds mist and lotion sachet or powder sachet. CMV, $40.00 MB.

Mist, 1959 – 1964. 3 oz., red plastic coated glass, gold crown cap. Came in red and gold box. CMV, $6.00 MB.

Persian Treasure Set, 1959 – 1960.
Fancy gold box with white satin lining holds mist, 2 oz. toilet water, perfume spray, and cream sachet. CMV, $60.00 MB.

Cologne, 1960 – 1963.
Red and gold box holds 4 oz. bottle with gold lettering and gold cap. CMV, $6.00 BO. $10.00 MB.

Body Powder, 1961 – 1963.
4 oz. red plastic bottle with gold cap, in red and gold box. CMV, $10.00 MB.

Beauty Dust Refill, 1960s.
Box holds plain paper refill pack with red powder puff. CMV, $6.00 MB.

Toilet Water, 1959 – 1961.
2 oz., gold cap, painted label. Came in red and gold box. CMV, $4.00 BO. $6.00 MB.

Persian Magic Set, 1961 – 1962.
Red and gold box holds Persian Wood 2 oz. cologne and cream sachet. CMV, $25.00 MB.

Beauty Dust, 1960 – 1966.
White plastic with red design around gold handle. CMV, $8.00 CO, mint. $12.00 MB.

Persian Wood Perfumed Skin Softener, 1959 – 1964.
5 oz. off-white glass bottom with straight sides. Red and gold cap with either curved or straight sides. CMV, $3.00 each, BO. $5.00 each, MB.

Persian Legend Set, 1961 – 1962.
Red and gold box with red satin lining holds mist and beauty dust. CMV, $40.00 MB.

Cologne, 1960 – 1962.
Red and gold flip-open box holds 4 oz. cologne. CMV, $20.00 MB.

Cologne, 1961 – 1966.
2 oz., clear glass, gold lettering, gold cap. In red and gold box. CMV, $4.00 BO. $6.00 MB.

Beauty Dust, 1962 – 1963.
Red paper sides with gold writing around sides and clear plastic top. Came in Fragrance Magic Sets only (See Women's Sets of the 1960s). CMV, $15.00 mint.

Perfumed Bath Oil, 1960 – 1966.
6 oz. red plastic bottle with gold cap. Came in red and gold box. CMV, $4.00 MB.

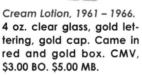

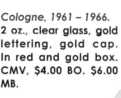

Cream Lotion, 1961 – 1966.
4 oz. clear glass, gold lettering, gold cap. Came in red and gold box. CMV, $3.00 BO. $5.00 MB.

Perfumed Talc, 1962 – 1968. Red and gold box holds red can with brass cap and trim. CMV, $4.00.

Intrigue Set, 1963 – 1964. Red and gold box holds mist, cream lotion, and perfumed cream rollette. CMV, $37.50 MB.

Perfume Oil, 1964 – 1966. Red and gold box holds ½ oz. bottle, white lettering and gold cap. CMV, $5.00 BO. $8.00 MB.

Perfumed Skin Softener, 1964 – 1966. 5 oz., white glass, round bottom, red and gold cap. CMV, $3.00 BO. $4.00 MB.

Cologne, 1962 – 1963. 2½ oz. clear glass, gold cap. Red label on front of flat sided bottle. Came in Refreshing Hours Set only (See Women's Sets of the 1960s). CMV, $10.00.

Perfume Mist, 1963 – 1967. 2 dram bottle, red base, white cap, in gold box. CMV, $4.00 MB.

Persian Wood Set, 1964. Red and gold box with white lining holds cream sachet and 1 dram perfume. CMV, $22.00 MB.

Perfume Oil for the Bath, 1963. ½ oz. bottle with gold cap, painted label. Came in red and gold box. CMV, $10.00 MB.

Cologne Mist, 1964 – 1976. 3 oz., red plastic coated glass, gold crown cap. Came in red and gold box. CMV, $1.00 BO. $2.00 MB.

Cream Sachet, 1975 – 1976. ⅔ oz., clear glass, red and gold cap. CMV, 50¢.

Pine/Royal Pine

Pine Soap, 1940 only. Special box holds three green bars of Pine soap. CMV, $45.00 MB.

Pine Soap Substitute, 1940. Three green bars of Pine soap came in brown and green box that was the Royal Pine set box. A letter from Avon stating the regular soap boxes were not available and Royal Pine set box was substituted was included. Rare, with letter. CMV, $45.00 MB with letter as shown.

Royal Pine Set, 1940 – 1943.
Pine cones on lid of box, holds two green bars of Pine soap and 6 oz. bottle of Pine bath oil with brown label. CMV, $60.00 MB.

Breath of Pine Set, 1940 – 1942.
Green and white box holds two green bars of Pine soap and 9 oz. bottle of Pine bath salts. CMV, $60.00 MB.

Breath of Pine Set, 1940.
Box holds 9 oz. bottle of Pine bath salts and two green bars of Pine soap. CMV, $60.00 MB.

Pine Soap Set, 1940 – 1959.
Green box with pine cone on lid holds three green round bars of Pine soap. CMV, $30.00 MB.

Towering Pine Set, 1941 – 1942.
Pine cones on lid of box, holds Apple Blossom body powder, green bar of Pine bath soap, and 6 oz. bottle of Pine bath oil with tulip A on label. CMV, $85.00 MB.

Pine Bath Oil, 1942 – 1951.
6 oz. flat sided bottle with turquoise cap. CMV, $22.00 BO, mint. $30.00 MB.

Royal Pine Set, 1946.
Beige box with pine cones and crest on lid, holds 6 oz. Royal Pine bath oil with brown label and two bars of Pine soap. Came in two different size boxes. CMV, $70.00 each set, MB.

Pine Bath Oil, 1944 – 1945.
6 oz. flat sided bottle with green cap and brown label. CMV, $20.00 BO. $25.00 MB.

Pine Bath Salts, 1953.
8 oz. clear glass jar, green lid, painted pine branch. Came in two different versions as shown. Both came in 1953 Royal Pine Set only. CMV, $30.00 each, mint.

Royal Pine Set, 1953.
Pine box holds one bar of Pine soap and 8 oz. jar with green lid and pine cone and branch painted on bottle. OSP, $1.25. CMV, $45.00.

Royal Pine Bath Salts, 1954 – 1957.
8 oz., clear glass with green lid. Green and brown label. CMV, $20.00 BO. $25.00 MB.

Royal Pine Set, 1954 – 1957.
Pine covered box holds 8 oz. jar with green lid of Royal Pine bath salts and green bar of Pine soap. CMV, $20.00 BO. $35.00 set.

Royal Pine Bath Oil, 1955 – 1957.
6 oz. flat sided bottle, green cap. OSP, $1.25. CMV, $20.00 BO. $25.00 MB.

Pine Soap, 1959.
Plain green box with gold printing on lid. Three green flat edge bars. CMV, $32.50 MB.

Pine Bath Oil, 1955 – 1956.
2 oz., pink cap, pink and white curtain label. Came in That's for Me Set only (See Women's Sets of the 1950s). CMV, $15.00.

Royal Pine Bath Oil, 1957 – 1959.
8 oz. bottle with green cap and pine cones on label in yellow, white, and green box. CMV, $10.00 MB.

Royal Pine Soap Set, 1959 – 1965.
Same design box and same design on soap as 1940 – 1959 set, only edge of soap is flat instead of round. CMV, $25.00 MB.

Pinehurst Set, 1955 – 1957.
Pine box holds two green bars of Pine soap and 4 oz. bottle of Pine bath oil with green cap. CMV, $55.00 MB.

Royal Pine Bath Oil, 1963 – 1968.
8 oz. green plastic bottle and cap. CMV, $3.00 MB.

Pine Bath Oil, 1955 – 1957.
4 oz. bottle with green cap. Came in Pinehurst Set only. CMV, $20.00.

Pretty Peach

Eau de Cologne, 1960s.
Foreign bottle. Peach cap and painted label. CMV, $10.00.
Hand Cream.
Foreign bottle. CMV, $6.00.

Cream Sachet, 1964 – 1967.
Yellow glass jar with peaches on lid. CMV, $5.00 jar only. $8.00 MB.

Peach Pomade, 1964 – 1967.
Foam peach with green leaf holds pomade lipstick. CMV, $18.00 MB.

Pretty Peach Soap, 1964 – 1966.
Pink box holds two peach halves and brown seed center soap. CMV, $25.00 MB.

Necklace, 1965.
Small peach on gold chain. Came in Peach Delight Set only. CMV, $20.00 necklace only. $25.00 on card.

Sachet Samples, 1964 – 1967.
Box holds 10 peach shaped samples of cream sachet packets. CMV, $5.00 box of 10.

Peach Surprise Set, 1964.
Pink and white box holds 2 oz. cologne with choice of 4 oz. bubble bath or cream lotion. CMV, $22.00 MB.

Soap on a Rope, 1964 – 1967.
5 oz. peach shaped soap on white rope. CMV, $20.00 MB.

"Soda" Cologne Mist, 1964 – 1967.
2 oz. pink plastic coated bottle with pink top with white flowers and blue straws. Came in two different silver stands. OSP, $2.50. CMV, $5.00 BO, mint. $8.00 each, MB.

Perfumed Talc, 1964 – 1967.
2½ oz. pink and white paper container. CMV, $8.00 MB.

Miss Avon Set, 1964 – 1965.
Blue and black plastic case holds cologne, bubble bath, perfumed talc, and 10 Lip Dew and talc samples in a bag. CMV, $50.00 set in blue case. $60.00 set MB.

Cream Lotion and Bubble Bath, 1964 – 1967.
4 oz. pink plastic bottle with peach on cap, painted label, pink box. CMV, $6.00 each, BO. $8.00 each, MB.

Beauty Dust, 1964 – 1967.
Pink and white cardboard box. CMV, $10.00 CO. $14.00 MB.

Cologne, 1964 – 1967.
2 oz. bottle with peach cap with green leaf and painted label. Pink box. CMV, $8.00 MB.

Just Peachy Set, 1964 – 1965.
Pink and white box holds soap on a rope and pomade. CMV, $45.00 MB.

Princess Set, 1965 – 1966.
Box holds talc and cream sachet. CMV, $20.00 MB.

Talc Puff, 1965 – 1966.
Pink box holds pink and white puff filled with powder. CMV, $2.00 puff only, mint. $6.00 MB.

Peach Delight Set, 1965.
Box holds Pretty Peach neck-lace, beauty dust, and co-logne. CMV, $55.00 set MB.

Peachy Kleen Set, 1966 – 1967.
Pink box holds pink and white sponge and soap. CMV, $9.00 soap and sponge. $15.00 set MB.

Peach Smooth Set, 1965.
Peach box holds two tubes of Pretty Peach hand cream. CMV, $5.00 TO, mint. $15.00 MB.

Quaintance

Powder Sachet, 1948 – 1956.
⁹/₁₀ oz., clear glass, white cap and painted label. Cap same as Bright Night without stars, but came this way. Very rare. CMV, $15.00 BO. $20.00 MB.

Body Powder, 1948 – 1956.
5 oz. red and white paper box, shaker top. CMV, $12.00 CO. $16.00 MB.

Cologne, 1948 – 1950.
2 oz. bottle with rose cap, painted label and ribbed corners. Came in Quaintance and Quaintance Bowknot Sets only. CMV, $20.00 MB.

Perfume, 1948 – 1950.
1 dram size with red rose cap, painted label in large or small lettering. Blue and white box. CMV, $50.00 MB.

Beauty Dust, 1948 – 1957.
Red rose on tin lid, white paper sides and tin bot-tom, white box. CMV, $12.00 beauty dust only, mint. $20.00 MB.

62nd Anniversary Cologne, 1948 only.
First issued in white lace design box. 4 oz. Given to reps for sell-ing 62 Avon items on 62nd anni-versary celebration. CMV, $65.00 MB.

Cologne, 1948 – 1956.
4 oz. clear glass, green painted label, ribbed corners, rose cap with green leaf. CMV, $10.00 BO. $15.00 MB.

Powder Sachet, 1948 – 1956.
⁹/₁₀ oz. or 1¼ oz., clear glass with red cap, painted label. CMV, $12.00 MB.

Powder Sachet, 1948 only.
⁹/₁₀ oz., clear glass with red cap and larger painted label. CMV, $20.00 MB. Also came in 1¼ oz. size with large size label. CMV, $20.00 MB.

Diary Perfume, 1949 – 1956.
3 dram glass bottle, painted label, rose flowered cap and green leaf. Box green felt. Diary has white cover with red rose and turquoise design. CMV, $100.00 MB.

Sachet, 63rd Birthday Box, 1949.
Regular issue powder sachet came in special issue Avon's "63rd Birthday" box. CMV, $15.00 MB as shown.

Gay Bonnet Set, 1948.
White hat shaped box with black ribbon and red rose around hat lid contains gold lipstick and 1 dram bottle of Quaintance perfume with rose cap. OSP, $2.35. CMV, $125.00 MB.

Diary Perfume Award, 1949.
Given to representatives during 63rd anniversary campaign for selling 63 pieces of Avon. Green felt cover trimmed in gold, holds 3 dram bottle with rose flowered cap and painted label, green leaf around neck (not shown in picture). Must have leaf to be mint. "63rd anniversary" inscribed on inside cover. CMV, $100.00 MB.

Left: Beauty Muff Set, 1949.
Red, white, and blue box with blue ribbon on lid contains white lamb's wool muff with 1 dram perfume with rose cap and gold lipstick. CMV, $135.00 MB.
Right: Beauty Muff Set, 1950.
Same set and box came with 1 dram gold scroll top perfume, shown. CMV, $65.00 MB.

Quaintance Set, 1948.
Blue and white box contains 2 oz. cologne and powder sachet. Both have red caps. CMV, $55.00 MB.

Bath Oil, 1949 – 1956.
4 oz., clear glass, white painted label. Rose on cap. CMV, $20.00 MB.

Buttons and Bows Song Sheet, 1949.
Green song sheet with words to help sell Quaintance products. 4¼" wide x 6½" high. CMV, $5.00.

Cream Lotion, 1949 – 1956.
4 oz., clear glass, white painted label. Rose cap. CMV, $15.00 MB.

Perfume, 1950.
White box with white lace trim holds 3 dram perfume with plain red cap and green leaf. CMV, $125.00 MB.

Rose Gay Set, 1950 – 1951.
Blue and white box with red rose holds body powder and 4 oz. cream lotion. CMV, $55.00 MB.

Harmony Set, 1952 – 1953.
Box with blue ribbon on clear plastic lid holds 4 oz. cream lotion and cologne. CMV, each 4 oz. cologne with rose cap, $20.00 mint. $50.00 set MB.

Leisure Hours Set, 1954 – 1955.
Blue and yellow fold-up box holds 4 oz. bath oil and cream lotion. CMV, $55.00.

Harmony Set, 1950 – 1951.
White box with blue ribbon over clear plastic lid holds 4 oz. cologne and body powder. CMV, $50.00 MB.

Toilet Water, 1953 – 1956.
2 oz. clear glass, green painted label, ribbed corners, rose cap with green leaf. CMV, $15.00 BO. $20.00 MB.

Bath Oil, 1955 – 1956.
2 oz., pink cap, pink and white label. Came in That's for Me set only (See Women's Sets of the 1950s). CMV, $15.00 mint.

Bowknot Set, 1950.
Box holds 2 oz. cologne and powder sachet. CMV, $55.00 MB.

Cream Sachet, 1953 – 1956.
White square glass jar with red rose on white cap. CMV, $12.00 MB.

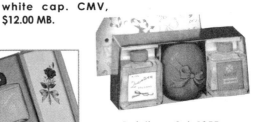

Daintiness Set, 1955.
White box with pink and blue ribbons, holds 2 oz. bottles of perfumed deodorant and cologne with blue caps and blue bar of soap. CMV, $55.00 MB.

Sachet Valentine Box, 1952.
Short issue box around Valentine's Day. Holds regular issue powder sachet. CMV, $22.00 in this box, mint.

Harmony Set, 1954 – 1955.
Blue and white flip-open box holds cologne and cream lotion. CMV, $50.00 MB.

Miss Quaintance Set, 1952 – 1953.
Blue and white octagonal box holds body powder and 4 oz. cream lotion. CMV, $50.00 MB.

Rosegay Set, 1954 – 1956.
Blue and white box holds 4 oz. cream lotion and body powder. CMV, $55.00 MB.

Soap Set, 1955 – 1956. Three blue bars with embossed bows. CMV, $40.00 MB.

Cologne, 1955 – 1956. 2 oz. bottle with blue cap, came in Daintiness Set and Bath Bouquet Set. CMV, $15.00. Quaintance cream lotion in same sets. CMV, $12.00.

Daintiness Set, 1956. White box with pink and blue ribbon holds 2 oz. bottles of cream lotion and cologne with blue caps and blue bar of soap. CMV, $60.00 MB.

Bath Bouquet Set, 1955. White and blue box with red rose on lid holds 2 oz. bottles of cream lotion and cologne with blue caps and blue bar of soap. CMV, $52.00 MB.

Rapture

Perfume Oil, 1964 – 1969. ½ oz., green glass and cap. CMV, $2.00 BO. $4.00 MB.

Powder Sachet, 1964 – 1966. ⁹/₁₀ oz., blue frosted glass with blue lid with two white doves. CMV, $6.00 MB.

Cologne, 1964 – 1971. 2 oz., blue glass and cap. CMV, $2.00 MB.

Rhapsody Set, 1964 – 1965. Powder sachet, 1 dram perfume, and 2 oz. cologne sit on blue velvet, trimmed in gold. Rapture mirror in center with two doves on mirror. CMV, $30.00 tray, set mint. $40.00 set MB.

Cream Sachet, 1964 – 1975. ⅔ oz., dark purple glass jar with two white doves on purple plastic lid. CMV, 50¢.

Cologne Mist, 1964 – 1974. 3 oz., turquoise plastic coated cap, all have gold letters. CMV, $1.00 MB. Pictured with regular issue box on right and special issue 1970 box on left. Add $2.00 for 1970 box.

Perfumed Skin Softener, 1964 – 1973. 5 oz., blue and gold lid. Blue painted over clear glass. CMV, $1.00. Also came blue painted over white milk glass. CMV, $2.00.

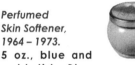

Beauty Dust, 1964 – 1970. **Light blue plastic, white doves on lid. CMV, $3.00 CO. $5.00 MB.**

Perfumed Bath Oil, 1965 – 1966. **6 oz., blue plastic bottle and cap. CMV, $1.00 MB.**

Cologne Mist, 1966 only. **2 oz., medium blue glass, gold trim. CMV, $2.00 MB.**
Cologne Mist, 1966 only. **2 oz., dark blue glass, no gold trim. CMV, $2.00 MB.**

Perfumed Cream Rollette, 1964 – 1965. **Gold cap, embossed 4A design on ⅓ oz. bottle. CMV, $2.00 MB.**

Cream Lotion, 1965 – 1968. **4 oz. blue plastic bottle and cap. CMV, $1.00 MB.**

Foaming Bath Oil, 1966 – 1972. **6 oz. blue plastic bottle and cap. CMV, $1.00.**

Perfumed Rollette, 1965 – 1969. **⅓ oz., blue ribbed glass, gold cap. CMV, $4.00 MB.**

Perfumed Talc, 1965 – 1972. **2¾ oz. blue can. CMV, $1.00 MB.**

Scented Hair Spray, 1966 – 1970. **7 oz. blue can. CMV, $3.00 MB.**

Perfumed Talc, 1965 – 1972. **Foreign perfumed talc is 2¾ oz. blue can, but shorter than U.S. can. CMV, $2.00 MB.**

Perfumed Soap, 1966 – 1967. **3 oz. soap in turquoise wrapper. CMV, $4.00.**

Soap, 1965 – 1968. **Blue box holds three blue bars with two doves embossed. CMV, $20.00 MB.**

Cologne Mist, 1965 – 1966. **2 oz., very light, appears almost frosted glass. CMV, $2.00 MB.**

Rapture Deluxe Set, 1965. **Turquoise box contains beauty dust, perfumed skin softener, and cologne mist. CMV, $32.50.**

Cologne, 1969 – 1972. **½ oz., green cap. CMV, $2.00 MB.**

Beauty Dust, 1971 – 1974. **6 oz., blue and gold cardboard. CMV, $4.00 MB.**

Perfume, 1966 – 1969.
1 oz. frosted glass bottle and stopper, trimmed in gold, green and white box. Gold neck tag. CMV, $20.00 BO. $30.00 MB.

Cream Sachet, 1966 – 1967.
Green painted glass with green paper band. Green and gold cap, gold base. Also came green painted over clear or milk glass. CMV, $2.00 MB.

Perfume Rollette, 1967 – 1968.
¹⁄₃ oz., ribbed glass, smooth gold cap. CMV, $2.00 MB.

Perfume, 1966 – 1969.
¹⁄₂ oz., frosted glass with gold plastic cap. Bottle trimmed in gold, green, and white box. Gold neck tag. CMV, $15.00 BO. $25.00 MB.

Cologne Mist, 1966 – 1971.
3 oz., green and gold plastic. Base is gold on older ones and green on newer ones. CMV, $3.00 gold base. $2.00 green base, MB.

Perfume Glace, 1967 – 1970.
Green and gold box holds green and gold glace compact. CMV, $5.00 compact only. $8.00 MB.

Beauty Dust, 1966 – 1973.
Green and gold plastic bottom, clear plastic lid with gold crown. Paper side older, CMV, $8.00 MB. Plastic side newer, CMV, $5.00 MB. $2.00 less each for no box.

Hand Mirror, 1966.
Green and gold metal, 4¹⁄₂" long. Came in Régence Gift Set. CMV, $7.00 mirror only. $10.00 MB.

Régence Gift Set, 1966.
Green box holds cream sachet, cologne mist, and green and gold hand mirror. CMV, $37.50 MB.

Perfumed Powder Mist, 1967 – 1972.
7 oz. green can with gold cap, painted label. CMV, $1.00 CO. $3.00 with paper label.

Cologne Mist Refill, 1966 – 1971.
3 oz., green plastic coated. CMV, $2.00 MB.

Cologne, 1967 – 1969.
2 oz., gold cap. CMV, $2.00 MB.

Perfumed Skin Softener, 1967 – 1968.
5 oz., green ribbed glass, small silver edge cap with gold center and plain green cap. CMV, $3.00 MB.

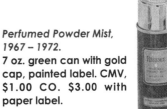

Cream Sachet, 1968.
²⁄₃ oz., clear glass painted green. Green and gold tone cap and base. Sides are smooth, no design. CMV, $4.00 MB.

Perfume Oil, 1968 – 1969.
½ oz., gold cap. Came with either clear bottom label or gold neck tag label. CMV, $4.00 MB.

Hair Spray, 1968 – 1971.
7 oz., green and gold with green cap. CMV, $3.00 MB.

Cologne, 1969 – 1971.
4 oz., gold cap. CMV, $2.00.

Cologne Silk, 1968 – 1970.
3 oz., gold cap, frosted glass bottle. CMV, $2.00 MB.

Perfumed Skin Softener, 1968 – 1971.
5 oz., ribbed glass, small silver edged cap. Gold center and multicolored cap. CMV, $2.00.

Foaming Bath Oil, 1969 – 1972.
6 oz., light plastic bottle with gold cap. CMV, $1.00 MB.

Skin So Soft, 1968 – 1970.
6 oz., gold cap. CMV, $2.00 MB.

Perfumed Talc, 1968 – 1972.
3½ oz., green paper box. CMV, $1.00.

Cologne, 1970 – 1971.
½ oz., clear glass bottle with gold cap. CMV, $2.00 MB.

Cream Sachet, 1968 – 1975.
Solid green glass, green plastic cap. CMV, $1.00. Also came green painted over clear or milk glass. Same CMV.

Perfume Rollette, 1969 – 1973.
⅓ oz., ribbed glass and green cap. CMV, $1.00 BO.

Perfumed Skin Softener, 1971 – 1974.
5 oz., ribbed glass, large silver edged, gold center and multicolored green cap. CMV, $3.00.

Rose Geranium

Liquid Soap Fragrance, 1942 only.
6 oz. flat sided bottle came in Rainbow Wings and Bath Bouquet Sets only (See Women's Sets of the 1940s). CMV, $45.00 MB.

Bath Oil, 1943 – 1948.
6 oz. flat sided bottle, pink cap. CMV, $20.00 BO. $25.00 MB.

Bath Oil, 1943 – 1950.
6 oz. flat sided bottle has Tulip A label, pink cap. CMV, $20.00 BO. $25.00 MB.

Bath Oil, 1957 – 1958.
8 oz. bottle with red cap.
CMV, $6.00 BO. $10.00 MB.

Soap Set, 1966 – 1967.
Flowered box holds four flower shaped
soaps. CMV, $20.00 MB.

After Bath Freshener, 1964 – 1968.
8 oz. glass bottle with rose colored cap,
red flowered box. CMV, $2.00 MB.
Perfumed Talc, 1964 – 1966.
3½ oz. rose covered paper container
with plastic shaker top. CMV, $1.00 MB.
Also came with upside down label.
CMV, $8.00.
Perfumed Soap, 1964 – 1966.
3 oz. bar with rose design wrapping.
CMV, $2.00.

Roses Roses

**Glow of Roses Perfumed
Candle, 1972 – 1973.**
4½" high, pink frosted
glass. CMV, $8.00 MB.

**Scent of Roses Decanter,
1972 – 1973.**
6 oz. red glass jar with
gold lid, filled with cologne
gelee. CMV, $2.00 MB.

**Dew of Roses Perfumed
Skin Softener, 1972 – 1973.**
5 oz. frosted pink glass jar
with gold lid. CMV, $1.00
MB.

**Scent of Roses Cologne
Gelee, 1972 – 1976.**
3 oz. clear or tinted glass
jar, gold lid. CMV, $1.00
MB.

**Mist of Roses Cologne
Mist, 1972 – 1977.**
3 oz. pink plastic
coated bottle, gold
cap. CMV, $1.00 MB.
**Foam of Roses
Creamy Bath Foam.**
5 oz. pink plastic
coated bottle, gold
cap. CMV, $1.00 MB.

**Touch of Roses
Perfumed Soap,
1972 – 1977.**
Pink box holds
three pink flow-
ered soaps. CMV,
$9.00 MB.

**Cream Sachet,
1972– 1975.**
²⁄₃ oz. pink glass jar
with pink rose on
gold lid. Also came
in clear glass. CMV,
$1.00.

**Perfumed Skin Softener,
1973 – 1976.**
5 oz., pink plastic with
pink and gold metal lid.
CMV, 25¢.

**Perfumed
Talc, 1974 – 1977.**
3½ oz., pink and
gray cardboard.
CMV, 25¢.

Soap, 1974 – 1975.
3 oz. pink soap,
pink wrapper with
floral band. CMV,
$2.00.

**Sachet of Roses
Cream Sachet,
1975 – 1978.**
⅓ oz., clear glass
with pink metal lid.
CMV, 50¢.

**Touch of Roses Soap,
1976 – 1978.**
3 oz. pink soap, pink
and gray wrapper. CMV,
$2.00.

Perfumed Soap Bar, 1976.
3 oz. bar wrapped in red
paper. Short issue. CMV,
$2.00.

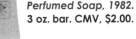

Perfumed Soap, 1982.
3 oz. bar. CMV, $2.00.

165

Silk & Honey ··

*Perfumed Soap,
1970 – 1976.
3 oz. bar, gold and
yellow wrapper.
CMV, $2.00.*

Bank, 1969.
Yellow plastic beehive
bank. CMV, $15.00 MB.

Bath Gelee, 1969 – 1970.
4 oz. gold frosted glass jar with
gold beehive lid and gold spoon.
CMV, $7.00 MB, with spoon.

Milk Bath, 1970 – 1971.
6 oz. gold plastic milk can
bottle with flowers around
neck. CMV, $4.00.

Small World ···

Small World Products, 1970 – 1973.
Left to right: Small World Sucker, 1970.
**Sent to representatives at introduction of Small World.
Red and yellow wrapper says "Avon Watch for the
Small World." CMV, $25.00 mint.**
Cologne (Splashu), 1970 – 1972.
2 oz., 4½" high. CMV, $7.00 MB.
Bubble Bath (Bubbly-O-Bath), 1970 – 1971.
5" high, 5 oz. green plastic bottle. CMV, $10.00 MB.
Love Cakes Soap, 1970 – 1973.
Three pink heart shaped bars in blue box. CMV, $9.00 MB.
Demi Stick, 1970 – 1973.
3" high with pink cap. CMV, $2.00 MB.
Pin Pal Perfume Glacé, 1970 – 1971.
Black hair, white and red body. CMV, $5.00 CO. $7.00 MB.
Non-tear Shampoo (Poolu), 1970 – 1971.
5½" high, red bottle, black hair. CMV, $7.00 MB.
Cologne Mist (Heidi), 1970 – 1971.
3 oz., 5" high, purple bottle, yellow hair. CMV, $6.00 MB.
Lipkins, 1970 – 1973.
**3" high with pink, yellow, and orange caps in Dutch Choco-
late, Tropical Fruit, or French Mint. CMV, $3.00 each, MB.**
Love Dove Cream Sachet, 1970 – 1973.
White jar and dove lid. CMV, $4.00 CO. $5.00 MB.

Cream Lotion (Wendy), 1971 – 1972.
**5 oz., 5" high cowgirl plastic bottle.
CMV, $8.00 MB.**
Bubble Bath (British Miss), 1971 – 1972.
4½" high, 3 oz. pink plastic bottle. CMV, $8.00 MB.
Cologne Mist (Gigi), 1971 – 1972.
**5" high, 5 oz. blue plastic coated bottle with
white collar and blue and red hat. CMV, $8.00 MB.**
Non-tear Shampoo (Senorita), 1971 – 1972.
**5" high, 5 oz. orange plastic bottle with pink flower in
hair on cap. CMV, $12.00 MB.**
Cream Sachet, 1971 – 1972.
**⅔ oz. white jar with pink and white lid.
CMV, $3.00 MB.**
Perfumed Talc, 1971 – 1973.
3½ oz. blue paper container. CMV, $4.00.
Small World Glacé Watch, 1971.
Orange with striped band. CMV, $15.00 MB.
Rollette, 1971 – 1972.
3" high, ⅓ oz., Indian design. CMV, $3.00.
Pin Pal Perfume Glacé, 1971 – 1972.
Blue and white polka dots. CMV, $6.00 MB.

Perfume, 1961 – 1963.
1 oz., pink jewel cap, jewels in glass around bottom of bottle. Has four butterflies on lid. CMV, $30.00 BO, mint. $60.00 MB.

Perfume Mist Award, 1961.
Given to each representative sending in an order during the 75th anniversary campaign. This was also the introduction to the new Somewhere fragrance. CMV, $15.00 MB.

Soap, 1962 – 1966.
Pink box holds three bars with embossed name. CMV, $24.00 MB.

Cologne Mist, 1961 – 1966.
3 oz., pink plastic coated glass, pink jeweled lid. CMV, $3.00 BO. $5.00 MB.

Powder Sachet, 1962 – 1966.
1¼ oz., pink glass bottom, pink jeweled lid. Also came in 9/10 oz. CMV, $4.00 BO. $6.00 MB.

Bath Oil, 1962 – 1966.
6 oz. pink plastic bottle and cap. CMV, $2.00 MB.

Cream Sachet, 1962 – 1966.
Pink glass and pink jeweled lid. Some came pink paint on milk glass. CMV, $1.00 CO. $3.00 MB.

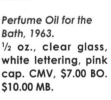

Perfume Oil for the Bath, 1963.
½ oz., clear glass, white lettering, pink cap. CMV, $7.00 BO. $10.00 MB.

Cologne, 1961 – 1966.
2 oz., pink jeweled lid. CMV, $3.00 BO. $5.00 MB.

Talc, 1962 – 1966.
2¾ oz. pink can and lid. CMV, $3.00 CO. $4.00 MB.

Cream Lotion, 1963 – 1966.
4 oz., pink lid without jewels. CMV, $3.00 BO. $5.00 MB.

Dusting Powder, 1961 – 1966.
Pink plastic bottom. Clear plastic top with pink jeweled crown handle. CMV, $5.00 CO. $10.00 MB.

Unforgettable Set, 1962 – 1963.
Pink, yellow, and blue box holds cologne mist, cream sachet, and beauty dust. CMV, $45.00 MB.

Dreams of Somewhere Set, 1964.
Box holds 2 dram bottle of perfume mist, 6 oz. beauty dust, and 4 oz. bottle of cream lotion. CMV, $40.00 MB.

Perfumed Soap, 1965.
3 oz. pink soap with pink and white wrapper. CMV, $4.00 mint.

Powder Sachet, 1966 – 1968.
9/10 oz., white glass, green label, white lid with gold band. Hard to find. CMV, $10.00 BO. $12.00 MB.

Perfume Mist, 1966 – 1968.
2 dram, white cap, green bottom. CMV, $2.00 MB.

Soap, 1966 – 1968.
Green and white box holds three bars. CMV, $18.00 MB.

Perfume Mist, 1964 – 1966.
White lid, pink bottom, gold band. CMV, $2.00 MB.

Left to right: Cream Sachet, 1966 – 1975.
White glass trimmed in green and gold. 2/3 oz. CMV, 50¢.
Skin Softener, 1966 – 1972.
Green and gold lid, 5 oz. glass jar. Came in green paint over clear glass. CMV, $1.00. Or green paint over white milk glass. CMV, $1.00.
Perfume Oil, 1966 – 1969.
1/2 oz., green label, gold cap. CMV, $4.00 BO. $6.00 MB.

Dream Castle Set, 1964.
Pink and white box holds 2 oz. bottle of cologne and cream sachet. CMV, $30.00 MB.

Scented Hair Spray, 1966 – 1971.
7 oz. green can. CMV, $3.00.
Soap, 1966 – 1967.
Single bar in green wrapper. CMV, $4.00.
Perfumed Talc, 1966 – 1972.
2¾ oz. green and white can, green cap. CMV, $1.00.

Perfumed Skin Softener, 1964 – 1966.
5 oz. pink glass jar with pink and gold lid. CMV, $2.00 MB.

Perfume Oil, 1964 – 1966.
1/2 oz., clear glass, white lettering, pink cap. CMV, $5.00 BO. $7.00 MB.

Cologne, 1966 – 1971.
2 oz., gold cap. CMV, $1.00.

Cologne Mist, 1966 – 1976.
3 oz., green plastic coated, gold cap, green label. CMV, $1.00.

Powder Sachet, 1967 only.
9/10 oz. white glass bottom, white and gold cap with green ribbon. Issued during bottle strike in 1967. Bottom is same as Wishing powder sachet. CMV, $15.00 CO. $20.00 MB.

Cologne, 1970 – 1971.
½ oz., gold cap. CMV, $1.00 BO. $2.00 MB.

Beauty Dust, 1967 – 1970.
White plastic with green around bottom. Gold handle. CMV, $6.00 CO. $10.00 MB.

Soap, 1968 – 1971.
Three white bars in green box. CMV, $15.00 MB.

Perfumed Talc, 1973 – 1976.
(Green And White Design)
3½ oz. cardboard, round container. CMV, $1.00.

Perfumed Talc, 1968.
3½ oz. green cardboard with gold trim. Came with Fluff Puff set. (See Women's Sets of the 1960s.) CMV, $2.00.

Cream Lotion, 1967 – 1968.
4 oz., gold cap. CMV, $2.00 MB.

Demi Stick, 1975 – 1976.
(Green And White Design)
CMV, 50¢.

Cream Sachet, 1976.
Gold and green lid. CMV, 50¢.

Fragrance Mist Sonnet Set, 1940 – 1942.
Blue and gold box holds 2 oz. toilet water (gold cap and label) and spray atomizer. Also came in other fragrances. See Fragrant Mist Set in Women's Sets of the 1940s. CMV, $35.00 BO, mint. $50.00 MB.

Toilet Water, 1941 only.
2 oz. purple cap and label. Two different labels. One has yellow dress on box and label and the other has green dress on box and label. CMV, $30.00 BO. $40.00 each, MB.

Toilet Water, 1941– 1946.
2 oz., gold ribbed cap and gold front label. CMV, $30.00 BO, mint. $35.00 MB.

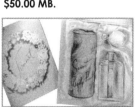

Sonnet Set, 1941 – 1942.
Satin lined lavender box holds 2 oz. toilet water with gold top atomizer and body powder. CMV, $75.00 MB.

Body Powder, 1941 – 1943.
Special issue box, angel on box, blue and white paper container with plastic shaker top. CMV, $18.00 CO. $25.00 MB as shown.

Body Powder, 1941 – 1943.
Flat sifter top, scroll box. CMV, $18.00 CO, mint. $22.00 MB.

Blue Bird Set, 1943 – 1944.
Blue and white box, blue satin lining holds feather design face powder, cardboard or plastic lipstick, and Sonnet or Apple Blossom body powder. CMV, $75.00 MB.

Perfumed Skin Softener, 1973 – 1978.
5 oz. plastic jar. CMV, 50¢.

Perfumed Powder Mist, 1973 – 1977.
Regular issue can came out with double stamp label on entire can. Rare. CMV, $5.00.

Cologne and Skin So Soft Bath Oil, 1973.
4 oz. clear glass bottles, caps are gold. Came in Treasure Chest set only (see Women's Sets of the 1970s). CMV, $4.00 each.

Perfumed Soap, 1972 – 1974.
Three pink 3 oz., round shaped bars of soap, in gold and white box. CMV, $6.00 MB.

Beauty Dust, 1973 – 1978.
6 oz., plastic puff. CMV, $2.00 CO. $5.00 MB.

Perfumed Soap, 1974 – 1975.
3 oz., white with multicolored center. CMV, $3.00.

Perfumed Powder Mist, 1973 – 1978.
7 oz. metal can, white cap. CMV, $1.00 MB.
Perfumed Talc, 1973 – 1978.
3½ oz. cardboard with plastic top and bottom. Rare upside down label. CMV, $5.00.

Perfumed Rollette, 1973 – 1978.
⅓ oz. bottle. CMV, $1.00 MB.

Perfumed Demi Stick, 1974 – 1978.
White and gold. CMV, $1.00.

Perfumed Soap, 1974 – 1977.
3 oz., three pink oblong shaped soap bars, in gold and white box. CMV, $5.00 MB.

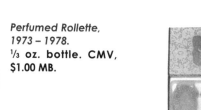

Cologne Mist, 1973 – 1978.
3 oz. spray bottle. First issue 1973. Issued with no gold ring around neck. CMV, $2.00. 1973 – 1978 issued with gold ring around neck. CMV, 50¢.

Powder Sachet, 1975 – 1978.
1¼ oz., white and gold cardboard. CMV, $1.00.

Cream Sachet, 1973 – 1978.
⅔ oz. jar. CMV, 50¢.

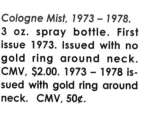

Perfumed Soap, 1976 – 1978.
3 oz. white bar with gold and white wrapper. CMV, $2.00.

Strawberry

Strawberry Fair Soap, 1969 – 1970. Red soap in yellow plastic basket with green grass, wrapped in cellophane and bow. CMV, $10.00 MB.

Porcelain Napkin Rings and Soap Set, 1978 – 1979. Box holds two porcelain napkin rings and one red strawberry shaped guest soap. Porcelain, made in Brazil. CMV, $10.00 MB set.

Porcelain Sugar Shaker and Perfumed Talc, 1979. Box holds white porcelain shaker and 3½ oz. box of strawberry perfumed talc. Made in Brazil. "Avon 1978" on bottom of shaker. CMV, $12.00 MB, set. Early orders and demos had 1978 on bottom of sugar shaker and regular issue had only "Avon" and no date on bottom. Talc only, CMV, $2.00. Shaker only, CMV, $8.00, no date. CMV, $10.00, 1978 date. Talc also came with upside down label from factory by mistake. CMV, $5.00 upside down label on talc.

Stawberries and Cream Bath Foam, 1970. 4 oz., white milk glass, red cap and design, or orange cap and design. CMV, $5.00 orange cap. $7.00 red cap.

Berry Nice Strawberry Compact, 1979 – 1980. Small red and green plastic, holds lip gloss. CMV, $3.00 MB.
Strawberry Fair Shower Soap, 1979 – 1980. Red strawberry soap on a green rope. CMV, $8.00 MB.

Bath Gelee, 1971 – 1972. 4 oz. red strawberry base and gold cap and spoon. CMV, $4.00 CO. $6.00 MB.
Guest Soaps, 1971 – 1972. Red box holds three strawberry soaps. CMV, $7.00 MB.
Bath Foam, 1971 – 1972. 4 oz., red glass and top, 6" high. CMV, $5.00 MB.

Porcelain Demi Cup Candlette Set, 1979 – 1980. Box holds 4" saucer and 2¼" high cup. Strawberry design. "Made in Brazil for Avon 1978" on bottom of each. CMV, $7.00 MB.

Swan Lake

Big Berry Strawberry, 1973 – 1974. 10 oz., red plastic with green cap top. Holds bath foam. CMV, $2.00 CO. $3.00 MB.

Bath Oil, 1947 – 1949. 6 oz. flat sided bottle, pink cap, painted label. CMV, $55.00 BO. $65.00 MB.

Cologne, 1947 – 1950. 4 oz., pink cap, painted label. CMV, $45.00 BO. $55.00 MB.

Body Powder, 1947 – 1949.
9 oz. blue, pink, and white paper box. Came with swan or ballerina on side. CMV, $30.00 CO. $35.00 MB. Also came in 4½ oz. size in sets. CMV, $30.00 mint.
Swan Lake Bath Salts, 1947 – 1949.
9 oz. blue, pink, and white paper box. CMV, $30.00 CO. $35.00 MB.

Swan Lake 3-Piece Set, 1947 – 1950.
Blue and white box holds 9 oz. blue boxes of bath salts and body powder, and 4 oz. cologne with white cap. CMV, $125.00 MB.

Swan Lake 2-Piece Set, 1947 – 1949.
Blue and white box holds 6 oz. bath oil and 9 oz. blue box of body powder. CMV, $100.00 MB.

To a Wild Rose

Perfume, 1950 – 1956.
Pink flowers on pink and blue box. 3 dram bottle with blue cap and flower around neck. CMV, $75.00 BO, with tag. $110.00 MB.

Body Powder, 1950 – 1955.
5 oz. blue paper container, two different bottoms. One is refillable from the bottom. Some issued as shown with "To a Wild Rose Body Powder" on side and some only say "Avon Body Powder." CMV, $15.00 CO. $20.00 MB.

Beauty Dust, 1950 – 1955.
Blue can with flowers on lid. CMV, $15.00 CO. $20.00 MB.

Toilet Water, 1950 – 1955.
2 oz., blue cap, with or without embossed roses. Three cornered bottle. CMV, $15.00 BO. $20.00 MB.

To a Wild Rose Set, 1950 – 1952.
Blue and pink box holds body powder and 4 oz. cologne. CMV, $60.00 MB.

Cream Sachet, 1950 – 1955.
Left: Blue cap with pink flowers, white glass, three cornered shape. CMV, $8.00 BO. $10.00 MB.
Right: Same shaped jar as one on right, only has blue lid as on the left jar. Lid will not interchange with jar on right. Also came with white lid, label on bottom, with no zip code, is older. Rare. CMV, $9.00 BO. $11.00 MB.

Cologne, 1950 – 1955.
4 oz., clear glass, blue cap, blue label. CMV, $16.00 BO. $20.00 MB.

Soap Set, 1952 – 1956.
White box holds three white bars. OSP, $1.50. CMV, $26.50.
Not shown: Soap Set, 1954.
Blue box of three bars. CMV, $30.00 MB.

Rose Petals Set, 1953 – 1954. Two clear glass bottles, blue caps, holds bath oil and cream lotion. CMV, $57.50 MB.

Cream Lotion, 1953 – 1955. 4 oz. blue cap and label, with or without embossed roses. CMV, $15.00 BO. $17.00 MB.

Petal of Beauty Set, 1953. Pink box holds blue and pink satin bag, all blue bag, or all pink bag with 4 oz. cologne and beauty dust with ⅝ dram perfume (small square bottle with ribbon tied around it inside beauty dust). CMV, $75.00 MB. Bag and contents only, $55.00. 1950 – 1952 set sold without ⅝ dram perfume. CMV, $50.00 in bag with no box mint. $65.00 MB.

Sachet, 1953 – 1955. 1¼ oz., blue cap with embossed flower on top. Blue box. CMV, $10.00 BO, mint. $15.00 MB.

Petal of Beauty Set, 1954 – 1955. Blue and pink box with blue ribbon around outside holds 4 oz. cologne and beauty dust. CMV, $62.50 MB.

Bath Oil, 1953 – 1955. 4 oz. bottle with blue cap, with or without embossed roses. Blue label. CMV, $17.00 BO. $20.00 MB.

Cologne or Cream Lotion, 1954. 2 oz. clear glass with blue caps. Came in Bath Bouquet Set. CMV, $17.50 each, mint.

Wild Roses Set, 1953. Body powder with cream sachet on top. Pink ribbon around set. CMV, $40.00 MB.

Bath Bouquet Set, 1954. Pink and blue box holds 2 oz. cologne and cream lotion (with blue caps) and white soap. CMV, $55.00 MB. One box has sleeve top and one has a lift-off lid. Came with and without flowers on bottom of box.

Miss Coed Set, 1954. Blue box holds three 2 oz. bottles of cologne, cream lotion, and bath oil. All have white caps. CMV, $17.50 each bottle. $75.00 set.

Cologne, Bath Oil, and Cream Lotion, 1954. Each 2 oz., clear glass with white cap, blue label. Came in Miss Coed Set only. CMV, $17.50 each.

Powder Sachet, 1953 – 1955. 1¼ oz., blue smooth top cap, blue label, clear glass. CMV, $12.00 BO. $15.00 MB.

Talc, 1954 – 1955. Blue can and cap with pink flowers. CMV, $8.00 MB.

Cream Sachet, 1955 – 1972. White glass, white lid with painted rose. CMV, $1.00 MB.

Perfume, 1955 – 1959. Pink and white box holds ½ oz. white glass bottle with pink cap and painted label. CMV, $35.00 BO. $70.00 MB.

Bath Oil, 1955 – 1956. 2 oz., pink cap and label. Came in That's for Me Set only (see Women's Sets of the 1950s). CMV, $15.00 mint.

Cologne or Cream Lotion, 1955. 2 oz., clear glass with white caps. Came in Bath Bouquet Set. CMV, $15.00 each, mint.

Cologne, 1955 – 1963. 4 oz. white glass bottle, pink cap, flowered paper border around base. CMV, $10.00 BO. $12.00 MB.

Beauty Dust, 1955 – 1959. Pink ball on top, trimmed in pink, tin lid and bottom. Sides cardboard. Specially packaged with ⅝ dram of To a Wild Rose perfume tied with a ribbon bow. OSP, $1.75. CMV, $12.00 CO. $16.00 MB.

Powder Sachet, 1955 – 1967. White glass, white lid with painted rose. Paper band around bottom with roses. Came in 9 oz. and 1¼ oz. sizes. CMV, $6.00 BO. $7.00 MB.

Adorable Set, 1955 – 1956. Pink and white box with pink flowers on top holds body powder and cream sachet. CMV, $35.00 MB.

Body Powder, 1955 – 1959. 4 oz., white glass and cap with rose on lid, paper label around bottom, pink letters. CMV, $10.00 BO. $13.00 MB.

Body Powder, 1955 – 1959. 4 oz., white glass and cap with rose on lid, paper label. CMV, $10.00 BO. $13.00 MB.

Bath Bouquet Set, 1955. White and pink box holds 2 oz. cologne and cream lotion with white caps and one bar of soap. CMV, $55.00 MB.

Sweethearts Set, 1955. Pink and white box holds beauty dust with pink ribbon and 4 oz. cologne. CMV, $55.00 MB.

Pink Bells Set, 1955.
Pink box holds two blue cans of talc. CMV, $25.00 MB.

Sweethearts Set, 1956.
White and pink box holds beauty dust and 4 oz. cologne. CMV, $47.50 MB.

Cream Lotion, 1956 – 1965.
4 oz., white glass, pink cap, paper label. CMV, $5.00 BO. $7.00 MB.

Anniversary Special Set, 1956.
Pink and white box holds two cans of talc. CMV, $20.00 MB.

Bath Oil or Cologne, 1956.
Both 2 oz. bottles with white caps. Came in 1956 Bath Bouquet Set only. CMV, $15.00 each, mint.

Toilet Water, 1956 – 1962.
2 oz., white glass, pink cap, paper flower band around base. CMV, $10.00 BO. $12.00 MB.

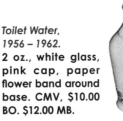

Bath Oil, 1956 – 1959.
4 oz. white glass bottle with pink cap. CMV, $10.00 BO. $12.00 MB. 2 oz. white glass bottle with pink cap, same label, came in Trilogy Set only. CMV, $15.00.

Adorable Set, 1956.
Pink and white box with pink ribbon on lid holds body powder and cream sachet. CMV, $35.00 MB.

Bath Bouquet Set, 1956.
White and pink box holds cologne and bath oil with white caps and one bar of soap. CMV, $55.00 MB. Also came with two bath oils as substitutes.

Lotion, 1957.
2 oz., white glass with paper label and pink cap. Came in Trilogy Set only. CMV, $16.00 mint.

Special Date Set, 1956.
Pink and gold box holds black lipstick, powder pak, and ½ oz. toilet water. CMV, $45.00 MB.

Talc, 1956 – 1962.
White can with pink flowers and cap. CMV, $5.00 CO. $7.00 MB. Add $4.00 for 1959 Christmas box.

Cologne, 1957.
2 oz., white glass with paper label, pink cap. Came in Trilogy Set only. CMV, $16.00 mint.

Spray Perfume Refill, 1960 – 1963. Box holds small metal refill. CMV, $2.00 refill only. $4.00 MB.

Soap Sets, 1957 – 1968.
Pink and white box holds three bars in two different size boxes. CMV, $25.00 MB, large box. $20.00 MB, small box.

Perfumed Skin Softener, 1959 – 1970. 5 oz., white glass, pink and white lid. CMV, $2.00.

Roses Adrift Set, 1957.
Pink and white box holds beauty dust, cream sachet, and cologne.
CMV, $52.50 MB.

Perfumed Bath Oil, 1959 – 1961. 8 oz. white plastic bottle with pink cap. CMV, $3.00 MB. *Not shown: Perfumed Bath Oil, 1961 – 1966.* Same, only 6 oz. size. CMV, $3.00 MB.

Cologne, 1960 – 1961.
Pink, green, and white Christmas box holds 4 oz. white glass bottle with pink cap and neck ribbon. No flower band around base, but also came with a paper flower band around base as shown. CMV, $25.00 in box pictured.

Trilogy Set, 1957.
Box holds three 2 oz. bottles of bath oil, cream lotion, and cologne.
CMV, $60.00 MB.

Cologne Mist, 1959 – 1975.
3 oz., white plastic coated with pink flower on cap. CMV, $2.00 MB.

A Spray of Roses Set, 1958.
Pink and white box holds cologne mist and cream sachet. CMV, $37.00 MB.

Cologne Mist, 1958 – 1959.
3 oz., white plastic coated over clear glass, pink cap. Came with or without embossed rose on lid. CMV, $15.00 MB.

Spray Perfume, 1960 – 1963.
Red, white, and gold box holds pink and white metal spray perfume with pink flowers. CMV, $7.00 spray only. $11.00 MB.

Cologne, 1960 – 1961.
Pink and white box holds 4 oz. white glass bottle, pink cap, painted label, pink silk ribbon on neck. Came with and without painted flowers around base. CMV, $15.00 BO with ribbon, mint. $17.00 MB.

Cologne, 1961 – 1968.
2 oz., white glass, pink letters and cap. Came with and without painted flowers around base, as shown. CMV, $3.00 each, MB.

Perfumed Talc, 1962 – 1972. 2¾ oz. white and pink can with pink cap. CMV, $1.00.

Beauty Dust, 1962 – 1963. Pink and green flowers, clear plastic top, cardboard. Came in Fragrance Magic Set only (See Women's Sets of the 1960s). CMV, $16.00 mint.

Beauty Dust, 1960 – 1970. White plastic, trimmed in pink. CMV, $4.00 CO. $6.00 MB.

Perfumed Mist, 1964 – 1968. 2 dram, pink and white, gold band. CMV, $2.00 CO. $4.00 MB.

Body Powder, 1961 – 1963. 4 oz. white hard plastic bottle, white lid with roses. Also came in 3 oz. size and with short issue pink cap. CMV, $12.00 pink cap. CMV, $8.00 BO. $10.00 MB.

Perfume Oil for the Bath, 1963. ½ oz., white glass, pink cap, pink and white box. CMV, $8.00 BO. $10.00 MB.
Not shown: Toilet Water, 1956. ½ oz. size. Same size and design as perfume oil shown. White glass with pink cap and lettering. Came in Special Date Set, rare. CMV, $27.00 mint.

Perfume Oil, 1964 – 1968. ½ oz., white glass, pink letters and cap. CMV, $6.00 BO. $8.00 MB.

Spray of Roses Set, 1961. White and pink box with pink satin lining holds beauty dust and cologne mist. CMV, $30.00 MB.

Holiday Roses Set, 1963 – 1964. Box holds beauty dust, splash cologne, and cream lotion, with paper labels. Same set in 1964 with painted labels. CMV, $37.00 each set, MB.

Lovely as a Rose Set, 1961. Pink and white box holds 2 oz. cologne and cream sachet. CMV, $20.00 MB.

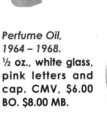

Wild Roses Set, 1964. Multi-pink flowered box holds 2 oz. bottle of cologne and cream sachet. CMV, $25.00 MB.

Cream Lotion, 1965 – 1968.
4 oz., painted label, white glass, pink cap. CMV, $5.00 MB.

Scented Hair Spray, 1966 – 1969.
7 oz., pink and white can, pink cap. CMV, $3.00.

Soap Set, 1969 – 1973.
Floral box holds three white bars. CMV, $7.00 MB.

Soap, 1966 – 1967.
3 oz. white embossed soap in pink and green wrapper. CMV, $4.00.

Perfumed Powder Mist, 1968 – 1973.
7 oz., pink and white can, two different labels. CMV, $4.00 each, paper label. $2.00 each, painted label.

Cologne, 1970 – 1971.
½ oz., white glass with pink cap and letters. CMV, $1.00 BO. $3.00 MB.

Foaming Bath Oil, 1966 – 1968.
6 oz. white plastic bottle with pink cap. CMV, $1.00 BO. $2.00 MB.

Talc, 1969.
2¾ oz. pink and white can, pink cap. Came in 1969 Perfumed Pair Set only. CMV, $2.00.

Cream Sachet, 1975 – 1976.
⅔ oz. clear glass jar, red and gold lid. CMV, 50¢.

Topaze

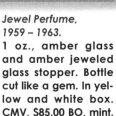

Jewel Perfume, 1959 – 1963.
1 oz., amber glass and amber jeweled glass stopper. Bottle cut like a gem. In yellow and white box. CMV, $85.00 BO, mint. $135.00 MB.

Perfume, 1935 only.
¼ oz., gold cap, gold and white label and box. "Introducing Topaze for the 50th wedding anniversary of Mr. and Mrs. D. H. McConnell." CMV, $50.00 BO. $70.00 MB.

Cologne, 1959 – 1963.
Gold cap. CMV, $4.00 BO. $8.00 in plain yellow box.

Spray Perfume, 1959 – 1963.
Yellow box holds 2 dram metal spray perfume, gold top and yellow bottom. CMV, $7.00 BO. $12.00 MB.

Gift Cologne, 1959 – 1961.
Gold cap, clear glass in yellow and gold satin lined box. CMV, $20.00 MB as shown.

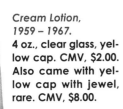

Cream Lotion,
1959 – 1967.
4 oz., clear glass, yellow cap. CMV, $2.00. Also came with yellow cap with jewel, rare. CMV, $8.00.

Treasure Set, 1960.
Box holds 2 oz. cologne and beauty dust. CMV, $40.00.

Body Powder,
1961 – 1963.
4 oz. yellow plastic bottle and cap. CMV, $4.00 BO. $6.00 MB.

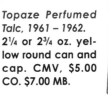

Topaze Perfumed Talc, 1961 – 1962.
2¼ or 2¾ oz. yellow round can and cap. CMV, $5.00 CO. $7.00 MB.

Cologne Mist, 1959 – 1968.
3 oz., yellow plastic coated, yellow jewel on lid, in round yellow box. CMV, $3.00 in round box. 1969 – 1976 issue came in square box, same bottle. CMV, $1.00.

Golden Topaze Set, 1960 – 1961.
Gold box with plastic cover holds cream sachet, cologne mist, and beauty dust. CMV, $40.00 MB.

Soap Set, 1961 – 1964.
Yellow box holds two bars of soap. CMV, $22.00 MB.

Powder Sachet,
1959 – 1967.
Both 9/10 oz., yellow glass, yellow caps. Common issue with large cap. CMV, $6.00 MB. CMV, $7.00 with small cap, MB.

Temple of Love Set, 1960 – 1961.
Yellow and gold. Holds yellow and white plastic holder. Came with ¾ oz. cream sachet. CMV, $10.00 holder only. $20.00 MB. $6.00 for ¾ oz. cream sachet only.

Golden Gem Set, 1961.
Gold box holds 2 oz. cologne and cream sachet in ¾ oz. size. CMV, $25.00 MB.

Cologne,
1960 – 1971.
Gold cap, painted label. CMV, $1.00 MB.

Cream Sachet,
1960 – 1975.
⅔ oz., yellow paint on clear or milk glass, yellow cap. CMV, 50¢.

Beauty Dust,
1960 – 1970.
Yellow plastic bottom, white lid with yellow jewel. CMV, $5.00 MB.

Bath Oil,
1961 – 1966.
6 oz. yellow plastic bottle and cap. CMV, $1.00.

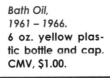

Jewel Set, 1961.
Gold box holds cologne mist and cream lotion. CMV, $30.00 MB.

Perfumed Talc,
1962 – 1974.
2¾ oz. yellow and white can, yellow cap. CMV, $1.00.

Perfume Mist,
1964 – 1968.
2 dram yellow bottle, white top with gold band, gold box. CMV, $2.00 BO. $4.00 MB.

Perfume Oil,
1963 – 1969.
½ oz., gold cap and painted label. CMV, $4.00 BO. $6.00 MB.

Perfumed Skin Softener,
1964 – 1972.
5 oz., yellow painted over white milk glass or clear glass, gold and white lid. CMV, $1.00 MB.

Column Soap Set, 1965 – 1966.
Holds three yellow bars. CMV, $25.00 MB.

Perfume Rollette,
1965 – 1969.
⅓ oz., ribbed carnival glass, gold cap. CMV, $2.00 MB.

Scented Hair Spray,
1966 – 1970.
7 oz. yellow can. CMV, $3.00.

Perfume Oil for the Bath, 1963.
½ oz., gold cap, painted label. CMV, $15.00 BO. $20.00 MB.

Setting Set, 1964.
Yellow box holds 2 oz. bottle of cologne and powder sachet. CMV, $25.00 MB.

Foaming Bath Oil,
1966 – 1973.
6 oz. yellow plastic bottle and cap. CMV, $1.00.

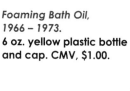

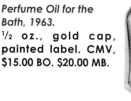

Elegance Set, 1963.
Gold and white box holds beauty dust, 4 oz. creme lotion, and 2 oz. cologne. CMV, $35.00 MB.

Princess Set, 1964.
Gold box holds 3 oz. cologne mist and 4 oz. cream lotion. CMV, $25.00 MB.

Cologne, 1970 – 1971.
⅓ oz., gold cap and painted label. CMV, $2.00 MB.

Unforgettable

Perfume Mist,
1964 – 1968.
2 dram, rose colored bottom, white cap, gold trim, all metal. CMV, $3.00 MB.

Perfume Oil, 1965 – 1969.
Left: Clear glass, gold cap, no neck trim.
Center left: Clear glass, gold cap, cutout gold neck trim.
Center right: Clear glass, gold cap, solid gold neck trim, scalloped edge.
Right: Solid gold neck trim with smooth edge. CMV, $4.00 each, BO, mint. $7.00 each, MB.

Beauty Dust, 1965 – 1970. Pink plastic trimmed in gold. CMV, $6.00 MB.

Skin Softener, 1965 – 1973. 5 oz., pink painted over clear or milk glass, pink and gold lid. CMV, $1.00.

Soap Set, 1965 – 1968. Orange box holds three orange soaps with gold centers. CMV, $20.00 MB.

Powder Sachet, 1965 only. *Left:* ⁹/₁₀ oz., pink glass, gold lettering, cap, and trim. Neck trim has cutout pattern. *Right:* ⁹/₁₀ oz., no trim. CMV, $6.00 each, MB.

Powder Sachet, 1965 only. 9 oz., pink glass, gold lettering, cap, and trim. No holes in trim. CMV, $6.00 MB.

Deluxe Set, 1965. Gold and white box holds beauty dust, cream sachet, and cologne mist. CMV, $32.50 MB.

Perfumed Soap, 1965. 3 oz., pink and gold wrapper. CMV, $4.00.

Cologne Mist, 1965 – 1976. 3 oz., pink plastic coated, gold cap. Two different gold trims around neck. CMV, $1.00 with holes in gold trim. $4.00 on solid gold neck trim.

Cream Sachet, 1965 – 1975. Pink painted over clear or milk glass bottom with gold plastic cap and gold trim. CMV, $1.00 MB.

Heirloom, 1965 – 1966. Gold and white tray holds ½ oz pink and gold cardboard perfumed talc. CMV, $15.00. ⁹/₁₀ oz. powder sachet, gold cap, and ½ oz. perfume oil with gold cap. CMV, $30.00 CO. $40.00 set MB.

Perfumed Talc, 1966 – 1974. 2¾ oz. pink can and cap. CMV, $1.00.

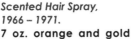

Scented Hair Spray, 1966 – 1971. 7 oz. orange and gold can. CMV, $3.00.

Cologne, 1966 – 1971. 2 oz., gold cap, painted label. CMV, $2.00.

Cream Lotion, 1966 – 1968. 4 oz., orange plastic bottle with gold cap. CMV, $2.00 MB.

Foaming Bath Oil, 1966 – 1972. 6 oz. orange plastic bottle with gold cap. CMV, $2.00 MB.

Powder Sachet, 1966 – 1968. ⁹/₁₀ oz. pink glass, gold pattern printing and gold cap. No neck trim. CMV, $6.00 MB.

Perfumed Powder Mist, 1968 – 1972. 7 oz. orange and gold can, two different labels painted on paper. CMV, $1.00 each, CO, painted label. $3.00 each, paper label.

Cologne, 1970 – 1971. ½ oz. with gold cap. CMV, $2.00 MB.

 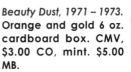

Beauty Dust, 1971 – 1973. Orange and gold 6 oz. cardboard box. CMV, $3.00 CO, mint. $5.00 MB.

Violet Bouquet

Representative Gift, 1945.
Avon's 59th anniversary gift to each representative. Violet colored net ribbon around white cap. 16 oz. crackle glass bottle. CMV, $100.00 BO. $175.00 with ribbon mint, MB.

Cologne, 1946 – 1949.
6 oz. bottle. Came in different colored caps. CMV, $50.00 BO, mint. $80.00 MB.

White Moiré

Body Powder, 1945 – 1949.
5 oz. or 4½ oz. size, blue and white paper container with plastic sifter top, came in blue and white box. CMV, $25.00 CO, mint. $30.00 MB.

Sachet, 1946.
White cap and small plain paper label. CMV, $20.00 BO. $25.00 MB.

Powder Sachet, 1946 – 1947.
1¼ oz., clear glass, white or blue plastic cap. CMV, $15.00 BO. $20.00 MB. Same label as 1948 – 1949 powder sachet.

Cologne, 1945 – 1949.
6 oz. bubble sided bottle with white or blue cap. Blue and white label. CMV, $50.00 BO. $75.00 MB.

Powder Sachet, 1948 – 1949.
1¼ oz., clear glass, blue and white label, blue cap. CMV, $15.00 BO. $20.00 MB.

Soap, 1946 – 1949.
Blue and white box, white bowtie soap. CMV, $50.00 MB.

White Moiré Set, 1945 – 1949.
Blue and white box with white silk bow on lid contains 6 oz. cologne with white cap and blue and white label, and 5 oz. body powder. Blue and white cardboard. CMV, $115.00 MB.

Sachet 60th Anniversary Box, 1946.
1¼ oz. regular issue bottle, white cap. Came in special issue blue and white box with white ribbon and blue and silver tag saying "Avon Diamond Anniversary 60th Year." CMV, $30.00 MB as shown.

Wishing

Cologne, 1947.
4 oz. bottle with gold cap, painted label. Same bottle as Golden Promise cologne. Came in fancy open front and top box. Given to Avon representatives for calling on 61 customers during 61st anniversary campaign during campaign 9, 1947. CMV, $85.00 BO. $110.00 MB.

Secret Wish Set, 1963 – 1965.
White box holds perfumed talc and 4 oz. cream lotion. CMV, $20.00 MB.

Perfumed Talc, 1963 – 1966.
2³⁄₄ oz. white can, gold lettering. CMV, $4.00.

Toilet Water, 1947 – 1949.
2 oz., white cap. CMV, $30.00 BO. $35.00 MB. Also came in gold 61st anniversary box. CMV, $40.00 MB.

Bubble Bath, 1963 – 1966.
4 oz. white plastic bottle and cap, white box. CMV, $3.00 BO. $5.00 MB.

Wishing Set, 1963 only.
White and gold box holds 2 oz. cologne and cream sachet. CMV, $25.00 MB.

Toilet Water, 1952.
2 oz., white cap. Same as Flowertime bottle. CMV, $25.00 BO. $30.00 MB.

Cologne Mist, 1963 – 1970.
2¹⁄₂ oz., white plastic coated, gold trim. Gold wishbone on neck, white box. CMV, $3.00 BO. $5.00 MB.

Beauty Dust, 1963 – 1967.
4 oz., white plastic trimmed in gold. CMV, $10.00 MB.

Cream Lotion, 1963 – 1967.
4 oz. white plastic bottle and cap. White box. CMV, $4.00 BO. $6.00 MB.

Cologne, 1963 – 1967.
2 oz., clear glass, white cap, gold lettering with gold wishbone on neck, white box. CMV, $4.00 BO. $7.00 MB.

Powder Sachets, 1964 – 1968.
Back two: ⁹⁄₁₀ oz., white glass bottom. Bottle on right has white plastic cap, bottle on left has yellow plastic cap, not faded. Both have wishbone in center of cap. White box. CMV, $10.00 yellow cap, $6.00 white cap, add $2.00 each, MB.
Cream Sachets, 1963 – 1970.
Front two: White glass bottom with white plastic cap, gold wishbone in center of cap. Also came with "Wishing" written on lid. CMV, $2.00 with wishbone, $15.00 with "Wishing" lettering.

**Perfume Oil,
1964 – 1967.**
½ oz., clear glass, white cap, gold lettering with small gold wishbone on gold string. White box. CMV, $8.00 BO. $10.00 MB.

Perfumed Pair, 1964.
White box holds perfumed talc and bar of soap in white wrapper. CMV, $19.00 MB.

**Wish Come True Set,
1963 – 1964.**
White and gold box holds bubble bath and 2 oz. cologne with wishbone on neck. CMV, $26.00 MB.

**Perfumed Soap,
1965 – 1966.**
3 oz. white soap with white and gold wrapper. CMV, $5.00 mint.

**Wishing Soap Set,
1963 – 1966.**
White box holds three white "Wishbone" embossed soaps. CMV, $25.00 MB.

Necklace, 1964 – 1965.
22K gold wishbone necklace came in Charm of Wishing Set only. CMV, $17.00 necklace only. $25.00 in small pink and white box.

Perfume Mist, 1965 – 1967.
2 dram, white metal, gold trim, white box. CMV, $4.00 MB.

Bath Oil, 1964 – 1966.
6 oz. white plastic bottle, gold lettering, white box. CMV, $7.00 BO. $10.00 MB.

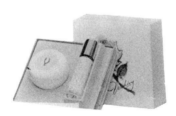

Duette Set, 1964 – 1965.
White, gold, and pink box holds cream rollette and cream sachet. CMV, $22.00 MB.

Date Set, 1965.
White and gold box holds perfumed skin softener, perfume rollette, and white vinyl covered date book. CMV, $32.50 MB.

**Perfumed Skin Softener,
1964 – 1969.**
5 oz. white glass jar with gold and white lid. CMV, $3.00 MB.

**Charm of Wishing Set,
1964 – 1965.**
Gold and white box holds beauty dust, cologne mist, and 22K gold plated wishbone necklace on 9" chain. CMV, $62.50 MB.

**Scented Hair Spray,
1966 – 1967.**
7 oz. white can with gold lettering and white cap. CMV, $5.00.

Talc, 1952 – 1953.
1²/₃ oz., cardboard. Came in sets only. CMV, $20.00.

Young Hearts, 1952 – 1954.
Left to right: 1 dram perfume, pink cap and painted label. Came in sets only. CMV, $60.00. ½ oz. Toilet water with pink cap and painted label. Came in sets only. CMV, $30.00. 1 oz. cologne with pink cap. Came in sets only. CMV, $30.00.

For Young Hearts Set Bottles, 1945 – 1946.
Each are 2 oz. frosted glass with pink caps. In Cotillion toilet water, cream lotion, and bubble bath. CMV, $20.00 each.

Cologne, 1952 – 1954.
2 oz., pink cap and painted label. CMV, $30.00 BO, mint.

Sachet, 1945 – 1946.
Box holds two pink lace net sachets with pink ribbons on each end and flower in the middle. Refills for the Young Hearts Set. CMV, $40.00 MB.

Bubble Bath, 1952 – 1954.
2 oz., pink cap and painted label. CMV, $30.00 BO, mint.

Rain Drops Set, 1952.
Red umbrella bag holds 1 oz. cologne, perfume, and cream lotion. All have pink caps. OSP, $2.95. CMV, $125.00 MB.

Kiddie Bubble Bath, 1952 – 1954.
2 oz. bottle with pink cap and white foam cat head on cap. Blue and white box, painted label. OSP, $1.10. CMV, $50.00 MB with foam head. $30.00 BO. Add $10.00 for foam head.

Honey Bun Set, 1952.
Pink and white eight-sided box holds toilet water and gold pomade lipstick. OSP, $1.19. CMV, $50.00 MB.

Sachet, 1945 – 1946.
One pink lace net with pink ribbons on each end. Came in For Young Hearts Set only. CMV, $25.00 MB.

For Young Hearts Set, 1945 – 1946.
Pink box holds three 2 oz. frosted glass bottles of Cotillion toilet water, cream lotion, and bubble bath. All have pink caps. Pink net sachet in top box. OSP, $3.75. CMV, $22.50 each bottle. $110.00 set MB. $20.00 for net sachet.

Kiddie Cologne, 1952 – 1953.
2 oz. bottle with white foam cat head over pink cap, painted label. Blue and white box. OSP, $1.25. CMV, $30.00 BO. $50.00 MB with cat head. Add $10.00 for foam head.

Rain Drops Set, 1953. Red umbrella hand-bag holds cologne, pomade, and cream lotion. Pink caps. OSP, $2.95. CMV, $95.00 set, MB.

'N Everything Nice Set, 1952. Box holds cream lotion, pink cap; polish remover, pink cap; nail polish, white cap. Also includes emery board and orange stick. OSP, $1.50. CMV, $60.00 MB.

Honey Bun Set, 1953. Blue and pink round box holds 2½ oz. toilet water with pink cap and gold pomade lipstick. CMV, $50.00 MB.

Kiddie Kologne, 1954 – 1955. 2 oz. bottle of cologne has pink cap with white foam dog head on cap, in yellow, white and blue box. OSP, $1.25. CMV, $25.00 BO. $50.00 MB. Add $15.00 for foam head on BO, mint.

Young Hearts Set, 1952. Blue, white, and pink box holds cologne, talc, and bubble bath. CMV, $85.00 MB.

Young Hearts Set, 1953. Blue and white box holds cologne, bubble bath, and talc. CMV, $100.00 MB.

Kiddie Bubble Bath, 1954 – 1955. White foam dog head on pink cap, in yellow, white and blue box. OSP, $1.10. CMV, $25.00 BO. Add $15.00 for foam head on BO, mint. $50.00 MB.

Cream Lotion, 1952 – 1953. 2 oz., pink cap. Came in sets only. CMV, $20.00 mint.

Talc, 1954 – 1955. Pink and white metal can. CMV, $25.00 mint.

Polish Remover, 1952 – 1953. 2 oz., pink cap. Came in 'N Everything Nice Set only. CMV, $20.00 mint.

'N Everything Nice Set, 1953. Box holds cream lo-tion, polish remover with pink caps, nail polish with white cap, emery board, and or-ange stick. Top differ-ent from back of lid. CMV, $65.00 MB.

Cologne, 1954 – 1955. Pink cap. CMV, $25.00 mint.

Bubble Bath, 1954 – 1955. CMV, $25.00 mint.

Honey Bun Set,
1954 – 1955.
Cologne and gold lipstick in white, blue, and yellow box. OSP, $1.19. CMV, $50.00 MB.

Neat and Sweet Set,
1954 – 1955.
Cologne and cream lotion with pink heart shaped soap. Pink caps in yellow, white, and blue box. OSP, $2.50. CMV, $85.00 MB. 1955 set came with green and gold spray atomizer. CMV, $95.00.

Cream Lotion, 1954.
Bottle has pink cap, in pink and white heart shaped box. OSP, 50¢. CMV, $20.00 BO. $25.00 MB.

Honey Bun Set, 1954.
Blue, white, and yellow box holds toilet water and gold pomade lipstick. CMV, $50.00 MB.

Beauty Dust,
1954 – 1955.
Blue, white, and yellow paper box. OSP, $1.19. CMV, $20.00 CO. $25.00 MB.

Little Doll Set, 1954 – 1955.
Plastic doll with blond hair. Blue dress is a zipper handbag containing cream lotion, cologne, and gold pomade. OSP, $2.95. CMV, $115.00 set MB.

Rain Drops Set,
1954 – 1955.
Red umbrella handbag holds cologne, pomade, and cream lotion. OSP, $3.25. CMV, $90.00 set MB.

Miss Fluffy Puff Set,
1954 – 1955.
Beauty dust and cologne in blue and pink. Pink cap in pink and white box. OSP, $2.35. CMV, $60.00 MB.

Young Hearts Set,
1954 – 1955.
Cologne, talc, and bubble bath with pink caps and pink hearts on label, in pink and white box. OSP, $1.95. CMV, $85.00 MB.

After Shaves and Colognes

After Shaving Lotion,
1932 – 1936.
4 oz., black caps. Two different yellow paper labels. CMV, $30.00 each, BO, mint. $40.00 MB.

After Shaving Lotion Sample, 1936 – 1940.
Maroon cap. "CPC" on back label. CMV, $35.00 mint.

After Shaving Lotion,
1936 – 1949.
4 oz., maroon cap, maroon and cream colored box. CMV, $22.00 BO. $30.00 MB.

Hair Tonic Sample, 1939. ¼ oz., maroon cap. CMV, $40.00 BO. $45.00 MB. *Not shown: Hair Lotion Sample, 1940s.* Same as ¼ oz. Hair Tonic. Same CMV.

Service Kit After Shave Bottle, 1951 – 1952. 4 oz., clear plastic with red cap. CMV, $12.00.

4A After Shave, 1964 – 1966. 6 oz. 4A painted on clear glass, black cap with gold mirror on top. CMV, $15.00 BO. $20.00 MB.

After Shave Lotion Sample, 1940 – 1949. ½ oz., maroon cap. CMV, $35.00.

After Shower for Men, 1959 – 1960. 8 oz., gold cap with gold foil on neck and gold neck cord with stagecoach on bottom. CMV, $30.00 with foil top and tag, mint. $40.00 MB.

After Shaves, 1965 – 1966. 2 oz. with 4A on black caps. Came in Island Lime, Blue Blazer, Leather, Tribute, Spicy, Bay Rum, Original, 4A After Shaves, Leather All Purpose Cologne, and After Shower Cologne. Came in Bureau Organizer, Fragrance Wardrobe, and After Shave Selection sets only. Ten different, CMV, $5.00 each, BO. $8.00 each, MB. Add $3.00 for Blue Blazer.

Cologne for Men, 1946 – 1949. 6 oz., maroon cap. Shield on paper label. CMV, $35.00 BO, mint. In two different maroon boxes, $50.00 each, MB.

Vigorate After Shave, 1959 – 1960. 8 oz., clear glass with white cap. Bottle indented on bottom with carriage. Box is black with red ribbon, gold bottom, plastic white insert on top with gold carriage. CMV, $20.00 BO, mint. $35.00 MB.

Gentlemen's Choice, 1969 – 1970. Red and silver box holds 2 oz. embossed bottles with silver, gold, and black caps. Came in Excalibur, Wild Country, Tribute, Leather, and Windjammer colognes. CMV, $4.00 BO. $6.00 MB.

Deodorant for Men, 1948 – 1949 2 oz., maroon cap and label. CMV, $10.00.

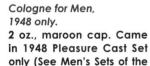

Cologne for Men, 1948 only. 2 oz., maroon cap. Came in 1948 Pleasure Cast Set only (See Men's Sets of the 1940s). CMV, $15.00.

Deluxe After Shave, "Wood Top," 1961 – 1963. 6 oz. Some have gold letters on bottle, some have gold paper labels. Came in Deluxe Electric Pre-Shave Lotion, Deluxe After Shave Lotion, After Shave Lotion Spicy, and Electric Pre-Shave Lotion Spicy. CMV, $20.00 BO, mint. $25.00 each MB. Four different fragrances.

Gentlemen's Selection, 1970.
2 oz. each, with gold caps. Came in cologne in Oland, Tribute, Excalibur, Leather, Wild Country, and Windjammer. CMV, $2.00 each, BO. $3.00 each, MB.

Cologne Spray for Men, 1970 – 1972.
4 oz. silver can with red cap in Leather; brown cap in Wild Country; and tan cap in Oland. These cans leaked and most boxes were ruined. CMV, $3.00 each MB.

Eagle Organizer Bottle, 1972.
3 oz., clear glass, eagle embossed, gold cap. Came in set only in Deep Woods and Tai Winds. CMV, $5.00 each.

Gift Cologne for Men, 1974 – 1975.
2 oz., clear glass with gold cap. Came in Wild Country, Deep Woods, Oland, or Tai Winds. CMV, $1.00 MB.

After Shave, 1975 – 1979.
5 oz., clear glass, brown cap. Came in Deep Woods, Everest, Oland, Tai Winds, Wild Country, and Clint. Different labels, same bottles. CMV, 50¢ each. Issued in 1981 – 1982 in 4 oz. size. Same shape in Wild Country, Weekend, Trazarra, and Clint. CMV, 50¢ each.

Gift Cologne for Men, 1975 – 1976.
2 oz., clear glass, gold cap. Choice of Wild Country, Tai Winds, Deep Woods, or Oland. CMV, $1.00 MB.

Gift Cologne for Men, 1976.
2 oz., came in Deep Woods, Tai Winds, Wild Country, Everest, or Oland. CMV, $1.00 MB.

Cologne Miniature for Men, 1977 – 1978.
5 oz., smoked glass, black cap. Came in Clint, Everest, or Wild Country. CMV, $2.00 MB.

Gift Cologne for Men, 1978 – 1979.
2 oz., clear glass, black cap. Held Everest, Clint, Wild Country, or Deep Woods cologne. CMV, $2.00 MB.

Cologne Miniature for Men, 1978 – 1979.
5 oz., clear glass, brown cap. Held Wild Country, Clint, Everest, or Trazarra cologne. CMV, $2.00 MB.

Cologne Accent for Men, 1979 – 1980.
½ oz., clear glass. Blue cap, blue and silver box. CMV, $2.00 MB.

Cologne for Men, 1979 – 1982.
3 oz., clear glass bottle. Gold caps. Choice of Brisk Spice, Cool Sage, Light Musk, or Crisp Lime. Came in box. CMV, $1.00 MB.

Gift Cologne for Men, 1980.
½ oz. black cap, clear glass. Choice of Trazarra, Wild Country, Clint, Weekend, Light Musk, Cool Sage, Brisk Spice, or Crisp Lime. CMV, $2.00 MB.

Country Christmas Cologne, 1982.
2 oz., ribbed, clear glass, green cap and box. Came in Country Christmas set only in men's cologne. CMV, $2.00 MB.

CJ Gift Edition Cologne,
1982 – 1983.
½ oz. mini cologne. Clear glass,
gray cap, Christmas box. CMV,
$2.00 MB.

Fragrance Traditions
Cologne for Men,
1995.
3²/₅ oz. glass stop-
pered bottles in
choice of Rugger,
Lover Boy, Clint,
Windjammer, or
Trazarra. Each bottle
and box has the introduction date for
the fragrance on the front. CMV, $1.00
each, MB, empty.

Holiday Vintage
Mini Colognes,
1995.
½ oz. ribbed glass
bottles, gold caps.
Special black box
with red stripes
sold only during
Christmas season
in 1995. Choice of
Aures 1985, Everest 1975, Legacy 1988,
Signet 1987, and Tai Winds 1971. Must
be in this red or black short issue box.
CMV, 50¢ each, MB.

Men's Miscellaneous Items

Automassage Shaving
Brush, 1915.
"Automassage" on
handle. Rubber cen-
ter of brush as shown.
This was not made for
CPC but sold by CPC
with a special offer for
CPC shaving powder.
OSP, 25¢. CMV, $30.00
brush only. $60.00 MB.

Talc for Men,
1929 only.
Green can. CMV,
$55.00 mint.

Shaving Stick,
1934 – 1936.
Nickel metal con-
tainer. CMV, $40.00
CO, mint. $50.00
MB.

Cream Shaving
Stick, 1915.
Gold or silvertone
metal can. Came
with soap stick,
"CPC" on lid. OSP,
25¢. CMV, $30.00
CO, mint. $55.00
MB.

Shaving Stick,
1929 – 1933.
Green metal can.
"CPC" on lid.
CMV, $50.00 CO,
mint. $60.00 MB.

Bayberry Shaving
Stick, 1923.
Three-piece nickel
metal container,
holds shaving soap.
OSP, 33¢. CMV,
$55.00 mint.

Talc for Men,
1930 – 1936.
Greenish yellow
can, black cap.
Came with plain
black cap and sifter
cap. CMV, $45.00
mint.

Styptic Cream, 1936 – 1949.
Maroon and ivory tube. CMV,
$8.00 TO. $15.00 MB.
Shaving Stick, 1936 – 1949.
Avon on maroon base on
soap stick. Maroon box. CMV,
$25.00 MB.

Hair Tonic Eau de Quinine, 1936 – 1938. For normal, dry, or oily hair. 6 oz., turquoise cap. CMV, $15.00 BO. $20.00 MB. Also came in 16 oz. size, $25.00 BO. $30.00 MB.

Talc for Men, 1943 – 1946. Maroon and ivory colored cardboard. Came with black octagonal cap as shown and also with maroon or black round cap. One on right has smooth top. You punched holes in it. CMV, $35.00 each, mint.

Talc for Men, 1949 – 1958. 2⅝ oz. green can, red cap. Also came in 2⅗ oz. size. CMV, $6.00 CO. $8.00 MB.

Hair Tonic, 1938 – 1939. 6 oz., clear glass, maroon cap and label. CMV, $30.00 BO, mint. $40.00 MB.

Lather and Brushless Shaving Cream, 1949 – 1959. Green tubes, flat red caps, used from 1949 to 1956. Tall red caps used 1957 – 1959. CMV, $8.00 each, TO, mint. $10.00 each, MB.

Hair Lotion, 1940 – 1949. 6 oz., maroon cap and box. CMV, $30.00 BO, mint. $40.00 MB. Some labels say "Formerly Hair Tonic."

Cream Hair Lotion, 1948 – 1949. 4 oz., maroon cap. CMV, $20.00 BO. $25.00 MB.

Shaving Stick, 1949 – 1957. Green and red box holds shaving soap stick with red plastic base. CMV, $15.00 MB.

Hair Lotion, 1940 only. 6 oz. glass bottle. Very short issue. Rare. CMV, $50.00 MB.

Shaving Bowl, 1949 – 1953. Wood shaving bowl, green label with red center handle. CMV, $35.00 bowl only. $45.00 MB.

Styptic Cream, 1949 – 1957. ⅓ oz. green tube with red cap. CMV, $10.00 TO. $15.00 MB.

Hand Guard and Hair Guard, 1951 – 1952. 2 oz., clear glass with blue cap; hair guard has red cap. Label is red, white, and black. Came in Changing of the Guard set only (See men's sets of the 1950s). CMV, $20.00 each.

Cream Hair Dress, 1949 – 1957. 2¼ oz. green tube and box. Came with flat or tall red cap. CMV, $15.00 MB.

Deodorant for Men, 1949 – 1958. 2 oz., red cap and green label. CMV, $6.00 MB.

Cologne for Men, 1949 – 1958. All three sizes have red caps and silver labels, 6 oz. size, 1949 – 1957. CMV, $10.00 MB. 4 oz. size, 1952 – 1957, came in sets only. Also with green label. CMV, $6.00. 2 oz. size, 1949 – 1958, CMV, $6.00.

Deodorant for Men Sample, 1949 – 1958. ½ oz. bottle with red cap, green label. CMV, $12.00 mint.

Shaving Cream Sample, 1949 – 1958. ¼ oz. green tubes of lather and brushless shaving creams, red caps. CMV, $6.00 each, mint. Also came in ½ oz. size sample tubes. CMV, $8.00 each, mint.

After Shave Lotion, 1949 – 1958. 4 oz. bottle with silver label and red cap. CMV, $7.00 MB.

Cologne for Men, 1952 – 1957. 4 oz. clear glass bottle with red cap. Label is green and red. CMV, $7.00.

Hair Lotion, 1949 – 1958. 4 oz., silver label and red cap. CMV, $7.00 BO. $12.00 MB.

Cologne for Men Sample, 1949 – 1958. ½ oz., red cap, silver label. CMV, $25.00 MB.

After Shaving Lotion Sample, 1949 – 1958. ½ oz., red cap, green label. CMV, $5.00.

Cream Hair Lotion, 1949 – 1958. 4 oz. bottle, silver label, red cap. CMV, $7.00 BO. $12.00 MB. Also came in after shave lotion, same bottle, 1953 – 1954. CMV, $15.00.

Shaving Bowl, 1953 – 1956. Wood shaving bowl, green label. No center handle. CMV, $30.00 bowl only. $40.00 MB.

First Class Male,
1953 – 1956.
6 oz. cologne
for men, red and
white box. CMV,
$25.00 MB as
shown.

Deodorant for Men,
1954 – 1957.
4 oz., red cap and green
label. Came in sets only.
CMV, $7.00 MB.

After Shave, 1957.
2 oz., silver label. Came
in Good Cheer set only
(see Men's Sets of the
1950s). CMV, $8.00.

Cologne for Men,
1953 – 1954.
4 oz., green label,
red cap. Came in
Before and After
Set only (see Men's
Sets of the 1950s).
CMV, $15.00.

Hand Guard and Hair Guard,
1954 – 1957.
2 oz., red cap on Hair Guard.
2 oz., green cap on Hand
Guard. Both came in Backfield
set and Touchdown set. Hair
Guard also came in Pigskin
Parade Set (see Men's Sets of
the 1950s). CMV, $18.00 each.

Hair Lotion,
1953 – 1954.
1 oz. bottle with red
cap and green label.
CMV, $20.00 BO.
$25.00 MB.

Cream Hair Lotion, 1955.
2 oz., clear glass, red
cap. Came in Space
Scout Set only (see
Men's Sets of the 1950s).
Rare. CMV, $25.00.

Triumph, 1957.
Special issue box holds 6 oz. cologne for men. Silver label, red
cap. CMV, $25.00 MB.

King for a Day, 1957.
Box holds 4 oz. bottle of
Electric Pre-Shave Lotion
or choice of cologne for
men or 4 oz. deodor-
ant for men. All had red
caps. CMV, $25.00 MB.

Cream Hair Lotion,
1953 – 1954.
1 oz. bottle with red
cap and green label.
CMV, $10.00 BO. $25.00
MB in trial size box.

Kwick Foaming Shave
Cream, 1955 – 1957.
10 oz. green and white
can, pointed red cap.
CMV, $4.00 CO. $7.00 MB.

Electric Pre-Shave
Lotion, 1957 – 1958.
4 oz., red cap, silver
label. CMV, $10.00
MB.

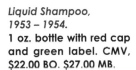

Liquid Shampoo,
1953 – 1954.
1 oz. bottle with red cap
and green label. CMV,
$22.00 BO. $27.00 MB.

Kwick Foaming Shave
Cream, 1957 – 1958.
10 oz. green and
white can, with flat
red top, red cap.
CMV, $4.00 CO. $7.00
MB.

Royal Order, 1957 only. Red and green box holds 6 oz. cologne for men. Silver label. CMV, $25.00 MB.

After Shave Lotion Sample, 1958 – 1962. ½ oz., red cap, black and white label. CMV, $8.00 MB.

Cream Hair Lotion, 1958 – 1962. 4 oz. white plastic bottle, red cap. CMV, $4.00 MB.

Foamy Bath for Cleaner Hides, 1957. 2 oz., red cap, cow hide on label. Came in Trading Post Set only (see Men's Sets of the 1950s). CMV, $20.00.

After Shaving Lotion, 1958. 2 oz., red cap. Came in sets only. CMV, $6.00 MB.

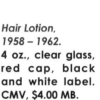

Hair Lotion, 1958 – 1962. 4 oz., clear glass, red cap, black and white label. CMV, $4.00 MB.

After Shaving Lotion, 1958 – 1962. 4 oz., red cap, black and white label. CMV, $4.00 MB.

Hair Trainer for Training Wild Hair, 1957. 2 oz., red cap, cow hide on label. Came in Trading Post Set only (see Men's Sets of the 1950s). CMV, $20.00.

Cologne for Men, 1958 – 1959. 4 oz., black glass, red cap. CMV, $10.00 BO. $15.00 MB.

Hair Guard and Hand Guard, 1958 only. Both 2 oz. bottles with red caps. Came in Avon Guard Set only (see Men's Sets of the 1950s). CMV, $16.00 Hand Guard. $20.00 Hair Guard.

Hair Trainer, 1957 – 1958. 6 oz. clear glass bottle with white or blue cap. Came in 1957 Hair Trainer Set (see Men's Sets of the 1950s). CMV, $20.00.

Cologne for Men, 1958. 2 oz., red cap, black and white label. Came in Happy Hours Set only (see Men's Sets of the 1950s). CMV, $7.00 BO.

Kwick Foaming Shave Cream, 1958 – 1962. 6 oz. black and white can, red cap. CMV, $6.00 MB.

Deodorant for Men, 1958 – 1962. 2 oz., red cap. CMV, $6.00 BO. $8.00 MB.

Hair Trainer, 1958 – 1974. 4 oz. red plastic bottle, white cap. CMV, $1.00.

Stand Up Hair Stick, 1958 – 1965.
Red and white container with white cap. CMV, $3.00 CO. $7.00 MB.

Spray Deodorant for Men, 1959 – 1962.
2¾ oz. white plastic bottle with red cap. CMV, $3.00 BO. $5.00 MB. 1½ oz. size in white plastic, red cap, came only in 1959 Lamplighter Set (see Men's Sets of the 1950s). CMV, $5.00.

After Shower Powder for Men, 1959 – 1962.
3 oz. black and white can, red cap. CMV, $7.00 MB.

After Shower for Men, 1959 – 1962.
4 oz., black glass, red or gold cap. CMV, $12.00 MB.

Stick Deodorant for Men, 1959 – 1961.
2¾ oz. black and red plastic container. Came with two different caps, one flat, one indented. CMV, $12.00 each, CO. $15.00 each, MB.

After Shower Sample, 1959 – 1962.
½ oz., black glass, red cap. CMV, $6.00.

Attention Cream Hair Dress, 1959 – 1962.
4 oz. red and white tube, red cap. CMV, $8.00 MB.

After Shower for Men, 1959 – 1960.
2 oz., black plastic bottle with red cap. CMV, $4.00 MB.

Left: Brushless Shaving Cream, 1959 – 1962.
5 oz. black and white tube, red cap. CMV, $7.00 MB.
Right: Lather Shaving Cream, 1959 – 1962.
5 oz. black and white tube, red cap. CMV, $8.00 MB.

After Shave, 1959 – 1960.
2 oz., red plastic bottle and cap. Came in 1959 Lamplighter Set (see Men's Sets of the 1950s). CMV, $4.00 MB.

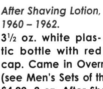

After Shaving Lotion, 1960 – 1962.
3½ oz. white plastic bottle with red cap. Came in Overnighter Set only (see Men's Sets of the 1960s). CMV, $4.00. 2 oz. After Shave, red plastic and cap as above came in 1959 Lamplighter Set. CMV, $4.00.

Electric Pre-Shave Lotion, 1959 – 1962.
4 oz., red cap, black and white label. CMV, $8.00 BO. $12.00 MB.

Talc for Men, 1959 only.
Black and white can, red cap. CMV, $12.00 MB.

Vigorate After Shave, 1960 – 1962.
4 oz. frosted glass bottle, gold or red caps. Two different painted labels. CMV, $10.00 each, BO. $15.00 each, MB.

After Shave for Dry and Sensitive Skin, 1960 – 1961.
2 oz., white plastic bottle with red cap. Also came in 2¾ oz. size. CMV, $7.00 BO. $10.00 MB.
Cream Hair Lotion, 1960 – 1961.
2 or 2¾ oz. white plastic bottle with red cap. Came in First Prize Set only (see Men's Sets of the 1960s). CMV, $7.00 MB.

Hair Trainer Boxes, 1958 – 1961. Left to right: **4 oz. red plastic bottle with 1958 box; 1962 box; 1960 – 1961. 1959 box came with boxer on front of box. CMV, $1.00 BO. Add $5.00 for each box mint.**

Roll On Deodorant for Men, 1960 – 1963. **1¾ oz., white plastic with red cap. CMV, $5.00 MB.**

Deluxe Stick Deodorant Normal, 1962 – 1963. **2½ oz. brown and gold plastic bottle. CMV, $8.00 MB.**

Stagecoach Embossed Bottle, 1960 – 1961.
2 oz., red or white caps. Came in First Prize Set (see Men's Sets of the 1960s) only in After Shower for Men, Vigorate, Deodorant for Men, After Shave Lotion, Electric Pre-Shave Lotion, or Liquid Hair Lotion. CMV, $10.00 BO. $18.00 MB.

Stick Deodorant for Men — A Spicy Fragrance, 1961 – 1962.
2¾ oz., brown and gold plastic holder. CMV, $9.00 CO. $11.00 MB.

Cream Hair Lotion, 1962 – 1965.
4 oz. white plastic bottle, red cap. CMV, $7.00 BO. $10.00 MB.

After Shower Powder — A Spicy Fragrance, 1961 only.
4 oz. brown can. CMV, $12.00 MB.

Stagecoach Embossed Bottle, 1960 – 1961.
8 oz. size with gold metal cap, came in Spice After Shave Lotion, After Shave Lotion, Vigorate, and After Shower for Men. CMV, $17.00, with indented gold cap. $25.00 MB.

Liquid Hair Lotion, 1962 – 1965.
4 oz. clear glass bottle, red cap. CMV, $8.00 BO. $12.00 MB.
Hair Trainer, 1962 – 1965.
4 oz. white plastic bottle, red cap. CMV, $7.00 BO. $10.00 MB.

After Shave After Shower Spray Lotion — A Spicy Fragrance, 1961 – 1962.
5½ oz. brown can, gold cap. CMV, $12.00 MB.

Stagecoach Embossed Bottle, 1961 only.
4 oz. size with white cap came in Spice After Shave Lotion. CMV, $10.00 BO. $14.00 MB.

*After Shave Lotion, Spicy,
1962 – 1965.
Electric Pre-Shave Lotion, Spicy.
Not shown: After Shower Cologne
for Men.
Original After Shave Lotion.
Vigorate After Shave Lotion.*
**Each bottle is 4 oz. size with red
cap. CMV, $7.00 each, MB.**

*Stand Up Hair Stick,
1962 – 1965.*
**1½ oz. white plas-
tic, red cap. CMV,
$3.00 MB.**

*After Shower Cologne
Spray, 1962.*
**5½ oz., white can and cap.
CMV, $7.00 MB.**

*Talc for Men, Spicy,
1962 – 1965.*
**3 oz. white can, red
cap. Also came in
3¹/₁₀ oz. size. CMV,
$7.00 MB.**

*Foam Shave
Cream, Spicy,
1962 – 1965.*
**6 oz. white can,
red cap. Came
in regular or
mentholated.
CMV, $4.00 BO.
$6.00 MB. Came with tall or flat red cap
as shown.**

*Deluxe Talc for Men,
1962 – 1963.*
**4 oz. brown can.
CMV, $8.00 CO.
$10.00 MB.**

Spray Deodorant for Men, 1962 – 1966.
**2¾ oz. white plastic bottle, red cap.
Came in gentle, normal, or plain. CMV,
$3.00 MB.**
*Liquid Deodorant for Men — Gentle or
Plain, 1962– 1965.*
**4 oz. and 2 oz. clear glass bottles, red
caps. CMV, $6.00, 2 oz. MB. $7.00, 4
oz. MB.**

*Roll On Deodorant for Men,
1963 – 1966.*
**1¾ oz. glass bottle, red cap.
CMV, $3.00 MB.**

*Deluxe Foam Shave
Cream, 1962 – 1963.*
**6 oz. brown can
and cap. Regular or
mentholated. CMV,
$8.00 MB.**

*After Shave for Dry or Sensitive Skin,
Spicy, 1962 – 1965.
Lather Shave Cream, Spicy,
1962 – 1965.*
**Both white tubes with red caps. CMV,
$3.00 each, TO. $6.00 each, MB.**
Lather Shave Cream, 1962 – 1963.
**4 oz. tube, red cap. CMV, $4.00 TO,
mint. $6.00 MB.**

*Deluxe After Shave
After Shower Spray,
1962 – 1963.*
**5½ oz. brown can, gold
cap. CMV, $8.00 MB.**

*Vigorate After Shave
After Shower Spray, 1963 – 1965.
Original After Shave
After Shower Spray, Spicy, 1963 – 1965.
After Shave After Shower
Spray, Spicy, 1963 – 1965.
After Shower Cologne Spray,
1963 – 1965.*
**5½ oz. each. White cans with red caps.
CMV, $4.00 each, MB.**

Men's Squeeze Bottles, 1963 – 1964.
2 oz. white plastic bottles with red caps and letters. Came in Vigorate, Spicy and Original After Shave Lotions, Electric Pre-Shave Lotion, Spicy Liquid Hair Lotion, Hair Trainer, Cream Hair Lotion, After Shower Cologne for Men, and Liquid Deodorant for Men, gentle or plain. Came only in 1964 Christmas Trio Set and 1965 Jolly Holly Day Set (see Men's Sets of the 1960s). CMV, $3.00 each.

After Shower Foam for Men, 1965 – 1967.
4 oz. silver can, black and red cap. Came in silver box. CMV, $4.00 BO. $6.00 MB.

Bath Oil for Men, 1965 – 1967.
4 oz., silver paint over clear glass, red cap and red Avon plastic tag on gold neck cord. Came in silver box. CMV, $7.00 MB.

All Purpose Skin Conditioner for Men, 1966 – 1968.
5 oz., black glass, tan lid, gold label. CMV, $5.00 MB.

Liquid Deodorant for Men, 1966 – 1970.
2 oz., red cap. CMV, $2.00 MB.

Original After Shave Spray, 1965 – 1966.
5½ oz. green can with red cap. CMV, $4.00 CO. $10.00 MB.

Hair Dress, 1966 – 1971.
4 oz. tubes in Cream, Clear, and Clear for Extra Control. CMV, $1.00 each, MB. Also came in 3 oz. tube. CMV, $1.00 MB.

Body Powder for Men, 1967 – 1968.
6 oz. maroon cardboard box. CMV, $8.00 CO, mint. $15.00 MB.

Original After Shave, 1965 – 1969.
4 oz., green label, red cap and red and green box. CMV, $4.00 BO. $6.00 MB.
Original Soap on a Rope, 1966 – 1968.
White bar with embossed carriage. CMV, $25.00 MB.

Liquid Hair Lotion, 1966 – 1970.
4 oz. clear glass bottle with white cap. CMV, $2.00 MB. 1970 – 1971 bottle is white, red cap, 6 oz. plastic. CMV, $1.00 MB.

Electric Pre-shave Lotion, 1966 – 1972.
4 oz., white cap. CMV, $1.00 MB.

Stick Deodorant for Men, 1968 – 1970.
2¼ oz., red, white, and black plastic. CMV, $2.00.

Cream Hair Lotion, 1966 – 1969.
4 oz. white plastic bottle with red cap and red label. Regular issue, CMV, $1.00 MB. Very short issue sold 1966 only with red cap and red label with black border. CMV, $2.00 MB.

Anti-perspirant Deodorant for Men, 1971 – 1974.
4 oz. red, white, and black can. CMV, $1.00 MB. With upside down label, CMV, $6.00 MB.
Stick Deodorant for Men, 1971 – 1974.
2¼ oz. red, white, and black can. CMV, $1.00.

Today's Man Shave Cream, 1975 – 1976.
5 oz., white with red and black design, black cap. CMV, $1.00 MB.

Top left: After Shave Soother, 1969 – 1972.
4 oz. frosted glass bottle with red cap. CMV, $2.00 MB.
Top center: Bath Oil, 1969 – 1972.
4 oz. black glass bottle, red cap. CMV, $2.00 MB.
Top right: Protective Hand Cream for Men, 1969 – 1972.
3 oz. black plastic tube with red cap. CMV, $2.00 MB.
Bottom: Skin Conditoner for Men, 1969 – 1973.
5 oz., black glass, red lid, and red and black label. CMV, $2.50 MB.

Today's Man Hand Conditioner, 1975 – 1976.
Plastic tube with black and red design, black cap. CMV, $1.00 MB.

Today's Man After Shave Face Conditioner, 1975 – 1976.
5 oz., white with red and black, black cap. CMV, $1.00 MB.

Men's Fragrance Lines

All men's product lines 1975 or newer are no longer collectible because of little or no interest and mass production. Only soaps and sets in this category are collectible after 1975.

Jug, 1962 – 1965.
8 oz., white painted bottom, green top over clear glass, black cap. Holds Bay Rum after shave. CMV, $7.00 BO, mint. $12.00 MB.

Bay Rum, 1936 – 1949.
4 oz., maroon cap. Two different labels. Both bottles have indented shoulders. Also came in 8 and 16 oz. sizes. CMV, $22.00 each, BO. $30.00 each, MB.

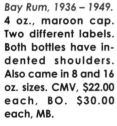

Soap Set, 1964 – 1965.
Green box holds two Bay Rum shaped soaps. CMV, $27.50 MB.

Bay Rum Gift Set, 1964.
Green box holds 4 oz. after shave with black cap and green 4 oz. paper talc for men. CMV, $35.00 MB.

Talc for Men, 1964 – 1965.
4 oz. green paper container. CMV, $10.00, mint.

After Shave, 1964 – 1965.
4 oz., clear glass, black cap. CMV, $10.00 MB.

Black Suede ························

Black Suede Products, 1980 – 1984.
Basic color is tan and black.
Gift Soap and Case, 1980 only.
Black plastic soap case and soap.
CMV, $5.00 MB.
Soap Bar.
CMV, $2.00 mint.
Soap on a Rope.
CMV, $5.00 MB. All other products,
25¢ each.

Blend 7 ·······························

Blend 7 Products, 1973 – 1974.
Right: Soap on a Rope, 1973 – 1976.
5 oz., yellow with black cord.
CMV, $6.00 MB.
All other products, 50¢ each.

Blue Blazer ························

After Shave, 1964 – 1968.
6 oz., blue glass with red square cap over small red
cap. Horses on labels, came in gold or silver and with
or without lines across horses. Some labels have 6 oz.
at bottom of horse label. CMV, $12.00 BO. $15.00 MB.
Soap on a Rope, 1964 – 1968.
Blue soap on white rope. CMV, $10.00 soap only, mint.
$20.00 MB.

After Shave Spray,
1964 – 1965.
Blue 6 oz. can, red cap.
CMV, $7.00 CO. $10.00 MB.
Not shown: Foam Shave
Cream, 1964 – 1965.
6 oz. blue can, red cap.
CMV, $7.00 CO. $10.00
MB.

Talc, 1964 – 1965.
3½ oz. blue paper box.
CMV, $9.00 CO. $12.00
MB.

Hair Dress, 1964 – 1967.
4 oz. blue tube, red cap.
CMV, $6.00 TO. $8.00 MB.

Blue Blazer I Set,
1964 – 1965.
Blue and red box holds
6 oz. after shave lotion
and soap on a rope.
CMV, $50.00 MB.

Blue Blazer II Set, 1964 – 1965.
Blue and red box holds talc and spray deodorant. CMV, $25.00 MB.

After Shave Towelettes, 1969 – 1972.
Pink and black box holds 100 sample packets. CMV, $7.00 MB or 10¢ per sample.

Spray Deodorant, 1964 – 1967.
2¾ oz. blue plastic bottles, red caps. One bottle has lines on horse design and one is plain. The plain one is hardest to find. CMV, $8.00. Different label on right. CMV, $7.00 with 2¾ oz. on front side.

After Shave Sample, 1969 – 1972.
Box of 10 samples. CMV, $1.50 MB.

Talc, 1969 – 1972.
3½ oz. pink and black paper container. CMV, $1.50.

Tie Tac, 1964.
Silver Blue Blazer emblem tie tac. Came in Blue Blazer Deluxe Set only. In blue and red box. CMV, $10.00 pin only. $22.00 MB.

After Shave, 1969.
4 oz. bottle with black cap, pink label. CMV, $2.00 BO, mint. $3.00 MB.

Blue Blazer Deluxe Set, 1965.
Blue and red box holds 6 oz. after shave, spray deodorant, and silver emblem tie tac. CMV, $67.50 MB.

After Shave, 1970 – 1972.
4 oz., black cap, pink label with black border around label. CMV, $2.00 MB.

Soap and Sponge Set, 1966 – 1967.
Red and blue box holds bar of blue soap and red and blue sponge. CMV, $22.50 MB.

Santa's Helper, 1970.
Green box holds 4 oz. after shave. Box came with foam stick-on decorations. CMV, $8.00 MB only.

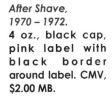

Clint ···

Center: Cologne, 1976 – 1979.
5 oz. bottle with "Clint" painted on front. CMV, $1.00 MB. Also came in 4 oz. size, same design and CMV.
Left: After Shave, 1977 – 1979.
5 oz. glass bottle, brown cap. CMV, $1.00.
Front: Shower Soap, 1977 – 1978.
Soap on green or white rope. CMV, $5.00 MB.
Right: Talc for Men.
3½ oz. CMV, $1.00.

Travel Kit Set, 1977.
Comes empty, gray, maroon and green bag. CMV, $8.00 MB.
Soap, 1977 – 1978.
3 oz. CMV, $1.50. All other Clint products, CMV, 25¢.

Gift Set, 1977 – 1978.
Gray and green box with outer sleeve. Came with soap on a rope and 5 oz. cologne. CMV, $12.00 MB.

Travel Set, 1977.
Cardboard 1½ oz. talc and 3 oz. shampoo in plastic bottle with maroon cap. CMV, $6.00 MB.

Deep Woods ···

Shower Soap on a Rope, 1972 – 1975. CMV, $6.00 MB.

After Shave, 1976 – 1979.
5 oz., brown cap. CMV, 50¢ MB.

Shower Soap on a Rope, 1976 – 1979. CMV, $6.00 MB.

Soap Bar, 1977 – 1978.
Brown wrapped soap, 3 oz. bar. CMV, $1.00 mint.
All other Deep Woods products, CMV, 50¢ each.

Everest ···

Soap on a Rope, 1975 – 1979.
Blue soap, white rope. CMV, $5.00 MB.
Soap Bar, 1977 – 1979
Blue wrapped 3 oz. bar. CMV, $1.00 mint.
All other Everest products, CMV, 50¢ each.

Excalibur

Cologne, 1969 – 1973.
6 oz., gold cap. Bottom of bottle appears to have rocks in glass. CMV, $6.00 MB. Rare issue came with sword pointing to right side, low end of rocks. CMV, $15.00 mint.

Island Lime After Shave, 1966 – 1969.
First issue, 6 oz., dark yellow basket weave. CMV, $12.00 MB, 1967 issue has light yellow weave on clear. 1968 issue has light green weave. CMV, $10.00 each, MB. All 1966 to 1968 are clear glass bottles. 1969 issue is green glass bottle and low issue. CMV, $20.00 MB. All have green and yellow caps. Came with small or large flowers on caps.

Island Lime After Shave, 1969 – 1973.
6 oz., green frosted glass and green cap with yellow letters. CMV, $1.50 MB. 1973 – 1974 issue has gold cap, green letters. CMV, $2.00 MB.

Soap on a Rope, 1969 – 1971.
Blue soap on a rope. CMV, $10.00 MB.

Spray Talc, 1970 – 1972.
7 oz. black can and cap. CMV, $1.00.

Island Lime Spray Talc, 1974 – 1976.
7 oz., green and yellow with dark green cap. CMV, $1.00 MB.

Leather

Island Lime

Island Lime Aerosol Deodorant, 1966 – 1967.
4 oz. green and yellow checked can and green cap. CMV, $3.00 MB.

Island Lime Soap, 1966 – 1968.
Green soap on a rope. Two different weave designs on soap. CMV, $22.00 each, MB.

Soap, 1966.
One bar in brown and red box. CMV, $18.00 MB.

All Purpose Cologne, 1966.
4 oz. black cap, red label. Came in Fox Hunt Set only (see Men's Sets of the 1960s). CMV, $10.00.

Leather Aerosol Deodorant, 1966 – 1967.
4 oz., tan and red can with black cap. CMV, $2.00 CO. $3.00 MB.

Leather After Shave Lotion, 1968.
3 oz., red cap, clear glass. Came in Boots and Saddle Set only (see Men's Sets of the 1960s). CMV, $5.00.

Leather Spray Talc, 1969 – 1972.
7 oz. tan and red can, black cap. CMV, $2.00.

Öland Spray Talc, 1970 – 1972.
7 oz. can with "O" on brown cap. Painted label on can is upside down. Can was filled and sold by Avon by mistake. CMV, $5.00.

Öland After Shave and Cologne, 1970.
3½ oz., clear glass bottles with gold caps. Came in Master Organizer Set only. (See Men's Sets of the 1970s). CMV, $5.00 each.

Öland ···

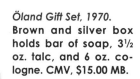

Öland Gift Set, 1970.
Brown and silver box holds bar of soap, 3½ oz. talc, and 6 oz. cologne. CMV, $15.00 MB.

Spicy ···

Spicy After Shave Samples, 1961.
Plastic sample tubes. Full box of 30. Same samples also came in Cream Hair Dress, Rich Moisture Cream, and Dew Kiss. CMV, 25¢ each sample or $7.00 for full box of 30 mint. Comes in two different boxes.

Öland Cologne, 1970 – 1977.
6 oz. embossed bottle with brown cap. CMV, $2.00 MB.
Öland Soap on a Rope, 1970 – 1977.
Tan bar of soap on green rope with plastic "O." CMV, $7.00 MB with plain rope (no "O"). CMV, $5.00 MB.
Öland Spray Talc, 1970 – 1977.
7 oz. brown spray can with brown cap. CMV, $1.00.

Spice After Shave Lotion Samples, 1961.
Small white envelope holds two plastic samples. CMV, $5.00 mint.

Soap Set, 1965 – 1966. Five brown bars. CMV, $22.50 MB.

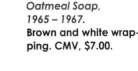

Oatmeal Soap, 1965 – 1967. Brown and white wrapping. CMV, $7.00.

Cologne Plus Spicy, 1965 – 1967. 2 oz., gold ribbed cap. CMV, $20.00 MB.

After Shave Lotion, 1965 – 1967. 4 oz., tan cap. CMV, $7.00 MB.

Spicy Three Set, 1965. Brown box holds two bars of Spicy oatmeal soap and Spicy talc for men. CMV, $22.50 MB.

After Shave Spray, 1965 – 1967. 5½ oz. bamboo style can, gold cap. CMV, $6.00 MB.

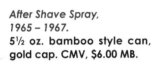

First Edition Spicy, 1965. Book type box holds 4 oz. after shave lotion and talc for men. CMV, $25.00 MB.

Talc for Men, 1965 – 1967. 3½ oz., bamboo style box. CMV, $5.00 MB.

Christmas Wreath, 1965. Gold box holds two 4 oz. bottles of after shave lotion with tan caps. CMV, $20.00 MB.

After Shave Spray, 1965 – 1967. 5½ oz., bamboo style can, tan cap. CMV, $5.00 MB.

Holiday Spice, 1965. Brown and white box holds talc for men and 4 oz. after shave lotion. CMV, $22.50 MB.

After Shave for Dry or Sensitive Skin, 1965 – 1967. 2 oz. tan and white tube, tan cap. CMV, $4.00 MB. Upside down label on right is rare. CMV, $8.00 MB.

Overnighter, 1965 – 1966. Brown vinyl zippered bag holds talc, 4 oz. after shave lotion, and bar of oatmeal soap for men. CMV, $25.00 MB.

Fore 'N After Spicy, 1966.
Spicy box holds 4 oz. electric pre-shave lotion and 4 oz. after shave lotion. White caps on both and wood grain paper labels. CMV, $22.00 MB.
Electric Pre-shave and After Shave Lotions, 1966.
4 oz. white caps and wood grain paper labels. Came in Fore 'N After Set only. CMV, $7.00 each.

Twice Spice, 1967.
Brown striped box holds 4 oz. after shave lotion and talc for men. CMV, $17.00 MB.

Spice O' Life Set, 1966 only.
Box holds talc for men and 4 oz. after shave lotion. Came out at Father's Day. CMV, $22.50 MB.

Spicy Treasures, 1968.
Brown chest type box holds 4 oz. after shave lotion and 3½ oz. talc for men. CMV, $17.00 MB.

After Shave, 1967 – 1974.
4 oz., clear glass, black cap. CMV, $1.00 MB. 4 oz. amber glass with black cap. CMV, $2.00 MB.

Sports Rally

Bracing Lotion, 1966 – 1968.
4 oz. glass bottle with blue cap. CMV, $2.00 MB.
Bracing Towelette, 1966 – 1968.
Blue and white box holds 12 packets. CMV, $2.00 MB.

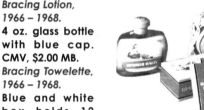

Soap on a Rope, 1966 – 1968.
4 oz. soap on white rope. CMV, $15.00 MB.
Aerosol Deodorant, 1966 – 1968.
4 oz. red, white, and blue can, white cap. CMV, $2.00 MB.

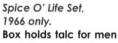

Talc for Men, 1967 – 1974.
3½ oz. brown and white container. CMV, $1.00 MB. Upside down label, CMV, $5.00 MB.

Hair Dress, 1966 – 1968.
4 oz. red and white tube, red cap. CMV, $3.00 MB.
All Purpose Talc, 1966 – 1968.
3½ oz. blue and white cardboard container. CMV, $2.00 MB.
Clear Skin Soap, 1966 – 1968.
Two bars with blue bands around them. CMV, $4.00 each bar. $10.00 set.
Clear Skin Lotion, 1966 – 1968.
4 oz. white plastic bottle, red cap. CMV, $1.00 MB.

After Shave for Dry or Sensitive Skin, 1967 – 1975.
2 oz. black, brown, and white tubes, brown or white cap. One has all white letters. CMV, $2.00. One has black over print on white letters. Hard to find. CMV, $4.00.

Oatmeal Soap, 1967 – 1976.
Large bath size and 3 oz. size in brown and white wrappers. OSP, 60¢ each. CMV, $2.00 each.

Tai Winds

Tai Winds Cologne, 1971 – 1979.
5 oz., green glass, blue-green cap and yellow ribbon. CMV, $1.00 MB.
Spray Talc, 1971 – 1976.
7 oz., blue-green and yellow can. CMV, $1.00.
After Shave, 1971 – 1975.
5 oz., clear glass, blue-green cap, yellow ribbon. CMV, $1.50 MB.
Soap on a Rope, 1972 – 1979.
Yellow soap on a rope. CMV, $6.00 MB.

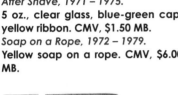

Tai Winds Gift Set, 1971 – 1972.
5 oz. green glass bottle with green cap. Yellow bands, 5 oz. embossed soap. CMV, $15.00 MB.

Tribute

Tribute After Shave Samples, 1963 – 1968.
Box holds 30 foil samples. CMV, $5.00 MB.

Tribute Aerosol Deodorant, 1963 – 1967.
3 oz. blue and silver can and cap. CMV, $6.00 MB. 4 oz. size, same can, 1967 only. CMV, $6.00 MB.

Tribute Cream Hair Dress, 1963 – 1966.
4 oz. blue and silver tube and cap. CMV, $8.00 MB.

Tribute Foam Shave Cream, 1963 – 1966.
6 oz. blue and silver can and cap. Came in regular and mentholated. CMV, $6.00 MB.

Tribute After Shave Lotion, 1963 – 1968.
6 oz., silver and blue cap. CMV, $6.00 mint.

Tribute Talc, 1963 – 1966.
4 oz. blue and silver can, blue cap. CMV, $6.00 mint.

Tribute After Shave After Shower Spray, 1963 – 1966.
5½ oz. blue and silver can and cap. CMV, $6.00 mint.

Tribute Gift Set No. 1, 1963 – 1964.
Blue and silver box holds talc, foam shave cream, and after shave after shower spray. CMV, $35.00 MB.

Tribute Gift Set No. 2, 1963 – 1964.
Blue and silver box holds 6 oz. after shave lotion, talc, and aerosol deodorant. CMV, $35.00 MB.

Tribute All Purpose Cologne, 1967 – 1968.
4 oz., blue and silver top, cap and neck tag. CMV, $12.00 MB. Later issues had no tags. CMV, $6.00 MB.

Tribute Soap, 1963 – 1966.
Single bar in blue box. CMV, $25.00 MB.

Tribute After Shave, 1968 – 1972.
4 oz., blue label, blue and silver cap. Same bottle also reads "After Shave Lotion" on label. CMV, $2.50 mint.

Tribute Cologne for Men, 1964 – 1966.
4 oz., blue and silver top, cap, and neck tag. CMV, $12.00 MB.

Tribute Spray Talc, 1969 – 1972.
7 oz. blue can. CMV, $1.00. Upside down label, rare. CMV, $10.00.

Wild Country ································

Tribute Shave Set, 1964 – 1965.
Blue box holds 6 oz. after shave lotion and can of foam shave cream. CMV, $35.00 MB.

Wild Country Soap on a Rope, 1967 – 1976.
Ivory colored bar with bull's head in center. Round. CMV, $6.00 MB. *Not shown: Soap on a Rope, 1976 – 1978.*
Squared sides, not round. CMV, $4.00 MB.

Wild Country Body Powder, 1967 – 1968.
6 oz. brown and white cardboard box. CMV, $8.00 mint. $12.00 MB.

Tribute Shampoo, 1964 – 1966.
Blue and silver tube. CMV, $5.00 MB. *Tribute Electric Pre-shave Lotion, 1963 – 1966.*
4 oz., blue and silver cap. CMV, $5.00 BO. $8.00 MB.

All Purpose Cologne, 1968 – 1980.
6 oz., silver cap and label. CMV, $1.00 MB.

Tribute Soap Set, 1966 – 1967.
Blue and silver box holds two white bars with blue and silver centers. CMV, $20.00 MB.

Spray Talc, 1969 – 1977.
7 oz. brown can. CMV, $2.00. With special upside down label, CMV, $5.00.

Cologne Spray, 1969 – 1970.
2½ oz. white coated plastic bottle with silver cap. CMV, $4.00 MB.

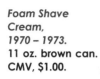

Foam Shave Cream, 1970 – 1973. 11 oz. brown can. CMV, $1.00.

Wild Country Products, 1976 – 1980. Most products for this design period, 25¢ each. Soap, $1.00. Belt Buckle, $3.00.

Travel Set, 1977. Box holds 1½ oz. talc and 3 oz. after shave in plastic bottle with brown cap. CMV, $5.00 MB.

Saddle Kit, 1970 – 1971. Brown and white cowhide kit holds 6 oz. cologne, foam shave cream, and spray talc. CMV, $12.00 MB.

After Shave, 1971 – 1976. 4 oz., silver label and black cap. CMV, $1.00.

Gift Soap, 1977 – 1978. Metal container holds 5 oz. bar of white soap. CMV, $6.00 MB. Also came with label printed upside down on bottom of can. CMV, $8.00.

Talc, 1971 – 1978. 3½ oz. brown shaker top container. CMV, 50¢. Reissued in 1978.

Roll-On Deodorant, 1978. 2 oz. white and brown plastic bottle. CMV, 50¢.

Deodorant, 1975 – 1977. 4 oz. brown and white can, white cap. CMV, 75¢. With upside down label, $8.00.

Protective Hand Cream, 1973 – 1974. 3 oz. brown and white plastic tube with brown cap. CMV, $1.00.

Pendant, 1978. Silver and ivory bull head. Neck chain for men. "Avon" on back. CMV, $4.00 MB.

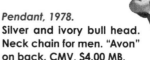

Windjammer

Spray Talc, 1968.
7 oz. blue can. CMV, $3.00 MB. Also came in 4 oz. size. CMV, $4.00 MB.

Cologne, 1968 – 1969.
5 oz. blue glass bottle and cap with ring. Painted label. CMV, $8.00 MB.

Cologne, 1969 – 1972.
5 oz., blue glass and cap with blue paper label. CMV, $3.50 MB.

Soap on a Rope, 1973.
Canadian. CMV, $12.00 MB.

Women's Colognes

All colognes 1975 or newer have little value to collectors. If they are not pictured in this book, we suggest you do not collect them. No new colognes will be added to this book 1984 or newer.

Headache Cologne, 1931 – 1936.
4 oz. ribbed glass bottle with dark blue cap and silver label. CMV, $50.00 BO. $60.00 MB.

Cologne Stick, Christmas Packaging, 1952 only.
Red and white candy striped cardboard, red ribbon top. CMV, $20.00 MB.

Inhalant Cologne, 1936 – 1940.
4 oz. bottle with turquoise cap and label. Turquoise and white box. CMV, $30.00 BO. $35.00 MB.

Cologne Sticks, 1952 – 1956.
Turquoise plastic, came in Golden Promise, Cotillion, Quaintance, Forever Spring, and To a Wild Rose. 1956 only, Nearness and Bright Night came in white plastic of same design. CMV, $10.00 each.

Cologne Stick, Christmas Packaging, 1953 – 1954.
Green and red on white cardboard, pink ribbon on top. CMV, $20.00 MB.

Refreshing Cologne, 1940 – 1941.
4 oz. bottle with turquoise cap and label. Turquoise box. CMV, $30.00 BO. $35.00 MB.

Cologne, 1953 – 1955.
½ oz. size with white cap and painted label. Came in Cupid's Bow, Fragrance Tie Ins, Fragrance Rainbow, and Special Date sets only (see Women's Sets of the 1950s). Came in Forever Spring, Cotillion, Quaintance, To a Wild Rose, and Bright Night. CMV, $10.00 each, mint.

Cologne Sticks, 1956 – 1958.
White plastic with colored caps. Came in Nearness, Bright Night, Cotillion, Quaintance, To a Wild Rose, and Forever Spring. Came in blue, white, and gold paper ornament at Christmas only. CMV, $6.00 stick only. $20.00 in ornament.

Beauty Dust Colognes, 1953 – 1955.
⅝ dram bottles with no labels and flat white or round white caps. Came in Beauty Dust at Christmas only. Each had a silk neck ribbon with gold edge. Quaintance, blue ribbon; To a Wild Rose, pink ribbon; Forever Spring, purple ribbon; Cotillion, pink ribbon; Nearness, pink ribbon; Elégante, red ribbon. CMV, $8.00 BO. $12.00 with ribbon.

Cologne Sticks, 1956 – 1958.
White plastic with colored caps. Gold, white, and red paper ornament package. Christmas only in 1957 – 1958. Came in Nearness, Elégante, Bright Night, To a Wild Rose, Forever Spring, and Cotillion. CMV, $6.00 stick only. $20.00 MB.

Fragrance Cologne, 1956.
3 dram bottle with white painted label and cap. Came in Fragrance Rainbow Set only in Nearness, Cotillion, Bright Night, and To a Wild Rose. CMV, $15.00 mint.

Snowflake Cologne, 1957 – 1958.
⅛ oz., round, white caps. Came in beauty dust only in Cotillion, Forever Spring, To a Wild Rose, Nearness, Elégante, and Bright Night. No labels on bottles. CMV, $9.00 each. Flat top bottle came in all beauty dust at Christmas 1963. CMV, $8.00 each.

Coin Fan Bottles, 1958.
½ oz., clear glass with turquoise caps. Box pink and gold. Came in either cologne or lotion sachet, choice of To a Wild Rose, Cotillion, Nearness, Forever Spring, Bright Night, Elégante, Here's My Heart, or Persian Wood. Came in Wishing Coin Set only (see Women's Sets of the 1950s). CMV, $8.00 each, MB.

Powder Box Cologne, 1956.
¹⁄₁₆ oz. Came in beauty dust only with ribbons attached. In Cotillion, Forever Spring, Golden Promise, To a Wild Rose, and Quaintance. CMV, $11.00 BO. $13.00 with ribbon, mint.

Gems in Crystal Colognes, 1957 only.
½ oz. bottle in two different shapes. Both came with pointed and flat top plastic caps. Each came in To a Wild Rose, Cotillion, Bright Night, and Nearness. Each has matching tops and labels. All came in Gems in Crystal Set only (see Women's Sets of the 1950s). CMV, $15.00, flat top. $18.00, pointed cap.

Flat Top Rocker Cologne, 1959 – 1962.
½ oz., flat plastic cap. Came in Persian Wood, Here's My Heart, Cotillion, To a Wild Rose, Topaze, Somewhere, Régence, Bright Night, and Nearness. CMV, $6.00 MB. Add $2.00 for Nearness and Bright Night.

Bath Classic, 1962 – 1963.
1½ oz., clear glass with gold design and gold cap. Came in Bath Classic Set only (see Women's Sets of the 1960s). Came in Somewhere, Cotillion, Topaze, Here's My Heart, Persian Wood, and To a Wild Rose. CMV, $10.00 BO, mint.

Fan Rocker, 1962 – 1963.
½ oz. cologne, gold cap with neck cord. Came in To a Wild Rose, Here's My Heart, Persian Wood, Cotillion, Somewhere, and Topaze. CMV, $6.00, with cord, MB.

Refreshing Hours Cologne, 1962 – 1963.
2½ oz., gold cap, front side of bottle is flat, trimmed in gold. Came in Somewhere, Topaze, Cotillion, Here's My Heart, Persian Wood, and To a Wild Rose. Came in Refreshing Hours Set only (see Women's Sets of the 1960s). CMV, $8.00 mint.

Heart Shaped Cologne, 1964 – 1966.
½ oz. bottle with gold band on plastic cap. Came in Unforgettable, Rapture, Occur!, Cotillion, Somewhere, Topaze, Here's My Heart, Persian Wood, To a Wild Rose, and Wishing. CMV, $5.00 MB.

Heart Shaped Eau de Cologne (Foreign).
No gold band around plastic cap. CMV, $8.00 MB.

Cologne Silk, 1966 – 1970.
3 oz. frosted glass bottle, gold cap, colored neck labels. Came in Here's My Heart, To a Wild Rose, Somewhere, Topaze, Cotillion, Unforgettable, Rapture, and Occur! CMV, $3.00 MB.

Gold Cap Rocker Cologne, 1967 – 1968.
½ oz., gold round cap. Came in Brocade, Regence, Unforgettable, Rapture, Occur!, Somewhere, Topaze, Cotillion, Here's My Heart, To a Wild Rose, Persian Wood, and Wishing. CMV, $4.00 MB.

Cologne, 1966.
Has embossed leaves in glass, gold cap. Came in Unforgettable, Rapture, Occur!, Somewhere, Topaze, Cotillion, Here's My Heart, To a Wild Rose, or Wishing. Came in red and gold box in Renaissance Trio Set only (see Women's Sets of the 1960s). CMV, $5.00 MB.

Cologne Gems, 1966 – 1969.
1 oz., clear glass with flat plastic top. Came in Cotillion, Rapture, Unforgettable, Somewhere, Occur!, Topaze, Here's My Heart, and To a Wild Rose. CMV, $5.00 MB.

Cologne Classic, 1967 – 1968.
4 oz. spiral bottle with gold cap. Came in Here's My Heart, To a Wild Rose, Somewhere, Topaze, Cotillion, Unforgettable, Rapture, and Occur! CMV, $5.00 MB.

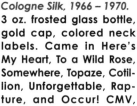

Cologne Riviera, 1968.
4 oz., silver cap and silver on bottle. Unscrew bottom of bottle and reverse metal to make stand for bottle. Came in Brocade and Régence. CMV, $7.00 MB.

Bud Vase Cologne, 1968 – 1969.
4 oz., gold neck trim, colored paper label. Came in Here's My Heart, To a Wild Rose, Somewhere, Topaze, Cotillion, Unforgettable, Rapture, and Occur! CMV, $3.00 MB.

Fragrances Fling Cologne, 1968 – 1969.
½ oz., gold cap. Came in Charisma, Brocade, Régence, Occur!, Unforgettable, Rapture, Somewhere, Topaze, Cotillion, Here's My Heart, To a Wild Rose, Wishing, and Persian Wood. CMV, $4.00 MB.

Dazzling Perfume, 1969 – 1975.
⅛ oz., gold cap. Came in Unforgettable, Rapture, Occur!, Somewhere, Topaze, Cotillion, Here's My Heart, To a Wild Rose, Charisma, Brocade, Régence, Bird of Paradise, Elusive, and Moonwind. CMV, $2.00 MB.

Minuette Cologne, 1969 – 1970.
½ oz., gold cap. Came in Elusive, Charisma, Brocade, Régence, Unforgettable, Rapture, Somewhere, Topaze, Occur!, and Cotillion. CMV, $2.00 MB.

Gift Cologne, 1969.
4 oz., gold cap. Came in Topaze, To a Wild Rose, Somewhere, Here's My Heart, Cotillion, and Rapture. CMV, $5.00 MB.

Minuette Colognes, 1970 – 1971.
5 oz. clear glass cologne bottles with gold caps. Came in Bird of Paradise, Elusive, Charisma, Brocade, Régence, Unforgettable, Rapture, Occur!, Somewhere, Topaze, To a Wild Rose, Cotillion, and Here's My Heart. CMV, $1.00 each, MB.

Demi Cologne, 1973 – 1975.
½ oz., clear glass, gold cap. Came in Imperial Garden, Patchwork, Sonnet, Moonwind, Roses Roses, Field Flowers, Bird of Paradise, Charisma, Unforgettable, Topaze, Occur!, and Here's My Heart. CMV, $1.00 MB.

Fragrance Facets, 1973.
½ oz., gold cap. Came in Brocade and all fragrances. CMV, $2.00 MB.

Be My Valentine Mini Cologne, 1984.
His and hers cologne in two separate half-heart boxes, ½ oz., clear glass, red cap on hers, black on his. Choice of Odyssey, Foxfire, Timeless, Candid, Ariane, Tasha, Pavi Elle, and Soft Musk for her; and Rugger Musk for Men, Black Suede, or Wild Country for him. CMV, $2.00 each, MB.

Cologne Mists and Sprays

All cologne mists and sprays 1975 or newer have little collector value. If they are not pictured in this book, we suggest you do not collect them. No new cologne mists or sprays will be added and all others 1975 or newer are not included.

Essence de Fleurs, 1957 – 1959.
1 oz., black plastic coated, gold and blue lid. Came in Nearness, Elégante, To a Wild Rose, Cotillion, Bright Night, and Forever Spring. CMV, $7.00 MB.
Spray Essence, 1959 – 1966.
1 oz., black plastic coated, gold and blue lid. Came in Cotillion, To a Wild Rose, Bright Night, Nearness, Persian Wood, and Here's My Heart. Also came in Somewhere, 1962 – 1966, and Rapture and Occur! from 1965 to 1966. CMV, $5.00 MB.

Cologne Mist, 1963 – 1966.
Embossed bottles with gold plastic caps, came with black and gold paper label, green and gold cloth type label, or green and white paper label. Held 2 oz. of Occur!, Somewhere, Topaze, Cotillion, Persian Wood, Here's My Heart or To a Wild Rose. CMV, $1.00 each, MB.

Spray Essence, 1967 – 1970.
1¼ oz. All had gold caps. Eight different fragrances with eight different colored bands around necks. Came in Unforgettable, Rapture, Occur!, Somewhere, Topaze, Cotillion, Here's My Heart, and To a Wild Rose. CMV, $4.00 each, MB.

Cologne Mist, 1968 – 1972.
2 oz., gold cap, gold and white band. Came in Here's My Heart, Topaze, To a Wild Rose, Somewhere, Cotillion, Occur!, Roses Roses, and Unforgettable. CMV, $1.00 MB.

Christmas Box, 1965.
Special issue box used by Avon at Xmas 1965 for several different products. Add $4.00 to value of product for this short issue box.

Cologne Special Issue Box, 1968.
Sold with choice of fragrance for a short period. CMV, $2.00 box.

Left: Crystal Glory, 1962– 1964.
Does not say "Spray Essence" on cap. Plastic gold top and base. 1 oz. refillable bottle. Came in Topaze, Somewhere, Cotillion, Here's My Heart, Persian Wood, and To a Wild Rose. CMV, $6.00 MB.
Not shown: Crystal Glory Spray Essence, 1962– 1964.
Gold top and base. Same fragrances as above. CMV, $6.00 MB.
Not shown: Silver Top Crystal Glory Spray Essence, 1962.
Metal on top and base is silver instead of gold. Rare. Same fragrances as above. CMV, $20.00 MB.
Right: Crystal Glory Refill, 1962 – 1964.
1 oz. spray bottle fits inside Crystal Glory bottle. Came in all fragrances above. CMV, $3.00 MB.

Cologne Mist, 1966 – 1968.
2 oz., gold cap with 4A design on cap. Came in Here's My Heart, To a Wild Rose, Somewhere, Topaze, Cotillion, Unforgettable, Rapture, or Occur! CMV, $1.00 each, BO. $2.00 each, MB.

Spray Essence, 1966 – 1967.
1¼ oz., plastic coated glass with gold cap. Came in Here's My Heart, To a Wild Rose, Wishing, Somewhere, Topaze, Cotillion, Rapture, Unforgettable, and Occur! CMV, $2.00 MB.

Cologne Mist, 1969 – 1970.
2 oz., gold cap, frosted glass. Came in Charisma, Brocade, Elusive, and Régence. CMV, $1.00 MB.

Purse Spray Essence, 1970 – 1976.
¼ oz. glass bottle with gold cap in Elusive, Charisma, Brocade, Régence, Unforgettable, Rapture, Occur!, Somewhere, Topaze, Cotillion, Bird of Paradise, or Hana Gasa. CMV, $1.00 MB.

Decorator Cologne Mist, 1972.
4 oz. plastic coated bottle in color to match fragrance. Long gold cap with top matching fragrance color. Came in Moonwind (deep blue), Charisma (crimson red), Bird of Paradise (pale blue), and Field Flowers (spring green). CMV, $3.00 each, MB.

Spray Essence, 1969 – 1971.
1¼ oz., gold cap, ribbed glass. Came in Charisma, Brocade, and Régence. CMV, $1.00 MB.

Cologne Mist, 1971 – 1975.
2 oz., silver top. Came in Bird of Paradise, Hana Gasa, Elusive, Charisma, Brocade, and Régence. CMV, $1.00 MB.

Cologne Mist Special Issue Box, 1974.
Sold with choice of fragrance for a short period. CMV, $2.00 box.

Cologne Special Issue Box, 1969.
Sold with choice of fragrance for a short period. CMV, $2.00 box.

Cologne Mist Special Issue Box, 1971.
Sold with choice of fragrance for a short period. CMV, $2.00 box.

Cologne Mist Special Issue Boxes.
Each came in choice of fragrance and was sold for a short period.
Left: Cologne Mist, 1975.
Inside left: Cologne Mist, 1975.
Inside right: Cologne Mist, 1976.
Right: Ultra Cologne Spray, 1978.
Add $3.00 to CMV of each bottle for each box shown.

Cream Sachets

Cream sachets 1975 or newer are not included in this book, and no new ones will be added due to little collector interest.

Cream Sachet Petites, 1956.
Plastic cream sachet came in Cotillion, Bright Night, Nearness, and To a Wild Rose. Came in Cream Sachet Petites Set only (see Women's Sets of the 1950s). Four different colors. CMV, $10.00 each, MB.

Cream Sachet, 1957.
White jar with green, yellow, or pink lid. Came in Cotillion, To a Wild Rose, Bright Night, or Nearness. Came in Over the Rainbow Set only (see Women's Sets of the 1950s). CMV, $8.00.

Cream Sachet Decor, 1960.
Ribbed clear plastic with removable bottom sold for 50¢ at Christmas with purchase of cream sachet in Bright Night, Nearness, Cotillion, To a Wild Rose, Persian Wood, or Here's My Heart. CMV, $8.00 holder only. $12.00 MB.

Magnolia Cream Sachet, 1974 – 1976.
Left: 2/3 oz., clear embossed glass with white lid and pink and yellow on flower. CMV, $1.00 MB.
Magnolia Demi Stick, 1974 – 1977.
Inside left: 3/16 oz., white with floral colored center. CMV, $1.00 MB.
Hyacinth Demi Stick, 1974– 1977.
Right: 3/16 oz., white with pink flowers. CMV, $1.00 MB.

Christmas Box, 1957.
Special issue at Christmas. Pink and white, came in choice of Cotillion, Forever Spring, Bright Night, To a Wild Rose, or Elégante. See bottle in each fragrance line and add $6.00 for this box.

Scentiments Cream Sachet, 1969.
½ oz. clear glass jar, gold lid, 4A design on lid. Came in Scentiments Set only (see Women's Sets of the 1960s) in Unforgettable, Rapture, Occur!, Somewhere, Topaze, or Cotillion. CMV, $4.00 BO.

Boxes.
Special short issue boxes came with cream sachets in several fragrances.
Left to right: 1956, 1964, 1958, 1954.
CMV, see bottle in each fragrance line and add $5.00 each for these boxes.

Cream Sachet Jars, 1973 – 1975.
Clear ribbed glass jars with colored borders on lid and colored flowers to match fragrances. 2/3 oz. Came in Gardenia, Violet, or Carnation. CMV, $1.00 each.

Christmas Box, 1958.
Special issue box came with choice of cream sachet in To A Wild Rose, Cotillion, Forever Spring, Nearness, Bright Night, or Elégante. CMV, see jar in each fragrance line and add $5.00 for this box.

Powder Sachets

Powder Sachet, 1930 – 1932.
Clear glass bottle with brass cap and silver and blue label. Came in Ariel and Jardin d'Amour. CMV, $60.00 mint.

Powder Sachet, 1934 – 1936.
1¼ oz. ribbed glass bottle with dark blue cap and silver and blue label. Came in Jardin d'Amour and Ariel. CMV, $28.00 each, BO, mint. $33.00 each, MB.

Powder Sachet, 1936 – 1938.
1¼ or 2 oz., ribbed glass with turquoise cap and label. Came in Ariel 1936 – 1938; Cotillion 1937 – 1938; Marionette 1938 only; Jardin d'Amour 1936 – 1938; or Jardin sachet. All prices are mint only. CMV, $20.00 each, BO. $25.00 each, MB.

Powder Sachet, 1939 – 1948.
1¼ oz. glass bottle with turquoise cap and label. Came in Jardin d'Amour 1939 – 1940; Ariel 1939 – 1942; Cotillion 1939 – 1946; Garden of Love, turquoise or black cap, 1940 – 1946; Attention 1942 – 1948; or Marionette 1939 – 1946. CMV, $10.00 each, BO. $15.00 each, MB.

Powder Sachet, 1944 – 1945.
1¼ oz. pink paper sachet box. Came in Attention, Garden of Love, Cotillion, or Marionette. Pink plastic flower on lid. CMV, $15.00 each, CO. $22.00 each, MB.

Christmas Box, 1952 only.
Special issue red and green box for all powder sachets at Christmas. Came in Cotillion, Golden Promise, Quaintance, and Flowertime. CMV, see bottle in each fragrance line and add $7.00 for this box.

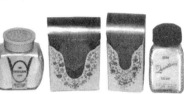

Valentine Gift Sachet, 1952.
Short issue box in red and white. Came in Flowertime, Golden Promise, Cotillion, and Quaintance. Cotillion came in same design, different shaped box. CMV, see bottle in each fragrance line and add $8.00 for this box.

Christmas Box, 1956.
Special issue Christmas box came with choice of six fragrances. Add $5.00 to CMV of bottle for this box.

Christmas Box, 1957.
Pyramid shaped box in pink, green, blue, and white. Came in To a Wild Rose, Forever Spring, Cotillion, Nearness, Bright Night, and Elégante powder sachet. Short issue, rare. See bottle in each fragrance line and add $8.00 for this box, mint.

Christmas Box, 1958.
Special issue pink and white box came with powder sachet in choice of To a Wild Rose, Cotillion, Forever Spring, Nearness, Bright Night, or Elégante. See jars in each fragrance line for CMV and add $5.00 for this box.

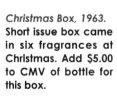

Christmas Box, 1963.
Short issue box came in six fragrances at Christmas. Add $5.00 to CMV of bottle for this box.

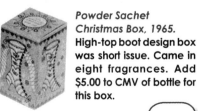

Powder Sachet Christmas Box, 1965.
High-top boot design box was short issue. Came in eight fragrances. Add $5.00 to CMV of bottle for this box.

Crown Top Powder Sachet, 1965 – 1966.
⁹/₁₀ oz. frosted bottle with gold cap. Came in Perfume Pillowette Set in Rapture, Wishing, Occur!, Lavender, Somewhere, Topaze, Cotillion, Here's My Heart, or To a Wild Rose. CMV, $8.00 MB.

Powder Sachet, 1969 – 1970.
1½ oz., painted red over clear glass, red neck bow with silver lid. Came in Cotillion, Charisma, Unforgettable, and To a Wild Rose. CMV, $7.00 MB.

Powder Sachet, 1970 – 1971.
Crystal-like glass bottle holds 1¼ oz. of powder sachet in Elusive, Charisma, Unforgettable, or Topaze. CMV, $6.00 MB.

Turn-of-Century Powder Sachet Shaker, 1973 – 1975.
1¼ oz., clear glass with solid gold cap. Came in Roses Roses, Charisma, or Unforgettable. CMV, $5.00 MB.

Powder Sachet Shaker, 1972 – 1973.
3½" high, 1¼ oz. white glass jar with gold cap. Came in Moonwind, Bird of Paradise, Unforgettable, or Field Flowers. CMV, $5.00 MB.

Perfumed Talcs

All talcs 1960 or newer have little value to collectors. If it is not in this book, we suggest you don't collect it unless you know it is 35 years old or older.

Christmas Box, 1958.
Special issue Christmas box for perfumed talc in choice of To a Wild Rose, Cotillion, Nearness, or Forever Spring. Check fragrance line for CMV on talc and add $7.00 for this box.

Christmas Box, 1959.
Short issue box in choice of six fragrances of talc. Add $7.00 CMV for this box to price of talc, MB.

Floral Perfumed Talc, 1959 – 1960.
Lavender and white can. Matching box. CMV, $7.00 MB.

Special Issue Christmas Boxes.
Left to right: 1966, 1967, 1969, 1970. Each came in choice of talc. Add $2.00 each box to CMV of the talc it holds.

1933 – 1934.
2 oz. ribbed bottle came in Trailing Arbutus, Vernafleur, Lily of the Valley, White Rose, or Lilac Vegetal. Black or blue cap. CMV, $50.00 BO, mint. $60.00 MB.

1935 – 1940.
2 oz., gold cap with "A" on top of cap. Blue and gold tulip label. "CPC" on back of label. Came in Cotillion, Vernafleur, Lily of the Valley, White Rose, Lilac, Trailing Arbutus, Marionette, and Lilac Vegetal. CMV, $35.00 BO, mint. $45.00 MB.

1940 only.
2 oz., plastic caps, blue and gold label with tulip. Came in Cotillion, Vernafleur, Lily of the Valley, White Rose, Lilac, Trailing Arbutus, Marionette, and Lilac Vegetal. CMV, $35.00 BO, mint. $45.00 MB.

1940 – 1946.
2 oz., gold ribbed cap and gold label. Also came with plastic cap. Came in Cotillion, Jasmine, Marionette, Lilac, Lily of the Valley, Trailing Arbutus, Apple Blossom, Sonnet, and Attention. CMV, $30.00 BO, mint. $40.00 MB.

Perfumes

All must be in new mint condition for CMV.

Gift Atomizer Perfume, 1931 – 1934.
1 oz. red glass bottle with screw-on metal top and white squeeze bulb. Came in Atomizer Set No. 6 only (see Women's Sets of the 1930s). Does not say Avon or CPC. Also comes in green glass. CMV, $45.00.

391 Perfume Flaconette, 1931 – 1933.
Small embossed bottle with glass stopper with long dabber. Brass cap with "391" on it. CMV, $85.00 BO. $95.00 MB.

Perfumes, 1933 – 1936.
Small six-sided bottles with silver label, and black caps. Came in Ariel, Bolero, Gardenia, Trailing Arbutus, 391, or Vernafleur. Came in Little Folks sets (see Little Folks Sets section) and Handkerchief Set (see Women's Sets of the 1930s). CMV, $45.00 each, mint.

391 Perfume, 1931 – 1933.
Silver and blue box holds 1 oz. bottle, glass stopper. Blue ribbon on neck. CMV, $125.00 BO. $150.00 MB.

391 Perfume, 1933 – 1936.
½ oz. ribbed glass bottle with black octagonal cap. Came in Gold Box sets (see Gold Box Sets section). CMV, $45.00 mint.

Ribbed Perfume, 1933 – 1936
½ oz. ribbed glass bottle with black octagonal cap and gold label. Came in Gold Box Set in Bolero, 391, Gardenia, Ariel, and Vernafleur (see Gold Box Sets section). CMV, $45.00 mint.

Tulip Perfume, 1934 – 1939.
7 dram glass stopper bottle, gold label with tulip. Came in Jardin d'Amour, Bolero, Cotillion, Ariel, Narcissus, Rose, Lily of the Valley, Trailing Arbutus, Gardenia, Sweet Pea, Marionette, Topaze, Courtship, or Lucy Hays. CMV, $100.00 BO. $125.00 MB.

Tulip Perfume, 1934 – 1939.
¼ oz. or 2 dram, gold cap and label with tulip. "CPC" on back of label and "Avon" on bottom of bottle. Came with two different labels as shown. Came in Jardin d'Amour, Bolero, Cotillion, Ariel, Narcissus, Rose, Lily of the Valley, Trailing Arbutus, Gardenia, Sweet Pea, Marionette, Courtship, Lucy Hays, and Topaze. CMV, $55.00 BO, mint. $65.00 MB.

Perfume, 1937 – 1946.
⅛ oz. bottle on right has flower on label with three branches on each side. Came in sets only in Gardenia, Cotillion, Narcissus, Trailing Arbutus, or Sweet Pea. CMV, $15.00 each. White, blue, red, green, or yellow plastic caps. 2 dram size or ¼ oz. on left came in 1939 – 1940 Gold Box Sets and Little Folks Sets in same fragrances and caps. CMV, $25.00 each.

Floral Perfume, 1940 – 1942.
⅜ oz., gold cap and label in gold speckled box. Came in Sweet Pea, Gardenia, Trailing Arbutus, or Lily of the Valley. CMV, $50.00 BO, mint. $80.00 MB.

Tulip Perfume, 1934 – 1939.
¼ oz., glass stopper, gold label with tulip. Came in Lucy Hays, Topaze, Jardin d'Amour, Bolero, Cotillion, Ariel, Narcissus, Rose, Lily of the Valley, Trailing Arbutus, Gardenia, Sweet Pea, Marionette, or Courtship. CMV, $75.00 BO. $90.00 MB.

Perfume, 1940 – 1942.
1 dram or ⅛ oz., gold cap and label. Came in Cotillion, Ballad, Gardenia, Garden of Love, Apple Blossom, Marionette, Trailing Arbutus, Lily of the Valley, or Sweet Pea. CMV, $25.00 BO, mint. $35.00 MB.

Perfume, 1940 – 1944.
⅛ oz., gold metal or plastic caps and gold labels. Came in Garden of Love, Gardenia, Marionette, Sweet Pea, Lily of the Valley, Trailing Arbutus, Ballad, Courtship, Apple Blossom, or Cotillion. CMV, $25.00 BO, mint. $30.00 MB.

Tulip Perfume, 1934 – 1939.
7 dram glass stopper, gold label with tulip. Came in Lucy Hays, Topaze, Jardin d'Amour, Bolero, Cotillion, Ariel, Narcissus, Rose, Lily of the Valley, Trailing Arbutus, Gardenia, Sweet Pea, Marionette, and Courtship. CMV, $100.00 BO, mint. $125.00 MB.

Bouquet Perfumes, 1940 – 1944.
3 dram, glass stopper, box has gold base and orange lid. Came in Garden of Love, Apple Blossom, Marionette, Courtship, or Cotillion. Gold neck tag. CMV, $100.00 BO, mint. $135.00 MB.

Valentine's Day Perfume, 1941.
1/8 oz. clear glass bottle with gold cap with Ballad perfume, red and white box. Came in several fragrances. CMV, $75.00 MB.

Bouquet Perfumes, 1944 only.
Blue and pink box holds 3 dram perfume, glass stopper. Came in Marionette, Cotillion, or Garden of Love. Gold neck tags. CMV, $100.00 with tag, BO. $140.00 MB.

Perfume, 1946 – 1953.
1/8 oz., flower on label, plastic cap. Came in Trailing Arbutus, Cotillion, Crimson Carnation, Quaintance, Lily of the Valley, or Sweet Pea. Came in Fair Lady, Your Charms, and Hairribbons sets (See Women's Sets of the 1940s). CMV, $15.00 each. Crimson Carnation and Sweet Pea, CMV, $25.00 mint. Same label came out on 5/8 dram size, "smaller bottle" but has no size on label. Same CMV.

Perfumes, 1941 – 1945.
1/8 oz., two different flat gold caps and also plastic caps. White paper label. Came in Courtship, Sweet Pea, Lily of the Valley, Trailing Arbutus, Marionette, American Ideal, Apple Blossom, Cotillion, Ballad, Gardenia, or Garden of Love. CMV, $30.00 BO, mint. $40.00 MB.

Bouquet Perfumes, 1945 – 1947.
Blue, pink, and white box holds 3 dram glass stopper bottle with gold neck tag. Came in Cotillion, Courtship, or Garden of Love. CMV, $100.00 with tag, BO. $125.00 MB.

Floral Perfumes, 1946 –1947.
Blue and white box holds 3 dram bottle with plastic cap. Came in Crimson Carnation, Gardenia, or Lily of the Valley. CMV, $45.00 BO. $75.00 MB. Crimson Carnation, CMV, $60.00 BO. $100.00 MB.

Perfume, 1941 – 1946.
1/8 oz., white paper label, gold metal caps and plastic caps. Came in Gardenia, Sweet Pea, Courtship, Apple Blossom, Cotillion, Trailing Arbutus, Lily of the Valley, Garden of Love, or Marionette. CMV, $25.00 BO. $30.00 MB.

Perfume, 1946 – 1950.
1/8 oz., clear glass, gold cap, painted label. Available in Crimson Carnation, Lily of the Valley, Gardenia, Cotillion, Golden Promise, Garden of Love, Ballad, Quaintance, or Flowertime. CMV, $20.00 BO. $25.00 MB.

Perfume, 1946 only.
1/8 oz., plastic cap. Came in Gardenia, Cotillion, Garden of Love, Lily of the Valley, Trailing Arbutus, or Sweet Pea. CMV, $25.00 each, BO. $30.00 each, MB.

Floral Perfumes, 1944 – 1945.
3 dram, gold caps and labels. Came in yellow feather design box in Trailing Arbutus, Cotillion, Gardenia, Sweet Pea, Lily of the Valley, or Marionette. Two different boxes. CMV, $45.00 each, BO, mint with tag. $90.00 each, MB.

Perfume,
1946 – 1950.
1/8 oz. or 1 dram, gold box, gold label. Some have metal gold caps. Came in Crimson Carnation, Lily of the Valley, Gardenia, Cotillion, Golden Promise, Garden of Love, Ballad, Quaintance, or Flowertime. CMV, $20.00. Crimson Carnation, $30.00. Add $7.00 each MB. Also came in Gold Box Set of 1947 – 1949 (See Gold Box Sets section).

Perfumes, 1950.
5/8 dram each. Quaintance, Cotillion, Golden Promise, or Luscious. Green, blue, pink, or yellow caps. Came in Avon Blossoms Set (see Women's Sets of the 1950s). CMV, $12.00 each, mint.

Perfumes (for size comparison only.)
Left to right: 2 dram or 1/4 oz.; 1/8 oz. or 1 dram; 5/8 dram; 5/8 dram.

Perfumes, 1950 – 1955.
1 dram ribbed bottles with gold caps came in Cotillion, Quaintance, Ballad, Golden Promise, Gardenia, Lily of the Valley, Forever Spring, and To a Wild Rose. CMV, $8.00 BO. $12.00 MB.

Perfumes, 1951 – 1953.
5/8 dram bottles with pink, yellow, green, or blue caps came in Cotillion, Quaintance, Forever Spring, Golden Promise, Luscious, or Lily of the Valley. Came in 1952 – 1953 House of Charms Set, 1951 Always Sweet Set, and Sweet As Honey Beehive Set (see Women's Sets of the 1950s). CMV, $12.00 each, mint.

With Love Perfumes, 1951 – 1952.
Pink heart box opens to 1 dram ribbed bottle and cap in Lily of the Valley, To a Wild Rose, Luscious, Quaintance, Golden Promise, Cotillion, Ballad, Flowertime, or Gardenia. CMV, $25.00 MB as shown.

Christmas Bell Perfume, 1951.
Gold bell box holds 1 dram, ribbed bottle and cap in Forever Spring, To a Wild Rose, Luscious, Cotillion, Flowertime, Quaintance, Golden Promise, Ballad, Gardenia, and Lily of the Valley. CMV, $25.00 MB as shown.

Perfume, 1951 – 1953.
1 dram vertical ribbed bottle and ribbed gold cap with scroll on cap. Came in Cotillion, Golden Promise, Quaintance, To a Wild Rose, or Forever Spring. CMV, $8.00 MB.

Valentine Perfumes, 1953.
1 dram, came in To a Wild Rose, Forever Spring, Cotillion, Golden Promise, or Quaintance. CMV, $25.00 MB as shown.

Perfume, 1953 – 1954.
Green and pink fold-out box holds 1 dram ribbed glass bottle with gold scroll cap. Came in To a Wild Rose, Cotillion, Forever Spring, Quaintance, Golden Promise, Luscious, or Ballad. CMV, $25.00 MB as shown.

Perfume, 1954 only.
5/8 dram, came in 1954 House of Charms Set only (see Women's Sets of the 1950s). Blue caps, pink, blue, and white labels. Came in Cotillion, Quaintance, To a Wild Rose, Golden Promise, Lily of the Valley. Rare. CMV, $22.00 each.

Perfumes, 1955 – 1959.
1 dram, clear smooth glass, gold scroll cap with felt like wrapper. Nearness, gray; Bright Night, black; Elégante, maroon; To a Wild Rose, pink; Forever Spring, green; or Cotillion, gold. Simulated grain leather, Luscious, First issue, 1950, tan; Here's My Heart, blue. CMV, $10.00 each, mint in wrapper. $5.00 BO. $12.00 MB.

Christmas Perfume, 1955.
1 dram, gold cap in red, white, blue, and gold Christmas box. Came in To a Wild Rose, Cotillion, Forever Spring, Golden Promise, Luscious, or Quaintance. CMV, $25.00 MB.

Top Style Perfume, 1959 – 1962.
Shown with general issue box. 1 dram, gold cap. Came in Topaze, Persian Wood, Here's My Heart, To a Wild Rose, Cotillion, Bright Night, or Nearness. CMV, $5.00 MB.

Perfume Gold Box, 1964 – 1965.
1 dram, 4A embossed gold box. Ribbed bottle, gold cap. Came in Somewhere, Topaze, Cotillion, Here's My Heart, Persian Wood, Occur!, To a Wild Rose, Wishing, Rapture, or Unforgettable. On left, same bottle sold in regular issue box, 1962 – 1966. CMV, $6.00 in gold box MB. 1965 Christmas special issue box on right. CMV, $8.00 MB, CMV, $3.00 regular issue box MB.

Top Style Christmas Perfume, 1959 – 1960.
Sold only at Christmas time in box shown. Came in all regular fragrances of Top Style perfume. CMV, $17.00 MB in this box only.

Gift Perfume, 1958.
1 dram smooth clear glass bottle, cap either smooth or embossed. Box is blue, white, and gold. Choice of Elégante, Nearness, Bright Night, Forever Spring, To a Wild Rose, or Cotillion. CMV, $5.00 BO. $20.00 MB as shown.

Golden Gift Perfume, 1961.
Blue, gold, and green box holds 1 dram top style perfume. Came in Cotillion, To a Wild Rose, Nearness, Bright Night, Somewhere, Here's My Heart, Persian Wood, or Topaze. CMV, $13.00 MB.

Perfume Rollettes, 1965 – 1969.
⅓ oz. glass bottles available in Somewhere, Topaze, Cotillion, Here's My Heart, To a Wild Rose, Wishing, Régence, Occur!, Rapture, Unforgettable, Brocade, or Persian Wood. Issued in carnival glass or clear ribbed glass. CMV, $2.00 clear MB. CMV, $6.00 carnival MB. Box pictured is 1966 Christmas box. Add $2.00 extra for this box.

Heart Perfume, 1963 – 1971.
1 oz., gold box, 4A insignia on glass stopper. Gold neck tag. Came in Unforgettable, Occur!, Somewhere, Topaze, Cotillion, Here's My Heart, Persian Wood, Rapture, or To a Wild Rose. CMV, $25.00 BO. $45.00 MB.

Rocker Perfume, 1959 – 1963.
White box holds 1 oz. bottle with flat glass stopper with 4A on top. Gold cord crisscrossed bottle with white tag label. Came in Here's My Heart, Persian Wood, To a Wild Rose, Bright Night, Nearness, or Cotillion. CMV, $25.00 BO, with mint tag. $35.00 MB.

Perfume Creme Rollette, 1963 – 1965.
4A embossed bottles with gold caps. Came in Here's My Heart, Persian Wood, To a Wild Rose, Cotillion, Somewhere, Topaze, Wishing, Occur!, or Rapture. CMV, $3.00 MB.

Perfume, 1966 – 1969.
½ oz., gold cap, metal leaves around base. White and gold box. Came in Unforgettable, Rapture, Occur!, Somewhere, Topaze, Cotillion, Here's My Heart, To a Wild Rose, or Wishing. CMV, $18.00 MB.

Perfume Flacon, 1966 – 1967.
1 dram, gold ribbed cap, ribbed glass. Came in Here's My Heart, Wishing, To a Wild Rose, Somewhere, Topaze, Cotillion, Unforgettable, Régence, Rapture, and Occur! CMV, $4.00 MB.

Perfume, 1969 – 1972.
½ oz., pink box holds jewel-like clear glass bottle, 4" high. Came in Elusive, Charisma, Brocade, Régence, Unforgettable, Rapture, Occur!, Somewhere, Topaze, or Cotillion. CMV, $13.00 MB.

Perfume, 1971.
½ oz. bottle with clear plastic top in a pink and gold box. Came in Somewhere, Topaze, Cotillion, Unforgettable, Rapture, Occur!, Régence, Brocade, Charisma, and Elusive. CMV, $16.00 MB.

Perfume Pendant, 1970.
Gold pendant with ruby teardrop, holds 1 dram liquid perfume. Came in Charisma, Elusive, Brocade, and Régence. CMV, $10.00 pendant only, mint. $15.00 MB.

Golden Moments Pendant Perfume, 1971 – 1972.
Antique brass pendant on 32" gold chain. Holds ⅛ oz. perfume in Moonwind, Bird of Paradise, Elusive, or Charisma. CMV, $10.00 pendant on chain, mint. $16.00 MB.

Scentiment Perfume Rollette, 1973 – 1974.
⅓ oz., white base with blue bird and pink flowers, gold trim and cap. Holds Moonwind, Patchwork, or Sonnet. CMV, $4.00 MB.

Scentiment Purse Spray Essence, 1974.
¼ oz., blue plastic coated bottom, white and pink bird design on paper label with gold cap. Came in Field Flowers, Bird of Paradise, or Charisma. CMV, $6.00 MB.

Ultra Perfume, 1984.
Gold box holds ⅗ oz. perfume, glass stopper. CMV, $4.00 MB.

Heart Strings Perfume Flacon, 1986
²⁄₁₁ oz., gold cap. CMV, $2.00 MB.

Perfume Pendant, 1972 – 1975.
Gold with two simulated half pearls, 32" chain. Came in Sonnet or Moonwind perfume. CMV, $5.00 pendant only. $10.00 MB.

Perfume Oils

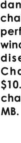

Jewel Perfume Oil, 1964 – 1965.
⅝ dram, gold cap. Came in Jewel Collection Set only (see Women's Sets of the 1960s). Came in Cotillion, Topaze, Persian Wood, Here's My Heart, or To a Wild Rose. CMV, $6.00 each, mint.

Bullet Perfume Oil, 1965.
⅝ dram, gold top. Came in Wishing, Somewhere, Occur!, Rapture, To a Wild Rose, Topaze, Unforgettable, Here's My Heart, or Cotillion. Came in Fragrance Ornaments Set only (see Women's Sets of the 1960s). CMV, $4.00 BO. $8.00 with holder.

Perfume Oil Petites (Pin Cushion), 1966.
⅝ dram, clear bottle, gold cap and label. Came in Perfume Oil Petites Pin Cushion Set only (See Women's Sets of the 1960s). Came in Somewhere, Wishing, Occur!, Rapture, Topaze, To a Wild Rose, Here's My Heart, Unforgettable, or Cotillion. CMV, $5.00 each, mint.

Perfume Oil, 1969 – 1973.
½ oz., gold cap. Came in Elusive, Rapture, Hana Gasa, Charisma, Brocade, Moonwind, Régence, Bird of Paradise, Unforgettable, or Occur! CMV, $3.00 MB.

Avon Bottles

Miscellaneous Avon bottles are very high production items and most collectors are no longer interested in them unless they are very old (1950s or older). We have removed all plastic bottles and most bottles back to the 1950s or newer from this book. They have little or no value to most collectors. All plastic Skin So Soft bottles have been dropped from this book because of no value to collectors. Boxes are very important to most collectors, and become more valuable with age 35 to 40 years old and older.

Rose Water, Glycerine and Benzoin, 1926.
4 oz. ribbed bottle with cork stopper, front and neck label. CMV, $60.00 BO. $75.00 MB. See CPC bottles section for different label.

Bath Salts, 1929 – 1930.
10 oz. bottle with metal lid, silver and blue label, ribbed glass sides. CMV, $60.00 BO. $75.00 MB.

Astringent, 1930 – 1936.
Came in 2 oz. and 4 oz. sizes. Both are ribbed glass bottles with dark blue caps and silver and blue labels. CMV, $35.00 each, BO. $40.00 each, MB.

Rose Water, Glycerine and Benzoin, 1930 – 1936.
4 oz. ribbed glass bottle, blue cap. CMV, $40.00 BO. $45.00 MB. Regular issue box in center. Add $5.00 for 1935 special issue Christmas box shown on right.

Liquid Powder, 1930 – 1936.
4 oz. ribbed glass bottle with dark blue cap, silver and blue label. CMV, $35.00 BO. $40.00 MB.

Lotus Cream, 1930.
4 oz. ribbed glass. Rare with flowered label. CMV, $50.00 BO. $60.00 MB.

Skin Freshener, 1930 – 1936.
2 or 4 oz. ribbed glass, blue or black cap. 2 oz. size came in sets only. CMV, $40.00 each, BO. $45.00 each, MB.

Lotus Cream, 1930 – 1936.
4 oz. ribbed glass bottle, blue cap. CMV, $35.00 BO. $40.00 MB.

Bath Salts, 1931 – 1933.
10 oz. ribbed glass bottle with blue lid, silver label. Two different labels. CMV, $40.00 BO. $60.00 MB.

Deodorant, 1931 – 1936.
2 oz. ribbed glass bottle with silver label and dark blue cap. CMV, $35.00 BO. $40.00 MB.

Hair Tonic Eau de Quinine for Oily Hair, 1931 – 1936.
1 pint. Silver metal cap. (For dry hair, same price and date). CMV, $40.00 BO. $45.00 MB.

Liquid Shampoo, 1930 – 1936.
1 pint, metal cap. CMV, $35.00 BO. $40.00 MB.

Hair Tonic Eau de Quinine, 1931 – 1936.
6 oz. ribbed glass bottle with dark blue cap with silver and blue label. Came in tonic for dry hair and for oily hair. CMV, $35.00 BO. $40.00 MB.

Wave Set, 1930 – 1936.
4 oz. ribbed glass bottle with dark blue cap, silver and blue label. CMV, $35.00 BO. $40.00 MB.

Liquid Shampoo, 1931 – 1936.
6 oz. ribbed glass bottle with dark blue cap and silver and blue label. CMV, $35.00 BO. $40.00 MB.

Brilliantine, 1931 – 1936.
2 oz. ribbed glass bottle with dark blue cap and silver and blue label. CMV, $40.00 BO mint. $45.00 MB.

Pre-Shampoo Oil, 1931 – 1936.
2 oz. ribbed glass bottle with dark blue cap, silver and blue label. CMV, $35.00 BO. $40.00 MB.

Witch Hazel, 1930 – 1936.
4 oz. ribbed glass bottle with dark blue plastic cap, green label. Also came in 8 and 16 oz. sizes. CMV, $40.00 BO. $45.00 MB.

Nail Polish, 1931 – 1936.
Ribbed glass bottle with black octagonal cap. Gray and blue box. CMV, $30.00 MB.

Bath Salts, 1933 – 1937.
8½ oz. ribbed glass jar with dark blue cap. Came in Ariel or Vernafleur from 1933 – 1937, Pine or Jasmine from 1935 – 1937. CMV, $40.00 BO. $60.00 MB.

Pre-shampoo Oil, 1936 – 1938.
2 oz. bottle with turquoise cap and label. CMV, $18.00 BO. $22.00 MB. Add $5.00 for CPC label on bottle in box.

Polish Remover and Cuticle Softener, 1931– 1936.
Both ½ oz., ribbed glass, black eight-sided caps. Silver labels. CMV, $25.00 each, BO. $30.00 MB.

Antiseptic, 1936 – 1940.
6 oz., metal cap. Turquoise box and label. CMV, $30.00 mint, BO. $35.00 MB.

Lotus Cream, 1936 – 1944.
4 oz., clear glass, green cap. CMV, $12.00 BO. $17.00 MB. Add $5.00 for CPC label on bottle in box. Came with two different labels and two different boxes.

Antiseptic, 1932 – 1936.
Metal cap, green label. 6 oz. size. CMV, $30.00 BO. $35.00 MB. Also came in 12 oz. size with same label. CMV, $35.00 BO. $40.00 MB.

Astringent, 1936 – 1954.
2 oz. and 4 oz. size with turquoise caps. CMV, $10.00 BO each, mint. $15.00 each, MB. Add $5.00 for CPC label.

Bath Salts Sample, 1933 – 1937.
Ribbed glass bottle with blue cap. Came in Ariel or Vernafleur. CMV, $60.00. Pine and Jasmine, CMV, $55.00 each.

Liquid Powder, Rachel or Peach, 1936 – 1941.
4 oz., green cap, clear glass. CMV, $15.00 BO. $20.00 MB. Add $5.00 for CPC label on box.

Bath Salts, 1936.
8½ – 9 oz. glass jars with turquoise lids from 1936 – 1944, small paper label. 9 oz. jars from 1943 – 1953 came in Ariel, 1936 – 1944, Pine 1936 – 1944 then 1946 – 1953, Vernafleur 1936 – 1944, Attention 1936 – 1944, and Jasmine 1936 – 1944 then 1946 – 1948. CMV $20.00 BO. $30.00 MB.

Witch Hazel, 1936 – 1948.
4 oz., green cap and label. Also came with black cap. CMV, $15.00 BO. $20.00 MB. Add $5.00 for CPC label on bottle in box. (Also came in 8 and 16 oz. sizes).

Polish Remover, 1936 – 1940.
Has *Good House-keeping* seal on turquoise and gold label. Black cap. CMV, $15.00 BO. $20.00 MB.

Skin Freshener, 1936 – 1954.
Left to right: 2 and 4 oz. bottles. Both 4 oz. bottles have two different labels. Turquoise caps. CMV, $5.00 BO. $10.00 MB.

Deodorant, 1936 – 1948.
2 oz., turquoise cap and label. CMV, $14.00 BO. $20.00 MB. Add $5.00 for CPC label on bottle in box. 1946 – 1948 came with black applicator with sponge end. CMV, $20.00 BO. $25.00 MB.

Polish Remover, 1936 – 1939.
½ oz. bottle, turquoise cap. CPC on label. CMV, $15.00 BO. $20.00 MB.

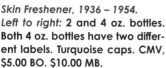

Brilliantine, 1936 – 1954.
2 oz., green cap and label, three different labels. CMV, $15.00 BO. $20.00 MB. Add $5.00 for CPC label.

Cuticle Softener, 1936 – 1939.
1⅛ oz. bottle with turquoise cap. CPC on label. CMV, $15.00 BO. $20.00 MB.

Liquid Shampoo, 1937 – 1950.
6 oz., turquoise cap. Indented top of bottle. CMV, $15.00 BO. $20.00 MB. Add $5.00 for CPC label on bottle in box.

Wave Set, 1936 – 1944.
4 oz. bottle with turquoise cap and label. CMV, $15.00 BO. $20.00 MB. Add $5.00 for CPC label on bottle in box.

Nail Polish, 1936 – 1937.
Clear glass with turquoise cap. CPC label. CMV, $15.00 BO. $20.00 MB.

Rose Water, Glycerine and Benzoin, 1936 – 1944.
4 oz. bottle with turquoise cap. CMV, $12.00 BO. $17.00 MB. Add $5.00 for CPC label on bottle in box.

Liquid Shampoo, 1937 – 1950.
1 pint size with raised pouring or flat metal or black cap. CMV, $20.00 BO. $25.00 MB. 1937 – 1939 has CPC label, $30.00.

Insect Repellent "Allied Products," 1941. 2 oz. clear bottle. Allied Products was war-time division of Avon Products. CMV, $30.00.

Liquid Shampoo, 1943 – 1945. 6 oz. round shoulder bottle, black cap. This bottle is rare with round shoulders. CMV, $30.00 BO. $35.00 MB.

Finishing Lotion, 1938 – 1950. 2 oz. clear glass bottle. CMV, $12.00 BO. $17.00 MB. Add $5.00 for CPC label on bottle.

Cream Lotion, 1942 – 1949. 6 oz., pink cap, back side of bottle is flat. Flowered box shown sold in 1942 only. CMV, $20.00 BO. $30.00 MB.

Leg Makeup, 1943 – 1949. 4 oz., clear glass with turquoise cap on left. Two different bottles as shown. CMV, $15.00 each, BO. $20.00 each, MB.

Nail Polish, 1938 – 1950. ½ oz. and ¼ oz. bottle came in polish remover, cream polish, cuticle softener, cuticle oil, oily polish remover, nail polish base, and top coat. 1946 – 1950, same bottles and labels with black caps. Also came in double coat, nail polish and cling-tite. CMV, $2.00 BO. $5.00 MB.

Cream Lotion, 1942 – 1943. Box shown sold 1942 – 1943 only. 6 oz. flat sided bottle with pink cap sold 1942 – 1949 as pictured. CMV, $20.00 BO, mint. $30.00 MB as shown.

Hand Lotion, 1943 – 1950. 4 oz., clear glass, turquoise cap. CMV, $3.00 BO. $7.00 MB.

Hand Lotion, Rose Water, Glycerine and Benzoin Lotion, 1942 only. 6 oz. flat sided bottle. Came in sets only. CMV, $20.00 mint.

Sun Cream, 1943 – 1948. 4 oz., clear glass, turquoise cap. CMV, $5.00 BO. $10.00 MB.

Antiseptic, 1940 – 1950. 6 oz. clear glass bottle with turquoise cap. Early issue had metal cap. Also came in 12 oz. size. CMV, $12.00, 6 oz. MB. CMV, $16.00, 12 oz. BO, $20.00 MB. Add $5.00 for CPC label.

Bath Salts, 1943 – 1945. 5 oz., white paper containers. Came in Attention, Jasmine, Pine, and Vernafleur. CMV, $25.00 each, CO, mint. $30.00 MB.

Liquid Deodorant, 1944 – 1945.
2 oz., turquoise cap with applicator. CMV, $20.00 BO. $25.00 MB.

Antiseptic Only, 1946.
6 oz. round bottle, black cap. Two different labels. Rare. CMV, $40.00 BO. $45.00 MB.

Hand Lotion, 1948.
2 oz. glass bottle with blue cap. Came in 1948 Hairribbons Set (see Cotillion section). CMV, $5.00.

Soapless Shampoo, 1946 – 1949.
6 oz., turquoise cap. CMV, $20.00 BO. $25.00 MB. Also came in 16 oz. round size with same label, 1946 – 1949. CMV, $20.00 BO. $25.00 MB.

Sun Lotion, 1949 – 1958.
4 oz. bottle with white cap. Montreal label to 1954. CMV, $11.00 Pasadena label, 1954 – 1958. CMV, $10.00 BO. $12.00 MB.

Bubble Bath, 1944 – 1948.
Blue and white box with pink ribbon holds 8 oz. bottle with blue cap and label. CMV, $35.00 BO, mint. $45.00 MB.

Double Dare Nail Polish, 1946 – 1947.
1 oz., black cap, red paper label. CMV, $8.00 BO $12.00 MB.

Hand Lotion, 1950 only.
4 oz., clear glass, turquoise cap and label. CMV, $7.00 BO. $12.00 MB.

Liquid Twin-Tone, 1944 – 1945.
2 oz. bottle. CMV, $15.00 BO. $20.00 MB.

Oily Polish Remover, 1946 – 1950.
2 oz. bottle with turquoise cap. CMV, $10.00 BO. $15.00 MB.

Hand Lotion, 1950.
4 oz., pink cap. Same bottle as Cotillion of that period. This was a substitute bottle. Rare. CMV, $7.00 BO. $12.00 MB.

Toilet Water, Cream Lotion, and Bubble Bath, 1945.
All are 2 oz. size, frosted glass and pink caps. Came in 1945 Young Hearts Set. CMV, $20.00 each. Toilet water is in Cotillion fragrance.

Bubble Bath, 1948 – 1951.
4 oz. bottle with blue cap. Round blue and pink box with top of bottle sticking through lid. CMV, $15.00 BO. $25.00 MB.

Cream Lotion,
1950 – 1951.
2 oz., clear glass with turquoise cap, label has red, yellow, and blue streamers. Came in 1951 Always Sweet Set and 1950 Jolly Surprise Set (see Women's Sets of the 1950s). CMV, $12.00.

Coconut Oil Shampoo,
1951 – 1955.
6 oz. bottle with turquoise cap and label. CMV, $12.00 BO. $17.00 MB.

Hand Lotion, 1951 – 1954.
4 oz., pink or white plastic cap, blue and pink label. CMV, $5.00 BO. $10.00 MB.

Nail Polish, 1950 – 1954.
½ oz. bottle with white cap and gold line through label. Came in nail polish, cuticle softener, cling-tite, oily polish remover, clear nail polish, and double coat. CMV, $3.00 each, MB.

Coconut Oil Shampoo,
1951 – 1955.
1 pint bottle with black pouring or flat black cap. CMV, $22.00 BO. $27.50 MB.

Cream Lotion, 1951.
2 oz. bottle with blue cap. Came in 1951 Always Sweet Set. CMV, $18.00.

Creme Hair Rinse,
1953 – 1955.
6 oz. clear glass bottle with green cap and label. CMV, $4.00 MB.

Oily Polish Remover,
1950 – 1953.
2 oz., white cap. CMV, $6.00 BO. $10.00 MB.

Bubble Bath,
1951 – 1958.
4 oz. bottle with blue cap. Square blue and pink box. CMV, $15.00 BO. $20.00 MB.

Skin Freshener,
1954 – 1958.
2 oz. bottle with turquoise cap and label. Came in Beautiful You Set, A Thing of Beauty Set, For Your Beauty Set, and Happy Traveler Set, with white cap (see Women's Sets of the 1950s). CMV, $2.00 MB.

Fashion Film, 1951 – 1954.
1 oz., white cap. CMV, $5.00 BO. $8.00 MB.

Foundation Lotion,
1950 – 1951.
2 oz. bottle with turquoise cap. Formerly called Finishing Lotion. CMV, $15.00 BO. $20.00 MB.

Astringent, 1954 – 1965.
4 oz. bottle with green cap and label. CMV, $1.00 BO. $2.00 MB.
Skin Freshener, 1954 – 1965.
4 oz. bottle with green cap and label. CMV, $1.00. 1965 bottle has "For Dry Skin" or "For Normal Skin" added to label. CMV, $2.00 MB.
Not shown: Astringent Freshener for Oily Skin, 1965.
Same 4 oz. bottle as 1954 – 1965 astringent, only name is changed. CMV, $2.00 MB.

Oily Polish Remover, 1955 – 1962. 2 oz., white cap and label. CMV, $4.00 MB.

Hand Lotion. 1954 – 1958. 4 oz., green cap and label. CMV, $1.00 BO. $2.00 MB.

Bath Salts, 1954 – 1957. 8 oz. bottle with turquoise cap and label. Came in Jasmine and Pine. CMV, $5.00 BO, mint. $7.00 MB.

Nail Polish, 1954 – 1958. With 4A design on label, came in long-last nail polish, cuticle softener, silvery base, top coat, or oily polish remover. CMV, $2.00 each, MB.

Creme Lotion Shampoo, 1954 – 1956. 6 oz. bottle with turquoise cap, painted label. 1956 label has 4A design. CMV, $4.00 MB.

Creme Lotion Shampoo, 1956 only. 6 oz., clear glass, green cap. CMV, $3.00 MB.

Fashion Film, 1954 – 1958. 1 oz., white cap. CMV, $3.00 BO. $5.00 MB.

Antiseptic Mouthwash, 1955 – 1959. 7 oz., white cap. Label says antiseptic only. CMV, $7.00 BO. $10.00 MB.

Liquid Coconut Oil Shampoo, 1956 – 1957. 6 oz. clear bottle with green cap, painted label. CMV, $3.00 MB.

Liquid Rouge, 1954 – 1959. 1/8 oz., gold embossed cap. CMV, $5.00 BO. $7.00 MB.

Skin Freshener, 1955. Rare 2 oz. glass bottle with embossed flowers around neck. Turquoise cap. Came in 1955 Happy Traveler Set only (See Women's Sets of the 1950s). CMV, $12.00 mint.

Creme Hair Rinse, 1956. 6 oz. bottle with white cap and painted label with 4A design. CMV, $3.00 MB.

Sun Lotion, 1954. 2 oz. bottle, white cap. Came in Camping Kit Set only (See Women's Sets of the 1950s). Rare. CMV, $22.00.

Sun Foam, 1955 – 1957. Peach colored can and cap. CMV, $3.00 CO. $6.00 MB.

Stick Deodorant, 1956 – 1961. Green cap and label on clear glass jar, two different caps. Older has 4A design on top and newer one has "New" spelled on lid. CMV, $6.00 each, CO. $9.00 each, MB.

Liquid Coconut Oil Shampoo, 1956 – 1957. 1 pint with green label and double pouring cap. CMV, $17.00 BO. $22.00 MB.

Liquid Rouge, 1959 – 1966. ¼ oz., smooth brass cap, two different labels. CMV, $3.00 BO. $5.00

Hand Lotion and Pump, 1963 – 1964. 8 oz., gold stripes on bottle, gold and white pump. Also came without gold neck band. CMV, $1.00 BO. $3.00 MB.

Beautiful Journey Bottles, 1957.
1 oz. clear glass bottles came in Beautiful Journey Set only (see Women's Sets of the 1950s). Pink caps. Came in hand lotion, skin freshener, deep clean, deodorant, and Cotillion cologne. CMV, $5.00 each.

Antiseptic Mouthwash, 1959 – 1968. 7 oz., white cap. CMV, $6.00 MB.

Lotion Lovely, 1964 – 1965. 8 oz., gold painted label. Came in Wishing, Here's My Heart, Persian Wood, To a Wild Rose, Somewhere, Topaze, Cotillion, Occur!, or Rapture. CMV, $1.00 BO. $4.00 MB.

Fashion Film, 1958 – 1961. 1 oz., pink cap. CMV, $4.00 BO. $7.00 MB.

Nail Clippers, 1960s.
"Avon" embossed on nail clipper. We have no information on this. Rare. CMV, $5.00.

Eye and Throat Oil, 1965 – 1972. 1 oz., gold cap, painted label. CMV, $1.00 MB.

Bath Oil, 1965.
Came in Bath Bouquet Set only (see Women's Sets of the 1960s). 2 oz., gold cap and label. Came in Rapture, Occur!, Somewhere, Topaze, Cotillion, Here's My Heart, To a Wild Rose, or Wishing. CMV, $3.00.

Dew Kiss, 1960 – 1966. 1½ oz., pink lid, gold string with pink and gold tag, with 4A design. CMV, $1.00 BO. $3.00 MB.

Insect Repellent, 1959 – 1965.
2 oz. bottle with red and white caps. CMV, $3.00 BO. $5.00 MB.

Stick Deodorant, 1961 – 1962. 1¾ oz., white cap, green glass jar with painted label. CMV, $5.00 CO. $9.00 MB.

Skin So Soft, 1966 – 1967. 1 oz., gold cap with painted leaf. Came in set of three only, in several fragrances: Unforgettable, Rapture, Occur!, Somewhere, Topaze, Cotillion, Here's My Heart, To a Wild Rose, or Wishing. CMV, $3.00 MB.

Ultra Sheer Liquid Foundation, 1966 – 1967.
1 oz., gold top, embossed bottle. CMV, $1.00 MB.
Not shown: Ultra Sheer Natural Veil, 1968 – 1974.
1 oz. embossed bottle, same as Liquid Foundation, only name changed. CMV, $1.00 MB.

Hair Color Colorant, 1969.
2 oz., brown glass with white cap. Has 4A on cap. CMV, $3.00.

Dew Kiss Decanter, 1973.
4 oz., clear glass with gold cap. CMV, $1.00 MB.

Eye and Throat Oil, 1967.
1 oz., gold cap. Issued during glass strike in 1967 only. Short issue. CMV, $2.00 BO. $4.00 MB.

Skin So Soft, 1970.
Clear glass container holds 2 oz. Skin So Soft, gold cap. Comes in Bird of Paradise, Elusive, Charisma, Brocade, Unforgettable, Field Flowers, Occur!, Rapture, or To a Wild Rose. CMV, $2.00 MB.

Dew Kiss Decanter, 1974.
4 oz., clear glass with gold cap. CMV, $1.00 MB.

Skin So Soft, 1969.
1 oz., gold cap and paper label. Came in Unforgettable, Rapture, Occur!, Somewhere, Topaze, Cotillion, To a Wild Rose, or Here's My Heart. CMV, $4.00 MB.

Color Perfect Hair Colorant, 1971 – 1972.
2 oz., brown glass with white cap. CMV, $1.50.

Proper Balance Vitamins, 1979 – 1981.
Three different, 60 and 100 count bottles. Proper balance for the whole family. Women's Vitality, Dieter's Support. CMV, $5.00 each, MB.

Skin So Soft Scented Bath Oil, 1969 – 1970.
2 oz., clear glass bottom, clear plastic top. This top is the same as the bottle in the Just Two Set from 1965 (see Women's Sets of the 1960s). Came in Charisma, Brocade, Rapture, Unforgettable, Occur!, Here's My Heart, Cotillion, To a Wild Rose, or Régence. CMV, $4.00 MB.

Skin So Soft, 1971 – 1972.
2 oz., seven layer glass bottle with gold cap. 4½" high. Came in Bird of Paradise, Elusive, Charisma, Brocade, or To a Wild Rose. CMV, $3.00 MB.

Vita-Mights for Kids, 1980 – 1981.
Vitamins for kids, bottle of 100 tablets. CMV, $7.00 MB.

Beauty Dust, Powders and Talc

All powders newer then 1975 are not pictured and have little or no value to collectors.

Dusting Powder, 1926 – 1929.
Gold metal can with black stripes. Came in Daphne, Vernafleur, Trailing Arbutus, California Rose, Baby Powder, and Super Rite Talcum. CMV, $40.00 CO. $50.00 MB.

Dusting Powder, 1930 – 1934.
8 oz. blue and silver square can. CMV, $30.00 CO, mint. $40.00 MB. Gold can, blue letters. CMV, $50.00 mint.

Tooth Powder, 1930 – 1936.
Green metal can. CMV, $25.00 CO, mint. $32.00 MB.

Dusting Powder, 1935 – 1936.
13 oz. metal gold colored can. Came in Bath Ensemble Set only (see Women's Sets of the 1930s). CMV, $35.00 mint. *Not shown: Dusting Powder, 1935 – 1936.*
Same as gold can only general issue was silver and blue can. CMV, $30.00 CO, mint. $40.00 MB.

Face Powder, 1930 – 1936.
Silver and blue paper box came in Ariel and Vernafleur. CMV, $12.00 CO, mint. $17.00 MB.

Elite Powder, 1931 – 1936.
Silver and blue can with blue cap is general issue. CMV, $25.00 CO. $30.00 MB. Family size 1 lb. tin can was issued 1934 – 1935. Add $5.00 MB.

Dusting Powder, 1936 – 1949.
13 oz. turquoise and beige can with "A" on top. First issue (1936 – 1939) has CPC on bottom. CMV, $30.00. 1940 – 1949 Avon Products label only, CMV, $20.00 CO. $25.00 MB. There are at least three different varieties of the 1936 – 1949 metal dusting powder. One has a deeply indented bottom, shiny silver, with CPC on it. Another has a slightly indented dull silver bottom, no CPC on it.

Smoker's Tooth Powder, 1932 – 1936.
Green cap. CMV, $25.00 CO. $35.00 MB.

Dusting Powder Refill, 1930 – 1936.
Gray box holds plain paper wrapped box of powder. CMV, $25.00 MB.

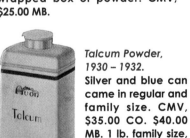

Talcum Powder, 1930 – 1932.
Silver and blue can came in regular and family size. CMV, $35.00 CO. $40.00 MB. 1 lb. family size, CMV, $35.00 CO. $45.00 MB.

Elite Powder, 1934 – 1935.
Same design and shape can as 1931 Elite powder. Came in sets only in gold and blue cans. CMV, $35.00 CO. $40.00 MB.

Dusting Powder Refill, 1936 – 1949.
Round cardboard container. Came in Jasmine or Avon dusting powder. CMV, $15.00 MB. Add $5.00 for CPC label.

Tooth Powder, 1936 – 1950. Turquoise and white metal can, silver cap. CMV, $10.00 CO. $15.00 MB.

Smoker's Tooth Powder, 1938 – 1949. Maroon and cream can. Came in men's sets only. CMV, $16.00 mint.

Face Powder, 1936 – 1939. 3" diameter, turquoise and cream cardboard container. Came in Cotillion, Ariel, or Vernafleur fragrance. Choice of natural, rose, peach, Rachel No. 1, Rachel No. 2, orchre, orchre-rose, or suntan shades. CMV, $6.00 CO. $10.00 MB.

Powder Puffs Refill, 1960s. Envelope holds two puff refills. CMV, $3.00.

Elite Powder, 1936 – 1948. Large family size, turquoise and white can. CMV, $25.00 CO. $30.00 MB.

Smoker's Tooth Powder Samples.
Top left: 1936 – 1940, small ¼ oz. turquoise and white can. CPC label, turquoise sifter cap. CMV, $35.00 mint.
Top right: 1940 – 1949. Same can, only has chrome lift-off cap. CMV, $30.00 mint.
Bottom left: Same can, has small chrome cap. CMV, $30.00.

Smoker's Tooth Powder, 1936 – 1949. Metal cap, 3½ oz. turquoise and white can. CMV, $16.00 CO. $20.00 MB.

Dusting Powder Puff, 1940s – 1950s. Envelope holds Avon puff. Rare. CMV, $10.00.

Elite Powder, 1936 – 1954. 2⁹⁄₁₀ oz. or 3 oz. size on right, turquoise and white cans, two different boxes. CMV, $10.00 CO. $14.00 MB. Add $3.00 for CPC label.

Tooth Powder, 1936 – 1949. Box holds 2¼ oz. turquoise and white can. Silver slide-open cap. CMV, $10.00 CO. $15.00 MB.

Talc for Men, 1936 – 1949. Maroon and cream can with maroon cap. CMV, $10.00 CO. $15.00 MB.

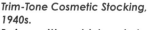

Trim-Tone Cosmetic Stocking, 1940s. Beige with gold band, turquoise box. CMV, $25.00 MB.

Dusting Powder Christmas Box, 1940 – 1941.
Special issue blue and white Christmas box holds regular issue metal can of dusting powder. CMV, $35.00 MB as shown.

Dusting Powder, 1943 – 1944. 13 oz. paper box, turquoise and ivory. War-time issue. CMV, $30.00 BO, mint. $35.00 MB.

Dusting Powder, 1943 – 1944. Turquoise and white paper box. War-time issue. CMV, $35.00 CO. $40.00 MB.

Dusting Powder Mother's Day Box, 1941.
Special issue lavender box with white lace holds regular issue dusting powder. Sold around Mother's Day. CMV, $35.00 MB as shown.

Dusting Powder Christmas Box, 1943. Outer box was special issue for Christmas. Holds square cardboard beauty dust. War-time issue. CMV, $50.00 MB as shown.

Elite Powder, 1943 – 1944. Turquoise and white paper boxes in family size. Large, CMV, $30.00. Regular size, CMV, $20.00. Three different caps: plastic cap, punch-out top, and punch-out top with paper top and bottom cover. Same CMV.

Elite Foot Powder, 1943 – 1944. Maroon and cream colored paper box. 2³⁄₄ oz. Black screw-on octagonal cap. War-time issue. CMV, $25.00 mint.

Left to right:
Beauty Dust, 1942 – 1948.
6 oz., blue feather design cardboard. Came in Avon beauty dust and Apple Blossom. CMV, $20.00 CO. $25.00 MB.
Face Powder, 1942 – 1948.
1³⁄₄ oz., blue feather design cardboard. CMV, $8.00 CO, mint. $12.00 MB.
Heavenlight Face Powder, 1946 – 1948.
2¹⁄₂ oz., same feather design paper box. CMV, $8.00 CO. $12.00 MB.
Rouge, 1942 – 1949.
Blue feather design, paper container. CMV, $5.00 CO. $8.00 MB.
Feather Design Lipstick, 1942 – 1946.
Blue plastic top and bottom with cardboard sides. Also came with red plastic top and bottom. CMV, $5.00 CO. $9.00 MB.

Elite Foot Powder, 1943 – 1944.
2³⁄₄ oz. maroon and white victory paper box. Flat punch-out top with paper lift-off lid. CMV, $25.00 mint.

Tooth Powder, 1943 – 1946. Flat metal top, paper side container. 3 oz., turquoise and white. CMV, $20.00 CO, mint. $25.00 MB.

Smoker's Tooth Powder, 1944 – 1946. Turquoise and white paper container. Plastic cap. CMV, $20.00 CO, mint. $25.00 MB.

Smoker's Tooth Powder, 1946 – 1950. 3½ oz. turquoise and white can, turquoise plastic cap. CMV, $14.00 CO. $19.00 MB.

Elite Powder, 1943 – 1946. 2¾ oz. or 3 oz. paper box. Turquoise and white. CMV, $18.00 CO, mint. $23.00 MB.

Ammoniated Tooth Powder, 1949 – 1955. 3 oz. turquoise and white can with turquoise lid. CMV, $10.00 CO. $15.00 MB.

Tooth Powder, 1943 – 1946. 3 oz. paper box. Turquoise and white. CMV, $20.00 CO, mint. $25.00 MB.

Heavenlight Face Powder, 1944. General issue feather design paper box. Shown in 1944 pink design box. 2½ oz. contents. Powder only sold in 1944 – 1948. CMV, $8.00, powder box only. $12.00 MB as shown.

Ammoniated Tooth Powder, 1949 only. 3 oz. turquoise can and tilt cap. This can with this style cap was a very short issue. CMV, $13.00 CO, mint. $20.00 MB.

Smoker's Tooth Powder, 1943 – 1946. 3½ oz. paper box with metal top and bottom. Turquoise and white. CMV, $20.00 CO, mint. $25.00 MB.

Beauty Dust Christmas Box, 1944. Special issue Christmas box. Holds feather design paper container of beauty dust. CMV, $22.00 beauty dust only, mint. $27.00 MB as shown.

Smoker's Tooth Powder, 1950 – 1954. 3½ oz. turquoise and white can, turquoise tilt cap. CMV, $14.00 CO. $19.00 MB.

Smoker's Tooth Powder, 1943 – 1946. Maroon and cream paper sides, tin top and bottom. CMV, $20.00 CO, mint. $25.00 MB.

Beauty Dust, 1945 – 1948. 6 oz., blue and white cardboard with lady's face on lid. Also contained Apple Blossom beauty dust. CMV, $25.00 CO. $30.00 MB.

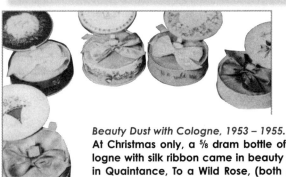

Beauty Dust with Cologne, 1953 – 1955.
At Christmas only, a ⅝ dram bottle of cologne with silk ribbon came in beauty dust in Quaintance, To a Wild Rose, (both pink and white), Golden Promise (blue), Forever Spring, or Cotillion. CMV, add $12.00 to price of beauty dust if bottle has ribbon and $10.00 without ribbon.

Sheer Mist Face Powder, 1955 – 1957.
Turquoise cardboard with white and pink flowers and gold 4A design on lid. CMV, $5.00 MB.
Not shown: Face Powder, 1960 – 1963.
Same design as Sheer Mist, only has plastic lid, no pink rim. CMV, $2.00 MB.

Beauty Dust with Cologne, 1957 – 1958.
At Christmas only, a ⅝ dram snowflake bottle with white round cap of cologne was given free with purchase of beauty dust. Matching neck ribbons on each bottle. Cotillion, Forever Spring, To a Wild Rose, Nearness, Elégante, or Bright Night. CMV, add $9.00 for each bottle with ribbon to price of beauty dust.

Beauty Dust with Cologne, 1956.
At Christmas only, a ⅝ dram bottle with white flat cap and neck ribbon came in beauty dust. Elégante with red ribbon, Nearness with lavender ribbon, Cotillion and To a Wild Rose with pink ribbons, Forever Spring with purple ribbon, or Quaintance with blue ribbon. Each ribbon has a gold edge. Add $12.00 to each beauty dust if bottle has ribbon.

Aqua Dent, 1958 – 1966.
7 oz. green can with white cap. CMV, $1.00 CO. $3.00 MB.

Powder-Pak Puffs Refill, 1940s.
Envelope holds two compact puff refills. CMV, $5.00 mint.

Powder Puff Compact Refills, 1960 – 1970s.
Two different puffs and packages for compacts. CMV, $3.00 each, mint.

Beauty Dust, 1960 – 1961.
3 oz. white plastic bottle, has paper label or painted label, turquoise cap. This came in Modern Simplicity Set only (see Women's Sets of the 1960s). Came in Cotillion, To a Wild Rose, or Here's My Heart. CMV, $5.00.

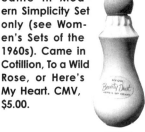

Antiseptic Powder, 1956 – 1962.
3 oz. gray and white can, red cap. CMV, $2.00 MB.

Sheer Mist Face Powder, 1958– 1959.
2½ oz. white cardboard box with pink rose on lid and pink rim around edge. CMV, $3.00 MB.

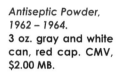

Fashion Finish Face Powder, 1963 – 1967.
1½ oz. white plastic box. CMV, $1.00 MB.

Antiseptic Powder, 1962 – 1964.
3 oz. gray and white can, red cap. CMV, $2.00 MB.

Beauty Dust Refill, 1965. White outer box holds colorful inner box with plain beauty dust re-fill. Came in choice of Persian Wood, Cotillion, To a Wild Rose, Some-where, Topaze, Occur!, Here's My Heart, or Rapture. CMV, $7.00 MB as shown.

Sachet Pillows, 1963.
Green and white holder contains powder sachet pillows. Came six to a pack. CMV for set of six, $5.00 mint.

Beauty Dust Demo, 1966 – 1968. White box, came in choice of beauty dust refill and different fragrance empty container. Both came boxed. Used by reps dur-ing campaign 10, 1966. CMV, $11.00 MB.

Heavy Duty Powdered Hand Cleanser, 1973 – 1976.
10 oz., blue, white, pink, and black card-board with plastic top and bottom. CMV, $1.00 mint.

Bath Bouquet Talc, 1965.
1½ oz. green paper box. Came in Bath Bou-quet Set only in all fragrances of that set (see Women's sets of the 1960s). CMV, $4.00 mint.

Compacts and Lipsticks

Compacts and lipsticks 1975 or newer are not included due to mass production and little collector interest.

CPC Eyebrow Pencils, 1916 – 1920.
Metal tubes. CMV, $15.00 each. $25.00 MB.

Compact, 1930 – 1932.
Silver metal compact in single and double size. CMV, $30.00 each, CO. $40.00 each, MB.

Dressing Table Rouge, 1930 – 1936.
Silver and blue paper box. CMV, $12.00 CO. $17.00 MB.

Single Rouge Compact, 1930 – 1936.
Blue and silver metal compact. OSP, 52¢. CMV, $20.00 CO. $25.00 MB.

*Eyelash Cream,
1930 – 1933.*
Blue compact with mirror, same as 1930 – 1936 rouge compacts. CMV, $20.00 CO. $25.00 MB.

*Nail White and Nail Cream,
1931 – 1936.*
Both small silver and blue or gold and blue cans. Came in manicure sets only. CMV, $8.00 mint.

Cream Rouge Compact, 1930 – 1936.
Blue metal compact. CMV, $20.00 CO. $25.00 MB.

Compact Refill, 1931 – 1936.
"Avon" on small and large size, blue and silver puff and refill cake. Came in gray box. CMV, $4.00 each, MB.

Double Compact, 1934 – 1936.
Blue and silver compact and puffs. CMV, $30.00 CO. $35.00 MB.

*Face Powder Sample,
1936 – 1942.*

Cream colored metal can. Came in Vernafleur or Ariel, in five shades. CMV, $5.00 CO. CPC label, add $2.00 MB.

Fan Compact, 1931 – 1933.
Silver and blue compact. CMV, $30.00 CO. $40.00 MB.

*Compact,
1932 – 1933.*
Octagonal shaped, blue and gold. Avon lid shown closed and open. Came in 1932 – 1933 Vanity Set only (see Women's Sets of the 1930s). CMV, $30.00 mint.

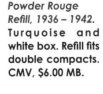

Dressing Table Rouge, 1936 – 1942.
Turquoise and gold cardboard with turquoise and white box. Came in five shades. CMV, $5.00 CO. $8.00 MB. Add $2.00 for CPC label.

*Lipstick,
1932 – 1936.*
Blue and silver metal tube. CMV, $20.00 CO. $25.00 MB.

Powder Rouge Refill, 1936 – 1942. **Turquoise and white box. Refill fits double compacts. CMV, $6.00 MB.**

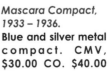

Triple Compact, 1931 – 1933.
Blue and silver compact. Avon on lid. CMV, $35.00 CO. $40.00 MB.

*Mascara Compact,
1933 – 1936.*
Blue and silver metal compact. CMV, $30.00 CO. $40.00 MB.

Cream Rouge Compacts, 1936 – 1942.
Turquoise and gold metal cases. CMV, $9.00 each, MB.
Not shown: Single Rouge Compact, 1936 – 1942.
Turquoise and gold metal case. CMV, $7.00 CO. $10.00 MB.

Nail White and Nail Cuticle Cream, 1937 – 1939.
Both turquoise and white small metal cans. Came in Manicure Set only. CMV, $7.00 mint.

Nail White Pencil, 1941 – 1948.
White plastic pencil in turquoise box. "Avon" on pencil. CMV, $2.00 pencil only. $5.00 MB.

Mascara Compact, 1936 – 1941.
Turquoise and gold. CMV, $12.00 CO. $15.00 MB.

Rouge Puffs Refills, 1940s.
Avon package held three small turquoise rouge double compact puffs. CMV, $3.00.

Bamboo Mascara Compact, 1941 – 1948.
Gold metal, bamboo design. Sold 1942 – 1943, then 1946 – 1948. CMV, $15.00 CO. $12.00 MB.
Bamboo Lipstick, 1941 – 1948.
Gold metal bamboo design. CMV, $6.00 CO. $8.00 MB.
Bamboo Single Rouge Compact, 1941 – 1948.
Gold metal, bamboo design. CMV, $7.00 CO. $9.00 MB.
Bamboo Cream Rouge Compact, 1941 – 1948.
Gold metal, bamboo design. CMV, $7.00 CO. $9.00 MB.

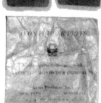

Powder Compact Puffs Refills, 1940s.
Avon package held two turquoise puff refills. CMV, $3.00 mint.

Lipstick, 1936 – 1941.
Turquoise and gold. CMV, $8.00 CO. $10.00 MB.

Compacts, 1936 – 1942.
Single and double compacts. Both turquoise and gold metal. CMV, $15.00 each, CO. $20.00 each, MB.

Bamboo Compacts, 1941 – 1949.
Gold metal, bamboo design. Double or single size, both in same design. Sold 1942 – 1943 then 1946 – 1949. CMV, $15.00 each, CO. $20.00 each, MB.

Face Powder Sample, 1942 – 1949.
Blue and white feather design, metal case or paper box in 1943 – 1946. CMV, $4.00 CO.

Lipstick, 1942 – 1946.
Blue feather design plastic lipstick. CMV, $4.00 lipstick only. $8.00 MB.

Mascara, 1943 – 1949.
Blue and white feather design paper box. CMV, $14.00 CO. $17.00 MB.

Chap-Check, 1956 – 1959.
Small white plastic tube, red cap. CMV, $3.00.

Chap-Check, 1960 – 1973.
Same colors as above, only longer tube. CMV, $1.00.

Heavenlight Compact, 1943 – 1945.
Blue plastic or metal compact with white feather, came in rouge or face powder. Rouge is smaller. CMV, $8.00 CO. $10.00 MB.
Not shown: Eyeshadow, 1945 – 1949.
Blue plastic compact with white feather. Same as 1943 rouge feather compact above. CMV, $7.00 CO. $9.00 MB.

Lipstick Refill, 1944.
Foil wrapped lipstick in plastic case, metal or paper case. Came in green and white box. Two different boxes. Some are white top, green bottom, or reversed. CMV, $10.00 MB.

Mascara, 1949 – 1952.
Gold metal case. CMV, $5.00 CO. $8.00 MB.

Flower Print Compact and Lipstick, 1967.
Four compacts with matching lipsticks. Designs are Sunflower, Daisy, Poppy, and Carnation. CMV, $3.00 each compact. $5.00 MB. CMV, $2.00 each lipstick. $3.00 MB. Also came in flower print nail polish.

Chapstick, 1943 – 1945.
Olive green metal case. "Lipstick Anti-Chap and Sunburn Protective Hot Climate." "Avon Products, Inc., New York" on label. Given to G.I.'s in World War II in first aid kit. CMV, $25.00.

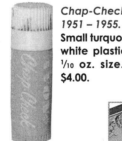

Chap-Check, 1951 – 1955.
Small turquoise and white plastic tube. 1/10 oz. size. CMV, $4.00.

Compact and Lipstick Deluxe, 1967 – 1969.
Gold compact. CMV, $8.00 MB. Gold lipstick. CMV, $5.00 MB.

Face Powder Compact, 1943 – 1944.
Feather design cardboard compact with mirror inside. 3½" across. CMV, $20.00 CO. $25.00 MB.

Jeweled Lipstick, 1954.
Gold Christmas box holds gold lipstick with jewel on top. CMV, $15.00 MB.
Jeweled Lipstick, 1954 – 1956.
Gold lipstick with white jewel on top. CMV, $8.00 MB.

Jeweled Lipstick, 1968 – 1969.
Gold lipstick with simulated diamonds. CMV, $6.00 MB.
Jeweled Compact, 1968 – 1969.
Gold powder compact with simulated diamonds. CMV, $12.00 MB.

Captivators Compacts and Lipsticks, 1969.
Leopard, zebra, and tiger design plastic compacts. CMV, $5.00 each, MB. Matching lipsticks, CMV, $3.00 each, MB.

Empress Lipstick, 1970 – 1971.
Green, blue, and gold lipstick. CMV, $3.00 MB.
Empress Compact, 1970 – 1971.
Green, blue, and gold compact. CMV, $5.00 MB.

Cream Jars

Violet Nutri-Cream, 1930 – 1934.
White jar, metal lid, silver and blue label. 2 or 4 oz. sizes. CMV, $30.00 jar only. $40.00 MB.

Tissue Cream, 1930 – 1934.
2 oz., ribbed white glass, metal lid, silver and blue label. CMV, $35.00 CO. $40.00 MB.

Bleach Cream, 1932 – 1933.
3 oz. frosted glass jar, metal lid, silver and blue label. CMV, $50.00 CO. $60.00 MB.

Cleansing Cream, 1930 – 1934.
4 oz. white glass ribbed jar with aluminum lid. Silver and blue label. CMV, $30.00 jar only, mint. $40.00 MB.

Rose Cold Cream, 1930 – 1934.
2 or 4 oz. white glass ribbed jars with aluminum lids. Silver and blue labels. CMV, $30.00 jar only. $40.00 MB.

Vanishing Cream, 1931.
2 oz. white glass jar with aluminum lid. Silver and blue label. CMV, $35.00 jar only. $40.00 MB.

Miscellaneous Cream Jars, 1933 – 1936.
Ribbed white glass jars with blue metal caps. Following came in 2 and 4 oz. sizes: Rose Cold Cream, Violet Nutri Cream; 4 oz. size only in Cleansing Cream; 2 oz. size only in Bleach Cream, Vanishing Cream, or Tissue Cream. CMV, $30.00 each, CO. $35.00 each, MB.

*Cream Deodorant,
1939 only.*
**White glass jar, turquoise
lid. Rare. CMV, $12.00 jar
only, mint. $16.00 MB.**

Cream Deodorant, 1936 – 1954.
**1 oz. white glass jar, turquoise lid. CMV, $7.00 jar only. $12.00
MB. Add $4.00 for CPC label.**

*Miscellaneous Cream Jars,
1936 – 1955.*
**This style bottle was sold from 1935 –
1955. Came in Tissue Cream, Rose Cold
Cream, Special Formula Cream, Foundation Cream, Violet Protective Cream,
All Purpose Cream, Bleach Cream,
Cleansing Cream, Night Cream, Violet Nutri Cream, Complexion Cream,
Super Rich Cream, 1947 Special Dry
Skin Cream, Vanishing Cream, and
1948 Facial Mask Cream. White glass
jars came in small, medium, and large
sizes with turquoise metal caps. Paper
caps were used 1943 – 1946. CMV,
$4.00 each. Add $3.00 each for turquoise paper caps. CMV, with CPC
labels on jar or box, 1936 – 1939, $8.00
jar only. $12.00 CPC label on box.**
*Not shown: Antiseptic Cream,
1954 – 1955.*
**3½ oz. large size jar only. CMV, $4.00
CO. $7.00 MB.**

*Nail and Cuticle
Cream, 1940 – 1950.*
**1 oz. white glass jar,
turquoise lid. CMV,
$5.00 CO. $8.00 MB.**

Rose Cold Cream Box, 1940.
**1¾ oz. jar came in special issue
box for reps to use as demonstrator only. Cost reps 10¢. CMV,
$20.00 MB as shown.**

*Rose Cold Cream Special
Issue Box, 1942.*
**Special issue blue and
pink rosebud box holds
regular issue large size
jar of Rose Cold Cream.
CMV, $25.00 MB.**

*Rose Cold Cream Special
Issue Box, 1941.*
**Special issue rose color box
with girl's face on side. Came
with regular issue middle size
jar of Rose Cold Cream for
10¢. with regular order. CMV,
$20.00 MB as shown.**

*Rose Cold Cream Box,
1939.*
**2 oz. white glass jar,
turquoise lid, in special
short issue design box.
CPC on box. CMV,
$25.00 MB as shown.**

*Twin-Tone Make-up,
Cream, 1943 – 1946.*
**1⅞ oz. white jar, tur-
quoise paper lid or
metal lid. CMV, $9.00
metal lid. $12.00
paper lid.**

*Twin-Tone Make-up
Cream, 1943 – 1946.*
**⅞ oz. white glass jar,
turquoise paper lid.
CMV, $10.00 CO.
$14.00 MB.**

Hand Cream, 1945 only.
3½ oz. clear glass jar, turquoise lid. Rare. CMV, $25.00 CO. $32.00 MB.

Cream Cake, 1948 – 1955.
Dove on top of pink lid. White glass bottom. CMV, $4.00 CO. $5.00 MB.

Rich Moisture Cream, 1954 – 1957.
Turquoise jar and cap in 2 oz. and 3½ oz. sizes. Came with two different size necks and caps. CMV, $2.00 each, jar only. $3.00 each, MB.

Color Pick-Up Liquid, 1946 – 1950.
1 oz. clear glass bottle with turquoise cap. CMV, $8.00 CO. $11.00 MB.

Nail Beauty, 1951 – 1954.
1 oz. white glass jar, white lid. CMV, $4.00 CO. $5.00 MB.

Color Pick-Up Cream, 1946 – 1954.
1⅞ oz. white glass jar with turquoise lid. CMV, $6.00 CO. $10.00 MB. Also came in 1 oz. jar. Same lid and jar.

Creme Shampoo, 1953.
4 oz. jar, very short issue. Rare. CMV, $10.00 jar only. $17.00 MB.

Left: Color Pick-Up Cream, 1955 – 1957.
White glass jar with pink lid. CMV, $4.00 jar only. $6.00 MB.
Inside left: White Velvet Cream, 1961 – 1965.
3½ oz. white glass jar with 4A on turquoise lid. CMV, $1.00 CO. $2.00 MB.
Inside right: Polish Remover Pads, 1963 – 1966.
White glass jar with red lid, holds 20 pads. CMV, $2.00 CO. $3.00 MB.
Right: Antiseptic Cream, 1954 – 1958.
3½ oz. white glass jar with gray lid. CMV, $2.00 CO. $3.00 MB.

Color Pick-Up Cream, 1946 – 1947.
Painted over Twin-Tone lid. 1⅞ oz. white glass jar with green lid. CMV, $12.00 BO. $16.00 MB.

Color Pick-Up Cream, 1946.
⅞ oz. white glass jar, turquoise lid. CMV, $15.00 CO. $18.00 MB.

Cream Deodorant, 1954 – 1959.
White glass jar, turquoise lid. CMV, $2.50 jar only. $4.00 MB.

Cake Make-up, 1947 – 1954.
1¾ oz., pink base, white cap. CMV, $3.00 CO. $5.00 MB.

Rich Moisture Cream, 1954.
1½ and 3½ oz. turquoise glass jar with turquoise plastic lid. CMV, $3.00 CO. $4.00 MB.

Avon Creams, 1954 – 1961.
Left to right: White glass jar with green lid and label. Came in: Hormone Cream, Super Rich Cream, Cleansing Cream, and Antiseptic Cream in large and small jars. CMV, $2.00 each, CO. $3.00 each, MB.

Nail Beauty,
1954 – 1957.
1 oz white jar with white lid. CMV, $3.00 CO. $4.00 MB.

Strawberry Cooler, 1956.
Frosted glass jar with strawberries on white lid. CMV, $2.00 CO. $3.00 MB.

Left: Skin So Soft Vanity Jar, 1973 – 1974.
5 oz., clear glass with antiqued gold lid. CMV, $2.00 MB.
Center: Cream Sachet Vanity Jar, 1973 – 1975.
1 oz., clear glass with antiqued silver lid. Holds Field Flowers, Charisma, or Topaze. CMV, $2.00 MB.
Right: Rich Moisture Cream Vanity Jar, 1973.
5 oz. clear glass with antiqued silver lid. CMV, $2.00 MB.

Cream Cake,
1955 – 1957.
"Avon" in center of pink lid, white glass bottom. CMV, $3.00 CO. $4.00 MB.

Cream Foundation, 1963 – 1966.
1 oz. white glass jar with white plastic lid with gold center. CMV, $1.00 MB.

Spray Cans

All spray cans 1960 and newer are mass produced and have little value to most collectors. We have not included most spray cans 1960 or newer for this reason. All Avon spray cans not pictured in this book 1960 or newer would not have a value over 25¢ each. We suggest you do not collect them unless they are very old. We suggest you collect 1950s and older in cans and jars.

Avon Net Hair Spray, 1954 – 1957.
Green and white, white caps. Came in 5 oz. size. CMV, $2.00 each, CO. $4.00 each, MB.

Moth Proofer, 1956 – 1960.
12 oz. red and white spray can, white cap. CMV, $2.00.
Not shown: Moth Proofer, 1968 – 1972.
11 oz. red and white spray can, white cap. CMV, $1.00.

Klean Air, 1956 – 1958.
12 oz. blue and white spray can with white cap. Mint scented. CMV, $5.00 mint. Also came in 3 oz. pink and white can, same shape. CMV, $3.00.

Lather Foam Shampoo, 1956.
Green cap and can, short issue. CMV, $3.00 mint.

Avon Net Liquid Hair Spray, 1957 – 1958.
White and pink spray can came in 5 and 11 oz. sizes. CMV, $5.00 each.
Avon Net for Fine Hair, 1958 – 1960.
5 oz. blue and white can and cap, CMV, $2.00.
Avon Net Regular, 1959 – 1964.
5 oz. pink and white can and cap. CMV, $2.00.

Smooth-flo Toothpaste, 1959 – 1961.
5½ oz. white, red, and gray metal can, red cap. CMV, $2.00.

Tubes

Tubes 1965 or newer are not included in this book due to mass production and little or no interest to most Avon collectors. Only fancy decorated or cute kids-type tubes are considered collectible after 1965. All tubes not pictured in this book, unless they are very old, should not be collected for future value. The abbreviation "TO" means "Tube Only."

Witch Hazel Cream, 1904.
OSP, 2 oz. tube, 25¢. OSP, 6 oz. tube, 50¢. CMV, $45.00 TO, mint. $50.00 MB.

Almond Cream Balm, 1908.
2 and 6 oz. size tubes. OSP, 25¢ and 50¢. CMV, $40.00 each, TO. $50.00 each, MB.

Almond Cream Balm, 1910.
Tube came in two sizes. OSP, 25¢ and 50¢. CMV, $40.00 TO, mint. $45.00 MB.

Almond Cream Balm, 1904.
OSP, 2 oz. tube, 25¢. OSP, 6 oz. tube, 50¢. CMV, $45.00 TO, mint. $50.00 MB.

Almond Cream Balm, 1908.
Metal tube. OSP, 50¢. CMV, $45.00 TO, mint. $55.00 MB.

Dental Cream, 1912.
Metal tube, paper label. OSP, 25¢. CMV, $50.00 TO, mint. $75.00 MB.

Witch Hazel Cream, 1908.
2 and 6 oz. size tubes. OSP, 25¢ and 50¢. CMV, $40.00 each, TO, mint. $50.00 each, MB.

Menthol Witch Hazel Cream, 1909.
2 oz. tube, first issue. OSP, 25¢. CMV, $45.00 TO. $50.00 MB.

Menthol Witch Hazel Cream, 1914.
OSP, 25¢. CMV, $40.00 TO, mint. $45.00 MB.

Menthol Witch Hazel Cream, 1914.
Small and large tube. OSP 25¢ and 50¢. CMV, $40.00 each, TO, mint. $45.00 each, MB.

Menthol Witch Hazel Cream, 1923.
Green tube. OSP, 33¢. CMV, $30.00 TO, mint. $35.00 MB.

Styptic Pencil, 1923.
White pencil. OSP, 10¢. CMV, $10.00 pencil only. $15.00 MB.

Dental Cream, 1915 – 1933.
OSP, 23¢. 1915 – 1923 tube was pink, 1923 – 1933 tube was light blue. CMV, $40.00 pink tube, mint. $35.00 blue tube, mint. Add $5.00 for box.

Cold Cream Tube, 1923.
Large or small tube. OSP, 23¢ and 45¢. CMV, $30.00 each, TO, mint. $40.00 each, MB.

Bayberry Shaving Cream Sample, 1925.
Small sample tube in sample box. Came with instruction sheet. CMV, $70.00 MB.

Sen-Den-Tal, 1921– 1933.
Yellow tube. OSP, 47¢. CMV, $30.00 TO, mint. $35.00 MB. Also came in small sample tube. CMV, $35.00 mint.

Bayberry Shaving Cream, 1923.
Green tube. OSP, 33¢. CMV, $35.00 TO, mint. $40.00 MB.

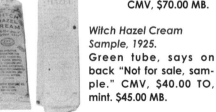

Witch Hazel Cream Sample, 1925.
Green tube, says on back "Not for sale, sample." CMV, $40.00 TO, mint. $45.00 MB.

Shampoo Cream, 1923.
Yellow tube. OSP, 48¢. CMV, $35.00 TO, mint. $40.00 MB.

Witch Hazel Cream, 1923.
Large or small green tube. OSP, 30¢ and 59¢. CMV, $35.00 each, TO, mint. $40.00 each, MB.

Bayberry Shaving Cream, 1923.
Green tube, came in Gentlemen's Shaving Set (See CPC Men's Sets). CMV, $35.00 TO, mint. $40.00 MB.

Styptic Pencil, 1925.
White stick in CPC box. Came in Humidor Shaving Set (See CPC Men's Sets). Box in French and English. CMV, $35.00 MB.

Menthol Witch Hazel Cream, 1930 – 1936. **Green and black tube. OSP, 50¢. CMV, $15.00 TO, mint. $25.00 MB.**

Hair Dress, 1931 – 1936. **Silver tube. OSP, 37¢. CMV, $20.00 TO, mint. $25.00 MB.**

Sen-Den-Tal, 1933 – 1936. **Green tube of toothpaste. OSP, 35¢. CMV, $20.00 TO, mint. $25.00 MB.**

Hand Cream Christmas Box, 1934. **Green and red box, short issue, held silver tube of hand cream. OSP, 10¢ with regular order. CMV, $25.00 MB as shown.**

Witch Hazel Cream, 1930 – 1936. **Green and black tube. OSP, 75¢. CMV, $15.00 TO, mint. $25.00 MB.**

Depilatory, 1931 – 1934. **Silver tube. OSP, 75¢. CMV, $12.00 TO, mint. $22.00 MB.**

Dental Cream No. 2, 1932 – 1936. **Green tube. OSP, 35¢. CMV, $25.00 MB.**

Hand Cream, 1934. **Regular issue, gray box held silver tube of hand cream. OSP, 52¢. CMV, $12.00 TO, mint. $20.00 MB.**

Bayberry Shaving Cream, 1930 – 1936. **Green tube. OSP, 35¢. CMV, $20.00 TO, mint. $25.00 MB.**

Dental Cream, 1933 – 1936. **Green tube. OSP, 25¢. CMV, $15.00 TO, mint. $20.00 MB.**

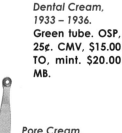

Pore Cream, 1930 – 1936. **Silver and blue tube. OSP, 78¢. CMV, $20.00 TO, mint. $25.00 MB.**

Hand Cream Introductory, 1934 – 1936. **Blue and silver tube. OSP, 52¢. CMV, $20.00 TO, mint. $25.00 MB as shown.**

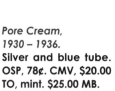

Brushless Shaving Cream, 1935 – 1936. Green and black tube, OSP, 51¢. CMV, $20.00 TO, mint. $25.00 MB.

Witch Hazel Cream, 1936 – 1944. Turquoise and white tube. OSP, 52¢. CMV, $12.00 TO, mint. $15.00 MB.

Hair Dress, 1936 – 1949. Maroon and ivory tube. OSP, 37¢. CMV, $15.00 TO, mint. $20.00 MB.

Toothpaste, 1935 – 1936. Red, white, and green tube. OSP, 23¢. CMV, $12.00 TO, mint. $22.00 MB as shown.

Menthol Witch Hazel Cream, 1936 – 1944. Maroon and ivory tube. OSP, 37¢. CMV, $15.00 TO, mint. $20.00 MB.

Cleansing Cream Sample, 1936. ¼ oz. tube, black or turquoise cap. CMV, $6.00. CPC label, add $4.00.

Hand Cream, Christmas Box, 1935. Silver tube of hand cream came in special issue Christmas box for 10¢ with regular order. CMV, $23.00 MB as shown. Same box came with Tulip "A" tube of Hand Cream on right in 1936. CMV, $20.00 MB.

Shaving Cream, 1936 – 1949. Maroon and ivory tube. OSP, 36¢. CMV, $15.00 TO, mint. $20.00 MB.

Pore Cream, 1936 – 1939. Turquoise and white tube. OSP, 78¢. CMV, $15.00 TO, mint. $20.00 MB.

Sen-Den-Tal, 1936 – 1942. Turquoise and white tube. OSP, 36¢. CMV, $15.00 TO, mint. $20.00 MB.

Brushless Shaving Cream, 1936 – 1949. Maroon and ivory tube. OSP, 41¢. CMV, $15.00 TO, mint. $20.00 MB.

Dental Cream, 1936 – 1944. Turquoise and white tube. OSP, 26¢. CMV, $7.00 TO, mint. $10.00 MB.

Toothpaste No. 2, 1936 – 1948. Turquoise and white tube. OSP, 23¢. CMV, $10.00 TO, mint. $15.00 MB.

Hand Cream, 1938. Cost 10¢ with each order, Feb. 1938. Bells on box. CMV, $25.00 MB as shown.

Toothbrush, 1940s – 1950s. Turquoise and white box with tulip A holds one Avon toothbrush. OSP, 50¢. CMV, $3.50 MB.

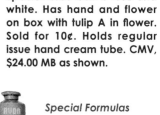

Toothpaste, 1936 – 1948. Turquoise and white tube. OSP, 23¢. CMV, $7.00 TO, mint. $12.00 MB.

Toothpaste Special Issue Box, 1938. Short issue box holds regular issue toothpaste. Cost 10¢ with regular order. CMV, $25.00 MB as shown.

Hand Cream Special Issue Box, 1940. Special issue box is rose and white. Has hand and flower on box with tulip A in flower. Sold for 10¢. Holds regular issue hand cream tube. CMV, $24.00 MB as shown.

Hand Cream Special Issue Box, 1939. Short issue box came with regular issue tube of hand cream for 10¢ with regular order. CMV, $24.00 MB as shown.

Special Formulas Cream, 1940 – 1943. Turquoise and white tube. OSP, 78¢. CMV, $9.00 TO, mint. $12.00 MB.

Hand Cream, 1937 – 1954. 2½ oz. turquoise and white tube. OSP, 52¢. CMV, $4.00 TO, mint. $8.00 MB.

Toothpaste Special Issue Box, 1937. Regular issue toothpaste came in special issue box for 10¢ with regular order. CMV, $22.00 MB as shown.

Toothpaste Special Box, 1939. OSP, 10¢ with order, October 1939. CMV, $25.00 MB as shown.

Toothpaste, 1940. Special box. OSP, 10¢ with order from rep in Sept. 1940. CMV, $22.00 MB as shown.

Smoker's Toothpaste, 1941 – 1950.
Maroon and cream tube. OSP, 39¢. CMV, $15.00 TO, mint. $18.00 MB.

Amber Cream Shampoo or Amber Gel, 1948 – 1950.
Turquoise and white tube with blue cap. CMV, $4.00 TO, mint. $8.00 MB.

Ammoniated Toothpaste, 1949 – 1955.
Green and white tube. OSP, 49¢. CMV, $5.00 TO, mint. $8.00 MB.

Hand Cream Special Issue Box, 1941.
Special issue flowered box holds regular issue tube of hand cream. Sold for 10¢ with regular order. CMV, $25.00 MB as shown.

Dental Cream, 1948 – 1953.
Red cap, red, white, and blue tube. OSP, 43¢. CMV, $4.00 TO, mint. $8.00 MB.

67th Anniversary Hand Cream Duo, 1953.
Box holds two, 2½ oz. tubes of hand cream. OSP, $1.10. CMV $20.00 MB.

Hand Cream Special Issue Box, 1942.
Special issue box with flower design holds regular issue tube of hand cream. OSP, 10¢. CMV, $22.00 MB as shown.

Hand Cream New Year Box, 1943.
Regular issue tube of hand cream. Came in special short issue flower designed box. Rare. OSP, 15¢. CMV $25.00 MB as shown.

Special Dry Skin Cream, 1948.
Night Cream, 1948.
Both tubes are blue, 2¼ oz. size. Came in 1948 Skin Care Demo Kit (see Samples and Demonstrator Kits section). Was never sold to public. Very rare. CMV, $20.00 each, mint, full.

Hand Cream Duo, 1953.
Box holds two tubes, 2½ oz. each, of hand cream. Turquoise and white. OSP, $1.18. CMV $20.00 MB.

Liquefying Cleansing Cream, 1947.
Fluffy Cleansing Cream, 1947.
Both tubes are pink, 2¼ oz. each. Came in 1947 Cleansing Cream Demo Kit only (see Samples and Demonstrator Kits section). Never sold to public. Very rare. CMV, $20.00 each.

Creme Shampoo, 1949 – 1958.
Green tube with blue or white cap. OSP, 59¢. CMV, $5.00 TO, mint. $8.00 MB.

Hand Cream Duo, 1953 only.
Two turquoise and white metal tubes of hand cream in Merry Christmas box. OSP, $1.10. CMV, $20.00 MB.

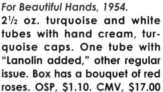

For Beautiful Hands, 1954.
2½ oz. turquoise and white tubes with hand cream, turquoise caps. One tube with "Lanolin added," other regular issue. Box has a bouquet of red roses. OSP, $1.10. CMV, $17.00 MB. In 1955 same box came with two tubes of hand cream like in the 1954 Hand Cream, Duo. CMV, $17.00 MB.

Creme Shampoo, 1955 – 1960.
Green and white tube. CMV, $6.00 TO. $10.00 MB.

Hand Cream, 1955 – 1962.
2½ oz., turquoise tube and cap. Flat cap sold 1955 – 1957 in a tube. Tall cap sold 1957 – 1962 in a 2 oz. tube. CMV, $2.00 TO. $3.00 MB, flat cap. $1.00 less on tall cap tubes.

Chlorophyll Toothpaste, 1953 – 1956.
Green and white tube, green cap. OSP, 49¢. CMV, $5.00 TO, mint. $8.00 MB.

Toothpaste, 1953 – 1956.
Blue and white tube, white cap. OSP, 49¢. CMV, $5.00 TO, mint. $8.00 MB. Also came in ¾ oz. sample tube. CMV, $5.00 mint.

Hand Cream Duo, 1954.
Christmas Special. Red and white box holds two green tubes of Avon hand cream. OSP, $1.10. CMV, $17.00 MB.

Doubly Yours Gift Box, 1955.
Special issue Christmas box holds two turquoise tubes of hand cream. OSP, 89¢. CMV, $17.00 MB.

Doubly Yours, 1954.
Rose box holds two tubes of Avon Hand Cream. OSP, $1.18. CMV, $17.00 MB.

Hand Cream with Lanolin, 1954.
2½ oz. tube. OSP, 59¢. CMV, $10.00 TO, mint. $12.00 MB.

Creme Shampoo, 1954 – 1955.
Green tube with white cap. OSP, 59¢. CMV, $6.00 TO, mint. $8.00 MB.

Hair Beauty, 1956.
Blue box holds two 2 oz. tubes of creme shampoo. OSP, $1.29. CMV, $20.00 MB.

For Beautiful Hands, 1956 only.
Blue flowered box holds two tubes of 2¾ oz. hand cream. OSP, $1.10. CMV, $16.00 MB.

Silicone Formula Cream, 1957 – 1961.
White tube, small turquoise cap. OSP, 98¢. CMV, $1.00 TO. $2.00 MB.

Creme Shampoo with Lanolin, 1960 – 1962.
Green and white box holds yellow tube with turquoise cap. CMV, $6.00 MB.

Moisturized Hand Cream, 1957 – 1967.
Pink and white tube, small white cap. OSP, 79¢. CMV, $1.00 TO. $2.00 MB.

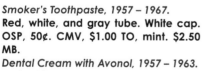

Merry Christmas Twin Favorites, 1956 only.
Green and red box holds two tubes of hand cream. OSP, $1.18. CMV, $18.00 MB.

Antiseptic Cream, 1957 – 1960.
1¾ oz. tube, white, gray, and red with red cap. OSP, 69¢. CMV, $1.00 TO. $2.00 MB.

Christmas Treasure Box, 1960 only.
Red and green box holds turquoise tube of hand cream. OSP, 69¢. CMV, $2.00 TO, mint. $7.00 MB as shown.

Cleansing Cream, 1957.
2½ oz. white tube with gray band, turquoise lettering. OSP, 59¢. CMV, $3.00 TO. $4.00 MB.

Merry Christmas Gift Boxes, 1958 – 1959.
Special issue gift box came with choice of moisturized hand cream, pink and white tube (OSP, 79¢), Avon hand cream, turquoise tube (OSP, 59¢), or Silicone Formula hand cream, white tube (OSP, 98¢). CMV, $10.00 each, MB as shown.

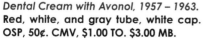 

Smoker's Toothpaste, 1957 – 1967.
Red, white, and gray tube. White cap. OSP, 50¢. CMV, $1.00 TO, mint. $2.50 MB.
Dental Cream with Avonol, 1957 – 1963.
Red, white, and gray tube, white cap. OSP, 50¢. CMV, $1.00 TO. $3.00 MB.

Creme Shampoo, 1959.
2⅖ oz. yellow tube and turquoise cap. Yellow and blue box. OSP, 69¢. CMV, $3.00 TO. $5.00 MB.

Cream Deodorant, 1960 – 1967.
OSP, 69¢. CMV, $1.50 TO. $2.00 MB.

Cream Hair Dress, 1962 – 1965.
4 oz. white tube. Red cap. Stagecoach on tube. OSP, 89¢. CMV, $4.00 TO. $6.00 MB.

Rosemint Facial Mask, 1962 – 1971.
3 oz. pink and white tube. CMV, $2.00 MB.

Hand Cream Christmas Packaging, 1964.
Special Christmas boxes in pink, blue, and white. Came with choice of green tube of 3 oz. Hand Cream, 4 oz. white plastic bottle of Hand Lotion, pink and white 3¾ oz. tube of Moisturized Hand Cream, and 2¼ oz. turquoise and white tube of Silicone Glove. CMV, $4.00 each, MB.

Hand Cream for Men Double Pak, 1966 – 1968.
Box holds two black and orange tubes. OSP, $2.50. CMV, $2.00 each, TO. $8.00 set, MB.

Care Deeply Hand Cream, 1974.
Two tubes, 4 oz. each in pink, blue, orange, and purple box. CMV, $4.00 MB.

Moisturized Hand Cream Christmas Box, 1963 only.
3¾ oz. pink and white tube pictured with special issue Christmas box. CMV, $1.00 TO, sold 1957 – 1967. CMV, $3.00 MB.

Smoker's Toothpaste, 1964 – 1967.
5 oz. white tube, blue cap. OSP, 79¢. CMV, $1.50 MB.

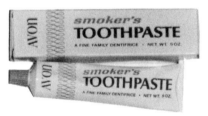

Take Along Hand Cream, 1980.
1 oz. tube in Vita Moist red design or Rich Moisture blue design. CMV, 50¢ each, MB.

Silicone Glove Christmas Box, 1963 only.
2¼ oz. turquoise and white tube in special issue Christmas box. CMV, $1.00 TO, sold 1960 – 1969. $3.00 MB.

Premium Toothpaste, 1964 – 1966.
5 oz. white tube, red cap. OSP, 89¢. CMV, $1.50 MB.

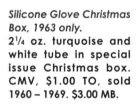

Hand Creams, 1963 – 1969.
3 oz. turquoise tubes, white caps. Top tube older, bottom tube newer. Two different labels. 1963 – 1969 and 1970 – 1973. CMV, $1.00 each.

Santa's Helper Hand Cream and Lip Balm, 1980.
Lip balm is green, red, and white. Care Deeply hand cream is red, white, and green. 1½ oz. tube. Sold together with no box. CMV, $2.00 mint set.

Hot Stuff, 1981 – 1982. Tanarifics tanning lotion. 3¾ oz. yellow tube. CMV, $1.00.

Seasonal Smoothers Hand Cream, 1982. 1½ oz. tubes in blue, red, or green. CMV, $1.00 each, MB.

Cool It, 1981 – 1982. Tanarifics tanning lotion. 3¾ oz. blue tube. CMV, $1.00.

Clearly Gentle Baby "Bear" Products, 1983. Each item has bear in blanket design.
Baby Bath.
1 oz. tube.
Baby Cream.
1 oz. tube.
Baby Oil.
1 oz. plastic bottle. CMV, 50¢ each, MB.

Clowning Around Body Soap, 1982. 1½ oz. tubes in red, yellow or blue. CMV, $1.00 each, MB.

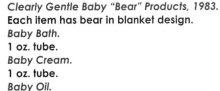

Rabbit Lip Balm and Hand Cream, 1983. Both have pink caps and rabbit on side. Hand cream is 1½ oz. tube. No box. CMV, $1.00 each.

Fruit-For-Alls Hand Creams and Lip Balms, 1981. Lip balms and 1½ oz. matching tubes of hand creams in strawberry, grape, or orange. CMV, $2.00 each set.

Stars and Stripes to Go After Tan Moisturizer, 1982 only. 1 oz. bottle, red cap. No box. CMV, $1.00.
Suntan Lotion. 1 oz. tube, red cap. No box. CMV, $1.00.

Samples and Demonstrator Kits

CPC Sales Manager's Demo Bag, 1913. Leather-bound straw bag used by early day Avon ladies to show their products. Measures 14" wide, 4" deep, 10" high. Does not say CPC on case. CMV, $75.00 mint. Also came with CPC Products label on inside lid. Same case design, only size is 17" x 11¼" x 4" deep. CMV, $100.00.

Delivery Bag, 1929. Black leatherette. CMV, $30.00.

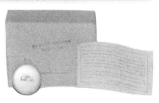

Face Powder Samples, 1930 – 1936. Plain box of 30 silver and blue metal samples. With CPC card inside. CMV, $30.00 MB.

Representative Demo Case, 1930s.
Black case held sets and demo products and catalog. $75.00 case only, mint.

Face Powder Sample, 1930 – 1936. Small silver can, came in Ariel or Vernafleur. CMV, $3.00 mint.

Perfume Sample, 1932.
Very small glass vial with cork stopper in envelope. Came in Gardenia, Jardin d'Amour, Bolero, Cotillion, Ariel, Narcissus, Rose, Lily of the Valley, Sweet Pea, or Trailing Arbutus. "CPC" on package. CMV, $18.00 each in envelope, mint.

Representative Demo Case, 1936.
Black case with metal mirror in lid. Handle is on opposite side of lid opening. Inner shelf is dark blue and lifts out of case. Storage area under shelf. Case came complete with 1936 sales catalog, ¼ oz. glass stopper perfume in Cotillion, metal cap, ¼ oz. perfume in Gardenia, blue and silver lipstick and rouge compact, silver box of face powder, ribbed glass bottle of skin freshener (2 oz.), astringent (2 oz.), Lotus Cream (4 oz.), and Rosewater, Glycerin and Benzoin (4 oz.). All with black caps. Also included 2 oz. jars of vanishing cream and tissue cream, and 4 oz. jars of cleansing cream. CMV, $700.00 MB, complete set.

Demo Bag, 1937. Simulated ostrich leather held Avon sales catalog and room for four demo packages. Used by Avon reps. CMV, $35.00 bag only, mint.

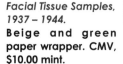

Facial Tissue Samples, 1937 – 1944. Beige and green paper wrapper. CMV, $10.00 mint.

Hand Cream Samples, 1938.
Box of 24, ¼ oz. turquoise and white tubes. CMV, $3.00 each tube. $100.00 mint, complete.
Cleansing Cream Samples, 1938.
Same box as hand cream samples. Box of 24, ¼ oz. tubes. CMV, $3.00 each tube, mint. $50.00 complete set.

Makeup Trio Demo Kit, 1936.
Brown box held 1¾ oz. box of Ariel Suntan Face Powder, turquoise and gold rouge compact in Crusader red, and matching lipstick in Crusader red. Came with fold-out display card. CMV, $60.00 MB.

New Customer Kit, 1936 – 1940. Turquoise box held 30 turquoise metal lipstick samples with 30 sample cards. CMV, $45.00 MB set, with all cards.

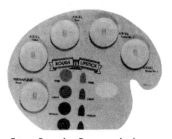

Face Powder Demonstrator Palette, 1938.
Board held five samples in Ariel and Vernafleur. CMV, $20.00 mint.

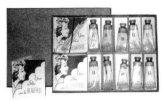

Lipstick Sample, 1938.
Came in another size and style card in 1940. This lipstick sample has a turquoise metal case. CMV, $1.00 on card, mint.

Cleansing Cream Sample Set, 1940s.
Box held 10 turquoise ¼ oz. sample tubes of cleansing cream. Also came with two stacks of "Your Skin Can Be Beautiful" pamphlets. CMV, $35.00 MB.

Face Powder Demo Palette, 1940s.
Green palette held five Tulip "A" metal samples in Ariel and Vernafleur. CMV, $32.00 mint.

Face Powder Demonstrator Palette, 1939.
Board held six different face powder samples with tulip A on lid, in Cotillion, Ariel, or Vernafleur. CMV, $20.00 mint.

Perfume Demo Kit, 1940 – 1941.
Green and gold box held three 1 dram bottles with colored caps. Perfume samples set used by representatives. Came in Marionette, Garden of Love, Cotillion, and Gardenia. CMV, $67.50 MB.

Face Powder Demonstrator Palette, 1940.
Board held eight metal samples. CMV, $20.00 mint.

Representative Demo Kit, 1940.
Box held jar of cleansing cream, night cream, foundation cream, and bottle of skin freshener. CMV, $55.00 MB.

Face Powder Demonstrator Palette, 1940.
Board held six metal samples in Ariel, Cotillion, and Vernafleur. CMV, $20.00 mint.

Facial Demo Kit, 1940s.
Green lid, box with pink base held white glass jars of cleansing cream, night cream, and foundation cream, and 4 oz. bottle of skin freshener. All have turquoise caps. Used by reps to demonstrate facial products. CMV, $50.00 MB.

Garden of Love Perfume Sample, 1940.
Small bottle with metal cap in sample envelope. Also came in Ballad, Trailing Arbutus, Cotillion, Gardenia, Merriment, Sweet Pea, Courtship, Lily of the Valley, and Jardin d'Amour. CMV, $18.00 each, in envelope only. Add $2.00 for "CPC" on envelope.

Heavenlight Face Powder Sample, 1940s.
Blue metal case, white feather on lid. CMV, $2.00 mint.

Face Powder Sample Box, 1940s.
Light green box held 30 plain blue face powder samples. "Avon" on back. CMV, $25.00 box complete, mint.

Lipstick Sample, 1940.
Similar to 1938 card, but different size. This lipstick has a gold metal case. CMV, $1.00 on card. 25¢ lipstick only.

Face Powder Sample, 1941.
One metal face powder sample of Tulip "A" design on round card. Silver back says "Avon Products 1 dollar." CMV, $6.00 mint.

Face Powder Sample Masterpiece, 1941.
Blue card held Tulip "A" metal samples of Rose and Ochre Rose. CMV, $7.00 mint.

Lipstick Demonstrator, 1940.
Box held 30 metal lipstick samples, with cards. CMV, $35.00 MB, with all 30 cards.

Facial Tissues Demo, 1940s.
Plain box of Avon tissues used as demo for reps. CMV, $20.00 mint.

Face Powder Samples, 1940 – 1950s.
Avon envelope held 10 sample packets of face powder. CMV, $3.00 mint.

Delivery Bag, 1941 – 1943.
Black imitation leather waterproof bag used by reps to deliver Avon products. Base of bag measures 15½" long, 7" wide, 10" high, and has a 21" zipper. Cost a rep $1.49. CMV, $15.00 mint.

Demonstrator Kit, 1940.
Box with gold Avon seal on lid held lipstick sample box, face powder palette, box of face powder, and 30 cotton puffs. CMV, $75.00 MB complete set.

Demo Kit — Christmas 1941.
For representatives only. CMV, $350.00 MB, complete.

Demonstrator Kit, 1942 only.
Box held a jar of cream deodorant and a bar of Lemonol soap. CMV, $50.00 MB.

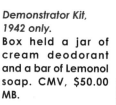

Cleansing Cream Demonstrator Kit, 1942.
Box held one jar and three sample tubes of cleansing cream. CMV, $40.00 MB.

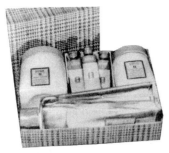

Facial Demonstrator Kit, 1942.
Box held three tubes of night cream, jar of night cream, foundation cream, and 4 oz. bottle of skin freshener. CMV, $55.00 MB.

Face Powder Samples, 1942.
Box held 30 blue feather design samples. CMV, $40.00 MB.

Delivery Bag Prize, 1944.
Black waterproof bag, zipper top, metal buttons on bottom. Given to reps for placing order of $150.00 or more. Used to deliver Avon products. CMV, $15.00 mint.

Gift Display Ensemble Demo, 1942.
A special hand carrying box used by reps at Christmas time. Came with several sets to show customers. To determine price of this kit, look up each set and get price. Then add $25.00 for the demo box.

Lipstick Demonstrator Case, 1942.
Box held 30 turquoise plastic or metal samples or 30 brass bamboo samples. Lady's face on top of box. CMV, $40.00 MB.

Heavenlight Face Powder Sample Palette, 1946.
Each pink sample has "Heavenlight" written across each top. CMV, $15.00 mint.

Face Powder Demonstrator Palette, 1942.
Board held eight paper box samples. CMV, $15.00 mint.

Delivery Bag, 1942.
Black leatherette. CMV, $20.00.

Face Powder Demonstrator Palette, Heavenlight, 1946 – 1949.
Blue board held nine feather design samples. CMV, $15.00 mint.

Face Powder Sample Set, 1942.
Box held 30 metal face powder samples. CMV, $1.00 each sample. $45.00 set MB. Also came with CPC Avon label. CMV, $65.00 set MB.

Gift Display Ensemble Demo, 1943.
A special hand carrying box used by reps at Christmas time to show Christmas sales items and sets. To determine the price of this kit, look up each set and get its price, then add $25.00 for this demo box.

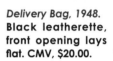

Heavenlight Face Powder Samples, 1946 – 1949.
Box held 30 feather design samples. Samples came in both cardboard and tin. CMV, $35.00 MB.

Perfume Samples, 1947 – 1950.
Small sample tubes with glass vials of perfume inside. Came in Gardenia, Lily of the Valley, Crimson Carnation, Luscious, Garden of Love, Ballad, Quaintance, and Golden Promise. CMV, $20.00 each with vials. Here's My Heart, Flowertime, Quaintance, and Cotillion. Came in pink or blue tubes. CMV, $15.00 each, mint.

Skin Care Demo Kit, 1948.
Demo box held blue 2¼ oz. tube of fluffy cleansing cream, 4 oz. bottle of skin freshener, and tube of special dry skin cream. Not sold to public. Used by reps as demonstrator. CMV, $55.00 MB.

Delivery Bag, 1948.
Black leatherette, front opening lays flat. CMV, $20.00.

Demonstrator Kit, 1946.
Box held tubes of toothpaste and hand cream, and bottle of antiseptic. CMV, $55.00 MB.

Lipstick Samples, 1947.
Red box held 30 brass samples. Also came in two boxes in a plain carton from Avon. CMV, $30.00. CMV, $60.00 box of two sets.

Shampoo Demo Kit, 1947.
Box held two bottles, soapless and liquid shampoo. For reps only. CMV, $55.00 mint.

Representative Demonstrator Kit, 1948.
Black leather kit. CMV, $90.00 mint.

Demonstrator Kit, 1949.
Demo box held tubes of hand cream and creme shampoo, and jar of perfumed deodorant. Used by reps to show products. CMV, $35.00 MB.

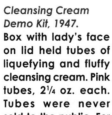

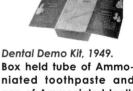

Cleansing Cream Demo Kit, 1947.
Box with lady's face on lid held tubes of liquefying and fluffy cleansing cream. Pink tubes, 2¼ oz. each. Tubes were never sold to the public. For reps only. Rare. CMV, $50.00 MB.

Hand Lotion and Hand Cream Demo Kit, 1948.
Demo box held tubes of hand cream and 4 oz. bottle of hand lotion. Not sold. Used by reps to sell products. CMV, $35.00 MB.

Dental Demo Kit, 1949.
Box held tube of Ammoniated toothpaste and can of Ammoniated tooth powder. Not sold to public. Used by reps to show products. CMV, $45.00 MB.

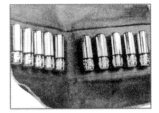

Face Powder Palette, 1949 – 1954.
Turquoise board held eight to 10 samples. CMV, $10.00 mint.

Lipstick Demonstrator Kit, 1949.
Black flannel roll-up kit held 10 gold full-size lipsticks. CMV, $30.00 mint.

Cologne Demonstrator Set, early 1950s.
1 dram bottles of Cotillion, Quaintance, Forever Spring, Golden Promise, and To a Wild Rose. In green and gold box. Came in five and six bottle sets. CMV, $17.00 MB.

Cream Cake Samples, 1949 – 1955.
Held six shades of cream cake. CMV, $8.00 mint.

Face Powder Samples, 1949 – 1955.
Green metal samples. CMV, $2.00 each, mint.

Cologne Samples, 1950.
Green box held six samples, colored lids. CMV, $12.00 MB.

Demonstration Tissues, 1949.
Small packet of Avon tissues for demonstrations. CMV, $12.00 mint.

Face Powder Palette Demonstrator, 1950s.
Board held 10 sample powders. Came in pink envelope. Used by reps. Same palette came in different envelopes. CMV, $10.00, with envelopes mint.

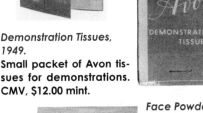

Lipstick Jewel Etched Samples, 1949 – early 1950s.
Box held 30 metal lipstick samples. CMV, $30.00 MB.

Flavor Buds Toothpaste Sample, 1950s.
Red and white box with foil tear-off samples. CMV, $7.00 MB.

Face Powder Demo Samples, 1949 – 1950.
Pink and white feather box held 50 demo packets of face powder. Used by reps. Packets are different. Not sold to the public. CMV, $15.00 MB.

Lipstick Packs, 1950s.
Two different packs of 10 brass lipsticks. CMV, $6.00 complete pack or 50 sample pack, brass. CMV, $15.00 complete.

Powder Sachet Packets, 1950s.
Came in all fragrances, 10 in an envelope. CMV, $1.00 each, or $7.00 for packet of 10, mint.

Delivery Bag, 1950s.
Black leatherette. CMV, $17.00 mint.

Cleansing Cream Demonstrator Kit, 1951.
Demo box held two white glass jars with turquoise lids of cleansing cream and one jar of night cream. Used by reps to show products. Came in two different boxes. CMV, $30.00 MB.

Skin Care Demo Kit, 1952.
Flip-open display box held one jar each of cleansing cream and night cream, and a bottle of skin freshener. Used by reps to show products. CMV, $50.00 MB.

Lipstick Demonstrator, 1952.
Box held four full-size gold embossed lipsticks and one refill. Used in the early to mid-1950s. CMV, $30.00 MB.

Pack Up Your Skin Troubles Demonstrator Kit, 1953.
Cardboard carrying case held jars of cleansing cream and tissue cream, and 4 oz. bottle of astringent. CMV, $55.00 MB.

Lipstick Demonstrator, 1953.
Green leatherette zippered case held five gold lipsticks. CMV, $27.50 mint.

Face Powder Palette, 1954 – 1955.
Turquoise board held 10 samples. CMV, $10.00 mint.

Birthday Cake, 1951.
Blue and white box held foam cake with five 1-dram ribbed perfumes in To A Wild Rose, Golden Promise, Cotillion, Quaintance, and Flowertime. This was a demonstrator kit, for reps. CMV, $90.00 cake and bottles only, mint. $125.00 MB.

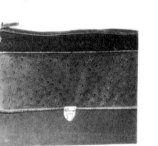

Sales Bag, 1953.
Black bag used by Avon reps in the early 1950s. CMV, $22.00 mint.

Lipstick Samples, 1951.
White plastic tray held 30 brass lipstick samples. CMV, $25.00 mint.

Hand Care Demonstrator Kit, 1953.
Box held two bottles of nail polish, one tube of hand cream, and one jar of nail beauty. CMV, $40.00 MB.

Skin Care Demonstrator, 1956.
Plastic case held plastic bottle of deep clean cleansing cream, 1 oz. glass bottle of skin freshener, two white jars of rich moisture and hormone creams, and plastic spoon. CMV, $37.50 MB.

Beauty Showcase Bag, Early 1960s.
Two tones, blue with black trim. Used by reps. CMV, $6.00.

Beauty Counselor Demo Kit Samples, 1956 – 1960.
Front row, left to right: White plastic jars with turquoise caps. Came in Vita Moist Cream, Strawberry Cooler, and Rich Moisture Cream. CMV, $6.00 each.
Back row, left to right: Skin freshener, clear glass, white cap, $10.00. Deep clean cleansing cream, white plastic, gold lettering, white cap. CMV, $6.00. Rouge jars, clear glass, white caps. CMV, $6.00 each.

Face Powder Demonstrator Palette, 1957.
Turquoise board held 10 samples with clear plastic tops. CMV, $10.00 mint.

Beauty Showcase Bag, late 1960s.
Two toned blue and blue trim. Used by reps. CMV, $5.00.

Nail Polish Demonstrator, 1957.
Six, ½-dram bottles with white caps. CMV, $20.00 MB.

Delivery Bag, 1960s.
Two toned blue, silver 4A emblem under handle. CMV, $6.00.

Cologne Demonstrator Set, 1956.
1 dram bottles of To a Wild Rose, Forever Spring, Bright Night, Nearness, Elégante, and Cotillion. All different color caps, in pink and gold box. CMV, $15.00 MB. Also released in Canada with all white caps. CMV, $15.00 MB.

Powder Samples, 1958.
14 samples, square container. CMV, $7.00 MB.

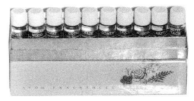

Fragrance Samples — Women's, 1960.
Pink and gold box held ten 1 dram bottles, white caps. CMV, $12.00 MB.

Harmony Rouge Samples, 1956.
Five sample bottles. CMV, $15.00.

Beauty Counselor Demo Kit, 1959 – 1960.
Black shoulder bag with outside pocket held removable turquoise and white plastic inner case with Avon and 4A design on lid containing three white plastic jars with turquoise lids holding ⁵⁄₁₁ oz. of rich moisture cream, Vita Moist Cream and Strawberry Cooler, 1 oz. glass bottle sample of skin freshener, 1¼ oz. white plastic sample bottle of deep clean cleansing cream, 17 sample bottles of liquid powder, five liquid rouge samples in small bottles, 45 gold metal lipstick samples, and 16 plastic shaker powder samples. CMV, $200.00 complete and mint.

Nosegay Lipstick Demo Kit, 1960.
White foam, pink ribbon and flowers. Held four white lipsticks. Came only in plum, orange, peach, and cherry blossom. Made up like flower bouquet. CMV, $65.00 mint.

Foundation Demonstrator, 1960s.
Clear glass bottles with white plastic lids.
Top to bottom: Six bottle set, 12 bottle set, 10 bottle set, eight bottle set. CMV, $5.00 all sets, MB.

Cream Hair Dress Samples, 1961.
Box of 30 tubes. CMV, 25¢ each tube. $5.00 MB.

Eyeshadow Demonstrator Card, 1960.
Six gold metal eyeshadow tubes. CMV, $2.00 mint.

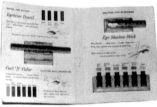

New Beauty for Eyes Demo Kit, 1960.
Cardboard card opened up with six brass lipstick samples, brass eyeshadow stick, eyebrow pencil, and Curl 'N' Color. Used by reps. CMV, $4.00 mint.

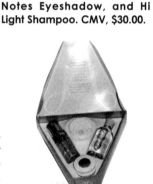

76th Anniversary Celebration Demo Kit, 1962.
Pink cardboard box held 2 oz. Cotillion cologne, Cotillion cream sachet, 2 oz. perfumed deodorant, 6 oz. Rosiest Spray Sachet, Silver Notes Eyeshadow, and Hi Light Shampoo. CMV, $30.00.

Men's After Shave Samples, 1960s.
Red and silver box, bottles have red caps. CMV, $10.00 MB.

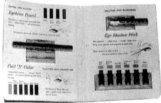

Lipstick Demonstrator, 1961.
A demonstrator piece sold to representatives for $1.35. Black plastic base with clear lucite dome. Came with silver deluxe lipstick with 4A on top (wrong lipstick shown in case). CMV, $22.00 MB.

77th Anniversary Demo Set, 1963.
Demo kit for Avon reps on 77th Anniversary. Top of box has rose in left corner and says "Celebrating Avon's 77th Anniversary." Box held 2 oz. cologne mist with 4As embossed on side, jar of cream foundation, 4 oz. Skin So Soft, and Petti Pat compact. CMV, $35.00 MB.

Lipstick Samples, 1960s – 1970s.
Turquoise plastic box held 40 white plastic lipstick samples. CMV, 10¢ each sample. $5.00 MB, complete.

Delivery Bag, 1960s.
Used by Avon reps. CMV, $25.00.

Tribute After Shave Samples, 1963. **Box of 10. CMV, $5.00.**

Fragrance Cologne Samples, 1965. **Pink and gold box held 10 cologne samples with white caps. CMV, $7.00 MB.**

Delivery Bag, 1970s. **White, blue, and green design used by Avon ladies. CMV, $6.00.**

Perfume Sample, 1964. **Small ⅛ oz. bottle, came in Occur!, Somewhere, Cotillion, Topaze, Here's My Heart, Persian Wood, and To a Wild Rose. CMV, $4.00 each.**

Occur! Cream Sachet Samples, 1965. **Box of 30. CMV, $5.00 each.**

Beauty Showcase Bag, 1970s. **Blue and green vinyl came with blue plastic holder for samples. CMV, $5.00 each. $10.00 for both.**

Eyeshadow Try-ons, 1964. **Demo paper container with 50 match samples, double sided. CMV, $6.00 mint. CMV, $5.00 mint.**

Liquid Powder Samples, 1967. **Box of 12 samples, clear plastic top. CMV, $5.00 MB.**

Representative's Demo Bag, 1970. **White background with bright colored flowers. Silver 4A emblem under handle. CMV, $6.00 mint.**

Bath Freshener Samples, 1968. **Colored caps, seven samples. CMV, $6.00 MB. 14 samples, white caps. CMV, $7.00 MB.**

Manager's Demo Kit, 1965. **White box held eye and face makeup. CMV, $55.00 MB.**

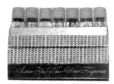

Cologne Samples, 1968. **Green box with woven design held seven samples, all have yellow caps. CMV, $5.00 MB.**

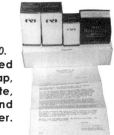

Prima Natura Products Introduction Demo Kit for Managers Only, 1970. **White Avon embossed box held Creme of Soap, Night Veil Concentrate, Toning Freshener, and Moisturizing Freshener. CMV, $25.00.**

Rep's Demo and Order Case, 1970.
Blue plastic snap-shut case. Had order pad and fragrance samples and color brochures. CMV, $10.00 mint.

Foundation Makeup Demo, 1973.
Box held seven bottles with white caps. Used by reps only. CMV, $3.00 MB.

Making Eyes Display, 1976.
Plastic base used by managers to display new turquoise color eye makeup products. Base held 12 powder eyeshadows, five dream eyeshadows, two eyeshadow wands, three mascaras, and three brow and liner pencils. CMV, 25¢ each, empty products. $5.00 base only. $25.00 MB as shown full.

Men's After Shave Samples, early 1970s.
Box is red woven design and black, bottles have red caps. Came with two different outer sleeves as shown on top. CMV, $6.00 each, MB.

Perfect Balance Manager's Demo Kit, 1974.
Contained Tissue-Off cleansing cream, Toning Freshener, night cream, Wash-Off cleansing lotion, Toning astringent, and night time moisturizer. CMV, $15.00 MB.

Custom Conditioner, 1971 – 1972.
¾ oz. bottle with white cap. Used in Avon beauty shops, for professional use only. CMV, $10.00.

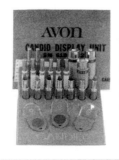

Delivery Bag, 1976.
Blue brocade bag used by Avon reps to deliver Avon products. CMV, $3.00
Beauty Showcase Demo Bag, 1976.
Used by Avon reps to carry Avon demonstration products. Matching blue brocade. CMV, $3.00.

Colorworks Demo Kit, 1977.
Silver and white box with outer sleeve held Oil Free Liquid Makeup, Oil Free Cheek blush, Super shine Lip Gloss, Lasting Eye Shadow and Lashes, Lashes Mascara. Used by Reps to sell new Colorworks products. Reps cost, $4.50. CMV, $8.00 complete MB.

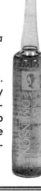

New Dimension Extra and Regular, 1971 – 1972.
¾ oz. glass bottle. Used in Avon beauty shops, for professional use only. Top of bottle must be broken to use contents. CMV, $10.00.

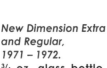

Candid Manager's Display Unit, 1976.
Orange plastic unit for Avon managers to display new Candid products. Base held seven Candid lipsticks, six eye colors, two mascaras, three cheek colors, and three 1½ oz. bottles of makeup. CMV, 25¢ each, empty items. $15.00 base only. $45.00 MB, complete full set.

Candid Makeup Demo Kit, 1977.
For reps only. Box lid "Candid" is in different position than regular set sold. Came with outer sleeve and says "(Not for Resale)" on back side. Box held five items: makeup, lip color, eye color, cheek color, and mascara with lash builders. CMV, $10.00 MB with outer sleeve only. Sold to public for $10.95. Same CMV.

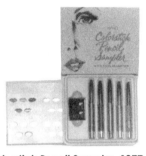

Colorstick Pencil Sampler, 1977.
Plastic base with sleeve lid held color chart and five Colorstick pencils and brown plastic two-hole pencil sharpener, marked "Avon." Used by reps to sell Colorstick products. CMV, $2.00 MB, complete.

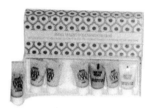

Foundation Makeup Duo, 1977.
Box held seven Even-Tone foundation tubes with white caps. Marked "not for resale" on back. CMV, $2.00 MB.

Fashion Makeup Group Collection, 1977.
Demo kit used by reps to sell Fashion Makeup products. Box is black and gold with white base. Outside sleeve. Cost rep $5.47. CMV, $8.00 MB, complete.

Moisture Secret Skin Care Kit, 1978.
White and pink plastic kit held pink plastic tubes of moisture secret enriched creme gel cleanser, enriched freshener, and enriched daytime moisturizer. All with PMB and pink plastic jar of enriched night concentre. All are trial size. Came with outer sleeve over kit. CMV, $6.00 MB.

Colorcreme Moisture Lipsticks Demo Set, 1978.
Fruit basket design box held 15 small white plastic sample lipsticks and one full-size lipstick in silver and blue tube. Box came with outer sleeve. CMV, $2.00 MB.

Fragrance Demo Kit, 1978 – 1983.
Plastic demo kit held six sample bottles of Avon fragrance. CMV, $2.00 mint.

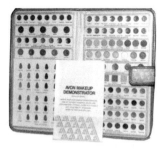

Makeup Demo Case, 1979.
Large tan vinyl case. CMV, $5.00 MB.

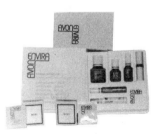

Envira Makeup Demo Kit and Products, 1979 – 1980.
Pink lid box with outer sleeve and white plastic inner base held one each of Envira products, which were also sold separately: Conditioning Make-up, Pure Color Blush, Gentle Eye Color, Pure Color Lipstick, Soft Eye Definer, and Conditioning Mascara. CMV, $7.50 complete set in demo box, mint.
Samples Conditioning Makeup.
Box of 10.
Samples of Pure Color Blush.
Box of 10. CMV, 25¢ each, all products listed.

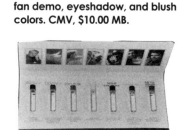

Fresh Look Makeup Demo Kit, 1979. Used by reps only. Peach color box. CMV, $8.00 MB.

Beauty Fluid Sample Kit, 1980. Given to President's Club member reps. Box has outer sleeve. Silver and brown box and sleeve. Held 3 oz. bottle of beauty fluid and pack of tissues. CMV, $12.00 MB.

Coordinates Makeup Demonstrator, 1983. Plastic display case used by Avon reps to show makeup products. Size 11" x 16". Red and white lipstick sample tubes, nail enamel fan demo, eyeshadow, and blush colors. CMV, $10.00 MB.

Moisture Secret Kit, 1980. Outer sleeve held white and pink plastic case, with four small pink plastic containers of creams. CMV, $7.00 MB.

Accolade Demo Kit, 1982. Carmel color plastic case held Accolade products for Avon managers. CMV, $20.00 mint.

Fragrance Sampler, 1984. Gold box held seven, one-inch vials of fragrance, four women's and three men's. CMV, $4.00 MB.

Versatilities Makeup Demo Kit, 1982. Gray box with sleeve and black box lid held black and gray lipstick and Versatilities nail polish and eye makeup. Used by reps for demo. CMV, $5.00 MB.

Time Control Demo Kit, 1980. Black and pink box and sleeve had small white hour glass and ¾ oz. plastic bottles of Time Control, plus six more bottles in box. Used by reps as demo kit. CMV, $8.00 MB.

Beauty Makeup Demo Kit. Came in gray box. CMV, $5.00 MB.

Paper Items

CPC Calling Card, 1896. Has list of products on back side and "CPC Co., 126 Chambers St., New York" on front. CMV, $25.00.

CPC Sales Catalog, 1896. Small 30-page booklet on products. Contains no pictures. Rare. CMV, $125.00.

CPC Catalog, 1898.
5" x 8" blue cover, 64 pages in blue paper. Used by CPC reps to sell products. Eureka trademark on back cover. Very rare. CMV, $225.00.

CPC Christmas Greeting Card, early 1900s.
1¢ postcard sent out at Christmas time. 126 Chambers Street, New York, is the return address. CMV, $25.00.

Letter from CPC, 1897.
Letter to CPC managers. On CPC letterhead. CMV, $45.00.

CPC Letterhead, 1896.
This letterhead is the same as on the CPC letter above. Shown here for better detail. CMV, $45.00 in good condition.

CPC Catalogs.
1900 CPC catalog shown at top left, bottom right 1908, and bottom left is 1915. Each one shows the item sold during that period by CPC and gives prices. 1915 was the last small catalog printed. 1916 they went to the large black hardbound color books. For comparison of size, the 1896 is 4½" wide and 6⅝" high. CMV, $150.00 each.

CPC Catalog, 1897.
62-page sales catalog. Very rare, hand-drawn illustration. CMV, $250.00.

Outlooks, 1905 – 1974.
Outlooks were first printed in 1905 and given only to sales reps of CPC and Avon. They showed new items coming out and also showed awards that could be won. The Outlook was discontinued in 1974 and the name was changed to Avon Calling. Outlooks were given for each sales campaign during the year. CMV, 1905 to 1930, $5.00 to $15.00; 1930 to 1939, $2.00 to $5.00; 1940 to 1949, $1.00 to $5.00; 1950 to 1959, $1.00 to $4.00; 1960 to 1965, $1.00 to $3.00; 1960 to 1969, 50¢ to $1.00; 1970 to 1976, 10¢ to 25¢ each.

CPC Catalog, 1898.
62-page sales catalog. Only has illustrations, not pictures of products. Very rare. CMV, $225.00.

CPC D. H. McConnell Letter, 1900s.
On CPC letterhead. Handwritten by D. H. McConnell, founder of Avon, to his factory workers. CMV for any handwritten D. H. McConnell letter dated 1890s to 1930s would be $25.00 to $50.00, depending on buyer. Note that most later years McConnell's signature is rubber stamped and not handwritten.

Shaving Pads, early 1900s.
Two different, lady and Joe Jefferson. CMV, $75.00 each.

CPC Calendar, 1910.
9" wide, 12⁵/₁₆" high. Printed in six colors. Given to all customers with orders of 75¢ or more. CMV, $300.00 in new condition.

Sales Manager's Contract, 1913.
Paper agreement for Avon ladies in early 1900s. Signed by D. H. McConnell, founder of Avon. CMV, $30.00.

CPC Ink Blotter, 1912.
Used by reps in the early 1900s. CMV, $40.00.

Depot Manager's Contract, CPC, 1909.
Paper agreement between CPC and sales lady. CMV, $45.00 mint.

Shaving Pad, 1908.
Girl holding flowers on cover. CMV, $75.00 mint.

The Woman Beautiful Booklet, 1909.
Small booklet on massage cream. CMV, $35.00.

CPC Calendar, 1912 – 1914.
3" x 6½" small calendar with gold embossed color picture. Both 1912 and 1914 calendars have the same picture, just different calendar dates. CMV, $200.00 in mint condition to $60.00 in fair condition.

Shaving Pad, 1915.
Lady with big flower on hat on cover. CMV, $75.00.

Instruction Manual, 1912.
Used by CPC sales managers. CMV, $50.00.

Panama-Pacific Gold Medal Certificate, 1915.
Paper certrificate for CPC Products at the Panama-Pacific International Exposition in 1915. CMV, $50.00.

CPC Calendar, 1909.
Given only to best CPC customers. CMV, $335.00 in new condition.

Shaving Pad, 1910.
This is the first color CPC shaving pad to be found. All the rest we know of are black and white. Rare. CMV, $100.00.

CPC Catalog, 1912.
64-page sales catalog used by reps. CMV, $150.00.

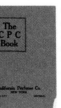

CPC Mail Order Catalog, 1916 – 1918.
4½" x 6", gray cover, 40-page booklet sent to customers in areas where CPC reps did not call. Rare. CMV, $150.00.

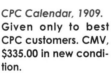

Baby Book, 1920.
CMV, $50.00.

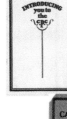

CPC Intro Booklet, 1928.
30-page booklet used by reps to start selling Avon. CMV, $30.00 mint.

CPC Prize Credit Certificate, 1928.
3" x 6" paper certificate for products in 1928. CMV, $35.00.

CPC Order Booklet, 1922.
Used by reps to keep records of their orders. CMV, $25.00 mint.

CPC Sales Catalogs, 1916 – 1929.
On bottom is black hardbound CPC sales catalog with 32 to 40 color pages. Book is 10½" x 16" in size. The hardbound book was first issued in 1916 in the big size and last used in 1921. Gold lettering on front. The top black catalog (1922 – 1929) is softcover and 34 pages in color. 10" x 14½" in size. These catalogs are usually not dated and are very hard to find. CMVs range from $25.00 in very bad condition to $150.00 for a mint, new condition catalog. Each year a new book was issued.

CPC Order Book, 1926.
Order book used by reps, shown with CPC envelope and announcement of new headquarters address in New York. CMV, $25.00 as shown.

CPC Customer List Booklet, 1928.
12 pages. CMV, $8.00 mint.

CPC Instruction Manual, 1920.
14-page booklet used to train early day Avon reps. Tells them how and what to do to be a sales lady for CPC. No pictures. CMV, $35.00.

Calopad Sanitary Napkins, 1926.
Cardboard box holds 12 napkins. Extremely Rare. Sold by CPC. CMV, $75.00 MB.

Order Books.
Left to right: 1920s, CPC on white cover. CMV, $20.00. 1930s, Tulip A design (white cover), CMV, $15.00. 1940s, script A design (blue cover). CMV, $10.00. 1950s, 4A design (green cover). CMV, $5.00. 1960s, 4A design (white cover). CMV, $2.00. All must be in new condition for CMV given.

Sales Brochures, 1920s – 1930s.
Fold-out color sales brochures given to customers by CPC and Avon representatives. Each one shows all items sold in regular sales catalog. These are rare.
Left to right: 1926, CMV, $40.00; 1929, CMV, $35.00; 1931 – 1936, CMV, $30.00.

Avon Christmas Catalogs.
Starting in the early 1930s through 1956, Avon printed special Christmas sales catalogs showing many gifts never sold at any other time. These catalogs are rare and hard to find. CMV, 1930s, $40.00 each. 1940s, $35.00 each. 1950s, $15.00 each.
Christmas Catalog, 1967.
Upper right, special hard-bound edition. CMV, $8.00 mint.

Avon Catalogs, 1930 – 1957.
Front row, left to right: 1930 – 1936, 10" x 7" dark blue, silver Avon on cover. CMV, $20.00 to $40.00 depending on condition. 1936 – 1948, 7¼" x 10½" size, green cover, gold tulip A. CMV, $20.00 to $35.00. 1948 – 1954, 7¼" x 10½" green cover, Avon in gold letters. CMV, $15.00 to $20.00.
Bottom row, left to right: 1954, a special gold cover catalog for Honor President's Award reps. CMV, $20.00 each. 1954 – 1957, general issue was green cover, 7½" x 10½", gold Avon and 4A design. CMV, $15.00. 1956 Honor Award, red cover catalog, gold Avon and 4A design. CMV, $15.00 Each of these catalogs was made to install or remove pages. The dates given reflect the years that each cover was issued. Each catalog was changed each year on the inner pages.

CPC Avon Five Hundred Club Certificates, 1930s.
Certificates given to representatives for selling $500.00 worth of Avon products. CMV, $25.00 each, mint.

CPC Five Hundred Club Certificate, 1929.
Sent to a representative when she completed $500.00 worth of net business. CMV, $25.00 mint.

Order Book, CPC/Avon, 1930.
CMV, $15.00 mint.

Customer List Booklet, 1930.
Eight pages. CMV, $5.00 mint.

McConnell Letter Book, 1930.
174 pages of letters from managers to D. H. McConnell, Avon founder. Rare. No price established.

Address Book, 1930s – 1940s.
Green leather, gold A design. CMV, $10.00.

Cleansing Tissues, 1930 – 1932.
Wrapped in cellophane. Package of 135 sheets. CMV, $15.00 mint.

CPC Sales Rep Contract, 1930s.
Used to sign up CPC reps for sales in early 1930s. Came in CPC Avon business envelope. Shown also with Customer List booklet and "Now You are in Business for Yourself" booklet. CMV, $25.00 complete as shown.

CPC Lady Introduction Card, 1930s.
3½" x 5¼" card used by reps to introduce themselves to customers. CMV, $8.00 mint.

Business Intro Book, 1935.
20-page booklet on how to be an Avon lady. Used by reps. CMV $10.00.

Avon Facial Tissues, 1937 – 1944.
Turquoise and white paper box. Rare. CMV, $40.00 mint, unopened.

Business Intro Book, 1931.
17-page booklet on how to be an Avon lady. Used by reps. CMV, $10.00.

Letter from Avon, 1936.
Miscellaneous letters from Avon may vary in price, depending on the year. Any letters personally signed by D. H. McConnell, founder of Avon, in his own handwriting should be worth at least $25.00. Letter shown is a copy. CMV, $15.00 mint.

Pocket Catalog, 1937.
A small fold-out leaflet brochure. CMV, $25.00 mint.

Facial Tissues, 1932 – 1936.
Box of 160 tissues. CMV, $40.00 mint.

50th Anniversary Gold Quill Pen and Letter, 1936.
Sent to representatives to announce the 50th year celebration. The circle stands for the "Avon Family Circle," the feather and quill indicated the opportunities to "Feather Your Nests." Comes complete with attached 50th anniversary letter. It folds in center. Did not come separate. CMV, $50.00 complete as pictured, mint.

Order Books.
Left to right: 1933, 1937, 1942, 1939 (green cover). CMV, $15.00 each, mint.

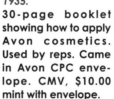

Avon's Tribute to Me, 1939.
Booklet presented to representatives during founders' campaign, July 1939. Filled with company history facts and pictures. CMV, $25.00, complete as shown.

Beauty Service Booklet, 1934.
24-page beauty tip book. CMV, $10.00.

Beauty Service Book, 1935.
30-page booklet showing how to apply Avon cosmetics. Used by reps. Came in Avon CPC envelope. CMV, $10.00 mint with envelope.

Paving the Way, 1937.
Booklet used by reps in the 1930s to help train them for better sales. Tulip A on cover. CMV, $8.00.

Ad Displays, 1950s.
Magazine advertising on hardbacks. CMV, $15.00 each.

Order Book, 1940.
Dark green cover for order book imprinted with tulip "A" and name of representative. Given for sales during 1940 Founder's Campaign. CMV, $15.00 book only, mint. $20.00 in envelope.

Promise to Myself Booklet, 1953.
23-page booklet published by Irene Nunemaker and Avon Products, Inc. CMV, $10.00.

Children's Color Books, 1960s – 1970s.
Small World, Mickey Mouse, I Wish I Could, and Peanuts. CMV, $7.00 each.

Avon War Time Hat, 1942.
Paper hat marked "Avon" on inside. CMV, $50.00.

Honor Award Book Cover, 1956.
Red plastic, gold design. CMV, $7.50.

Rose Stamps, 1961.
Page of 75 rose stamps for Avon rep use in C-2-1961. Stamps say "Avon 75th Year." CMV, $20.00.

Great Oak Booklet, 1945.
20-page, blue cover. Given to reps in 1945. Written by D.H. McConnell, founder of CPC, in 1903. Came with letter from Russell Rooks, who became president of Avon. Rare. CMV, $50.00 with letter.

Call Tag Pads, 1958.
Pad of tear-off sheets left by Avon lady. CMV, $3.00 pad.

Order Book, 1960.
CMV, $2.00.

Manager's Sales Meeting Notebook, 1962.
Campaigns 15,16,17, and 18 sales meeting plans. Red and white Christmas tree cover. CMV, $25.00.

Manager's Information Booklet, 1945.
8¼" x 9", 18-page booklet for managers to give new Avon reps general information on Avon products. The cover of this booklet is the same artwork Avon Products used to make the 1977 National Association of Avon Clubs plate advertised in C26-77 Avon Calling. CMV, $20.00.

Order Books, 1960s – 1970s.
Miscellaneous Avon order books used by reps. CMV, 50¢ each.

Calendar, 1967. "Avon Calling" calendar. CMV, $8.00 mint.

Place Mats, 1971.
Four Seasons, Robert Woods signed plastic place mats for Avon. Had choice of one of the four when you bought certain products. CMV, $3.00 each.

George Washington Representative Gift Letter, 1976.
Folder (on left) and a copy of a letter George Washington wrote from Mt. Vernon. Given at sales meeting in February. CMV, $5.00 mint.

Designer's Collection Christmas Card Catalogue Demonstrator, 1971.
Large spiral bound picture album holds one each of 36 different Christmas cards sold by Avon in 1971. CMV, $45.00 album only, no cards. Never sold to public. $75.00 complete, mint with all 36 cards.

Heritage Almanac, 1975.
1975 calendar given to district managers only. Duplicate of 1929 calendar, each page shows different Outlook. Limited edition, 2,678 given. CMV, $25.00.

Hong Kong Catalog, 1978.
Avon sales catalog from Hong Kong. CMV, $9.00.

Designer's Collection Christmas Cards, 1971.
Box of 25 Avon Christmas cards, all the same design. Came in 36 different designs. No. 1 shown. Back of each card marked "Avon Products, Inc." and gives the card number. CMV, 50¢ to $1.00 each card.
Not shown: Designer's Collection Christmas Card Sample Set, 1971.
Box of 36 different Avon Christmas cards used by Avon reps for sales. Short issue. CMV, $35.00 complete set.

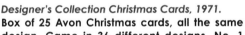

Avon Calendar, 1979 – 1980.
Large Avon calendar given to customers by Avon reps. Came in big envelope each year. CMV, $1.00 each, mint in envelope.

Perfection

Harmless Coloring Set, 1895 – 1920.
Set of eight ½ oz. bottles with cork stoppers. Came in wood box. Lemon, chocolate, lilac, coffee, orange, red, violet, and green. CMV, $45.00 each bottle. $400.00 set MB.

Olive Oil, 1895.
8 oz. glass bottle with cork stopper. CMV, $85.00 BO, mint. $105.00 MB. Also came in 1 pt., 1 qt., ½ gal., and 1 gal. sizes. CMV, $125.00 each, rare.

Fruit Flavoring Extracts, 1898.
2 oz., clear glass. "Fruit Flavors California Perfume Co." embossed on back
side of each bottle. Cork stoppers.
CMV, $110.00 each, BO, mint. $130.00
each, MB.

Furniture Polish, 1904.
8 oz glass bottle.
This bottle may be
dark amber glass or
clear. Eureka trade-
mark on neck label.
Cork stopper. CMV,
$100.00 BO, mint.
$150.00 MB.

Silver Plate Polish, 1906.
4 oz. glass bottle with
metal cap. CMV, $100.00
BO. $125.00 MB.

Flavoring Extract, 1900 – 1912.
2 oz. bottle shown is same as 4 oz. bottle. Paper label. Came in almond, banana, blood orange, celery, cinnamon,
cloves, lemon, nutmeg, onion, orange,
peach, pear, peppermint, pineapple,
pistachio, quince, jamaica ginger,
raspberry rose, strawberry, vanilla, or
wintergreen. CMV, $85.00 BO, mint.
$100.00 MB. Also came in 16 oz., 1 qt.
½ gal., and 1 gal. sizes. CMV, $125.00
each, BO. $150.00 each, MB.

Olive Oil, 1905.
16 oz. bottle.
CMV, $100.00
mint, rare.

Flavoring Extract, 1905 – 1908.
8 oz. and 16 oz. bottles, glass
stoppers. Came in all flavors
listed under smaller bottles of
1900 flavoring extracts. CMV,
$150.00 BO. $175.00 MB.

**Vegetable Color
Sample, 1900.**
Small clear glass vial
with cork stopper.
CMV, $50.00 mint.

**Carpet Renovator,
1906.**
Box holds one bar
of soap. CMV,
$85.00 MB.

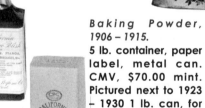

**Baking Pow-
der, 1906.**
½ lb. or 1 lb.
can. CMV,
$100.00 mint.

**Food Flavoring Dem-
onstrator Set, 1900.**
Straw covered
wood case holds
20 bottles of food flavoring extracts. CMV,
$1,500.00 complete set mint.

**Baking Powder,
1906 – 1915.**
5 lb. container, paper
label, metal can.
CMV, $70.00 mint.
Pictured next to 1923
– 1930 1 lb. can, for
size comparison.

CPC Furniture Polish, 1906.
8 oz. bottle with cork stopper.
Came as round or square bottle, same label. CMV, $100.00
each, BO. $125.00 each, MB.

Nutmeg Flavoring, 1906.
2 oz., cork stopper. Eureka trademark label. CMV, $100.00 mint.

"Extra Concentrated" Vanilla Extract, 1906.
2 oz. or 4 oz. glass bottle with cork stopper. CMV, $100.00 BO. $125.00 MB.

Flavoring Extracts, 1908.
Came in 1, 2, 4, and 8 oz. sizes with cork stoppers. Also came in 1 pt. and 1 qt. with glass stoppers. Flavors are almond, banana, celery, cinnamon, jamaica, ginger, lemon, maple, nutmeg, orange, onion, peppermint, pineapple, pistachio, raspberry, rose, strawberry, vanilla, tonka and vanillin, vanilla pure, and wintergreen. The 2 oz. bottles are embossed "California Perfume Co. Fruit Flavors" on back side, paper labels on front. OSP, 1 oz., 25¢. 2 oz., 45¢. 4 oz., 90¢. 8 oz., $1.75. 16 oz., $3.25. CMV, $100.00 each, mint with label. CMV, $125.00 each, MB. Embossed bottle with no label, $35.00. CMV, 1 pt. and 1 qt. sizes, $125.00 each, BO. $150.00 each, MB, with label and glass stopper.

Vanilla, Tonka and Vanillin Flavor Extract, 1910.
2 or 4 oz. glass bottle, cork stopper. Came in 17 flavors. CMV, $100.00 BO, mint. $125.00 MB.

Fruit Flavoring, 1908.
2 oz., embossed "Fruit California Perfume Co. Flavors." Had paper label on reverse side. CMV, $40.00 BO. $100.00 mint with paper label. $125.00 MB. Some came with reversed "A" in California. Add $5.00 for reversed "A."

Raspberry Flavor, 1908.
1 oz., CPC New York Label. CMV, $50.00 BO. $75.00 MB.

Food Flavoring Demonstrator Set, 1909.
Black leather covered wood case holds 24, 1 oz. bottles of food flavoring. OSP, $2.00 to reps. CMV, $1,800.00 complete and mint with all labels.

Extract of Lemon, 1908.
16 oz., glass stopper. CMV, $150.00 BO, mint. $175.00 MB.

Vegetable Coloring, 1908.
2 oz. or 4 oz., clear glass. Front white paper label. Embossed "Fruit Flavors" on back side. CMV, $100.00 BO, mint. $125.00 MB.

Vanilla, Tonka and Vanillin Flavor Sample, 1910.
Small sample bottle, clear glass, cork stopper. CMV, $100.00 BO, mint. $125.00 MB.

Flavoring Extract Set, 1912.
Black leather grain case with double handles and snaps. Holds 20, one-ounce bottles of food flavor extract. Used by reps to show products. CMV, $1,500.00 complete set, mint.

Furniture Polish, 1915.
8 oz. clear glass bottle, cork stopper. CMV, $85.00 BO, mint. $100.00 MB. Same label is on rare amber bottle.

Harmless Colors Set, 1910 – 1915.
Wood box, slide-open lid, holds 8½ oz. bottles with cork stoppers: red, chocolate, green, coffee, lemon, velvet, orange, and lilac. Labels on tops of corks only. CMV, $350.00 MB.

Furniture Polish, 1915.
8 oz. amber glass, cork stopper. Very rare. CMV, $150.00 BO, mint. $175.00 MB.

Maplex Flavoring, 1914 – 1918.
1 oz. clear glass bottle with cork stopper. Maplex was used to make syrup to make homemade ice cream. This is the only bottle of Maplex we have seen. Very rare. CMV, $75.00 BO. $100.00 MB.

Furniture Polish, 1912.
8 oz. (½ pint) bottle, cork stopper, clear glass. CMV, $100.00 BO. $125.00 MB.

Carpet Renovator Soap, 1915 – 1920.
Paper box with one bar of carpet soap, two different boxes shown. First issued about 1893. CMV, $90.00 each, mint.

Food Flavoring Set, 1914.
Box holds 2 oz. bottle of vanilla tonka, a 2 oz. bottle of lemon, and four 1 oz. bottles of any other flavor. CMV, $450.00 MB, set.

Furniture Polish, 1912.
8 oz. bottle, cork stopper, label also read "for automobile bodies." CMV, $100.00 BO, mint. $125.00 MB.

Shoe-White, 1915.
Box holds 5 oz. sack of Shoe-White powder. CMV, $90.00 MB.

Olive Oil, 1915.
8 oz. glass bottle with cork stopper. CMV, $90.00 BO, mint. $110.00 MB. Also came in 16 oz., 1 qt., ½ gal., and 1 gal. sizes. Rare. CMV, $100.00 each, BO. $125.00 each, MB.

Baking Powder, 1915.
16 oz. container. CMV, $65.00 CO, mint. $80.00 MB. Also came in 1 lb. and 5 lb. sizes. CMV, $100.00 each, mint.

Furniture Polish, 1916.
12 oz. metal can with green label. CMV, $65.00 CO, mint. $80.00 MB. Also came in 1 qt. and ½ gal. sizes. CMV, $75.00 each, mint.

Root Beer Extract, 1915.
2 oz., cork stopper, clear glass. Very rare. CMV, $100.00 BO, mint. $125.00 MB.

CPC Silver Cream Polish, 1918.
6 oz. jar, metal lid. CMV, $85.00 mint.

CPC Easyday or Simplex Automatic Clothes Washer, 1918.
Made of pure zinc. Washer is 11" high and 9" in diameter. Has Easyday name on top and "Pat. July 4, 1916." CMV, $100.00.

Harmless Red Coloring, 1915.
2 oz., clear glass, cork stopper. CMV, $75.00 BO, mint with label. $90.00 MB.

Perfection Blue Coloring, 1919.
1 oz., black and white label. Cork stopper. New York-Montreal label. CMV, $75.00 mint.

Furniture Polish Sample, 1915.
2 oz., clear glass. Very rare. CMV, $70.00 mint.

CPC Marvel Electric Silver Cleaner, 1918.
Metal plate has Marvel name and "Pat. Jan. 11, 1910." CMV, $75.00.

Jamaica Ginger Flavoring, 1919.
1 oz., cork stopper. CMV, $75.00 mint.

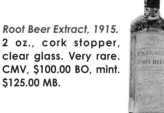

Harmless Colors Set, 1915.
Wood box with slide-open lid, paper label on top. Holds eight, ½ oz. bottles with cork stoppers. Paper labels on top of cork and front of bottles also. Came in chocolate, lemon, green, red, coffee, violet, lilac, and orange. CMV, $350.00 MB.

Left: Savory Coloring, 1920.
3 oz. clear glass bottle, cork stopper. Rare in this size. CMV, $80.00 BO, with mint label. $100.00 MB.
Right: Savory Coloring, 1920.
8 oz., clear glass. Cork stopper. Rare In this size. CMV, $125.00 BO, mint. $150.00 MB.

Spots-Out, 1920.
Metal can. CMV, $70.00 CO, mint. $85.00 MB.

Shoe White, 1920.
Green box holds 5 oz. sack of pow-der. CMV, $100.00 MB.

Concentrated Coloring, 1920 – 1930.
2 oz. No coloring listed on label. Cork stopper. CMV, $45.00 BO, mint. $55.00 MB.

Harmless Colors Set, 1920.
Cardboard box holds eight, ½ oz. bottles with cork stoppers: red, choc-olate, green, coffee, lemon, velvet, orange, and lilac. CMV, $300.00 MB.

Kwick Cleaning Pol-ish Sample, 1922.
Small sample can is-sued for one month on introduction of this product. Rare. CMV, $75.00.

No Alcohol Flavor in Tubes, 1920 – 1921.
Metal tubes came in small and large sizes, available in flavors as set. CMV, $40.00 small tube. $45.00 large tube, mint.
No Alcohol Flavoring Set, 1920 – 1921.
Set came with five small tubes and one large tube. Choice of vanilla, lemon, pineapple, banana, maple, almond, orange, strawberry, jamaica ginger, peppermint, nutmeg, wintergreen, cin-namon, rose, celery onion, pistachio, or raspberry. CMV, $200.00 MB.

Kwick Cleaning Polish, 1922.
8 oz. metal can, brown label. CMV, $55.00 CO. $70.00 MB. Also came in 16 oz. can. CMV, $60.00 CO, mint. $75.00 MB.

Perfection Coloring Set, 1920 – 1930.
Bottles of green, yellow, blue, and brown in ½ oz. sizes. Red in 2 oz. size. All have cork stoppers. Came with CPC Cook Booklet. CMV, $250.00 MB.

Silver Cream Polish, 1923.
8 oz. metal can. CMV, $40.00 mint. 16 oz. can, CMV, $45.00 mint. Add $5.00 MB.

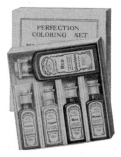

Flavoring Extract Set, 1920.
Box holds two 2 oz. bottles and four 1 oz. bottles of any flavor desired. 1, 2 and 4 oz. bottles shown. CMV, $450.00 set MB.

Mothicide, 1923.
½ lb. metal can, 3¼" across. Paper label in English and French. CMV, $40.00 mint.

Spots-Out, 1923.
8 oz. metal can. CMV, $40.00 mint. 16 oz. can not shown. CMV, $45.00 mint. Add $10.00 each, MB.

Supreme Huile d'Olive Oil, 1923.
Green and yellow can in 1 pt. size. CMV, $60.00 CO, mint. $75.00 MB. Also came in 1 qt. size can. CMV, $70.00 CO, mint. $85.00 MB.

Lemon and Orange Flavor Extracts, 1923 – 1930.
2 oz. clear glasss bottles with green labels and cork stoppers. CMV, $50.00 each, BO. $65.00 each, MB.

Baking Powder, 1923 – 1930.
1 lb. can. Also came in ½ lb. and 5 lb. sizes. CMV, $60.00 CO, mint. $65.00 MB.

No Alcohol Flavors, 1923.
Lemon and vanilla only, in small and large size tubes. CMV, $30.00 each, TO, mint. $40.00 each, MB.

Savory Coloring, 1923 – 1930.
4 oz. bottles with yellow labels and brown letters, cork stoppers. Came in red, yellow, blue, brown, and green. CMV, $45.00 each with mint label. $55.00 MB. ½ oz. bottle came in Coloring Set only. CMV same as above.

Concentrated Flavoring Extract, 1923 – 1930.
8 oz., with handle. Same label as 1923 – 1930 extracts. This bottle is very rare with handle. Label in poor condition. CMV, $75.00 mint.

Flavoring Extract, 1923 – 1930.
2 oz. clear glass bottle, cork stopper. Came in lemon, orange, grape, cherry, raspberry, and loganberry. CMV, $50.00 BO. $60.00 MB.

Fruit Flavors Brochure, 1923.
Introducing new line of CPC Perfection fruit flavors. 1 page. CMV, $20.00.

Mothicide, 1925.
Metal cans. Paper label around bottom can is in English and French. CMV, $50.00 each, metal cans at top, mint. Right can, CMV, $60.00 mint. CMV, $20.00 as shown with spots.

Mothicide, 1925.
½ lb. metal can with blue label. CMV, $50.00 CO, mint. $65.00 MB.

Liquid Spots-Out, 1925 – 1929.
4 oz. clear glass bottle, black cork cap, blue label. CMV, $45.00 BO, mint. $50.00 MB.

Powdered Cleaner, 1928 – 1931.
12 oz. blue box. CMV, $75.00 CO, mint. $90.00 MB.

Cake Chest Product Box, 1930s.
CPC box with list of all contents that came in Perfection Cake Chest. CMV, $15.00 box only.

Kwick Metal Polish, 1925.
½ lb. metal can with brown label. CMV, $45.00 CO, mint. $60.00 MB.

Avon Powdered Cleaner Sample, 1928 – 1931.
Small blue, orange, and white paper box. 3 oz. size sample. CPC on label, rare. CMV, $100.00 mint.

Food Coloring Directions, 1930s.
Came in Perfection Food Coloring sets. CPC on back. CMV, $15.00 mint.

Furniture Polish, 1925.
12 oz. metal cans with blue labels. OSP, 48¢ each. Also came in 32 oz. blue metal can. Back labels in French on both cans. CMV, $70.00 each, CO, mint. $85.00 each, MB. Can on right has a different cap.

Perfection Spots-Out Liquid, 1929.
4 oz. bottle with CPC on black cork stopper and blue label. CMV, $40.00 BO. $45.00 MB.

Liquid Shoe White, 1928 – 1930.
4 oz. glass bottle with cork stopper. CMV, $45.00 BO, mint. $50.00 MB.

Auto Lustre, 1930 – 1933.
Blue 1 pt. can. CMV, $75.00 CO, mint. $90.00 MB.

Auto Lustre Sample, 1930 – 1933.
1 oz. blue metal can. Rare. CMV, $90.00.

Perfection Flavoring Extract Set, 1930 – 1934.
In orange, brown, and white can, has 2 oz. vanilla and 1⅕ oz. each of almond, lemon, peppermint, and wintergreen extracts. All have cork stoppers. CMV, $15.00 CO, mint. $125.00 set, mint.

**Recipe Books,
1930s – 1940s.**
Came in food coloring or flavoring sets. At least four different booklets. CMV, $15.00 each, mint. 1920 far right, CMV, $25.00.

Spots-Out, 1931 – 1941.
½ lb. orange, brown, and white can. CMV, $20.00 CO, mint. $25.00 MB.

**Furniture Polish,
1931 – 1936.**
12 oz. brown, orange, and white can. CMV, $20.00 CO. $30.00 MB.

Coloring Set, 1930 – 1934.
Brown and orange paper box. Red coloring in 2 oz. size; brown, blue, yellow, and green coloring in ½ oz. size. All have cork stoppers. CMV, $20.00 CO, mint. $160.00 MB.

**Liquid Shoe White,
1931 – 1935.**
4 oz. bottle with cork stopper. Brown, orange, and white label. CMV, $25.00 BO. $30.00 MB.

**Prepared Starch,
1931 – 1941.**
6 oz. brown, orange, and white can sold 1931 – 1936. CMV, $25.00 CO. $30.00 MB. Same can in 8 oz. size sold 1936 – 1941, two different labels as shown. CMV, $20.00 CO. $25.00 MB.

**Silver Cream Polish,
1931 – 1941.**
½ lb. brown, orange, and white can. CMV, $25.00 CO, mint. $30.00 MB.

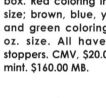

**Kwick Metal Polish,
1931 – 1941.**
½ lb. orange, brown, and white can. CMV, $30.00 CO. $35.00 MB.

**Mothicide,
1931 – 1941.**
½ lb. orange, brown, and white can. CMV, $20.00 CO, mint. $25.00 MB. Add $5.00 for CPC label.

**Powdered Cleaner,
1931– 1934.**
Red, white, and blue, 16 oz. CMV, $75.00 CO, mint. $90.00 MB.

**Liquid Spots Out,
1931 – 1934.**
4 oz. size. "CPC" on cork stopper. CMV, $32.50 BO. $40.00 MB.

Perfection Laundry Crystals, 1931 – 1936.
Brown, orange, and white paper box. CMV, $30.00 MB.

**Machine Oil,
1931 – 1941.**
3 oz. brown, orange, and white can. Two different labels. CMV, $12.50 CO, mint. $18.00 MB.

Olive Oil, 1931 – 1941.
1 pt., orange, brown, and white can. Two different labels. CMV, $35.00 CO. $45.00 MB.

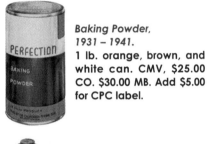

Baking Powder, 1931 – 1941.
1 lb. orange, brown, and white can. CMV, $25.00 CO. $30.00 MB. Add $5.00 for CPC label.

Cake Chest, 1933 – 1938.
Blue and gold cake pan, 10½" diameter, contained Perfection coloring set with metal caps and can of Perfection baking powder. Bottles contained lemon, maple, black walnut, almond, and vanilla flavorings. Also contained recipe book. "Avon Perfection" in bottom of cake pan. CMV, $50.00 chest only, mint. $70.00 MB. $135.00 MB, complete set.

Flavoring Extracts, 1934 – 1941.
8 oz. bottles. Came in vanilla, tonka, lemon, almond, orange, peppermint, wintergreen, pure vanilla, black walnut, and maple. CMV, $25.00 BO. $35.00 MB.

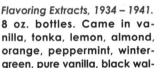

Savory Coloring, 1931 – 1934.
4 oz., cork stopper. CPC label. CMV, $30.00 BO. $35.00 MB.

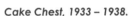

Liquid Spots Out, 1934 – 1941.
4 oz. bottle. Orange, brown, and white label. Black cap. CMV, $25.00 BO. $30.00 MB.

Extracts, 1934 – 1941.
Metal caps on ½, 2, 4, and 8 oz. bottles. Flavors are vanilla, tonka, lemon, almond, orange, peppermint, wintergreen, pure vanilla, black walnut, and maple. CMV, $12.50, each, 2 oz. and 4 oz.; $20.00, for 8 oz.; $12.00 for ½ oz. size.

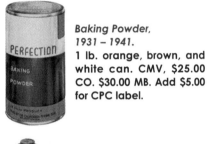

Auto Polish, 1933 – 1936.
1 pt. brown, orange, and white can. Two different labels. Rare. CMV, $40.00 CO. $50.00 MB.

Powdered Cleaner, 1934 – 1941.
16 oz. orange, brown, and white can. Two different labels. Cardboard sides, metal bottom. CMV, $20.00 each, CO, mint. $25.00 each, MB.

Mending Cement, 1933 – 1941.
Brown, orange, and white tube. CMV, $10.00 TO, mint. $12.00 MB.

Laundry Crystals, Perfumed, 1934 – 1936.
Brown, white, and orange box holds 13 white crystals. CMV, $30.00 mint.

Coloring, 1934 – 1941.
½ oz. bottles in green, yellow, blue, and brown. Came in Coloring Set. CMV, $15.00 each. 2 oz. size in same colors, plus red. CMV, $17.00. 4 oz. size in Savory Coloring. All have metal caps. CMV, $17.00. Add $3.00 each, MB.

Vanilla Tonka Sample, 1934 – 1939.
¼ oz. size, 2⅜" high, metal cap. Shown next to ½ oz. size, on left that came in food flavor sets. CMV, $25.00 ¼ oz. size sample, mint. CMV, $15.00 ½ oz. size, mint.

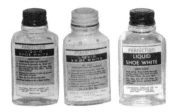

Liquid Shoe White Samples, 1935 – 1941.
½ oz., black caps. "CPC" on labels. CMV, $40.00 each. Also with Avon Products label only, white cap. CMV, $25.00 each.

Laundry Crystals, Perfumed, 1938 – 1941.
Brown, orange, and white paper sides, tin tops and bottoms. Tops cut out to be used as banks. Held 13 crystals. Came with Avon and CPC labels. CMV, $30.00, Avon label. $40.00, CPC label.

Perfection Coloring Set, 1934 – 1941.
Orange, brown, and white metal can held four, ½ oz. bottles of blue, yellow, brown and green coloring, and 2 oz. bottle of red. All have plain metal caps, or all color caps. Rare. Came with Perfection recipe booklet. CMV, $15.00 CO, mint. $75.00 MB.

Furniture Polish, 1936 – 1941.
12 and 32 oz. brown, orange, and white cans. Three different labels. CMV, $15.00 CO, 12 oz. $20.00 MB. CMV, $20.00 CO. 32 oz. size. $25.00 each, MB.

Baking Powder Samples, 1936 – 1941.
On right, orange, brown, and white 1 oz. can, 2¼" high. Shown with two different size samples. Rare. CMV, $40.00 each, mint.

Cake Chest, 1938 – 1941.
Gold, red, brown, and black cake chest. Contained can of baking powder, coloring set of 4 oz. vanilla extract, 2 oz. each of lemon and almond extracts, and 2 oz. each of black walnut and maple flavors. All have metal caps. Also came with recipe book. "Avon Perfection" in bottom of cake pan. CMV, $35.00 chest only, mint. $135.00 complete set, MB.

Flavoring Extract Set, 1934 – 1941.
Orange, brown, and white metal can holds four, ½ oz. bottles in wintergreen, peppermint, almond, and lemon, and a 2 oz. bottle of maple. All have metal caps. Came with Perfection recipe booklet. CMV, $12.00 booklet only. CMV, $15.00 CO, mint. $75.00 MB.

Vanilla, Tonka Vanillin Special Issue Box, 1937.
Regular issue 2 oz. bottle in special issue box for 15¢ with regular order. CMV, $25.00 MB as shown.

Imitation Vanillan Coumarin, Vanillin, and Tonka Sample, 1939 – 1941.
¼ oz. bottle, metal cap. CMV, $25.00 mint.

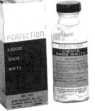

Liquid Shoe White, 1935 – 1941.
Box holds 4 oz. bottle with brown cap. Brown, orange, and white label. CMV, $25.00 BO. $30.00 MB.

Lemon Extract, 1937.
2 oz. bottle, metal cap. CMV, $15.00 BO. $25.00 MB.

Imitation Vanillin, Coumarin, Vanilla, and Tonka Flavor, 1939 – 1941. 4 oz., red cap. CMV, $15.00 BO. $20.00 MB.

Spots-Out, 1941 – 1943. 8 oz. green, brown, and white labeled can. Sold 1941 – 1943, then 1946 – 1948. CMV, $20.00 CO. $25.00 MB.

Powdered Cleaners, 1941 – 1943, then 1946 – 1957. 16 oz. paper sides with metal tops and bottoms. Green, bronze, and white. CMV, $15.00 each, CO. $20.00 each, MB. Five different labels and a Canadian label.

Silver Cream Polish, 1941 – 1952. Green, brown, and white 8 oz. can. Sold 1941 – 1943, then 1946 – 1952. CMV, $15.00 CO, mint. $20.00 MB.

Liquid Shoe White Sample, 1941 – 1957. 3/4 oz., white cap, green and brown label. CMV, $35.00.

Furniture Polish, 1941. Green, bronze, and white metal cans. 12 oz. can, 1941 – 1943, then 1946 – 1948. CMV, $12.00 CO. $15.00 MB. 16 oz. can, 1948 – 1951. CMV, $12.00. 32 oz. can, 1941 – 1943. CMV, $25.00. Add $5.00 MB.

Mothicide, 1941– 1943, then 1946 – 1954. 8 oz. metal can. Green, bronze, and white label. OSP, 55¢. CMV, $20.00 CO. $30.00 MB.

Prepared Starch , 1941 – 1948. 8 oz. brown, green, and white can. Two different labels. Shiny or painted top. CMV, $20.00 each, CO, mint. $25.00 each, MB. 1943 – 1946 had paper sides. CMV, $20.00 mint.

Laundry Crystals (Perfumed), 1941 – 1948. Green, brown, and white cans with green lids held 13 crystals. Metal tops and bottoms and paper sides. Sold 1941 – 1946. All metal sold 1946 – 1948. CMV, $20.00 each, mint.

Samples, 1941. Perfection flavor sample came 20 in a box for 50¢. Baking powder came 16 in a box for 50¢. CMV, flavoring bottle, $20.00 each. Baking powder, $45.00 each.

Liquid Shoe White, 1941 – 1957. 4 oz., green smooth or threaded cap. Two different labels. CMV, $10.00 BO. $15.00 MB.

Machine Oil, 1941 – 1948. 3 oz. brown, green, and white can. Sold 1941 – 1943, then 1946 – 1948. CMV, $10.00 CO. $15.00 MB.

Baking Powder, 1941 – 1943, then 1946 – 1948.
16 oz. red and white can, cardboard sides, metal top or all metal can and top. CMV, $20.00 CO, mint. $25.00 MB. 1946 – 1948 came in all metal can. Screw-on lid. Rare. CMV, $50.00.

Savoury Coloring, 1941 – 1948.
4 oz. bottle with the word "Savoury" spelled different. Regular spelling is "Savory." CMV, $15.00 BO. $18.00 MB.

Food Coloring, 1941 – 1948.
Red plastic caps. Savory coloring came in 4 oz. bottle. Red, yellow, blue, brown, and green coloring came in 2 oz. bottles. All but red and Savory coloring came in ½ oz. bottles in coloring set. CMV, $12.00 each size, BO. $15.00 each, MB.

Flavoring Set, 1941 – 1948.
Red, white, and bronze can holds 2 oz. bottle of vanilla, and ½ oz. bottles of maple, black walnut, almond, and lemon. All have red plastic caps. CMV, $60.00 complete set, mint. Set came with Avon recipe booklet in can. Add $10.00 for recipe booklet. $12.00 CO, mint.

Kwick Metal Polish, 1941 – 1948.
8 oz. green, brown, and white can. Sold 1941 – 1943, then 1946 – 1948. CMV, $35.00 CO. $45.00 MB.

Mending Cement, 1941 – 1948.
White, green, and brown tube. CMV, $10.00 TO, mint. $12.00 MB.

Flavoring Extracts, 1941 – 1948.
Vanilla and lemon came in 2 and 4 oz. sizes. 2 oz. size only in maple, black walnut, orange, peppermint, almond, and wintergreen. All have red plastic caps. CMV, $9.00 each. ½ oz. size came in Extract Set only. CMV, $12.00 each, BO. $15.00 each, MB.

Silver Cream Polish, 1943.
Stick-on white and green label over name of other products on can. Used during shortage of products during the war. CMV, $25.00 mint with label shown.

Cake Chest, 1941 – 1942.
Brown and red designed cake chest has coloring set in can, 2 oz. bottles of lemon and almond extract, 2 oz. bottles of maple and black walnut flavoring, and 4 oz. bottle of vanilla. All bottles have red plastic caps. Can of baking powder, recipe book, and cake chest are same as 1938 to 1941. "Avon Perfection" in bottom of cake pan. CMV, $35.00 chest only, mint. $110.00 MB, complete set.

Coloring Set, 1941 – 1948.
Orange, brown, and white can holds 2 oz. red coloring and ½ oz. each of yellow, brown, blue, and green colorings, red plastic caps. CMV, $65.00 MB. Set came with Avon recipe booklet. Add $10.00 for recipe booklet. $15.00 CO, mint. This set also came in 1934 – 1941 can, but can is marked "Avon" and not "CPC." Came with red caps and 1941 – 1948 labels. CMV, $70.00 MB. Same set came in 1942, but with matching caps to color content. Rare. CMV, $85.00 set, MB.

Baking Powder,
1943 – 1946.
16 oz. paper container used during the war. CMV, $40.00 mint.

Furniture Polish, 1944 only.
12 oz. bottle, black cap. CMV, $40.00 BO. $50.00 MB.

Spots-Out, 1943 – 1946.
9½ oz. glass jar, white metal lid. CMV, $22.00 CO. $27.00 MB.
Kwick Metal Polish, 1943 – 1946.
11 oz. glass jar with white metal cap. Rare. CMV, $40.00 CO. $50.00 MB.
Silver Cream Polish, 1943 – 1946.
10½ oz. glass jar with white metal lid. CMV, $22.00 CO. $27.00 MB.

Mothicide,
1943 – 1946.
Glass jar with white lid, green and white. CMV, $20.00 CO. $30.00 MB.

Liquid Spots Out, 1946 – 1958.
4 oz., green smooth or threaded cap. Two different labels. One box brown and one box bronze. CMV, $15.00 BO. $20.00 MB.

Powdered Cleaner,
1943 – 1946.
16 oz. paper can, green, bronze, and white. CMV, $20.00 CO, mint. $25.00 MB.

Mothicide, 1954 – 1957.
8½ oz. bronze metal can, green top, three different edges on lid. Sold 1954 – 1957. CMV, $10.00. Red metal can sold 1957 only. CMV, $12.00 CO. $16.00 MB.

Furniture Polish,
1943 – 1946.
12 oz. bottle, metal cap. Two different labels. Green and white or white and bronze label. CMV, $22.00 BO. $30.00 MB. Add $5.00 for green and white label.

Laundry Crystals (Perfumed),
1943 – 1946.
All cardboard wartime packaging. Also came with white top and bottom. Four different labels. CMV, $30.00 mint.

Kwick Metal Polish,
1954 – 1957.
Green and brown 13 oz. can on right. Two different lids. CMV, $30.00 mint.

Left: Machine Oil, 1943 – 1946.
3 oz. smooth side glass, metal cap. CMV, $20.00 BO. $25.00 MB.
Right: Machine Oil, "Ribbed Side."
Short issue, 3 oz. ribbed sided bottle, metal cap. Came in two different boxes as shown. CMV, $25.00 BO. $30.00 MB.

Facial Set, 1933 – 1936.
Silver and blue box contains 2 oz. jar of cleansing cream and 1 oz. jar of tissue cream, one bottle of astringent, a silver box of Ariel face powder, and a package of tissues. CMV, $110.00 MB.

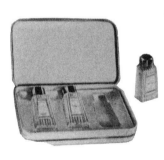

Facial Set, 1936 – 1937.
Turquoise flip-up box holds Ariel face powder, 2 oz. jars of cleansing cream and tissue cream, and a 2 oz. bottle of astringent. All products are marked "CPC." Also came with packet of tissues. CMV, $50.00 MB.

Facial Set, 1937 – 1938.
Green box contains choice of 2 oz. bottle of skin freshener or astringent, green caps, 2 oz. jar of cleansing cream, 1 oz. jar of tissue cream, and Ariel or Vernafleur face powder. CMV, $65.00 MB.

Facial Set, 1938 – 1940.
Green box holds 4 oz. bottles of astringent and lotus cream, jars of tissue cream and cleansing cream, and box of face powder in Ariel or Cotillion. CMV, $65.00 MB.

Facial Set, 1941 – 1948.
Green box contains jar of cleansing cream, foundation cream, and night cream with green lids, skin freshener (2 oz., green cap), and box of face powder (blue and white feather design), and two packs of Avon facial tissues. Jars had green or white metal lids. CMV, $50.00 MB. Add $10.00 set for white lids.

Facial Set for Dry Skin, 1949 – 1954.
Green box contains Fluffy cleansing cream, skin freshener, special dry skin cream, and lipstick.
Same Set for Oily Skin.
Contained liquifying cleansing cream, astringent, night cream, and lipstick. CMV, $50.00 MB, each set.

Gold Box Set, 1932.
Metal gold with black strips. Can holds 3½ oz. ribbed glass bottles of 391, Ariel, and Vernafleur perfumes. All have black octagonal caps. This is the same metal can as the 1925 – 1930 manicure set. CMV, $140.00 MB.

Gold Box Set, 1933 – 1936.
Gold box contained three, ½-oz. bottles of Vernafleur, Ariel, 391, Bolero, or Gardenia. Black caps. CMV, $125.00 MB.

Gold Box Set, 1937 – 1938.
Gold box holds three, 1/8-oz. bottles of Cotillion, Narcissus, and Gardenia perfumes. CMV, $85.00 MB.

Gold Box Set, 1941 – 1944.
Pink and gold box contains 1/8 oz. perfumes in Gardenia, Cotillion, and Trailing Arbutus. White caps, pink and gold box. CMV, $90.00 MB.

Gold Box, 1945 – 1946.
Pink and white box holds three, 1/8-oz. bottles in Crimson Carnation, Gardenia and Cotillion perfumes. CMV, $85.00 MB.

Gold Box, 1939 – 1940.
Gold open front box holds three bottles of perfume in Gardenia, Cotillion, Narcissus, or Trailing Arbutus. White plastic caps on all. CMV, $90.00 MB.

Gold Box, 1944.
Ribbons and flower design box holds three, 1/8-oz. perfumes in Trailing Arbutus, Cotillion, and Gardenia. CMV, $90.00 MB.

Gold Box Set, 1947 – 1948.
Three, 1/8-oz. perfume bottles, gold caps, pink labels. Ballad, Garden of Love, or Cotillion. OSP, $2.50. CMV, $85.00 MB.

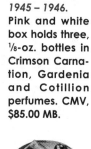

Gold Box Set, 1949.
Turquoise plastic bottom with gold insert, clear plastic lid, contains three 1 dram bottles of Cotillion, Flowertime, and Golden Promise perfumes. All have gold caps and labels. CMV, $80.00 MB.

Makeup Ensemble Sets

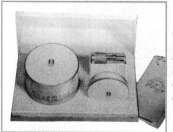

Makeup Ensemble, 1939 – 1940.
Box holds can of face powder in choice of Cotillion, Ariel, or Vernafleur, and table rouge in green and gold boxes. Lipstick in green and gold. CMV, $40.00 MB.

Makeup Ensemble, 1941 – 1942.
Box contains face powder, rouge in feather design, and turquoise and gold lipstick. CMV, $40.00 MB.

Makeup Ensemble, 1946 only.
Pink and blue feather design box holds gold bamboo lipstick, rouge, and box of face powder. CMV, $45.00 MB.

Makeup Ensemble, 1948.
Same as 1947 makeup ensemble except lipstick is gold with swirl design around bottom. CMV, $45.00 MB.

Makeup Ensemble, 1943 – 1944.
Blue and pink box holds feathered box of face powder, rouge, and plastic or cardboard lipstick. CMV, $40.00 MB.

Makeup Ensemble, 1949 – 1951.
Blue, pink, and white box contains face powder, gold lipstick, and rouge. Eiffel Tower on box. CMV, $35.00 MB.

Makeup Ensemble, 1945.
Lipstick designed box holds feather design face powder, lipstick, and rouge. Also came with metal bamboo lipstick. CMV, $37.00 MB.

Makeup Ensemble, 1947 only.
White and pink box with Eiffel Tower on box holds pink and blue feather design powder, with bamboo lipstick and rouge OSP, $2.35. CMV, $45.00 MB.

Makeup Ensemble, 1952 – 1953.
Turquoise and gold box holds compact, lipstick, and face powder or powder pak. CMV, $35.00 MB.

Manicure Sets

Warning! Grading condition is paramount on sets. CMV can vary 50% to 90% on condition.

Manicure Set No. 1, 1930.
Silver box holds two small bottles of nail polish remover. Black caps. Booklet, "What Story Do Your Hands Tell?" came with set. CMV, $65.00 MB.

Manicure Set No. 2, 1931 – 1936.
Silver box holds three small ribbed glass bottles of polish remover, nail polish, and cuticle softener. All have black caps. Two small silver cans of nail white and nail cream, one fingernail file, and booklet, "What Story Do Your Hands Tell?" were included. CMV, $110.00 MB. Same set also came with no stripe on box and two different listings inside box.

Manicure Set No. 1,
1936 – 1937.
Green and white box held
bottles of nail polish and polish
remover with two rolls of cotton
and booklet, "What Story Do
Your Hands Tell?" CMV, $45.00
MB.

Twosome Set,
1938 – 1949.
Turquoise and white box
held ½ oz. bottle of nail
polish and ½ oz. of bot-
tle cuticle softener, two
cotton rolls, and book-
let, "What Story Do Your
Hands Tell?" CPC on
box in 1938 – 1939. Add
$5.00 for CPC box. CMV,
$30.00.

Manicure Set No. 1, 1938 – 1949.
Turquoise box held ½ oz. bottles of nail polish
and cream polish, two cotton rolls, and booklet, "What Story Do Your Hands Tell?" CPC on
box, two different boxes. Some say "Manicure
Set No. 1" at top of box and some at bottom
of box. Add $5.00 for CPC box. CMV, $30.00
MB.

Royal Windsor Set,
1941 – 1944.
Blue box held choice of ½ oz.
bottle of nail polish base and
½ oz. bottle of cream polish, or ½ oz. top coat. CMV,
$17.00 MB as shown.

Manicure Set No. 2, 1937.
Turquoise and white lid, gold inside box. Held cans of nail white
and nail cream, bottles of nail
polish remover, cuticle softener,
and nail polish, orange stick, nail
file, three cotton rolls in glass tube,
and booklet, "What Story Do Your
Hands Tell?" CMV, $80.00 MB.

Nail Polish Threesome, 1938 – 1949.
Turquoise and white box holds ½ oz.
bottle of double coat, ½ oz. bottle of
nail polish, ½ oz. bottle of oily polish remover, two rolls of cotton, and booklet.
CMV, $42.50.

Threesome Set, 1942 – 1943.
Pink and white box held three
small bottles with turquoise
caps of cream polish, nail polish
base, and oily polish remover.
Came with story booklet on
hands. CMV, $40.00 MB.

Manicure Set No. 2,
1938 – 1939.
Brown case holds orange
stick, nail file, can of nail
white, nail cream, and
bottles of cuticle softener,
cream polish, and polish remover. CMV, $60.00 MB.

Manicure Set No. 2, 1940.
Brown case holds fingernail file,
orange stick, white Avon nail
white pencil, ½ oz. bottles of
clear or cream nail polish, polish
remover, cuticle softener, and
cuticle oil. Turquoise or black
caps. CMV, $60.00 MB.
Not shown: Manicure Set Deluxe,
1941 – 1943.
Same set as above, only name
changed. CMV, $60.00 MB.

Manicure Set Deluxe, 1944 – 1949.
Black and red bag held five bottles of nail polish, top coat, nail polish base, cuticle softener, and oily polish remover. All have black or turquoise caps. Also included white nail white pencil, orange stick, and two nail files. CMV, $45.00 MB.

Manicure Set Deluxe, 1949.
Same black and red bag as 1944 – 1949 Manicure Set Deluxe, only held four bottles with turquoise caps in Cling-Tite nail polish, nail polish remover, and cuticle softener. CMV, $40.00 MB.

Manicure Set Deluxe, 1953 – 1954.
Gray case held ½ oz. bottles of cuticle softener, nail polish, double coat, and 2 oz. oily polish remover. White caps on all. CMV, $25.00 MB.

Nail Polish Twosome, 1945 – 1950.
Turquoise box held ½ oz. bottles of cream polish and cuticle softener, and small 30-page booklet. CMV $30.00 MB.

Deluxe Manicure Set, 1950 – 1951.
Black and red box held three, ½ oz. bottles of nail polish, ½ oz. bottle of clear nail polish, ½ oz. bottle of cuticle softener, one orange stick, one white nail white pencil, and a booklet. CMV, $25.00 MB.

Deluxe Manicure Set, 1955.
White plastic case with gold dots and red lining held oily nail polish remover, cuticle softener, Silvery Base, and choice of nail enamel. All white caps. Also includes emery board. CMV, $25.00 MB.

Avon Threesome Set, 1950 – 1952.
Red and white box held three nail polish bottles with white caps. CMV, $30.00 MB.

Avon Threesome Set, 1948 – 1949.
Red, white, and green tray with green box held three ½ oz. bottles with white caps of oily polish remover, Cling-Tite, and nail polish. CMV, $30.00 MB.

Deluxe Manicure Set, 1950 – 1952.
Black and red bag holds bottles of cuticle softener, nail polish, oily polish remover, and Cling-Tite. CMV, $25.00 MB.

Little Favorite Set, 1955.
Plastic turquoise case held bottles of nail polish, oily polish remover, and cuticle softener. All had white caps. CMV, $20.00 MB.

Polka Dot Set, 1956 – 1957.
Red and white plastic case holds ½ oz. bottles of nail polish, top coat, and 2 oz. oily polish remover. CMV, $20.00 MB.

Color Bar Set, 1958.
White plastic tray held four bottles of nail polish or Silvery Base, top coat, and cuticle softener. Mix or match. CMV, $15.00 complete set. $20.00 MB.

Deluxe Manicure Set, 1960 – 1961.
Black vinyl case held Silvery Base, oily polish remover, cuticle softener, top coat, and cream nail polish. All have white caps. $20.00 MB.

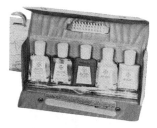

Manicure Set Deluxe, 1956 – 1957.
Pink plastic container holds ½ oz. bottles of polish remover, cuticle softener, Silvery Base, top coat, and polish. All have white caps. CMV, $25.00 MB.

Manicure Deluxe Set, 1959.
Box held cuticle softener, Silvery Coat, oily polish remover, top coat, and cream polish. CMV, $25.00 MB.

Manicure Kit, 1966.
Gold and white plastic case held one bottle of nail enamel, long last base coat, enamel set, cuticle remover cream, nail beauty, 10 nail enamel remover pads, emery board, and orange stick. CMV, $15.00 MB, complete set.

Color Change Set, 1957.
Pink, turquoise, and gold design on white plastic case, held 2 oz. bottles, white caps, of oily polish remover, top coat, and nail polish. CMV, $20.00 MB.

Manicure Petite Set, 1960 – 1961.
Black vinyl case held top coat, oily polish remover, and cream or pearl nail polish. White caps. CMV, $15.00 MB.

Manicure Beauti-Kit, 1968 – 1969.
Black and white vinyl case holds ½ oz. bottles of nail enamels, 1 oz. plastic tube cuticle conditioner, 1 oz. plastic tube cuticle remover, 10 enamel remover pads, ½ oz. bottle of enamel set, long-last top coat, and emery boards. Red plastic tray. CMV, $8.00 MB.

Nail Buffer Set, 1974.
Box held ¼ oz. tube of nail buffing cream and nail buffer. CMV, $1.50 MB.

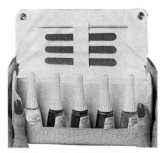

Nail Care Kit, 1978 – 1979.
Same as on right, only beige color alligator grain case. CMV, $5.00 MB.

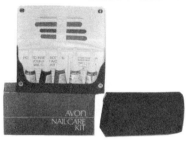

Nail Care Kit, 1979 – 1980.
Blue plastic kit held five bottles of nail care products, three emery boards, and one cuticle stick. CMV, $5.00 complete, MB.

Perfume Pair Sets

Perfume Pair, 1962.
Box held 2¼ oz. can of perfumed talc and perfumed soap in Somewhere, Topaze, Cotillion, Persian Wood, Here's My Heart, or To a Wild Rose. CMV, $15.00 MB.

Perfume Pair, 1964.
Box held perfumed talc and soap in Here's My Heart, Persian Wood, To a Wild Rose, Somewhere, Topaze, or Cotillion. CMV, $14.00 MB.

Perfume Pair, 1967.
Box contained perfumed talc and matching soap. Came in Unforgettable, Here's My Heart, To a Wild Rose, Somewhere, Topaze, Cotillion, Rapture, or Occur! CMV, $10.00 MB.

Perfume Pair, 1963.
Gold and white with perfumed talc and bar of soap in To a Wild Rose, Here's My Heart, Persian Wood, Topaze, Somewhere, or Cotillion. CMV, $14.00 each set, MB.

Perfume Pair, 1966.
Brown, gold, and white box held 2¾ oz. perfumed talc and wrapped soap in Unforgettable, Rapture, Occur!, Cotillion, Somewhere, Topaze, Here's My Heart, To a Wild Rose, or Wishing. CMV, $12.00 MB.

Perfume Pair, 1968.
Box holds 2¾ oz. can of talc and matching soap in Brocade, Régence, Unforgettable, Hawaiian White Ginger, Honeysuckle, or To a Wild Rose. CMV, $8.00 MB.

Perfume Pair, 1969.
Box held perfumed talc and bar of soap in Charisma, Brocade, Blue Lotus, White Ginger, Honeysuckle, or To a Wild Rose. CMV, $8.00 MB.

Perfume Pair, 1970.
Each box contained perfumed talc and matching soap in Hawaiian White Ginger, Honeysuckle, Elusive, Blue Lotus, Bird of Paradise, or Charisma. CMV, $8.00 MB.

Perfume Pair, 1974 – 1975.
1½ oz. perfumed talc and ½ oz. cologne. Choice of Roses Roses, Unforgettable, Cotillion, Sonnet, or Moonwind. Came in two different boxes. CMV, $6.00 MB.

Purse Sets

Evening Charm Set, 1949.
Black purse held gold compact, lipstick, and 1 dram bottle in gold metal case with Golden Promise perfume. Also came with beige purse. CMV, $30.00 MB.

Evening Charm Set, 1952.
Gold purse held 1 dram perfume, lipstick, and gold deluxe compact. CMV, $30.00 MB.

Evening Charm Purse, 1953.
Gold purse held 1 dram perfume, lipstick, and gold deluxe compact. CMV, $30.00 MB.

Evening Charm Set, 1954.
Choice of black velvet or white brocade purse with 1 dram perfume, gold deluxe compact, and jeweled lipstick. Both have zipper tops. CMV, $30.00 MB.

Evening Charm Set, 1951.
Brocade handbag or black satin bag with gold trim. Came with same contents as 1953 Evening Charm Set. CMV, $6.00 purse only. $30.00 MB, complete set.

Evening Charm Set, 1953.
Choice of black velvet bag or brocade bag. Came with 1 dram embossed top perfume, gold deluxe compact, and gold jeweled lipstick. CMV, $35.00 MB.

Dress Up Set, 1955.
Black and gold purse with gold satin lining held 1 dram perfume, jeweled lipstick, and deluxe gold compact. CMV, $30.00 MB.

Evening Charm Set, 1955.
Gold brocade purse, Avon tag inside. Also came in matching black satin bag. Held 2 dram embossed top perfume, gold deluxe compact, and gold jeweled lipstick. CMV, $30.00 MB.

In Style Set, 1957.
Black satin purse held Persian Wood spray perfume, white compact, gold lipstick, and black coin purse. CMV, $30.00 MB.

Going Steady Set, 1960.
Gray bag held white compact and lipstick. Purse does not say Avon on it. CMV, $10.00 MB.

Dress Up Set, 1955 – 1956.
Black and gold reversible purse held 1 dram perfume, gold compact, and jeweled lipstick. CMV, $30.00 MB.

Makeup Tuck In Set, 1957.
Black striped purse contained pink powder-pak, liquid rouge, and lipstick. CMV, $30.00 MB.

High Style Set, 1960.
Blue satin lined bag held gold deluxe compact and lipstick. CMV, $20.00 MB.

On the Avenue Set, 1958.
Black purse held Top Style lipstick and Top Style compact with Here's My Heart or Persian Wood spray perfume. CMV, $30.00 MB.

Modern Mood Set, 1961.
Gold and white sequin bag held deluxe lipstick and compact. CMV, $20.00 MB.

Lady Fair Set, 1956.
Gold box held 1 dram perfume, gold lipstick, and red leather billfold. CMV, $35.00 MB.

Around Town Set, 1956.
Black leather bag held gold lipstick, powder compact, 1 dram perfume, and cologne stick. CMV, $30.00 MB.

Pak Purse Set, 1959.
White leather purse held lipstick, 1 dram perfume, and compact. OSP, $8.95. CMV, $20.00 MB.

Deluxe Twin Set, 1962.
Blue clutch bag held deluxe compact and lipstick. CMV, $20.00 MB.

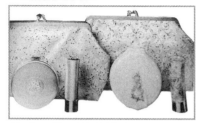

Modern Mood Set, 1963.
Gold and white or pink and gold purse held deluxe compact and lipstick. *Left:* CMV, $17.50 MB. *Right:* pearl pink compact and floral fashion lipstick. CMV, $20.00 MB.

Beauty Bound Set, 1964.
Black leather handbag, deluxe compact and lipstick, and choice of creme rollette. CMV, $30.00 MB. *Not shown: Beauty Bound Set, 1965.*
Same set as 1964, with perfume rollette instead of creme rollette. CMV, $30.00 MB.

Purse Companions Set, 1964.
Brocade beige purse with pockets to hold floral fashion lipstick and cameo compact. Same set in 1965, only with cameo lipstick. CMV, $20.00 each set, MB.

Evening Lights Purse Set, 1965.
White box with gold purse came with deluxe compact, lipstick, and perfume rollette. CMV, $20.00 MB.

Men's Sets of the 1930s

Warning! Grading condition is paramount on sets. CMV can vary up to 90% on condition.

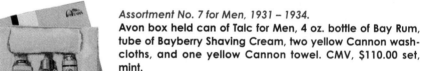

Christmas Boxes, 1930.
Special issue boxes came with seven different Avon sets at Christmas, 1931. CMV, $25.00 added to price of set for this box.

Assortment No. 7 for Men, 1931 – 1934.
Avon box held can of Talc for Men, 4 oz. bottle of Bay Rum, tube of Bayberry Shaving Cream, two yellow Cannon washcloths, and one yellow Cannon towel. CMV, $110.00 set, mint.

Shaving Cabinet, 1930 – 1934.
White enamel cabinet with mirror on door. Cabinet is 8" high, 6½" wide, and 2⅜" deep. Label on door reads "Gem Micromatic Shaving Cabinet, Avon Products." CMV, $90.00 cabinet, empty, mint.

Assortment for Men, 1931 – 1936.
Green box held tube of shaving cream and green can Talc for Men with choice of 4 oz. Bay Rum or 2 oz. Lilac Vegetal. Both versions shown. CMV, $110.00 MB.

Hair Treatment Set for Men, 1931 – 1935.
6 oz. Liquid Shampoo, 2 oz. Pre-Shampoo oil, and 6 oz. Hair Tonic, all with blue caps. Silver tube of Hair Dress also included. White box. CMV, $135.00 MB.

Men's Travel Kit, 1933 – 1936.
Black leather case, 7¼" x 6½" x 2". Held green tube of Bayberry Shaving Cream, 4 oz. After Shave Lotion, Styptic Pencil, and green can of Talc for Men. CMV, $110.00 MB.

Men's Shaving Set, 1934 – 1935.
Wood grain box held 4 oz. After Shave Lotion, can of Talc for Men, Smoker's Tooth Powder, and tube of Bayberry Shaving Cream. CMV, $175.00 set.

Assortment for Men No. 1 and No. 2, 1936.
Avon box held can of Talc for Men, tube of Bayberry Shaving Cream, and choice of ribbed glass bottle After Shave or Bay Rum. CMV, $110.00 MB.

Men's Packages, 1936 – 1937.
Maroon box held can of Talc for Men, 4 oz. After Shave Lotion, turquoise can of Smoker's Tooth Powder, and tube of Shaving Cream. CMV, $100.00 MB.

Men's Travel Kit, 1936 – 1938.
Leather case, 7¼" x 6½" x 2". Held 4 oz. After Shave Lotion, Talc for Men, Shaving Cream, and tube of Styptic. CMV, $90.00 mint.

Assortment for Men, 1936 – 1937.
Wood grain paper box held tube of shaving cream and can of Talc for Men with choice of 4 oz. Bay Rum or After Shave Lotion. CMV, $85.00 MB.

Not shown: Esquire Set or Country Club Set, 1938 – 1939.
Same set as above and same price, only name changed. CMV, $85.00 MB.

Brushless Shaving Set, 1937 – 1939.
Speckled box held 4 oz. After Shave Lotion, maroon can of Talc for Men, and tube of Brushless Shaving Cream. CMV, $85.00 MB.

Headliner for Boys, 1938 – 1939.
Maroon and gray striped box held tubes of Hair Dress and toothpaste with toothbrush. CMV, $65.00 mint.

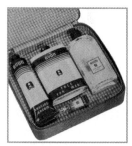

Travel Kit for Men, 1938.
Tan leather like case with zipper. Held tube of Styptic Cream, 4 oz. After Shave Lotion, tube of shaving cream, and can of Talc for Men. CMV, $80.00 MB.

Valet Set, 1938 – 1939.
Speckled box held 4 oz. After Shave, maroon can of Talc for Men, Smoker's Tooth Powder, and tube of shaving cream. CMV, $100.00 set, mint.

Men's Travel Kit, 1938 – 1940.
Brown leather zipper case held maroon can of Talc for Men, tube of shaving cream, tube of Styptic, and 4 oz. After Shave Lotion. CMV, $85.00 MB.

Smoker's Trio, 1938 – 1939.
Green box held 6 oz. Antiseptic, toothbrush, and green can of Smoker's Tooth Powder. CMV, $85.00 MB.

Women's Sets of the 1930s

Warning! Grading condition is paramount on sets. CMV can vary up to 90% on condition.

Assortment Set for Women, 1931 – 1932.
Contained two bars of Vernafleur toilet soap, blue and silver can of Avon dusting powder, bottle of Vernafleur bath salts, one bath towel, and two washcloths. All in orange and blue box. CMV, $160.00 MB.

Vanity Book Set, 1931 – 1932.
Silver and blue box contained blue and silver compact and lipstick. CMV, $80.00 MB. Also came in Christmas box. CMV, $90.00 MB.

Vanity Set, 1932 – 1933.
Gray velvet lined box contained blue and gold double compact and lipstick. CMV, $70.00 MB.

Hair Treatment Set for Women, 1931 – 1935.
Contained Liquid Shampoo, Pre-Shampoo Oil, Wave Set, and Hair Tonic. All have blue plastic caps, blue and white box. CMV, $180.00 MB.

Atomizer Set No. 6, 1931 – 1933.
Blue and silver box contained red 1 oz. glass bottle with atomizer with Vernafleur perfume in 1 oz. bottle with cork stopper. Set came in two different boxes. CMV, $160.00 MB.

Perfume Handkerchief Set, 1933 – 1936.
Contained two small bottles of Ariel and 391 perfume or Bolero with black caps, and four handkerchiefs under green and red flower cutout. CMV, $85.00 MB.

Vanity Book Set, 1933.
Silver and blue box contained blue and silver double compact and lipstick. CMV, $75.00 MB.

Gift Set No. 21, 1933 – 1935.
Contained boxes of silver and blue face powder and table rouge, and blue lipstick. Green, white, and red box. CMV, $65.00 MB.

Christmas Perfume Set, 1933.
Small blue box with winter snow scene held four octagonal shaped perfumes with black caps. Came in choice perfumes. Very rare. CMV, $275.00.

Trio Set, 1934 – 1935.
Red and blue box contained Trailing Arbutus toilet water, Daphne talcum, and Ariel sachet. CMV, $115.00 MB.

Gift Set No. 19, 1934.
Red and green box contained deluxe hairbrush, toothpaste, one bar of Savona soap, bottle of antiseptic, and tube of Dental Cream No. 2. CMV, $110.00 MB.

Gift Set No. 24, 1934.
Holly decorated box contained box of face powder, rouge, and jar of vanishing cream. CMV, $85.00 MB.

Gift Set No. 36, 1934.
Red and green box contained bottle of Rosewater, Glycerine, and Benzoin, Lily of the Valley toilet water, can of Daphne talcum, and Vernafleur bath salts. CMV, $175.00 MB.

Christmas Set No. 49, 1934.
Red and green holly design box held two white and green linen hand towels, 4 oz. bottle of Vanilla Tonka, and Vanilla Extract in box with tube of mending cement in box. Rare set. Comes with outer sleeves with "Set No. 49" on sleeve. CMV, $115.00 MB with sleeve.

Vanity Book Set, 1934 – 1935.
Blue and silver box held blue and silver compact and lipstick. CMV, $70.00 MB.

Threesome Set, 1934 – 1935.
Silver and blue box contained compact, face powder, and 2 dram bottle of Bolero perfume. CMV, $110.00 MB.

Gift Set W, 1935.
Box contained nail polish, lipstick, rouge compact, and polish remover. CMV, $105.00 MB.

Gift Set F, 1935.
Red and gold box contained blue compact, face powder in Ariel or Vernafleur, and lipstick. CMV, $85.00 MB.

Gift Set B, 1935.
Box contained blue and silver lipstick and rouge compact and 2 dram bottle of Trailing Arbutus perfume. CMV, $95.00 MB.

Gift Set A, 1935.
Satin lined box contained face powder in Ariel or Vernafleur and 2 dram bottle of Gardenia perfume with gold ribbed cap. CMV, $85.00 MB.

Gift Set D, 1935.
Blue and yellow box contained choice of Ariel or Vernafleur face powder in silver and blue box and 2 dram Ariel perfume with gold cap and Ariel sachet with silver label. CMV, $105.00 MB.

Gift Set K, 1935.
Box contained blue compact, 2 dram perfume in Gardenia, and blue and silver lipstick. CMV, $115.00 MB.

Bath Ensemble Set, 1935.
Box contained Jasmine bath salts, two bars of Jasmine bath soap, Avon dusting powder in silver can, and bottle of Trailing Arbutus toilet water. CMV, $185.00 MB.

Bath Ensemble Set, 1936 – 1939.
Plaid box held 9 oz. Jasmine bath salts, 2 oz. Trailing Arbutus toilet water, two bars of Jasmine soap, and can of beauty dust. CMV, $160.00 MB.

Handkerchief Set, 1936 only.
Avon box held 2 perfume bottles of Bolero and Ariel. CMV, $90.00 MB.

Threesome Set, 1936 – 1937.
Box held green and gold compact, box of face powder, and glass stopper 3 dram bottle of Bolero perfume. CMV, $115.00 MB.

Powder Compact Set, 1936 – 1937.
Box held face powder and green and gold compact. CMV, $50.00 MB.
Not shown: Aristocrat Set, 1938.
Same set as Powder Compact Set, only name changed in 1938. CMV, $50.00 MB.

Vanity Book Set, 1936 – 1937.
Satin lined box held green and gold compact and lipstick. CMV, $50.00 MB.
Not shown: Sports Wise Set, 1938 – 1940.
Same set as 1936 – 1937 Vanity Book Set, only name changed. CMV, $50.00 MB.

Trio Gift Set, 1936.
Box held 2 oz. Trailing Arbutus toilet water with tulip label and gold ribbed cap, silver can of Daphne talcum, and ribbed glass Ariel powder sachet. CMV, $115.00 MB.

Gift Set D, 1936.
Blue and yellow box contained Ariel or Vernafleur face powder in green and gold and 2 dram Ariel perfume with gold cap and Ariel powder sachet with black cap. CMV, $90.00 MB.

Gift Set No. 21, 1936 – 1937.
Striped box held turquoise and white box of face powder, turquoise and white cake rouge, and turquoise and gold lipstick. CMV, $60.00 MB.

Gift Set K, 1936 – 1937.
Blue and gold box held green and gold lipstick and compact and 2 dram perfume with gold cap. CMV, $90.00 MB.
Not shown: Empress Set, 1938.
Same set as Gift Set K, only name is changed. CMV, $90.00 MB.

Gift Set F, 1936 – 1937.
Box held green and gold compact, lipstick, and box of face powder in Ariel or Vernafleur. CMV, $60.00 MB.
Not shown: Mastercraft Set, 1938.
Same set as Gift Set F, only name changed in 1938. CMV, $60.00 MB.

Bath Duet, 1937 – 1939.
Box held turquoise and white can of Daphne talcum with choice of bath salts in Jasmine, Pine, Ariel, or Vernafleur. CMV, $55.00 MB.

Gift Set B, 1936 – 1937.
Green and silver box held green and gold lipstick and rouge, and 3 dram Trailing Arbutus perfume with gold cap. CMV, $90.00 MB.

Gift Set A, 1936 – 1937.
Box held face powder and 3 dram size of Ariel, Vernafleur, or Gardenia perfume with gold cap. CMV, $75.00 MB.

Gift Set W, 1936 – 1937.
Satin lined box held two ribbed bottles of nail polish and polish remover, green and gold lipstick, and rouge. CMV, $80.00 MB.

Perfume Handkerchief Set, 1937 – 1938.
Two ⅛ oz. bottles of Gardenia and Cotillion Perfume on four colored handkerchiefs. CMV, $70.00 MB.

Harmony Set, 1937.
Blue and white box contained Lily of the Valley toilet water with gold cap and label, white milk glass jar with turquoise cap of Rose Cold Cream, and turquoise and white tube of hand cream. CMV, $75.00 MB.

Lyric Set, 1937.
White and gold box held turquoise and white can of Trailing Arbutus toilet water, turquoise and white can of Daphne talcum, and white jar of cold cream with turquoise lid. CMV, $75.00 MB.

Charmer Set, 1938 – 1941.
Satin lined box contained lipstick, mascara, and rouge. All green and gold. CMV, $60.00 MB.

Wings to Beauty Set, 1938 – 1940.
Hinged lid box held 4 oz. bottle of Lotus Cream and choice of Ariel or Cotillion face powder and choice of astringent or skin freshener. CMV, $75.00 MB.

Beauty Kit for Fingers, 1938 – 1939.
Green box held bar of Lemonal soap, turquoise tube of hand cream, bottle of polish remover, and cream or nail polish. Same set also came in gold design box as substitute. CMV, $75.00 MB.

Fair Lady Set, 1939 – 1942.
Green, yellow, and white flowered box with gold base held four perfumes in Narcissus, Gardenia, Cotillion, Trailing Arbutus, or Sweet Pea. Each came with different colored caps. CMV, $100.00 MB.

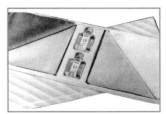

Handkerchief Set, 1939 only.
Gardenia and Cotillion perfumes with four handkerchiefs. CMV, $75.00 MB.

Spectator Set, 1939.
Turquoise and white box held 2 dram bottle with gold cap of Trailing Arbutus perfume, lipstick, and rouge compact. CMV, $80.00 MB.

Mayfair Set, 1939.
Blue lid box held 2 dram glass stopper bottle of Bolero perfume, box of face powder, and turquoise double compact. CMV, $110.00 MB.

Colonial Set, 1939.
Blue and gold box held 2 dram Gardenia perfume and face powder in choice of Ariel or Cotillion. CMV, $75.00 MB.

Warning! Grading condition is paramount on sets. CMV can vary up to 90% on condition.

Country Club Set, 1939 – 1941.
Box held 4 oz. bottle of after shave, tube of shaving cream, and can of talc for men. CMV, $80.00 MB.

Brushless Shave Set, 1940 – 1942.
Maroon and ivory box with man fishing, contained bottle of after shaving lotion, maroon can of talc for men, and tube of brushless shaving cream. CMV, $85.00 MB.

Commodore Set, 1940 – 1942.
Maroon and ivory box held 4 oz. after shaving lotion, maroon can of talc for men, and two white handkerchiefs. CMV, $90.00 MB.

Valet Set, 1940 – 1942.
Maroon and white box held 4 oz. after shaving lotion, maroon cans of talc for men, smoker's tooth powder, and tube of shaving cream. CMV, $100.00 MB.

Olympic Set, 1940 – 1946.
Maroon and ivory box held 6 oz. bottle of hair lotion, tube of shaving cream, and 4 oz. after shave lotion. CMV, $95.00 MB.

Army and Navy Kit, 1941 – 1942.
Blue and red box with eagle on lid, held 4 oz. after shave lotion, maroon tube of brushless shaving cream, and maroon can of elite powder. Each in maroon and ivory boxes. CMV, $90.00 MB.

Country Club Set, 1940 – 1942.
Maroon and ivory box held 4 oz. after shaving lotion, maroon can of talc for men, and tube of shaving cream. CMV, $90.00 MB.

Esquire Set, 1940 – 1941.
Maroon box held 4 oz. bottle of Bay Rum, tube of shaving cream, and can of talc for men. CMV, $90.00 MB.

The Traveler Set, 1941 – 1945.
Maroon and ivory box held 4 oz. after shaving lotion, maroon tubes of smoker's toothpaste, and shaving cream. OSP, $1.10. CMV, $75.00 MB.

Men's Traveler's Set,
1941 – 1942.
Brown leather snap case with maroon and black stripes inside case and lid. Held 4 oz. after shaving lotion, 3½ oz. tube of brushless shaving cream, maroon 2⅝ oz. can of talc for men, and tube of styptic cream. All products came in original maroon and ivory boxes. CMV, $100.00 MB, set.

Army and Navy Kit,
1943 – 1946.
Blue and red box held tube of brushless shaving cream, maroon paper box of Elite foot powder, and paper carton of tooth powder. CMV, $100.00 MB.

Country Club Set, 1943 – 1946.
Maroon and white box held 4 oz. after shave lotion, 2⅝ oz. paper box of talc for men, and 3 oz. tube of shaving cream. Talc came with flat paper top lid or cap lid as shown. CMV, $90.00 MB.

Valet Set, 1943 – 1945.
Maroon and ivory box held 4 oz. after shave lotion, 3 oz. tube in box of Shaving Cream, 2⅝ oz. paper talc, and 3½ oz. paper side, tin flat top and bottom can of smoker's tooth powder. OSP, $1.85. CMV, $115.00 MB.

Country Club Set, 1943 – 1946.
Maroon and white box held 4 oz. after shave lotion, maroon flat top paper box of talc for men, and tube of shaving cream. CMV, $90.00 MB.

Army and Navy Kit,
1943.
Blue box with eagle held turquoise can of Elite powder, 4 oz. bottle of after shave, and maroon tube of brushless shaving cream. CMV, $85.00 MB.

Commodore Set,
1943 – 1946.
Maroon and white box held 4 oz. after shave lotion, two white handkerchiefs, and maroon paper box of talc for men. CMV $90.00 MB.

Brushless Shave Set, 1943 – 1946.
Maroon and white box held tube of brushless shave cream, 4 oz. after shave lotion, and maroon paper box of talc for men. OSP, $1.35. CMV, $90.00 MB.

Valet Set, 1945 – 1946.
Maroon and ivory box held 4 oz. after shave lotion, tube of shaving cream, talc for men, and smoker's tooth powder. Both came in maroon paper containers with flat top lids or pouring lids with caps. OSP, $2.00. CMV, $125.00 MB.

Modern Knight,
1946 – 1949.
Maroon and white box held 2 oz. deodorant for men, can of talc for men, and 4 oz. after shaving lotion. CMV, $95.00 MB.

Brushless Shave Set,
1946 – 1949.
Maroon and white box held can of talc for men, tube of brushless shaving cream, and 4 oz. after shaving lotion. CMV, $85.00 MB.

Men's Travel Kit, 1946 – 1949.
Brown flip-open leather case held can of talc for men, 4 oz. after shaving lotion, styptic cream, and choice of tube of shaving cream or brushless shaving cream. CMV, $85.00 MB.

Valet Set, 1946 – 1949.
Maroon box held maroon can of smoker's tooth powder, talc for men, 4 oz. after shaving lotion, and tube of shaving cream. CMV, $90.00 MB.

Olympic Set, 1946 – 1949.
Maroon and white box held tube of shaving cream, 6 oz. bottle of hair lotion, and 4 oz. after shaving lotion. OSP, $1.65. CMV, $95.00 MB.

Traveler Kit,
1946 – 1949.
Maroon and white box held 4 oz. after shaving lotion and maroon tubes of smoker's toothpaste and shaving cream. OSP, $1.25. CMV, $75.00 MB.

Country Club Set,
1946 – 1949.
Maroon and white box held tube of shaving cream, 4 oz. after shaving lotion, and can of talc for men. CMV, $85.00 MB.

Pleasure Cast Set, 1948.
Blue box held 2 oz. bottles with maroon caps in deodorant for men and tube of brushless or regular shaving cream. CMV, $75.00 MB.

Women's Sets of the 1940s

Warning! Grading condition is paramount on sets. CMV can vary up to 90% on condition.

Mayfair Set, 1940.
Blue box contained 1 dram perfume with gold cap, green and gold compacts, and box of face powder in Ariel or Cotillion. CMV, $75.00 MB.

Milady Set,
1940 – 1941.
Satin lined box contained two small bottles of perfume in Gardenia, Cotillion, Apple Blossom, or Ballad, and white lace edged hanky. CMV, $85.00 MB.

Mr. and Mrs. Set,
1940 – 1943.
Blue and pink box contained smoker's tooth powder, after shaving lotion for men, Cotillion toilet water, and Cotillion talcum for women. CMV, $140.00 MB.

Spectator Set, 1940.
Box contained green and gold rouge, 1 dram Garden of Love perfume with gold cap, and green and gold lipstick. CMV, $65.00 MB.

Bath Duet Set, 1940 – 1943.
Blue, pink, and white box held can of Daphne or Cotillion talc and choice of Jasmine, Pine, Ariel, or Vernafleur bath salts. CMV, $60.00 MB.

Merriment Set, 1940 – 1942.
Rouge, lipstick, and eyebrow pencil. All green and gold. CMV, $45.00 MB.

Tandem Set, 1941.
Box held gold bamboo compact and turquoise and gold lipstick. CMV, $50.00 MB.

Colonial Set, 1940.
Blue box held 1 dram Garden of Love perfume, gold cap and label, and box of face powder. CMV, $55.00 MB.

Handkerchief Set, 1940 – 1942.
Box held white, pink, blue, and yellow handkerchiefs, 1/8 oz. Cotillion perfume with red cap, and Gardenia perfume with blue cap. CMV, $60.00 MB.

Wings to Beauty Set, 1941.
Red designed box contained choice of two 2 oz. skin conditioners, astringents, finishing lotions, or Lotus creams, and box of face powder. CMV, $55.00 MB.

Colonial Set, 1940 – 1941.
Feather face powder and Garden of Love perfume in blue box. CMV, $60.00 MB.

Fragrant Mist Set, 1940 – 1942.
Blue and gold box held 2 oz. toilet water with gold or plastic cap and label, and spray atomizer. Came in Cotillion, Marionette, Sonnet, Jasmine, or Apple Blossom. CMV, $50.00 MB.

Reception Set, 1941– 1942.
Satin lined box held gold compact, blue box of face powder, and 1/8 oz. perfume. CMV, $75.00 MB.

Orchid Set, 1940.
Red and white box, green and gold lipstick and rouge, and cream polish with green cap. CMV, $55.00.

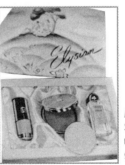

Elysian Set, 1941 – 1942.
Satin lined box contained lipstick, rouge, and 1 dram perfume with gold cap. CMV, $85.00 MB.

Minuet Set, 1942.
Box with music notes on lid, satin lined, held lipstick, powder compact, rouge, and face powder. All are blue and white feather design. CMV, $75.00 MB.

Tandem Set, 1942.
Same as 1941 Tandem Set, only with matching bamboo lipstick. CMV, $50.00 MB.

Peek-a-Boo Set, 1943.
Pink and blue box with yellow satin lining held blue and white feather design cardboard compact, cardboard lipstick, and rouge. CMV, $65.00 MB.

Colonial Days Set, 1943.
6 oz. clear glass bottle, pink cap, cream lotion, and cardboard body powder, shaker cap. CMV, $65.00 MB.

Bath Bouquet Set, 1943 – 1944.
Blue box held 6 oz. bottle of Rose Geranium bath oil and Apple Blossom beauty dust. CMV, $75.00 MB.

Rainbow Wings Set, 1943 – 1944.
Box held 6 oz. bottles of cream lotion and Rose Geranium bath oil with pink caps. Both bottles are flat on one side. Butterflies on box. CMV, $65.00 MB.

Minuet Set, 1943 – 1944.
Pink and blue box with yellow satin lining held blue plastic rouge compact, cardboard feather design lipstick, Cotillion perfume with gold cap and neck tag, and blue satin sachet pillowette. CMV, $110.00 MB.

Little Jewels Set, 1944 – 1945.
Pink box held three paper powder sachets in 1¼ oz. Cotillion, Attention, or Garden of Love. OSP, $3.25. CMV, $65.00 MB.

Peek-a-Boo Set, 1944 only.
Blue, white, and pink box with yellow satin lining held cardboard compact covered with pink satin and white net, cake rouge in blue plastic compact, and cardboard feather design lipstick. CMV, $60.00 MB.

Fair Lady Set, 1945 – 1947.
Blue and white box held four small bottles with colored caps of perfume in Cotillion, Lily of the Valley, Gardenia, Garden of Love, Trailing Arbutus, and Sweet Pea. Also came with all blue caps. CMV, $75.00 MB.

Rainbow Wings Set, 1945 – 1946.
Pink box held two, 6 oz. flat sided bottles of cream lotion and Rose Geranium bath oil. Pink net ribbon on top of box. CMV, $75.00 MB with net.

Double Dare Set, 1946.
Red and gold box held bottle of Double Dare nail polish and gold bamboo lipstick. CMV, $50.00 MB.

That's for Me Set, 1947 – 1949.
Multicolored box contained choice of cream cake or cake makeup, gold lipstick, and ½ oz. bottle nail polish. CMV, $40.00 MB.

Color Cluster Set, 1948.
Red and gold box contained gold lipstick, gold rouge, and ½ oz. bottle of nail polish with green cap. CMV, $45.00 MB.

Leading Lady Set, 1946 only.
Red, blue, and gold box held bamboo lipstick and nail polish. CMV, $45.00 MB.

Perfumed Deodorant Set, 1947 – 1954.
Turquoise box held two, 2 oz. bottles of perfumed deodorant. CMV, $15.00 set MB.

Color Magic Three-Piece Set, 1949 – 1950.
Multicolored box held gold lipstick, gold rouge, and ½ oz. bottle of nail polish with green cap. CMV, $50.00 MB.

Fair Lady Set, 1948 – 1949.
Pink and blue box contained four, ⅛ oz. perfumes in Lily of the Valley, Garden of Love, Quaintance, Gardenia, and Cotillion. All have blue caps. CMV, $85.00 MB.

Color Cluster Set, 1946 – 1947.
Red and gold box held gold bamboo lipstick and rouge with ½ oz. nail polish with black cap. CMV, $50.00 MB.

Beauty Basket Set, 1947.
Straw basket with pink ribbon held two, 6 oz. bottles of Avon cream lotion and Rose Gardenia bath oil. Both bottles are flat on the back side and have pink caps. OSP, $2.00. CMV, $55.00 basket with bottles mint. $75.00 MB.

Beauty Mark, 1948.
Red and gold box contained gold lipstick and ½ oz. nail polish with green cap. CMV, $40.00 MB.

Color Magic Two-Piece Set, 1949 – 1950.
Multicolored box contained gold lipstick and ½ oz. bottle of nail polish with green cap. CMV, $40.00 MB.

Warning! Grading condition is paramount on sets. CMV can vary up to 90% on condition.

Valet Set, 1949 – 1950.
Green box with choice of green can talc for men or shaving soap and 4 oz. cologne for men. CMV, $50.00 MB.

Commodore Set, 1949 – 1953.
Stagecoach on green flip-open box held 2 oz. cologne, 2 oz. deodorant for men, and green tube of brushless or lather shaving cream. CMV, $55.00 MB.

Avon Service Kit, 1951 – 1952.
Red and green box held canvas apron with 4 oz. plastic bottle of after shaving lotion with red cap, Dr. Zabriskie's soap, tube of brushless shaving cream, toothpaste, toothbrush, and comb. CMV, $55.00 MB.

Hi Podner Set, 1950 – 1951.
White box held two red leatherette cowboy cuffs with tubes of cream hair dress, ammoniated toothpaste or dental cream, and toothbrush. CMV, $70.00 MB.
Not shown: Hi Podner Set, 1952.
Same, except tube of cream hair dress was replaced with green tube of creme shampoo. CMV, $70.00 MB.

Pleasure Shave Set, 1949 – 1951.
Green box held green can of talc for men, wood shaving bowl, and 4 oz. after shave lotion with silver label. CMV, $75.00 MB.

Deluxe Trio Set, 1949 – 1951.
Stagecoach on green flip-open box with green and red inner box. Held choice of 4 oz. cream or liquid hair lotion, 2 oz. deodorant for men, and 2 oz. cologne for men. CMV, $60.00 MB.
Not shown: Deluxe Trio Set, 1952.
Same as 1949 set, only has green removable lid. CMV, $60.00 MB.

Young Man Set, 1950.
Red, white, and green box held tubes of cream hair dress and creme shampoo, comb, and nail file in brown leather case. CMV, $60.00 MB.

Classic Set, 1951.
Green box held 4 oz. choice of liquid or cream hair lotion, tan bar of soap, and 2 oz. deodorant. CMV, $65.00 set MB.

Country Club Set, 1949 – 1951.
Green flip-open box with red inner box, held green can of talc for men, 4 oz. after shaving lotion, and choice of lather or brushless shaving cream. CMV, $55.00 MB.

Valet Set, 1951.
Green flip-open box held 2 oz. deodorant for men, tube of brushless or lather shaving cream, and 4 oz. cream or liquid hair lotion. CMV, $50.00 MB.

Changing of the Guard Set, 1952.
Red, white, and blue guard house box held 2 oz. hair guard with red cap. Came with outer box. CMV, $70.00 MB.

Avon Classic Set, 1952 – 1953.
Silver and green box held 2 oz. deodorant for men, green talc for men, and 4 oz. cologne for men. CMV, $55.00 MB.

Man's Sample Case Set, 1953.
Very rare brown leather case had three partitions inside to hold a Gillette brass razor, ½ oz. green sample tube of brushless shaving cream, ¾ oz. blue, white, and green sample toothpaste tubes, 1 oz. bottle of liquid shampoo with green label, 1 oz. bottle of cream hair lotion with green label, ½ oz. bottle of shaving lotion with green label, ½ oz. bottle of deodorant for men with green label, and ½ oz. bottle of cologne for men with silver label. All bottles have red caps. CMV, $125.00 complete set, mint.

Pleasure Shave Set, 1952 – 1954.
Green box with red and white barber pole held two tubes of shaving cream in choice of brushless or lather. CMV, $25.00 MB.

Deluxe Trio Set, 1953 – 1956.
Tan leatherette bag held 2 oz. cologne for men and 2 oz. deodorant for men, and choice of 4 oz. cream or liquid hair lotion. "Avon" on bag. Fold-open top, no zipper. CMV, $45.00.

Country Club Set, 1952 – 1953.
Stagecoach on green box lid with inner box in red. Held green talc for men, 4 oz. after shave lotion, and tube of brushless or lather shave cream. CMV, $55.00 MB.

Men's Traveling Kit, 1953 – 1955.
Choice of brown leatherette or plaid case. Held 4 oz. after shave lotion, 2 oz. deodorant for men, styptic cream, green can of talc for men, and tube of lather shaving cream. CMV, $55.00 MB.

U.S. Male Set, 1952 – 1953.
Green and white mailbox, choice of two, 4 oz. after shave lotions or 4 oz. after shave lotion and 2 oz. deodorant for men. CMV, $40.00 MB.

Avon Service Kit, 1953 – 1954.
Green and red box held tan plastic apron with 4 oz. plastic bottle of after shaving lotion with red cap, tube of brushless shaving cream, chlorophyll toothpaste, Dr. Zabriskie's soap, comb, and toothbrush. CMV, $55.00 MB.

Two Suiter Set, 1953 – 1954.
Two different olive tan boxes with airlines painted on sides. Held choice of two, 2 oz. deodorants for men or one, 2 oz. deodorant and 4 oz. after shave, or 2 oz. deodorant and 2 oz. cologne for men. Sold around Father's Day. CMV, $60.00 MB, light color box. $70.00 MB, dark color box.

Kingpin Set, 1953.
Red and green box held two, 4 oz. bottles of after shave lotion wrapped in green Kingpin wrappings. CMV, $45.00 MB.

Rough 'n Ready Set, 1953.
White, red, and green box held 4 oz. cream hair lotion, chap check, and Dr. Zabriskie's soap. CMV, $47.50 MB.

Space Ship Set, 1953.
Blue box held plastic spaceship with tubes of chlorophyll toothpaste, creme shampoo, and toothbrush. CMV, $60.00 MB.

Smooth Shaving Set, 1954.
Green tubes with red caps, had choice of brushless or lather shaving cream. CMV, $25.00 MB.

Backfield Set, 1954.
Red and green box held 2 oz. bottle of hair guard with red cap, 2 oz. hand guard with green cap, tube of chap check, and small brown football soap. CMV, $70.00 MB.

Parade Dress Set, 1953 – 1954.
Red, white, and blue soldier box held 1 oz. bottle of liquid shampoo, 1 oz. cream or liquid hair lotion, and one bar of Dr. Zabriskie's Soap. CMV, $75.00 MB. Set also came with two shampoos and one hair lotion with no soap. Same CMV.

Before and After Set, 1953 – 1954.
Silver, white, and green box opened up to 4 oz. cologne for men and choice of cream or liquid hair lotion. CMV, $45.00 MB.

Personal Note Set, 1954 – 1956.
Green and red box held 4 oz. cologne and deodorant for men with green label and gold ball point pen. CMV, $60.00 MB.

Quartet Set, 1953 – 1954.
Green and red box held two tubes of shave cream, brushless or lather, 2 oz. deodorant for men with green label, and 4 oz. after shave lotion with silver label. CMV, $60.00 MB.

Pleasure Cast No. 1 Set, 1954. Red and white box held 2 oz. deodorant for men and 4 oz. after shave lotion. CMV, $35.00 MB.

Good Morning Set, 1955 – 1956. Red box with geese held choice of two, 4 oz. bottles of cream or liquid hair lotion. CMV, $26.00 MB.

Country Club Set, 1954 – 1955. Red box held green can of talc for men, 4 oz. after shaving lotion, and tube of brushless or lather shaving cream. CMV, $60.00 MB.

Pigskin Parade Set, 1955. Red and green box held tube of creme shampoo, youth's toothbrush, chap check, 2 oz. bottle of hair guard, and a plastic football. CMV, $65.00 MB.

Pleasure Cast No. 2 Set, 1954. Green and white box held 4 oz. after shave lotion and green can of talc. CMV, $35.00 MB.

Classic Set, 1954. Red and white box with horse head on box held green can of talc for men, 2 oz. deodorant with green label, and 4 oz. cologne with silver label. All have red caps. Rare. CMV, $80.00.

Sport-Wise Set, 1954. Red, white, and green box held two 4 oz. bottles of after shave lotions. OSP, $1.18. CMV, $30.00 MB.

Shave Bowl Set, 1955 – 1956. Bronze box held wood shave bowl and bronze 4 oz. deodorant for men. CMV, $55.00 MB.

Penny Arcade Set, 1954 – 1955. Red and white box with center foil mirror held tubes of cream hair dress, creme shampoo, and chlorophyll toothpaste, toothbrush, and chap check. CMV, $70.00 MB.

Black Sheep, 1954 – 1956. Red, white, green, and black box held black sheep soap with gold bell on neck, 4 oz. cologne for men, and 4 oz. deodorant for men. CMV, $100.00 MB.

Pleasure Cast Set, 1955. Green and white box held two 4 oz. bottles of after shaving lotion. CMV, $30.00 MB.

Flying High No. 1 and No. 2 Set, 1955.
Red and green box had 4 oz. after shave lotion and 4 oz. deodorant for men. No. 2 box had 4 oz. deodorant for men and green can of talc for men. CMV, $35.00 each set, MB.

The Traveler Set, 1956.
Brown leatherette bag held choice of shaving cream in Kwick, lather, or brushless, 4 oz. after shaving lotion, green can talc for men, 2 oz. deodorant for men, and styptic cream. CMV, $50.00 MB.

Top o' the Mornin' Set, 1956.
Red, white, green, and silver box held can of Kwick Foaming shave cream and 2 oz. after shave lotion. CMV, $45.00 MB.

Touchdown Set, 1956 – 1957.
Green, red, and gold box held 2 oz. bottles of hair guard with red caps, hand guard with green cap, and small football soap. CMV, $65.00 MB.

Round the Corner Set, 1955.
Red and white striped box held 2 oz. deodorant for men and can of Kwick Foaming shave cream. CMV, $35.00 MB.

Before and After Set, 1956.
Red and silver box held 4 oz. electric pre-shave lotion and 4 oz. after shave lotion. CMV, $30.00 MB.

Attention Set, 1957.
Red and green box held two, 4 oz. bottles in after shave lotion and choice of liquid or cream hair lotion. CMV, $35.00 MB.

Space Scout Set, 1955.
Blue box held wall charts of planets, toothbrush, white toothpaste, bottle of hair guard, tube of antiseptic cream, and chap check. CMV, $60.00 MB.

Overnighter Set, 1956 – 1957.
Brown alligator type bag held 2 oz. after shaving lotion, 2 oz. deodorant for men, and choice of 4 oz. cream or liquid hair lotion. CMV, $45.00 MB.

Saturday Night Set, 1955.
Plaid box held 4 oz. deodorant for men, plaid bowtie, and choice of 4 oz. cream or liquid hair lotion. CMV, $50.00 MB.
Not shown: Varsity Set, 1956.
Same as Saturday Night Set, only name changed. CMV, $50.00 MB.

More Love Than Money Set, 1956.
Red, black, and gold box held 4 oz. cologne for men, 4 oz. after shave lotion, and 2 oz. deodorant for men. Brown leather wallet with a new 1956 penny in it. CMV, $55.00 MB.

Country Club Set, 1956.
Came in green box with golf ball and red flag on lid and red lined box. Same contents as 1954 set. CMV, $60.00 MB.

Sailing, Sailing Set, 1957.
4 oz., clear glass, red cap, silver label. Choice of any two bottles of after shaving lotion, electric pre-shave lotion, or deodorant for men. CMV, $30.00 MB.

Trading Post Set, 1957.
Red and brown box held 2 oz. bottles of foamy bath and hair trainer. Both have red caps. CMV, $40.00 MB.

Hair Trainer and Comb Set, 1957.
6 oz. bottle, white or blue cap, red and white label. Came in box with comb. CMV, $25.00 BO. $40.00 MB.

Refreshing Hours Set, 1957.
Red and green hourglass box held 4 oz. after shaving lotion and 4 oz. deodorant for men. CMV, $30.00 MB.

Money Isn't Everything Set, 1957.
Red box with "money" written all over lid, held 4 oz. cologne for men, 4 oz. after shave lotion, and 2 oz. deodorant for men, plus brown leather billfold. CMV, $60.00 MB.

Man's World Set, 1957.
Box had choice of two cream or liquid hair lotions in 4 oz. size. CMV, $30.00 MB.

Good Cheer Set, 1957.
Man playing bass fiddle on green and red box. 2 oz. bottles of cologne, deodorant, and after shave lotions. All had red caps. CMV, $45.00 MB.

Send Off Set, 1957.
Red, white, and black box held two 4 oz. after shave lotions. CMV, $30.00 MB.

Father's Sail Day Special Set No. 1, 1957.
Box with sailboat held two 4 oz. bottles of after shave with silver labels. Also came with choice of 4 oz. after shave and green can of talc for men or 4 oz. deodorant and 4 oz. after shave lotion. CMV, $35.00 MB.

Merrily Set, 1957.
Red, white, and green box held can of Kwick Foaming shave cream, 2 oz. deodorant for men, and 2 oz. after shave lotion. CMV, $30.00 MB.

Holiday Holly Set, 1957.
Green and white box held 4 oz. after shave lotion and green can of talc for men. CMV, $30.00 MB.

Neat Traveler Set, 1958.
Tan soft leather case held 2 oz. deodorant for men, 4 oz. after shaving lotion, choice of Kwick Foaming, lather, or brushless shaving creams or electric pre-shave lotion, and choice of cream or liquid hair lotions. CMV, $45.00 MB.

Modern Decoy Set, 1958.
Blue and brown box with ducks on lid held silver Paper Mate Capri pen, 4 oz. cream hair lotion, and choice of 4 oz. after shave lotion, cologne, deodorant, or electric pre-shave lotion. CMV, $40.00 MB.

New Day Set, 1957.
Red top box held 4 oz. electric pre-shave lotion and 4 oz. after shaving lotion. CMV, $30.00 MB.

Happy Hours Substitute Set, 1958.
Outer sleeve marked "Happy Hours Sub" held tan vinyl case with 2 oz. cologne, after shave lotion, and deodorant. This is a rare set. Factory ran out of regular issue boxes and used overnighter cases for short period. Must have outer sleeves. CMV, $45.00 MB, set.

Stagecoach Set, 1958.
Yellow stagecoach box held 2 oz. bottles of hair trainer and foamy bath. Both have red caps. CMV, $40.00 MB.

Cufflinks Set, 1957.
Black velour covered box held two gold cufflinks and 4 oz. cologne and deodorant for men. CMV, $55.00 MB.

On the Go Set, 1957.
Brown leatherette bag held green can of talc for men, 2 oz. deodorant for men, 4 oz. after shave lotion, and can of shaving cream in choice of Kwick Foaming lather, brushless, or electric pre-shave lotions. CMV, $50.00 MB.

Overniter Set, 1958.
Tan case held 2 oz. deodorant for men, 2 oz. after shaving lotion, and choice of 4 oz. liquid or cream hair lotion. CMV, $35.00 MB.

Happy Hours Set, 1958.
Cuckoo clock on black and brown box. 2 oz. cologne, deodorant, and after shave lotion. All have red caps. CMV, $40.00 MB.

Avon Guard Set, 1958.
Red and blue box held bottles of hair guard and hand guard with red caps. White Avon rocket soap sits on top of bottles. CMV, $65.00 MB.

Out in Front Set, 1959.
Box with soldier on horse held 4 oz. cream or liquid hair lotion and 2¾ oz. spray deodorant for men in white plastic bottles. CMV, $30.00 MB.

Triumph Set, 1959.
Triumph box held choice of five combinations of two, 4 oz. after shave lotions or electric pre-shave lotion, and after shave lotion or after shave lotion and after shower powder for men. CMV, $30.00 each set, MB. Same set with electric pre-shave lotion and after shower for men in black glass, or after shower powder for men and after shower for men in black glass. CMV, $30.00 MB, each set.

Lamplighter Set, 1959 – 1960.
Lamp post on covered box held 2 oz. bottle of after shave lotion, 1½ oz. white plastic bottle of spray deodorant for men, and 2 oz. black plastic bottle of after shower for men. All have red caps. CMV, $45.00 MB.

Coat of Arms Set, 1958.
Red, white, blue, and gold box held 6 oz. Kwick Foaming shave cream, 2 oz. deodorant for men, and 2 oz. after shave lotion. CMV, $40.00 MB.

Grooming Guards Set, 1959.
Black flip-open box with red inner box held can of after shower powder for men, 2 oz. spray deodorant for men in white plastic, tube of Attention cream hair dress, and choice of 4 oz. after shower for men or after shaving lotion. CMV, $60.00 MB.

Captain of the Guard Set, 1959.
White tube of cream hair dress with red cap and white plastic bottle of spray deodorant for men with red cap. CMV, $40.00.

Carollers Set, 1959 – 1960.
Christmas box with red and gold base held red and black stick deodorant for men, black and white can of after shower powder for men, and choice of 4 oz. black glass bottle of after shower for men, electric pre-shave lotion, or after shave lotion. CMV, $55.00 MB.

Women's Sets of the 1950s

Warning! Grading condition is paramount on sets. CMV can vary up to 90% on condition.

Fragrant Mist, 1950.
Turquoise and gold box held 2 oz. toilet water with green and gold atomizer in the choice of Flowertime, Cotillion, Lily of the Valley, or Wishing. CMV, $50.00 MB.

Avonette Set, 1950 – 1951.
Blue and white brocade bag held 1 dram perfume and deluxe gold lipstick. CMV, $18.00 CO. $25.00 MB.

Avon Blossoms Set, 1950.
Four ⅛ oz. or ⅝ dram perfume bottles set in white foam with wire fence behind it. Flowers around bottles. Plastic caps. Quaintance, Cotillion, Luscious and Golden Promise. CMV, $85.00 set only. $100.00 MB.

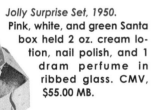

Jolly Surprise Set, 1950.
Pink, white, and green Santa box held 2 oz. cream lotion, nail polish, and 1 dram perfume in ribbed glass. CMV, $55.00 MB.

Lady Fair Set, 1950 – 1951.
Red, white, and silver box held gold deluxe lipstick and bottle of nail polish. CMV, $30.00 MB.

Adorable Set, 1950.
Foam holder had powder pak and gold lipstick. Trimmed in blue feathers and pink ribbon and flowers. Came in green box. CMV, $35.00 mint as shown.

Adorable Set, 1950 – 1951.
White box held blue satin with white lace pillow with powder pak and lipstick inside. CMV, $35.00 MB.

High Fashion Set, 1950 – 1954.
Black case with white satin lining held 1 dram perfume, gold lipstick, gold compact, and gold rouge compact. CMV, $45.00 MB.

Home Permanent Refill Kit, 1951.
Kit contained 4 oz. permanent wave lotion. CMV, $25.00 BO. Neutralizer and end tissues. CMV, $45.00 MB set.

Happy Vacation Special Gift Bag Set, 1951.
Folder had plastic bag and Avon tie tag to hold cream deodorant, toothpaste, toothbrush, and Cotillion talcum, all boxed. CMV, $7.00 as pictured.

Special Set, 1951.
Blue and pink Christmas box held two bottles of hand lotion. CMV, $30.00 MB.

Fragrant Mist Set, 1951 – 1952.
Turquoise box with pink and gold inside held 2 oz. toilet water and 1 dram perfume in choice of Cotillion, Flowertime, and Lily of the Valley. OSP, $2.75. CMV, $50.00 MB.

Sweet As Honey Set, 1951.
Foam beehive held four, ⅝ dram bottles of perfume in Cotillion, Quaintance, Golden Promise, Luscious, Forever Spring, and To a Wild Rose. All have different colored caps. CMV, $90.00 beehive and bottles only, mint. $115.00 MB.

Time for Beauty Set, 1952.
Blue, white, and pink box with pink ribbon held gold lipstick and nail polish. CMV, $30.00 MB.

Twin Pak Set, 1952 – 1953.
Silver box held two bottles of hand lotion. White caps, red ribbon on box. OSP, $1.10. CMV, $30.00 MB.

Avonette Set, 1953 – 1954.
Black case held 1 dram perfume and gold deluxe lipstick. CMV, $20.00 CO. $25.00 MB.

House of Charms Set, 1952 – 1953.
With windows open you found four, ⅛ oz. or ⅝ dram bottles of perfume: Lily of the Valley, Cotillion, Golden Promise, or Quaintance. In pink box, all blue caps. CMV, $100.00 MB.

Sunny Hours Set, 1952 – 1953.
White umbrella held 1 dram perfume and deluxe gold lipstick. CMV, $30.00 umbrella and contents only, mint. $50.00 MB.

Happy Vacation Set, 1953.
Plastic bag and tie string says "Avon Happy Vacation." Bag held Cotillion talc, toothpaste, cream deodorant, and tube of ammoniated toothpaste. CMV, $60.00 MB.

Precious Pear Set, 1953.
Gold bell box held 1 dram perfume in Golden Promise, Quaintance, Cotillion, To a Wild Rose and Forever Spring. CMV, $75.00 MB.

Holiday Fashion Set, 1953.
White box held two gold fashion lipsticks in green holly leaves. CMV, $25.00 MB.

Gadabouts Set, 1952 – 1953.
Gold and white box held turquoise compact and cologne stick. CMV, $25.00 MB.

Avonette Set, 1952.
Gold pouch held two tubes, choice of lipstick and 1 dram perfume. CMV, $20.00 MB.

Fragrance Tie-Ins Set, 1953.
White box with bows held four, ½ oz. bottles with white caps. Came in Cotillion, Forever Spring, Quaintance, and To a Wild Rose cologne. CMV, $70.00 MB.

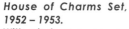

Christmas Angels Sets, 1953 – 1955.
Blue and white box held gold lipstick and cream sachet in To a Wild Rose, Quaintance, Cotillion, Forever Spring, or Golden Promise. To a Wild Rose sold 1955 only and 1953 – 1954 came with older three corner white jar with blue cap. Both are same CMV. CMV, $30.00 MB.

Fragrance Rainbow Set, 1954.
Flowers on top of box. Choice of Cotillion, To a Wild Rose, Forever Spring, or Quaintance cologne in ½ oz. bottles, white caps and painted labels. CMV, $70.00 MB.

Little Lambs Set, 1954 – 1956.
Box held two lamb soaps and can of baby powder. Two different boxes. One has two lambs and the other has two lambs holding an umbrella. CMV, $80.00 each set, MB.

Lady Belle Set, 1954 – 1955.
White bell shaped box trimmed in blue and gold had two, 1 dram perfumes. Ribbed glass with gold cap. Choice of Cotillion, To a Wild Rose, Golden Promise, Quaintance, Bright Night, or Forever Spring. CMV, $60.00 MB.

House of Charms Perfumes.
Shown only to identify size and labels. Left square bottle is 1954 set only. Center bottle has same label as short one on left, issued in 1953 – 1954. Right one was issued in 1952 – 1953 sets only.

Silver Wings Set, 1954.
Box held cream sachet and body powder in choice of To a Wild Rose, Quaintance, Golden Promise, or Forever Spring. CMV, $40.00 each set, MB.

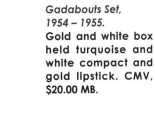

Gadabouts Set, 1954 – 1955.
Gold and white box held turquoise and white compact and gold lipstick. CMV, $20.00 MB.

Concertina Set, 1954.
Two gold fashion lipsticks in red, white, and green box. CMV, $35.00 MB.

House of Charms Set, 1954.
Pink box held four ⅝ dram bottles of perfume with turquoise or white caps. Choice of To a Wild Rose, Cotillion, Golden Promise, or Quaintance. CMV, $110.00 MB.

Beauty Pair Set, 1954.
Red and gold box held gold deluxe lipstick and nail polish. CMV, $25.00 MB.

Color Corsage Set, 1954 – 1955.
Turquoise box of face powder with gold lipstick on top. CMV, $25.00 MB.

Two Loves Set, 1955.
Red, white, blue, and gold Christmas tree ornament box held two gold fashion lipsticks. CMV, $35.00 MB.

For Your Loveliness Set, 1954 – 1955.
Green and silver box held 3½ oz. jar of moisture cream and choice of 4 oz. bottle of hand lotion or skin freshener. CMV, $20.00 MB.

Jeweled Lipstick, 1955.
Blue and gold box with gold lipstick with pearl and rhinestones on top. CMV, $20.00 MB.

Showers of Stars Set, 1955.
Silver box with fluff on top held cream sachet and body powder in choice of Golden Promise, Quaintance, and Forever Spring. CMV, $40.00 MB.

Camping Kit, 1954.
Navy blue cotton twill drawstring bag. Came with 2 oz. sun lotion, chap check, antiseptic cream, and choice of creme shampoo or cream hair dress. $50.00 MB complete set.

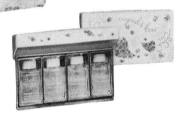

Charmer Set, 1955.
White, gold, and red brocade case held jeweled lipstick and 1 dram perfume. CMV, $25.00 mint.

Hand Beauty Set, 1954.
Red box held two bottles of hand lotion. CMV, $20.00 MB.

Fashion Jewels Set, 1954 – 1955.
Black velvet case held 1 dram perfume, jeweled lipstick, and gold compact. CMV, $40.00 MB.

Cupid's Bow Set, 1955.
White and pink box held four, ½ oz. bottles of cologne with white caps: Bright Night, To a Wild Rose, Quaintance, and Cotillion. CMV, $70.00 MB.

Bath Delights Set, 1955.
Box held bottle of Avon bubble bath and choice of body powder in Golden Promise, Quaintance, or Forever Spring. CMV, $50.00 MB.

Happy Traveler Set, 1954.
Black and white bag held perfumed deodorant, hand cream, rich moisture cream, skin freshener, cleansing cream, and a plastic jar. CMV, $35.00 MB.

That's for Me Set, 1955 – 1956.
Pink box held four, 2 oz. bottles with pink caps of bath oil: Quaintance, To a Wild Rose, Cotillion, and Pine. CMV, $85.00 MB.

Foam 'N' Spray Set, 1955.
Green box held can of Avon hair spray and 6 oz. bottle of creme lotion shampoo. CMV, $20.00 MB.

Two Loves Set, 1956. Box held two black lipsticks. CMV, $25.00 MB.

Special Date Set, 1955.
Blue and white box held gold lipstick, two different powder paks, and ½ oz. Cotillion toilet water. CMV, $40.00 MB.

Special Nail Care Set, 1955 – 1957.
Red and white box contained Silvery Base and Top Coat. CMV, $10.00 MB.

Top Style Set, 1955 – 1956.
Box held gold lipstick, ½ oz. nail polish, and liquid rouge. CMV, $25.00 MB.

Fragrance Rainbow Set, 1956.
Box held four, 3 dram bottles with white painted caps. Came in To a Wild Rose, Nearness, Bright Night, Cotillion, Quaintance, and Forever Spring. CMV, $75.00 MB.

Hand Beauty Set, 1955.
Pink box held two 4 oz. bottles of hand lotion with turquoise caps. CMV, $20.00 MB.

Happy Traveler Set, 1955 – 1956.
Black bag with pink and blue stripes held cleansing cream, skin freshener, rich moisture cream, hand cream, flowing cream deodorant, one empty plastic jar, and a pack of tissues. CMV, $35.00 MB.

Two Loves Sets, 1956 – 1960.
Matching boxes hold cologne mist and cream sachet in To a Wild Rose, or Here's My Heart. CMV, $23.00. 1959 only for Persian Wood, CMV, $27.00. Bright Night, CMV, $30.00. Nearness, CMV, $25.00.

Beauty Bound Set, 1955 – 1956.
Turquoise and white plastic compact and jeweled lipstick. Box pink and turquoise. CMV, $20.00 MB.

Happy Traveler Set, 1955.
Black zipper bag with pink and blue stripes. Came with pack of Kleenex tissues, two turquoise and white plastic jars, tubes of hand cream and cleansing cream, and a rare 2 oz. bottle of skin freshener with turquoise cap. CMV, $35.00 mint. $40.00 MB.

Cream Sachet Petites Set, 1956.
Gold box held four plastic cream sachets in blue boxes. Came in Cotillion, Bright Night, Nearness, or To a Wild Rose. CMV, $55.00 set. $10.00 each jar, MB.

Shower of Freshness Set, 1956.
Turquoise and white box held two bottles of perfumed deodorant. CMV, $15.00 MB.

Over the Rainbow Set, 1957.
Blue box held four cream sachet jars in Cotillion, To a Wild Rose, Bright Night, and Nearness. Jars are white glass with green and yellow and have two pink lids. CMV, $8.00 each jar. $50.00 set MB. $55.00 MB with outer box as shown.

Singing Bells Set, 1956.
White bell box held two cans of talc in Cotillion or To a Wild Rose. CMV, $20.00 MB.

Two Loves Set, 1957.
Red Christmas tree hang-on box came with black fashion lipstick and liquid rouge. CMV, $35.00 MB.

Modern Mood Set, 1957.
Pink and gold box held two cans of talc in choice of Cotillion or To a Wild Rose. Same box in blue and gold held two cans of talc in choice of Nearness or Forever Spring. OSP, $1.29. CMV, $25.00 each set, MB.

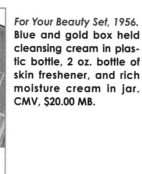

For Your Beauty Set, 1956.
Blue and gold box held cleansing cream in plastic bottle, 2 oz. bottle of skin freshener, and rich moisture cream in jar. CMV, $20.00 MB.

Beauty Pair Set, 1957.
White, blue, and yellow box with two black and pink fashion lipsticks. CMV, $30.00 MB.

Tri Color Set, 1957.
Blue and white box held Nearness or choice of cream sachet, gold satin sheen lipstick, and white leather purse trimmed in gold. CMV, $45.00 MB.

Gems in Crystal Set, 1957.
½ oz. bottles of Nearness, Bright Night, Cotillion, and To a Wild Rose. Pointed plastic caps. CMV, with flat top caps $65.00. With pointed caps, $75.00 MB.

Doubly Yours Set, 1956.
Blue and gold box held two bottles of hand lotion. CMV, $20.00 MB.

Avon Jewels Set, 1957.
Box contained liquid rouge, nail polish, and long life gold lipstick. CMV, $25.00 MB.

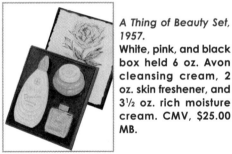

A Thing of Beauty Set, 1957.
White, pink, and black box held 6 oz. Avon cleansing cream, 2 oz. skin freshener, and 3½ oz. rich moisture cream. CMV, $25.00 MB.

Classic Style Set, 1958.
Black and gold box held Top Style lipstick and gold Top Style compact. CMV, $20.00 MB.

Fashion Firsts Set, 1958.
White and gold box held two light tan fashion lipsticks. CMV, $15.00 MB.

Beautiful Journey Set, 1957.
Pink zippered bag held 1 oz. bottles of Cotillion cologne, deep clean cleansing cream, deodorant, hand lotion, skin freshener, and ½ oz. jar of rich moisture cream, with peach colored caps. $10.00 each, BO. $15.00 Cotillion cologne. $7.00 rich moisture cream. CMV, $70.00 set MB.

Wishing Coin Trio Set, 1958.
Blue and gold box. Held choice of cream sachet, lotion sachet, and ½ oz. cologne in To a Wild Rose, Cotillion, Nearness, Forever Spring, Bright Night, Elégante, Here's My Heart, and Persian Wood fragrances. Blue caps on all. CMV, $40.00 MB.

Safe Journey Set, 1958.
Gold and white zippered travel kit held six plastic containers of perfumed talc, hand lotion, lotion sachet, cleansing cream, rich moisture cream, and deodorant. CMV, $35.00 mint.

Bouquet of Freshness Set, 1957.
Pink and lavender box held two, 2 oz. bottles of perfumed deodorant. CMV, $15.00 MB.

Makeup Mates Set, 1958.
Green box held lipstick and face powder. CMV, $20.00 MB.

Touch of Paris Set, 1958.
Box held white lipstick and compact. CMV, $15.00 MB.

Dramatic Moments Set, 1958.
Essence de Fleurs cologne mist and paper box of powder in blue box. Came in To a Wild Rose, Cotillion, Forever Spring. Nearness, Elégante, and Bright Night. CMV. $40.00 MB.

Beautiful You Set, 1958.
Pink and white box with lady's face held 3½ oz. rich moisture cream, 2 oz. of skin freshener, and rich moisture suds or deep clean. CMV, $20.00 MB.

Top Style Beauty Set, 1959.
Red and white box held lipstick and 1 dram perfume Top Style perfume. CMV, $25.00 MB.

Clear-it Skin Care Kit, 1959.
White box held shampoo and lotion in white plastic bottles and bar of Clear Skin soap. CMV, $20.00 MB.

2 Lips Set, 1959.
Two white enamel lipsticks, white box with pink and gold design. CMV, $15.00 MB.

Pearl Favorites Set, 1959.
Blue, green, and white box held white compact and white enamel lipstick. CMV, $20.00 MB.

Men's Sets of the 1960s

Warning! Grading condition is paramount on sets. CMV can vary up to 90% on condition.

Travel Deluxe Set, 1959 – 1960.
Brown leather case held after shave lotion, choice of spray deodorant for men, 4 oz. hair lotion in cream or liquid or Attention, and choice of shave cream in Kwick foaming, lather, or brushless, or electric pre-shave lotion. CMV, $35.00 MB.

Overnighter Set, 1960 – 1962.
Tan plastic travel case held after shaving lotion, roll-on deodorant for men, and cream hair lotion or hair trainer. CMV, $25.00 MB.

Dashing Sleighs Set, 1960 – 1961.
Black, gold, and red box held 4 oz. plastic bottle of cream hair lotion, can of after shower powder for men, roll-on deodorant for men, and choice of Vigorate or after shower for men in 8 oz. embossed stagecoach bottle. CMV, $62.50 MB.

First Prize Set, 1960.
Black, gold, and red box held three 2 oz. embossed stagecoach bottles in choice of after shower for men, Vigorate after shaving lotion, cream hair lotion, deodorant for men, liquid hair lotion, electric pre-shave lotion, or after shave for dry or sensitive skin. CMV, $55.00 MB set of three with outer sleeve.

Gold Medallion Gift Set, 1961.
Gold box held three individual men's grooming products in 2 oz. glass or plastic bottles. Glass bottles are: Spicy after shave lotion, Vigorate after shaving lotion, after shaving lotion, after shower lotion, electric pre-shave lotion, liquid hair lotion, and deodorant for men. Plastic bottles are: after shave for dry sensitive skin and cream hair lotion. Set of three bottles. CMV, $55.00 MB with outer sleeve.

For Gentlemen Set, 1961.
Black, gold, and red box held 4 oz. plastic cream hair lotion, roll-on deodorant for men, choice of Vigorate or after shower for men in 8 oz. embossed stage-coach bottle, and choice of 6 oz. Kwick foaming shave cream or 4 oz. electric pre-shave lotion. CMV, $62.50 each set MB. Two different sets are shown.

Travel Deluxe Set, 1962.
Tan plastic bag with front and top zipper. Held only two items, after shave lotion and roll-on deodorant, as pictured. Outer sleeve lists contents. CMV, $35.00 MB.

Under the Mistletoe Set, 1962 – 1963.
Green box held 4 oz. electric pre-shave lotion Spicy and after shave lotion Spicy. Red caps. CMV, $20.00 MB.

Deluxe Set for Men, 1962 – 1963.
Brown and gold box held can of deluxe foam shave cream, deluxe after shave, after shower spray, and deluxe stick deodorant (normal). Box has outer sleeve. CMV, $45.00 MB.

Good Cheer Set, 1962 – 1963.
Red and gold box held Spicy talc for men and choice of Spicy or original after shave lotion. CMV, $20.00 MB.

Christmas Classic Set, 1962 – 1963.
Blue box held choice of two 4 oz. bottles of Vigorate after shave lotion, after shower cologne for men, or original after shave lotion. CMV, $20.00 MB.

Holly Time Set, 1962 – 1963.
Red, white, and green box held choice of two plastic bottles in cream hair lotion, or liquid hair lotion in glass bottle. CMV, $20.00 MB.

Christmas Day Set, 1962 – 1963.
Partridge box held 4 oz. liquid deodorant for men (gentle) and choice of Spicy or original after shave lotion. CMV, $15.00 MB.

Jolly Holly Day Set, 1963.
Green and white box held three 2 oz. white plastic bottles with red caps in choice of Vigorate, Spicy, and original after shave lotions, electric pre-shave lotion, liquid or cream hair lotion, hair trainer, after shower cologne for men, and liquid deodorant for men (gentle). CMV, $15.00 MB.

Holiday Greetings Set, 1964.
Gold box held 4 oz. bottle of electric pre-shave lotion (Spicy) and after shave lotion (Spicy). CMV, $20.00 MB.

Christmas Morning Set, 1964.
Red and gold box held two, 4 oz. bottles of after shave lotion (original) and liquid deodorant for men (Spicy). CMV, $15.00 MB.

Men's Travel Kit, 1963 – 1964.
Black leather bag held can of after shave, after shower spray (Spicy), tube of cream hair dress, toothbrush, smoker's toothpaste, spray deodorant for men, and choice of foam shave cream, Spicy, or electric pre-shave lotion. CMV, $32.50 MB.

Holly Star Set, 1964.
Red, white, and green box held 4 oz. of after shave lotion, (Spicy) and 3 oz. talc for men, (Spicy). CMV, $20.00 MB.

Christmas Call Set, 1965.
Red box held two 4 oz. bottles of original after shave lotion, with red caps. CMV, $20.00 MB.

Christmas Trio for Men Set, 1964.
Winter scene box held three, 2 oz. red and white plastic bottles of any three of: Spicy after shave lotion, original after shave lotion, Vigorate after shave lotion, after shower cologne, Spicy electric pre-shave lotion, liquid deodorant for men, liquid hair lotion, cream hair lotion, or hair trainer. CMV, $15.00 MB.

Santa's Team Set, 1964 only.
Blue box held 4 oz. each of after shave lotion (Spicy) and liquid deodorant for men. CMV, $20.00 MB.

Men's Fragrance Wardrobe Set, 1965.
Red box held three, 2 oz. bottles of after shave lotion in choice of Set A: Leather, Blue Blazer, after shower cologne; Set B: Leather, Tribute, Spicy; Set C: "4-A," Tribute, original; or Set D: Spicy, Bay Rum, original. CMV, $33.00 each set, boxed with sleeve.

Original Set, 1965.
Horse box held two 4 oz. bottles of original after shave with red caps. CMV, $20.00 MB.

King for a Day, 1965.
Box held three white plastic bottles with red caps in choice of any three after shave lotions. Spicy, Original, and Vigorate after shave, after shower cologne for men, cream or liquid hair lotion, liquid deodorant for men, or electric pre-shave lotion. CMV, $15.00 MB.

Fragrance Chest, 1966 – 1967.
Brown chest type box held four, 1 oz. bottles with silver caps of after shave lotion in Tribute, blue glass; Leather in amber glass; Spicy in clear glass; Island Lime in green glass. CMV, $40.00 MB. $37.00 as pictured with outer sleeve.

Bureau Organizer, 1966 – 1967.
Wood grain plastic tray is 12¼" x 5¼". Came with 2 oz. bottles with black 4A embossed caps in Tribute after shave lotion, Blue Blazer after shave, Spicy after shave, and Leather all purpose cologne. CMV, $15.00 tray. $50.00 MB.

Fox Hunt Set, 1966.
Fox hunt box held two, 4 oz. bottles with black caps in Leather all purpose cologne. CMV, $30.00 MB.

Men's Travel Kit, 1966.
Brown travel bag held smoker's toothpaste, clear hair dress, Spicy after shave lotion, Spicy talc for men, aerosol deodorant, and choice of electric pre-shave lotion or foam shave cream in regular or mentholated. CMV, $30.00 MB.

After Shave Selection Set, 1966.
Father's Day box held three, 2 oz. bottles in choice of Leather all purpose lotion for men, Blue Blazer, Island Lime, Tribute, after shave lotion Spicy, Bay Rum, and original and 4A after shave lotions. CMV, $33.00 boxed with outer sleeve.

Men's After Shave Choice Set, 1967 – 1968.
Black box held 2 oz. after shave lotion in Wild Country with silver cap; Leather with gold cap; and Tribute with blue cap. Late issue set came with all silver or gold caps. CMV, $18.00 MB.

Smart Move Set, 1967.
Orange and black box held three, 2 oz. plastic bottles of after shave, original or Spicy in red, Tribute or Spicy in black. White bottle came in both original or Spicy. CMV, $20.00 MB.

Tag-alongs Set, 1967.
Box held 3½ oz. red plastic bottle of after shave lotion (Spicy) and tan 3 oz. plastic bottle of Squeeze Spray deodorant. Both have black caps. CMV, $3.00 each, bottles only. $12.00 MB.

Gentleman's Collection Set, 1968.
Brown plastic box held three, 2 oz. bottles with gold, silver, and bronze caps. Came in Leather, Windjammer, and Wild Country cologne. CMV, $20.00 MB.

Boots and Saddle Set, 1968.
Cowhide type box held 3 oz. bottles of Leather after shave lotion with red cap and Wild Country after shave lotion with black cap. CMV, $15.00 MB.

Structured for Men Set, 1969.
Silver box held black plastic stair-step base with 3 oz. bottles of Glass, Wood, and Steel colognes. CMV, $10.00 bottles and base only. $15.00 MB.

After Shave Caddy, 1968.
6 oz. rectangular bottle with silver cap and top fits in brown plastic box. Came in Leather and Island Lime after shave. CMV, $14.00 MB.

Cologne Trilogy Set, 1969 – 1970.
Brown and gold plastic box held three, 1½ oz. bottles with gold caps and labels in Wild Country, Windjammer, and Excalibur colognes. Box is 6" high. CMV, $18.00 MB.

The Traveler Set, 1969.
Box held two plastic bottles in Bravo or Spicy after shave and squeeze spray deodorant. CMV, $10.00 MB.

Overnighter Set, 1968.
Black box held 3 oz. white plastic bottle of Squeeze Spray deodorant and 3½ oz. black plastic bottle of Spicy after shave lotion. CMV, $10.00 MB.

Women's Sets of the 1960s

Warning! Grading condition is paramount on sets. CMV can vary up to 90% on condition.

Paris Mood Set, 1959 – 1960.
Gift set came with spray essence, beauty dust, and cream sachet in Persian Wood, Here's My Heart, Cotillion, To a Wild Rose, Bright Night, and Nearness fragrances. CMV, $47.00 MB.

On the Wing Set, 1959 – 1960.
Blue plastic bag held choice of perfumed talc in Here's My Heart, Persian Wood, To a Wild Rose, Nearness, Cotillion, or Floral; Skin freshener, deep clean; and choice of 2 oz. plastic bottle of Vita Moist or 1½ oz. jar of Rich Moisture cream. CMV, $30.00 MB.

Gift Magic Set, 1960.
Flat rocker bottles in same set that sold in 1967 – 1968 with round cap rocker bottles. CMV, $20.00 MB.

Making Eyes Set, 1961 – 1962.
Blue and green box with checkerboard top held eyeshadow stick, Curl 'N' Color, and eyebrow pencil. Box came with outside sleeve. CMV, $15.00 MB.

Lady's Choice Set, 1960.
Matching boxes hold 4 oz. cologne and beauty dust in Cotillion, Persian Wood, To a Wild Rose, or Here's My Heart. CMV, $40.00 each set, MB.

Party Fun Set, 1960.
Blue and gold box held gold lipstick and 1 dram perfume in Topaze, Here's My Heart, Persian Wood, Cotillion, To a Wild Rose, Bright Night, or Nearness. CMV, $20.00 MB.

Modern Simplicity Set, 1960 – 1961.
Lavender blue and white box contained soap, 4 oz. bath oil, and 3 oz. beauty dust in choice of Cotillion, To a Wild Rose, or Here's My Heart. CMV, $45.00 MB.

Beguiling Set, 1960.
Multicolored box held spray essence and cream sachet in Bright Night, Nearness, To a Wild Rose, Cotillion, Here's My Heart, or Persian Wood. CMV, $15.00 MB.

Manicure Tray Set, 1962 – 1964.
Clear plastic, "Avon" on bottom, 4A design. Came with 3 oz. bottle of Oily Polish Remover, ½ oz. bottles of Nail Polish and Base Coat or Double Coat, and two tubes of Cuticle Remover and Nail Beauty. CMV, $3.00 tray only. $15.00 MB, complete set.

Classic Harmony Set, 1960.
Red, white, and gold box held Top Style lipstick compact and perfume. Came in choice of shades and fragrances. CMV, $25.00 each.

Golden Rings Set, 1960.
Red and gold box held two pink and white lipsticks. CMV, $15.00 MB.

Fragrance Magic Set, 1962 – 1963.
Matching boxes held cologne mist and beauty dust with clear plastic top. Came in To a Wild Rose, Persian Wood, Here's My Heart, Somewhere, Cotillion, and Topaze. CMV, $35.00 each, MB.

Color Trick Set, 1962.
Blue and gold foil box had two black Fashion lipstick tubes, gold bottoms. CMV, $15.00 MB.

Bath Classic Set, 1962 – 1963.
1½ oz., gold design, gold cap, in gold box with large red powder puff. Box has clear plastic top. Cologne came in Somewhere, Cotillion, Topaze, Here's My Heart, Persian Wood, or To a Wild Rose. CMV, $35.00 MB.

Tote Along Set, 1962.
Tapestry bag held 4 oz. cologne and cream lotion, cream sachet, and three cakes of wrapped soap in Somewhere, Topaze, Cotillion, Here's My Heart, Persian Wood, or To a Wild Rose. CMV, $32.00 MB.

Clever Match Set, 1962.
Pink and red box held black lipstick and nail polish with white cap. 1961 set is the same, only has white plastic lipstick with pink flowered top. CMV, $10.00 MB.

Fragrance Gems Set, 1962 – 1963.
Box held creme sachet and cream lotion in Topaze, Cotillion, Somewhere, Persian Wood, Here's My Heart, or To a Wild Rose. CMV, $12.00 MB.

Flower Fantasies Set, 1963 – 1964.
Cream sachet and cream rollette in Here's My Heart, Persian Wood, To a Wild Rose, Cotillion, Somewhere, Topaze, or Occur! CMV, $17.00 MB.

Hawaiian Delights Set, 1962 – 1963.
Box held four bottles of nail polish with white caps. CMV, $15.00 MB.

Fashion Twin Set, 1962.
Blue and white silk cosmetic case held gold and black compact and lipstick. CMV, $15.00 MB.

Fashion Star Set, 1963.
Blue, pink, and white box held two Fashion lipsticks. CMV, $10.00 MB.

Refreshing Hours Set, 1962 – 1963.
Red and white box held 2¾ oz. can of perfumed talc and 2½ oz. bottle of cologne in Somewhere, Topaze, Cotillion, Here's My Heart, Persian Wood, or To a Wild Rose. CMV, $25.00 each set.

Bath Bouquet Set, 1962.
White and gold box held 6 oz. pink and white plastic bottle of bath oil and wrapped soap in Somewhere, Cotillion, Here's My Heart, Topaze, Persian Wood, Royal Jasmine, Rose Geranium, Royal Pine, Floral, or To a Wild Rose. CMV, $12.00 MB.

Color Note Set, 1963.
Gold and white box held bottle of nail polish and pink Fashion lipstick. CMV, $10.00 MB.

Bath Bouquet Set, 1963.
8 oz. plastic bottle of bath oil and soap in Royal Jasmine, Royal Pine, or Rose Geranium. CMV, $10.00 MB.

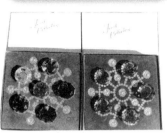

Jewel Collection Set, 1964.
Left: With six gem shaped bottles of perfume oil and gold caps. Blue and gold box. Somewhere, Topaze, Cotillion, Persian Wood, Here's My Heart, and To a Wild Rose. CMV, $35.00 MB.
Jewel Collection — Canadian Set, 1964.
Right: Box is same as American set, only center bottle hole is not punched out. Came in Somewhere, Topaze, Cotillion, Here's My Heart, and To a Wild Rose in perfume oils, ⁵/₈ dram each. Very rare set. CMV, $100.00 MB.

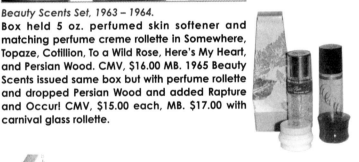

Beauty Scents Set, 1963 – 1964.
Box held 5 oz. perfumed skin softener and matching perfume creme rollette in Somewhere, Topaze, Cotillion, To a Wild Rose, Here's My Heart, and Persian Wood. CMV, $16.00 MB. 1965 Beauty Scents issued same box but with perfume rollette and dropped Persian Wood and added Rapture and Occur! CMV, $15.00 each, MB. $17.00 with carnival glass rollette.

Bath Bouquet Set, 1963.
Gift box held 8 oz. plastic bottle of bath oil and soap in Lily of the Valley or Lilac. CMV, $10.00 each, MB.

Floral Enchantment Set, 1963 – 1964.
Floral box held cologne mist and cream sachet in Occur!, Persian Wood, Here's My Heart, To a Wild Rose, Topaze, Somewhere, and Cotillion. Came with two different bottles. CMV, $15.00 MB.

Fragrance Gold Set, 1964.
Box held three heart shaped ½ oz. colognes in Occur!, Somewhere, Wishing, Topaze, Cotillion, Here's My Heart, Persian Wood, or To a Wild Rose. CMV, $20.00 MB.

Touch-up Twins Set, 1963 – 1964.
Multicolored box held perfume cream rollette in Here's My Heart, Persian Wood, To a Wild Rose, Somewhere, Topaze, Cotillion, or Occur! CMV, $17.00 MB.

Woman's Travel Kit, 1963 – 1964.
White floral bag held moisturized hand cream, perfumed talc, 4 oz. Skin So Soft, 2 oz. perfumed deodorant, and choice of night cream. CMV, $25.00 MB.

Decoration Gift Set, 1964.
Purple, gold, and white box held cream sachet and spray essence in Here's My Heart, Persian Wood, To a Wild Rose, Somewhere, Cotillion, or Topaze. CMV, $15.00 MB.

Vanity Showcase Set, 1964 – 1965.
Silver and gold plastic holder. "Avon" on bottom. Came with 1 dram ribbed perfume and deluxe silver lipstick with 4A on top. CMV, $9.00 in box holder only. $20.00 complete set.

Pair Tree Set, 1964.
Gold, white, and blue box held nail polish and floral lipstick. CMV, $15.00 MB.

Flower Bath Set, 1964.
Talc and two bars of soap in choice of Lily of the Valley, Lilac, Jasmine, or Rose Geranium. CMV, $10.00 MB.

Color Garden Set, 1964.
Red and white floral box held four nail polish bottles with white caps. Came with pearl or cream polish only. CMV, $20.00 MB.

Bath Mates Set, 1964 – 1965.
Box held 4 oz. bottle of Skin So Soft bath oil and cakes of soap. CMV, $11.00 MB.

Fragrance Fortune Set, 1964.
Matching boxes hold 2 oz. cologne and ½ oz. perfume oil in Somewhere, Here's My Heart, Cotillion, To a Wild Rose, Persian Wood, or Topaze. CMV, $30.00 MB.

Golden Arch Set, 1964.
Gold arch box held two floral Fashion lipsticks. CMV, $17.50 MB.

Bath Bouquet Set, 1964.
Pink and white plastic 6 oz. bottle of perfumed bath oil and perfumed soap in Topaze, Somewhere, To a Wild Rose, Persian Wood, Here's My Heart, or Cotillion fragrances. CMV, $10.00 each, MB.

Fragrance Ornaments Set, 1965.
Three bottles of ⅝ dram perfume oil. White paper trimmed in gold. Gold and white box. Set A: Wishing, Somewhere, Occur!; Set B: Rapture, Topaze, To a Wild Rose; Set C: Unforgettable, Here's My Heart, Cotillion. CMV, $35.00 MB.

Fragrance Favorites Set, 1965.
Box held three heart shaped ½ oz. colognes in Unforgettable, Rapture, Occur!, Cotillion, Somewhere, Topaze, Here's My Heart, Persian Wood, To a Wild Rose, or Wishing. CMV, $20.00 MB.

Fragrance Gold Duet, 1965.
Two heart shaped ½ oz. colognes in gold and white box. Came in Rapture, Occur!, Cotillion, Somewhere, Topaze, Here's My Heart, Persian Wood, To a Wild Rose, Wishing, or Unforgettable. CMV, $20.00 MB.

Star Attractions Set, 1965.
Box contained ½ oz. cologne and metal lipstick in Rapture, Occur!, Somewhere, Topaze, Cotillion, Here's My Heart, Persian Wood, To a Wild Rose, or Wishing. CMV, $20.00 MB.

Golden Vanity Set, 1965 – 1966.
Gold metal stand with removable mirror in center. Came with perfume rollette and gold refillable lipstick. CMV, $15.00 stand with mirror only. $30.00 MB, complete set.

Flower Fantasy Set, 1965.
Floral box held cream sachet and perfume rollette in To a Wild Rose, Wishing, Somewhere, Cotillion, Topaze, or Occur! CMV, $15.00 each, MB. $18.00 with carnival glass rollette.

Perfumed Pillowettes Set, 1965.
Box contained two sachet pillows and gold top powder sachet in Occur!, Somewhere, Cotillion, Topaze, Here's My Heart, To a Wild Rose, and Wishing. CMV, $22.00 MB.

Just Two Set, 1965.
3 oz. each, Tribute after shave, black glass, andclear Rapture cologne with gold tags. CMV, $15.00 each, BO, with tag. $50.00 MB.

Fashion Twins Set, 1965. Multicolored box held two Cameo lipsticks. CMV, $10.00 MB.

Touch-up Twins Set, 1965.
Angel box held deluxe lipstick and perfume rollette in Here's My Heart, Wishing, To a Wild Rose, Somewhere, Topaze, Cotillion, Rapture, or Occur! CMV, $10.00. Add $2.00 for carnival glass rollette.

Bath Bouquet Set, 1965.
Green box contained 1½ oz. green cardboard talc, 2 oz. bath oil, and ½ oz. cologne in Here's My Heart, To a Wild Rose, Wishing, Somewhere, Topaze, Cotillion, Rapture, or Occur! CMV, $35.00 MB.

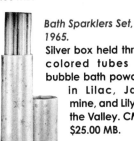

Bath Sparklers Set, 1965.
Silver box held three colored tubes of bubble bath powder in Lilac, Jasmine, and Lily of the Valley. CMV $25.00 MB.

Floral Talc Trio, 1965.
Floral box held three, 3½ oz. talc in Lily of the Valley, Lilac, and Jasmine. CMV, $10.00 MB.

Women's Travel Kit, 1965 – 1966.
Yellow floral "hat box" contained cream deodorant, Skin So Soft hand cream, white Velex Cleansing cream, Hormone cream, Rich Moisture cream, Vita Moisture, and Cream Supreme. CMV, $6.00 hat box only. $15.00 MB, complete set.

Cologne Gems Set, 1966 – 1967.
Gold and white box contained two 1 oz. Gem colognes, clear glass with plastic caps. Came in Unforgettable, Rapture, Occur!, Somewhere, Topaze, Cotillion, Here's My Heart, or To a Wild Rose. CMV, $12.00 MB.

Manicure Tray, 1965 – 1966.
White plastic tray and tissue holder. Came with pink box of Kleenex tissues with 4A design on box. 8½" x 6" x 3". CMV, $5.00, tray only. $7.00 MB Avon Kleenex box, mint. $15.00 MB, complete set.

Shower Mates Set, 1965.
Green and white box held 4 oz. can of after shower foam and two bars of Skin So Soft soap. CMV, $11.00 MB.

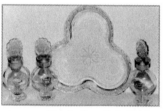

Fragrance Vanity Tray Set, 1966.
Three hearts on tray. ½ oz. cologne, heart shaped bottles on glass tray with Avon insignia. CMV, $3.00 tray. $4.00 MB. Colognes, CMV, $2.00 each, BO. $4.00 each, MB. CMV, $20.00 MB set.

Pretty Notions Set, 1965.
Pink vinyl case contained pink compact and Cameo lipstick. CMV, $4.00 set only. $6.00 MB.

Perfume Oil Petites Set Pincushion, 1966.
Gold box with red velvet pincushion top and inner box held three ⅝ dram heart shaped bottles with gold caps and labels. Came in choice of Wishing, Somewhere, Occur, Rapture, To a Wild Rose, Here's My Heart, Unforgettable, or Cotillion. CMV, $35.00 MB.

Candy Cane Twins Set, 1966.
Candy cane box held two Cameo lipsticks. CMV, $20.00 MB.

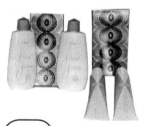

Double Pak Set, 1965.
Box in green, pink, and red foil design. Came with choice of two tubes of moisturized hand cream, or Avon hand cream or silicone glove or bottles of hand lotion as shown. CMV, $10.00 MB.

Renaissance Trio, 1966 – 1967.
Box held three boxes with ½ oz. colognes in Unforgettable, Rapture, Occur!, Somewhere, Topaze, Cotillion, Here's My Heart, To a Wild Rose, or Wishing. CMV, $20.00 MB.

Sleigh Mates Set, 1966.
Red and gold box held Fashion Cameo lipstick and bottle of nail enamel. CMV, $20.00 MB.

Fragrance Trio Set, 1966.
Box held three bottles of Skin So Soft, 1 oz. each, gold caps. In choice of Unforgettable, Rapture, Occur!, Somewhere, Topaze, Cotillion, Here's My Heart, To a Wild Rose, or Wishing. CMV, $12.00 MB.

Merry Liptints Set, 1967.
Red flocked sleeve held two white and gold Encore lipsticks with boxes to match sleeve but not flocked. CMV, $9.00 MB.

Gift Magic Set, 1967 – 1968.
3½ oz. clear glass rocker bottle with gold label and lid. Box red and purple with gold and white sleeve. Came in choice of Brocade, Régence, Unforgettable, Rapture, Occur!, Somewhere, Topaze, Cotillion, Here's My Heart, To a Wild Rose, Wishing, or Persian Wood. CMV, $15.00 MB.

Fragrance Duette Set, 1966.
Blue and gold box held 2 oz. splash-on cologne and perfume rollette in Occur!, Rapture, or Unforgettable. CMV, $15.00 MB.

Fragrance Chimes Set, 1966.
Red and gold box held perfumed talc and cream sachet in Rapture, Occur!, Unforgettable, Somewhere, Topaze, Cotillion, Here's My Heart, To a Wild Rose, and Wishing. CMV, $10.00 MB.

Manicure Tray Set, 1967.
Dark brown plastic tray with 4A design. Came with tubes of Nail Beauty and Cuticle Remover, ½ oz. bottles of Double Coat and Nail Enamel with white caps, and box of 10 enamel remover pads, one orange stick, and one emery board. CMV, $5.00 tray only. $16.00 MB, complete set. Also came in amber color tray. CMV, $10.00 tray.

Two Loves Set. 1967.
Gold and green box had cream sachet and perfume rollette in Unforgettable, Rapture, Occur!, Somewhere, To a Wild Rose, Topaze, Cotillion, or Here's My Heart. CMV, $13.00 MB.

Bath Luxury Set, 1966 – 1967.
Box held 4 oz. bottle of Skin So Soft and pink bath sponge. Came with two different sponges, coarse as shown or fine grain. CMV, $11.00 MB.

Merry Fingertips Set, 1967.
Pink velvet box held two bottles of nail polish. CMV, $10.00 MB.

Floral Medley Set, 1967.
Floral box contained perfumed talc and cream sachet in Honeysuckle, Jasmine, Lily of the Valley, or Lilac. CMV, $10.00 MB, each set.

Keepsakes Set, 1967 – 1968
Gold, floral, and white box held 3 oz. cologne mist and perfume rollette in Occur!, Rapture, or Unforgettable. CMV, $10.00 MB.

Roll-a-Fluff Set, 1967 – 1970. Fluff held 3½ oz. beauty dust. Red puff is Charisma. Green puff is Régence. White puff is Brocade. Gold tops and handles. CMV, $15.00 MB.

Vanity Tray Set, 1968. Brown plastic tray. Came with brown plastic fashion lipstick and perfume rollette in choice of Unforgettable, Rapture, Occur!, Here's My Heart, or To a Wild Rose. CMV, $6.00 tray only, MB. $11.00 complete set, MB.

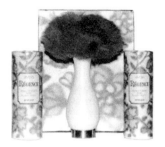

Fluff Puff Set, 1967.
Issued during bottle strike. Green box held two boxes of 3½ oz. powder. White plastic bottle, gold base and pink puff. Does not say Avon. Came in Unforgettable, To a Wild Rose, Cotillion, or Régence. CMV, $18.00 MB. Régence came in dark pink and light pink and green. Green is rare. CMV, $25.00 MB, green only.

Skin So Soft Compliments Set, 1967. Box held 3 oz. box of Satin Talc and two bars of Skin So Soft soap. CMV, $9.00 MB.

Splash and Spray Set, 1968. Purse size cologne spray and 2½ oz. splash cologne bottle with refill funnel. Both trimmed in gold. Gold box. Came in Brocade, Régence, Unforgettable, Somewhere, or Topaze. CMV, $20.00 MB.

Fluff Puff Set, 1967.
Floral box contained one puff and beauty dust. White plastic. Came in Unforgettable, To a Wild Rose, Cotillion, and Régence. CMV, $12.00 MB. Also came in white puff Régence. CMV, $20.00.

Fragrance Fling Trio, 1968.
½ oz. cologne bottles, gold caps. Set of three. Came in Occur!, Charisma, Brocade, Régence, Unforgettable, Rapture, Somewhere, Topaze, Cotillion, Here's My Heart, Wishing, To a Wild Rose, or Persian Wood. CMV, $15.00 MB.

Fluff Puffs Set, 1968. 3½ oz. talc and matching puff came in Somewhere with green puff, Honeysuckle with yellow puff, Here's My Heart with blue puff, and To a Wild Rose with pink puff. CMV, $10.00 MB.

Golden Heirloom Chest Set, 1968. 6" long gold metal, glass lid. Red velvet in bottom of chest. "Avon" on bottom. Came in perfume rollette in Brocade or Régence and deluxe refillable gold lipstick. Came in pink box. CMV, $25.00 chest only. $35.00 complete set in box.

Fluff Puff Set, 1969.
Cardboard talc, blue and gold design on white, puff white with marbleized handle, white knob with 4A. Came in three different colors: Rapture, turquoise; Occur!, yellow; and Unforgettable, coral. CMV, $10.00 MB.

Skin So Soft Smoothies Set, 1968.
Box held 4 oz. bottle of Skin So Soft and 3 oz. Satin Talc. CMV, $8.00 MB.

Scentiments Set, 1969.
Box held ½ oz. clear glass container with gold cap with cream sachet in Unforgettable, Rapture, Occur!, Somewhere, Topaze, or Cotillion with 4A embossed soap. CMV, $10.00 MB. Each fragrance came with different color soap.

Scentiments Set, 1968 – 1969.
Gold, white, and silver box held cream sachet and perfume rollette in Brocade, Régence, Unforgettable, Rapture, Occur, Somewhere, Topaze, or Cotillion. CMV, $12.00 MB.

Two Loves Set, 1969.
Red and gold box with red felt inside held perfume rollette and cream sachet in Charisma, Brocade, or Régence. Brocade is gray inside box. CMV, $12.00 each set.

Hair Color Set, 1969.
2 oz. brown glass bottle of hair color and 2 oz. white plastic bottle of cream developer in blue box. Short issue. CMV, $16.00 MB.

Men's Sets of the 1970s

Warning! Grading condition is paramount on sets. CMV can vary up to 90% on condition.

American Eagle Bureau Organizer Set, 1972.
Plastic case, wood carved like finish. Case held two, 3 oz. clear glass bottles with embossed eagles and a 5 oz. bar of soap. One has cologne and one after shave. Came in Deep Woods or Tai Winds. CMV, $40.00 MB.

Master Organizer Set, 1970.
Wood grain plastic flip-open box, held choice of 3½ oz. cologne or after shave in Öland with tan bar of soap, or Excalibur with blue bar of soap. CMV, $50.00 MB. Only 14,000 sets made.

Collector's Organizer Set, 1971 only.
Plastic brown duck held two, 3 oz. bottles of cologne and after shave. Tai Winds and Wild Country. Painted duck design on bottles and gold caps. One yellow bar of duck soap. CMV, $35.00 MB.

Whale Organizer Set, 1973.
Brown plastic whale held two, 3 oz. ivory milk glass bottles and 5 oz. bar of soap. Came in Blend 7 or Deep Woods after shave and cologne. CMV, $45.00 MB.

Travel Set for Men, 1974 – 1975.
Brown box held 3 oz. white plastic bottle with white cap. Choice of Deep Woods, Wild Country, Öland, or Spicy after shave and 1½ oz. brown plastic bottle, white cap, of talc in choice of same fragrances. Short issue. CMV, $5.00 MB.

Wild Mallard Set, 1978.
Brown and green ceramic organizer and white Clint soap on a rope. Bottom says "Made in Brazil for Avon, May 1978." CMV, $16.00 items only. $20.00 MB. Also came with no date.

Fragrance Gift Set for Men, 1979.
Box held choice of after shave in plastic bottles in Cool Sage, Brisk Spice, or Light Musk, or the same fragrances in cologne in glass bottles and matching talcs. CMV, $4.00 cologne set glass, MB. CMV, $3.00 cologne set plastic, MB.

Women's Sets of the 1970s

Warning! Grading condition is paramount on sets. CMV can vary up to 90% on condition.

Lights and Shadows Cologne Set, 1969 – 1972.
Lights is clear glass and gold cap. Shadows is smoked glass and cap. 2 oz. each. CMV, $6.00 MB.

Ultra Fluff Set, 1970.
Box held 3½ oz. beauty dust, ⅛ oz. perfume, Lamb's Wool Puff, and white pedestal dish in Brocade, Charisma, or Régence. CMV, $12.00 MB.

Original Body Salon Permanent Wave Set, 1971.
Pink box held 4 oz. bottle of neutralizer and waving lotion. Used only in Avon beauty salons. Not sold. CMV, $12.00 MB.

Two Loves Set, 1970.
Cream sachet and perfume rollette in Elusive in pink and gold box, Bird of Paradise in turquoise and gold box, and Charisma in red and gold box with white, gold, or red liner. CMV, $12.00 each, MB.

Sophisticurl Set, 1971.
A salon permanent wave used only in Avon beauty salons. Box held 4 oz. bottle of waving lotion and 3¾ oz. white tube of neutralizer. CMV, $10.00 MB, set.

Hair Perfect Set, 1971 – 1974.
Blue and white box held 2 oz. brown glass bottle of Color Perfect and 2 oz. white plastic bottle of cream developer. CMV, $4.00 MB.

Built-in Body Salon Permanent Wave Set, 1971.
White box held 4 oz. bottle of waving lotion and 4 oz. bottle of neutralizer. Used only in Avon beauty salons and not sold. CMV, $12.00 MB.

Curl Supreme Salon Permanent Wave Set, 1971.
Purple box held 3¾ oz. white tube of neutralizer and 4 oz. bottle of waving lotion. Used only in Avon beauty salons. Not sold. CMV, $12.00 MB.

Treasure Chest Set, 1973.
White plastic chest with deep purple velour inside and on top. Bottles are clear glass with white on fronts and gold roses and gold caps. One bottle held 4 oz. Skin So Soft, other held 4 oz. cologne in Moonwind or Sonnet. Soap is 5 oz. and came in Moonwind (blue) or Sonnet (pink). CMV, $27.50 MB.

Minuette Duet Set, 1973.
5 oz. cologne in clear bottle with gold cap. 1½ oz. talc in paper cylinder with Christmas scene. Came in set of Unforgettable, To a Wild Rose, Occur!, Somewhere, Topaze, or Cotillion. CMV, $5.00 MB.

Fragrance Treasures Set, 1973 – 1975.
⅔ oz. clear glass cream sachet with pink and gold lid. Pink and gold soap wrapper and box. Choice of Sonnet, Charisma, or Moonwind. CMV, $4.00 MB.

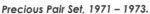

Precious Pair Set, 1971 – 1973.
Multicolored box held matching 1½ oz. perfumed talc and ½ oz. cologne in Occur!, Rapture, Unforgettable, Somewhere, Topaze, or Cotillion. CMV, $5.00 MB.

Unspoken Ultra Gift Set, 1976 – 1977.
Box came with 1⅘ oz. Ultra cologne spray and ⅓ oz. Ultra perfume rollette. CMV, $8.00 MB.

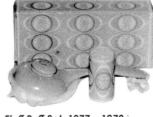

Fluff Puff Set, 1977 – 1978.
Perfumed talc dispenser. Pink plastic holder, approximately 11½" long. Came with 2 oz. cardboard talc in Roses Roses or Sonnet. CMV, $5.00 MB.

Fragrance Fancy Set, 1972 – 1975.
Pink, blue, and white. Had ⅓ oz. rollette and 1½ oz. perfumed talc. Choice of Unforgettable, Somewhere, Cotillion, Occur!, Topaze, Here's My Heart, or Rapture. CMV, $4.00 MB.

Timeless Gift Set, 1976.
Amber bottle with gold cap. Box yellow and gold. Contains Ultra cream sachet and cologne mist. CMV, $10.00 MB.

Emprise Perfume, 1977 – 1980.
Box held ¼ oz. bottle with glass stopper with plastic base seal. CMV, $4.00 BO. $6.00 MB.

Emprise Ultra Gift Set, 1977 – 1978.
Box came with 1⅘ oz. Ultra cologne spray and ⅓ oz. Ultra purse concentre. CMV, $5.00 MB.

Sweet Honesty Gift Set, 1977 – 1978.
Came with 2 oz. cologne and two perfumed soaps. CMV, $7.00 MB.

Timeless Ultra Gift Set, 1977 – 1978.
Box came with 1⅘ oz. Ultra cologne spray and ⅓ oz. Ultra perfume rollette. CMV, $8.00 MB.

Fragrant Notions Set, 1978 – 1979.
Floral design box with gold and blue felt inner box held ⅓ oz. bottle, gold cap, and porcelain thimble with "Avon" stamped in bottom. Box came with outside sleeve. Choice of Ariane or Timeless cologne. CMV, $5.00 MB.

Men's Sets of the 1980s

Left: Men's Fragrance Duo Set, 1980.
Brown box held choice of 5 oz. after shave and 1½ oz. talc in Wild Country, Trazarra, Weekend, or Clint. CMV, $4.00 each set, MB.
Right: Naturals After Shave Sampler Set, 1980 – 1981.
Box held three plastic bottles of Brisk Spice, Crisp Lime, and Light Musk After Shave. CMV, $2.00 MB.

Traveler Gift Set, 1981.
Green and red box with deer held 1½ oz. deer decor talc and 2 oz. plastic after shave in own box, in choice of Weekend, Wild Country, or Black Suede. CMV, $5.00 MB.

Country Christmas Collection for Him Set, 1982.
Green plastic box with green outer sleeve, held matching bar of soap, 1½ oz. talc, 2 oz. ribbed clear glass bottle, green cap cologne in choice of Clint, Weekend, Black Suede, or Wild Country. CMV, $12.00 MB, with sleeve.

Buckaroo Gift Set for Boys, 1981.
Brown leather look box held 2 oz. Buckaroo talc and matching tan 2 oz. plastic bottle of Buckaroo cologne for boys. CMV, $8.00 MB.

Naturals After Shave and Soap Set, 1981.
Wood look box held 3 oz. plastic bottle and bar of soap to match box. Choice of Crisp Lime, Brisk Spice, or Light Musk. CMV, $5.00 MB.

Howdy Pardners Set, 1982 – 1983.
Box held 2 oz. talc and 2 oz. plastic bottle of Buckaroo cologne with two-piece blue cowboy hat cap. CMV, $7.00 MB.

Gift Collection for Men Set, 1984. Triangle box held 1 oz. talc, deodorant, and after shave conditioner. Choice of Wild Country, Cordovan, Musk for Men, or Black Suede. CMV, $2.00 MB.

Gentlemen's Gift Collection, 1986. Box held 3½ oz. talc and 3 oz. cologne in choice of Wild Country, Musk for Men, or Black Suede. CMV, $6.00 MB, set.

Holiday Traditions Deluxe Gift Set, 1987. Box held 3 oz. bottles of men's cologne and after shave and soap dish. Same set as in 1989 Avon Classic Gift Set, only different box. CMV, $10.00.

Men's Traveler Gift Set, 1985. Box held 2 oz. after shave deodorant and small bar of soap. Choice of Black Suede, Wild Country, Cordovan, or Musk for Men. CMV, $4.00 MB.

Aures Gift Set, 1986. Box held 4 oz. Aures after shave and soap on a rope. CMV, $7.00 MB. *American Classic Gift Set, 1986.* Box held 4 oz. American Classic after shave and soap on a rope. CMV, $7.00 MB.

Signet Gift Set, 1988. Box held 3½ oz. cologne and ballpoint pen. CMV, $15.00 MB.

Gentlemen's Gift Set, 1985. Box held 3 oz. cologne in flannel pouch and can of talc. Choice of Cordovan, Black Suede, Musk for Men, or Wild Country. CMV, $6.00 MB, set.

Féraud pour Homme Gift Set, 1986. Black box held 2½ oz. after shave and razor with clear black plastic handle. CMV, $10.00 MB.

Brisk Spice Gift Set, 1988. Box held soap on a rope and 4½ oz. cologne. CMV, $8.00 MB.

Féraud pour Homme Gift Set, 1985. Box held cologne, soap, and talc. CMV, $10.00 MB.

Féraud pour Homme Gift Set, 1987. Black box held gray, black, and white necktie and 2½ oz. cologne. CMV, $16.00 MB.

Legacy Gift Sets, 1988. Box held sunglasses and choice of after shave or cologne. CMV, $12.00 each, MB.

Black Suede Key Ring Gift Set, 1989.
Box held cologne, keyring, and talc. CMV, $12.00 MB.

Gentlemen's Gift Collection, 1989.
Gift box held 3³/₁₀ oz. talc and 3 oz. cologne. CMV, $5.00 MB.

Wild Country Gift Set, 1989.
Box held tin box with choice of Wild Country or Wild Country Musk in cologne, deodorant, or after shave conditioner. CMV, $10.00 MB.

Avon Classic Gift Set, 1989.
Box held soap, cologne, and after shave. CMV, $10.00 MB.

Women's Sets of the 1980s

Warning! Grading condition is paramount on sets. CMV can vary up to 95% on condition.

Color Creme and Ultra Wear Gift Set, 1980.
Blue and red box held blue and silver Color Creme moisture lipstick and Ultra Wear nail enamel. Each item in own box inside set box. CMV, $4.00 MB.

Holiday Tapestry Gift Set, 1981.
Red and green handle carry box held green and red tapestry design 1½ oz. talc and 1⅘ oz. cologne spray in choice of Occur!, Topaze, Moonwind, Charisma, Sweet Honesty, or Zany. Colognes come in their own boxes. CMV, $5.00 MB, set.

Holiday Gift Soap Set, 1981.
Red and green handle box held three bars of soap in gold wrappers. Choice of mix and match in Tasha, Foxfire, Odyssey, Candid, Timeless, Unspoken, Ariane, or Emprise. CMV, $7.00 MB, set.

Floral Accents Gift Set, 1982.
Box held 1 oz. cologne and matching trim handkerchief. Choice of Wild Jasmine or Honeysuckle in yellow trim; Hawaiian White Ginger or Field Flowers in green trim; or Roses Roses or Sweet Honesty in pink trim. CMV $5.00 each set, MB.

Holiday Gift Set Ultra, 1981.
Red and green carry box held gold 1½ oz. talc and 1 oz. Ultra cologne spray in gold box. Choice of Timeless, Candid, Ariane, Tempo, or Tasha. CMV, $5.00 MB.

Envira Skin Care Kit, 1982.
Handle carton held ½ oz. tube of conditioning cleansing cream and ½ oz. plastic bottles of clarifying toner and protective moisturizing lotion. Short issue. CMV, $2.00 mint set.

Gold Stamps Set, 1982.
Blue and gold box sleeve held small bottle of golden fixative and small container of beauty dust and plastic stamps. CMV, $6.00 MB.

Going to Grandma's House Set, 1982.
Carton box held 1¼ oz. white plastic bottles with turquoise caps of bubble bath for children and Little Blossom Whisper Soft cologne, and one small green child's toothbrush. CMV, $5.00 MB.

Nurtura Get Acquainted Pack Set, 1982.
Carry carton held tube of 2½ oz. Replenishing body cream, ¼ oz. eye cream, and 1 oz. jar of replenishing cream. Short issue. CMV, $4.00 mint set.

Halloween Make a Face Kit, 1982.
Carton box held jar of Make a Face Base, blue lid, and three pomettes of face color: orange, black, and blue. CMV, $6.00 MB.

Toccara Deluxe Gift Set, 1982.
Blue box held white bar of soap and jar of renewable creme cologne. Short issue. CMV, $9.00 MB.

Coordinates Set, 1982.
White and red box held small red checked bag marked "Avon." Came with choice of two of four different coordinates makeup products. Lipstick and nail enamel shown. Each boxed separately. CMV, $4.50 MB, set.

Switch Gift Set, 1982.
Blue sleeve over red box. Held 7 oz. New Vitality shampoo, 10 oz. Care Deeply lotion, Lots O' Lash, Ultra Wear eyeshadow, and 3 oz. Beauty Fluid. This set was given to first people around U.S. to call in on radio advertisement to switch to Avon products. Rare. CMV, $15.00 MB.

Country Christmas Collection for Her Set, 1982.
Red and tan plastic box and outer sleeve held matching soap, talc and ⅓ oz. cologne. Choice of Odyssey, Timeless, Tasha, Foxfire, Ariane, or Candid. CMV, $9.00 MB.

Nail Accents Set, 1982.
Yellow container box held ½ oz. top shield and packet of three sheets of decals. CMV, $3.00 MB.

Apple Blossom Time Set, 1983.
Fancy box from early Avon days held ½ oz. bottle of Apple Blossom cologne. Box has outer sleeve. CMV, $7.00 MB.

Roaring Twenties Set, 1983.
½ oz. bottle of Trailing Arbutus cologne. Fancy blue and gold box. CMV, $7.00 MB with outer sleeve.

Gilded Perfume Set, 1985.
Gold and black box held ⅓ oz. cologne and ⅗ oz. perfume in Pavi Elle, Soft Musk, or Odyssey. CMV, $6.00 MB.

Fantasque Elegant Evening Set, 1985.
Black box held ⅓ oz. cologne and black earrings. CMV, $10.00 MB.

Gay Nineties Set, 1983.
Fancy box from early Avon days held ½ oz. White Lilac cologne. Box has outer sleeve. CMV, $7.00 MB.

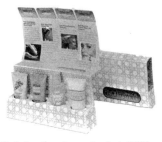

Celebration Sampler Set, 1983.
Trial size products given to customers for one campaign only for $7.50 purchase. Box held trial size tubes of Care Deeply Hand Cream, Aqua Clean Shower Gel, Nurtura Creamy Wash Off Cleanser, and small bottle of Naturally Gentle Shampoo. CMV, $5.00 set MB.

Pearls & Lace Classic Collection Set, 1985.
Pink box held 1½ oz. cologne spray and pair of pearlized earrings. CMV, $8.00 MB.

Vivage Radiance Gift Set, 1985.
Box held blue earrings and ⅓ oz. cologne. CMV, $7.00 MB.

Soft Musk Gilded Perfume Set, 1985.
Box held ¹⁄₁₆ oz. perfume and ⅓ oz. cologne. CMV, $7.00 MB.

Fantasque Gift Collection Set, 1983.
Black box, gray plastic liner held Eau de Cologne Flacon spray, 5 oz. perfumed Body Veil, and ½ oz. perfumed Bath Essence. CMV, $6.50 MB.

Gift Collection for Women, 1984.
Triangle box held 1 oz. bath foam, talc, and 1 oz. cologne. Choice of Pavi Elle, Odyssey, or Soft Musk. CMV, $3.00 MB.

Celebration of Beauty Set, 1985.
Black plastic box held makeup. CMV, $4.00 MB.

Imari Gift Set, 1986. Maroon box held ⅓ oz. cologne purse spray and pair of red and gold enamel-like earrings. CMV, $5.00 MB.

Somersaults Pastel Talc and Puff Sets, 1986. 2 oz. talc with Tallulah in pink, Zippy in yellow, and Miss Pear in green puff. CMV, $3.00 each, MB.

Fragrance Treasures Set, 1987. Box held 1 oz. cologne spray and 5 oz. perfumed beauty dust. CMV, $4.00 MB.

Pearls & Lace Fragrant Treasure Gift Set, 1986. Pink box held eight bath pearls and ⅓ oz. cologne. CMV, $3.00 MB.

Lavender Floral Gift Set, 1987. Box held 4 oz. Lavender Floral toilet water and bar of soap. CMV, $5.00 MB.

Fragrance Luxuries Set, 1987. Box held 1 oz. cologne spray and 5¾ oz. shimmering body lotion. CMV, $4.00 MB.

Fragrance Duet Collection Set, 1986. Box held ⅓ oz. cologne spray and 1½ oz. perfumed talc in choice of Soft Musk, Pavi Elle, Odyssey, or Pearls and Lace. CMV, $4.00 MB.

Nutrafresh Gift Set, 1987. Box held tubes of Cleansing Buffing Gel, After Bath Moisturizer, and 1 oz. bar of soap. CMV, $5.00 MB.

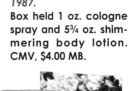

English Country Gift Set, 1988. Box held 1 oz. cologne spray and beauty dust. CMV, $3.00 MB.

Fantasque Gift Set, 1986. Black box held 1 oz. cologne spray and two bars of soap. CMV, $5.00 MB.

Silk Taffeta Gift Set, 1986. Box held two square goldtone earrings and ⅓ oz. cologne spray in choice of Soft Musk, Pavi Elle, Odyssey, or Pearls and Lace. CMV, $4.00 MB.

Fragrance Indulgences Set, 1987. Box held 1 oz. cologne spray and jar of perfumed skin softener. CMV, $4.00 MB.

Creme de la Fleur Gift Set, 1988. Box held 4 oz. creme bath and two bars of soap. CMV, $6.00 MB.

Imari Holiday Trio Gift Set, 1988.
Maroon box held soap, talc, and cologne spray. CMV, $6.00 MB.

Facets Gift Set, 1988.
Blue box held cologne spray and ¼ oz. perfume. CMV, $5.00 MB.

Breathless Sensual Treasures Gift Set, 1988.
Box held cologne spray and body veil. CMV, $4.00 MB.
Fifth Avenue Fragrance Essentials Gift Set, 1988.
Box held body lotion, cologne spray, and talc. CMV, $4.00 MB.

Men's Sets of the 1990s

All newer sets of the 1980s and 1990s are priced empty of liquids and reflect collector value, not what they sold for new from Avon. Many sets sold by Avon in the 1990s are very short issue and may be very hot collectibles in the future. This applies to men's and women's sets. All sets must come in a box with a lid to be collectible.

Men's Cologne Sampler Gift Set, 1990.
Box held ½ oz. cologne in Wild Country, Musk, and Black Suede. CMV, $4.00 MB.

Grooming Traveler Gift Set, 1991.
Box held choice of 1¾ oz. deodorant talc, 2 oz. after shave conditioner, 2 oz. after shave lotion, and 2 oz. roll-on deodorant. Short issue. CMV, $3.00 MB.

My First Shave Kit Set, 1991.
Box held 2 oz. after shave and gray plastic toy shaver. CMV, $7.00 MB.

Clean Up Hitter Gift Set, 1990.
Box held 2 oz. baseball soap and bat toothbrush. CMV, $5.00 MB.

Black Suede Address Book Gift Set, 1991.
Box held black and silver address book, 3¼ oz. cologne, and 4 oz. after shave conditioner. Short issue. CMV, $7.00 MB.

Avon Sports Car Gift Set, 1991.
10½" x 5" black plastic car caddy held choice of 3³/₁₀ oz. cologne or 2 oz. after shave conditioner. Black box. Short issue. CMV, $7.00 MB.

Black Suede Army Knife Gift Set, 1992.
Box held black Swiss style knife, 2¼" long, Black Suede cologne, after shave conditioner, and roll-on deodorant. CMV, $7.00 MB.

Undeniable for Men Toiletry Gift Set, 1992.
Nylon zipper bag held cologne, after shave conditioner, and deodorant talc. CMV, $6.00 MB, set.

Triumph Toiletry Kit Gift Set, 1992.
Black and red nylon bag, 9½" long, held full-size Triumph cologne, talc, and after shave conditioner. CMV, $3.00 MB.

Hip Pack Gift Set, 1992.
Black nylon hip bag held 4 oz. after shave conditioner, 2 oz. roll-on deodorant, and cologne in choice of Black Suede, Everafter for Men, Musk for Men, or Wild Country. CMV, $5.00 set.

Hot Line Spring Fling Set for Boys, 1992.
Round box held tube of shampoo, bar of soap, and ½ oz. cologne. CMV, $5.00 MB.

Shaving Essentials Gift Set, 1993.
Black and gray box held 3¼ oz. cologne, 4 oz. shaving cream, and plastic and metal razor. Choice of Triumph or Black Suede. CMV, $5.00 MB.

Men's Fragrance Gift Tin Set, 1993.
Box held 4¾" high round tin can with world map on side. Held 2 oz. cologne, soap on a rope, and 2 oz. tube of after shave conditioner. Choice of Black Suede or Undeniable for Men. CMV, $5.00 MB, set.

Totally Musk for Men/Women Set, 1993.
Box held 4¼ oz. sample size bottles of Soft Musk cologne, Night Magic Evening Musk, Musk for Men, and Wild Country Musk. CMV, $5.00 MB.

Grooming Trio Gift Set, 1993.
Wire basket held men's soap on a rope, roll-on deodorant, and 3⅖ oz. cologne in Trail Blazer or Undeniable for Men. CMV, $7.00 MB.

Wild Country Belt Buckle Gift Set, 1993.
Box held 4 oz. cologne, 4 oz. after shave conditioner, and metal Wild Country belt buckle. Very short issue. CMV, $6.00 MB.

Black Suede Pen and Pencil Gift Set, 1994.
Box held black pen and pencil set, 3¼ oz. cologne, 4 oz. after shave conditioner, and talc. CMV, $6.00 MB.

Sea Zone Marine Fresh Gift Set,1994. Blue box held 3²/₅ oz. Sea Zone co- logne, after shave soother, body talc, and 5 oz. Marine Fresh soap. CMV, $5.00 MB.

Valentine Gift Set for Men, 1995. Six different colored boxes held men's co- logne and after shave conditioner in choice of Black Suede, Sea Zone, Musk for Men, Trail Blazer, Wild Country, or Triumph. CMV, $4.00 MB, each set.

Grooming Trio Collection Set, 1996. Different boxes held 3 oz. natural spray co- logne, 3½ oz. deodor- ant talc, and after shave conditioner. Choice of Triumph or Wild Country. Sold through brochure only. CMV, $10.00 each set, MB.

Traveler Gift Sets, 1994. Zippered travel bags, 9³/₄" long, 6¹/₄" wide, 6" high, held 3²/₅ oz. cologne, 2 oz. after shave conditioner, and 2 oz. roll-on deodorant in choice of Trail Blazer or Tri- umph. CMV, $5.00 each set, MB.

Trailblazer Utility Box Gift Set, 1995. Blue plastic tool- box held 3²/₅ oz. Trail Blazer cologne, after shave conditioner, and roll-on antiper- spirant. Box size 9¹/₄" long, 5³/₄" wide, 4¹/₂" high. Short issue set. CMV, $17.00 MB, set.

Mesmerize for Men Deluxe Gift Set, 1996. Blue box held soap on a rope, 3²/₅ oz. co- logne spray, and 4¹/₅ oz. tub of after shave conditioner. CMV, $20.00 MB, set.

Canister Gift Set, 1994. Black cardboard round weights and measures canister box held 2 oz. men's cologne and 2 oz. tube of after shave con- ditioner. Choice of eight fragrances. Sold two times only. CMV, $8.00 MB, set.

Black Suede Holiday Classic Gift Set, 1995. Box held black and gold pen and pencil set, soap on a rope, deodorant talc, and 3¹/₄ oz. Black Suede co- logne. Short issue set. CMV, $17.00 MB, set.

Classical Canister Gift Set, 1994. Black round marbleized box held 2 oz. mini co- logne, 2 oz. after shave conditioner, and 5 oz. soap on a rope. Choice of Triumph or Black Suede. Short issue. CMV, $6.00 MB.

Triumph Holiday Gift Pack Set, 1995. Box held 3²/₅ oz. Triumph cologne and after shave. CMV, $17.00 set MB.

Black Suede Classic Wallet Gift Set, 1996. Box held 3²/₅ oz. cologne splash, 5 oz. soap on a rope, and black leather wallet. CMV, $20.00 MB, set.

Black Suede Cologne High-lights Collection Set, 1996. Black and white and gray box held 3²/₅ oz. cologne splash, 3¹/₂ oz. deodorant talc, 4¹/₅ oz. alcohol free after shave conditioner, and personal size black and gray flashlight. CMV, $18.00 MB, set.

It's Got to Be MAXX Gift Set, 1997. Red box held cologne spray and after shave cooling gel. CMV, $15.00 MB, set.

Black Suede Classic Duo Gift Set, 1997. Black and gray box held 3²/₅ oz. cologne spray and 3²/₅ oz. after shave lotion. Very short issue. CMV, $15.00 MB, set.

Wild Country Rugged Trio Gift Set, 1997. Tan tin box held 3 oz. cologne spray, 3¹/₂ oz. deodorant body talc, and 2 oz. roll-on antiperspirant deodorant. CMV, $15.00 MB, set.

Women's Sets of the 1990s

Warning! 1980s and 1990s open basket sets are not collectible. All sets must be boxed with lid and Avon name needs to be on the box to be considered collectible.

Minnie 'n Me Gift Set, 1990. Box held Minnie 'n Me 2 oz. talc and 2 oz. tube of bubble bath. CMV, $5.00 MB.

Beguiling Holiday Gift Set, 1990.
Imari Holiday Gift Set, 1990.
Both sets came in blue and gold tin boxes. Each held cologne spray, body talc, and body creme. Also came in Night Magic Evening Musk or Soft Musk. CMV, $7.00 each, MB.

Imari Fantasy Creation Gift Set, 1991.
Box held 21" wide fan with stand and 1¹/₅ oz. cologne. Short Issue. CMV, $10.00 MB.

Beauty Time Manicure Set, 1990.
Pink box held two bottles of nail polish and one tube of hand cream. CMV, $5.00 MB.

Beauty Time Makeup Kit, 1990. Pink heart box held three Crayola makeup sticks. CMV, $5.00 MB.

Holiday Celebrations Gift Set, 1991. Bamboo chest box held cologne spray, talc, and perfumed skin softener in choice of fragrances. Short issue. CMV, $6.00 MB.

Floral Print Tin Gift Set, 1991.
8" x 6¾" x 3¾" flowered tin box had choice of Imari, Night Magic Evening Musk, or Soft Musk with cologne spray, perfumed talc, and perfumed skin softener. CMV, $7.00 each set, MB.

Floral Fantasies Nail Care Set, 1991.
Red and white flowered round box held nail brush, emery board, nail advantage, nail strengthener, and cuticle repair cream. CMV, $4.00 MB.

Mother's Day Cozy Cottage Set, 1991.
House shaped box held choice of four fragrances in perfumed skin softener, cologne spray, and talc. Short issue. CMV, $4.00 MB.

Loving Sentiments Bouquet Gift Set, 1991.
Black and pink rose box held ½ oz. cologne splash in choice of six fragrances. CMV, $5.00 MB.

Enchanted Castle Gift Set, 1991.
Castle box held Shimmering cologne rollette, hand cream, and bubble bath. CMV, $5.00 MB.

Luxury Gift Set, 1991.
4" x 8" round flowered box. Fragrance choice of Imari, Everafter, Splendor, or Beguiling in cologne spray, body creme, and perfumed talc. Short issue. CMV, $5.00 each set, MB.

Love Struck Gift Set, 1992.
7½" red wicker heart box held choice of Imari, Everafter, or Beguiling, in Eau de Cologne spray, body creme, and body talc. Short issue. CMV, $5.00 MB, set.

Decorative Holiday Gift Set, 1992.
Winter ice skating scene on metal box, 8½" x 6¼" x 3½". Choice of seven ladies' fragrances with cologne spray, silky moisture lotion, and satin cologne rollette. CMV, $7.00 MB, set.

Imari Elegance Gift Set, 1992.
Box held Imari Eau de Cologne spray, purse spray, and hand cream. CMV, $5.00 MB.

Jewel of Love Gift Card, 1992.
Flower fold-out display box held ½ oz. mini cologne. Short issue. CMV, $5.00 MB.

Fragrance Keepsake Gift Set, 1992.
Flowered box, 8" x 5" x 2¼", held choice of four fragrances with three bars of soap, 1 oz. cologne spray, and 2 oz. tube of body creme. CMV, $7.00 MB, set.

Bathosaurus Gift Set, 1992.
Box held 2½" dinosaur brush and tubes of non-tear shampoo and gritty hand cleanser. CMV, $6.00 MB.

Enchanted Evening Gift Set, 1992.
Colorful hexagon box, 6½" across, held limited edition perfume, Eau de Cologne spray, and fragrance body creme in Undeniable fragrance. CMV, $5.00 MB, set.

Pink Bubble Gum Gift Set, 1993.
Box held 1½ oz. tubes of bubble bath, body lotion, non-tear shampoo, and lip balm. CMV, $5.00 MB.

Kaleidoscope Spring Fling Set for Girls, 1992.
Pink and yellow box held tube of shampoo, soap, and ½ oz. cologne. CMV, $6.00 MB.

Imari Luxury Gift Set, 1993.
Red and gold box held 1⅕ oz cologne spray and ½ oz. cream sachet in red plastic tray, 7¼" x 10". CMV, $5.00 MB.

Victorian Promise Gift Set, 1992.
Tin can held 3½ oz. cologne spray, 3½ oz. perfumed talc, and 5 oz. skin softener in choice of lady's fragrance. CMV, $6.00 MB.

Inspire Fragrance Gift Set, 1993.
Box held crystal heart pendant on 20" chain and 1⁷⁄₁₀ oz. Inspire cologne. Sold one time only. CMV, $8.00 MB.

Blossom Garden Manicure Set, 1992.
Display box came with three bottles of nail tint. CMV, $5.00 MB.

Contrast Fashion Fragrance Gift Set, 1993.
Black and white polka dot box with red ribbon held 1⁷⁄₁₀ oz. cologne spray and 5 oz. skin softener. CMV, $6.00 MB.

Practice Makes Perrfect Gift Set, 1992.
Pink and blue ballet plastic purse held 1½ oz. tubes of non-tear shampoo and bubble bath and box of Kitty Ballerina soap. CMV, $6.00 MB.

Mesmerize Enchanting Gift Set, 1993.
Blue box held solid brass bowl, potpourri, and 1⁷⁄₁₀ oz. cologne spray. CMV, $10.00 MB.

Festive Hat Box Gift Set, 1993.
Red octagonal box held choice of 1½ oz. cologne spray or perfumed skin softener. CMV, $5.00 MB.

Fragrance Elegance Gift Set, 1993.
Blue and pink box, 7½" x 3¼", held cologne spray and body talc in choice of Mesmerize, Imari, Inspire, or Undeniable. CMV, $5.00 MB.

Parfums Creatifs Demo Set, 1993.
Purple box held three spray toilet waters in Casbah, C'est Moi, and Perle Noire. Sold only to reps to demonstrate to customers. CMV, $7.00 MB, set.

Holiday Elegance Lipstick Set, 1993.
Red box held four red lipsticks. CMV, $3.00 MB.

Bubble Bath Gift Set, 1993.
Box held six, 1 oz. plastic bottles of bubble bath. CMV, $2.00 MB.

Billowing Bubbles Gift Set, 1993.
Pink box held 8 oz. plastic bubble bath and 5 oz. pink soap on a rope. CMV, $4.00 MB.

Beauty and the Beast Vanity Set, 1993.
Box held hand mirror, nail tint, and lip gloss. CMV, $5.00 MB.

Parfum Gift Set, 1993.
Pink box held ¼ oz. perfume in frosted glass bottle with glass stopper. Choice of Lahana, Mesmerize, or Contrast. CMV, $10.00 MB.

Peppermint Rose Gift Set, 1993.
Pink box held 1 oz. talc, 1½ oz. body lotion, and 1 oz. rose soap. CMV, $6.00 MB.

Imari Fragrant Treasures Gift Set, 1994.
Red and gold box held 1⅕ oz. cologne spray and 5 oz. perfumed dusting powder. CMV, $6.00 MB.

Cabbage Patch Kids Tea Set, 1994.
Box held plastic tea set for kids. CMV, $8.00 MB, set.

Perle Noire Collection du Soir Set, 1994.
Black and gold box held 1⅔ oz. Eau de Toilette and perfumed body talc. Lid has gold tassel. CMV, $5.00 MB.
Casbah Luxurious Holiday Collection Set, 1994.
Box held 2" long blue and gold earrings and 1⁷⁄₁₀ oz. Casbah Eau de Toilette spray. CMV, $6.00 MB.

*Tranquil Moments Aroma-
therapy Iridescent Gift Set,
1994.*
Box held 6 oz. body lotion
and 8 oz. Foam bath. Both
sets sold two times only.
CMV, $3.00 MB.

*Night Magic Evening Delights
Gift Set, 1994.*
Blue box held 1½ oz cologne
spray, 5 oz. perfumed skin softener, and ⅓ purse spray. CMV,
$5.00 MB.

*Small Luxuries Fragrance
Collection, 1994.*
Gold and black box held
small size colognes in Pro-
vocative, Mesmerize, Imari,
and Undeniable. CMV, $6.00
MB.

*Bubble Bath Trial Size Gift Set,
1994.*
Box held six different 1 oz. plastic bubble bath samples. CMV,
$2.00 MB.

*Mesmerize Beautiful
Enchantment Gift Set, 1994.*
Blue box held 1⁷/₁₀ oz. cologne
spray in a blue zippered cosmetic purse, gold trim. CMV,
$5.00 MB.

*Holiday Lipstick Collection Set,
1994.*
Box held four different lipsticks
from choice of 16 shades. CMV,
$3.00 MB.

*Soothing Seas Trial
Size Set, 1994.*
Blue and white
box held ½ oz. size
foaming bath salts,
nourishing body
cream, polishing
bath, shower gel,
and smoothing talc.
CMV, $3.00 MB.

*Sentimental Treasures Fragrance
Collection, 1994.*
Box held four, ½ oz. colognes: Cotillion, Sonnet, Somewhere, and Unspoken. CMV, $7.00 MB, set.

Halloween Makeup Kit, 1994.
Box held four face and body
makeup sticks. CMV, $4.00 MB.

*Tranquil Moments
Trial Size Set, 1994.*
Purple and white
box held 1 oz. foam
bath, 1 oz. body lo-
tion, ½ oz. bath and
shower gel, and ½
oz. talc. CMV, $3.00
MB.

*Undeniable Holiday
Elegance Purse Spray
Gift Set, 1994.*
Box held 1⁷/₁₀ oz. co-
logne spray, 5 oz.
body creme, and ⅓
oz. purse spray. CMV,
$5.00 MB.

*Soothing Seas Aromatherapy
Gift Set, 1994.*
Box held jar of bath salts and
tube of bath gel. CMV, $3.00
MB.

Mesmerize Sophisti-
cated Elegance Gift
Set, 1995.
Blue box held 1⁷⁄₁₀
oz. Mesmerize co-
logne spray and
matching blue pen
and pencil set.
CMV, $17.00 MB.

Avon Essentials Gift Set, 1994.
Pink and white rose carton held
any two products in choice of
rose shower gel or rose hand and
body lotion. Short issue. CMV,
$3.00 MB, set.

"Just Like Mom" Gift Set, 1996.
Box held Sweet Honesty 2 oz. perfumed body lotion, 2 oz. cologne
splash, and ½ oz. perfumed body
talc. CMV, $6.00 MB, set.

The Baby-sitters Club
Fragrance Gift Set,
1994.
Set held cologne rol-
lette, white soap, and
4 oz. body cream.
CMV, $6.00 MB.

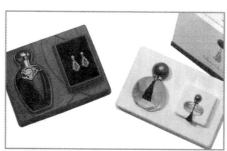

Left: Mesmerize Sparkling
Gift Set, 1995.
Blue box held 1⁷⁄₁₀ oz. co-
logne spray and gold tone
earrings with faux sapphires.
CMV, $17.00 MB.
Right: Far Away Gift Set, 1995.
Box held 1⁷⁄₁₀ oz. Far Away
Eau de Parfume Spray and
⅛ oz. mini parfum. CMV,
$18.00 MB.

Classic Perfume Collection Set,
1995.
Red box held miniature ⅛ oz.
bottles of perfume in Soft Musk,
Lahana, Imari, Night Magic
Evening Musk, and Mesmerize.
CMV, $5.00 MB.

Imari Elegant Treasures
Gift Set, 1996.
Box held 1⅕ oz. Eau de
Cologne spray and ce-
ramic trinket box, 3¼"
long, 2½" wide, 1½" high,
in Imari red color. CMV,
$17.00 MB, set.

Mesmerize Gift Set, 1996.
Blue box held 1⁷⁄₁₀ oz. cologne
spray, 5 oz. body crème, and 3½
oz. body talc. CMV, $17.00 MB, set.

Imari Holiday Riches
Gift Set, 1995.
Box held ⅓ oz. Parfum and
5 oz. Rich Indulgence Body
Crème. CMV, $20.00 MB.

Holiday Trio Gift Set, 1996.
Different boxes held 1 oz. cologne spray, 3½ oz. body talc,
and 5 oz. skin softener. Came
in choice of Candid, Timeless,
or Sweet Honesty. Sold in one
brochure only. CMV, $10.00
each MB, set.

Holiday Trio Gift Sets, 1997.
Different boxes held skin softener, body talc, and 1 oz. cologne spray. Choice of Sweet Honesty or Pearls and Lace. CMV, $10.00 each set, MB. Sold one time only.

Vanilla Soft Musk Glimmering Delights Gift Set, 1997.
Box held frosted glass candleholder and 1½ oz. cologne spray. CMV, $13.00 MB, set.

Fragrant Memories Gift Set, 1997.
Silvertone tin box with flower design lid held 1 oz. cologne spray and 2 oz. body lotion. Choice of Somewhere, Here's My Heart, Inspire, or Cotillion. CMV, $13.00 each set, MB.

Imari Rich Indulgence Holiday Gift Set, 1997.
Red box held Eau de cologne, body talc, bath and shower gel, and body lotion. CMV, $20.00 MB, set.

Night Magic Evening Musk Sensuous Occasions Gift Set, 1997.
Blue tin box held 1½ oz. cologne spray and 5 oz. perfumed skin softener. CMV, $12.00 MB, set.

Mesmerize Enchanting Trio Gift Set, 1997.
Blue box held body crème, body talc, and 1 oz. cologne spray. Sold one time only. CMV, $10.00 MB, set.

Barbie Glamour Girl Gift Set, 1997.
Pink and white box held ²⁵/₃₂ oz. Barbie cologne, 1½ oz. body powder, and 2 oz. hand and body cream. CMV, $10.00 MB, set.

Sunny Sky Bright Light Candle Set, 1997.
Box held 1 oz. Eau de Toilette spray, and two terra cotta candleholders, one yellow and one blue, 1¾" high each. Also included two tealight candles. CMV, $13.50 MB, set.

Fragrant Delights Gift Sets, 1998.
Same design box held 1 oz. cologne spray, 2⅔ oz. body talc, and 5 oz. skin softener/body crème in choice of Imari, Vanilla Soft Musk, Candid, or Timeless. Sold one time only. CMV, $10.00 each set, MB.

Stockholders' Gift Sets

Stockholders' gifts were specially packaged Avon items sent to each shareholder of Avon stock at Christmas each year. A special stockholder's greeting card was sent with each gift and a stockholder's gift is not mint or complete without this card. They were first sent in 1957 and discontinued at Christmas 1973. They are considered quite hard to find and rare.

There are only two years of stockholders' gifts not shown: The 1957 set with Persian Wood perfume mist and beauty dust, and the 1959 set with Topaze spray perfume and cologne mist.

1958.
Satin lined box with large ribbon across lid and stockholder's card. Held Here's My Heart beauty dust, sachet lotion, and Top Style lipstick. CMV, $70.00 MB.

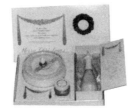

1961.
Box with stockholder's Christmas card, held Cotillion beauty dust, cream sachet, and cologne mist. This set is the same as the 1961 – 1962 Cotillion Debut, only with special card. CMV, $65.00 MB.

1964.
White flip-open box with 4A design on both sides of lid, held 4A after shave and Rapture 2 oz. cologne. With stockholder's card. CMV, $65.00 MB.

Topaze Treasure, 1960.
Yellow and gold satin lined box held Topaze beauty dust and 2 oz. cologne. Came with stockholder's card. This was a general issue gift that was also sold. CMV, $40.00 MB. $60.00 MB with stockholder's card.

1962.
Flip-open box with Avon printed all over lid. Held Bay Rum jug after shave and Skin So Soft bud vase. With stockholder's card. CMV, $70.00 MB.

1965.
Box with stockholder's card and Just Two Set. CMV, $80.00 MB.

1963.
Box opened in center with double lid to show 3 oz. Occur! cologne mist and Tribute after shave. Stockholder's card included. CMV, $55.00 MB.

Régence Cologne Mist, 1966.
White, green, and gold box. Given to stockholders on introduction of Régence. Says "Your introduction to a fragrance masterpiece by Avon." CMV, $45.00 MB.

1971.
White foam box with blue felt band. Contained Moonwind cologne mist. CMV, $30.00 MB with card.

1967.
Brown Brocade design box held "First Edition" book after shave and Brocade 4 oz. cologne. CMV, $45.00 MB.

1970.
Bird of Paradise cologne mist in foam box. Gold band around box. Came with card from Avon. CMV, $30.00 MB with card.

Deep Woods, **1972.**
Brown foam box shaped like a log, card on top, with brown ribbon and gold sticker, contained Deep Woods cologne. CMV, $30.00 MB.

1968.
Short pony in Windjammer and Charisma cologne mist, set in white foam. CMV, $40.00 MB.

Meeting Gifts, 1970s.
A special wrapped Avon product is given to each stockholder attending the annual Avon stockholder's meeting. Each gift comes with a special card which states "With the compliments of the Board of Directors, Officers and Employees of Avon Products, Inc." CMV, $15.00 to $20.00 each, mint with card.

1969.
Pink foam box held Elusive cologne mist and perfume rollette. Ribbon around box. CMV, $30.00 MB.

Imperial Gardens, 1973.
Cream sachet in white styrofoam with orange and gold ribbon. With card. CMV, $18.00 MB.

Men's Decanters — Transportation Series

Box prices: All containers are priced empty but in mint new condition. For 1960s, deduct $3.00 each, no box. For 1970s, deduct $2.00 each, no box. For 1980s and 1990s, deduct $1.00 to $2.00 each, no box.

Sterling Six, 1968 – 1970.
7 oz., came in four different shades of amber glass, black tire cap, rough top roof. Came in Spicy, Tribute, or Leather after shave. OSP, $4.00. CMV, $12.00 MB. Smooth top in very light amber glass. CMV, $45.00 MB.

Gold Cadillac, 1969 – 1973.
6 oz. gold paint over clear glass. Came in Öland, Wild Country, or Leather after shave. CMV, $16.00 MB.

Covered Wagon, 1970 – 1971.
6 oz., 4½" long. Dark amber glass bottom, white painted top and gold cap. Came in Spicy and Wild Country after shave. CMV, $12.00 MB.

Straight 8, 1969 – 1971.
5 oz. dark green glass with black trunk cap. No. 8 on hood. Came in Wild Country, Windjammer, or Island Lime after shave. Label says "Avon for Men." CMV, $12.00 MB.
Not shown: Straight 8, 1973 – 1975.
5 oz., green glass. Came in Wild Country and Island Lime after shave. Label says "Avon, Keep out of reach of children." CMV, $12.00 MB.

Captain's Pride, 1970.
6 oz. bottle with ship decal, tan cap and blue neck label. Sits on black plastic stand. Came in Öland and Windjammer after shave. CMV, $8.00 MB.

Electric Charger, 1970 – 1972.
5 oz. black glass with red cap and red side decals. Came in Spicy, Leather, or Wild Country after shave. CMV, $11.00 MB.

Spirit of St. Louis, 1970 – 1972.
6 oz. silver paint over clear glass. Came in Windjammer and Excalibur after shave. 7½" long. CMV, $14.00 MB.

Touring T, 1969 – 1970.
6½" long, 6 oz. black glass with black plastic top and tire cap. Came in Excalibur or Tribute after shave. CMV, $14.00 MB.

Stagecoach, 1970 – 1977.
5 oz. dark amber glass with gold cap. Came in Wild Country, Tai Winds, or Öland after shave. 1977 issue has "R" on bottom for reissue and hard to find silver cap. CMV, $10.00 MB, reissue. CMV, $11.00 MB, regular issue.

Packard Roadster, 1970 – 1972.
6 oz., light amber glass and matching plastic rumble seat cap. Came in Öland and Leather cologne. 6½" long. CMV, $13.00 MB.

Silver Duesenberg, 1970 – 1972.
6 oz. silver paint over clear glass. Came in Öland and Wild Country after shave. CMV, $15.00 MB.

Volkswagen Bug — Black, 1970 – 1972.
4 oz. black glass with black plastic cap. Held Wild Country, Spicy, or Electric pre-shave lotion. CMV, $10.00 MB.

Super Cycle, 1971 – 1972.
4 oz., gray glass. Came in Wild Country, Island Lime, or Sports Rally bracing lotion. CMV, $12.00 MB.

Volkswagen Bug — Red, 1972.
4 oz., painted red with red cap. Came in Öland or Wild Country after shave or Sports Rally bracing lotion. CMV, $10.00 MB.

Side Wheeler, 1971 – 1972.
5 oz., dark amber glass, black plastic stacks, silver cap, brown label. Came in Wild Country or Spicy after shave. CMV, $12.00 MB. Re-issued in 1976 in Tai Winds, gold cap, white label, same CMV.

Stanley Steamer, 1971 – 1972.
5 oz. deep blue or light blue glass bottle with black plastic seats and tire cap. Came in Wild Country or Windjammer after shave. CMV, $12.00 MB.

First Volunteer, 1971 – 1972.
6 oz., gold coated over clear glass. Came in Öland or Tai Winds cologne. CMV, $15.00 MB.

General 4-4-0, 1971 – 1972.
5½ oz., dark blue glass and cap. Came in Tai Winds or Wild Country after shave. CMV, $15.00 MB.

Mini-bike, 1972 – 1973.
4 oz., light amber glass coated over clear glass with light amber plastic wheel and silver handlebars with yellow grips. Came in Wild Country after shave, Sure Winner bracing lotion, or Protein hair lotion for men. CMV, $10.00 MB.

Dune Buggy, 1971 – 1973.
5 oz., blue glass, silver motor cap. Came in Spicy after shave, liquid hair lotion, and Sports Rally bracing lotion. CMV, $11.00 MB.

The Camper, 1972 – 1974.
5 oz. green glass truck with after shave. 4 oz. talc in beige plastic camper. Came in Deep Woods or Öland. CMV, $14.00 MB.

Avon Open Golf Cart, 1972 – 1975.
5½" long green glass bottle with green plastic front end, red plastic golf bags. Held 5 oz. Wild Country or Windjammer after shave. Came in light or darker green glass. CMV, $12.00 MB.

Station Wagon, 1971 – 1973.
6 oz. green glass car with tan plastic top. Came in Wild Country or Tai Winds after shave. CMV, $14.00 MB.

Rolls Royce, 1972 – 1975.
6 oz. beige painted over glass with dark brown and silver plastic parts. Came in Deep Woods or Tai Winds after shave. CMV, $14.00 MB.

Maxwell '23 Decanter, 1972 – 1974.
6 oz., green glass with beige plastic top and trunk over cap. Came in Deep Woods or Tribute cologne or after shave. CMV, $12.00 MB.

Sure Winner Racing Car, 1972 – 1975.
5½ oz. blue glass with blue cap. Came in Sure Winner bracing lotion or Wild Country. CMV, $10.00 MB.

Harvester Tractor, 1973 – 1975.
5½ oz., amber glass with amber plastic front. Held Wild Country after shave or protein hair lotion for men. CMV, $14.00 MB.

Model A, 1972 – 1974.
4 oz., yellow painted over clear glass, yellow cap. Held Wild Country or Leather after shave. CMV, $11.00 MB.

Big Mack, 1973 – 1975.
6 oz., green glass with beige bed. Held Öland or Windjammer after shave. CMV, $10.00 MB.

Country Vendor, 1973.
5 oz., brown glass with brown plastic top, has picture of fruits and vegetables on side. Held Wild Country or Avon Spicy after shave. CMV, $12.00 MB.

Jaguar Decanter, 1973 – 1976.
5 oz., jade green glass with green plastic trunk over cap. Held Deep Woods or Wild Country after shave. CMV, $12.00 MB.

Sterling Six II, 1973 – 1974.
7 oz., green glass with white tire cap. Came in Wild Country or Tai Winds after shave. CMV, $10.00 MB.

Reo Depot Wagon, 1972 – 1973.
5" long, 5 oz. amber glass with black plastic top and cap. Held Tai Winds or Öland after shave lotion. CMV, $13.00 MB.

Volkswagen Bug — Blue, 1973 – 1974.
4 oz., light blue painted with plastic cap. Held Öland or Windjammer after shave. CMV, $10.00 MB.

American Schooner, 1972 – 1973.
4½ oz., blue glass with blue plastic end over cap. Some are blue painted over clear glass. Came in Öland or Spicy after shave. CMV, $13.00 MB.

Road Runner Decanter, 1973 – 1974.
5½ oz., blue glass with blue plastic front wheel, silver handlebars with black grips. Held Sure Winner bracing lotion or Wild Country after shave. CMV, $10.00 MB.

1902 Haynes Apperson, 1973 – 1974.
4½ oz., green glass with green plastic front over cap, silver tiller steering rod. Held Blend 7 or Tai Winds after shave. CMV, $11.00 MB.

Atlantic 4-4-2 Decanter, 1973 – 1975.
5 oz., silver over clear glass with silver plastic parts. Held Deep Woods or Leather after shave or cologne. CMV, $15.00 MB.

Gone Fishing Decanter, 1973 – 1974.
5 oz. light blue boat with white plastic man, yellow fishing rod. Came in Tai Winds or Spicy. CMV, $13.00 MB.

Ferrari '53, 1974 – 1975.
2 oz. dark amber glass with plastic closure. Came in Wild Country after shave or Avon protein hair lotion for men. CMV, $10.00 MB.

Thunderbird '55, 1974 – 1975.
2 oz., blue glass with blue plastic closure. Came in Wild Country or Deep Woods after shave. CMV, $10.00 MB.

Stock Car Racer, 1974 – 1975.
5 oz., blue glass with blue plastic cap. Held Wild Country after shave or Electric pre-shave lotion. CMV, $10.00 MB.

Bugatti '27, 1974 – 1975.
6½ oz., black glass with chrome colored plastic trim. Came in Wild Country or Deep Woods cologne or after shave. CMV, $14.00 MB.

'37 Cord, 1974 – 1976.
7 oz., yellow painted with yellow plastic cap and black plastic top. Came in Tai Winds or Wild Country after shave. CMV, $14.00 MB.

Snowmobile, 1974 – 1975.
4 oz., blue glass with yellow plastic front and back runners. Came in Öland or Windjammer after shave. CMV, $11.00 MB.

1914 Stutz Bearcat, 1974 – 1977.
6 oz., red painted with black plastic seats and cap. Came in Öland or Blend 7 after shave. CMV, $10.00 MB.

1936 MG Decanter, 1974 – 1975.
5 oz., red painted with red plastic cap and white plastic top. Came in Blend 7, Tai Winds, or Wild Country after shave. CMV, $10.00 MB.

Army Jeep, 1974 – 1975.
4 oz., olive drab green with plastic closure. Came with Wild Country or Avon Spicy after shave. CMV, $10.00 MB.

Super Cycle II, 1974 – 1975.
Issued in blue glass. Came in Wild Country or Spicy after shave. CMV, $12.00 MB.

Golden Rocket 0-2-2, 1974 – 1976.
6 oz., smoky gold over clear glass with gold plastic cap. Came in Tai Winds or Wild Country after shave. CMV, $10.00 MB. Factory reject from factory had indented sides and gold coated. CMV, $20.00.

The Thomas Flyer 1908, 1974 – 1975.
6 oz., white painted glass with red and blue plastic parts with white tire cap on back. Came in Wild Country or Öland after shave. CMV, $12.00 MB.

Cable Car Decanter, 1974 – 1975.
4 oz., green painted over clear glass, plastic green and white top. Came in Wild Country or Avon Leather. CMV, $14.00 MB.

Pierce Arrow '33, 1975 – 1977.
5 oz., dark blue sprayed glass with beige plastic cap. Came in Wild Country or Deep Woods after shave. CMV, $10.00 MB.

Triumph TR-3 '56, 1975 – 1976.
2 oz., blue-green glass with plastic cap. Came with Spicy or Wild Country after shave. CMV, $10.00 MB.

Studebaker '51, 1975 – 1976.
2 oz., blue glass with blue plastic parts. Held Avon Spicy or Wild Country. CMV, $10.00 MB.

Corvette Stingray '65, 1975.
2 oz., green glass with green plastic cap. Held Wild Country, Deep Woods, or Avon Spicy after shave. CMV, $11.00 MB.

'55 Chevy, 1975 – 1976.
5 oz., sprayed green glass with white plastic parts. Held Wild Country or Electric pre-shave lotion. CMV, $12.00 MB.

1910 Fire Fighter, 1975.
6 oz., painted over glass with red plastic back. Came in Wild Country or Tai Winds after shave. CMV, $10.00 MB.

Volkswagen Bus, 1975 – 1976.
5 oz., red painted glass with silver gray motorcycle plastic closure. Set of four "decorate-it-yourself" labels come with each decanter. Came with Tai Winds after shave or Sure Winner bracing lotion. CMV, $12.00 MB.

Big Rig, 1975 – 1976.
3½ oz., blue glass cab with 6 oz. white and blue plastic trailer. Cab held after shave, trailer held talc in Wild Country or Deep Woods. CMV, $16.00 MB.

Chrysler Town & Country '48, 1976.
4¼ oz., off-red painted over clear glass. Beige plastic top. Came in Everest or Wild Country. CMV, $12.00 MB.

Greyhound Bus '31, 1976 – 1977.
5 oz., blue painted over clear glass. Blue plastic front cap. White plastic roof will pop off. Came in Avon Spicy or Everest. CMV $10.00 MB.

Mustang '64, 1976 – 1978.
2 oz., blue glass and blue tail cap. Came in Spicy or Tai Winds. CMV, $10.00 MB.

Porsche Decanter '68, 1976.
2 oz., amber glass with amber plastic cap. Held Wild Country or Spicy after shave. CMV, $10.00 MB.

'36 Ford, 1976 – 1977.
5 oz., orange paint over clear glass. Plastic stick-on hubcaps and grill. Came in Tai Winds or Öland. CMV, $11.00 MB.

Cannonball Express 4-6-0, 1976 – 1977.
3¼ oz., black glass, black cap. Came in Deep Woods or Wild Country after shave. CMV, $12.00 MB.

Extra Special Male, 1977– 1979.
3 oz., blue glass, dark blue cap and white plastic roof. Separate American eagle and red striped stick-on decals. Came in Deep Woods or Everest after shave. CMV, $11.00 MB.

1926 Checker Cab, 1977 – 1978.
5 oz., yellow painted over clear glass. Black plastic trunk cap and top. Stick-on decal hubcaps, bumper and checker design. Came in Everest or Wild Country. CMV, $11.00 MB.

Highway King, 1977 – 1979.
4 oz., green glass bottle with white plastic center connection piece. Rear section is 6½ oz. white plastic talc bottle. Came in Wild Country or Everest. CMV, $14.00 MB.

Viking Discoverer, 1977 – 1979.
4 oz., blue-green glass and matching plastic cap. Red and white metal sail. Black plastic sail post. Came in Wild Country or Everest. CMV, $13.00 MB.

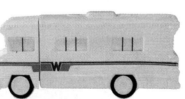

Winnebago Motor Home, 1978 – 1979.
5 oz., white painted over clear glass. Stick-on trim decals. Held Wild Country or Deep Woods after shave. CMV, $13.00 MB.

Red Sentinel Fire Truck, 1978 – 1979.
Four-piece decanter. Engine is 3½ oz. clear glass painted red. Held Wild Country or Deep Woods after shave. Plastic hook and ladder center section and 6 oz. rear red plastic section held talc. Came with stick-on decals. CMV, $15.00 MB.

1973 Ford Ranger Pick-up, 1978 – 1979.
5 oz., blue paint over clear glass, blue plastic bed cap. Stick-on decals. Came in Wild Country or Deep woods. CMV, $11.00 MB.

Stanley Steamer, 1978.
5 oz., silver paint over clear glass. Came in Tai Winds or Deep Woods after shave. CMV, $14.00 MB.

Touring T Silver, 1978.
6 oz., silver plated over clear glass. "May, 1978" on bottom. Came in Deep Woods or Everest. CMV, $14.00 MB.

Buick Skylark '53, 1979 – 1980.
4 oz., emerald green glass and cap. Stick-on decals. Came in Clint or Everest after shave. CMV, $12.00 MB.

Jeep Renegade, 1981 – 1982.
3 oz., black glass, stick-on decals. Tan plastic top. Black cap. Sure Winner bracing lotion or Trazarra cologne. CMV, $10.00 MB.

Sterling Six Silver, 1978.
7 oz., plated silver over clear glass. Came in Tai Winds or Deep Woods after shave. "May 1978" on bottom. CMV, $12.00 MB.

Vantastic, 1979 – 1980.
5 oz., burgundy glass. Stick-on decals. Came in Wild Country or Everest after shave. CMV, $10.00 MB.

Auburn Boattail Speedster, 1983 – 1984.
First in series. Black and red ceramic car figurine. 8½" long. Dated 1983. CMV, $30.00 MB.

Train 1876 Centennial Express Decanter, 1978 – 1986.
5½ oz., dark green glass with stick-on trim decals. Held Wild Country or Everest after shave. CMV, $13.00 MB. Reissued in 1986.

Cement Mixer, 1979 – 1980.
Three-piece bottle. Front section is dark amber glass. Came in Wild Country or Everest after shave. Center plastic section connects to 6 oz. pale yellow plastic rear section bottle, held talc. Included stick-on decals. CMV, $14.00 MB.

Goodyear Blimp, 1978.
2 oz., silver-gray paint over clear glass, blue letters. Came in Everest or Wild Country after shave. CMV, $11.00 MB.

Volkswagen Rabbit, 1980 – 1982.
3 oz., blue glass and blue plastic cap. Came with silver stick-on windows and hubcaps. Choice of Light Musk cologne or Sure Winner bracing lotion. CMV, $10.00 MB.

Pewter Car Collection, 1984.
Wood bases with '63 Corvette, '63 Riviera, '55 Thunderbird, '57 Chrysler 300, and '64 Mustang. CMV, $15.00 each, MB.

1937 Cord Car, 1984.
9" long, yellow. CMV, $30.00 MB.

Historic Flight "1903 Flyer," 1986.
3¾" high pewter plane. Wood base. CMV, $20.00 MB.

Spirit of St. Louis, 1986.
4½" wide pewter plane with wood base. CMV, $20.00 MB.

Four Wheel Drive Decanter, 1987.
3 oz., black glass. Stick-on decals. Held after shave. CMV, $9.00 MB.

Corvette Decanter, 1988.
3 oz., black glass. Held after shave. CMV, $8.00 MB.

Speedboat Decanter, 1989.
7" long, blue glass with stick-on decals. Held after shave. CMV, $10.00 MB.

10-Four Truck Decanter, 1989.
2½ oz., held after shave. CMV, $10.00 MB.

Classic Sports Car Decanter, 1990.
2 oz., blue glass car with stick-on decals. Held Wild Country after shave. CMV, $8.00 MB.

Blue Comet Lionel Classic Train, 1991.
Blue porcelain train figurine on wood base with name plate. Base size, 9¾" x 3¾". CMV, $45.00 MB.

No. 381E Locomotive, 1992.
Green porcelain train on 9¾" x 3¾" wood base with metal plaque. CMV, $45.00 MB.

"Lionel" Santa Fe F3 Diesel Engine, 1992.
Third in series of Lionel trains. Train engine is 9" long x 2¼" high. Red and silver painted porcelain figurine on a wood base with brass plaque. CMV, $45.00 MB.

700E Hudson Locomotive, 1993.
Black porcelain train is 9" long, 1½" wide, and 2¼" high. Wood base is 10½" x 4". CMV, $45.00 MB.

Jeep Decanter Gift Set, 1993.
Box held 3 oz. blue glass jeep decanter with tan plastic top and multi-function pocketknife. Jeep held Trailblazer cologne. CMV, $20.00 MB, set. Jeep only, $10.00 mint.

1964½ Mustang Decanter, 1994.
3 oz. green glass bottle and cap held Wild Country cologne. 5½" long. CMV, $7.00 MB.

Lionel GG-1 Electric Engine Train, 1994.
Made of Hartford porcelain. 9" long, 2¾" high, on wood base with brass name plate. Base is 10½" x 4". CMV, $45.00 MB.

Ford Edsel 1958 Decanter, 1995.
3 oz., blue-green glass, held original after shave. 5¼" long. CMV, $10.00 MB.

Thunderbird 1955 Ford, 1995.
3 oz., blue glass. Held Sea Zone after shave. 5¼" long. CMV, $10.00 MB.

Classic Car Collection,
1930s Roadster, 1995.
First in series. 7" long wood base held removable yellow and black diecast metal car. Tires and doors move. CMV, $15.00 MB.

Classic Car Collection,
1950s Sports Convertible, 1996.
Second in series. Red metal convertible with plastic parts. 6¼" long wood base is dated. CMV, $15.00 MB.

Classic Car Collection,
1930s Touring Sedan, 1996.
Third, and last in series. Diecast blue metal car, 4½" long by 1½" high. Doors open, tires move. Wood base. CMV, $15.00 MB.

Hot Wheels, 1997.
Father and son collector pack. Mattel package of two diecast metal cars marked "Avon." Choice of Mercedes, Mustang, or Corvette. Each set of cars must be in the package and unopened to be an Avon collectible. CMV for this set and all future Hot Wheels sets marked "Avon." CMV, $6.00 each set, mint, unopened.

Top: American 4-4-0 Locomotive, 1999.
Red and black resin figurine. Wood base.
Bottom: Great Northern F-7 Locomotive, 1999.
Black and yellowish resin. Wood base. Both are 6¼" long and 2¼" high. CMV, $45.00 each, MB.

1958 Ford Edsel, 2000.
5½" long, held 2½ oz. after shave. Amber glass. Sold twice. CMV, $5.00 MB, empty.

1955 Ford Thunderbird Decanter, 2000. 5½" long, amber glass. Held 2½ oz. Wild Country after shave. CMV, $5.00 MB.

1964½ Ford Mustang Decanter, 2000. 5½" long, amber glass. Held 2½ oz. Mesmerize for Men after shave. CMV, $5.00 MB.

Top left: 1949 Lincoln Cosmopolitan, 2001. *Top right: 1942 Lincoln Continental, Cabriolet, 2001.* *Bottom right: 1969 Mustang, Mach 1, 2001.* Each glass car bottle held 3⅖ oz. of after shave. Each car is 5½" long. CMV, $8.00 each, BO. $10.00 each, MB.

Men's Decanters

Close Harmony (Barber Bottle), 1963. 8 oz. white glass bottle, gold painted letters and neck band. White cap with or without tip. Came in Spicy or original after shave, Vigorate, and after shower cologne. CMV, $15.00 BO, mint. $25.00 MB.

Decisions, 1965. 8 oz., red painted labels, black caps with red centers that say "Panic Buttons." Came in Spicy after shave lotion. CMV, $16.00 BO. $22.00 MB.

Royal Orb, 1965 – 1966. 8 oz. round bottle, gold cap, red felt around neck. Came in Spicy or original after shave. Red letters painted on bottle, common issue. CMV, $23.00 BO, mint. $30.00 MB. White letter orb is rare. CMV, $75.00.

Bay Rum Keg, 1965 – 1967. 6 oz., brown and silver paint over clear glass bottle. CMV, $15.00 BO. $22.00 MB.

Captain's Choice, 1964 – 1965. 8 oz., green glass with green paper label, gold cap. Came in Spicy and original after shave lotion, Electric pre-shave lotion, Spicy after shower cologne for men, and Vigorate after shave lotion. CMV, $11.00 BO. $15.00 MB.

Boot, Silver Top, 1965 – 1966. 8 oz., amber glass, silver cap with hook on cap. Came in Leather all purpose lotion for men. CMV, $10.00 MB.

Tall Pony Post, 1966 – 1967. 8 oz., green glass with gold cap and nose ring. Held Island Lime, Tribute, or Leather after shave. CMV, $12.00 BO. $18.00 MB.

Viking Horn, 1966.
7 oz., dark amber glass with gold cap and decoration. Came in Spicy, Blue Blazer, or original after shave. CMV, $16.00 BO. $22.00 MB.

Top Dollar Soap on a Rope, 1966 – 1967.
White 1886 dollar soap. CMV, $30.00 MB.
Dollars 'N' Scents, 1966 – 1967.
8 oz. white glass bottle with green dollar painted on silver cap. Came in Spicy after shave. Red rubber band around bottle. CMV, $15.00 BO, mint. $22.00 MB.

Twenty Paces, 1967 – 1969.
3 oz. each, 10" long. Gold paint over clear glass, gold caps. Red paper labels on ends of barrels. Came in all purpose cologne, Wild Country, or Leather after shave. CMV, $50.00 brown box lined with red. $120.00 black lined box. $160.00 blue lined box. Very rare gun with raised sight did not break off in glass mold. CMV, $100.00, raised sight gun only. Regular issue guns, $15.00 each, mint.

Defender Cannon, 1966.
6 oz., 9½" long, amber glass, brown plastic stand, gold cap, gold center band, small paper label. Came in Leather, Island Lime, or Tribute after shave. CMV, $20.00, bottle and stand, mint. $26.00 MB.

Alpine Flask, 1966 – 1967.
8 oz., 8¾" high, brown glass, gold cap and neck chain. Came in Spicy, original, Blue Blazer or Leather after shave. CMV, $28.00 BO, mint. $33.00 MB.

Mallard Duck, 1967 – 1968.
6 oz., green glass, silver head. Came in Spicy, Tribute, Blue Blazer, or Windjammer after shave. CMV, $13.00 MB.

Casey's Lantern, 1966 – 1967.
10 oz., gold paint on clear glass bottle, gold cap. Came in Leather after shave in red window and Island Lime in green window. CMV, $45.00 BO, amber and green; $35.00 BO, red. $55.00 MB, amber and green; $45.00 MB, red.

Pipe Dream Clear Test, 1967.
6 oz. clear glass factory test bottle. Very rare. CMV, $250.00.

Pipe Dream, 1967.
6 oz., dark amber glass, black cap, tan plastic base. Came in Spicy, Tribute, or Leather after shave. CMV, $17.00 BO. $22.00 MB.

Boot Spray Cologne, 1967 – 1970.
3 oz., tan plastic coated with black cap. Came in Leather all purpose cologne in early issues. CMV, $5.00 MB. Leather cologne spray in later issues. CMV, $5.00 MB.

Tribute Silver Warrior, 1967.
6" high, 6 oz., silver and blue paint over clear glass, silver cap. Came in Tribute after shave. CMV, $23.00 MB. All blue glass, $30.00 mint.

Gavel, 1967 – 1968.
5 oz., dark amber glass with brown plastic handle. 8" long. Came in Island Lime, Original, or Spicy. CMV, $14.00 BO. $20.00 MB.

Western Choice (Steer Horns), 1967.
Brown plastic base with red center. Held 2 – 3 bottles with silver caps. Came in Wild Country and Leather after shave. CMV, $17.00 BO, mint. $25.00 MB.

First Edition, 1967 – 1968.
6 oz., gold cap. Came in Bay Rum, Wild Country, or Leather after shave. CMV, $12.00 MB.

Short Pony Decanter, 1968 – 1969.
4 oz., green glass, gold cap. Came with Wild Country, Windjammer, Spicy, Leather, or Electric pre-shave. CMV, $10.00 MB.

Opening Play, 1968 – 1969.
6 oz. each, 4" high. Gold caps, white plastic face guards. Came in Sports Rally bracing lotion, Spicy, or Wild Country after shave. Shiny gold over blue glass was issued one campaign only. CMV, $25.00 BO, shiny gold. $30.00 MB. Dull gold over blue glass with blue stripe, CMV, $13.00 MB. Dull gold over blue glass, no stripe, CMV, $16.00 MB.

Scimitar, 1968 – 1969.
10" long, 6 oz., gold paint with red windows over clear glass, gold cap. Came in Tribute or Windjammer after shave lotion. CMV, $20.00 BO, mint. $25.00 MB.

Tribute Ribbed Warrior, 1968 – 1971.
6" high, 6 oz., frosted glass, silver cap. Came in Tribute cologne. CMV, $12.00 MB.

Town Pump, 1968 – 1969.
8" high black glass bottle with gold cap and plastic shoehorn. Held 6 oz. of Leather, Windjammer, or Wild Country. CMV, $13.00 MB.

Daylight Shaving Time, 1968 – 1970.
6 oz. gold paint over clear glass. Came in Spicy, Wild Country, Windjammer, Bravo, or Leather after shave. CMV, $16.00 MB.

Snoopy Surprise, 1969 – 1971.
5 oz., 5½" high. White glass with blue or yellow hat and black ears. Came in Wild Country, Excalibur after shave, or Sports Rally bracing lotion. CMV, $12.00 MB.

Wise Choice Owl, 1969 – 1970.
4 oz., silver top, light amber bottom. Came with Excalibur or Leather after shave. CMV, $11.00 MB.

King Pin, 1969 – 1970.
4 oz., 6½" high. White glass and cap, red label. Came in Wild Country or Bravo after shave. CMV, $10.00 MB.

*Avon Calling for Men,
1969 – 1970.*
8½" high, 6 oz., gold
paint over clear glass,
gold cap, black
mouthpiece, black
plastic earpiece. Held
1¼ oz. talc. Came
with Wild Country or
Leather cologne. CMV,
$16.00 MB.

Avon Classics, 1969.
6 oz. each, Leather in clear or
dark amber glass; Wild Country
in light or dark amber glass or
clear glass; Tribute after shave
in clear glass, or light or dark
amber glass. All bottle caps or
labels must match color, gold
or silver. CMV, $12.00 each,
MB.

First Down, 1970.
5 oz., brown glass, white
plastic base. Came in
Wild Country or Sports
Rally bracing lotion.
CMV, $10.00 MB.
*Not shown: First Down,
1973 – 1974.*
5 oz., brown glass, white
base. Came in Deep
Woods or Sure Winner
bracing lotion. CMV,
$10.00 MB.

*Weather-or-Not,
1969 – 1971.*
5 oz., dark amber
glass, regular issue on
left, gold cap. Came in
Leather, Öland, Tribute,
Wild Country, or Spicy
after shave. There are
five different thermom-
eters starting with 20
below, 10 below, 0, 10
above, and 20 above.
All same price. CMV,
$14.00 MB.

Man's World, 1969 – 1970.
Brown plastic stand held
6 oz. globe. Gold paint
over clear glass, gold
cap. Came in Bravo,
Windjammer, or Trib-
ute after shave. 4" high.
CMV, $15.00 MB.

Futura, 1969.
5 oz., 7½" high, sil-
ver paint over clear
glass, silver cap.
Came in Excalibur
or Wild Country co-
logne. CMV, $13.00
BO, mint. $16.00 MB.

*Washington Bottle,
1970 – 1972.*
5½" high, 4 oz. bottle with
gold eagle cap. Held
Spicy or Tribute after
shave. CMV, $7.00 MB.

*"The Swinger" Golf Bag,
1969 – 1971.*
5 oz., black glass,
red and silver clubs.
Came in Wild Country
or Bravo after shave.
CMV, $13.00 MB.

*Pot Belly Stove,
1970 – 1971.*
5" high, 5 oz.
black glass bot-
tle with black
cap. Came in
Bravo or Excali-
bur after shave.
CMV, $11.00
MB.

Inkwell, 1969 – 1970.
6 oz., amber with purple
tint, black cap, with gold
or silver pen. Came with
Windjammer or Spicy after
shave. CMV, $14.00 MB.

*Capitol Decanter,
1970 – 1972.*
5 oz., amber glass or
clear glass, coated
amber, gold cap.
Came in Leather or
Tribute after shave.
CMV, $11.00 MB.

First Class Male, 1970 – 1971. 4½" high, 4 oz., blue glass with red cap. Came in Bravo or Wild Country after shave or liquid hair lotion. CMV, $10.00 MB.

Liberty Dollar, 1970 – 1972. 6 oz., silver paint over clear glass, silver cap with eagle. 6" high. Came in Öland and Tribute after shave. CMV, $12.00 MB. Rare gold bottle, CMV, $40.00 MB.

Bucking Bronco, 1971 – 1972. 6 oz., dark amber glass horse with bronze plastic cowboy cap. Came in Öland or Excalibur. CMV, $11.00 MB.

It's a Blast, 1970 – 1971. 5 oz., 8½" high, gold paint over clear glass, black rubber horn on cap. Came in Öland or Windjammer after shave. CMV, $15.00 MB.

Paid Stamp, 1970 – 1971. 5" high, dark amber glass with black cap and red rubber "paid" stamp on bottom. Held 4 oz. of Spicy or Windjammer after shave. CMV, $11.00 MB.

Boot, Gold Top, 1971 – 1972. 8 oz., amber glass, no hook on cap. Came in Leather all purpose cologne for men. CMV, $8.00 MB. Gold top boot with hook on cap is 1966 – 1971 with Leather cologne. CMV, $9.00 MB.

Duck After Shave, 1971. 3 oz. glass bottles with gold caps and ducks painted on sides. Came in Collector's Organizer Set only in Tai Winds or Wild Country after shave. CMV, $4.00 each.

Angler, 1970. 5 oz., 4½" high, blue glass with silver reel cap and trim. Came in Windjammer or Wild Country after shave. CMV, $13.00 MB.

Pipe Full Decanter, 1971 – 1972. 2 oz., brown glass with black stem. Held Spicy, Öland, Tai Winds, or Excalibur after shave. CMV, $10.00 MB.

Indian Head Penny, 1970 – 1972. 4 oz., 4" high. Bronze paint and cap over clear glass. Came in Bravo, Tribute, or Excalibur after shave. CMV, $12.00 MB.

Pony Express, 1971 – 1972. 5 oz., brown glass with copper colored man on cap. Came in Leather or Wild Country after shave. CMV, $11.00 MB.

American Eagle, 1971 – 1972. 6" high, dark amber glass with silver eagle head. Held 5 oz. Öland or Windjammer after shave. CMV, $11.00 MB. *Not shown: American Eagle, 1973 – 1975.* Black glass eagle with dark gold head. CMV, $9.00 MB.

Buffalo Nickel, 1971 – 1972.
5 oz., plated over clear glass with matching cap. Came in Spicy, Wild Country after shave, or liquid hair lotion. CMV, $12.00 MB.

Lincoln Bottle,
1971 – 1972.
5½" high, 4 oz. bottle with gold eagle cap. Held Wild Country or Leather after shave. CMV, $7.00 MB.

Twenty Dollar Gold Piece,
1971 – 1972.
6 oz., gold paint over clear glass. Gold cap. Came in Windjammer after shave or Electric pre-shave lotion. CMV, $12.00 MB.

Bulldog Pipe, 1972 – 1973.
6 oz., cream colored milk glass with black stem. Came in Wild Country or Öland after shave or cologne. CMV, $12.00 MB.

Liberty Bell, 1971 – 1972.
5 oz., light amber glass coated over clear glass, brown cap. Came in Tribute or Öland after shave or cologne. CMV, $11.00 MB.

Pony Post,
1972 – 1973.
5 oz., bronze paint over clear glass with bronze cap and nose ring. Held Tai Winds or Leather after shave. CMV, $10.00 MB.

Western Saddle, 1971 – 1972.
5 oz., brown glass with brown cap, sits on beige fence. Came in Wild Country or Leather after shave. CMV, $13.00 MB.

Fielder's Choice,
1971 – 1972.
5 oz., dark amber glass, black cap. Came in Sports Rally bracing lotion, liquid hair trainer, or Wild Country after shave. CMV, $12.00 MB.

Pipe Full Decanter,
1972 – 1974.
2 oz., light green glass with brown plastic stem. Held Tai Winds or Spicy after shave. CMV, $10.00 MB.

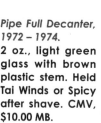

Tribute Ribbed Warrior,
1971 – 1973.
6" high, 6 oz., clear ribbed glass, silver cap. Came in Tribute cologne. CMV, $12.00 MB.

World's Greatest Dad Decanter, 1971.
4 oz., clear glass, red cap. Came in Spicy or Tribute after shave or Electric pre-shave lotion. CMV, $4.00 MB.

Old Faithful,
1972 – 1973.
5 oz., brown glass with brown plastic head and gold keg. Held Wild Country or Spicy after shave. CMV, $11.00 MB.

Pheasant,
1972 – 1974.
5 oz., brown glass with green plastic head. Held Öland or Leather after shave. CMV, $12.00 MB.

Smart Move, 1971 – 1972.
Came in Tribune or Öland cologne (CMV, $9.00 MB), Wild Country after shave, or protein hair/scalp conditioner. CMV, $7.00 MB.

Indian Chieftain, 1972 – 1975.
4 oz., brown glass with gold cap. Came in Spicy after shave or protein hair lotion for men. CMV, $9.00 MB.

Big Game Rhino, 1972 – 1973.
4 oz., green glass with green plastic head over cap. Came in Spicy or Tai Winds after shave. CMV, $10.00 MB.

Blacksmith's Anvil, 1972 – 1973.
4 oz., black glass with silver cap. Came in Deep Woods or Leather after shave. CMV, $10.00 MB.

Radio, 1972 – 1973.
5" high, dark amber glass with gold cap and paper dial on front. Held 5 oz. liquid hair lotion, Wild Country, or Spicy after shave. CMV, $10.00 MB.

Sea Trophy, 1972.
5½ oz., light blue glass with plastic blue head cap. Came in Wild Country or Windjammer after shave. CMV, $14.00 MB.

Chess Pieces, "Brown" (The Original Set).
3 oz., dark amber glass with silver toned tops. Pieces needed for one side are two Smart Moves, one King, one Queen, two Rooks, two Bishops, and eight Pawns. Early issue chess pieces do not have to have names on labels.
The King, 1972 – 1973.
Came in Tai Winds or Öland after shave. CMV, $9.00 MB.
The King, 1973 – 1978.
Came in Wild Country or Öland. CMV, $7.00 MB.
The Queen, 1973 – 1974.
Came in Tai Winds or Öland after shave. CMV, $8.00 MB.
The Queen, 1974 – 1978.
Came in Wild Country or Deep Woods after shave. CMV, $7.00 MB.
The Rook, 1973 – 1974
Came in Öland or Spicy after shave. CMV, $8.00 MB.
The Rook, 1974 – 1978.
Came in Wild Country, Blend 7, or protein hair lotion for men. CMV, $7.00 MB.
The Bishop, 1974 – 1978.
Came in Wild Country, Blend 7, or protein hair lotion for men. CMV, $7.00 MB.

The Pawn, 1974 – 1978.
Came in Wild Country, Öland, or Electric pre-shave lotion. CMV, $9.00 MB.

Chess Pieces (The Opposing Set).
3 oz., silver over clear or amber glass with amber plastic tips. CMV, $7.00 MB. Pawns, CMV, $9.00 MB. Silver over clear are hard to find. Pieces needed for one side are two Smart Moves, one King, one Queen, two Rooks, two Bishops, and eight Pawns.
Smart Move II, 1975 – 1978.
Came in Wild Country after shave, protein hair lotion, or protein hair/scalp conditioner for men.
The King II, 1975 – 1978.
Came in Spicy after shave or protein hair lotion.
The Queen II, 1975 – 1978.
Came in Spicy after shave or protein hair/scalp conditioner.
The Rook II, 1975 – 1978.
Came in Wild Country after shave or protein hair lotion for men.
The Bishop II, 1975 – 1978.
Came in Spicy after shave or protein hair lotion for men. CMV, $7.00 MB.
The Pawn II, 1975 – 1978.
Came in Spicy after shave or protein hair/scalp conditioner for men.

Piano, 1972.
4" high, 4 oz., dark amber glass piano with white music stack cap. Held Tai Winds or Tribute after shave lotion. CMV, $11.00 MB.

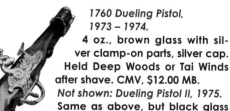

1760 Dueling Pistol, 1973 – 1974.
4 oz., brown glass with silver clamp-on parts, silver cap. Held Deep Woods or Tai Winds after shave. CMV, $12.00 MB.
Not shown: Dueling Pistol II, 1975. Same as above, but black glass and gold plastic parts. Came in Wild Country or Tai Winds. CMV, $12.00 MB.

Western Boot, 1973 – 1975.
5 oz., dark amber glass bottle, silver cap and clamp-on spurs. Came in Wild Country or Leather. CMV, $9.00 MB.

Big Whistle Decanter, 1972.
4 oz., blue glass with silver cap. Came in Tai Winds or Spicy after shave or Electric pre-shave lotion. CMV, $10.00 MB.

At Point Decanter, 1973 – 1974.
5 oz., reddish brown glass with reddish brown plastic head. Came in Deep Woods or Tribute. CMV, $11.00 MB.

Dutch Pipe, 1973 – 1974.
2 oz., white milk glass, blue design, silver handle and cap. Came in Tribute or Tai Winds cologne. CMV, $12.00 MB.

Canada Goose, 1973 – 1974.
5 oz., brown glass with black plastic head. Held Deep Woods, Wild Country, or Everest after shave or cologne. CMV, $12.00 MB. Reissued in 1976 in smaller box in after shave only. Same CMV.

Ten-point Buck, 1973 – 1974.
6 oz., reddish brown glass with reddish brown plastic head and gold antlers. Held Wild Country or Leather after shave. CMV, $12.00 MB.

Pony Post Miniature, 1973 – 1974.
1½ oz., clear glass with gold cap and ring. Held Öland or Spicy after shave. CMV, $7.00 MB.

Collector's Pipe, 1973 – 1974.
3 oz., brown glass with black stem. Held Deep Woods or Windjammer after shave or cologne. CMV, $10.00 MB.

Classic Lion, 1973 – 1975.
8 oz., green glass with green plastic head. Held Wild Country, Tribute after shave, or Deep Woods Emollient after shave. CMV, $10.00 MB.

Quail Decanter, 1973 – 1975.
5½ oz., brown glass, gold cap. Came in Blend 7, Deep Woods, or Wild Country after shave. CMV, $10.00 MB.

Homestead Decanter, 1973 – 1974.
4 oz., brown glass with gray plastic chimney over cap. Held Wild Country after shave or Electric pre-shave. CMV, $10.00 MB.

Pass Play, 1973 – 1975.
5 oz., blue glass with white soft plastic top over cap. Came in Sure Winner bracing lotion or Wild Country after shave. CMV, $13.00.

Whale Organizer Bottles, 1973.
3 oz., ivory milk glass with dark blue design. Held after shave and cologne in Deep Woods or Blend 7. Sold only in Whale Organizer. CMV, $8.00 each.

Sure Winner Baseball, 1973 – 1974.
White ball with dark blue lettering, blue base. Contained liquid hair trainer. CMV, $8.00 MB.

President Lincoln, 1973.
6 oz., white spray over clear glass, white plastic head. Held Wild Country or Tai Winds after shave. CMV, $12.00 MB.

Eight Ball Decanter, 1973.
3 oz., black glass with black cap and white "8." Came in Spicy after shave, protein lotion for men, or Electric pre-shave lotion. CMV $9.00 MB.

Long Drive, 1973 – 1975.
4 oz., brown glass with black cap. Held Deep Woods after shave or Electric pre-shave lotion. CMV, $9.00 MB.

Rainbow Trout, 1973 – 1974.
Plastic head over cap. Held Deep Woods or Tai Winds. CMV, $12.00 MB.

Auto Lantern Decanter, 1973.
Shiny gold with amber windows. Left bottle held 5 oz. Öland or Deep Woods after shave. Right base held 1¼ oz. Öland or Deep Woods talc. CMV, $15.00 MB.

Tee-off Decanter, 1973 – 1975.
3 oz., white golf ball on a plastic yellow tee, fits into a green plastic green. Held protein hair lotion for men. CMV, $9.00 MB.

"Avon Calling" 1905 Decanter, 1973.
7 oz., brown glass with brown plastic top, has gold bell and black plastic receiver. Held 7 oz. after shave and ¾ oz. talc. Came in Wild Country or Spicy. CMV, $16.00 MB.

Super Shaver, 1973.
4 oz., blue glass with gray plastic top. Held Sure Winner bracing lotion or Spicy after shave. CMV, $9.00 MB.

Marine Binoculars, 1973 – 1974.
Black over clear glass with gold caps. One side held 4 oz. Tai Winds or Tribute cologne, other side held 4 oz. Tai Winds or Tribute after shave. CMV, $12.00 MB.

Bottled by Avon (Seltzer), 1973. 5 oz., clear glass with silver lift-off cap, held Öland or Windjammer after shave. CMV, $9.00 MB.

Mallard-in-Flight, 1974 – 1976. 5 oz., amber glass with green plastic head. Held Wild Country or Tai Winds cologne or after shave. CMV, $11.00 MB.

Indian Tepee Decanter, 1974 – 1975. 4 oz., amber glass with brown plastic cap. Held Wild Country or Spicy. CMV, $8.00 MB.

American Eagle Pipe, 1974 – 1975. 5 oz., dark amber glass with gold plastic top and black handle. Held Wild Country or Tai Winds cologne. CMV, $12.00 MB.

Wild Turkey, 1974 – 1976. 6 oz., amber glass with silver and red plastic head. Held Wild Country or Deep Woods after shave. CMV, $10.00 MB.

Calabash Pipe, 1974 – 1975. 3 oz., yellow gold sprayed glass with yellow gold plastic cap and black plastic stand. Held Wild Country or Deep Woods after shave. CMV, $12.00 MB.

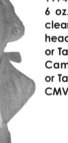

President Washington, 1974 – 1976. 6 oz., white spray over clear glass, white plastic head. Held Wild Country or Tai Winds after shave. Came in Deep Woods or Tai Winds after shave. CMV, $9.00 MB.

Barber Pole, 1974 – 1975. 3 oz., white milk glass with red and blue paper striped label and white plastic cap. Held protein hair/scalp conditioner or Wild Country after shave. CMV, $10.00 MB.

Corncob Pipe, 1974 – 1975. 3 oz., amber glass with black plastic stem. Held Wild Country or Spicy. CMV, $10.00 MB.

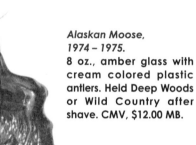

Alaskan Moose, 1974 – 1975. 8 oz., amber glass with cream colored plastic antlers. Held Deep Woods or Wild Country after shave. CMV, $12.00 MB.

Benjamin Franklin, 1974 – 1976. 6 oz., white spray over clear glass, white plastic head. Held Wild Country or Tai Winds after shave. CMV, $9.00 MB.

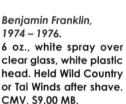

Electric Guitar Decanter, 1974 – 1975. 6 oz., brown glass with silver plastic handle. Came in Sure Winner bracing lotion or Wild Country after shave. CMV, $14.00 MB.

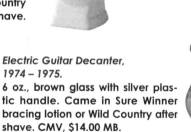

After Shave on Tap, 1974 – 1975.
5 oz., dark amber glass with gold plastic spigot cap. Held Wild Country or Öland after shave. CMV, $9.00 MB.
Not shown: After Shave on Tap, 1976.
5 oz., amber glass, red spigot cap. Held Spicy or Wild Country. CMV, $9.00 MB.

Colt Revolver 1851, 1975 – 1976.
3 oz., amber glass with silver plastic barrel. Held Wild Country or Deep Woods after shave. CMV, $12.00 MB.

American Buffalo, 1975 – 1976.
5 oz., amber glass with amber plastic head and ivory horns. Held Wild Country or Deep Woods after shave. CMV, $10.00 MB.

Triple Crown, 1974 – 1976.
4 oz., brown glass with red plastic cap. Held Spicy after shave or protein hair/scalp conditioner. CMV, $9.00 MB.

Longhorn Steer, 1975 – 1976.
5 oz., dark amber glass with amber plastic head, ivory horns. Held Wild Country or Tai Winds after shave. CMV, $11.00 MB.

Revolutionary Cannon, 1975 – 1976.
2 oz., bronze spray over glass with plastic cap. Held Spicy or Blend 7 after shave. CMV, $10.00 MB.

Whale Oil Lantern, 1974 – 1975.
5 oz., green glass with silver toned plastic top and base. Held Wild Country, Öland, or Tai Winds. CMV, $10.00 MB.

Noble Prince, 1975 – 1977.
4 oz., brown glass with plastic head. Held Wild Country after shave or Electric pre-shave lotion. CMV, $10.00 MB.

Ram's Head, 1975 – 1976.
5 oz., white opal glass on brown plastic base. Held Wild Country or Blend 7 after shave. CMV, $7.00 MB.

Stop 'n Go, 1974.
4 oz., green glass with green cap. Held Wild Country or Spicy after shave. CMV, $8.00 MB.

Sport of Kings Decanter, 1975.
5 oz., amber glass with plastic head. Held Wild Country, Spicy, or Leather after shave. CMV, $11.00 MB.

Minuteman, 1975 – 1976.
4 oz., white opal glass with plastic top. Held Wild Country or Tai Winds after shave. CMV, $10.00 MB.

*Theodore Roosevelt,
1975 – 1976.*
6 oz., white paint over clear glass. Came in Wild Country or Tai Winds after shave. CMV, $10.00 MB.

*Totem Pole Decanter,
1975.*
6 oz., dark amber glass with plastic cap. Held Wild Country, Deep Woods, or Spicy after shave. CMV, $11.00 MB.

Spark Plug Decanter, 1975.
1½ oz., white milk glass with gray cap. Held Wild Country, Tai Winds, or Spicy after shave. CMV, $6.00 MB.

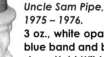

*Uncle Sam Pipe,
1975 – 1976.*
3 oz., white opal glass with blue band and blue plastic stem. Held Wild Country or Deep Woods after shave. CMV, $10.00 MB.

*Perfect Drive,
1975 – 1976.*
4 oz., green glass with white plastic top over cap. Held Spicy after shave or protein hair/scalp conditioner. CMV, $13.00 MB.

*Avon on the Air,
1975 – 1976.*
3 oz., black glass with silver plastic stand. Held Wild Country, Deep Woods, or Spicy after shave. CMV, $8.00 MB.

*No Parking Fire Plug,
1975 – 1976.*
6 oz., red painted glass with red cap. Came in Wild Country after shave or Electric pre-shave lotion. CMV, $10.00 MB.

Stop! Decanter, 1975.
5 oz., red plastic with white plastic base. Held Wild Country after shave or Sweet Honesty after bath freshener. CMV, $4.00, no box.

*Pony Express Rider Pipe,
1975 – 1976.*
3 oz., white milk glass with black plastic stem. Held Wild Country or Tai Winds cologne. CMV, $10.00 MB.

*Fire Alarm Box,
1975 – 1976.*
4 oz., red painted glass with black cap. Came in Spicy after shave, protein hair lotion, or Electric pre-shave lotion. CMV, $9.00 MB.

Star Signs Decanter, 1975.
4 oz., black glass with gold cap. Came in Sweet Honesty cologne or Wild Country after shave. Came blank with choice of one of 12 Zodiac stickers to apply. CMV, $6.00 each, MB.

*Wild Mustang Pipe,
1976 – 1977.*
3 oz., white paint over clear glass. Held Wild Country or Deep Woods cologne. CMV, $12.00 MB.

1780 Blunderbuss Pistol, 1976.
12½" long, 5½ oz., dark amber glass, gold cap, and plastic trigger. Came in Everest or Wild Country. CMV, $13.00 MB.

Arctic King, 1976 – 1979.
5 oz., blue glass bottle, silver bear cap. Came in Everest only. CMV, $8.00 MB.

NFL Decanter, 1976 – 1977.
Came with your choice of National Football League team emblem out of 28 member clubs. Came in Wild Country or Sure Winner bracing lotion. 6 oz. black glass with silver top. CMV, $10.00 MB.

Wilderness Classic, 1976 – 1977.
6 oz., silver plated over clear glass. Silver plastic head. Came in Sweet Honesty or Deep Woods. CMV, $13.00 MB.

Bold Eagle, 1976 – 1978.
3 oz., gold plated over clear glass, gold top. Came in Tai Winds or Wild Country. CMV, $8.00 MB.

Motocross Helmet, 1976 – 1978
6 oz., white plastic bottle with stick-on decals, blue plastic face guard cap. Came in Wild Country or protein hair lotion for men. CMV, $9.00 MB.

Capitol Decanter, 1976 – 1977.
4½ oz., white milk glass with white cap and gold tip. Came in Spicy or Wild Country after shave. CMV, $10.00 MB.

Bloodhound Pipe, 1976.
5 oz., light tan paint over clear glass, brown and silver cap. Came in Wild Country or Deep Woods after shave. CMV, $11.00 MB.

Big Bolt, 1976 – 1977.
2 oz., silver plated over clear glass. Silver cap. Came in Deep Woods or Wild Country. CMV, $7.00 MB.

Good Shot, 1976 – 1980.
2 oz. plastic bottles, gold caps. Red bottle in Wild Country or Brisk Spice after shave, and yellow bottle in Deep Woods or Cool Sage after shave. CMV, $6.00 MB. Add $5.00 for cap on wrong end.

Chief Pontiac Car Ornament Classic, 1976.
4 oz., black ribbed glass with silver Indian. Came in Tai Winds or Deep Woods after shave. CMV, $11.00 MB.

Duracell Super Charge, 1976 – 1978.
1½ oz., black glass with bronze and silver cap. Came in Spicy or Everest. CMV, $7.00 MB.

Remember When Gas Pump, 1976 – 1977. 4 oz., red painted over clear glass. Red and white plastic cap. Came in Deep Woods or Wild Country. CMV, $16.00 MB.

Captain's Lantern 1864, 1976 – 1977. 7 oz., black glass with black plastic cap and gold ring. Came in Wild Country or Öland after shave. CMV, $10.00 MB.

Pheasant Decanter, 1977. Same bottle as 1972 – 1974 issue, only came in Deep Woods or Wild Country, and box is smaller than early issue. CMV, $11.00 MB.

One Good Turn "Screwdriver," 1976. 4 oz., clear glass, silver cap. Came in Tai Winds or Spicy. CMV, $9.00 MB.

Majestic Elephant, 1977. 5½ oz., gray painted over clear glass. Gray head cap. Came in Wild Country or Deep Woods. CMV, $11.00 MB.

Thomas Jefferson, 1977 – 1978. 5 oz., white paint over clear glass. White head cap. Came in Wild Country or Everest after shave. CMV, $10.00 MB.

Barber Shop Brush, 1976. 1½ oz., brown glass with black and white plastic brush cap. Came in Tai Winds or Wild Country cologne. CMV, $9.00 MB.

Faithful Laddie, 1977 – 1979. 4 oz., light amber glass and amber head cap. Came in Wild Country or Deep Woods. CMV, $9.00 MB.

Wild West Bullet, 1977 – 1978. 1½ oz., bronze plated over clear glass. Silver top. Wild Country or Everest. CMV, $6.00 MB.

Liberty Bell, 1976. 5 oz., sprayed bronze with bronze cap. Came in Öland or Deep Woods after shave. CMV, $10.00 MB.

Kodiak Bear, 1977. 6 oz., dark amber glass and head. Came in Wild Country or Deep Woods. CMV, $9.00 MB.

Mixed Doubles Tennis Ball, 1977 – 1978. 3 oz., light green flock over clear glass. Green cap base. Came in Sweet Honesty body splash or Spicy. CMV, $8.00 MB.

Sure Catch, 1977.
1 oz., white milk glass, with red cap, yellow tassel, and black eyes. Came in Spicy or Wild Country. CMV, $7.00 MB.

Right Connection "Fuse," 1977.
1½ oz., clear glass, with gold and brown cap. Came in Öland or Wild Country. CMV, $7.00 MB.

Coleman Lantern, 1977 – 1979.
5 oz., green painted over clear glass. Green cap, silver bail handle. Came in Wild Country or Deep Woods. CMV, $10.00 MB.

Desk Caddy, 1977 – 1980.
Brown cork desk caddy holder, silver top, made in Spain. Held 4 oz. clear glass bottle of Clint cologne, red letters, silver cap, or Wild Country. CMV, $8.00 MB.

Juke Box, 1977 – 1978.
4½ oz., amber glass, silver top. Came in Sweet Honesty or Wild Country. Came with decals. CMV, $9.00 MB.

Firm Grip, 1977 – 1978.
1½ oz., silver plated clear glass. Came in Wild Country or Everest. CMV, $8.00 MB.

Just A Twist, 1977 – 1978.
2 oz., silver plated over clear glass. Came in Sweet Honesty or Deep Woods. CMV, $8.00 MB.

Derringer, 1977.
2 oz., gold plated over amber glass. Came in Deep Woods or Wild Country. CMV, $11.00 MB.

Weather Vane, 1977 – 1978.
4 oz., red painted over clear glass. Silver top with black horse weather vane. Came in Wild Country or Deep Woods. CMV, $8.00 MB.

Thomas Jefferson Handgun, 1978 – 1979.
10" long, 2½ oz., dark amber glass with gold and silver plastic cap. Held Deep Woods or Everest cologne. CMV, $11.00 MB.

Hard Hat, 1977 – 1978.
4 oz., yellow paint over clear glass. Yellow plastic base. Came with seven decals. Came in Everest or Deep Woods. CMV, $8.00 MB.

NBA Decanter, 1977 – 1980.
6 oz., dark amber glass. Silver top. Came with your choice of individual NBA team labels. Came in Wild Country or Sure Winner bracing lotion. CMV, $10.00 MB.

Breaker 19, 1977 – 1979.
2 oz. black glass with black and silver plastic cap. Wild Country or Sweet Honesty. CMV, $7.00 MB.

Strike Decanter, 1978 – 1979.
4 oz., white milk glass, white cap. Red painted on AMF designs. Came in Sweet Honesty or Wild Country. CMV, $7.00 MB.

Get the Message Decanter, 1978 – 1979.
3 oz., black glass with silver and black plastic top. Came in Clint or Sweet Honesty. CMV, $9.00 MB.

Smooth Going Oil Can, 1978.
1½ oz., silver plated over clear glass. Came in Deep Woods or Everest after shave. CMV, $8.00 MB.

Domino Decanter, 1978 – 1979.
1½ oz., black glass with white spots. Held Everest or Tai Winds after shave. CMV, $6.00 MB.

Little Brown Jug Decanter, 1978 – 1979.
Brown glass, tan plastic cap, beige painted sides. Held 2 oz. Deep Woods or Tai Winds after shave. CMV, $5.00 MB.

"Hammer" on the Mark Decanter, 1978.
8½" long, dark amber glass with silver top. Held 2½ oz. of Everest, or Wild Country or Deep Woods after shave. CMV, $9.00 MB.

1850 Pepperbox Pistol, 1979.
3 oz., silver plated over clear glass barrel bottle with gold and brown plastic handle cap. Came in Everest or Tai Winds. CMV, $8.00 BO. $11.00 MB.
Not shown: Pepperbox Pistol, 1982 – 1983.
Reissued in gold tone instead of silver. Came in Clint or Wild Country. CMV, $12.00 MB.

Quaker State Powered Hand Cleanser, 1978 – 1979.
12 oz., cardboard sides and gold plastic top and bottom. Held heavy duty powdered hand cleanser. CMV, $4.00 MB.

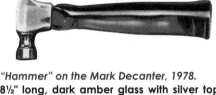

On the Level Decanter, 1978.
3 oz., silver coated over clear glass. Held Everest or Deep Woods after shave. CMV, $7.00 MB.

Weekend Decision Maker Decanter, 1978 – 1979.
3 oz., green and white painted over clear glass. Green top. Held Wild Country or Tai Winds after shave. CMV, $6.00 MB.

Super Shift, 1978.
4 oz., black glass bottle with silver and black shifter cap. Came in Sure Winner bracing Lotion or Everest cologne. 7" high. CMV, $9.00 MB.

Thermos Plaid Brand Decanter, 1978 – 1979.
3 oz., white milk glass. Red cap and plaid design. Held Wild Country after shave or Sweet Honesty body splash. CMV, $7.00 MB.

Remember When Gas Pump, 1979 – 1980.
4 oz., clear glass painted yellow, white top, yellow cap. Came in Light Musk or Cool Sage. CMV, $20.00 MB.

Volcanic Repeating Pistol Decanter, 1979 – 1980.
2 oz., silver coated over clear glass. Silver and pearl plastic handle. Held Wild Country or Brisk Spice cologne. CMV, $12.00 MB.

President Lincoln, Bronze, 1979.
6 oz., bronze tone over clear glass. Dated 1979 on bottom. Also came with no date on bottom. Held Deep Woods or Everest after shave. CMV, $11.00 MB.

President Washington, Bronze, 1979.
6 oz., bronze tone over clear glass. Dated 1979 on bottom. Held Wild Country or Tai Winds after shave. CMV, $11.00 MB.

It All Adds Up (Calculator), 1979 – 1980.
4 oz., black glass. Held Deep Woods after shave or Sweet Honesty body splash. CMV, $8.00 MB.

No Cause for Alarm Decanter, 1979 – 1980.
4 oz., silver plated over clear glass. Silver plastic top. Came in Deep Woods or Tai Winds. CMV, $9.00 MB.

Super Sleuth Magnifier, 1979.
10" long. Bottom is dark amber glass and top is real magnifying glass. Came in Wild Country or Everest after shave. CMV, $9.00 MB.

Country Lantern, 1979.
4 oz., clear glass painted red. Red wire handle. Held Wild Country or Deep Woods after shave. CMV, $9.00 MB.

Gentlemen's Talc, 1979.
3¾ oz., green can. Held Clint, Trazarra, or Wild Country talc. CMV, $2.00 mint, no box.

Dutch Boy Heavy Duty Powder Hand Cleanser, 1979 – 1980.
12 oz., blue and white paper sides. Yellow plastic top, gray bottom. No box. CMV, $4.00 mint.

Bath Brew Decanter, 1979 – 1980.
4 oz., dark amber glass, gold cap. Brown box. Held Wild Country bubble bath. CMV, $4.00 MB.

On Tap Mug Decanter, 1979.
4 oz., clear glass with white plastic top. Held Wild Country or Deep Woods after shave. CMV, $8.00 MB.

Paul Revere Bell Decanter, 1979.
4 oz., clear glass painted gold. Brown and silver handle. 1979 stamped in bottom. Held Clint after shave or Sweet Honesty body splash. CMV, $9.00 MB.

Philadelphia Derringer, 1980 – 1982.
2 oz., dark amber glass with gray stick-on parts and gold trim. Came in Light Musk or Brisk Spice after shave. CMV, $12.00 MB.

Rookie Cologne for Boys, 1980 – 1981.
2½ oz., clear glass. Red cap and label. CMV, $2.00 MB.

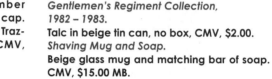

Time for Dad Mini Cologne, 1990.
⅓ oz. bottle with Avon clock on face. Short issue. CMV, $2.00 MB.

Avon's Finest Decanter, 1980 – 1981.
2 oz., dark amber glass. Gold tone cap. Came in Clint or Trazarra cologne. CMV, $3.00 MB.

Gentlemen's Regiment Collection, 1982 – 1983.
Talc in beige tin can, no box, CMV, $2.00.
Shaving Mug and Soap.
Beige glass mug and matching bar of soap. CMV, $15.00 MB.
Shaving Brush.
Beige plastic brush. CMV, $3.00 MB.
after shave Decanter.
4½ oz., clear glass painted beige. Gold cap. Fragrance choice was Wild Country or Black Suede. CMV, $6.00 MB.

Opening Play Decanter, 1995.
Dated 1995, 6 oz., clear glass, blue cap and face guard. Held Triumph cologne. CMV, $8.00 MB.

Boots 'n Saddle Decanter, 1980 – 1981.
7½" high, 7 oz., dark amber glass. Silver label, brown leather look wraparound label. Choice of Wild Country or Weekend after shave. CMV, $4.00 MB.

Miniature Volcanic Repeater Pistol Decanter, 1986.
1.4 oz., amber glass. CMV, $12.00 MB.

Dad's Pride and Joy Picture Frame, 1982 – 1983.
6½" long, clear glass. Holds pictures. CMV, $8.00 MB.

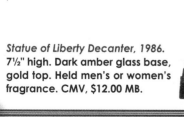

Statue of Liberty Decanter, 1986.
7½" high. Dark amber glass base, gold top. Held men's or women's fragrance. CMV, $12.00 MB.

Handkerchief Savings Bank, 1988.
Ben Franklin, 4½" high metal bank with white handkerchief inside. CMV, $4.00 MB.

U.S. Olympic Team Decanter, 1996.
5 oz. frosted glass, gold cap. Held Triumph cologne. CMV, $8.00 MB.

Stein – Silver, 1965.
8 oz., silver paint over clear glass, silver cap. Came in Tribute, Spicy, Blue Blazer, or 4A after shave. CMV, $13.00 MB.

Stein – Silver, 1968.
6 oz., silver paint over clear glass, silver cap. Came in Spicy, Windjammer, or Tribute after shave. CMV, $13.00 MB.

Tall Ships Short Stein, 1977.
Smaller stein on right was sold in test area and was later changed to larger regular issue size on left. Both marked "Avon" on bottom and numbered. CMV, $60.00 MB, small stein.

Car Classics Stein, 1979 – 1980.
9" high ceramic stein made in Brazil and numbered on the bottom. Came with 8 oz. plastic bottle of Trazarra cologne. CMV, $40.00 MB.

Hunter's Stein, 1972.
8 oz., nickel plated over clear glass, had gray and black plastic bottle inside. Held Deep Woods or Wild Country after shave. CMV, $15.00 MB.

Iron Horse Shaving Mug, 1974 – 1976.
White milk glass mug held 7 oz. plastic bottle with gold cap. Came in Blend 7, Deep Woods, or Leather after shave. CMV, $3.00 mug only. $7.00 MB.

Tall Ships Stein, 1977.
Ceramic stein, pewter handle and lid. Came with 8 oz. red plastic bottle of Clint or brown plastic bottle of Wild Country cologne for men. Silver cap. Each stein was handmade in Brazil and numbered on the bottom. CMV, $40.00 MB.

Western Roundup Stein, 1980.
8½" high. Made in Brazil and numbered on the bottom. Ceramic, metal top. Came with 8 oz. plastic bottle of Wild Country or Trazarra cologne. CMV, $40.00 MB.

Collector's Stein, 1976 – 1979.
Handmade ceramic blue stein. Made in Brazil and numbered on bottom. Came with 8 oz. plastic bottle of Everest or Wild Country. CMV, $40.00 MB.

Sporting Stein, 1978.
9" tall, ceramic stein marked on bottom "Made in Brazil for Avon Products 1978." Came with choice of 8 oz. Trazarra or Wild Country cologne with gold cap in red plastic bottle. Each stein is numbered on the bottom. CMV, $35.00 MB.

Casey at the Bat Tankard, 1980.
6" high, beige opaque glass. Came with a 4 oz. Casey plastic bottle of Wild Country or Weekend after shave. CMV, $16.00 MB.

Flying Classics Ceramic Stein, 1981. Sixth in series. 9½" high blue ceramic stein made in Brazil and numbered on the bottom. Sold empty. Metal top. CMV, $38.00 MB.

Sporting Miniature Stein, 1983 – 1984. 5" tall ceramic stein. Hunting scene on side. CMV, $15.00 MB.

Age of the Iron Horse Miniature Stein, 1985. 5¼" high ceramic stein. CMV, $15.00 MB.

Great American Football Stein, 1982 – 1983. 9" high ceramic stein, made in Brazil. Metal flip top. CMV, $40.00 MB.

Western Roundup Miniature Stein, 1983 – 1984. 5" miniature ceramic tan and white stein, made in Brazil and numbered on bottom. Cowboys on side. CMV, $15.00 MB.

"The Blacksmith" Stein, 1985. 8½" high, ceramic stein, pewter top, made in Brazil and numbered on bottom. CMV, $50.00 MB.

Collector's Stein Miniature Stein, 1983 – 1984. Blue and white 5" miniature stein, moose and goat on side. CMV, $15.00 MB.

Wright Brothers Mug, 1985. 3" high. Hand-painted porcelain mug. CMV, $16.00 MB.

Age of the Iron Horse Stein, 1982 – 1984. 8½" ceramic stein made in Brazil. Numbered and dated. Metal top. Has train design on side. Sold empty. CMV, $40.00 MB.

Big Shot Mug — Test Area, 1983. Chrome plated brass jigger, about 2½" high. Came with or without stick-on initials. Sold only in test area in Midwest. CMV, $40.00 in white test box.

Miniature Steins, 1982 – 1983. 4½" to 5½" high ceramic steins. Choice of Tall Ships, Vintage Cars, or Flying Classics. Each numbered and dated 1982. CMV, $15.00 each, MB.

Great American Baseball Stein, 1984. Ceramic stein, 8¾" high, metal top, made in Brazil. CMV, $40.00 MB.

Lewis and Clark Mug, 1985. Hand-painted porcelain mug. 3" high. CMV, $16.00 MB.

"The Shipbuilder" Stein, 1986.
Ceramic, 8½" high, numbered on bottom. Pewter lid. CMV, $50.00 MB.

Firefighter's Stein, 1989.
9" high ceramic stein. Gold bell lid and trim. CMV, $55.00 MB.

Great Dogs Outdoor Stein, 1991.
9" ceramic stein with pewter lid. Hunting dogs on side. Tan, brown, and green. CMV, $45.00 MB.

Gold Rush Stein, 1987.
8½" high ceramic stein, gold trim. CMV, $40.00 MB.

Fishing Stein, 1990.
8½" high ceramic fish stein. CMV, $45.00 MB.

Indians of the American Frontier Stein, 1988.
9" high ceramic stein. Indian design. CMV, $40.00 MB.

American Armed Forces Stein, 1990.
9¼" high ceramic stein with pewter lid, bald eagle on top. CMV, $45.00 MB.

Conquest of Space Stein, 1991.
9¾" blue ceramic stein with pewter lid, astronaut on top. Numbered and dated on bottom. CMV, $45.00 MB.

Ducks of the American Wilderness Stein, 1988.
8¾" high ceramic stein. Duck on top of lid. CMV, $45.00 MB.

Endangered Species Miniature Steins, 1990.
American bald eagle or Asian elephant 5¼" ceramic miniature steins with pewter lids. CMV, $20.00 each, MB.

Winner's Circle Stein, 1992.
10" high ceramic horse racing stein with pewter lid. CMV, $45.00 MB.

Racing Car Stein, 1989.
9¼" high ceramic stein. Has pewter race car on lid. CMV, $50.00 MB.

Giant Panda Miniature Stein, 1991.
Jaguar Miniature Stein, 1991.
Both ceramic steins are 5½" high with pewter lids. CMV, $20.00 each, MB.

Christopher Columbus Stein, 1992.
12" high ceramic stein with pewter lid. Dated and numbered on bottom. CMV, $45.00 MB.

Country and Western Music Stein, 1994.
8¼" high brown ceramic stein with pewter lid. Numbered and dated. CMV. $40.00 MB.

Salute to the Postal Service Stein, 1996.
9½" high ceramic stein with pewter lid. Dated and numbered on bottom. CMV, $45.00 MB.

Mountain Zebra Stein, 1992.
Sperm Whale Stein, 1992.
Both ceramic steins are 5½" high. Pewter lids. CMV, $20.00 each, MB.

Father Christmas Stein, 1994.
9½" high ceramic stein with pewter lid. Numbered and dated. CMV, $40.00 MB.

Christmas Carol Stein, 1996.
9½" high tan ceramic stein with pewter lid. Dated on bottom. CMV, $45.00 MB.

Wildlife Stein, 1995.
9½" high ceramic stein with pewter lid. Eagle on top of lid. Dated on bottom. CMV, $45.00 MB.

Century of Basketball Stein, 1993.
Ceramic stein, 9½" high. Pewter lid. CMV, $55.00 MB.

Majestic Forest Tankard, 1995.
6½" high, clear glass with deer's head on top of pewter lid. CMV, $20.00 MB.

Endangered Wetlands Tankard, 1996.
6" tall etched glass tankard with duck pewter lid. CMV, $25.00 MB.

Wild West Stein, 1993.
8½" high ceramic stein with pewter lid. Indian chief on top of lid. CMV, $50.00 MB.

Knights of the Realm Stein, 1995.
King Arthur on side of 9½" ceramic blue stein. CMV, $50.00 MB.

American Eagle Tankard, 1997.
7¼" high clear glass mug with eagle on side. Pewter lid. CMV, $20.00 MB.

Tribute to Rescue Workers Stein, 1997.
9½" high blue and gray stoneware stein. Pewter lid. CMV, $45.00 MB.

America the Beautiful Stein, 1998.
9½" high stoneware stein. Pewter lid. Dated 1998. CMV, $45.00 MB.

Tribute to the North American Wolf Stein, 1997.
9½" high ceramic stein with pewter lid. Wolf on top of lid. CMV, $45.00 MB.

Babe Ruth, "Legend of the Century" Stein, 1999.
9" high ceramic stein. Pewter lid. Came with numbered certificate. CMV, $45.00 MB.

Arctic Odyssey Stein, 2001.
9½" high blue and white ceramic stein with polar bear on the side. Pewter lid with ceramic walrus on top. CMV, $45.00 MB.

Harley-Davidson Stein, 2000.
9" high ceramic embossed stein. Pewter lid. Numbered on bottom. CMV, $50.00 MB.

Millennium Stein, 2000.
9" high ceramic stein with pewter lid. Numbered and dated. CMV, $45.00 MB.

Clydesdale Stein, 2002.
Anheuser Busch ceramic embossed stein. Pewter lid has eagle on top. Came with certificate of authenticity. CMV, $50.00 MB.

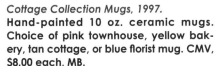

Cottage Collection Mugs, 1997.
Hand-painted 10 oz. ceramic mugs. Choice of pink townhouse, yellow bakery, tan cottage, or blue florist mug. CMV, $8.00 each, MB.

Great Kings of Africa Stein, 1997.
Ceramic stein is 5¾" high. With '"SHAKA," "AKHENATON," and "HANNIBAL" on three sides of mug. CMV, $20.00 MB.

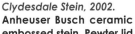

American Animal Steins, 2000 – 2003.
Series of four, 6¼" high ceramic steins. No lids.
Bald Eagle, 2000. Wolf, 2001. Cougar, 2002. Mustang, 2003.
CMV, $15.00 each, MB.

America the Beautiful Stein, 2002.
11" high ceramic stein with Statue of Liberty on the side and on pewter lid. CMV, $50.00 MB.

John Deere Stein, 2003.
9½" high ceramic stein with pewter lid. OSP, $50.00. CMV, $50.00 MB.

Dale Earnhardt, Jr. Stein, 2004.
9½" high stoneware stein with pewter and stoneware lid. OSP, $50.00. CMV, $40.00 MB.

Wildlife Tankard, 2002.
7½" high, 5" wide, clear glass. Etched glass with deer on the sides. Embossed pewter lid. CMV, $20.00 MB.
Sports Tankard, 2002.
7½" high, clear glass with etched glass baseball, football, and golf design. Embossed pewter lid. CMV, $20.00 MB.

African Serengeti Stein, 2005.
10" high ceramic stein. Pewter and ceramic lid. OSP, $50.00. CMV, $40.00 MB.

The Star Wars Stein (2004), NFL Classic Glass Tankard, Michael Jordan Tankard, and Winston Cup Tankard are not marked Avon and are not included here. It is recommended to collect only items marked "Avon."

Figurines

Warning! Precious Moments and Cherished Teddies figurines are made by Enesco, not Avon Products, Inc. They are not marked Avon on the product. They are not included in this book. Consult Precious Moments books for information. Department 56 and Thomas Kinkade figurines are also not included, since they are not marked Avon.

Jennifer Figurine, 1973.
Left: Girl with pastel turquoise dress and hat. 1973 embossed in ceramic and printed on box. Some came with flowers in center of hat and some with flowers on the right side of hat. Both issued from Springdale, Ohio branch only. CMV, $45.00.
Right: My Pet Figurine, 1973.
Girl with white kitten. 1973 embossed in ceramic and printed on box. CMV, $40.00 MB.

"Sharing the Christmas Spirit" Figurine, 1981.
First in Christmas Memories Series. Dated 1981. 6" high. CMV, $45.00 MB.

Best Friends Porcelain Figurine, 1981.
6" high boy figurine. Dated 1981. One made in Taiwan and one in Japan. CMV, $19.00 MB.

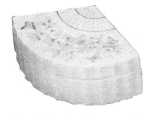

Butterfly Fantasy Treasure Fan, 1980 – 1981.
Fan shaped porcelain box. Dated 1980 on bottom. CMV, $13.00 MB. Add $5.00 for backward printed bottom label.

Mother's Love Figurine, 1981.
5½" high porcelain girl figurine holding a baby. Bottom tan painted label is dated 1981. Made in Taiwan sticker is tan. CMV, $19.00 MB.

Christmas Thimble, 1981.
Issued in 1982, but dated 1981 on outside and 1980 inside. CMV, $9.00 MB.

McConnell's Corner Town Shoppers, 1982.
3" high ceramic figurine. Bottom says "Christmas, 1982." CMV, $10.00 MB.

Wishful Thoughts, 1982 – 1983.
5½" high porcelain figurine. Blue and white. CMV, $15.00 MB.

Mother's Love Figurine (Advance), 1981.
Factory sample. About 75 were given by Avon Products, Inc. to collectors at the tenth annual National Association of Avon Collectors Convention in Long Beach, California, in 1991. These factory samples do not have Avon label on bottom and are ¼" higher. Made in Taiwan, label is green. Rare. Came in plain box. CMV, $100.00 mint.

American Heirloom Porcelain Bowl, 1981.
6" across, 4" high, white bowl. "Independence Day 1981" on bottom. Came with black plastic base. CMV, $20.00 MB.

McConnell's Corner General Store, 1982.
5½" ceramic box, roof lifts off. Dated "Christmas 1982." CMV, $25.00 MB.

Mother's Love Figurine Test Product, 1981.
Twenty-four of these porcelain figurines were given to Avon collectors at the tenth annual National Association of Avon Collectors Convention on the *Queen Mary* ship in June 1981. It is not in the regular issue box and is not marked on the bottom. Came with letter from Avon. Very rare. CMV, $150.00 with letter and plain box.

"Keeping the Christmas Tradition" Figurine, 1982.
Second in Christmas Memories Series. Hand painted porcelain figurine dated 1982. CMV, $45.00 MB.

American Fashion Thimbles, 1982 – 1986.
Eight different hand-painted porcelain ladies in 1890s to 1940s designs. CMV, $12.00 each, MB.
Thimble, 1938. CMV, $35.00 MB.
Thimble, 1947. CMV, $35.00 MB.
American Fashion Thimble Display Rack, 1983.
12½" long mahogany rack with eight pegs. Can hang on wall or sit on shelf. CMV, $13.00 MB.

A Sweet Remembrance, 1982.
4¼" porcelain box. "Valentine's Day 1982" on bottom. "A Token of Love" on inside with a gold foil-wrapped chocolate. Short issue. CMV, $15.00 MB.

Eagle — Pride of America Figurine, 1982 – 1983.
7¾" high porcelain eagle figurine. CMV, $30.00 MB.

Mother's Day Figurine, "Cherished Moments," 1983 – 1984.
4" high, hand-painted porcelain girl figurine. CMV, $18.00 MB.

Bunny Luv Ceramic Box, 1982.
Ceramic top and bottom. Rabbit on lid. Sold empty. CMV, $12.00 MB.

Christmas Thimble, 1982.
White porcelain, dated 1982. CMV, $9.00 MB.

Vivian Leigh Figurine, 1983 – 1984.
First in Images of Hollywood Series of porcelain figurines. 4½" high. Vivian Leigh as Scarlett O'Hara. CMV, $45.00 MB.

Mother's Day Figurine, "Little Things," 1983 – 1984.
3¾" high, hand-painted porcelain boy figurine. CMV, $18.00 MB.

Mother's Day Figurine, "Cherished Moments," 1983 – 1984.
4" high, hand-painted porcelain girl figurine. CMV, $18.00 MB.

American Heirloom Porcelain Bowl, 1983 – 1984.
6" across, 4" high porcelain bowl. Plastic stand. Flower design on bowl. CMV, $17.00 MB.

Mr. and Mrs. Claus Sugar Bowl and Creamer, 1983 – 1984.
Red, white, and green ceramic sugar bowl and creamer. CMV, $13.00 each, MB.

"Enjoying the Night Before Christmas" Figurine, 1983.
Third in Christmas Memories series. 5½" high hand-painted porcelain figurine. Dated Christmas 1983. CMV, $45.00 MB.

Christmas Thimble, 1983.
Small white porcelain thimble with decal. "1983 Christmas" in gold. CMV, $9.00 MB.

"Memories" Music Box, 1983 – 1984.
White, 4¼" long porcelain box with music box in lid. CMV, $27.50 MB.

Clark Gable Figurine, 1984 – 1985.
Second figurine in Images of Hollywood Series. Clark Gable as Rhett Butler. 5¾" high. CMV, $60.00 MB.

Mother's Touch Figurine, 1984.
Shiny glaze porcelain. Mother's Day figurine. CMV, $35.00 MB.

Duck Series, 1983 – 1984.
Six different hand-painted metal ducks. 4" long, 2" high. Mallard, canvasback, wood duck, bufflehead, green winged teal, and pintail. CMV, $13.00 each, MB.
Duck Display Rack, 1983 – 1984.
12½" long, two-tier wood rack to display all six duck figurines. CMV, $25.00 MB.

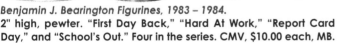

Benjamin J. Bearington Figurines, 1983 – 1984.
2" high, pewter. "First Day Back," "Hard At Work," "Report Card Day," and "School's Out." Four in the series. CMV, $10.00 each, MB.

Porcelain Cat Figurines, 1984.
Choice of four porcelain cat figurines: Siamese, Tabby, Calico, or Persian. CMV, $8.00 each, MB.

Fred Astaire Figurine, 1984.
Third in Images of Hollywood Series. 6¾" high, porcelain. CMV, $40.00 MB.

Ginger Rogers Figurine, 1984.
Fourth in Images of Hollywood Series. 6" high, porcelain. CMV, $40.00 MB.

"Celebrating the Joy of Giving" Figurine, 1984.
Fourth in Christmas Memories series. 6⅜" high, porcelain. Dated Christmas 1984. CMV, $50.00 MB.

Christmas Thimble, 1984. Porcelain, dated Christmas 1984. CMV, $8.00 MB.

"Father's Arms" Figurine, 1984. Wood base. Pewter figurine. CMV, $12.00 MB.

Joy to the World Musical Figurine, 1985. Small porcelain figurine, music base. CMV, $20.00 MB.

Easter Charm Figurine, 1985. 4" high, porcelain. Dated Easter 1985. CMV, $15.00 MB.

Statue of Liberty Centennial Bowl, 1985. 6" porcelain white bowl. Wood base. CMV, $20.00 MB.

Judy Garland Figurine, 1985. 5½" high, porcelain. CMV, $40.00 MB.

Bunny Luv Collection, 1984 – 1994. All are white ceramic: Napkin Holder, 1990, CMV, $8.00; Trinket Dish, 1985, CMV, $8.00; Bunny Picture Frame, 1988, CMV, $8.00; Bunny Country Planter, 1989, blue flowers around planter. CMV, $10.00. Bunny Dessert Plate, 1994, 7" basket weave plate. CMV, $10.00.

Cardinal Figurine, 1985. Red porcelain bird. CMV, $32.00 MB.

Country Village Canister Set, 1985. White pottery canisters by Pfaltzgraff. Marked "Avon" on bottom. CMV, $50.00 MB, set of three.

Magnolia, Seasons in Bloom Flower Figurine, 1986. Yellow, white, and green porcelain flower, Avon label. CMV, $28.00 MB.

Bear Cookie Jar, 1985. Brown ceramic cookie jar. CMV, $25.00.

John Wayne Figurine, 1985. 7¼" porcelain figurine. The great American hero. CMV, $60.00 MB.

Poinsettia, Seasons in Bloom Flower Figurine, 1986. Red porcelain flower. Avon label. CMV, $28.00 MB.

Christmas Tree Pomander, 1986.
9" high green ceramic tree. Came with wax chips. CMV, $17.00 MB.

Jessie Wilcox Smith Figurines, 1986.
3½" wide porcelain figurines. "Be Mine, Valentine," "Spring-time," and "Helping Mom." CMV, $28.00 each, MB.

"Giving Thanks" Figurine, 1986.
3¼" wide porcelain figurine by Jessie Wilcox Smith. CMV, $27.00 MB.

We Wish You a Merry Christmas Figurine, 1986.
3½" wide porcelain figurine with music base. CMV, $18.00 MB.

A Winter Snow Figurine, 1986.
Porcelain figurine by Jessie Wilcox Smith. CMV, $27.00 MB.

Baby Bear Bank, 1986.
Ceramic blue and tan bank with small green and white bear blanket. Came with iron-on letters. CMV, $7.00 MB.

"Summer Fun" Figurine, 1986.
3½" wide porcelain figurine by Jessie Wilcox Smith. CMV, $27.00 MB.

Bunny Bud Vase, 1986.
3½" high, porcelain. Came empty. CMV, $9.00 MB.

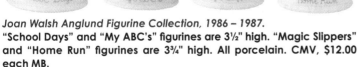

Summer Bride Figurine, 1986.
6" high, white porcelain. CMV, $25.00 MB.

Joan Walsh Anglund Figurine Collection, 1986 – 1987.
"School Days" and "My ABC's" figurines are 3½" high. "Magic Slippers" and "Home Run" figurines are 3¾" high. All porcelain. CMV, $12.00 each MB.

Bluebird Figurine, 1986.
Blue, orange, and white porcelain bird. CMV, $32.00 MB.

Joan Walsh Anglund Figurines, 1987.
Choice of "Christmas Wishes" (boy) or "The Night Before" (girl). Hand painted porcelain. 4" high. CMV, $15.00 each, MB.

Elvis Presley Figurine, 1987.
6½" high, hand-painted porcelain. CMV, $60.00 MB.

Forest Friends Figurines, 1988.
2" high, hand-painted. "Easter Fun," "Sunday Best," and "Springtime Stroll." CMV, $5.00 each, MB.

Hummingbird Porcelain Figurine, 1989.
7½" high, hand-painted porcelain. CMV, $60.00 MB.

Beary Cute Bear Bank, 1990.
6" high ceramic bank. CMV, $8.00 MB.

Forest Friends Miniature Figurines, 1987.
Choice of "Story Time," "Sleigh Ride," or "All Tucked In." 2" high x 2¼" wide each. CMV, $5.00 each.

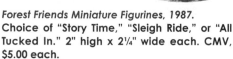

Iris Flower Figurine, 1987.
8" long porcelain Iris. Marked "Avon." CMV, $35.00 MB.

Peace Rose Figurine, 1987.
7" long, porcelain yellow rose. Marked "Avon." CMV, $35.00 MB.

Mother's Love Bunny Figurine, 1990.
Hand-painted porcelain. Baby, 1¼" high. Mother, 2½" high. CMV, $10.00 MB, set.

Native American Duck Figurine Collection, 1989.
Six different hand-painted, hand cast plaster duck figurines. Choice of Wood Duck, Goldeneye Duck, Widgeon Duck, Mallard Duck, Hooded Merganser (not shown), or Blue Winged Teal (not shown). All are 3" to 3¾" long. CMV, $13.00 each, MB.
Not shown: Native American Duck Collection Shelves, 1989.
Set of two 12" wood shelves to hold all six ducks. CMV, $15.00 MB, set.

Panda Sweetheart Figurines, 1990.
Boy and girl, hand-painted porcelain. 2½" high each. CMV, $10.00 MB, set.

Holiday Hugs Bear Figurine Set, 1990.
Papa Bear and Mama Bear with baby. Both 2⅝" high and dated on bottom. CMV, $10.00 MB.

Passing Down the Dream Figurine, 1991.
3¾" high porcelain. Choice of white or black men. CMV, $20.00 each, MB.

Silent Night Crystal Church, 1992.
5" high lead crystal church. Gold tone base. Top lights up with batteries. CMV, $19.00 MB.

"Kittens Sharing," 1992.
2½" high porcelain kittens. First in Best Buddies Series. CMV, $10.00 MB, set.

"God Bless My Dolly" Figurine, 1990.
3" high, porcelain in choice of black or white girl. CMV, $15.00 each, MB.

"Puppies Playing Ball," 1992.
2¼" high porcelain puppies. Second in Best Buddies Series. CMV, $10.00 MB, set.

Country Purr-fection Sugar and Creamer Set, 1991.
4½" high, ceramic cats, marked "Avon." CMV, $25.00 MB.
Country Purr-fection Salt and Pepper Set, 1992.
3" high, ceramic kitten salt and pepper shakers. CMV, $17.00 MB, set.
Country Purr-fection Teapot, 1992.
11" high, mother cat ceramic teapot. CMV, $50.00 MB.

"Friends for Keeps" Figurine, 1991.
3¼" high, porcelain. Tender Memories Series. Black or white child and pup. CMV, $15.00 each, MB.

"Mice-skating," 1992.
2¾" high porcelain mice. Third in Best Buddies Series. CMV, $10.00 MB, set.

"Purr-fect Love" Figurines, 1991.
Tender Memories Series. Black or white child porcelain figurines with kittens. 3¼" high. CMV, $15.00 each, MB.

Bunny Sugar and Creamer Set, 1992.
Ceramic basket weave design. CMV, $20.00 MB.
Bunny Candy Dish, 1991.
5½" wide x 2½" high, ceramic. CMV, $13.00 MB.

"Squirrels Clowning Around," 1992.
2¾" high gray and brown porcelain squirrels. Fourth in Best Buddies Series. CMV, $10.00 MB, set.

M. I. Hummel Crystal Trinket Box, 1993. **24% lead crystal box, 4" x 4" round. CMV, $20.00 MB.**

Crystal Sleigh Centerpiece, 1993. **Lead crystal sleigh, 6¾" wide, 3½" deep, 4¾" high. CMV, $20.00 MB.**

Circus Bear Collection, 1993. **Four different bisque porcelain figurines.** *Pierre the Ring Master.* **4½" high.** *Bettina the Ballerina.* **5¼" high.** *Marcello the Magician.* **4¼" high.** *Ulysses the Unicyclist.* **4¼" high. CMV, $20.00 each, MB.**

Santa Porcelain Figurine, 1993. **5¾" high, red and white porcelain figurine. CMV, $35.00 MB.**

Magic of Christmas Santa Rocker, 1993. **7¼" high, 4¾" wide. Made of plastic. Santa rocks and talks. Battery operated. CMV, $25.00 MB.**

Carousel Wonderland Miniatures Collection, 1993. **Each 3" high porcelain figurine is signed by artist Kathy Jeffers. Four in set. CMV, $10.00 each, MB.**

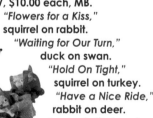

"Flowers for a Kiss," **squirrel on rabbit.** *"Waiting for Our Turn,"* **duck on swan.** *"Hold On Tight,"* **squirrel on turkey.** *"Have a Nice Ride,"* **rabbit on deer. A wood display stand for this collection was also issued in 1993, 13½" long, 4¾" wide, 7" high. $17.00 MB.**

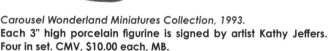

Precious Baby Treasures, 1993. **Lead crystal bootie, 2½" long. Baby carriage, 2¾" long. CMV, $15.00 each, MB.**

Bunny Collection Mug, 1993. **3½" high, white and green basket weave design mug. CMV, $10.00 MB.**

Sunny Cottage Land Figurines, 1994.
Set of three Hartford porcelain figurines, sold separately. *Left to right:* Manor, 3" wide, 2½" high; Shop, 3" wide, 2¼" high; Bakery, 2¾" wide, 2¾" high. CMV, $13.00 each, MB.

"Cat in Basket," 1994.
Second in Crystal Cats Series. 2¾" high, 2¼" wide. CMV, $15.00 MB.

Santa's Elves Collection, 1994.
Hartford porcelain figurines: Elf with Teddy Bear; Elf Wrapping Present; Elf with Rocking Horse. 2½" to 3" high each. CMV, $7.00 each, MB.

Santa Town Figurines, 1994.
Three porcelain houses with seven watt lights inside. Electric cord on each. Reindeer Lodge, Elves' Workshop, and Santa's House. CMV, $13.00 each, MB.

Alphabet Block, Crystal, 1994.
1¾" high, 1¾" wide, lead crystal glass block. Marked "Avon." CMV, $15.00 MB.

Country Quartet Figurines, 1994.
Hand-painted porcelain and polyester resin: Otis Owl, 3¼" high; Roscoe Raccoon, 3½" high. Four different figurines. CMV, $13.00 each, MB.
Bandstand Wood Stand.
8¾" high, 4½" deep, 8¾" wide. CMV, $15.00 MB.

Santa Porcelain Figurine, 1994.
"Father Christmas." Second in series. 7" high, porcelain, red and white figurine. Marked "Avon." CMV, $30.00 MB.

Ribbons and Lace Box, 1994.
2¼" high, 3" across, porcelain. Lace ribbon on top. CMV, $10.00 MB.

Teddy Bear, Crystal, 1994.
2½" high, 2½" wide lead crystal teddy bear. CMV, $15.00 MB.

Mother's Day Figurine, "A Mother's Love," 1995.
Porcelain figurine, 5½" high, 5¼" long. Dated on bottom. CMV, $20.00 MB.

"Sitting Cat," 1994.
First in Crystal Cats Series. 2¼" wide, 3" high. CMV, $15.00 MB.

Days of the Week Bear Collections, 1994.
Seven Hartford porcelain bears, each 2" to 3" high, for each day of the week. CMV, $10.00 each, MB.

Season's Treasures Teapots, 1995.
Small hand-painted porcelain teapots. Four different — Peony, Tulip, Sunflower, and Rose. CMV, $20.00 each, MB.

Mr. and Mrs. Santa Claus Salt and Pepper Shakers, 1995.
2¾" high ceramic shakers. CMV, $10.00 MB, pair.

Santa Porcelain Figurine, 1995.
7" high porcelain Santa and girl, dated 1995. Choice of white or black Santa and child. CMV, $25.00 each, MB.

"Cat on Pillow," 1995.
Lead crystal cat is 2¾" high x 2¼" wide. Third in Crystal Cats Series. CMV, $15.00 MB.

Kwanzaa Figurine, 1996.
7½" high, by 6⅜" wide. Black mother and father ceramic figurine. CMV, $30.00 MB.

Season's Harvest Miniature Teapots, 1996.
Small hand-painted porcelain teapots, 3" to 4" high. Choice of "Eggplant" (purple and green), "Red Pepper" (red and green), "Squash" (yellow and green), and "Asparagus" (green and yellow). Dated on bottom of each. CMV, $17.00 each, MB.

Cottage Collection Spice Jars, 1997.
Twelve different small ceramic jars, 3½" high. Roof lids, stick-on spice labels. CMV, $8.00 each, MB. Add $15.00 for the off-white wood spice rack.

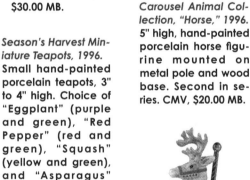

Carousel Animal Collection, "Lion," 1997.
Hand-painted porcelain lion on metal pole and wood base. 5¼" high. Dated 1997 on bottom. Fourth and last in this series. CMV, $20.00 MB.

Carousel Animal Collection, "Rabbit," 1996.
4⅞" high porcelain rabbit sits on wood base and metal poll. First in series of four. CMV, $20.00 MB.

Carousel Animal Collection, "Horse," 1996.
5" high, hand-painted porcelain horse figurine mounted on metal pole and wood base. Second in series. CMV, $20.00 MB.

Carousel Animal Collection, "Reindeer," 1996.
Hand-painted porcelain deer figurine on metal pole and wood base. 5½" high. Third in series. CMV, $20.00 MB.

Charming Thimble Collection #1, 1999.
First in series. 2¼" each, hand-painted porcelain and resin thimbles. Choice of cat, bear, or bunny. CMV, $5.00 each, MB.

Mother's Gift Figurine, 2002.
Moments and Memories porcelain figurine. 6¼" high, 4" wide. Sits on wood base. Pink dress and white hat. Also came in black lady with blue dress and pink hat. CMV, $20.00 MB.

Egyptian Royalty Figurines, "Pharaoh and Queen," 1997.
6½" high, made of cold cast resin. Dated 1997. CMV, $20.00 each, MB.

Essence of Motherhood Figurine, 1997.
10" high, cold cast resin. Black mother and child in white gown and hat. 4" base dated 1997. CMV, $20.00 MB.

Charming Thimble Collection #2, 1999.
Second in series. 2" each, hand-painted porcelain and resin thimbles. Choice of lion and lamb, angel, or dove thimbles. CMV, $5.00 each, MB.

Sleigh Ride Figurine, 2002.
Moments and Memories porcelain figurine sits on wood base. 8½" long, 4½" high, 2⅜" wide. CMV, $20.00 MB.

Negro League Baseball Figurines, 1997.
Josh Gibson and Satchel Paige. Both are 6" high, made of cold cast resin, and dated 1997 on bases. CMV, $20.00 each, MB.

Charming Thimble Collection #3, 2000.
Third in series. 2¼" high each, hand painted frosted glass thimbles. Choice of hummingbird, butterfly, or bumblebee thimbles. CMV, $5.00 each, MB.

Top: Porcelain Flowers with Hummingbird Figurines, 2003.
Bisque porcelain, 4" long, 3¾" high. One with pink flowers and one with white flowers. CMV, $10.00 each, MB.
Bottom left: Monarch Butterfly with Rose, 2003.
Porcelain pink rose and butterfly. CMV, $10.00 MB.
Bottom right: Tiger Swallowtail Butterfly Iris Flower Figurine, 2003.
3½" high, bisque porcelain. Lavender and white Iris flower. CMV, $10.00 MB.

Norman Rockwell "Triple Self Portrait" Figurine, 1999.
5" high, 4" wide, hand-painted resin figurine. CMV, $30.00 MB.

Spring Stroll Figurine, 2002.
Moments and Memories porcelain figurines. 9" high, 3" base. Choice of black or white lady. Blue dress with pink and white trim. CMV, $20.00 each, MB.

"Autumn Leaves" Angel Figurines, 2006.
6½" high hand-painted porcelain angels with plastic wings.
"Stargazer Lily" Angel Figurines, 2006.
6½" high porcelain angels with plastic wings, pearl accents.
"Sunflower" Angel Figurines, 2006.
6½" high porcelain angels with plastic wings. Yellow and green dresses.
"White Poinsettia" Angel Figurines, 2007.
6½" high porcelain angels with plastic wings.
Each set is marked "Avon" on the bottom. Choice of black or white angels in each set. OSP, $15.00 each. CMV, $10.00 each, MB.

Iridescent Swirl Angels, 2007.
White porcelain angels with choice of green trim angel holding a lute or pink trim angel holding a lyre. Each is 4¾" high and 2¼" wide. CMV, $6.00 each, MB.

Women's Decanters and Collectibles

What's hot is any decanter or figurine that's made of glass or ceramic. It has to look like something. This is what collectors are after today. What's not hot are plain looking bottles of no particular shape. Almost all plastic bottles, wall tiles, and wall decorations, plain tin can items, jars, fabric items such as sachet pillows etc., ceramic items not marked Avon on bottom, and kitchen items that have no shape are not very popular with collectors.

Avon collecting is 40 years old as we know it, and the Avon product line has expanded well beyond most people's abilities to collect everything in Avon's product line. There are thousands of products to collect. Choose the ones that appeal to most collectors and you should have a buyer when you decide to sell your collection in years to come.

This book has been researched to include all products that are hot with most collectors. Some new products not shown in this book fall in the category of new collectibles. There are over 500,000 Avon representatives, who provide more than ample supplies to collectors. It will take several (up to 30 or more) years for almost any new products to become scarce and start to rise in value due to supply and demand. Keep this in mind when buying new collectibles. Only the older products are true collectibles. This is why the CPC items, the first Avon products, are so scarce and have risen so high in value.

Candy products from Avon are not in this book unless they come in a figurine-type container. Boxes of candy will not be considered collectible as it easily melts, and is dangerous when it gets old and could cause harm to children. We suggest you buy this type of product to use, not to collect.

Most new items in this book 10 years old or less are listed below their original selling prices from Avon Products, Inc.

Skin So Soft Decanter, 1962 – 1963.
5¾ oz., gold neck string with white label, pink and white box. CMV, $5.00 BO, mint with tag. $12.00 MB.

Bath Urn (Cruet), 1963 – 1964.
8 oz., white glass top and bottle. Perfumed bath oil in Somewhere, Topaze, Cotillion, Here's My Heart, Persian Wood, or To a Wild Rose. CMV, $6.00 bottle with label. $12.00 MB.

Skin So Soft Decanter, 1964.
6 oz., gold crown top, gold neck tag. CMV, $6.00 BO, mint with tag. $12.00 MB.

Skin So Soft Decanter, 1965 – 1966.
10 oz. bottle with gold painted glass stopper. First issue came with solid painted gold around center. Later issue did not have this band. CMV, $12.00 MB, no solid band. $13.00 MB, solid band.

Skin So Soft Decanter, 1966.
10 oz. bottle with glass and cork stopper. 10" high. CMV, $12.00 MB.

Key Note Perfume Decanter, 1967.
¼ oz. glass key with gold plastic cap. 4A design on cap. Choice of Here's My Heart, To a Wild Rose, Somewhere, Topaze, Cotillion, Unforgettable, Rapture, or Occur! CMV, $12.00 key only, mint. $20.00 MB.

Icicle Perfume, 1967 – 1968.
1 dram, gold cap. Came in Here's My Heart, To a Wild Rose, Somewhere, Topaze, Cotillion, Unforgettable, Rapture, Occur!, or Régence. With gold neck label. CMV, $8.00 MB.

Christmas Ornaments, 1967.
Round, 4 oz. bubble bath. Came in gold, silver, red, or green. Silver caps. CMV, $14.00 MB, $9.00 BO mint.

Bath Seasons, 1967.
3 oz. bottles of foaming oil. Each has white glass and top. Orange design in Honeysuckle; green design in Lily of the Valley; lavender design in Lilac; yellow design in Jasmine. Matching ribbons on each. CMV, $10.00 each, MB.

Skin So Soft Decanter, 1967.
8 oz. bottle with glass and cork stopper. 11" high. CMV, $12.00 MB.

Snail Perfume, 1968 – 1969.
¼ oz., gold cap, clear glass. Came in Charisma, Brocade, Régence, Unforgettable, Rapture, and Occur! CMV, $8.00 BO. $14.00 MB.

Christmas Sparklers, 1968 – 1969.
4 oz. containers of bubble bath. Came in gold, green, blue, and red with gold caps. Two sides of bottle are indented. CMV, $10.00 BO, mint. $13.00 MB.
Not shown: Christmas Sparkler, Purple, 1968.
4 oz., painted over clear glass, gold cap. CMV, $25.00 mint. Sold only in West Coast area.

Christmas Trees, 1968 – 1970.
4 oz. bottles of bubble bath. Came in red, green, gold, or silver painted over clear glass. CMV, $8.00 BO, mint. $12.00 MB.

Salt Shakers, 1968 – 1970.
3 oz., bottles came with pink, purple, or yellow flowers and ribbons, in Hawaiian White Ginger, Honeysuckle, and Lilac bath oils. CMV, $10.00 each, MB.

Blue Demi-Cup, 1968 – 1970.
3 oz., white glass, blue cap and design. Some came with gold top with blue lid. Came in Brocade, Topaze, or Unforgettable. CMV, $9.00 MB.

Dolphin,
1968 – 1969.
8 oz., frosted glass with gold tail cap. CMV, $11.00 MB.

Christmas Cologne,
1969 – 1970.
3 oz. each. Unforgettable is silver and pink; Occur! is gold and blue; Somewhere is silver and green; Topaze is bronze and yellow. CMV, $10.00 BO, mint. $12.00 MB.

Bath Seasons, 1969.
3 oz. bath oil. Came in Charisma or Brocade. Black milk glass with silver cap and base. CMV, $6.00 MB.

Golden Angel Bath Oil,
1968 – 1969.
4 oz. gold bottle, gold paper wings. Gold and white cap. CMV, $12.00 MB.

Pyramid of Fragrance, 1969.
Top is ⅛ oz. perfume, gold cap. Center is 2 oz. cologne. Bottom is 2 – 3 oz. cream sachet in black glass. 6" high. Came in Charisma, Brocade, or Régence. CMV, $12.50 BO, mint. $20.00 MB.

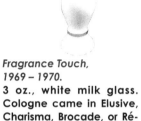

Fragrance Touch,
1969 – 1970.
3 oz., white milk glass. Cologne came in Elusive, Charisma, Brocade, or Régence. CMV, $7.00 MB.

Classic Decanter,
1969 – 1970.
8 oz. white glass bottle with gold cap. 11" high, filled with Skin So Soft bath oil. CMV, $10.00 MB.

Demi-Cups, 1969 – 1970.
3 oz., white milk glass. Charisma has red cap and design. Régence has green cap and design. CMV, $9.00 each, MB.

Petit Fleur Cologne,
1969 – 1970.
1 oz., gold cap. Shaped like flower. Came in Elusive, Brocade, Charisma, or Régence. CMV, $9.00 MB.

Love Bird Perfume,
1969 – 1970.
¼ oz., frosted bird with silver cap. 2½" long. Came in Charisma, Elusive, Brocade, Régence, Unforgettable, Rapture, or Occur! CMV, $10.00 MB.

To a Wild Rose Demi-Cup, 1969.
3 oz., white glass, red rose, pink cap. 6½" high. Contained foaming bath oil. CMV, $10.00 MB.

Bow Tie Perfume, 1970.
⅛ oz., clear glass. Shape of bow with gold cap. Came in Charisma or Cotillion. CMV, $7.00 mint.

Perfume Petite Mouse, 1970.
Frosted glass, gold head and tail, held ¼ oz. perfume in Elusive, Charisma, Brocade, Régence, Unforgettable, Rapture, or Occur! CMV, $12.00 BO. $18.00 MB.

Seahorse, 1970 – 1972.
Clear glass, 6 oz., held Skin So Soft, gold cap. CMV, $10.00 MB.

Keepsake Cream Sachet, 1970 – 1973.
5½" high, gold metal tree lid on ⅔ oz. frosted glass jar. Came in Bird of Paradise, Elusive, Charisma, Brocade, or Régence. CMV, $8.00 MB.

Bird of Paradise Cologne Decanter, 1970 – 1972.
8" high, 5 oz., clear glass, gold head. CMV, $12.00 MB.

Courting Lamp, 1970 – 1971.
5 oz., blue glass base with white milk glass shade and blue velvet ribbon. Held Elusive, Brocade, Charisma, Hana Gasa, or Régence. CMV, $10.00 BO. $14.00 MB.

Picture Frame Cologne, 1970 – 1971.
4 oz., gold paint on clear glass. Gold cap and gold plastic frame to hold bottle. Came in Elusive, Charisma, Brocade, or Régence. CMV, $13.00 mint. $17.00 MB.

Looking Glass Decanter, 1970 – 1972.
6½" high, clear glass mirror. Frame held 1½ oz. cologne in Bird of Paradise, Elusive, Charisma, Brocade, Régence, Unforgettable, Rapture, Occur!, Somewhere, Topaze, Cotillion, Here's My Heart, or To a Wild Rose. With gold handle cap. CMV, $13.00 MB.

Eiffel Tower, 1970.
3 oz., 9" high, clear glass with gold cap. Came in Occur!, Rapture, Somewhere, Topaze, Cotillion, or Unforgettable. CMV, $12.00 MB.

Royal Vase, 1970.
3 oz. blue cologne bottle in Elusive, Charisma, Brocade, or Régence. CMV, $6.00 MB.

Leisure Hours, 1970 – 1972.
5 oz. white milk glass bottle contained foaming bath oil in six fragrances. Gold cap. CMV, $10.00 MB.

Ruby Bud Vase, 1970 – 1971.
3 oz., red box held ruby glass vase filled with Unforgettable, Rapture, Occur!, Somewhere, Topaze, or Cotillion. CMV, $7.00 MB.

Lavender & Lace, 1970 – 1972.
Lavender and white box held 1⁷⁄₁₀ oz. white glass bottle of Lavender cologne with lavender ribbon. A lavender and white lace handkerchief came with it. CMV, $3.00 BO with ribbon. $8.00 MB, set.

Scent with Love Decanter, 1971 – 1972.
¼ oz. frosted glass with gold ink pen cap. White and gold label around bottle. Came in Field Flowers, Moonwind, Bird of Paradise, Charisma, or Elusive. CMV, $10.00 BO. $14.00 MB.

Treasure Turtle, 1971 – 1973.
1 oz. brown glass turtle with gold head. Held Field Flowers, Hana Gasa, Bird of Paradise, Elusive, Charisma, Brocade, Unforgettable, Rapture, Occur! Somewhere, Topaze, Cotillion, Here's My Heart, or Persian Wood. CMV, $10.00 MB.

Fashion Figurine, 1971 – 1972.
4 oz., white plastic top and white painted bottom, over clear glass. 6" high. Came in Field Flowers, Elusive, Bird of Paradise, or Brocade. CMV, $13.00 MB.

Sea Maiden Skin So Soft, 1971 – 1972.
6 oz., gold cap, clear glass, 10" high. CMV, $10.00 MB.

Sitting Pretty, 1971 – 1973.
4 oz., white milk glass with gold cat cap. Came in Topaze, Rapture, Cotillion, Somewhere, or Persian Wood. CMV, $9.00 MB.

Bath Urn, 1971 – 1973.
5 oz., white glass and cap with gold top plate. Held foaming bath oil in Elusive or Charisma, or bath foam in Lemon Velvet or Silk & Honey. 6" high. CMV, $7.00 MB.

Koffee Klatch, 1971 – 1974.
5 oz., yellow paint over clear glass pot with gold top. Held foaming bath oil in Field Flowers, Honeysuckle, or Lilac, or Lemon Velvet bath foam. CMV, $8.00 MB.

Fragrance Hours, 1971 – 1973.
6 oz., ivory glass grandfather clock, gold cap. Held Bird of Paradise, Field Flowers, Charisma, or Elusive. CMV, $125.00 MB.

Dutch Treat Demi-Cups, 1971.
3 oz. white glass bottles filled with cream lotion in Honeysuckle (yellow cap), Blue Lotus (blue cap), or Hawaiian White Ginger (pink cap, not shown). Each also came with white caps. CMV, $8.00 each, MB.

Ming Cat, 1971.
6 oz., white glass and head, blue trim and neck ribbon. Came in Moonwind, Bird of Paradise, Elusive, or Charisma. CMV, $10.00 MB.

French Telephone, 1971.
6 oz., white milk glass base with gold cap and trim. Held foaming bath oil. Center of receiver held ¼ oz. of perfume in frosted glass. Came in Moonwind, Bird of Paradise, Elusive, or Charisma. CMV, $30.00 MB.

Cornucopia, 1971 – 1976.
6 oz., white glass, gold cap. 5½" high. CMV, $10.00 MB.

Victoriana Pitcher and Bowl, 1971 – 1972.
6 oz. turquoise glass pitcher with Skin So Soft bath oil and turquoise glass bowl with Avon bottom. Some bowls have double Avon stamp on bottom. CMV, $10.00 no box. $12.00 MB. $14.00 with double stamp on bottom.

Flamingo, 1971 – 1972.
5 oz. clear bird shaped bottle with gold cap. 10" tall. Came in Bird of Paradise, Elusive, Charisma, or Brocade. CMV, $7.00 MB.

Song Bird, 1971 – 1972.
1½ oz., clear glass with gold base cap. Came in Unforgettable, Topaze, Occur!, Here's My Heart, or Cotillion. CMV, $6.00 MB.

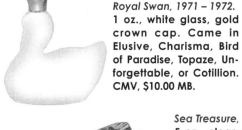

Royal Swan, 1971 – 1972.
1 oz., white glass, gold crown cap. Came in Elusive, Charisma, Bird of Paradise, Topaze, Unforgettable, or Cotillion. CMV, $10.00 MB.

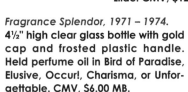

Sea Treasure, 1971 – 1972.
5 oz., clear glass coated iridescent seashell shaped bottle, gold cap. 7" long. Came in Field Flowers, Charisma, Honeysuckle, or Lilac. CMV, $12.00 MB.

Fragrance Splendor, 1971 – 1974.
4½" high clear glass bottle with gold cap and frosted plastic handle. Held perfume oil in Bird of Paradise, Elusive, Occur!, Charisma, or Unforgettable. CMV, $6.00 MB.

Parlor Lamp, 1971 – 1972.
Two sections. Gold cap over 3 oz. cologne top section in light amber iridescent glass. Yellow frosted glass bottom with talc. 6½" high. Held Bird of Paradise, Elusive, Charisma, Régence, or Moonwind. CMV, $12.00 BO. $15.00 MB.

Aladdin's Lamp, 1971 – 1973.
7½" long, 6 oz. green glass bottle with gold cap. Held foaming bath oil in Charisma, Bird of Paradise, Elusive, Occur!, or Unforgettable. CMV, $11.00 MB.

Cologne Elegante, 1971 – 1972.
4 oz., gold sprayed over clear glass and red rose on gold cap. 12" high. Came in Bird of Paradise, Hana Gasa, Elusive, Charisma, or Moonwind. CMV, $10.00 MB.

Emerald Bud Vase, 1971.
3 oz., green glass and glass top, 9" high. Came in Topaze, Occur!, Unforgettable, Here's My Heart, or To a Wild Rose. CMV, $4.00 MB.

Purse Petite Cologne, 1971.
1½ oz. embossed bottle with gold trim and cap and chain. Came in Elusive, Charisma, Bird of Paradise, Field Flowers, or Hana Gasa. CMV, $10.00 MB.

Keepsake Cream Sachet, 1971 – 1973.
6½" high, gold lid on marbleized glass jar with flower in colors. OSP, $5.00 Came in Moonwind, Bird of Paradise, Field Flowers, Elusive, or Charisma. CMV, $7.00 MB.

Cologne Royal, 1972 – 1974.
1 oz., clear glass, gold cap. Came in Field Flowers, Roses Roses, Bird of Paradise, Sonnet, Charisma, Unforgettable, or Somewhere. CMV, $6.00 MB.

Pineapple Petite, 1972 – 1974.
1 oz., clear glass, gold cap. Came in Roses Roses, Charisma, Elusive, Brocade, or Régence. CMV, $5.00 MB. Reissued in 1977 in Field Flowers and Unforgettable. Same CMV.

Dream Garden,
1972 – 1973.
½ oz., pink frosted glass with gold cap. Came in Moonwind, Bird of Paradise, Charisma, Elusive, or Unforgettable perfume oil. CMV, $12.00 BO. $15.00 MB.

Small Wonder Perfume,
1972 – 1973.
⅛ oz., frosted glass with gold cap. Held Field Flowers, Bird of Paradise, or Charisma. CMV, $8.00 MB.

Victorian Lady, 1972 – 1973.
5 oz., white milk glass, white plastic cap. Came in Bird of Paradise, Unforgettable, Occur!, or Charisma foaming bath oil. CMV, $10.00 MB.

Petite Piglet, 1972.
2" long, embossed clear glass with gold cap. Held ¼ oz. perfume in Field Flowers, Bird of Paradise, Elusive, or Charisma. CMV, $11.00 MB.

Roaring Twenties Fashion Figurine, 1972 – 1974.
3 oz., purple painted over clear glass with plastic purple top. Came in Unforgettable, Topaze, Somewhere, or Cotillion. CMV, $10.00 MB.

Elizabethan Fashion Figurine, 1972.
4 oz., pink painted glass bottom over clear glass with pink plastic top. 6" high. Came in Moonwind, Charisma, Field Flowers, or Bird of Paradise cologne. CMV, $20.00 MB. Also came pink painted over white milk glass. Remove cap to see difference. CMV, $15.00.

Little Girl Blue,
1972 – 1973.
3 oz., blue painted glass with blue plastic cap. Came in Brocade, Unforgettable, Somewhere, or Cotillion. CMV, $10.00 MB.

Compote Decanter,
1972 – 1975.
5 oz., white milk glass bottle, gold cap. Came in Moonwind, Field Flowers, Elusive, or Brocade. CMV, $8.00 MB.

Royal Coach, 1972 – 1973.
5 oz., white milk glass, gold cap. Held Moonwind, Bird of Paradise, Charisma, or Field Flowers foaming bath oil. CMV, $10.00 MB.

Victorian Manor, 1972 – 1973.
5 oz., white painted over clear glass with pink plastic roof. Held Roses Roses, Bird of Paradise, Unforgettable, or Cotillion. CMV, $10.00 MB.

Hobnail Decanter,
1972 – 1974.
5 oz., white opal glass. Came in Moonwind, Elusive, Roses Roses, or Lemon Velvet bath foam. CMV, $6.00 MB.

Sweet Shoppe Pincushion, 1972 – 1974.
1 oz., white milk glass bottom with white plastic back with hot pink pincushion seat. Came in Sonnet, Moonwind, Field Flowers, Roses Roses, Bird of Paradise, or Charisma. CMV, $8.00 MB.

Enchanted Hours,
1972 – 1973.
5 oz. blue glass bottle with gold cap. Came in Roses Roses, Charisma, Unforgettable, or Somewhere cologne. CMV, $10.00 MB.

Kitten Little, 1972 – 1976.
3½" high white glass bottle held 1½ oz. cologne in Occur!, Topaze, Unforgettable, Somewhere, or Cotillion. CMV, $7.00 MB.

Grecian Pitcher, 1972 – 1976.
6½" high, 5 oz. white glass bottle and white stopper held Skin So Soft. CMV, $10.00 MB.

Victoriana Powder Sachet, 1972 – 1974.
1½ oz. turquoise glass jar and lid. Came in Moonwind or Field Flowers. CMV, $8.00 MB.
Victoriana Dish and Soap, 1972 – 1973.
Turquoise glass dish with white soap. CMV, $3.00 dish only. $9.00 MB.

Left: Armoire, 1972 – 1975.
7" high, 5 oz. white glass bottle with gold cap. Choice of Field Flowers, Bird of Paradise, Elusive, or Charisma bath oil. Came in Field Flowers, Charisma, or Bird of Paradise only in 1975. CMV, $10.00 MB.
Right: Secretaire, 1972 – 1975.
7" high, pink paint over clear glass, gold cap. Held 5 oz. of foaming bath oil in Moonwind, Charisma, Brocade, Lilac, or Lemon Velvet. CMV, $11.00 MB.

Swan Lake, 1972 – 1976.
8" high, 3 oz. white glass bottle with white cap. Came in Bird of Paradise, Charisma, Elusive, or Moonwind. CMV, $8.00 MB.

Country Store Coffee Mill, 1972 – 1976.
5 oz., ivory milk glass, white plastic cap and plastic handles on side with gold rim. Came in Sonnet, Moonwind, Bird of Paradise, or Charisma cologne. CMV, $10.00 MB. Came in two different size boxes.

Little Dutch Kettle, 1972 – 1973.
5 oz., orange painted clear glass with gold cap. Came in Cotillion or Honeysuckle foaming bath oil, or Lemon Velvet bath foam. CMV, $7.00 MB.

Precious Owl, 1972 – 1974.
1½ oz., white bottle with gold eyes. Came in Moonwind, Field Flowers, Charisma, or Roses Roses. CMV, $5.00 MB.

Sea-Green Bud Vase, 1972 – 1973.
5 oz., 9" high green glass bottle held foaming bath oil in Field Flowers, Honeysuckle, or Bird of Paradise. CMV, $4.00 MB.

Butterfly, 1972 – 1973.
1½ oz., 3½" high, gold cap with two prongs. Held cologne in Occur!, Topaze, Unforgettable, Somewhere, or Here's My Heart. CMV, $8.00 MB. Reissued in 1976 in Field Flowers and Sweet Honesty. Same CMV.

Tiffany Lamp, 1972 – 1974.
5 oz., brown glass base with pink shade, pink and orange flowers, and green leaves on lavender background. Came in Sonnet, Moonwind, Field Flowers, or Roses Roses. CMV, $12.00 MB, Also came in pink and yellow flowers on shade, or all white flowers. CMV, $13.00 MB.

Bon Bon, "White," 1972 – 1973.
1 oz., white milk glass with white cap. Held Unforgettable, Topaze, Occur!, Cotillion, or Here's My Heart cologne. CMV, $10.00 MB.

Emollient Freshener for After Bath, 1972 – 1974.
6 oz., clear glass with gold cap, held Sonnet, Charisma, Imperial Garden, or Moonwind pearlescent liquid. CMV, $2.00 MB.

Fashion Boot Pincushion, 1972 – 1976.
5½" tall, blue milk glass with lavender bow and velvet cushion that fits over cap. Held 4 oz. cologne in Roses Roses, Charisma, Sonnet, or Moonwind. CMV, $8.00 MB.

Royal Apple Cologne, 1972 – 1973.
3 oz., frosted red glass with gold cap. Came in four fragrances. CMV, $7.00 MB.

Period Piece, 1972 – 1973.
½ oz., frosted glass. Came in Moonwind, Bird of Paradise, Charisma, or Elusive. Came with Charisma or Bird of Paradise in 1976. CMV, $7.00 MB.

Nile Blue Bath Urn, 1972 – 1974.
6 oz., deep blue glass with gold trim. CMV, $5.00 MB.
Not shown: Nile Green Bath Urn, 1975.
Same as above, only green glass. CMV, $5.00 MB.

Golden Thimble, 1972 – 1974.
2 oz., clear glass with gold cap. Came in Bird of Paradise, Brocade, Charisma, or Elusive cologne. CMV, $5.00 MB.

Remember When School Desk, 1972 – 1974.
4 oz., black glass with light brown plastic seat front and desk top, red apple for cap. Came in Rapture, Here's My Heart, Cotillion, or Somewhere cologne. CMV, $8.00 MB.

Courting Carriage, 1973 – 1974.
1 oz., clear glass, gold cap. Came in Moonwind, Sonnet, Field Flowers, or Flower Talk. CMV, $7.00 MB.

Snowman Petite Perfume, 1973.
¼ oz., textured glass with pink eyes, mouth, and scarf. Gold cap. Came in Cotillion, Bird of Paradise, or Field Flowers. CMV, $8.00 MB.

Precious Slipper, 1973 – 1974.
¼ oz., frosted glass bottle with gold cap. Came in Sonnet or Moonwind. CMV, $8.00 MB.

Victorian Fashion Figurine, 1973 – 1974.
4 oz., light green (some call it blue or aqua), painted over clear glass base with green plastic top. Came in Charisma, Field Flowers, or Bird of Paradise cologne. CMV, $30.00 MB.

Little Kate, 1973 – 1974.
3 oz., pastel orange painted glass with orange plastic hat over cap. Came in Bird of Paradise, Charisma, or Unforgettable. CMV, $11.00 MB.

Dutch Girl Figurine, 1973 – 1974.
3 oz., blue painted with light blue plastic top. Came in Unforgettable, Topaze, or Somewhere. CMV, $12.00 MB.

Snow Bird, 1973 – 1974.
1½ oz., white milk glass, white plastic cap. Came in Patchwork, Moonwind, or Sonnet cream sachet. CMV, $6.00 MB.

Flower Maiden, 1973 – 1974.
4 oz., yellow skirt painted over clear glass with white plastic top. Came in Unforgettable, Somewhere, Topaze, or Cotillion. Foreign issue had blue skirt. CMV, $11.00 MB.

Crystal Facets, 1973 – 1975. 3 oz., clear glass. Choice of Roses Roses or Field Flowers. CMV, $4.00 MB.

Venetian Pitcher Cologne Mist, 1973 – 1975. 3 oz. blue plastic coated bottle with silver plastic top. Came in Imperial Garden, Patchwork, Sonnet, or Moonwind. CMV, $5.00 MB.

Regal Peacock, 1973 – 1974. 4 oz., blue glass with gold cap. Came in Patchwork, Sonnet, or Moonwind. CMV, $11.00 MB.

Partridge, 1973 – 1975. 5 oz. white milk glass with white plastic lid. Came in Unforgettable, Topaze, Occur!, or Somewhere. CMV, $6.00 MB.

Country Kitchen, 1973 – 1975. 6 oz., white milk glass with red plastic head. Holds moisturized hand lotion. CMV, $8.00 MB.

Sea Spirit, 1973 – 1976. 5 oz., light green glass with green plastic tail over cap. Held Elusive, Topaze, or Cotillion. CMV, $7.00 MB.

Love Song, 1973 – 1975. 6 oz. frosted glass with gold cap. Held Skin So Soft bath oil. CMV, $6.00 MB.

Hobnail Bud Vase, 1973 – 1974. 4 oz., white milk glass with red and yellow roses. Held Charisma, Topaze, or Roses Roses cologne. Also came in 4¾ oz. size. CMV, $6.00 MB.

Bath Treasure Snail, 1973 – 1976. 6 oz., clear glass with gold head. Held Skin So Soft. CMV, $10.00 MB.

Beautiful Awakening, 1973 – 1974. 3 oz., gold painted over clear glass front paper clock face, gold cap. Came in Elusive, Roses Roses, or Topaze. CMV, $8.00 MB.

Dolphin Miniature, 1973 – 1974. 1½ oz., clear glass, gold tail. Held Charisma, Bird of Paradise, or Field Flowers cologne. CMV, $6.00 MB.

Enchanted Frog Cream Sachet, 1973 – 1976. 1¼ oz., cream colored milk glass with cream colored plastic lid. Came in Sonnet, Moonwind, or Occur! CMV, $5.00 MB.

Kitten Petite, 1973 – 1974. 1½ oz., amber glass ball with white plastic cat for cap. Came in Sonnet or Moonwind. CMV, $7.00 MB.

Hearth Lamp, 1973 – 1976. 8 oz., black glass with gold handle, daisies around neck with yellow and white shade. Held Roses Roses, Bird of Paradise, or Elusive. CMV, $12.00 MB.

Floral Bud Vase, 1973 – 1975. 5 oz., white milk glass. Held Roses Roses or Lemon Velvet bath foam, or Field Flowers or Honeysuckle foaming bath oil. CMV, $6.00 MB.

Creamery Decanter, 1973 – 1975. 8 oz., yellow painted over clear glass with brown basket of blue and orange flowers. Held Roses Roses, Field Flowers, or Bird of Paradise hand and body cream lotion. CMV, $10.00 MB.

Chimney Lamp, 1973 – 1974. 2 oz., clear glass bottom with white plastic shade with pink flowers. Held Patchwork, Sonnet, or Moonwind. CMV, $6.00 MB.

Suzette, 1973 – 1976. 5 oz., cream colored milk glass with cream colored plastic head and a pink-lavender bow around neck. Held Field Flowers, Bird of Paradise, or Cotillion foaming bath oil. CMV, $10.00 MB.

Amber Cruet, 1973 – 1975. 6 oz., light amber ribbed glass. Held Field Flowers, Bird of Paradise, or Charisma foaming bath oil. CMV, $4.00 MB. Came only in Field Flowers and Bird of Paradise in 1975.

Queen of Scots, 1973 – 1976. 1 oz., white milk glass, white plastic head. Came in Sweet Honesty, Unforgettable, Somewhere, Cotillion, or Here's My Heart. CMV, $7.00 MB.

Seahorse Miniature Cologne, 1973 – 1976. 1½ oz., clear glass, gold cap. Came in Unforgettable, Here's My Heart, or Cotillion. CMV, $7.00 MB.

Garnet Bud Vase, 1973 – 1976. 3 oz., garnet colored translucent glass bottle and stopper. Came in Occur!, Somewhere, Topaze, or To a Wild Rose cologne. CMV, $5.00 MB.

Dachshund, 1973 – 1974. 1½ oz., frosted glass, gold cap. Came in Unforgettable, Somewhere, Topaze, or Cotillion. CMV, $7.00 MB.

Bon Bon, "Black," 1973. 1 oz., black milk glass with black plastic cap. Held Field Flowers, Bird of Paradise, Roses Roses, or Elusive. CMV, $10.00 MB.

Hurricane Lamp, 1973 – 1974. 6 oz., white milk glass bottom with clear glass shade, gold cap. Held Roses Roses, Field Flowers, Bird of Paradise, or Charisma cologne. CMV, $13.00 MB.

Pineapple, 1973 – 1974. 10 oz., clear glass with green plastic leaves, dispenser top. Held moisturized hand lotion. CMV, $5.00 MB.

Grape Bud Vase, 1973.
6 oz., grape frosted glass. Held Skin So Soft. CMV, $5.00 MB.

Country Charm Butter Churn, 1973 – 1974.
½ oz., clear glass, gold bands and cap. Came in Field Flowers, Elusive, Occur!, or Somewhere cologne. CMV, $6.00 MB.

Dear Friends, 1974.
4 oz., pink painted with light pink plastic top. Came in Field Flowers, Bird of Paradise, or Roses Roses cologne. CMV, $13.00 MB.

Bell Jar, 1973 – 1975.
5 oz., clear glass with bouquet of pink and white flowers. Had gold cap and base with pink ribbon. Held Field Flowers, Bird of Paradise, Charisma, or Brocade cologne. CMV, $9.00 MB. Sold only in Field Flowers, Bird of Paradise, and Charisma in 1976. Same CMV.

Victorian Washstand, 1973 – 1974.
4 oz., buff painted with gray plastic simulated marble top with blue pitcher and bowl for cap. Came in Field Flowers, Bird of Paradise, or Charisma foaming bath oil. CMV, $8.00 MB.

18th Century Classic Figurine, Young Girl, 1974 – 1975.
4 oz., white sprayed glass with white plastic head. Choice of Sonnet or Moonwind cologne or foaming bath oil. CMV, $9.00 MB.

Cruet Cologne, 1973 – 1974.
8 oz., clear glass with glass stopper and flat dish. Held Imperial Garden, Patchwork, Sonnet, or Moonwind cologne. CMV, $10.00 MB.

Precious Swan Perfume, 1974 – 1976.
⅛ oz., frosted glass with gold cap. Came in Field Flowers, Bird of Paradise, or Charisma. CMV, $7.00 MB.

One Dram Perfume, 1974 – 1976.
Clear glass with gold cap. Came in Bird of Paradise, Charisma, Field Flowers, Sonnet, Moonwind, or Imperial Garden. CMV, $3.00 MB.

Left: Apothecary Bottle, 1973 – 1974.
8 oz. Spicy after shave in light brown glass with gold cap.
Center: Apothecary Bottle, 1973 – 1976.
8 oz. Lemon Velvet moisturized friction lotion in light yellow glass with gold cap. Also came in light green or blue-green glass.
Right: Apothecary Bottle, 1973.
8 oz. Breath Fresh in dark green with gold cap. CMV, $7.00 each, MB.

Strawberry Fair Perfume, 1974 – 1975.
⅛ oz., red glass, silver cap. Came in Moonwind, Charisma, or Sonnet. CMV, $6.00 MB.

18th Century Classic Figurine, Young Boy, 1974 – 1975.
4 oz., white sprayed glass with white plastic head. Choice of Sonnet or Moonwind cologne or foaming bath oil. CMV, $9.00 MB.

Pretty Girl Pink, 1974 – 1975. 6 oz., glass sprayed pink base with light pink top. Held Unforgettable, Topaze, Occur!, or Somewhere cologne. CMV, $10.00 MB.

Gay Nineties, 1974. 3 oz., orange sprayed bottle with white top and orange hat. Held Unforgettable, Topaze, or Somewhere. CMV, $13.00 MB.

Sweet Dreams, 1974. 3 oz., sprayed white bottom with blue top. Held Pink and Pretty or Sweet Honesty cologne. CMV, $15.00 MB.

Robin Red-Breast, 1974 – 1975. 2 oz., red frosted glass with silver plastic top. Held Charisma, Roses Roses, or Bird of Paradise. CMV, $6.00 MB.

Owl Fancy, 1974 – 1976. 4 oz., clear glass. Came in Raining Violets or Roses Roses. CMV, $4.00 MB.

Heavenly Angel, 1974 – 1975. 2 oz., clear glass with white top. Held Occur!, Unforgettable, Somewhere, Here's My Heart, or Sweet Honesty cologne. CMV, $7.00 MB.

Yule Tree, 1974 – 1979. 3 oz., green with plastic with green plastic top and gold star. Came in Sonnet, Moonwind, or Field Flowers cologne. CMV, $6.00 MB.

Perfume Concentre, 1974 – 1976. 1 oz., clear glass with gold cap. Came in Imperial Garden, Moonwind, Sonnet, Charisma, or Bird of Paradise. CMV, $4.00 MB.

Unicorn, 1974 – 1975. 2 oz., clear glass with gold cap. Came in Field Flowers, Charisma, Bird of Paradise, or Brocade. CMV, $7.00 MB.

La Belle Telephone, 1974 – 1976. 1 oz. Held clear glass with gold top. Held Moonwind, Sonnet, or Charisma perfume concentre. CMV, $9.00 MB.

Swiss Mouse, 1974 – 1975. 3 oz., frosted glass, gold cap. Held Roses Roses, Field Flowers, or Bird of Paradise cologne. CMV, $7.00 MB.

Buttercup Candlestick, 1974. 6 oz., white milk glass, yellow and white flowers. Held Moonwind, Sonnet, or Imperial Garden cologne. First issue has yellow band around neck. CMV, $9.00 MB. Later issue was plain with no band on neck and yellow or brown decals. CMV, $8.00 MB.

Buttercup Flower Holder, 1974. 5 oz., milk glass with plastic white top. Held Moonwind, Imperial Garden, or Sonnet. CMV, $6.00 MB.

Buttercup Salt Shaker, 1974.
1½ oz., white milk glass with yellow and white flowers, yellow plastic cap. Came in Moonwind, Sonnet, or Imperial Garden. CMV, $3.00 MB.

Kitten's Hideaway, 1974 – 1976.
1 oz., amber basket, white plastic kitten cap. Came in Field Flowers, Bird of Paradise, or Charisma cream sachet. CMV, $6.00 MB.

Royal Pekinese, 1974 – 1975.
1½ oz., white glass and white plastic head. Came in Unforgettable, Somewhere, or Topaze. CMV, $7.00 MB.

Ming Blue Lamp, 1974 – 1976.
5 oz., blue glass lamp, white plastic shade with gold tip. Held Charisma, Bird of Paradise, or Field Flowers foaming bath oil. CMV, $8.00 MB.

Leisure Hours Miniature, 1974.
1½ oz., white milk glass bottle, gold cap. Held Field Flowers, Bird of Paradise, or Charisma cologne. CMV, $6.00 MB.

Song of the Sea, 1974 – 1975.
Held bath pearls. Aqua colored glass with plastic head. Held Moonwind, Sonnet, or Imperial Garden. CMV, $8.00 MB.

Courting Rose, 1974.
1½ oz., red glass rose with gold cap and stem. Came in Moonwind, Sonnet, or Imperial Garden. Later issue painted red over clear glass. CMV, $7.00 each, MB.

Royal Swan, 1974.
1 oz., blue glass with gold crown cap. Came in Unforgettable, Topaze, Cotillion, or Here's My Heart. CMV, $10.00 MB.

Parisian Garden, 1974 – 1975.
⅓ oz., white milk glass with gold cap. Came in Sonnet, Moonwind, or Charisma perfume. CMV, $5.00 MB.

Sweet Treat Cologne, 1974 – 1976.
White and brown painted glass with red cap. Came in Pink and Pretty cologne. CMV, $4.00 MB.

Lady Spaniel, 1974 – 1976.
1½ oz., opal glass with plastic head. Held Patchwork, Sonnet, or Moonwind cologne. CMV, $7.00 MB.

Evening Glow, 1974 – 1975.
⅓ oz., white milk glass with green flowers, white and gold plastic cap. Came in Moonwind, Sonnet, or Charisma. CMV, $7.00 MB.

Venetian Blue, 1974 – 1976.
Frosted turquoise glass with turquoise plastic lid and gold tip. Held 75 bath pearls. Came in Moonwind, Sonnet, or Imperial Garden. CMV, $6.00 MB.

Honey Bear Baby,
1974 – 1976.
4 oz., yellow painted glass with blue plastic bear on lid. CMV, $4.00 MB.

Precious Turtle,
1975 – 1976.
²/₃ oz. gold jar with plastic lid. Came in Patchwork or Roses Roses cream sachet. CMV, $6.00 MB.

Dovecote, 1974 – 1976.
4 oz., clear glass with gold roof and two white doves. Held Field Flowers, Bird of Paradise, Charisma, or Roses Roses cologne. CMV, $4.00 MB.

Regency Decanter,
1974 – 1975.
6 oz., clear glass filled with Skin So Soft bath oil. CMV, $3.00 MB.

Breath Fresh Apothecary Decanter, 1974.
8 oz., clear glass with gold cap. Held Breath Fresh mouthwash. CMV, $3.00 MB.

Ladybug Perfume Decanter, 1975 – 1976.
¹/₈ oz., frosted glass with gold cap. Choice of Sonnet, Moonwind, or Patchwork. CMV, $7.00 MB.

Sewing Notions,
1975.
1 oz., pink and white glass with silver cap. Held Sweet Honesty, To a Wild Rose, or Cotillion. CMV, $5.00 MB.

Victorian Sewing Basket,
1974 – 1976.
5 oz., white milk glass basket jar with lavender plastic, gold cord held pink flower. Came in Roses Roses, Bird of Paradise, or Charisma perfumed Skin So Soft. CMV, $3.00 MB.

Persian Pitcher,
1974 – 1976.
6 oz., blue glass. Held Bird of Paradise, Charisma, or Elusive foaming bath oil. CMV, $3.00 MB.

Castleford Collection Emollient Bath Pearls,
1974 – 1976.
Held 60 bath pearls. Clear glass. Came in Imperial Garden, Sonnet, or Moonwind. CMV, $3.00 MB.

Crystalier Cologne,
1975.
2 oz., clear glass. Filled with Field Flowers, Bird of Paradise, or Roses Roses cologne. CMV, $4.00 MB.

Baroque Cream Sachet, 1974.
2 oz., white milk glass with gold top and bottom. Came in Imperial Garden, Sonnet, or Moonwind. CMV, $7.00 MB.

Teatime Powder Sachet, 1974 – 1975.
1¼ oz., frosted white with gold cap. Held Moonwind, Sonnet, or Roses Roses. CMV, $7.00 MB.

Baby Owl,
1975 – 1977.
1 oz., clear glass, gold cap. Held Sweet Honesty or Occur! cologne. CMV, $5.00 MB.

Pert Penguin,
1975 – 1976.
1 oz., clear glass, gold cap. Held Field Flowers or Cotillion cologne. CMV, $5.00 MB.

Garden Girl, 1975.
4 oz., sprayed frosted glass with yellow plastic top. Held Sweet Honesty, Somewhere, Cotillion, or To a Wild Rose. CMV, $12.00 MB.

Fly-a-Balloon,
1975 – 1977.
3 oz., glass sprayed blue with light blue top and red plastic balloon. Held Moonwind or Bird of Paradise cologne. CMV, $8.00 MB.

Scottish Lass, 1975.
4 oz., blue with red, green, and blue plaid skirt, blue plastic top. Held Sweet Honesty, Bird of Paradise, Roses Roses, or Cotillion cologne. CMV, $10.00 MB.

Spanish Senorita,
1975 – 1976.
4 oz., red base with white designs and pink plastic top. Held Moonwind, To a Wild Rose, or Topaze cologne. CMV, $12.00 MB.

Flight to Beauty, 1975.
5 oz. glass jar with white frosted top. Held Rich Moisture or Vita-Moist Cream or Skin So Soft. CMV, $4.00 MB.

Touch of Christmas,
1975.
1 oz., green glass with red cap. Held Unforgettable or Imperial Garden. CMV, $4.00 MB. Reissued in 1979 in Zany and Here's My Heart. Same CMV.

Crystal Tree Cologne, 1975.
3 oz., clear glass with gold plastic star cap. Held Moonwind or Sonnet. CMV, $8.00 MB.

Handy Frog,
1975 – 1976.
8 oz., white milk glass with red cap. CMV, $8.00 MB.

Snow Bunny, 1975 – 1976.
3 oz., clear glass with gold cap. Held Moonwind, Charisma, Bird of Paradise, or Sweet Honesty cologne. CMV, $6.00 MB.

High-buttoned Shoe, 1975 – 1976. 2 oz., clear glass with gold cap. Held Occur! or Unforgettable cologne. CMV, $6.00 MB.

Tabatha, 1975 – 1976. 3 oz., black glass and plastic. Held Imperial Garden, Bird of Paradise, or Cotillion cologne. CMV, $8.00 MB.

Butterfly Garden Bud Vase, 1975 – 1976. 6 oz., black glazed glass with gold stopper. Held Roses Roses, Bird of Paradise, or Topaze cologne. CMV, $5.00 MB.

Good Luck Elephant, 1975 – 1976. 1½ oz., frosted glass, gold cap. Held Sonnet, Imperial Garden, or Patchwork cologne. CMV, $7.00 MB.

Blue Eyes, 1975 – 1976. 1½ oz., opal glass with blue rhinestone eyes. Available in Topaze or Sweet Honesty cologne. CMV, $7.00 MB.

Charm Light, 1975 – 1976. ⅞ oz. cream sachet in white shade and 2 oz. cologne in pink base. Held Imperial Garden, Sonnet, or Moonwind. CMV, $8.00 MB.

Fostoria Compote, 1975 – 1976. Held 12 Skin So Soft capsules. Clear glass with glass top. CMV, $3.00 MB.

Mansion Lamp, 1975 – 1976. 6 oz., blue glass with white plastic top. Held Bird of Paradise or Moonwind cologne. CMV, $10.00 MB.

Liquid Milk Bath, 1975 – 1976. 6 oz., frosted glass bottle with gold cap. Held Imperial Garden, Sonnet, or Moonwind. CMV, $5.00 MB.

Bird of Happiness, 1975 – 1976. 1½ oz., light blue glass, gold cap. Held Charisma, Topaze, Occur!, or Unforgettable cologne. CMV, $5.00 MB.

Crystalique Cologne, 1975. 4 oz., clear glass with glass stopper. Held Moonwind, Sonnet, or Imperial Garden. CMV, $5.00 MB.

Kitten Little, 1975 – 1976. 1½ oz., black glass with black head. Held Sweet Honesty, Bird of Paradise, or Roses Roses. CMV, $7.00 MB.

Empire Green Bud Vase, 1975. 3 oz., green glass with silver base. Held Moonwind, Sonnet, or Imperial Garden cologne. CMV, $4.00 MB.

Sea Legend Decanter, 1975 – 1976. 6 oz., clear glass with white cap. Held Moonwind or Sonnet foaming bath oil or Roses Roses creamy bath foam. CMV, $4.00 MB.

Golden Flamingo, 1975.
6 oz., clear glass with gold flamingo on front. Held Bird of Paradise, Charisma, or Field Flowers foaming bath oil. CMV, $3.00 MB.

Pear Lumiere, 1975 – 1976.
2 oz., clear glass and plastic with gold leaf. Held Roses Roses, Charisma, or Bird of Paradise cologne. CMV, $5.00 MB.

Bridal Moments, 1976 – 1979.
5 oz., white paint over clear glass. White plastic top. Came in Sweet Honesty or Unforgettable cologne. CMV, $10.00 MB.

Athena Bath Urn, 1975 – 1976.
6 oz., clear glass. Held Field Flowers or Bird of Paradise foaming bath oil, or Roses Roses cream bath foam. CMV, $4.00 MB.

Song of Love, 1975 – 1976.
2 oz., clear glass, clear plastic top with white bird. Held Bird of Paradise, Charisma, or Sweet Honesty. Issued with blue base and blue top in Moonwind and Here's My Heart in 1976. CMV, $3.00 MB.

Betsy Ross, 1976.
4 oz., white painted over clear glass. Came in Sonnet or Topaze cologne. Sold during two campaigns only. CMV, $7.00 MB. Also came white painted over white milk glass. Remove cap to see color of bottle. CMV, $20.00 MB. The regular issue Betsy Ross bottle was one of the all-time biggest sellers in Avon history.

Country Style Coffee Pot, 1975 – 1976.
10 oz., yellow speckled paint over clear glass. Came with yellow and white pump top. Came with moisturized hand lotion. CMV, $7.00 MB.

Castleford Collection Cologne Gelee, 1975 – 1976.
4 oz., glass, held Raining Violets, Roses Roses, or Apple Blossoms cologne gelee. CMV, $3.00 MB.

Winter Garden, 1975 – 1976.
6 oz., clear glass with gold cap. Held Here's My Heart, Topaze, or Occur! cologne. CMV, $3.00 MB.

California Perfume Co. Anniversary Keepsake Cologne, 1975.
Issued in honor of 89th anniversary. 1⁷/₁₀ oz. bottle, pink ribbon and gold cap. Came in Charisma or Sweet Honesty cologne. Sold during two campaigns only. CMV, $6.00 BO. $8.00 MB. First issue, Avon President's Club reps received this bottle with 4A design under bottom label. Regular issue had "Avon" on bottom. CMV for 4A design and "M" for managers. Given to managers only. CMV, $15.00 MB.

Magic Pumpkin Coach,
1976 – 1977.
1 oz., clear glass, gold cap. Came in Bird of Paradise or Occur! cologne. CMV, $6.00 MB.

Library Lamp,
1976 – 1977.
4 oz., gold plated base over clear glass, gold cap. Came in Topaze or Charisma cologne. CMV, $10.00 MB.

Lucky Penny Lip Gloss,
1976 – 1980.
2" diameter, copper colored. Contained two colors of lip gloss. CMV, $1.00 no box. $2.00 MB. Reissued in 1980 with "R" on bottom.

Teddy Bear,
1976 – 1978.
¾ oz., frosted glass, gold cap. Came in Sweet Honesty or Topaze. CMV, $6.00 MB.

Catch-a-Fish,
1976 – 1978.
3 oz., dark tan, painted over clear glass, light tan plastic top, yellow hat and brown plastic, removable pole. Came in Field Flowers or Sonnet cologne. CMV, $11.00 MB.

Hearthside,
1976 – 1977.
⅔ oz., bronze plated over clear glass. Came in Sweet Honesty or Occur! CMV, $6.00 MB.

Precious Doe,
1976 – 1978.
½ oz., frosted glass bottle. Came in Field Flowers or Sweet Honesty. CMV, $5.00 MB.

American Belle,
1976 – 1978.
4 oz., yellow dull paint over clear glass, yellow cap. Came in Cotillion or Sonnet cologne. CMV, $9.00 MB.

Golden Angel,
1976 – 1977.
1 oz., gold plated over clear glass. White angel head cap. Came in Sweet Honesty or Occur! CMV, $7.00 MB.

Graceful Giraffe, 1976.
1½ oz., clear glass with plastic top. Held Topaze or To a Wild Rose cologne. CMV, $6.00 MB.

Little Bo Peep Decanter, 1976 – 1978.
2 oz., white dull paint over white milk glass base, white plastic top and can. Came in Sweet Honesty or Unforgettable cologne. CMV, $9.00 MB.

Fairytale Frog, 1976.
1 oz., clear glass with gold frog cap. Choice of Sweet Honesty or Sonnet cologne. CMV, $5.00 MB.

Heartscent Cream Sachet,
1976 – 1977.
⅔ oz., white glass bottom with white plastic top. Gold dove design. Came in Charisma, Occur!, or Roses Roses. CMV, $4.00 MB.

Lovable Seal,
1976 – 1977.
1 oz., frosted glass, gold cap. Came in Cotillion or Here's My Heart. CMV, $5.00 MB.

Princess of Yorkshire,
1976 – 1978.
1 oz., off-white over milk glass. Came in Sweet Honesty or Topaze cologne. CMV, $5.00 MB.

Christmas Surprise, 1976.
1 oz., green glass boot. Came in Sweet Honesty, Moonwind, Charisma, or Topaze cologne. Red or silver cap. CMV, $3.00 MB.

Silver Dove Ornament, 1976.
½ oz. bottle with gold or silver cap. Came in silver metal bird holder marked "Christmas '76" on both sides and "Avon" on inside. Came in Bird of Paradise or Occur! cologne. CMV, $6.00 MB.

Crystal Point Salt Shaker,
1976 – 1977.
1½ oz., blue glass. Held Sonnet or Cotillion cologne. CMV, $4.00 MB.

Country Charm,
1976 – 1977.
4⁴/₅ oz., white milk glass, yellow stove window. Green and white plastic top. Came in Field Flowers or Sonnet. CMV, $10.00 MB.

CPC Anniversary Keepsake Cologne, 1976.
1⁷/₁₀ oz. clear glass bottle, gold cap. Bottle is embossed on back side, "Avon 90th Anniversary Keepsake." Came in Moonwind or Cotillion cologne. Sold during two campaigns only. CMV, $8.00 MB.

Snow Owl,
1976 – 1977.
1¼ oz., frosted glass base and frosted plastic head with blue eyes. Came in Moonwind or Sonnet. Label in blue lettering. CMV, $6.00 MB.

Country Jug,
1976 – 1978.
10 oz., gray painted over clear glass. Blue and gray plastic pump. Came with almond scented hand lotion. CMV, $5.00 MB.

Treasure Turtle, 1977.
1 oz., clear glass turtle with gold cap. Came in Sweet Honesty or Charisma cologne. "Avon" on bottom and "R" for reissue on tail. CMV, $7.00 MB.

Sitting Pretty,
1976 – 1977.
1½ oz., white milk glass base, white plastic top. Came in Charisma or Topaze. Pink ribbons painted on each corner. CMV, $8.00 MB.

Enchanted Apple,
1976 – 1978.
⅔ oz., gold plated over clear glass. Gold top. Came in Charisma or Sonnet. CMV, $4.00 MB.

Emerald Prince Frog,
1977 – 1979.
1 oz., green frosted paint over clear glass. Came in Sweet Honesty or Moonwind cologne. CMV, $7.00 MB.

Christmas Candle Cologne Decanter, 1977. 1 oz., green glass. Came in Charisma, Sweet Honesty, Topaze, or Moonwind. CMV, $5.00 MB.

Roll-a-Hoop, 1977 – 1978. 3¾ oz., dull pink painted over clear glass base. Light pink plastic top, white plastic hoop. Came in Field Flowers or Cotillion cologne. CMV, $11.00 MB.

Baby Hippo, 1977 – 1980. 1 oz., frosted glass with silver head. Came in Sweet Honesty or Topaze cologne. CMV, $7.00 MB.

Song of Spring, 1977. 1 oz., frosted glass with frosted plastic bird bath top. Blue plastic bird attachment. Came in Sweet Honesty or Topaze. CMV, $6.00 MB.

Dutch Maid, 1977 – 1979. 4 oz., blue painted base over clear glass, flower design and blue plastic top. Came in Sonnet or Moonwind cologne. CMV, $10.00 MB.

Little Lamb, 1977 – 1978, ¾ oz., white milk glass, white head. Came in Sweet Honesty or Topaze cologne. CMV, $6.00 MB.

Felina Fluffles, 1977 – 1978. 2 oz., blue paint over clear glass, white plastic top, blue ribbon on head. Pink cheeks. Came in Pink and Pretty cologne. CMV, $8.00 MB.

Mary Mary, 1977 – 1979. 2 oz., frosted white over milk glass and white plastic top. Came in Sweet Honesty or Topaze. CMV, $10.00 MB.

Silver Swirls Salt Shaker, 1977 – 1979. 3 oz., silver plated over clear glass. Silver top. Came in Sweet Honesty or Topaze cologne. CMV, $4.00 MB.

Skip-a-Rope, 1977. 4 oz., yellow sprayed glass with yellow plastic top and white plastic rope. Held Sweet Honesty, Bird of Paradise, or Roses Roses cologne. CMV, $8.00 MB.

Skater's Waltz — Red, 1977 – 1978. 4 oz., red flock on clear glass and pink plastic tip. Came in Moonwind or Charisma cologne. CMV, $11.00 MB.
Skater's Waltz — Blue, 1979 – 1980. 4 oz., blue flock base over clear glass. Light blue plastic top. Held Charisma or Cotillion cologne. CMV, $11.00 MB.

Island Parakeet, 1977 – 1978.
1½ oz., blue glass base and blue and yellow plastic top. Approximately 4½" high. Came in Moonwind or Charisma cologne. CMV, $7.00 MB.

Golden Harvest, 1977 – 1980.
10 oz., ear of corn, clear and green glass bottle. Gold and plastic pump top. Came with Avon almond scented hand lotion. CMV, $6.00 MB.

Oriental Peony Vase, 1977.
1½ oz., red paint over clear glass with gold design. Came in Sweet Honesty or Moonwind. CMV, $7.00 MB.

Dr. Hoot, 1977 – 1979.
4 oz., white milk glass owl with blue plastic cap and white, gold, or green tassel. Came in Sweet Honesty or Wild Country. CMV, $7.00 MB.
Not shown: Dr. Hoot, 1975 – 1976.
4 oz., opal white glass, black cap, gold tassel. Held Wild Country after shave or Sweet Honesty cologne. CMV, $8.00 MB.

Courting Rose, 1977.
1½ oz., amber coated over clear glass, rose bottle with gold top. Came in Roses Roses or Moonwind cologne. CMV, $6.00 MB.

Royal Elephant, 1977 – 1979.
½ oz., white milk glass with gold snap-on top. Came in Charisma or Topaze. CMV, $6.00 MB.

Tree Mouse, 1977 – 1979.
⅔ oz., clear glass and clear plastic top. Gold mouse. Came in Sweet Honesty or Charisma. CMV, $4.00 MB.

Country Talc Shaker, 1977 – 1979.
3 oz., gray and blue speckled metal can shaker top. Came In Sweet Honesty or Charisma perfumed talc. CMV, $3.00 MB.

Fuzzy Bear, 1977 – 1979.
Tan flock over clear glass base and head. Came in Sweet Honesty or Occur! CMV, $6.00 MB.

Silver Pear, 1977.
⅔ oz., silver plated over clear glass. Silver top. Came in Sweet Honesty or Charisma. CMV, $4.00 MB.

California Perfume Co. Anniversary Keepsake, 1977 – 1978.
3¾ oz. blue can sold to public with "Avon 1977" on the bottom. CMV, $2.00 MB. Was also given to Avon reps during 91st anniversary with "Anniversary Celebration Avon 1977" on the bottom. CMV, $6.00 MB. Came in Roses Roses or Trailing Arbutus talc.

Autumn Aster Decanter,
1978 – 1980.
¾ oz., clear glass, gold cap. Held Topaze or Sun Blossoms cologne. CMV, $4.00 MB.

Proud Groom,
1978 – 1980.
2 oz., white painted over clear glass. Held Sweet Honesty or Unforgettable cologne. CMV, $9.00 MB.

On the Avenue,
1978 – 1979.
2 oz., blue painted over clear glass. Pink plastic top with lavender hat. White detachable umbrella. Held Topaze or Unforgettable cologne. CMV, $8.00 BO. $10.00 MB.

Dogwood Demi Decanter, 1978 – 1980.
¾ oz., flower shaped bottle, gold flower lid. Came in Apple Blossom, Moonwind, or Topaze cologne. CMV, $4.00 MB.

Good Fairy,
1978 – 1980.
3 oz., clear glass painted blue. Blue plastic top. Plastic wand. Blue and pink fabric purse and wings. Held Delicate Daisies cologne. CMV, $9.00 MB.

Garden Girl,
1978 – 1979.
4 oz., pink painted over clear glass. Held Charisma or Sweet Honesty cologne. CMV, $10.00 MB.

Little Miss Muffet,
1978 – 1980.
2 oz., white painted over milk glass. Came in Sweet Honesty or Topaze. CMV, $8.00 MB.

Dapper Snowman,
1978 – 1979.
1 oz., white milk glass with black painted spots and black hat cap. Held Moonwind or Sweet Honesty cologne. Brown, blue, and red neck scarf. CMV, $4.00 MB.

Church Mouse Bride,
1978 – 1979.
Plastic top with separate white veil. Came in Delicate Daisies cologne. Base is white dull paint over milk glass. CMV $8.00 MB.
Church Mouse Groom, 1979 – 1980.
¾ oz., white glass, white plastic top. Held Delicate Daisies cologne. CMV, $6.00 MB.

Angel Song Decanter,
1978 – 1979.
1 oz., frosted glass base with off-white plastic top. Held Here's My Heart or Charisma cologne. CMV, $8.00 MB.
Angel Song with Mandolin,
1979 – 1980.
1 oz., frosted over clear glass. White plastic top. Held Moonwind or Unforgettable cologne. CMV, $7.00 MB.

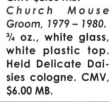

**Jolly Santa,
1978 – 1979.**
1 oz., clear glass, white painted beard. Red cap. Came in Here's My Heart or Topaze cologne. CMV, $3.00.

**Sniffy "Skunk,"
1978 – 1980.**
1¼ oz., black glass, white trim. Held Sweet Honesty or Topaze cologne. CMV, $6.00 MB.

**Royal Siamese Cat,
1978 – 1979.**
Light gray paint over clear glass. 4½ oz., gray plastic head has blue glass jewel eyes. Came in Cotillion or Moonwind cologne. CMV, $8.00 MB.

**Heavenly Music,
1978 – 1980.**
1 oz., clear glass, gold cap. Held Charisma or Topaze cologne. CMV, $4.00 MB.

**Victoriana Soap Dish,
1978.**
Blue marbleized glass, white soap. "May 1978" on bottom. CMV, $10.00 MB, with soap.

**Little Burro,
1978 – 1979.**
1 oz., light gray glass. Straw hat with red or pink flower. Held Sweet Honesty or Charisma cologne. CMV, $5.00 MB.

Victoriana Pitcher and Bowl, 1978.
Blue marbleized glass bowl and 6 oz. pitcher. Held bubble bath. "May 1978" on bottom. CMV, $9.00 MB.

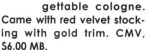

**Peek a Mouse Christmas Stocking,
1978 – 1979.**
1¼ oz., green glass with gold mouse cap. Held Sweet Honesty or Unforgettable cologne. Came with red velvet stocking with gold trim. CMV, $6.00 MB.

**Honey Bee,
1978 – 1980.**
1¼ oz., amber coated over clear glass. Gold bee on lid. Held Honeysuckle or Moonwind cologne. CMV, $4.00 MB.

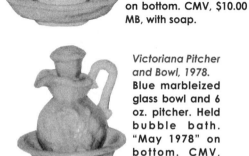

Love Bird, 1978.
1½ oz., milk glass bottle with gold cap. Came in Charisma or Moonwind cologne. CMV, $5.00 MB.

Kangaroo Two, 1978 – 1979.
8" red calico stuffed kangaroo with Avon tag. Green neck ribbon. Came with ¾ oz. frosted glass kangaroo bottle with gold head. Held Topaze or Sweet Honesty cologne. CMV, $4.00 BO. Stuffed toy, $5.00 mint. $10.00 MB for both.

**Baby Bassett Decanter,
1978 – 1979.**
1¼ oz., amber glass and matching plastic head. Held Topaze or Sweet Honesty cologne. CMV, $3.00 MB.

Hudson Manor Collection,
1978 – 1979.
Saltcellar Candle and Spoon.
Silver plated. Came with glass lined candle. Bottom says "HMC Avon Silver Plate" on both pieces. Silver and white box. CMV, $12.00 MB.
Silver Plated Dish and Satin Sachet.
6" silver plated dish with red satin sachet pillow. Bottom of dish says "Avon Silver Plate HMC, Italy." CMV, $10.00 MB.
Silver Plated Hostess Bell.
5½" high silver plated bell. "Avon Silver Plate HMC" on bottom. CMV, $15.00 MB.
Silver Plated Bud Vase and Scented Rose.
8" high silver plated bud vase. Came with long stemmed fabric rose and two Roses Roses pellets. CMV, $10.00 MB.

Scentiments Cologne,
1978 – 1979.
2 oz., clear glass. Came with pink card on front to write your own message. Came in Sweet Honesty or Here's My Heart cologne. CMV, $4.00 MB.

Vintage Year, "Champaign Year,"
1978 – 1979.
2 oz., green glass, gold cap. "1979" embossed on bottom. Came in Sweet Honesty or Wild Country cologne. Green and gold box. CMV, $4.00 MB.

Golden Bamboo Vase,
1978 – 1979.
1 oz., yellow painted over clear glass, black cap, base. Came in Moonwind or Sweet Honesty cologne. CMV, $5.00 MB.

Country Creamery "Milk Can,"
1978 – 1979.
10 oz., white painted over clear glass. Held moisturized hand lotion. CMV, $3.00 MB.

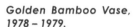

Silver Fawn,
1978 – 1979.
½ oz., silver coated over clear glass. Choice of Sweet Honesty or Charisma cologne. CMV, $5.00 BO. $6.00 MB.

CPC Anniversary Keepsake,
1978 – 1979.
1½ oz., clear glass. Old style CPC label and design. Pink neck ribbon. Came in Trailing Arbutus, Sweet Honesty, or Somewhere cologne. CMV, $5.00 MB.

Sea Fantasy Bud Vase, 1978 – 1979.
6 oz. bottle. Gold and white fish and seaweed design on both sides. Came in three colors. Held Skin So Soft bath oil, bubble bath, or Smooth as Silk. CMV, $4.00 MB.

Dingo Boot, 1978 – 1979.
6 oz., camel tan plastic bottle and cap. Choice of Sweet Honesty body splash or Wild Country after shave. CMV, $2.00 MB.

Scentimental Doll, Adorable Abigail,
1979 – 1980.
4½ oz., clear glass painted beige. Beige plastic top. Came in Régence or Sweet Honesty cologne. CMV, $11.00 MB.

**Mrs. Quackles,
1979 – 1980**
2 oz., clear glass painted off white. Off-white plastic top with white lace and green bonnet. Came in Delicate Daisies cologne. CMV, $7.00 MB.

**Little Jack Horner,
1979 – 1980.**
1½ oz., white glass painted white frosted. Came in Topaze or Roses Roses cologne. CMV, $9.00 MB.

**Festive Facets Decanter,
1979 – 1980.**
1 oz., gold caps. Came in Charisma (red glass), Sweet Honesty (green glass), and Here's My Heart (blue glass). CMV, $6.00 each, MB.

**Sweet Tooth Terrier,
1979 – 1980.**
1 oz., white glass and white plastic top. Came in Topaze or Cotillion cologne. CMV, $7.00 MB.

**Sweet Dreams,
1979 – 1980.**
1¼ oz., blue frosted over clear glass. White plastic boy's head cap. Held Zany or Somewhere cologne. CMV, $7.00 MB.

**Golden Notes (Canary),
1979 – 1980.**
1¾ oz., clear glass coated light yellow, yellow head. Came in Charisma or Moonwind cologne. CMV, $5.00 MB.

**Wedding Flower Maiden,
1979 – 1980.**
1¾ oz., white painted over clear glass. Held Unforgettable or Sweet Honesty cologne. CMV, $9.00 MB.

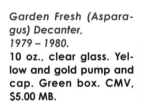

**Garden Fresh (Asparagus) Decanter,
1979 – 1980.**
10 oz., clear glass. Yellow and gold pump and cap. Green box. CMV, $5.00 MB.

**Fuzzy Bunny,
1979 – 1980.**
1 oz., clear glass coated with white flock. Pink ears, orange carrot. Held Sweet Honesty or Honeysuckle cologne. CMV, $6.00 MB.

**Tug-a-Brella,
1979 – 1980.**
2½ oz., clear glass painted yellow, plastic top. Black plastic umbrella on wire. Held Moonwind or Cotillion cologne. CMV, $11.00 MB.

**Merry Christmas Tree Hostess Set,
1979.**
9" high ceramic green tree. Came with Mountain Pine fragrance wax chips and rag doll and Teddy Bear ceramic salt and pepper shakers. This was a very short issue for Christmas 1979. CMV, $30.00 MB, set.

Pretty Piglet, 1979 – 1980.
¾ oz., clear glass. Held Roses Roses, pink cap; Honeysuckle, yellow cap; or Hawaiian White Ginger, blue-green cap. Fabric flowers around necks. CMV, $5.00 MB.

Merry Mouse, 1979 – 1980.
¾ oz., white milk glass bottle and head. Stick-on holly leaf. Choice of Zany or Cotillion cologne. CMV, $6.00 MB.

Christmas Bells, 1979 – 1980.
1 oz., red glass. Silver cap. Held Topaze or Sweet Honesty cologne. CMV, $3.00 MB.

Monkey Shines, 1979 – 1980.
1 oz., clear glass painted light gray, brown eyes and ears. Red cap and neck strap. Held Sonnet or Moonwind cologne. CMV, $6.00 MB.

Precious Chickadee, 1979 – 1980.
1 oz., white glass. Red and white cap. Came in Here's My Heart or Sun Blossoms cologne. CMV, $5.00 MB.

Red Cardinal, 1979 – 1980.
2 oz., clear glass painted red. Red cap. Held Bird of Paradise or Charisma cologne. CMV, $6.00 MB.

Bon Bon, 1979 – 1980.
¾ oz., dark amber glass. Pink and green top came with Sweet Honesty cologne, or Cotillion with yellow and green top. CMV, $5.00 MB.

Snug Cub, 1979 – 1980.
1 oz., milk glass. Green cap. Pink and green paint. Came in Occur! or Sweet Honesty cologne. CMV, $5.00 MB. Reissued in 1987 with green cap. Same CMV.

Snow Owl Powder Sachet II, 1979 – 1980.
1¼ oz., frosted glass. Held Moonwind or Timeless powder sachet. Blue Rhinestone eyes. Label in black lettering. CMV, $7.00 MB.

Gentle Foal, 1979 – 1980.
1½ oz., dark amber glass and plastic head. Came in Charisma or Sun Blossoms cologne. CMV, $5.00 MB.

Rocking Horse Tree Ornament, 1979 – 1980.
¾ oz., clear glass rocker shaped bottle with gold plastic rocking horse top. Bottom of horse says "1979." Held Sweet Honesty or Moonwind cologne. CMV, $7.00 MB.

Cute Cookie, 1979 – 1980. 1 oz., dark amber glass. Pink cap and point. Held Hello Sunshine cologne. CMV, $3.00 MB.

Charming Chipmunk, 1979 – 1980. 5 oz., clear glass painted frosted peach color. Held Field Flowers or Sweet Honesty. CMV, $4.00 MB.

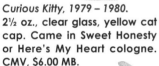

Curious Kitty, 1979 – 1980. 2½ oz., clear glass, yellow cat cap. Came in Sweet Honesty or Here's My Heart cologne. CMV, $6.00 MB.

Flower Fancy, 1979 – 1980. 1¼ oz., clear glass, gold flower cap. Held Field Flowers or Roses Roses. CMV, $5.00 MB.

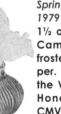

Spring Song, 1979 – 1980. 1½ oz., clear glass. Came with plastic frosted flower stopper. Came in Lily of the Valley or Sweet Honesty cologne. CMV, $6.00 MB.

Avonshire Bath Oil Decanter, 1979. 6 oz., clear glass painted blue and white. Held Skin So Soft. "R" on bottom for reissue and dated May 1979. CMV, $8.00 MB.

Avonshire Hostess Soaps, 1979. Blue box held three white bars. CMV, $9.00 MB. See page 88 for more products.

Anniversary Keepsake Eau de Toilette, 1979. Large 8 oz. clear glass bottle. "CPC" embossed on back side. "Avon 1979" on bottom. Gold cap. Pink and green box. Came in Trailing Arbutus cologne. Pink neck ribbon. CMV, $10.00 MB.

Lady Skater Perfumed Talc, 1979 – 1980. 3¾ oz., gold top can. Red cap. Choice of Ariane or Sweet Honesty talc. CMV, $2.00 mint. No box issued.

Gentleman Skater Talc for Men, 1979 – 1980. 3¾ oz., gold top can. Blue cap. Choice of Clint or Trazarra talc. CMV, $2.00 mint. No box issued.

Avonshire Decanter, 1979. 6 oz., clear glass painted blue and white. Held Charisma or Somewhere cologne. "R" on bottom for reissue, and dated May 1979. CMV, $9.00 MB.

Country Style Coffee Pot, 1979 – 1980. Came in special color of box. 10 oz., clear glass painted red, green, blue, or yellow. Held moisturized hand lotion. Came with matching hand pump. CMV, $8.00 MB.

Anniversary Keepsake CPC Flacon, 1979.
¾ oz., clear glass. Silver cap has 1979 on top. Came with Sweet Honesty or Trailing Arbutus cologne. CMV, $8.00 MB.

Christmas Soldier, 1980.
¾ oz., clear glass, gold cap. Choice of Sportif, Sweet Honesty, Charisma, or Moonwind. CMV, $6.00 MB.

Little Dream Girl, 1980 – 1981.
1¼ oz., aqua paint over clear glass. Cream color top. Choice of Sweet Honesty or Occur! cologne. CMV, $5.00 MB.

Rollin' Great Roller Skate, 1980 – 1981.
2 oz., glass, red top. Choice of Zany or Lover Boy cologne. CMV, $5.00 MB.

Owl Miniature, 1980 – 1981.
⅜ oz., clear glass, gold owl cap. Choice of Tasha, Ariane, Candid, or Timeless. CMV, $5.00 MB.

Bundle of Fun, 1980 – 1981.
¾ oz., light blue paint over clear glass. Sits on red plastic sled. Choice of Hello Sunshine cologne or Sure Winner bracing lotion. CMV, $5.00 MB.

Song of Christmas, 1980.
¼ oz., frosted glass. Red cap. Choice of Moonwind, Sweet Honesty, or Bird of Paradise. CMV, $4.00 MB.

Seahorse Miniature, 1980 – 1981.
½ oz., clear glass, gold cap. Choice of Sweet Honesty, Charisma, Occur!, or Moonwind. CMV, $5.00 MB.

Cologne-Go-Round, 1980.
½ oz., clear glass, gold cap. Choice of Roses Roses, Honeysuckle, Hawaiian White Ginger, or Field Flowers. CMV, $4.00 MB.

Porcelain Floral Bouquet, 1980.
4" high, dated 1980 on bottom. CMV, $18.00 MB.

Huggable Hippo, 1980.
1¾ oz., white glass. Red hat. Held Zany cologne or Light Musk after shave. Came with card of stick-on decals. CMV, $5.00 MB.

Green-Blue-Brown-Eyed Susan Compact, 1980.
Three different color centers with yellow flower rim. CMV, $2.00 each, MB.

Flower Mouse, 1980 – 1981.
¾ oz., dull red paint over clear glass and white and yellow mouse cap. Choice of Cotillion or Zany cologne. CMV, $4.00 MB.

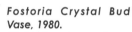

Fostoria Crystal Bud Vase, 1980.
6" high, clear glass. Dated 1980 on bottom. Came with white scented carnation. CMV, $13.00 MB.

Precious Hearts, 1980.
Heart embossed clear glass, 5 oz. gold tone cap. Came in Here's My Heart, Unforgettable, Moonwind, Topaze, or Sweet Honesty. CMV, $2.00 MB.

Frisky Friends, 1981.
Three different frosted 1 oz. glass cats. Blue cap bottle contained Honeysuckle, yellow cap bottle had Roses Roses, and pink cap bottle held Hawaiian White Ginger. CMV, $6.00 each, MB.

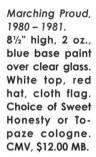

Marching Proud, 1980 – 1981.
8½" high, 2 oz., blue base paint over clear glass. White top, red hat, cloth flag. Choice of Sweet Honesty or Topaze cologne. CMV, $12.00 MB.

Fluffy Chick, 1980.
1 oz., clear glass, yellow flock coated. Held Hello Sunshine cologne. CMV, $4.00 MB.

Heavenly Angel, 1981.
½ oz., blue glass angel, silver cap. Choice of Ariane, Candid, or Timeless. Red box dated 1981. CMV, $4.00 MB.

Fluttering Fancy, 1980.
1 oz., clear glass with pink butterfly on yellow frosted plastic cap. Held Sweet Honesty or Charisma cologne. CMV, $5.00 MB.

Love Chimes, 1981 – 1982.
½ oz., clear glass, bell shape, gold cap. Choice of Roses Roses, Charisma, Moonwind, or Sweet Honesty. CMV, $3.00 MB.

Crystal Clear Hostess Decanter, 1980 – 1981.
Clear glass jar and glass lid, Avon stainless spoon. Came in 5½ oz. Strawberry bubble bath gelee. CMV, $6.00 MB.

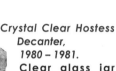

Bearing Gifts Lip Balm, 1981 – 1982.
Small fuzzy bear, head turns, held red and green lip balm in red box. CMV, $5.00 MB.

Winged Princess, 1981.
½ oz., swan shaped iridescent glass, gold cap. Choice of Occur!, Charisma, or Sweet Honesty. Box dated 1981. CMV, $4.00 MB.

Oops Cologne Decanter, 1981.
White glass, brown spots. Ice cream bottle with tan plastic cone top. 1½ oz., came with Sweet Honesty or Country Breeze. CMV, $6.00 MB.

Prima Ballerina, 1981.
Pink frosted glass over clear glass, 1 oz. Choice of Zany or Sweet Honesty. Bottle and box label dated 1981. CMV, $7.00 MB.

Holiday Hostess Collection Platter, 1981.
11" clear glass, holly and berry decal. Plate does not say Avon. CMV, $15.00 MB.
Holiday Hostess Compote, 1981.
4" high, clear glass, holly decoration. "Avon" on bottom. CMV, $12.00 MB.
Holiday Hostess Candlesticks, 1981.
3" high, clear glass, holly decoration. "Avon" on bottom. Set of two. CMV, $12.00 MB, set.

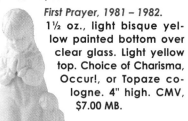

First Prayer, 1981 – 1982.
1½ oz., light bisque yellow painted bottom over clear glass. Light yellow top. Choice of Charisma, Occur!, or Topaze cologne. 4" high. CMV, $7.00 MB.

Ultra Crystal Cologne, 1981 – 1982.
Gray box held 2 oz. clear glass and glass cap. Choice of Tasha, Foxfire, Timeless, or Ariane. CMV, $3.00 MB. See Women's Soaps and Candles sections for other Ultra Crystal collections.

Precious Priscilla, 1982 – 1983.
3 oz., pale pink paint over clear glass. Plastic head top. Held Sweet Honesty or Moonwind. CMV, $10.00 MB.

Nostalgic Glow, 1981 – 1982.
1 oz., clear glass lamp bottom, blue plastic shade top. Choice of Moonwind, Wild Jasmine, or Topaze. CMV, $6.00 MB.

Stylish Lady Decanter, 1982 – 1983.
8 oz., white glass pig with white and pink pump top. Choice of Country Orchard liquid cleanser or moisturized hand lotion. CMV, $9.00 MB.

Big Spender, 1981 – 1982.
1 oz., green glass, silver cap. Light Musk for men or Sweet Honesty cologne. CMV, $5.00 MB.

Nature's Best Wooden Display Spoon Holder, 1981 – 1982.
Made of wood, 3½" x 7". Does not say Avon. Came in Avon box. CMV, $7.00 MB.
Nature's Best Collector's Spoons, 1981 – 1982.
Four different stainless spoons with Avon on them. 5" long, in flannel pouch. Porcelain inlaid with fruit — strawberries, oranges, plums, and raspberries. CMV, $10.00 each, MB.

Anniversary Keepsake — Men, 1981 – 1982.
Replica of California Perfume Co. Bay Rum after shave. 3 oz., clear glass with glass top in plastic cork. Came to Avon managers as a demo, empty and marked "Not for Sale." CMV, $6.00 MB.

Soft Swirls Bath Decanter, 1981 – 1982.
8 oz., clear glass, frosted cap. Choice of Smooth as Silk bath oil or Skin So Soft. CMV, $8.00 MB.

American Heirloom Ships Decanter, 1981 – 1982.
6 oz., clear glass top. Choice of Wild Country after shave or Sweet Honesty body splash. CMV, $9.00 MB.

Anniversary Keepsake — Women, 1981 – 1982.
3 oz., clear glass CPC replica of 1908 design. Held White Lilac cologne. Dated 1981. CMV, $6.00 MB. Came to Avon managers as a demo, empty and marked "Not for Sale." CMV, $10.00 MB.

Huggable Hop-a-Long, 1982. 1 oz., green glass frog. Plastic hat. Came with 20 stick-on decals. Choice of Sweet Honesty for girls or Light Musk for boys. CMV, $5.00 MB.

Humpty Dumpty Bank, 1982. Box held ceramic bank made in Korea for Avon. Dated 1982. Sold empty. 5" high. CMV, $7.00 MB.

Crystallique Tree, 1982. ½ oz. clear glass tree bottle with bronze color cap. Choice of Foxfire, Timeless, or Odyssey cologne. CMV, $3.00 MB.

Autumn Scurry Squirrel, 1982 – 1983. ½ oz., clear glass squirrel, gold cap. Choice of Moonwind, Topaze, or Charisma cologne. CMV, $2.00 MB.

Pierrette Cologne, 1982 – 1983. 1¾ oz. bottle, black and white. Choice of Charisma or Occur! CMV, $10.00 MB.

Pierrot Cologne, 1982 – 1983. 1¾ oz. bottle, black and white. Choice of Charisma or Occur! CMV, $10.00 MB.

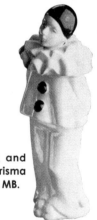

Fragrance Notables, 1982. ½ oz., clear glass with ribbon design. Red cap and box. Choice of Wild Jasmine, Occur!, Moonwind, Charisma, Topaze, or Sweet Honesty cologne. CMV, $2.00 MB.

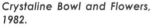

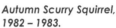

Emerald Accent Collection Decanter, 1982 – 1983. 10" high, clear glass, green glass stopper. CMV, $15.00 MB.
Emerald Accent Collection Cordial Glasses. Set of two clear glasses with green glass stems, 4½" high. CMV, $13.00 MB, set.
Emerald Accent Collection Serving Tray. 11½" long green glass tray. CMV, $15.00 MB.

Crystaline Bowl and Flowers, 1982. Pink box held 5" long glass bowl with plastic insert to hold artificial flowers. Came with fragrance tablet. CMV, $12.00 MB.

McConnell's Corner Town Tree, 1982. 8" high ceramic tree, green and white. Dated "Christmas 1982." CMV, $13.00 MB.

Lip Topping Lip Gloss, 1982 – 1983.
Tin box held choice of Chocolate Fudge or Butterscotch. CMV, $1.00 each.

Gingerbread Cottage, 1983 – 1984.
½ oz., dark amber glass, pink cap. Choice of Sweet Honesty or Charisma cologne. 2" high. CMV, $2.00 MB.

Pierre Decanter, 1984.
8 oz., white glass pig. Cloth apron on front. Held Care Deeply hand lotion. CMV, $5.00 MB.

Write Touch Mouse, 1982 – 1983.
1 oz., green glass and white plastic mouse with stick-on decals. Choice of Sweet Honesty or Charisma cologne. CMV, $6.00 MB.

Fragrance Keepsake, 1983.
½ oz., fan shaped clear glass, with rose red cap. Choice of Somewhere, Here's My Heart, Régence, Rapture, Persian Wood, Brocade, or Cotillion. CMV, $2.00 MB.

Statue of Liberty Brass Stamp, 1985.
"1886 – 1986" on wood base. CMV, $7.00 MB.

Mom's Pride and Joy Picture Frame, 1983.
6½" x 2", clear glass frame. CMV, $10.00 MB.

Hospitality Spoon Series, 1985.
Wood rack with four spoons — Italian Grapes, German Maiden, Scottish Thistle, and American Pineapple. CMV, $6.00 each piece. $30.00 MB, set with rack.

Heart Strings Decanter, 1983.
½ oz., red glass with gold cap. Choice of three fragrances. CMV, $3.00 MB.

Country Chicken, 1987.
9½ oz., white ceramic bottle with pump. Held hand lotion. CMV, $4.00 MB.

Angel's Melody Decanter, 1987. 8" high angel. Held 3 oz. of cologne. CMV, $8.00 MB.

Gift of Love Crystal Box, 1988. 1¼" high, 2¾" wide glass box. CMV, $10.00 MB.

Crystal Treasure Box, 1990. 2¾" square, 1¾" high, clear lead crystal box. CMV, $12.00 MB.

Meadow Blossoms Decanter, 1987. 1¾ oz. frosted glass bottle, porcelain flower top. Held cologne. CMV, $8.00 MB.

Country Goose Decanter, 1988. 4¾" high. Held 1¾ oz. cologne. Ceramic goose head. Wicker hat, cotton dress. CMV, $8.00 MB.

Seashell Decanter, 1990. 2 oz. seashell. Held Skin So Soft bath oil. CMV, $4.00 MB.

Hearts from the Heart, 1987. Heart shaped lead crystal dish and eight pink heart shaped bath pearls. CMV, $8.00 MB.

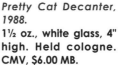

Pretty Cat Decanter, 1988. 1½ oz., white glass, 4" high. Held cologne. CMV, $6.00 MB.

Delicate Wings Butterfly Box, 1992. Lead crystal dish and lid. 4½" x 3¼" x 1¼". Short issue. CMV, $10.00 MB.

Purrfect Cat, 1987. 1½ oz. cologne. Black glass. CMV, $5.00 MB.

Forget Me Not Box, 1989. Heart shaped porcelain box and matching pin. CMV, $8.00 MB.

Be My Valentine Cologne Splash, 1995. Red box held ½ oz., heart shaped bottle, gold cap. Choice of nine fragrances. Sold two times only. Must be in box shown. CMV, $2.00 MB.

Confections Jar, 1988. Lead crystal glass jar, 5¾" high. CMV, $15.00 MB.

American Favorites Porcelain Spoon Collection, 1989. Porcelain spoons on wood rack. Daffodil, Day Lily, Rose, and Pansy. CMV, $10.00 each, MB. $5.00 MB, rack.

Atlanta "Olympic" Decanter, 1996. 7¾" high, 5 oz., frosted glass with gold flame cap. Held Imari cologne. CMV, $20.00 MB.

Nativity Figurines

The Donkey, 1984.
3" high. CMV, $20.00 MB.

Holy Family, 1981.
Mary, 4" high; Joseph, 6" high; Baby Jesus in manger, 2½" long. CMV, $47.50 MB, set of three.

The Shepherd, 1983.
6½" high. CMV, $22.50 MB.

The Camel, 1984.
4¾" high. CMV, $28.00 MB.

The Magi (Three Wise Men), 1982.
Kaspar, 7½"; Melchior, 4½"; Balthasar, 6½". CMV, $25.00 each, MB.

The Shepherd Boy, 1983.
4¾" high. CMV, $22.00 MB.

Nativity Ornament Collection, 1985.
All white porcelain. The Three Magi, the Holy Family, and the Shepherd. CMV, $12.00 each, MB.

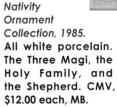

Heavenly Blessings Nativity Collection, 1986 – 1989.
All hand-painted pastel porcelain figurines, marked "Avon."
The Three Magi: Balthasar, 3½" high, Kaspar, 3¾" high, Melchior, 3½" high. CMV, $10.00 each, MB. *"Little Drummer Boy,"* 3¼" high, CMV, $10.00 MB. Angel, 3" high. CMV, $10.00 MB. Boy Angel, 2½" high, CMV, $10.00 MB. *The Holy Family:* Mary, 2½" high, Baby Jesus in Manger, 2½" long, Joseph, 3¼" high. Sold as set of three. CMV, $25.00 MB, set. Camel, 3¼" high. CMV, $10.00 MB. Donkey, 2¾" high. CMV, $10.00 MB. Sheep, 1¾" high. CMV, $10.00 MB.

Holy Family Nativity Figurines, 1986.
Porcelain figurines, 2½" to 3¾" high. Mary, Joseph, and Baby Jesus in manger. Set of three. CMV, $47.00 MB, set.

The Sheep, 1983.
4" long. CMV, $16.00 MB.

Nativity Angel and Stable, 1985.
White porcelain angel and plastic stable. CMV, $75.00 MB, set.

The Cow, 1987.
5½" long. CMV, $20.00 MB.

The Cherub, 1989.
3" high. CMV, $25.00 MB.

Poor Man, 1990.
3½" high. CMV, $35.00 MB.

*Standing Angel,
1987.*
6" high. CMV,
$25.00 MB.

*Woman with Water
Jar, 1990.*
6¾" high. CMV, $35.00
MB.

O Holy Night Three Kings Set, 1989.
Hand painted bisque porcelain.
Melchior and Balthasar each 3½"
high. Kaspar is 2⅝" high. CMV,
$15.00 each, MB.

*O Holy Night Nativity
Collection, 1989.*
Made of porcelain.
Background creche,
5¼" high. CMV, $15.00
MB. Baby Jesus, 1⅝"
long, Mary, 2¾" high,
Joseph, 3½" high. Set
of three. CMV, $25.00
MB, set.

*Nativity Wood Stand,
1988.*
11" wide. CMV, $25.00
MB.

Children in Prayer, 1991.
4" high. CMV, $30.00 MB.

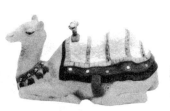

Gabriel, 1992.
7" high. CMV,
$65.00 MB.

*O Holy Night Nativity Set — Camel, Shepherd
Boy, and Lamb, 1990.*
Both are bisque porcelain and dated on bottom.
CMV, $13.00 each, MB.

The Innkeeper, 1988.
4½" high. CMV, $25.00
MB.

Nativity Collection, The Blessed Family, 1992.
High glazed porcelain figurines. Baby Jesus, 2" high; Mary, 4" high; and Joseph, 6¾" high. Set of three. CMV, $50.00 MB, set.

Bethlehem Nativity, "Ox," 1994.
4¾" long, 2¾" high porcelain ox, dated 1994. CMV, $20.00 MB.
Bethlehem Nativity, "Camel," 1994.
5½" long, 4" high porcelain camel with blue blanket, dated 1994. CMV, $25.00 MB.

Nativity Heirloom Collection, "Holy Family," 1996.
Hand-painted resin and dated 1996. Joseph, 4¾" high; Mary, 3½" high; Baby Jesus, 1¼" high, 2½" long. Sold as set of three. CMV, $35.00 MB, set.

Bethlehem Nativity Collection, The Magi, 1993.
Three blue painted shiny porcelain figurines. Gaspar, 6½" high; Melchior, 6½" high, Balthasar, 4¾" high. CMV, $35.00 each, MB.

Nativity Heirloom Collection, "Magi," 1996.
Melchior, 5" high, Gaspar, 4⅛" high, Balthasar, 3¼" high. Sold as set of three. CMV, $35.00 MB, set.

Shepherd with Lamb, 1993.
6" high, bisque porcelain. CMV, $25.00 MB.

Nativity Heirloom Collection, "Angel," 1996.
Hand-painted resin, 5" high. Dated 1996 on bottom. CMV, $15.00 MB.

Child's Nativity Collection, "My First Christmas Story," 1993 – 1995.
All are made of plastic and are 1½" to 3" high. Three different sets. Holy Family in choice of white or black family, Baby Jesus, Mary, and Joseph. The Wise Men, three different men. The Animals, Cow, Donkey, and Sheep. CMV, $10.00 each set, MB.

Nativity Heirloom Collection, "Shepherds," 1996.
Hand-painted resin. Each is dated 1996. "Praying Shepherd," 4¾" high; "Boy," 4¼" high; and "Lamb," 1½" high. Sold as set of three. CMV, $35.00 MB, set.

Nativity, "Divine Ornament," 2000.
3½" high manger scene on gold cord. It has a battery and plays *Silent Night*, and the star lights up on top of the manger. CMV, $10.00 MB.

Nativity Drummer Boy and Donkey Figurine, 2003.
Porcelain, 4" high, 3" wide. OSP, $10.00. CMV, $10.00 MB.

Nativity, "Christmas Blessings," 2005.
6¼" high, white bisque, gold trim. OSP, $15.00. CMV, $15.00 MB.

All pieces are painted bisque porcelain.
Left: Nativity, "Three Kings," 2002 – 2003.
6" high, 5" wide.
Center: Nativity "Holy Family," 2002 – 2003.
8" high, 6" wide. Joseph, Mary, and Baby Jesus in the manger.
Right: Nativity "Shepherds," 2002 – 2003.
6" high, 4" wide. Avon sold these as a set or by the piece. They fit together as one scene. CMV, $20.00 each piece. $50.00 MB, set of three.

Christmas Ornaments

All Avon Christmas tree ornaments must be marked "Avon" and dated to be collectible. Avon has made a lot of tree ornaments but most are not marked Avon or dated. Warning! Precious Moments and Cherished Teddies ornaments are made by Enesco, not Avon Products, Inc. They are not marked Avon on the product. They are not included in this book. Consult Precious Moments or Cherished Teddies books for information.

Melvin P. Merrymouse, 1982.
Small plastic mouse dressed as Santa. Back of mirror says "Avon Christmas, 1982." CMV, $10.00 MB.

Christmas Remembrance, Wreath, 1980.
White ceramic, gold tassel. Dated 1980. 3" across. First in series. CMV, $10.00 MB.

Christmas Remembrance, Dove, 1981.
White ceramic, gold cord. Second in series. CMV, $10.00 MB.

Christmas Remembrance, Angel, 1982.
White ceramic angel, gold tassel. Came in white felt bag. Third in series. CMV, $10.00 MB.

Merry Christmas Ornament Card, 1985.
Christmas card held 3" porcelain ornament. CMV, $8.00 MB.

Peace Dove, 1989.
3½" silver plate ornament with small dove in the center. Dated 1989. CMV, $10.00 MB.

Melvin P. Merrymouse Keepsake Ornament, 1983.
2¾" high, Santa mouse on sleigh. Dated 1983. Plastic, second in series. CMV, $8.00 MB.

Christmas Remembrance, Snowflake, 1983.
White porcelain snowflake dated 1983. 2½" wide, gold tassel. Fourth in series. CMV, $10.00 MB.

"Baby's First Christmas," 1986.
4" high, white porcelain, by Joan Walsh Anglund. CMV, $10.00 MB.

Christmas Tree Ornament, 1987.
Clear lead crystal, dated 1987. Gold tassel. CMV, $10.00 MB.

Sparkling Angel, 1990.
Silver plate angel with gold 1990 star. 3¼" high. CMV, $10.00 MB.

Captured Moments Frame Ornament, 1983.
Green and red plastic wreath. Photo could be slid into center. 4" across. CMV, $5.00 MB.

Fostoria Ornaments, 1985.
Christmas village, Christmas tree, or angel ornament. CMV, $7.00 each, MB.

Baby's First Christmas, "Love From Above," 1989.
Quarter moon and baby porcelain ornament. Dated 1989. 3½" high. CMV, $12.00 MB.

"Baby's First Christmas," 1991.
"First Christmas Together," 1991.
Both ornaments are white bisque porcelain and dated 1991. CMV, $10.00 each, MB.

"Our First Christmas Together," 1992. 3" bisque porcelain. Dated 1992. CMV, $10.00 MB.

"Baby's First Christmas," 1992. Bisque porcelain, 3¾" high. Baby carriage. Dated 1992. CMV, $10.00 MB.

"Dashing Through the Snow," 1992 3⅝" silver plate deer ornament. Dated 1992. Came with flannel pouch. CMV, $10.00 MB.

"First Christmas Together," 1993. Two kittens in porcelain white and gold socks. Dated 1993. CMV, $10.00 MB.

"Baby's First Christmas," 1993. 3", white bisque porcelain with green ribbon. Dated 1993. CMV, $10.00 MB.

"Father Christmas," 1993. 3½" high, pewter in red felt pouch. First in series. CMV, $10.00.

"Our First Christmas Together," 1994. 4" high, 3¼" wide, porcelain. Dated and marked "Avon." CMV, $10.00 MB.

"Baby's First Christmas," 1994. 4" high, 2¼" wide, porcelain. Dated and marked "Avon." CMV, $10.00 MB.

"Santa's Arrival," 1994. 3½" high, pewter. Red bag. CMV, $10.00 MB.

"St. Nicholas," 1995. Red felt bag held pewter Santa, dated 1995 and marked Avon. 3" long, 2¾" high. CMV, $10.00.

"Baby's First Christmas," 1995. 3½" high, pink, white, and blue. Dated 1995. CMV, $10.00 MB.

Commemorative Christmas Tree Ornament, 1995. Brass oval, 2½" wide, 3" high. Says "Christmas 1995." CMV, $15.00 MB.

Santa Ornament, 1996. 2⅜" wide, 3¼" high, pewter. Dated 1996. CMV $10.00 MB.

"Baby's First Christmas," 1996.
Bisque porcelain, dated 1996. 4⅛" high, 2⅜" wide. CMV, $10.00 MB.

Season's Joy, 1997.
White resin ornaments, 4½" high each. Choice of "Mother and Child," "Angel," or "Nativity." CMV, $8.00 each, MB.

Barbie, Marzipan Nutcracker, 1999.
Third in series. 5¾" high, porcelain, with green fabric ballet dress. Choice of black or white. Came with Avon certificate of authenticity. CMV, $15.00 MB.

"Baby's First Christmas," 1997.
4" high, porcelain. Dated 1997. CMV, $8.00 MB.

Barbie, Swan Queen, 1998.
Second in series. 5" high, porcelain, with fabric and lace ballet dress. Choice of black or white. Came with Avon certificate of authenticity. CMV, $15.00 MB.

Peaceful Millennium Ornament, 2000.
3½", pewter, on red cord. Dated 2000 and marked "Avon" on the back. CMV, $10.00 MB.

Santa, 1997.
4" wide, pewter, dated 1997. Came in a felt pouch. CMV, $8.00 MB.

Star of Bethlehem Nativity Ornament, 1998.
3" porcelain, with Madonna and Child on gold ribbon. Cubic zirconia embedded as the star. Marked "Avon" and dated 1998 on back. CMV, $10.00 MB.

Barbie, Sugar Plum Fairy, 1997.
First in series. 5½" high, porcelain. Fabric skirt. Came with Avon certificate of authenticity. CMV, $15.00 MB.

Season of Peace, 1999.
2½" high, 2¼" wide pewter, with red hanging ribbon. Dated 1999. CMV, $10.00 MB.

Partridge Ornament, 2001.
3½" pewter. Dated 2001 on front and marked "Avon" on back. Blue cord. CMV, $10.00 MB.

"Visit with Santa,"
2001.
2¾", porcelain.
Gold trim. CMV,
$5.00 MB.

Reindeer, 2006.
4" high, pewter, marked
"Avon" and dated 2006.
OSP, $10.00. CMV,
$10.00.

Sleigh, 2003.
3" wide, porcelain,
dated 2003. OSP,
$6.00. CMV, $6.00.

Angel, 2002.
3½" pewter.
Dated 2002 on
front and marked
"Avon" on back.
Blue cord. CMV,
$10.00 MB.

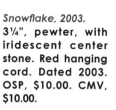

Snowflake, 2003.
3¼", pewter, with
iridescent center
stone. Red hanging
cord. Dated 2003.
OSP, $10.00. CMV,
$10.00.

Berta Hummel "Perfect
Fit" Ornament, 2002.
3¼" x 2¾", bisque por-
celain. Made only for
Avon. Dated 2002.
Marked "Berta Hummel"
on back. CMV, $15.00
MB.

Wreath, 2005.
3½" high, 2½" wide.
Dated 2005. Came in
red velvet-like pouch.
OSP, $10.00. CMV,
$10.00.

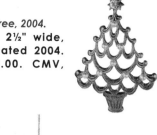

Present, 2006.
3½" high, porcelain.
OSP, $7.00. CMV,
$7.00.

Hot Air Balloon, 2002.
3½" high, porcelain.
Music chip plays Jingle
Bells. CMV, $8.00 MB.

Christmas Tree, 2004.
3¼" high, 2½" wide,
pewter. Dated 2004.
OSP, $10.00. CMV,
$10.00 MB.

Rocking Horse, 2002.
3½" high, porcelain.
Music chip plays Jin-
gle Bells. CMV, $8.00
MB.

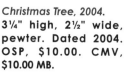

"Key for Santa,"
2006.
4" long, gold tone.
Red hanging rib-
bon. CMV, $5.00.

Christmas Tree, 2003.
3" high, porcelain.
Dated 2003. OSP,
$6.00. CMV, $6.00.

Stocking, 2006.
3½" high, porcelain.
OSP, $7.00. CMV,
$7.00.

Dolls, Porcelain

The only Avon dolls that will be featured in this book are those with porcelain heads, hands, and feet. Stuffed dolls are not included. See the Mrs. Albee and Avon Lady Doll Awards section for Mrs. P.F.E. Albee Barbie dolls. See the Christmas Ornaments section for Barbie ornaments. All Barbie dolls from Avon must be in their Avon boxes to be collectible.

American Heirloom Doll, 1981. 11" high fabric doll with porcelain head. Blue ribbon around waist. CMV, $16.00 MB.

Rapunzel Fairy Tale Doll, 1986. 8" tall doll with porcelain head, feet, and hands. Lavender dress, gold trim. Blonde hair. CMV, $25.00 MB.

Southern Bell Porcelain Doll, 1988. 8¼" high, pink and blue dress, on metal stand. CMV, $30.00 MB.

Victorian Collector Doll, 1983 – 1984. 8" high, nineteenth century doll with porcelain head, arms, and legs. Came with metal stand. Fancy box. CMV, $25.00 MB.

Snow Angel Tree Topper Doll, 1986. 10½" high. Head and hands are porcelain. Blue lace dress. CMV, $12.00 MB.

Roaring Twenties Doll, 1989. 8" high porcelain doll, black dress. Feather boa. On metal stand. CMV, $30.00 MB.

Cinderella Fairy Tale Doll, 1984. 9¼" high, porcelain face, hands, and feet. Blue dress. Blonde hair. On stand. CMV, $25.00 MB.

Early American Doll, 1987. 8½" doll with green skirt, white apron. CMV, $18.00 MB.

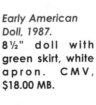

Fairy Princess Porcelain Doll, 1989. 8½" high, blue and white dress. On metal stand. CMV, $30.00 MB.

Little Red Riding Hood Doll, 1985. 8¼" high, porcelain face, hands, and feet. Red cape, on metal stand. CMV, $25.00 MB.

Victorian Fashion of American Times Porcelain Doll, 1987. 8¾" high, on metal stand. CMV, $25.00 MB.

Colleen from Ireland International Doll, 1990. First in series. Porcelain doll, 8" high, on metal stand. CMV, $35.00 MB.

Lupita Mexican International Doll, 1990.
Second in series. 8" tall doll with porcelain head, feet, and hands. On metal stand. CMV, $35.00 MB.

"Ballet Recital," 1991. 9¾" tall child has porcelain face, arms, and legs. Pink satin ballet dress. Metal stand. First in Childhood Dreams Series. CMV, $35.00 MB.

"Howdy Partner," 1993. Fifth in Childhood Dreams Series. Cowboy doll has porcelain head, hands, and feet. 10" high, on metal stand. CMV, $40.00 MB.

Masako International Doll, 1990.
Third in series. 9" high Japanese doll on metal stand. Has porcelain head, hands, and feet. CMV, $35.00 MB.

"Grand Slammers," 1991. Second in Childhood Dreams Series. 9½" high. First male doll made by Avon. Porcelain face, legs, and arms. Wood bat, metal stand. CMV, $35.00 MB.
"Grand Slammers," 1993. Female version of 1991 doll. Porcelain face, legs, and arms. Wood bat, metal stand. CMV, $35.00 MB.

Nigerian Adama International Doll, 1990.
Fourth in series. 8½" high doll. Porcelain head, hands, and feet. On metal stand. CMV, $35.00 MB.

"Skating Party," 1991.
Third in Childhood Dreams Series. 9" tall porcelain doll. Knit fabric clothes. CMV, $35.00 MB.

"Sunday Best," 1993. Sixth in Childhood Dreams Series. 9" high black doll. Porcelain arms, head, and legs. On metal stand. CMV, $40.00 MB.

Tasime Sioux Woman International Doll, 1991.
Last in International Doll series. 9" high. Face, arms, and legs are porcelain. Fabric body and clothes. Metal stand. CMV, $35.00 MB.

"Kitty Love," 1993. Fourth in Childhood Dreams Series. Porcelain head, arms, and legs. Fabric body, purple dress. Metal stand. 9¼" high doll. CMV, $40.00 MB.

"Favorite Dolly," 1993. Seventh in Childhood Dreams Series. 9½" tall, porcelain head, hands, and legs. Red coat, black and white checkered dress. On metal stand. CMV, $40.00 MB.

"Grand Slammers," 1994.
Eighth in Childhood Dreams Series. 9½" tall black baseball doll. Came with ball and wooden bat. Porcelain head, arms, and legs. On metal stand. CMV, $40.00 MB.

"First Day of School," 1995.
Third in Tender Memories Series. 14" high, black or white doll. Red and white dress. On metal stand. Dated 1995. CMV, $40.00 MB.

African Princess and Prince, 1996.
Each 14" high doll has yellow and reddish brown dress and hats. With metal display stands. Each is dated 1996. CMV, $30.00 each, MB.

"Ballet Recital," 1994.
Ninth in Childhood Dreams Series. 9½" tall black ballet doll. Porcelain head, arms, and legs. On metal stand. Pink lace dress. CMV, $40.00 MB.

"Batter Up," 1995.
Fourth in Tender Memories Series. 14" tall. Black or white doll. Porcelain look vinyl head, hands, and legs. Fabric body, blue, green, and white uniform. Doll is numbered and marked "AVON." Metal stand. CMV, $40.00 MB.

Barbie Doll, 1996.
First in a series made only for Avon. Came in white or black doll. Pink dress with yellow hat and waist ribbon. Yellow shoes. 11½" tall. CMV, $35.00 MB.

"First School Play," "Angel" Doll, 1994.
First in Tender Memories Series. 14" tall doll with porcelain look vinyl head, hands, and legs. Fabric body. Metal stand, white and gold dress. CMV, $40.00 MB.

Menelik African Prince Doll, 1995.
11½" high doll. Orange clothes. CMV, $13.00 MB.

Barbie Doll, "Winter Velvet," 1996.
Made only for Avon. 11½" tall doll with dark blue velvet outer dress with silver brocade trim. Blue high heels. Came with necklace, earrings, ring, and brush for hair. On display stand. Choice of black or white doll. Short issue. CMV, $40.00 MB.

Girl Scout Doll, 1995.
Second in Tender Memories Series. 14" high Girl Scout doll in green scout outfit. Choice of white or black doll. CMV, $40.00 MB.

"Little Bo Peep," 1996.
First in Story Time Doll Collection. 12" tall doll with miniature white lamb. Pink and white dress. Choice of white or black doll. CMV, $30.00 MB.

Huggy Bean Doll, 1997.
12" tall, bright yellow dress and hat. CMV, $20.00 MB.

Barbie Doll, "Winter Splendor," 1998.
11½" vinyl doll on metal stand. Velvet red dress bottom, black satin top, black gloves. Display box. Choice of black or white doll. CMV, $35.00 MB.

North African Inspired Doll, 1997.
14" high Moroccan doll on metal stand. Dated 1997. CMV, $40.00 MB.

Barbie Doll, "Spring Tea Party," 1998.
11½" tall doll on plastic stand. Rainbow shaded long polyester dress. Choice of blonde, brunette, or black doll. CMV, $40.00 MB.

Barbie Doll, "Lemon Lime Sorbet," 1999.
Barbie Doll, "Strawberry Sorbet," 1999.
Both dolls are vinyl, 11½" high, on display stands. Black is lemon design, green dress or green pants. White is strawberry design, pink dress or pink pants. CMV, $25.00 each, MB.

Barbie Doll, "Spring Petals," 1997.
Made only for Avon. 11½" tall with pink dress. Came in blonde, brunette, and African version. CMV, $40.00 MB.

Barbie Doll, "Avon Representative," 1999.
11½" vinyl doll on metal stand. Sold to Avon reps. Came with display box. Choice of black, white, or Spanish. CMV, $50.00 MB.

Barbie Doll, "Winter Rhapsody," 1997.
Made only for Avon by Mattel. Pink and black dress, white fur, on metal stand. Doll is 11½" high. Choice of blonde, brunette, or black doll. Came in gold display box. CMV, $45.00 MB.

Barbie Doll, "Snow Sensation," 1999.
11½" vinyl doll on metal stand. Blue and white dress with white fur trim and muff. Choice of black or white doll. Nice display box. Came with miniature musical snow globe that plays *The Nutcracker Suite*. CMV, $45.00 MB.

Special Memories Doll, 1999.
First in series. 16½" high porcelain doll. Metal stand. Straw hat and pigtails with straw basket in right hand and watering can in left hand. Choice of black "Bridget Lee" or white "Sarah Rose." CMV, $25.00 each, MB.

"Victorian Skater" Dolls, 1999. Second in Special Memories Series. 16" high porcelain dolls. Metal stands. Choice of black "Cecilia" with red velvet dress and hat or white "Angelique" with blue velvet dress and hat. Both have white trim. CMV, $25.00 each, MB.

Holiday Doll, 2000. Fifth in Special Memories Series. 16" high porcelain face and hands. Metal stand. Choice of "Adrienne" with green coat, "Cassandra" with yellow coat, or "Blanche" with red coat. Each has black hat and matching coat on dog. CMV, $30.00 each, MB.

Barbie Doll, "Angelic Inspirations," 2000. 11½" high vinyl angel doll on metal stand. Gold dress and wings with white net trim. White dove in hand. Choice of black or white doll. CMV, $30.00 each, MB.

Barbie Doll, "Victorian Skater," 2000. First musical base Barbie from Avon. Doll stands 11½" high on 2" music base. Burgundy velvet dress and cap and white faux fur trim. Ice skates on feet. Choice of white or black doll. CMV, $35.00 each, MB.

"Spring Tea" Doll, 2000. Third in Special Memories Series. 14" high porcelain doll. Teapot in left hand and cup and saucer in right hand. Choice of black "Olivia" in light green dress or white "Christina" in pink dress. Metal stands. CMV, $25.00 each, MB.

Barbie Doll, "Blushing Bride," 2000. 11½" vinyl doll on metal stand. White satin dress and white lace trim. Choice of white or black doll. CMV, $30.00 each, MB.

Barbie Doll, "Ballet Masquerade," 2001. 11½" vinyl doll in brocade and satin dress with feathers. Came with stand and display box. Choice of black, white, or Spanish. CMV, $40.00 each, MB.

Mother and Child Doll, 2000. Fourth in Special Memories Series. 16" high porcelain doll with white dress. Choice of black "Joyce," white "Margaret," or Spanish "Marisol." Came with certificate of authenticity. CMV, $30.00 each, MB.

Glorious Angel Doll, 2000. 10" high, porcelain face and hands. Metal stand. Choice of "Christina," "Katrina," or "Shana." CMV, $20.00 each, MB.

Holiday Radiance Doll, 2001.
Special Memories Series. 16" high, porcelain face and hands. Metal stand. Each doll has white fur hat and fur trim cape. "Sonia" in white dress, "Lorraine" in green dress, "Isabel" in burgundy dress. CMV, $30.00 each, MB.

Barbie Doll, "Simply Charming," 2002.
Vinyl doll with green dress and pink trim. Choice of black, white, or Spanish doll. Came with small gold tone charm bracelet. Display box. CMV, $35.00 each, MB.

Barbie Doll, "Hooray For Holly-wood," 2002.
11½" vinyl doll. Fancy gold display box. Barbie has gold satin dress and fur cape. Choice of black, white, or Spanish. CMV, $20.00 doll without box. $50.00 each, MB.

Barbie Doll, "Winter Reflection," 2002.
11½" high vinyl doll with white glittery dress with fur trim. Choice of black, white, or Spanish. Came with stand and display box. CMV, $40.00 each, MB.

Mother's Day Doll, 2001.
Special Memories Series. 14" high, porcelain face and hands. Sits on wooden chair holding baby doll. Choice of black, white, or Span-ish. CMV, $30.00 each, MB.

Barbie Doll, "Timeless Silhouette," 2001.
11½" high vinyl doll. Pink and black trim dress. Display box and stand. Choice of black, white, or Spanish. CMV, $35.00 each, MB.

Belle Doll, 2002.
Disney doll from *Beauty and the Beast.* 14" high, with stand. "Avon" on box. Pink satin dress and burgundy cape with white fur trim. CMV, $30.00 MB.

Barbie Doll, "Sterling Sil-ver Rose," 2003.
11½" high vinyl Barbie dolls designed by Bob Mackie. Choice of white, black, or Hispanic. OSP, $70.00 each. CMV, $50.00 each, MB.

Barbie Doll, "Victorian Tea," 2003.
11½" high vinyl doll with white dress and pink trim with straw hat. Metal stand. Display box also came with small porcelain tea set. CMV, $40.00 MB.

Barbie Doll, "Angelic Har-mony" 2002.
11½" high vinyl doll on metal stand. Choice of black, white, or Spanish doll. CMV, $30.00 each, MB.

*Barbie Doll, "Glamorous Gala,"
2003.*
11½" vinyl doll. Choice of white,
black, or Hispanic. OSP, $40.00
each. CMV, $40.00 each, MB.

*Barbie Doll, "Ring in the
New Year," 2003.*
11½" vinyl doll with
brocade dress. Came
in storybook-style box
with see-through panel.
OSP, $37.00. CMV,
$35.00 MB.

*Barbie Doll, "Exotic In-
trigue," 2004.*
11½" tall plastic doll.
Choice of white, black,
or Hispanic doll. OSP,
$50.00 each. CMV,
$40.00 each, MB.

*Barbie Doll, "Talk of the Town,"
2004.*
11½" high plastic doll and
white dog. Choice of white,
black, or Hispanic. OSP, $40.00
each. CMV, $40.00 each, MB.

Eggs

*Butterfly Fantasy Treasure Egg,
1974 – 1980.*
5½" long, white porcelain,
multicolored butterfly decals.
Sold empty. "1974" stamped
on bottom. Sold 1974 – 1975
then reissued in 1978. The 1978
issue had an "R" for reissue on
bottom and the big butterfly
on top is much lighter than the
1974 issue. CMV, $25.00 MB for
1974 issue. CMV, $15.00 MB
for reissue. 1979 – 1980 issue
has "R" 1979 on bottom, CMV,
$15.00 MB. Also came with
bottom label upside down or
backwards, add $6.00 to CMV.

*Oriental Egg, Peach
Orchard, 1974 – 1975.*
1 oz., white opal
glass with green
marbleized plastic
base. Came in Impe-
rial Garden, Sonnet
Moonwind, or Patch-
work perfume con-
centre. CMV, $7.00
egg only. $10.00 MB.

*Oriental Egg, Chinese
Pheasant, 1975.*
1 oz., white opal
glass, black plas-
tic base. Came in
Imperial Garden,
Charisma, or Bird of
Paradise cologne.
CMV, $7.00 egg only.
$10.00 MB.

*Oriental Egg,
Delicate Blossoms,
1975 – 1976.*
1 oz., light blue opal
glass with blue-green
plastic base. Came
in Patchwork, Sonnet,
or Charisma cologne.
CMV, $7.00 egg only.
$10.00 MB.

*Oriental Egg, Chinese Pheasant,
1975.*
Upside down label mistake made
at factory. Upside down bottle
only, CMV, $18.00.

Four Seasons Egg Series, 1984.
Four different porcelain eggs with wood bases. Winter, Spring, Summer, and Autumn. CMV, $10.00 each, MB.

Majestic Crystal Egg, 1993.
24% lead crystal egg, 3" high. With pewter stand. Total height, 4½". CMV, $30.00 MB.

Winter's Treasure Egg, 1987.
3" high porcelain egg. 1" wood base. CMV, $10.00 MB.

Autumn's Color Egg, 1987.
3" high porcelain egg on wood base. CMV, $10.00 MB.

Summer's Roses Egg, 1988.
3" high porcelain egg. 1" wood base. CMV, $10.00 MB.

Spring Brilliance Egg, 1988.
3" porcelain egg on 1" wood base. CMV, $10.00 MB.

Season's Treasures Egg Collection, 1994.
4¾" high Hartford Porcelain egg and base. Choice of four different eggs. Floral Bouquet, Seashells of Summer, Fruit Harvest, and Birds of Joy. CMV, $10.00 each, MB.

Spring Flowers Buttermint Egg Tin, 1995.
6" long, 3½" wide, 4" deep multicolored tin egg held 10 oz. of buttermint candy. CMV, $5.00 MB.

Sparkling Crystal Egg, 2000.
3" high solid lead crystal egg sits on lead crystal base. CMV, $12.00 MB.

Hummingbird Crystal

All hummingbird crystal is 24% lead crystal. Each piece has the hummingbird and flower design.

Hurricane Lamp, 1982 – 1984.
This was sold by Avon with the name "Gallery Original" on the base. CMV, $40.00 MB.

Candleholders, 1984.
Also sold by Gallery through Avon. Set of two. CMV, $30.00 MB, set.

Footed Cake Plate, 1985.
12" glass cake plate with 3" footed glass stand. CMV, $75.00 MB.
Champagne Glasses, 1985 – 1994.
9" high each. Came in box of two. CMV, $26.00 MB, set.

Bell, 1985.
Clear glass and etched frosted design. CMV, $12.00 MB.

Covered Dish, 1989.
Lead crystal, 5" wide dish. CMV, $30.00 MB.

Serving Bowl, 1993.
24% lead crystal bowl is 8³⁄₈" across by 4¼" high. CMV, $35.00 MB.

Vase, 1986.
7½" high vase. CMV, $27.00 MB.

Bud Vase, 1990.
9½" high, clear lead crystal glass. CMV, $25.00 MB.

Dinner Plate, 1993.
10½" lead crystal plate. CMV, $23.00 MB.

Ornament, 1986.
3½" lead crystal ornament has "1986" on it. CMV, $12.00 MB.

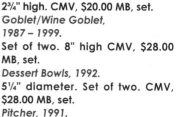

Candleholders, 1987.
Set of two — each 4¼" wide, 2⁵⁄₈" high. CMV, $20.00 MB, set.

Platter, 1992.
12½" in diameter. CMV, $40.00 MB.
Dessert Plates, 1988 – 2000.
Set of two. 7¾" diameter. CMV, $25.00 MB, set.
Dessert Plate, 2000.
Sold one plate only. CMV, $15.00 MB.
Wine Glass, 1992.
Set of two. 7½" high. CMV, $28.00 MB.
Wine Glass, 1999.
Set of two. 6½" high. CMV, $25.00 MB, set.

Salt and Pepper Shakers, 1991.
2¾" high. CMV, $20.00 MB, set.
Goblet/Wine Goblet, 1987 – 1999.
Set of two. 8" high CMV, $28.00 MB, set.
Dessert Bowls, 1992.
5¼" diameter. Set of two. CMV, $28.00 MB, set.
Pitcher, 1991.
8" high. CMV, $35.00 MB.

Beverage Glasses, 1994.
7¾" high crystal glasses. Set of two. Frosted bases. CMV, $30.00 MB, set.

Cup and Saucer Set, 1994.
Cup, 2½" high, 3½" wide. Saucer, 5¾" wide. CMV, $25.00 MB, set.

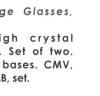

Soup/Salad Bowl, 1995.
8½" wide, 1¼" high crystal bowl. CMV, $23.00 MB.

Bud Vase, 1999.
7" high lead crystal vase. Smaller and different shape than 1990 issue bud vase. Embossed with hummingbird. CMV, $15.00 MB.

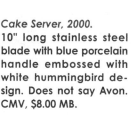

Cake Server, 2000.
10" long stainless steel blade with blue porcelain handle embossed with white hummingbird design. Does not say Avon. CMV, $8.00 MB.

Cape Cod

Cruet, 1975 – 1980.
5 oz., held Skin So Soft. CMV, $10.00 MB.

Wine Goblet, 1976 – 1982.
Came with candle. CMV, $7.00 MB. Also issued to reps with "President's Celebration 1976" embossed on bottom. CMV, $10.00 MB.

Dessert Bowl and Guest Soaps, 1978 – 1980.
CMV, $13.00 MB.

Water Goblet, 1976 – 1980.
Came with candle. CMV, $14.00 MB.

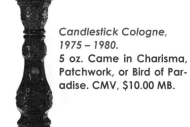

Candlestick Cologne, 1975 – 1980.
5 oz. Came in Charisma, Patchwork, or Bird of Paradise. CMV, $10.00 MB.

Wine Decanter, 1977 – 1980.
16 oz., held bubble bath. CMV, $28.00 MB.

Salt Shaker, 1978 – 1980.
"May 1978" on bottom. CMV, $7.00 MB.
Salt and Pepper Shaker Set, 1984.
Set of two. Not dated on bottom. CMV, $24.00 MB.

1876 Hostess Bell, 1979 – 1980. 6½" high. "Christmas 1979" on bottom. CMV, $15.00 MB. Also came in clear glass coated red.

Pedestal Mug, 1982 – 1984. Box held two ruby red glass mugs, 5" high each. CMV, $14.00 MB, set of two.

Water Pitcher, 1984. 8¼" high. CMV, $50.00 MB.

Dessert Plate, 1980. Box of two plates marked "Avon." CMV, $10.00 MB, set of two.

Dessert Bowl, 1982. 5" diameter. CMV, $12.00 MB.

Hurricane Candleholder, 1985. CMV, $20.00 MB.

Sugar Bowl, 1980 – 1983. 3½" high. Came with three sachet tablets. CMV, $10.00 MB.

Dinner Plate, 1982 – 1983. Full size dinner plate. CMV, $32.00 MB.

Creamer Candle, 1981 – 1984. 4" high. Held candle. Also came in 1983 without candle. CMV, $10.00 MB.

Covered Butter Dish, 1983 – 1984. 7" long. CMV, $20.00 MB.

Dessert Server, 1981 – 1984. 8" long, ruby red plastic handle. Stainless blade made by Regent Sheffield for Avon. CMV, $25.00 MB.

Candleholders, 1983 – 1984. ¾" wide, two in a box. CMV, $10.00 MB, set of two.

Flower Vase, 1985. 8" tall. CMV, $29.00 MB.

Condiment Dish, 1985.
CMV, $20.00 MB.

Serving Platter, 1986.
10¾" x 13½". CMV, $70.00 MB.

Serving Bowl, 1986.
8¾". Some bowls came with "Centennial Edition 1886 – 1986" on bottom of bowl. CMV, $25.00 MB. Add $5.00 for 1886 – 1986 edition.

Candy Dish, 1987.
6" wide, 3½" high. CMV, $20.00 MB.

Two Tier Server, 1987.
9¾" high. Brass handle. CMV, $65.00 MB.

Footed Glass, 1988.
3¾", came in set of two. CMV, $12.00 MB, set.

Footed Sauce (Gravy) Boat, 1988.
8" long. CMV, $25.00 MB.

Heart Box, 1989.
4" wide. CMV, $22.00 MB.

Napkin Rings, 1989.
1½". Set of four. CMV, $45.00 MB, set.

Tall Beverage Glass, 1990.
Came in set of two. 5½" tall. CMV, $20.00 MB, set.

Christmas Ornament, 1990.
3¼" wide, box. Back says "Christmas 1990." CMV, $20.00 MB.

Cup and Saucer, 1990.
Cup, 3½" high. Saucer, 5¾" wide. CMV, $19.00 MB.

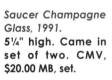

Saucer Champagne Glass, 1991.
5¼" high. Came in set of two. CMV, $20.00 MB, set.

Soup/Cereal Bowl, 1991.
7½" wide. CMV, $20.00 MB.

Pedestal Cake Plate, 1991.
Red glass cake stand, 3¼" high, 10¾" diameter. CMV, $65.00 MB.

Elegant Wine Glass, 1992
5¼" high, 4½ oz. Came in set of two. CMV, $16.00 each. $32.00 MB, set.

Bread and Butter Dish, 1992.
5¾". This is the 37th item in the Cape Cod Collection Avon started in 1975. Came in set of two. CMV, $13.00 MB, set.

Pie Plate Server, 1992.
Thirty-eighth piece in Cape Cod Collection. 10⅞" wide. CMV, $30.00 MB.

Bells

Fragrance Bell, 1965 – 1966.
4 oz., clear glass, plastic handle, neck tag. Came in Rapture, Occur!, Somewhere, Topaze, Cotillion, Here's My Heart, To a Wild Rose, or Wishing. CMV, $15.00 bell with tag. $20.00 MB.

Hobnail Bell, 1973 – 1974.
2 oz., white milk glass with gold handle and gold bell underneath. Held Unforgettable, Topaze, Here's My Heart, To a Wild Rose, or Sweet Honesty. CMV, $12.00 MB.

Hospitality Bell, 1976 – 1977.
Silver top, 3¾ oz., blue glass bottom. Came in Moonwind or Roses Roses cologne. "Avon 1976" stamped on bottom. CMV, $10.00 MB.

Christmas Bells, 1974 – 1975.
1 oz., red painted glass with gold cap. Came in Topaze, Occur!, Cotillion, To a Wild Rose, or Sweet Honesty. CMV, $8.00 MB.

Fragrance Bell, 1968 – 1969.
1 oz., gold handle. Bell actually rings. Came in Charisma, Brocade, Régence, Unforgettable, Rapture, Occur!, Somewhere, Topaze, Cotillion, Here's My Heart, To a Wild Rose, or Wishing. CMV, $15.00 bell with tag. $20.00 MB.

Crystal Song Bell, 1975 – 1976.
4 oz., red glass with frosted bow and handle. Held Timeless or Sonnet. CMV, $10.00 MB.

Rosepoint Bell, 1978.
4 oz., clear glass, clear plastic top. Came in Charisma or Roses Roses cologne. CMV, $10.00 MB.

Emerald Bell, 1978 – 1979. 3¾ oz., light green glass. Gold and green plastic cap. Bottom has "Avon 1978" embossed. Came in Sweet Honesty or Roses Roses cologne. CMV, $10.00 MB.

Moonlight Glow Annual Bell, 1981 – 1982. 3 oz. glass bell, frosted top. Choice of Moonwind or Topaze. CMV, $10.00 MB.

Avon Country Porcelain Bell, 1985. 3¼" high, porcelain. CMV, $10.00 MB.

Joyous Bell, 1978. Light blue frosted over clear glass. Silver cap. Came in Charisma or Topaze cologne. In blue and white box. CMV, $10.00 MB.

Tapestry Collection Bell, 1981. 5" high white porcelain bell. Dated 1981. Dove on top of bell. CMV, $15.00 MB.

Christmas Bell, 1985. Wood handle, porcelain, dated Christmas 1985. CMV, $15.00 MB.

Good Luck Bell, 1983. 4½" high, porcelain elf on flower bell. CMV, $15.00 MB.

Heavenly Cherub Hostess Bell, 1979 – 1980. 3¾ oz., clear glass painted frosted tan. Gold plastic handle. "1979" embossed on bottom. Came in Topaze or Bird of Paradise cologne. CMV, $10.00 MB.

Treasured Moments Bell, 1984. Fostoria glass. 5" high. CMV, $11.00 MB.

Birthday Bell, 1986. 5¾" high clear lead crystal bell. Choice of 12 different flowers and birthstones on bells. CMV, $12.00 MB.

Crystal Snowflake Christmas Bell, 1980. 3¾ oz., clear glass. Bottom label dated 1980. Choice of Charisma, Topaze, Occur!, or Cotillion cologne. CMV, $8.00 MB.

Bunny Bell, 1984. 3" high ceramic rabbit bell. CMV, $10.00 MB.

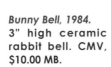

Christmas Bell, 1986. White porcelain bell, 5" high, dated 1986. Gold trim. CMV, $15.00 MB.

Christmas Bell, 1987. 4¾" high porcelain bell. CMV, $15.00 MB.

Floral Bouquet Crystal Bell, 1989. 6" high lead crystal bell. CMV, $23.00 MB.

"Garland of Greetings" Bell, 1991. 4¾" high red and green porcelain bell with teddy bear handle. CMV, $20.00 MB.

A Mother's Love Porcelain Bell, 1988. 3" high porcelain bell. CMV, $10.00 MB.

Under the Mistletoe Christmas Bell, 1989. Porcelain bell, 5½" high. CMV, $20.00 MB.

Love Crystal Bell, 1991. 4¼" high, clear lead crystal, frosted Cupid top and red heart clapper. CMV, $17.00 MB.

Heart Song Crystal Bell, 1988. 4¾" high clear glass bell. Red heart top dated 1988. CMV, $13.00 MB.

Crystal Butterfly Bell, 1990. Lead crystal bell, 6½" high, butterfly decals. CMV, $15.00 MB.

Spring Chimes Porcelain Bell, 1991. 6" pink porcelain bell and pink ribbons. CMV, $18.00 MB.

Giving Thanks Bell, 1990. 4½" high porcelain pumpkin bell. CMV, $15.00 MB.

Harvest Bounty Crystal Bell, 1988. 6½" lead crystal bell. Hand painted porcelain handle. CMV, $15.00 MB.

"Waiting for Santa" Bell, 1990. 5½" high porcelain bell. CMV, $20.00 MB.

Hearts and Flowers Crystal Bell, 1992. 4½" high lead crystal bell with pink and white flowered handle. Dated 1992. CMV, $20.00 MB.

Floral Fantasy Crystal Bell, 1992.
6" lead crystal bell. Stain glass design. CMV, $20.00 MB.

Basket of Love Crystal Bell, 1994.
4¾" high lead crystal bell. White, pink, and green plastic basket handle dated 1994 and marked "Avon." CMV, $20.00 MB.

Hummingbird and Flower Bell, 2000.
5¼" high, hand-painted lavender, green, white, and yellow porcelain hummingbird bell. CMV, $10.00 MB.

"Avon Heavenly Notes" Christmas Bell, 1992.
5½" high, blue porcelain bell with angel handle. Dated 1992. CMV, $20.00 MB.

"Love's Beginnings" Porcelain Bell, 1995.
4½" high, 2¾" wide pink porcelain bell. Dated and marked "Avon." CMV, $17.00 MB.

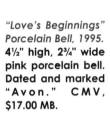

Heart's Delight Porcelain Bell, 1993.
4⅜" high porcelain bell in red and green strawberry shape. CMV, $17.00 MB.

"Sounds of Christmas" Bell, 1995.
4" high, 2½" wide, white, red, and green porcelain bell. CMV, $17.00 MB.

Cardinal and Flower Bell, 2000.
6¼" high. Red bird on white porcelain bell. CMV, $10.00 MB.

"Soloist" Crystal Bell, 1994.
5" high lead crystal bell. Choir boy, frosted handle. Signed "M.I. Hummel" and marked "Avon." CMV, $25.00 MB.

Marjolein Bastin Mini Bird Bells, 1997.
Miniature 2¾" high bells made of hand-painted resin. Choice of Cardinal (flowerpot), Sparrow (Birchbark birdhouse), Redbreast (thatched roof birdhouse), or Bullfinch (watering can). CMV, $10.00 each, MB.

Cherub Porcelain Bell, 2003.
4" high porcelain bell. CMV, $8.00 MB.

Perfume Glace

All Perfume Glace that are made of plastic are not collectible, and are not shown.

Perfume Jewel Glace, 1965 – 1966.
Gold and white box contained gold locket. Came as pin or on a chain with solid perfume in Unforgettable, Rapture, Occur!, Somewhere, Topaze, Cotillion, Here's My Heart, To a Wild Rose, or Wishing. CMV, $17.00 each, MB.

Pillbox Perfume Glace, 1967.
Black and gold with red rose on top. Came in Occur!, Rapture, Unforgettable, Somewhere, Topaze, Cotillion, Here's My Heart, or To a Wild Rose. CMV, $15.00 MB.

Golden Charmer Locket, 1968 – 1970.
Gold locket held perfume glace in Somewhere, Topaze, Cotillion, Here's My Heart, To a Wild Rose, Unforgettable, Rapture, Occur!, Brocade, or Régence. CMV, $14.00 MB.

Golden Leaf Pin, 1969 – 1970.
Blue box contained gold leaf pin with pearl at stem. Perfume glace came in Elusive, Charisma, Brocade, Régence, Unforgettable, Rapture, Occur!, Topaze, Somewhere, or Cotillion. Same pin also issued without glace. CMV, $11.00 MB.

Perfume Glace Necklace, 1966 – 1967.
Silver with black stone and gold with brown stone. Came in Unforgettable, Rapture, Somewhere, Cotillion, Topaze, To a Wild Rose, Here's My Heart, or Wishing. CMV, $17.00 each, MB.

Owl Pin Perfume Glace, 1968 – 1969.
Gold metal pin with green eyes. Green and gold box. Came in Unforgettable, Brocade, Régence, Rapture, Occur!, Cotillion, Here's My Heart, or To a Wild Rose. CMV, $12.00 MB.

Cameo Ring and Pin, 1970.
Both are perfume glace. Came in Elusive, Charisma, Brocade, Régence, or Bird of Paradise. CMV, $15.00 each, MB.

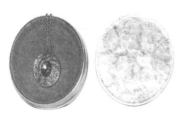

Perfume Glace Necklace, 1966 – 1967.
Special issue gold round box. Came with either silver with black stone or gold necklace with brown stone. CMV, $20.00 as shown.

Daisy Pin Perfume Glace, 1969.
White and gold pin Charisma, Brocade, Régence, Rapture, Occur!, Unforgettable, Somewhere, Topaze, or Cotillion. CMV, $10.00 MB.

Ring of Pearls Glace, 1969 – 1970.
Perfume glace ring is gold with white pearls. Came in Charisma, Régence, or Brocade. CMV, $10.00 MB.

Flower Basket Perfume Glace, 1970 – 1971.
1½" x 1¼", gold tone. Choice of Bird of Paradise, Elusive, Charisma, Brocade, or Régence. CMV, $10.00 MB.

Memory Book Perfume Glace, 1971 – 1975.
½" long gold book. Choice of Moonwind, Elusive, Brocade, Régence, or Bird of Paradise perfume glace. CMV, $10.00 MB.

Baby Grand Piano Perfume Glace, 1971 – 1972.
2" wide gold piano. Came in same fragrances as Memory Book. CMV, $14.00 MB.

Mandolin Perfume Glace, 1971 – 1972.
2½" long gold mandolin. Choice of Moonwind, Elusive, Charisma, Brocade, Régence, or Bird of Paradise perfume glace. CMV, $14.00 MB.

Tortoise Perfume Glace, 1971 – 1975.
2½" long gold turtle with turquoise back. Came in same fragrances as Mandolin. CMV, $10.00 MB.

Plates, Miscellaneous

Metal plates are not collectible and are not shown.

Cardinal North American Songbird Plate, 1974 – 1976.
10" ceramic plate. Gold and green letters on back, story of the cardinal. CMV, $20.00 MB.

Freedom Plate, 1974 – 1977.
9" ceramic plate, blue trim with gold edge. Blue printing on back. Made by Wedgwood, England, for Avon. CMV, $20.00 MB.

Betsy Ross Plate, 1973 – 1977.
White with colored scene, gold trim and lettering. 9" plate. Came with paper, tribute to Betsy Ross. CMV, $20.00 MB.

Tenderness Plate, 1974 – 1975.
9¼" ironstone plate. Blue and white with gold edge. Made in Spain for Avon by Pontesa. The plate was sold to the public with the word "Pontesa" on the back side in blue letters. This was also awarded to Avon reps. Plate was also sold with no inscription on back. No. 1 (regular issue) — all blue lettering on back of plate, No. 2 (reps award) — all blue lettering including Pontesa logo. No. 3 (reps award) — all blue lettering on back of plate except the Pontesa logo, which is red. CMV, $20.00 MB, regular issue. $25.00 MB, rep plate.

"Pink Roses" Cup and Saucer, 1974.
White china with pink flowers and green leaves with gold trim. Made by Stoke-on-Trent, England. CMV, $12.00 MB. Also came with double printed letters on bottom. CMV, $20.00 MB.

"Blue Blossoms" Cup and Saucer, 1974. White china with blue and pink flowers and 22K gold trim. Made in England. CMV, $12.00 MB.

Baby Keepsake Spoon and Bowl Set, 1984. 6¼" porcelain bowl and 5" spoon. CMV, $14.00 MB.

Cupid's Message Porcelain Dish, 1984. White heart shaped dish with angel. "Love" in red letters. Red box. CMV, $10.00 MB.

Gentle Moments Plate, 1975 – 1977. 8¾" ceramic plate. Green letters on back. Made by Wedgwood, England. CMV, $20.00 MB.

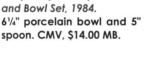

Christmas Lights Dessert Plate, 1985. 7" white ceramic plate with Christmas lights design. CMV, $7.00 MB.

Children's Personal Touch Plate, 1982 – 1983. 7⅝" ceramic plate. CMV, $12.00 MB.

Baked with Love, Plate, 1982 – 1983. 9" porcelain plate dated 1982. CMV, $20.00 MB.

European Tradition Cup and Saucer Collection, 1984 – 1985.
France, circa 1750.
2½" cup and 4½" saucer. Pink and white porcelain. CMV, $15.00 MB.
Germany, circa 1700.
Yellow and white porcelain. CMV, $15.00 MB.
Netherlands, circa 1650.
Blue and white porcelain. CMV, $15.00 MB.
Florence, circa 1560.
Blue and white porcelain. CMV, $15.00 MB.

Sweet Dreams Keepsake Plate, 1983. 7⅝" porcelain plate. CMV, $15.00 MB.

American Portraits Plate Collection, 1985.
Set of six 4½" porcelain plates. Choice of The East, The West, The Rockies, The Southwest, The Midwest, or The South. CMV, $8.00 each, MB.

Abigail Adams Plate, 1985.
9" porcelain plate. Wood stand. CMV, $20.00 MB.

Classic Wedding Plate, 1986.
9" bisque porcelain plate with two doves on face. Gold trim. CMV, $15.00 MB.

Images of Hollywood, Chorus Line Plate, 1986.
8" porcelain plate. Came with or without wood music box stand. Add $5.00 for music box base. CMV, $20.00 MB.

Moments of Victory Plate Collection, 1985.
Set of four different 7" porcelain plates: baseball, football, basketball, or hockey. CMV, $8.00 each, MB.

The Four Seasons Calendar Plate, 1987.
9" porcelain plate. CMV, $15.00 MB.

12 Days of Christmas Collection, 1985.
All white porcelain.
Candleholders.
CMV, $11.00 MB, pair.
Dessert Plates.
Set of four. CMV $20.00 MB, set.
Mugs.
Set of four. CMV, $16.00 MB, set.

Images of Hollywood, Singin' in the Rain Plate, 1986.
8" porcelain plate. Came with or without wood base music box. CMV, $18.00 MB. Add $5.00 for music box base.

Bouquet of Love Plate, 1987.
7" white porcelain bisque plate. CMV, $10.00 MB.

School is a New Beginning Plate, 1986.
5" porcelain plate. CMV, $8.00 MB.

Images of Hollywood, Easter Parade Plate, 1986.
8" porcelain plate came with or without wood base music stand that plays *Easter Parade*. CMV, $18.00 MB. Add $5.00 for music box base.

Holy Family Plate, 1991.
First in series. 8½" blue and white porcelain nativity scene plate. CMV, $22.50 MB.

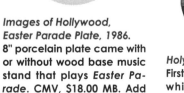

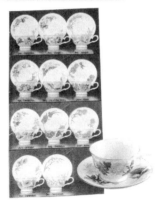

"The Last Supper" Plate, 1994.
Fourth in series. 8¼" blue and white porcelain plate. Dated 1994. CMV, $25.00 MB.

Keepsake Baby Plate, 1992.
5" plate with white or black child. Porcelain, trimmed in 22K gold. Plastic display stand. CMV, $10.00 each, MB.

"My Easter Bonnet" Easter Plate, 1995.
5" porcelain plate dated 1995. Fifth in Easter Plates Series. CMV, $10.00 MB.

Cups and Saucers — Avon Blossoms of the Month Series, 1991.
Porcelain flowered cups and 5½" saucers. Twelve different for 1991. Jan. – Carnation; Feb. – Violet; Mar. – Jonquil; April – Sweet Pea; May – Lily of the Valley; June – Rose; July – Larkspur; Aug. – Gladiola; Sept. – Aster; Oct. – Calendula; Nov. – Chrysanthemum; Dec. – Narcissus. Each marked "Avon" and dated. CMV, $20.00 each, MB.

"Easter Parade" Plate, 1993.
5" porcelain plate, "Easter 1993." Plastic stand. Third in Easter Plates Series. CMV, $10.00 MB.

Martin Luther King Jr., Plate, 1995.
5" porcelain plate, came with plastic stand. CMV, $10.00 MB.

"Springtime Stroll" Easter Plate, 1991.
5" porcelain plate with rabbit family strolling. Trimmed in 22K gold. CMV, $10.00 MB.

"Bless the Little Children" Plate, 1992.
Second in series. 8½" blue porcelain plate with date on back. CMV, $22.50 MB.

Jesus Feeds the Multitude, 1993.
Third in series. 8⅜" blue porcelain plate. CMV, $25.00 MB.

Joyous Occasions Anniversary Plate, 1995.
8¼" porcelain plate with flowers. Says "Happy Anniversary" on front. CMV, $20.00 MB.

"Colorful Moments" Easter Plate, 1992.
5" porcelain plate with rabbits coloring eggs. Second in Easter Plates Series. Plastic stand. CMV, $10.00 MB.

"All Dressed Up" Easter Plate, 1994.
5" porcelain plate says "Easter 1994," rabbit family on front side. Fourth in Easter Plates Series. CMV, $10.00 MB.

"Easter Bouquet"
Easter Plate, 1996.
5" porcelain plate. Dated 1996. Sixth in Easter Plates Series. CMV, $13.00 MB.

Sisters in Spirit Plate, 1996.
8" blue, red, and yellow porcelain African plate. CMV, $20.00 MB.

The Olympic Woman Plate, 1996.
5" blue plate with red and white letters, for Atlanta Olympics. Dated 1996. CMV, $13.00 MB.

Team USA Olympic Plate, 1996.
5" blue and white porcelain plate. Dated 1996. CMV, $13.00 MB.

M.I. Hummel "Angel" Plate, 1996.
8½" lead crystal plate dated 1996. CMV, $30.00 MB.

African Ancestry Last Supper Plate, 1997.
8" porcelain plate dated 1997. Plastic stand. CMV, $20.00 MB.

Plates, Christmas

Metal plates are not collectible and are not shown.

Christmas on the Farm, 1973.
This is Avon's first Christmas plate. 9", ceramic. White with colored scene, turquoise border, gold edge and lettering. CMV, $55.00 MB.

Christmas Plate, "Betsy Ross" Error, 1973.
Factory mistake. 1973 Christmas plate has inscription on back for Betsy Ross plate. Very rare. CMV, $100.00.

Country Church, 1974.
9" ceramic plate. Second in a series of Christmas plates by Avon. Made by Wedgwood, England. Blue writing on back. Blue and white front, gold edge. CMV, $40.00 MB. Rare issue came without "Christmas 1974" on front of plate. CMV, $75.00 MB.

Skaters on the Pond, 1975.
8¾" ceramic green and white plate. Green letters on the back. Made by Wedgwood, England, for Avon. This plate was not sold until the 1976 Christmas season. CMV, $20.00 MB. Some have "1976" on back. Add $10.00.

Christmas Plate Test, 1976.
8¾" test plate. Does not say Avon. "Christmas 1976" along rim on front six times in gold. Was never sold by Avon. Came from factory. Has blue border. CMV, $75.00.

"Bringing Home the Tree," 1976.
9" blue ceramic plate, gold edge. Blue printing on back. Made by Wedgwood, England, for Avon. CMV, $20.00 MB. Some have 1975 on back. Add $10.00.

"Carollers in the Snow," 1977.
8¾" ceramic blue and white plate, gold edge. Blue letters on back. Made by Wedgwood, England, for Avon. CMV, $20.00 MB.

"Trimming the Tree," 1978.
8⅝" ceramic plate. Turquoise rim with gold edge trim. Made for Avon by Enoch Wedgwood in England. CMV, $20.00 MB.

Christmas Plate — 15 Year, 1978.
Same plate as 15 year anniversary plate, inscribed on back. CMV, $50.00.

"Dashing Through the Snow," 1979.
8¾" blue and white ceramic plate with gold trim. "Christmas 1979" on front. Back of plate says "Made for Avon Products by Enoch Wedgwood in England." CMV, $20.00 MB.

"Country Christmas," 1980.
9" ceramic Christmas plate. CMV, $25.00 MB.

"Enjoying the Night Before Christmas," 1983.
9" porcelain plate. CMV, $20.00 MB.

"Sharing the Christmas Spirit," 1981.
9" porcelain plate has two kids carrying Christmas tree. "Christmas 1981" on front. CMV, $20.00 MB. Left: Rare issue came with no "Christmas 1981" on front. CMV, $75.00.

"Keeping the Christmas Tradition," 1982.
9" ceramic plate, back says "Christmas Memories, 1982." Came in green and gold box. CMV, $25.00 MB.

"Celebrating the Joy of Giving," 1984.
9" porcelain decal plate. CMV, $25.00 MB.

"A Child's Christmas," 1985. 7¾", white bisque porcelain. CMV, $30.00 MB.

"Together for Christmas," 1989. Bears on 8" wide. porcelain plate. CMV, $25.00 MB.

"A Child's Christmas," 1986. 8" porcelain plate with snowman and 2 kids. CMV, $35.00 MB.

"Bringing Christmas Home," 1990. 8" porcelain plate. "Christmas 1990" on front. CMV, $25.00 MB.

"The Wonder of Christmas," 1994. 8¼" porcelain plate. Dated 1994. CMV, $30.00 MB.

"Magic that Santa Brings," 1987. 8" porcelain plate. CMV, $25.00 MB.

"Perfect Harmony," 1991. 8" porcelain plate. CMV, $25.00 MB.

"Trimming the Tree," 1995. 8¼" blue porcelain plate, dated 1995. CMV, $25.00 MB.

"Home for the Holidays," 1988. 8" porcelain plate. CMV, $25.00 MB.

"Sharing Christmas with Friends," 1992. 8" porcelain plate. Animals decorating Christmas tree. CMV, $30.00 MB.

"Santa's Loving Touch," 1996. 8¼" porcelain plate, dated 1996. Stand not included. CMV, $35.00 MB.

Miniature Christmas Plates, 1989. First issued in 1989. The 1978, 1979, and 1980 Christmas plates in 3" size. CMV, $10.00 each, MB.

"Special Christmas Delivery," 1993. 8" porcelain plate. Santa and reindeer. CMV, $25.00 MB.

"Heavenly Dreams,"
1997.
8¼" porcelain plate, dated 1997. Choice of white or black angel on plate. CMV, $25.00 each, MB.

"A Visit with Santa," 2001. 8¼" porcelain plate. "Christmas 2001" in English or Spanish on the front. Santa Claus bear and baby bears on front. Gold trim. CMV, $20.00 MB.

"Greetings from Santa,"
1998.
8¼" blue porcelain plate with Santa sitting on moon. "Avon" and dated 1998 on plate. Choice of black or white Santa on plate. CMV, $20.00 MB.

"Snowy Winter," 2002. 8¼" blue and white porcelain plate. Gold trim. "Christmas 2002" on the front and "Avon" on the back. Came with plate stand. CMV, $20.00 MB.

"Santa's Tender Moment,"
1999.
8¼" porcelain plate. Marked "Avon" and dated 1999 on back. Choice of black or white Santa. CMV, $20.00 MB.

"Coming to Town," 2003. 8¼" porcelain plate with Santa and his sleigh. Came with plastic stand. OSP, $20.00. CMV, $20.00 MB.

"Trimming the Tree with Friends," 2004. 8¼" porcelain plate with plastic stand. OSP, $15.00. CMV, $15.00 MB.

"Christmas Dreams," 2000.
8¼" porcelain plate. Three different scenes of two kids asleep. Choice of black, white, or Spanish children. "Christmas 2000" on front of plate and "Avon" on the back. Came with plate stand. CMV, $20.00 each, MB.

"Angel Lights,"
2005.
8¼" ceramic plate, dated 2005. Came with plastic stand. OSP, $15.00. CMV, $15.00 MB.

"Storytime with Santa," 2006. 8¼" porcelain plate. 22K gold trim. Choice of black or white Santa. OSP, $20.00. CMV, $20.00 MB.

The 2002 Cherished Teddies Mother's Day plate is made by Enesco, not Avon Products, Inc., and is not shown.

"Cherished Moments Last Forever," 1981.
First in series. 5" porcelain plate dated 1981, with stand. CMV, $15.00 MB.

"A New Tooth," 1986. 5" porcelain plate. Choice of white or black mother and child. CMV, $35.00 each, MB.

Mother's Day Plate, 1990. **"A Message from the Heart," 1990.** 5" porcelain plate, with stand. CMV, $15.00 MB.

"Little Things Mean a Lot," 1982.
5" ceramic plate. Came in yellow box and plastic plate stand. CMV, $15.00 MB. Same plate given to President's Club reps. Label on back reads "January 1982 President's Club Luncheon." CMV, $15.00 MB.

"A Mother Is Love," 1987. 5" porcelain plate. CMV, $15.00 MB.

"Love Makes All Things Grow," 1991. 5" porcelain plate with plastic stand. CMV, $15.00 MB.

Mother's Day Plates, 1983 and 1984. 5" ceramic plates. Both dated on back. 1983 says "Love is a Song for Mother." 1984 says "Love Comes in All Sizes." CMV, $15.00 each, MB.

"A Mother's Work is Never Done," 1988. 5", ceramic. Choice of black or white child and doll. CMV, $15.00 each, MB.

"Special Creation of Love," 1985. 5" porcelain plate, choice of white or black mother and child. CMV, $15.00 each, MB.

"Loving is Caring," 1989. 5" plate with stand. CMV, $15.00 MB.

"How Do You Wrap Love," 1992. 5" porcelain plate, dated 1992. CMV, $15.00 MB.

"Tender Moments," 1997. 5" porcelain plate designed by Helene Levellee and dated 1997. Choice of white or black mother and child. CMV, $15.00 each, MB.

"Recipe for Love," 1993. 5" porcelain plate. Plastic stand. CMV, $15.00 MB.

"Special Moments," 1998. 5" porcelain plate with choice of black or white mother and daughter. Dated 1998. Came with white plastic stand. CMV, $15.00 each, MB.

"Love on Parade," 1994. 5" porcelain plate. Dated 1994. CMV, $15.00 MB.

"Blossoms of Love," 2001. 5" porcelain plate. Three different designs for black, white, or Spanish. CMV, $10.00 each, MB.

"A Mother's Love," 1995. 8¼" porcelain plate with choice of black or white mother and child. CMV, $20.00 each, MB.

"Pride and Joy," 1999. 5" porcelain plate. Came with white plastic stand. "Avon" and "1999" on plate. Choice of black or white mother and children. CMV, $12.00 each, MB.

"Love... It's A Gift!" 1996. 5" porcelain plate has Mama Bear and two babies on front. Came with plastic stand. CMV, $15.00 MB.

"A Mother's Love," 2000. 5" porcelain plate. Came with white plastic stand. "Avon" and "2000" on plate. Choice of white or black mother and children. CMV, $12.00 each, MB.

"Motherly Love," 2003.
5¼" porcelain plate with three different designs for black, white, or Spanish. Gold trim and plastic stand. 2003 date and "Mother's Day" on front. "Avon" on back. CMV, $10.00 each, MB.

"A Mother's Love," 2005.
5¼" porcelain plates. Choice of white, black, or Hispanic mother and child. Came with plastic stands. All three plates are different. OSP, $10.00 each. CMV, $10.00 each, MB.

"Mother and Child," 2006.
5¼" porcelain plate. Choice of black or white mother and child. OSP, $10.00 each. CMV, $10.00 each, MB.

Mother's Day Plates, 2004.
5¼" porcelain plates. Three different plates. White, "Sunny Day," black, "Sleepy Time," and Hispanic, "Amor Maternal." OSP, $10.00 each. CMV, $10.00 each, MB.

"Place in the Heart," 2007.
5¼" porcelain plates. Choice of white, black, or Hispanic mother and child. Came with plastic stands. OSP, $10.00 each. CMV, $10.00 each, MB.

Candles

All wax candles are hard to keep clean and in mint condition. They are not selling as well as in the past. Wax taper or tin can candles are not shown. Keep these thoughts in mind when buying and collecting candles. Candle refills and wax chips are no longer considered collectible. There is little resale interest to most collectors in these items. The abbreviation "CO" means "Candle Only," in this section.

White Milk Glass Candle,
1964 – 1966.
CMV, $12.00 CO. $17.00 MB.

Amber Glass Candle,
1965 – 1966.
Amber paint over clear glass. CMV, $15.00 CO. $20.00 MB.

Red Glass Candle,
1965 – 1966.
Red paint over clear glass. CMV, $15.00 CO. $20.00 MB. Dark red 1968 glass candle, not painted. CMV, $50.00.

White and Gold Candle, 1966 – 1967.
White glass top and bottom with gold band. Top makes stand for base. CMV, $15.00 CO. $20.00 MB.

Regence Candle, 1967.
Gold paint over clear glass with green paper band. Lid makes base for bottom. CMV, $20.00 CO, mint. $25.00 MB.

Fostoria Salt Cellar Candle, 1969 – 1970, and 1981.
Clear glass with small silver spoon. CMV, $7.00 CO. $10.00 MB. Reissued in 1981 with "R" on bottom of foot for reissue. CMV, $10.00 MB.

Candlestick Cologne, 1966.
3 oz., silver coated over clear glass. Silver cap. Came in Occur!, Rapture, or Unforgettable. CMV, $15.00 each, CO, mint. $25.00 each, MB.

Regence Candle, 1968 – 1969.
Green glass candleholder with gold handle and base. CMV, $20.00 CO. $25.00 MB.

Wassail Bowl Candle, 1969 – 1970.
Silver paint over red glass with silver spoon. CMV, $18.00 MB.

Frosted Glass Candle, 1967.
Gold band around edge. Lid makes stand for base. CMV, $15.00 CO. $20.00 MB.

Golden Apple Candle, 1968 – 1969.
Shiny gold over clear glass. CMV, $18.00 CO, mint. $25.00 MB.

First Christmas Candle, 1967 – 1972.
All shiny gold, red inside. 1967 had label on bottom and no Avon. 1972 Reissue had Avon on bottom and no label. CMV, $10.00 CO. $15.00 MB.

Silver Apple Candle, 1968.
Factory test sample same as gold apple, only in shiny silver over clear glass. Was not filled. CMV, $50.00 on silver top and bottom. Silver bottom with gold top, CMV, $35.00 mint.

Crystal Candleier, 1969 – 1970.
7" high, clear glass with blue crystals inside, gold handle on glass lid. CMV, $12.00 CO. $15.00 MB.

Gold and White Candle, 1969 – 1970. Painted gold and white over clear glass, lid makes stand for base. CMV, $15.00 CO. $20.00 MB.

Nesting Dove Candle, 1970. White base glass and lid with dove on top. CMV, $15.00 MB.

Water Lily Fragrance Candle, 1972 – 1973. Green lily pad base with white plastic petals with yellow center candle. CMV, $8.00 CO. $10.00 MB.

Crystallite Cologne Candle, 1970 – 1971. Clear glass bottle with gold cap held 4 oz. cologne in Unforgettable, Rapture, Occur!, Somewhere, Topaze, or Cotillion. CMV, $10.00 MB.

Floral Fragrance Candles, 1971 – 1975. Metal gold leaf stand and pink or yellow flower candle. CMV, $12.00 each, MB.

Candlestick Cologne, 1972 – 1975. 5 oz., silver painted over clear glass with silver cap. Came in Moonwind, Field Flowers, Bird of Paradise, or Roses Roses. 1975 came only in Imperial Garden, Moonwind, or Sonnet. CMV, $8.00 BO. $12.00 MB.

Danish Modern Candle, 1970. Stainless steel candleholder with red candle. CMV, $6.00 MB, with candle.

Floral Medley Perfumed Candles, 1971 – 1972. Box held yellow and purple frosted glass candleholders. CMV, $10.00 MB, set.

Turtle Candle, 1972. White glass turtle candle with green glass shell top. CMV, $12.00 MB.

Candlestick Cologne, 1970 – 1971. 4 oz. red glass bottle, gold cap. Held Elusive, Charisma, Brocade, Régence, or Bird of Paradise. CMV, $8.00 MB. Also came in smoked red glass. Appears much darker than red glass issue. It looks smoky red. CMV, $15.00 MB.

Dynasty Perfumed Candle, 1971 – 1972. 6" high, white glass jar and lid. CMV, $15.00, CO. $20.00 MB.

Mushroom Candle, 1972. White glass candle with pink glass mushroom top. CMV, $11.00 MB.

Crystal Glow Perfumed Candleholder, *1972 – 1973.*
Clear glass. Came in Moonwind, Bird of Paradise, Elusive, Charisma, Brocade, Régence, Wassail, Bayberry, Frankincense & Myrrh, or Roses Roses. CMV, $12.00 MB.

Potpourri Fragrance Candle, *1972 – 1973.*
White milk glass, came with potpourri candle. CMV, $10.00 MB.

China Teapot Candle, 1972 – 1973.
White china with blue flower design or without decal. Thousands came from factory, not sold by Avon, with or without decals, some decals were on front, some on back. Factory rejects, CMV, $9.00 each. Came from Avon with Roses Roses, Moonwind, Bird of Paradise, Elusive, Charisma, Brocade, Régence, Wassail, Bayberry, or Frankincense & Myrrh candles. CMV, $15.00 MB.

Flaming Tulip Fragrance Candle, 1973.
Red candle in Floral Medley fragrance. Gold holder. CMV, $10.00 MB.

Regency Candlestick Cologne, *1973 – 1974.*
4 oz., clear glass. Came in Bird of Paradise, Charisma, Elusive, or Roses Roses. CMV, $8.00 CO. $11.00 MB.

Fostoria Perfumed Candleholder, 1973.
Clear glass. Came with Patchwork, Sonnet, Moonwind, Roses Roses, Charisma, Bird of Paradise, Bayberry, Wassail, or Frankincense & Myrrh candles. CMV, $8.00, CO. $10.00 MB.

Hearts and Flowers Fragrance Candle, *1973 – 1974.*
White milk glass with red, green, and pink design. Came in Floral Medley fragrance. CMV, $10.00 MB.

Hobnail Patio Candle, *1973.*
White milk base, clear glass top. Came with Sonnet, Moonwind, Roses Roses, Bird of Paradise, Charisma, Wassail, Bayberry, or Frankincense & Myrrh candles. CMV, $12.00 MB.

Ovalique Perfume Candleholder, *1974 – 1975.*
4" high, clear gloss, choice of Sonnet, Moonwind, Patchwork, Roses Roses, Charisma, Bird of Paradise, Bayberry, Frankincense & Myrrh, or Wassail. CMV, $10.00 MB.

Golden Pine Cone Fragrance Candlette, *1974 – 1975.*
Gold toned glass. Came in Bayberry only. CMV, $8.00 MB.

Kitchen Crock Fragrance Candlette, 1974 – 1975.
Yellow crock with red, yellow, and blue flowers with cork cap. Came in Meadow Morn fragrance. CMV, $8.00 MB.

Grapefruit Fragrance Candle, 1974 – 1976.
Yellow wax with red center. Has grapefruit fragrance. CMV, $5.00 MB.

Lotus Blossom Perfumed Candleholder, *1974 – 1975.*
Black glass with green and white design. Available in: Bayberry, Frankincense & Myrrh, Wassail, Sonnet, Moonwind, Roses Roses, Bird of Paradise, or Charisma. CMV, $15.00 CO. $20.00 MB.

Facets of Light Fragrance Candlette, *1975 – 1976.*
4" high, clear glass. Came with Bayberry candle but any refill candlette will fit. CMV, $8.00 MB.

Washington Goblet Fostoria Candleholder, *1975 – 1977.*
Blue glass by Fostoria. Came with Frankincense & Myrrh or Floral Medley candle. CMV, $14.00 MB.

Dynamite Fragrance Candlette, *1975 – 1976.*
Red and white. CMV, $8.00 MB.

Black-eyed Susan Fragrance Candle, *1975 – 1976.*
Yellow wax with brown center. Wild Flowers fragrance. CMV, $5.00 MB.

Opalique Candlestick Cologne, *1976 – 1977.*
5 oz. swirl glass and cap. Came in Charisma or Sweet Honesty. $8.00 BO. CMV, $10.00 MB.

Terra Cotta Bird Candlette, *1976 – 1977.*
Reddish brown clay bird candleholder. "Avon" on bottom. CMV, $5.00 MB.

Cologne and Candlelight, *1975 – 1976.*
2 oz., clear glass with gold cap and clear plastic collar. Held Imperial Garden, Roses Roses, or Charisma. CMV, $6.00 MB.

Enchanted Mushroom Fragrance Candle, *1975.*
White wax shell/yellow cover. Meadow Morn fragrance. CMV, $4.00 MB.

Mount Vernon Sauce Pitcher, *1977 – 1979.*
Approximately 5½" high. Blue Fostoria glass. Came with Floral Medley perfumed candle. Refillable. "Avon" on bottom. CMV, $12.00 pitcher only. $16.00 MB.

Fostoria Candlelight Basket Candleholder, *1975.*
Clear glass, gold handle. Choice of Sonnet, Moonwind, Patchwork, Charisma, Roses Roses, Bird of Paradise, Wassail, Frankincense & Myrrh, or Bayberry candle refill. CMV, $10.00 CO. $12.00 MB.

Sleigh Light Fragrance Candle, *1975 – 1976.*
4" high, red and green. Bayberry scented. CMV, $4.00 MB.

Catnip Fragrance Candle, *1975 – 1976.*
4" high, yellow plastic. Floral Medley fragrance. CMV, $7.00 MB.

Martha Washington Goblet, *1976 – 1977.*
Blue glass Fostoria candleholder. CMV, $14.00 MB.

Gingerbread House Fragrance Candle, *1977 – 1979.*
Brown and white wax candle. Came in Frankincense & Myrrh fragrance. CMV, $3.00 no box. $5.00 MB.

Dove in Flight Candlette, 1977 – 1978.
Clear glass dove candleholder. Came in Meadow Morn fragrance candlette. Refillable. CMV, $10.00 MB.

Bunny Ceramic Planter Candleholder, 1977 – 1979.
Three different rabbits. One made in Brazil and recesses on bottom; one flat bottom made in U.S. and lighter in weight; 1978 issue, same flat bottom, only different type letters on bottom. Came with Floral Medley or Roses Roses perfumed candle. CMV, $10.00 each, rabbit only. $12.00 each, MB.

Tender Blossom Candle, 1977 – 1980.
Light pink wax base with dark pink inner candle. CMV, $4.00 MB.

Heart and Diamond Fostoria Loving Cup Perfumed Candleholder, 1978.
Approximately 7" high, clear Fostoria glass. Came with Floral Medley perfumed candle. Embossed with "Avon 1978" on its base. Refillable. CMV, $10.00 glass only. $15.00 MB.

Heart and Diamond Candlestick, 1978 – 1979.
7" high, heart embossed Fostoria clear glass candle. "Avon 1979" on bottom. Came with long red candle for one end or turn it over and insert the small glass candleholder on other end. Came in red box. CMV, $13.00 MB.

Bright Chipmunk Candlette, 1978 – 1979.
Clear glass candleholder. Refillable. CMV, $9.00 MB.

Fresh Aroma Smoker's Candle, 1978 – 1979.
Non-refillable brown wax like pipe with black plastic and chrome top. Bottom cardboard label. CMV, $8.00 MB.

Plum Pudding Candle, 1978 – 1979.
4" high brown, green, and white candle. Bottom label. CMV $6.00 MB.

Winter Lights Candlette, 1978 – 1979.
Clear glass square candleholder. Held glass candlette. "Avon" on bottom of both. CMV, $10.00 MB.

Sparkling Turtle Candlette, 1978 – 1979.
4½" long, clear glass turtle. CMV, $9.00 MB.

Revolutionary Soldier Smoker's Candle, 1979 – 1980.
Clear or dark amber glass. Clear harder to find. Red and gold box. CMV, $8.00 MB.

Shimmering Peacock Candle, 1979 – 1980. Box held clear glass peacock. CMV, $11.00 MB.

Country Spice Candle, 1979 – 1980. Light blue-green glass jar and lid. Wire bale. Came with candle inside. CMV, $9.00 MB.

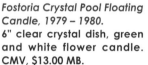

Fostoria Crystal Pool Floating Candle, 1979 – 1980. 6" clear crystal dish, green and white flower candle. CMV, $13.00 MB.

Sparkling Swirl Clearfire Candle, 1980 – 1982. Clear glass, 5⅛" high. CMV, $11.00 MB.

Mrs. Snowlight Candle, 1979 – 1981. White, red, and green wax candle. CMV, $4.00 MB.

Flowerfrost Collection Water Goblet Candlette, 1979 – 1980. Frosted glass goblet held glass candle insert. CMV, $11.00 MB.

Sherbet Dessert Candle, 1980 – 1982. 5" high, clear glass. Came with red, yellow, or pink candle. CMV, $8.00 MB.

Winter Wonderland Centerpiece Candle, 1979 – 1980. White wax base, green wax trees, red and white wax house. Center held glass candlette. CMV, $10.00 MB.

Bunny Ceramic Planter Candleholder, 1979 – 1980. Made of ceramic in Brazil for Avon. Green, pink, and yellow flowers. Brown eyes, pink inner ears. Came with Floral Medley or Spiced Garden candle. CMV, $15.00 MB.

Personally Yours Fragrance Candle, 1980 – 1982. Clear glass with refillable candle. Came with sheet of stick-on gold letters. CMV, $12.00 MB.

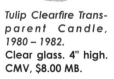

Garden Bounty Candle, 1979 – 1980. Beige and pink cart, red candle. CMV, $8.00 MB.

Tulip Clearfire Transparent Candle, 1980 – 1982. Clear glass. 4" high. CMV, $8.00 MB.

Star Bright Fragrance Candle, 1980 – 1981. Icy clear glass, held refillable candle. CMV, $8.00 MB.

Floral Light Candle Refill, 1980 – 1981. Came in lavender, green, or yellow wax. Flower shaped. CMV, $4.00 MB.

Crystal Glow Clearfire Candle, 1980. Clear glass. "Avon" on bottom under candle. CMV, $10.00 MB.

Sunny Bunny Ceramic Candleholder, 1981 – 1982. 5½" high ceramic candleholder dated 1981. CMV, $15.00 MB.

Bunny Bright Ceramic Candle, 1980. White ceramic with pink and green trim. "1980 Avon" on bottom. CMV, $12.00 MB.

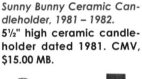

Floral Light Fragrance Candle, 1980 – 1981. Clear glass flower shaped base held flower shaped candle refill. CMV, $7.00 MB.

Christmas Charmer Candlestick, 1981. Small white, red, and green girl, plastic candleholder. Remove top sleeve to fit small bottle of cologne with red cap. Choice of Zany or Charisma ⅓ oz. cologne, red box. CMV, $7.00 MB, set.

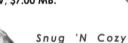

Snug 'N Cozy "Cat" Fragrance Candle, 1980 – 1982. Clear glass cat candleholder. CMV, $10.00 MB.

Holiday Candle Dish and Wreath, 1980. Clear glass candleholder, red candle and holly wreath. CMV, $9.00 MB.

Glow of Christmas Candle, 1980. White wax with red center refillable candle. CMV, $6.00 MB.

Ultra Crystal Candle, 1981 – 1982. 2½" high, clear glass. Gray box. CMV, $10.00 MB.

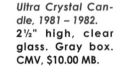

Harvest Time Fragrance Candle, 1980 – 1981. Tan wax candle, 6" high. CMV, $4.00 MB.

Chesapeake Collection Jigger Candle, 1981. Amber glass dog head candle, candle in bottom. CMV, $12.00 MB.

Ultra Shimmer Candle, 1981 – 1982. 2½" high, clear glass, octagonal shaped. Gold box. CMV, $9.00 MB.

**Hot Choco-lite Candle,
1981 – 1982.**
Beige or white color wax cup with brown chocolate smelling candle. CMV, $4.00 MB.

Love Light Clearfire Candle, 1982.
Clear ribbed glass heart shaped candle. CMV, $10.00 MB.

Snuggly Mouse Candleholder, 1983.
Ceramic mouse holder base, 4¼" wide. Came with 6" red candle. CMV, $6.00 MB.

**Pitkin Hat Candle,
1981 – 1982.**
Blue swirled glass hat held candle. Came in green box. CMV, $8.00 MB.

American Heirloom Candlestick and Candle, 1982 – 1984.
Pewter metal candlestick and 6" red candle. CMV, $5.00 MB.

**Glistening Tree Clearfire Candle,
1981 – 1982.**
4½" high clear ribbed glass tree shaped candle. CMV, $10.00 MB.

**Toccara Special Edition Candle,
1982 – 1983.**
Clear cut glass Fostoria candle. Blue box. CMV, $10.00 MB.

**Coral Glow Candle,
1983 – 1984.**
Clear glass conch shell design candle. CMV, $12.00 MB.

**Gem Glow Candle,
1981 – 1982.**
Clear glass, multi-faceted. Came with green, amber, or red filled candle. CMV, $10.00 MB.

**Harvest Glow Candle,
1982 – 1983.**
Clear glass pumpkin shaped candle and lid. CMV, $10.00 MB.

**Holiday Floating Candles,
1983.**
Box of two candles in choice of red poinsettia flowers or green and red wreaths, 2½" wide each. CMV, $4.00 MB, set.

**Carolling Trio Candles,
1981 – 1982.**
Came in separate boxes. Melodic Mouse, Howling Hound, or Crooning Cat candles. CMV, $3.00 each, MB.

Spice Cupboard Candle, 1982.
1½" high clear glass refillable candle. CMV, $5.00 MB.

Mr. Snowlight Candle, 1981.
5½" high, white wax, green trim. CMV, $5.00 MB.

Ho Ho Glow "Santa" Candle, 1982 – 1983.
5" ceramic red, white, and black Santa candle. CMV, $16.00 MB.

Year to Year Birthday Candle, 1983 – 1984.
4½" ceramic clown candleholder with yellow candle, 1, 2, 3, and 4 on sides. CMV, $10.00 MB.

Sparkling Jewel Stackable Candles, 1984.
Green or blue glass. CMV, $5.00 each, MB.

Christmas Fun Candle Gift Set, 1985.
Green horse, white doll, and red soldier wax candles. CMV, $4.00 MB, set.

Porcelain Angels Candleholder, 1985.
5" high, white porcelain. Empty. CMV, $10.00 MB.

Autumn Impressions Candle, 1984.
2¼" high, clear glass. CMV, $4.00 MB.

Summer Lights Indoor-Outdoor Candle, 1984.
2¼" high, green glass. CMV, $5.00 MB.

Shimmering Glass Convertible Candleholder, 1985.
2¾" high, clear glass. Held big candle on one side, flip it over to hold taper candle. CMV, $5.00 MB.

Country Fresh Candle, 1985.
Chicken, on egg candle with blue or red base. CMV, $4.00 MB.

Joyous Message Candles, 1985.
Three elf wax candles, 1½" high each. CMV, $3.00 MB, set.

Personal Creation Candle, 1985.
Glistening Creation Candle, 1985.
Both glass candles, same style. Different boxes and candle mix. CMV, $6.00 each, MB.

Country Jam Candles, 1985.
2" high, clear glass. Cloth covers over lids. Came in Black Raspberry, Mint, Orange, and Strawberry. CMV, $4.00 each, MB.

Soft Rose Floating Candles, 1985.
Box held white, pink, and red flower candles. CMV, $6.00 MB, set.

Anniversary Taper Candleholder, 1985.
Small, porcelain, doves and flowers. CMV, $8.00 MB.

Glistening Glow Candle, 1986.
Clear glass candle. CMV, $6.00 MB.

Gingerbread House Candle, 1986.
Ceramic house held glass cup candle. CMV, $16.00 MB.

Clearfire Tulip Cup Candle, 1986. Clear glass. 4" high. CMV, $5.00 MB.

Crystal Candle, 1987. Clear pressed cut crystal glass. Pear or apple shaped. CMV, $8.00 each, MB.

North Pole Pals Candles, 1988. Reindeer, penguin, and polar bear candles. Also used as tree ornaments. CMV, $3.00 each, MB.

Jolly Santa Candle, 1986. 5½" high Santa wax candle. CMV, $5.00 MB.

Bunny Taper Candleholders, 1987. Two small ceramic rabbit candleholders. CMV, $10.00 MB.

Dove Candleholders, 1986. Two white bisque porcelain candleholders. CMV, $9.00 MB.

Bunny Patch Candle, 1988. 6" tall wax rabbit candle. CMV, $3.00 MB.

Fireplace Friends Candleholder, 1988. 3½" high fireplace has candleholder on back side. CMV, $10.00 MB.

Egg Candles, Marbleized, 1987. 2¼" high, swirl wax candles. OSP, $3.50 for set of three. CMV, $2.00 each.

Three Wee Teddy Candles, 1987. Three 1½" high bear candles on one wick. Cut separate. CMV, $4.00 set or $1.00 each, mint.

Nature's Friend Candleholder, 1988. Hand-painted ceramic squirrel held scented candle. CMV, $8.00 MB.

Trinket Box "Seashell" Candle, 1987. Small ceramic 3½" pearlized seashell. CMV, $7.00 MB.

Christmas Teddy Candle, 1988. 3" high bear candle. CMV, $3.00 MB.

Natural Home Scents Townhouse Candle, 1988. 4¾" high ceramic townhouse candle. CMV, $18.00 MB.

Glitter and Glow Holiday Candles, 1989.
Red or gold metallic candles. CMV, $5.00 MB, set.

St. Nick's Starlit Journey Glass Candleholder, 1991.
5" x 5" frosted glass candleholder came with two white bayberry tealight candles. CMV, $10.00 MB.

Glowing Angel Crystal Candlesticks, 1992.
Set of two lead cut crystal angel candleholders, 7" high. CMV, $30.00 MB, set.

Fireside Friends Candleholder, 1992.
3" high ceramic candleholder and candle. CMV, $8.00 MB.

Holiday Dove Candleholders, 1993.
White porcelain doves. 4½" long, 2¾" high. Candles came separate. Set of two. CMV, $15.00 MB, set.

Glistening Star Crystal Candleholders, 1993.
2" x 2" lead crystal. Set of two. CMV, $8.00 MB, set.

Romantic Lights Scented Candle, 1994.
2¾" x 3¼" lead crystal scented candle. Four fragrances. CMV, $4.00 each, MB.

M.I. Hummel Crystal Candlesticks, 1995.
Set of two frosted lead crystal angels, 3½" high. Does not come with taper candles. CMV, $30.00 MB, set.

Cupid Candleholder, 1995.
3¼" high, white glazed porcelain cupid candle with red votive candle. CMV, $7.00 MB.

Christmas Traditions Glassware Hurricane Candle, 1995.
7⅝" high glass candleholder. Came with four white candles. CMV, $20.00 MB.

Trick or Treat Trio Candle Set, 1995.
Three Halloween wax candles, 2¾" high. CMV, $3.00 set of three, MB.

Easter Candles, 1997.
4¾" high wax candles with choice of bunny, lamb, or duck. CMV, $2.00 each, MB.

Berry Candles, 1997.
3½" high, 3" wide berry wax candles in metal buckets. Choice of blackberry, strawberry, or blueberry. CMV, $3.00 each, MB.

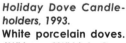

486

Left to right:
Hummingbird Candle, 2003.
First in series.
Summertime Delight Candle, 2003.
Second in series.
Winter Carousel Candle, 2003.
Third in series.

Charming Birdhouse Trio Candle, 2003.
Fourth in series.
Each candle is a clear glass jar with decal design on sides and a resin lid. Each is 6" high. CMV, $10.00 each, MB.

Angel Collector Candles, 2003.
Luminous Treasures Series. 6¾" high. Glass bottom decals, clear glass jars with resin angel lids. Marked "Avon." Choice of black or white angel. CMV, $10.00 each, MB.

Children's Decanters and Toys

Children's toys and collectibles continue to be popular with many collectors. Almost all children's toys are plastic, which are about the only plastic items in the book truly collectible. All children's items must be in new mint condition. If they are not, I suggest you do not buy them. Be sure to read What's Hot and What's Not in the introduction section of this book.

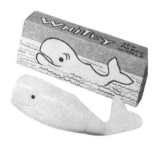

Avonville Slugger, 1961 – 1962.
6 oz. tan plastic bat held shampoo. CMV, $12.00 BO. $17.00 MB.

Pig in a Poke, 1960 – 1962.
8 oz. pink plastic pig held bubble bath. Came in pink bag. CMV, $9.00 BO. $14.00 BO with bag. $18.00 MB.

Whitey the Whale, 1959 – 1962.
8 oz., white plastic whale held bubble bath. CMV, $10.00 BO. $15.00 MB.

A Winner, 1960 – 1962.
4 oz. maroon plastic boxing gloves with white caps. Tied together with white plastic cord. Hand guard and hair guard. CMV, $7.00 each, BO. $20.00 MB.

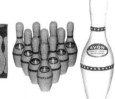

Clean as a Whistle, 1960 – 1961.
8 oz., red and white plastic bottle, real whistle cap. Came in bubble bath. CMV, $10.00 BO. $15.00 MB.

Frilly Duck, 1960 – 1962.
3 oz., yellow plastic duck with blue cap. Came in baby oil, baby lotion, and Tot 'N' Tyke shampoo. CMV, $10.00 BO. $13.00 MB.

Bowling Pin, 1960 – 1962.
4 oz., white plastic trimmed in red. Came in Vigorate, liquid deodorant, hand guard, hair trainer, after shaving lotion, after shower for men, liquid hair lotion, shampoo, cream hair lotion, or Electric pre-shave. Ten different. CMV, $10.00 each, BO. $15.00 each, MB. Vigorate, $15.00 BO, $20.00 MB.

Left: Land Ho! 1961 – 1962.
8 oz., blue and white plastic telescope held hair trainer. CMV, $12.00 BO, mint. $17.00 MB.
Right: Naughty-Less, 1961 – 1962.
8 oz., red and white submarine with white and blue cap. Held bubble bath. CMV, $15.00 BO, mint. $20.00 MB.

Little Helper Iron, 1962 – 1964.
8 oz., blue plastic iron with white handle. Held bubble bath. CMV, $13.00 BO, mint. $17.00 MB.

Bubble Bunny, 1964 – 1965.
Pink and white rabbit puppet with 6 oz. tube of bubble bath gel. CMV, $5.00 puppet only. $11.00 MB.

Aqua Car, 1964 – 1965.
8 oz., red and white plastic bottle of bubble bath. CMV, $10.00 BO. $15.00 MB.

Lil Folks Time, 1961 – 1964.
8 oz., yellow and white plastic clock with yellow cap and red hands. Held bubble bath. CMV, $8.00 BO. $11.00 MB.

Watering Can, 1962 – 1964.
8 oz., yellow plastic bottle. Held bubble bath. Blue cap. CMV, $13.00 BO, mint. $17.00 MB.

Lil Tom Turtles, 1961 – 1963.
3 oz., plastic turtles. Each has white hat. Yellow held baby shampoo, blue held baby oil, and red held baby lotion. CMV, $15.00 each, MB.

First Mate Shampoo, 1963 – 1964.
8 oz., blue and white plastic sailor with white hat. CMV, $11.00 BO. $15.00 MB.
Captain's Bubble Bath, 1963 – 1964.
8 oz., white, yellow, and black plastic bottle with blue hat. CMV, $11.00 BO. $15.00 MB.

Packy the Elephant, 1964 – 1965.
3 oz. each. Each has white hat. Blue held baby oil, yellow held baby shampoo, red held baby lotion. CMV, $10.00 each, BO, red and blue, $15.00 MB. $15.00 BO, yellow, $20.00 MB.

Six Shooter, 1962 – 1963.
6 oz., gray and white plastic gun with "No Tears" shampoo. CMV, $18.00 BO, mint. $24.00 MB.

Humpty Dumpty, 1963 – 1965.
8 oz. plastic bottle of bubble bath. Blue bottom, white top, black belt. CMV, $9.00 MB, $5.00 BO.

Santa's Chimney, 1964 – 1965.
Red and white box held 5 oz. of powdered bubble bath. Top of box makes a puzzle game. CMV, $20.00 MB.

Concertina, 1962 – 1965.
8 oz., red and yellow plastic squeeze bottle with musical cap. Held bubble bath. CMV, $12.00 BO. $15.00 MB.

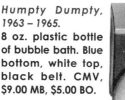

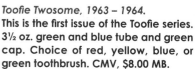

Toofie Twosome, 1963 – 1964.
This is the first issue of the Toofie series. 3½ oz. green and blue tube and green cap. Choice of red, yellow, blue, or green toothbrush. CMV, $8.00 MB.

Toy Soldiers, 1964.
4 oz. each. Red, white, and blue plastic bottles, black caps. Came in hair trainer, shampoo, hand lotion, and bubble bath. CMV, $12.00 each, MB.

Very Own Telephone, 1964 – 1965.
6 oz., red plastic telephone and base. Held baby shampoo. CMV, $9.00 BO. $13.00 MB.

Mr. Many Moods, 1965 – 1966.
6 oz., white plastic bottle with blue and yellow hat, red nose and mouth, and black eyes. Held shampoo. CMV, $8.00 BO $10.00 MB.

Bugle, 1965.
6 oz., blue plastic bugle with yellow cap. Held Tot 'N' Tyke shampoo. CMV, $10.00 BO. $15.00 MB.

Fife, 1965.
6 oz., yellow plastic bottle with red cap. Came in hand lotion or hair trainer. CMV, $10.00 BO. $15.00 MB.

Cuckoo Clock, 1965 – 1966.
10 oz., red, white, and blue plastic clock held bubble bath. CMV, $8.00 BO. $10.00 MB.

Safe Sam, 1965.
8 oz. red and black plastic safe held bubble bath. CMV, $8.00, BO. $11.00 MB.

Topsy Turvey Clown, 1965 only.
10 oz., red, white, and yellow plastic clown. Blue hat, black feet. Held bubble bath. CMV, $12.00 BO, mint. $16.00 MB.

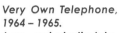

Jet Plane, 1965 only.
3 oz., red, white, and blue plastic tube with white plastic wings came in gel bubble bath, children's gel shampoo, or hair trainer. CMV, $10.00 BO, mint. $15.00 MB.

Freddie the Frog, 1965 – 1966.
Green rubber frog with yellow hat and eyes, pink lips, and green soap. CMV, $5.00 frog only. $10.00 MB, with soap.

First Down, 1965 – 1967.
Large box held real junior size football and 6 oz. brown football soap on a rope. CMV, $10.00 MB, soap. $15.00 ball. $30.00 MB, set.

Perry the Penguin, 1966 – 1967.
Black and white penguin soap dish and white soap. CMV, $12.00 MB, set.

Three Bears, 1966 – 1967.
Each 4¾" high, 3 oz. White plastic bottles with blue caps. Papa Bear held baby oil. CMV, $10.00 BO. $14.00 MB. Mama Bear held baby lotion, Baby Bear held shampoo. CMV, $8.00 each, BO. $12.00 each, MB.

Spinning Top, 1966 – 1967.
4 oz., red and white top held bubble bath. Yellow top spinner. CMV, $6.00 BO. $10.00 MB.

Whistle Tots, 1966 – 1967.
6¾" high, 4 oz. white plastic bottles with whistle caps. Red cap fireman held Tot 'N' Tyke shampoo. Blue cap policeman held hair trainer, and green clown held bubble bath. CMV, $7.00 each, BO, mint. $10.00 each, MB.

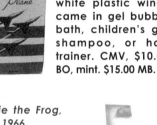

School Days, 1966 – 1967. 8 oz., red and white plastic ruler held non-tear shampoo. Yellow cap. CMV, $7.00 BO. $10.00 MB.

Ring Around Rosie, 1966 – 1967. Pink rubber elephant (sticks on wall) with blue bar of Avon soap. CMV, $4.00 elephant only. $6.00 soap only. $15.00 MB.

Good Habit Rabbit, 1967. 3 oz., 4½" high. White plastic rabbit, green hat and orange carrot. Came in Tot 'N' Tyke shampoo. CMV, $8.00 BO. $12.00 MB.

Globe Bank, 1966 – 1967. 10 oz., blue plastic globe held bubble bath. Black base. Included five different colored sets of stick-on countries. North America came in orange, blue, tan, pink, or yellow. CMV, $10.00 BO. $16.00 MB.

Little Champ, 1967 – 1968. ½ oz., each with white caps. Blue boxing glove held non-tear shampoo, yellow glove held hair trainer. CMV, $5.00 each glove. $17.00 MB.

Little Missy Rolling Pin, 1966 – 1967. 12" long, 8 oz., pink plastic center with orange ends. Held non-tear shampoo. CMV, $9.00 BO, mint. $13.00 MB.

Wash Aweigh Soap and Dish, 1966 – 1967. Green plastic boat dish and yellow anchor soap on a rope. CMV, $6.00 boat. $9.00 anchor soap. $20.00 MB, set.

Paddle 'N' Ball Set, 1966 – 1967. 6 oz., tan plastic paddle with red cap. Held shampoo. Rubber ball hooked to paddle. 8" long, 4½" wide. CMV, $15.00 MB.

Mr. Lion, 1967. 4 oz., white plastic bottle with red bubble pipe over white cap. Held bubble bath. CMV, $6.00 BO. $8.00 MB.

Tin Man, 1967. 4 oz. ,white plastic bottle with blue bubble pipe over white cap. Held non-tear shampoo. CMV, $6.00 BO. $8.00 MB.

Straw Man, 1967. 4 oz., white plastic bottle with yellow bubble pipe over white cap. Held hand lotion. CMV, $6.00 BO. $8.00 MB.

Toofie the Tiger, 1966 – 1967. 3½ oz., green and orange tube, green cap, toothbrush. CMV, $6.00 MB.

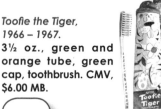

Three Little Pigs, 1967 – 1968. 3 oz., each, 4½" high. Blue pig with yellow hat held bubble bath, yellow pig with green hat held baby shampoo, and pink pig with pink hat held baby lotion. CMV, $6.00 each, BO. $9.00 each, MB.

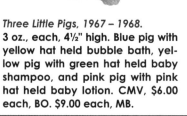

*Santa's Helper,
1967 – 1968.*
**Red and white
sponge with 6
oz. tube of gel
bubble bath.
CMV, $8.00 MB.**

*Bird Feeder,
1967 – 1968.*
**11" high, black and
white plastic center
with red base and
yellow top. Held 7½
oz. powdered bubble
bath. CMV, $8.00 BO.
$12.00 MB.**

Gaylord Gator, 1967 – 1969.
**10" long green and yellow rubber
soap dish with yellow soap. CMV,
$3.00 gator only. $10.00 MB, set.**

*Little Red Riding Hood,
1968.*
**4 oz., yellow plastic
bottle, red cap. Held
bubble bath. CMV,
$2.00 BO. $6.00 MB,
with glasses.**

*Smiley the Whale,
1967 – 1968.*
**9" blue plastic whale held
9 oz. bubble bath. CMV,
$6.00 BO. $9.00 MB.**

Snoopy Soap Dish, 1968 – 1976.
**White bar of Avon soap sits in black
and white plastic soap dish. CMV,
$2.00 Snoopy only. $6.00 MB.**

Wolf, 1968.
**4 oz., yellow and
blue plastic bottle,
green cap, held
non-tear sham-
poo. CMV, $2.00
BO. $6.00 MB with
white fang teeth.**

*Tic Toc Tiger,
1967 – 1969.*
**8 oz., orange and
white plastic clock
with yellow cap and
hands, held bubble
bath. CMV, $6.00 BO.
$9.00 MB.**

*Charlie Brown,
1968 – 1972.*
**4 oz., red, white,
and black plastic
bottle of non-tear
shampoo. CMV,
$3.00 BO. $5.00
MB.**

*Mr. Presto Chango,
1968.*
**6 oz. yellow plas-
tic bottle with red
hat, black eyes,
and pink lips. Held
non-tear shampoo.
CMV, $6.00 BO.
$8.00 MB.**

*Toofie Toothpaste,
1967 – 1968.*
**3½ oz. white tube with rac-
coon and pink cap, tooth-
brush, and pink and white
box. CMV, $6.00 MB.**

*Space Age,
1968 – 1969.*
**4 oz., silver and yel-
low plastic rocket
held liquid hair
trainer. CMV, $3.00
BO. $5.00 MB.**

*Tub Talk Telephone,
1967 – 1968.*
**6 oz., yellow telephone
with red cap and
holder. Held Tot 'N'
Tyke shampoo. CMV,
$8.00 BO. $11.00 MB.**

Linus, 1968 – 1974.
**Red, white, and green
plastic 4 oz. tube of gel
bubble bath with red,
white, and black plas-
tic Linus, plastic holder.
CMV, $3.00 Linus and
tube only. $5.00 MB.**

Milk Bath, 1968 – 1969.
**6 oz. pink plastic milk
can held powdered
bubble bath. CMV,
$3.00 BO. $5.00 MB.**

Tic Toc Turtle,
1968 – 1969.
8 oz., 5½" high. Green turtle, yellow clock face with pink hands. Held bubble bath. CMV, $6.00 BO. $9.00 MB.

One, Two, Lace My Shoe,
1968 – 1969.
8 oz. bubble bath. Pink plastic shoe with orange tie-on and yellow cap. Green or yellow roof. CMV, $6.00 BO. $9.00 MB.

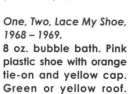

Little Lamb Baby Lotion, 1968 – 1969.
3 oz., white plastic lamb with blue cap. CMV, $7.00 MB.

Little Red Schoolhouse, 1968 – 1969.
3 oz. red plastic school with yellow cap. Contained bubble bath. CMV, $8.00 MB.

Snoopy and Doghouse,
1969 – 1972.
8 oz., white plastic dog and red plastic 3" high doghouse, held non-tear shampoo. CMV, $3.00 BO. $5.00 MB.

Scrub Mug,
1968 – 1969.
6 oz., blue plastic mug with blue brush lid. Held liquid soap. CMV, $6.00 MB.

Lucy Mug, 1969 – 1970.
5 oz., white glass, yellow top and label. White cap, non-tear shampoo. CMV, $8.00 MB.

Charlie Brown Mug,
1969 – 1970.
5 oz., white glass, blue top and label. White cap, bubble bath. CMV, $8.00 MB.

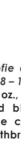

Toofie on Guard,
1968 – 1969.
3½ oz., red, white, and blue tube, blue cap. Avon toothbrush. CMV, $5.00 MB.

Tub Catch,
1968 – 1969.
2 ft. long yellow rod and reel held 6 oz. bubble bath. Pink, green, and blue plastic fish. CMV, $9.00 MB.

Easter Dec-a-Doo,
1968 – 1969.
8 oz., pink and yellow plastic egg held bubble bath. Came with stick-on decorations. CMV, $4.00 BO. $6.00 MB.

Mary Non-tear shampoo,
1968 – 1969.
3 oz. pink plastic bottle. CMV, $8.00 MB.

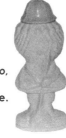

Snoopy the Flying Ace, 1969.
4 oz., 6" high white plastic with blue hat, yellow glasses, held bubble bath. CMV, $2.00 BO. $5.00 MB.

Snoopy Mug,
1969 – 1972.
5 oz., white glass, 5" high. Came with red or blue top. Blue top is more rare. Also came with oval or round decal. CMV, $7.00 MB, red top. $9.00 MB, blue top.

Jumpin' Jiminy, 1969 – 1973. 8 oz., 6" high, green, red, and yellow pull toy with yellow cap. Held bubble bath. CMV, $3.00 BO. $5.00 MB.

Chief Scrubem, 1969 – 1970. 4 oz., red and yellow plastic Indian held liquid soap. CMV, $6.00 MB.

Bo Bo the Elephant, 1970. 5 oz., light or dark pink plastic bottle of non-tear shampoo. CMV, $3.00 BO. $5.00 MB.

Wrist Wash Bubble Bath, 1969 – 1970. 2 oz., orange plastic clock with blue cap. CMV, $4.00 BO. $6.00 MB.

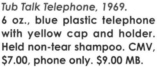

Ring 'em Up Clean, 1970 – 1972. 8 oz., orange plastic bottle with red or white cap held non-tear shampoo. CMV, $3.00 BO. $5.00 MB.

Birdhouse, 1969. 7" high, orange plastic bottom with tan roof. Held 8 oz. of powdered bubble bath. CMV, $7.00 BO. $9.00 MB.

Tub Talk Telephone, 1969. 6 oz., blue plastic telephone with yellow cap and holder. Held non-tear shampoo. CMV, $7.00, phone only. $9.00 MB.

Mad Hatter, 1970. 6 oz., bronze plastic with pink hat and clock. Held bubble bath. CMV, $4.00 BO. $6.00 MB.

Freddie the Frog, 1969 – 1970. Green rubber frog soap dish and green vest soap. Pink lips and pink band around hat. CMV $3.00 frog only. $10.00 MB, with soap.

Toofie Toothpaste, 1969 – 1970. 3½ oz. blue and green tube with pink cap and toothbrush in blue and green box. CMV, $2.00 BO. $5.00 MB.

Mickey Mouse, 1969 – 1971. 4½ oz., red pants, black and white plastic Mickey with yellow feet. Held bubble bath. CMV, $5.00 BO. $7.00 MB.

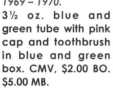

Lucy, 1970 – 1972. 4 oz., red, white, and black plastic bottle held bubble bath. CMV, $3.00 BO. $5.00 MB.

Concertina, 1970 – 1972. 8 oz., blue and yellow plastic squeeze bottle. Held bubble bath. Musical cap with pink strap. CMV, $6.00 BO. $8.00 MB.

S.S. Suds, *1970 – 1971.*
8 oz., blue and white plastic boat held non-tear shampoo. CMV, $5.00 BO. $7.00 MB.

Clean Shot, *1970 – 1972.*
Orange net held orange basketball sponge and one bar of Clean Shot soap. CMV, $8.00 MB, set.

Schroeder, *1970 – 1972.*
6 oz., red, white, black, and yellow plastic bottle held bubble bath, in piano shaped box. CMV, $4.00 BO. $9.00 MB, in piano box.

Pluto, *1970 – 1971.*
4 oz., yellow and black plastic dog with red collar. Held non-tear shampoo. CMV, $5.00 BO. $7.00 MB.

Reginald G. Raccoon III,
1970 – 1971.
Black, brown, and white rubber soap dish and 3 oz. pink vest soap. CMV, $10.00 MB, set.

Linus, *1970 – 1972.*
4 oz., red, white, and black plastic bottle held non-tear shampoo. CMV, $6.00 MB.

Topsy Turvey,
1970 – 1972.
4 oz. green plastic bottle with white cap held bubble bath. CMV, $1.00 BO. $2.00 MB.

Moon Flight Game, *1970 – 1972.*
4 oz., white space capsule held non-tear shampoo. Came with black game sheet. CMV, $6.00 MB, set.

Snoopy Comb and Brush Set,
1971 – 1975.
5½" long black and white brush and white comb. CMV, $5.00 MB.

Freddy the Frog Mug,
1970.
5 oz., white glass mug with red or orange top and white cap. Held bubble bath. CMV, $9.00 MB.
Gaylord Gator Mug,
1970 – 1972.
5 oz., white glass mug with yellow top and white cap. Held non-tear shampoo. CMV, $9.00 MB.

Splash Down Bubble Bath, *1970 – 1971.*
8 oz., white plastic bottle with red cap and yellow base ring. Came with three plastic toss rings. CMV, $5.00 MB.

Snoopy's Bubble Tub,
1971 – 1972.
5" long, 12 oz., blue and white plastic tub bottle held bubble bath. CMV, $4.00 BO. $7.00 MB.

Peanuts Pals Shampoo, 1971 – 1972.
6 oz., plastic white, red, and black bottle with yellow cap. 6" high. CMV, $3.00 BO. $6.00 MB.

Barney Beaver Soap Dish and Soap, 1971 – 1972.
10½" long, brown soap dish and brown "vest" soap. CMV, $10.00 MB.

Pop-a-Duck, 1971 – 1972.
6 oz., blue plastic bottle held bubble bath. Three plastic ducks and ball. CMV, $3.00 MB, complete set.

Mr. Robottle, 1971 – 1972.
8" high plastic bottle with blue body and red legs and arms. Silver and yellow cap. Held bubble bath. Came with white plastic wrench to put together. CMV, $7.00 MB.

Kanga Winks, 1971 – 1972.
7" high yellow and orange plastic bottle with pink hat, held 8 oz. of bubble bath. Box also held black and white plastic target and package of 16 plastic chips for tiddlywinks. CMV, $8.00 MB, set.

Maze Game, 1971 – 1972.
6 oz. green plastic bottle, white cap. Held non-tear shampoo. CMV, $5.00 MB.

Toofie Toothpaste, 1971 – 1973.
3½ oz. yellow and orange tube and box. CMV, $2.00 TO. $3.00 MB.

Choo-Choo Train, 1971 – 1972.
Puffer Chugger is 3" long green plastic bottle with yellow cap and nose. CMV, $4.00 MB. Soap coach is 4" long plastic soap dish with yellow bar of soap. CMV, $3.00 soap coach only. $6.00 MB with soap. Caboose is pink plastic bottle, 3" long with non-tear shampoo. Held bubble bath. CMV, $4.00 MB.

Huggy Bear, 1971 – 1972.
8 oz. brown plastic bottle with lace-up vest, held bubble bath. CMV, $5.00 MB.

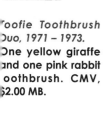

Toofie Toothbrush Duo, 1971 – 1973.
One yellow giraffe and one pink rabbit toothbrush. CMV, $2.00 MB.

Hickory Dickory Clock, 1971 – 1972.
5½" high, 8 oz. yellow plastic cheese clock with orange face and pink hands, purple mouse cap. Contained non-tear shampoo. CMV, $6.00 MB.

Aristocat, 1971 – 1972.
4 oz., gray cat with pink collar held non-tear shampoo. CMV, $5.00 MB.

Cluck-a-Doo, 1971. 8 oz., yellow bottle, pink hat. Came with stick-on decals. Held bubble bath. CMV, $5.00 MB.

Blouse Mouse, 1972. Green and pink. Also came green with white trim. CMV, $4.00.

Lip Pop Colas, 1973 – 1974. ⅛ oz. plastic tube with plastic top. Came in Cherry (light red case), Cola (brown case), or Strawberry (pink case) lip pomade. Strawberry and Cherry also came in solid red plastic, rare. CMV, $7.00. Others, CMV, $3.00 BO. $4.00 MB.

Charlie Brown Comb and Brush, 1972. 4½" long, red, black, and white with white comb. CMV, $5.00 MB.

Sniffy Pin Pal, 1972 – 1975. Black, white, and pink. CMV, $3.00.

Randy Pandy Soap Dish, 1972 – 1974. Black, white, and pink rubber soap dish and 3 oz. white soap. CMV, $10.00 MB, set.

Snoopy Come Home Soap Dish and Soap, 1973 – 1974. 6" long, brown raft with white sail, 3 oz. brown soap. CMV $6.00 MB.

Red Streak Boat, 1972 – 1973. 5 oz., red plastic boat, white cap. Held bubble bath. CMV, $3.00 BO. $5.00 MB.

Love Locket Glace, 1972. CMV, $2.00 locket only. $3.00 MB.

Bo Bo the Elephant, 1973 – 1974. 6 oz., pink plastic with squeeze head. Filled with baby shampoo. CMV, $3.00 BO. $5.00 MB.

Ball and Cup, 1972 – 1973. 4 oz., blue bottom with green cup and ball. Held shampoo. CMV, $2.00 BO. $4.00 MB.

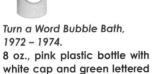

Turn a Word Bubble Bath, 1972 – 1974. 8 oz., pink plastic bottle with white cap and green lettered sides. CMV, $3.00 MB.

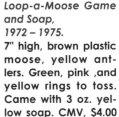

Loop-a-Moose Game and Soap, 1972 – 1975. 7" high, brown plastic moose, yellow antlers. Green, pink ,and yellow rings to toss. Came with 3 oz. yellow soap. CMV, $4.00 MB.

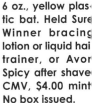

Sure Winner Slugger Decanter, 1973. 6 oz., yellow plastic bat. Held Sure Winner bracing lotion or liquid hair trainer, or Avon Spicy after shave. CMV, $4.00 mint. No box issued.

Snoopy's Snow Flyer, 1973.
10 oz., red, white, and black. Held bubble bath. CMV, $3.00 BO. $5.00 MB.

Safety Pin Decanter, 1973 – 1974.
8 oz., yellow plastic filled with baby lotion. CMV, $5.00 MB.

Children's Fun Jewelry, Fly-a-Kite, 1973.
Red, white, and blue. CMV, $3.00 pin only. $5.00 MB.

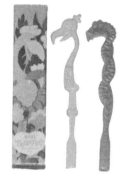

Grid Kid Brush and Comb, 1973 – 1974.
4½" long, red, black, and white with white comb. CMV, $5.00 MB.

Toofie Toothbrush Duo, 1973 – 1974. Pack of two, green worm and yellow bird. CMV, $2.00 MB.

Barney Beaver Toothbrushes and Holder, 1973.
4" high, brown plastic with white and blue shirt. Held pink and blue toothbrushes. Came with a sticker to put on wall. CMV, $4.00 MB.

Clancy the Clown Soap Holder and Soap, 1973 – 1974.
Orange, pink, and white clown held green and white or pink and orange 3 oz. soap. CMV, $8.00 MB.

Children's Fun Jewelry, Fuzzy Bug, 1973 – 1974.
Blue with green fur. CMV, $3.00 pin only. $5.00 MB.

Children's Fun Jewelry, Luv-a-Ducky, 1973.
Yellow and orange. CMV, $3.00 pin only. $5.00 MB.

"I Love Toofie" Toothbrushes and Holder, 1973.
5" high, white and pink, held red and blue toothbrushes. Came with sticker to put on wall. CMV, $4.00 MB.

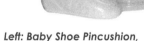

Left: Baby Shoe Pincushion, 1973 – 1974.
7 oz., white plastic with pink pincushion and blue bow. Filled with baby lotion. CMV, $5.00 MB.
Right: Sunny Bunny Baby Pomander, 1973 – 1976.
Wax figurine with Nursery Fresh fragrance. CMV, $6.00 MB.

Children's Fun Jewelry, Pandy Bear Pin, 1973.
Black and white. CMV, $3.00 pin only. $5.00 MB.

Children's Fun Jewelry, Perkey Parrot, 1973.
Red and green. CMV, $3.00 pin only. $5.00 MB.

Roto-boat Floating Soap Dish and Soap, 1973 – 1975.
9" long blue and white boat with red rudder. Held 3 oz. blue soap. CMV, $8.00 MB. Reissued with "R" on bottom.

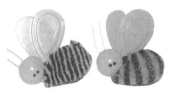

Bumbley Bee Pins, 1973 – 1974.
Yellow with black stripes. One with big stripes and one with narrow stripes. CMV, $4.00 each. $6.00 MB, set.

Funny Bunny, 1973 – 1974.
Pink and white. CMV, $4.00.

Calico Cat, 1973.
Red with white dots. Also came in red without dots. CMV, $4.00.
Not shown: Calico Cat, 1974 – 1975.
Blue with white dots. Also came in blue without dots on bottom half. CMV, $3.00 each.

Elphie the Elephant, 1973.
Yellow and pink. CMV, $4.00.

Gingerbread Pin Pal, 1973.
Brown and pink. Also came in brown and white. CMV, $5.00 pink, $6.00 white. Add $1.00 each, MB.

Reggie Raccoon Hairbrush and Comb, 1973.
6½" long, tan and black, with tan comb. CMV, $4.00 MB.

Topsy Turtle Floating Soap Dish and Soap, 1973 – 1974.
7" long, green rubber soap dish with 3 oz. pink soap. CMV, $8.00 MB. Reissued in 1979. Some came with light green body and dark green head. Also came with matching body and head.

Soap Boat, Floating Soap Dish and Soap, 1973 – 1974.
7½" long blue and red boat with white sail and white soap. CMV, $10.00 MB.

Little Wiggly Game and Bubble Bath, 1973.
8 oz., green with pink legs, red and yellow hoops. Held bubble bath. CMV, $3.00 MB.

Ice Cream Lip Pomade, 1974 – 1976.
⅛ oz., white plastic bottom with light pink, dark pink, or red top for cherry, strawberry, or tutti-frutti flavors. CMV, $4.00 MB.

Ice Cream Cone Lip Pomade, 1974 – 1976.
Yellow cones with different color tops for cherry, strawberry, tutti-frutti, mint, or chocolate flavors. CMV, $3.00 BO. $4.00 MB.

By the Jug, 1974 – 1975.
Each 10 oz., beige plastic. Strawberry bath foam, astringent, or Balsam shampoo. Brown caps look like corks. No boxes issued. CMV, $1.00 each.

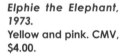

Snoopy's Ski Team,
1974 – 1975.
7 oz., white plastic bottle, red skis, yellow "Woodstock." Held bubble bath. CMV, $5.00 MB.

Ted E. Bear Toothbrush Holder,
1974 – 1975.
Box held tan, pink, and white plastic holder and pink and white Avon toothbrushes. CMV, $3.00 MB.

Rapid Rabbit Pin Pal,
1974 – 1975.
White, pink, and green plastic. Feet swing. Filled with perfumed glace. CMV, $2.00 pin only. $3.00 MB.

Slugger Brush,
1974 – 1975.
7" long, brown and black plastic. CMV, $3.00 MB.

Lovable Leo,
1974 – 1976.
10 oz., yellow plastic, pink cap. Held children's shampoo. CMV, $3.00 MB.

Myrtle Turtle Pin Pal,
1974.
Green and pink plastic. Filled with perfumed glace. CMV, $2.00 pin only. $3.00 MB.

Grid Kid Liquid Hair Trainer, 1974 – 1975.
8 oz., red, black, and white plastic. CMV, $3.00 MB.

Sure Winner Catcher's Mitt, 1974 – 1975.
6 oz., brown plastic with brown cap. Held Avon liquid hair trainer. CMV, $3.00 MB.

Minute Mouse Pin,
1974 – 1975.
White with blue clock, orange hands and numbers. CMV, $3.00 MB.

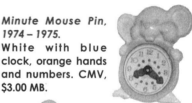

Lickety Stick Mouse Pin,
1974 – 1976.
White plastic with green hat and pink striped stick. CMV, $3.00 MB.

Cub Scout Knife Brush and Comb,
1974 – 1978.
Blue and silver plastic comb. Cub Scout gold label on top. CMV, $3.00 MB.

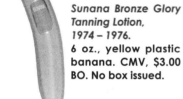

Sunana Bronze Glory Tanning Lotion,
1974 – 1976.
6 oz., yellow plastic banana. CMV, $3.00 BO. No box issued.

Toofie Train, 1974 – 1975.
Red plastic train, yellow plastic cup. Red and blue Toofie toothbrushes and yellow with red cap Toofie toothpaste. CMV, $5.00, items only. $7.00 MB.

Quack and Doodle Floating Soap Dish and Soap,
1974 – 1975.
Yellow rubber with yellow soap. CMV, $7.00 MB.

Blue Moo Pin Pal, 1974.
Blue and pink. CMV, $3.00.

Super Shoe, 1974 – 1976.
6 oz., white plastic shoe with blue plastic toe section cap. Held Sure Winner liquid hair trainer or Sure Winner bracing lotion. CMV, $3.00 MB.
Just for Kicks, 1974 – 1975.
7 oz., black and white plastic shoe with black plastic cap. Held Spicy or Sure Winner bracing lotion. CMV, $4.00 MB.

Hot Dog! Brush and Comb, 1975 – 1976.
Yellow and red plastic comb. CMV, $3.00 MB.

Precious Lamb Baby Lotion, 1975 – 1976.
6 oz., white plastic lamb with blue bow. Held baby lotion. CMV, $4.00 MB.

Wee Willy Winter Pin Pal Glace,
1974 – 1975.
White snowman with pink hat, scarf, and mittens. CMV, $4.00 MB.

Woodstock Brush and Comb,
1975 – 1978.
Yellow plastic brush, green comb. CMV, $2.00 MB.

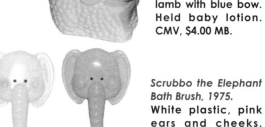

Scrubbo the Elephant Bath Brush, 1975.
White plastic, pink ears and cheeks. CMV, $2.00 MB. 1976 issue was all pink plastic. Each is 8" long. CMV, $2.00 each, MB.

Sunny Fresh Orange Glace Necklace, 1974 – 1975.
Orange and yellow with green cord. CMV, $4.00 MB.

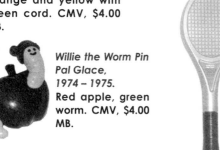

Willie the Worm Pin Pal Glace,
1974 – 1975.
Red apple, green worm. CMV, $4.00 MB.

Tennis Anyone?
1975 – 1976.
5 oz., gray and black plastic. Held Sweet Honesty after bath freshener or Spicy after shave. CMV, $3.00 MB.

Tortoise 'N' Hare Toothbrush Duo,
1975 – 1976.
Green tortoise and yellow hare. CMV, $2.00 MB.

Nutshell Color Magic Lipstick, 1974 – 1975.
Peanut shaped case came in Pink Sorcery (blue lipstick) or Peach Sorcery (green lipstick). CMV, $3.00 MB.

Arch E. Bear Brush and Comb,
1975 – 1976.
Red, white, and blue brush with white comb. CMV, $3.00 MB.

Brontosaurus Bubble Bath, 1975 – 1976.
10 oz., blue-gray plastic. CMV, $3.00 BO. $5.00 MB.

Winkie Blink Clock Bubble Bath, 1975 – 1976. 8 oz., yellow with blue clock hands and blue cap. CMV, $4.00 MB.

Puppy Love Pin Pal Glace, 1975. Beige dog with black ears and pink pillow. CMV, $4.00 MB.

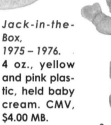

Rockabye Pony Decanter, 1975 – 1976. 6 oz., yellow plastic. Held Clearly Gentle baby lotion. CMV, $4.00 MB.

Bobbin' Robin Pin, 1975 – 1976. White cage, red bird (bird movable). CMV, $3.00 MB.

Peter Patches Pin Pal Glace, 1975 – 1976. Yellow with red and blue trim. CMV, $4.00 MB.

Jack-in-the-Box, 1975 – 1976. 4 oz., yellow and pink plastic, held baby cream. CMV, $4.00 MB.

Sunbonnet Sue Demi Stick, 1975 – 1977. 3/16 oz., red and white plastic. Pink and Pretty fragrance. CMV, $3.00 MB.

Pedal Pusher Pin, 1975 – 1976. Blue elephant with green jacket and pink bike. CMV, $3.00 MB.

Chicken Little Pin Pal Glace, 1975. Yellow chicken with pink flower and green leaf. CMV, $4.00.

School Days Pencil Lip Pomade, 1975 – 1976. 1/8 oz., red, white, and yellow plastic. Choice of strawberry, cherry, or tutti-frutti. CMV, $3.00 MB.

Magic Rabbit Pin, 1975 – 1976. White and pink rabbit with gray hat. CMV, $3.00 MB.

Rock-a-Roo Pin Pal Glace, 1975 – 1977. Pink with dark pink rocking pouch. CMV, $3.00 MB.

Sweet Lips Lip Gloss Cookie, 1975 – 1976. Brown plastic with two shades of lip gloss. CMV, $3.00 MB.

Great Catch, Charlie Brown, Soap Holder and Soap, 1975 – 1976. Red, white, black, and brown plastic. CMV, $8.00 MB.

Paddlewog Frog Floating Soap Dish and Soap, 1975 – 1976. Green plastic with pink propeller and yellow soap. CMV, $8.00 MB.

Spotty to the Rescue Toothbrush Holder, 1976 – 1977. Red, white, and black plastic toothbrush holder held two Avon toothbrushes. CMV, $3.00 MB.

School Days Ruler Comb,
1976 – 1979.
Box held yellow plastic 6"
ruler comb. CMV, $2.00 MB.

Tyrannosaurus Rex,
1976 – 1978.
4 oz., green plastic bottle,
green rubber head.
Held bubble bath.
CMV, $3.00 MB.

Giraffabath
Bath Brush,
1977 – 1979.
Orange and
beige plastic.
Blue eyes. CMV,
$3.00 MB.

Toofie Tiger Tooth-
brushes and Holder,
1976.
Yellow, black, white,
and pink. One pink
and one white tooth-
brush. CMV, $3.00 MB.

Custom Car, 1976 – 1978.
7 oz., blue plastic bottle with red
tire cap. Filled with bubble bath.
CMV, $3.00 MB.

Batman Styling
Brush,
1977 – 1978.
Blue, gray, and
black plastic
brush. CMV, $5.00
MB.

Jack in a Box Glace,
1976.
White plastic with pink
and green trim. CMV,
$3.00 MB.

Orangatan, 1976.
6 oz., orange shaped
and colored plastic
bottle. Held suntan lo-
tion. CMV, $2.00. No
box issued.

Superman Styling
Brush, 1977.
Red and blue
plastic brush.
CMV, $5.00 MB.

Cotton Tail Glace,
1976 – 1978.
Yellow and pink with
white tail. CMV, $3.00
MB.

Ice Cream
Comb,
1977 – 1978.
Orange plastic
comb with pink
and brown ice
cream and red
cherry on top.
CMV, $2.00 MB.

Randy Pandy Soap
Dish and Soap,
1976 – 1977.
Black, light blue,
and red rubber
soap dish and 3
oz. blue and white
soap. CMV (Panda
only), $2.00. $7.00
MB, set.

Reggie Raccoon Hair-
brush and Comb,
1977.
6¼" long. Brown,
white, pink, and
black brush and
comb. CMV,
$2.00 MB.

Wally Walrus Toothbrush Holder
and Toothbrush, 1977 – 1978.
Adhesive back holder sticks
to wall. Came with two child
sized Avon toothbrushes in
red and white. Plastic holder
is blue and red with white hat
and trim. CMV, $2.00 MB.

Funburger Lip Gloss,
1977 – 1978.
Came in Frostlight
Rose or Frostlight
Coral lip gloss.
Brown plastic. CMV,
$2.00 MB.

Chick a Peek Glace,
1977.
Yellow plastic back
and chick with purple
egg. CMV, $3.00 MB.

Sunnyshine Up,
1978 – 1979.
White plastic base with
yellow screw-on egg lid.
CMV, $2.00 MB.

Finger Puppet, Millicent
Mouse Demi Stick,
1977 – 1978.
Came with Pink and Pretty
fragrance demi stick. CMV,
$5.00 MB.

Kiss 'N' Makeup Lip Gloss
Compact, 1977 – 1979.
Came with Frostlight Peach
and Frostlight Pink lip gloss.
Red plastic container. CMV,
$1.00.

On the Run "Jogging Shoe,"
1978 – 1979.
6 oz., blue plastic with white
stripes. Held Wild Country
after shave or Sweet Honesty
body splash. CMV, $4.00 MB.

Finger Puppet, Glow
Worm,
1977 – 1979.
Came with Care
Deeply lip balm.
White rubber top
with purple spots.
CMV, $5.00 MB.

Scrub Away Nail Brush and
Soap, 1977 – 1978.
3 oz. soap, pink brush shaped
like Pink Pearl eraser. CMV,
$8.00 MB.

Finger Puppet,
Gilroy the Ghost,
1977 – 1978.
Came with Care
Deeply lip balm. White
and black rubber top
with black, green, and
white demi stick. CMV,
$5.00 MB.

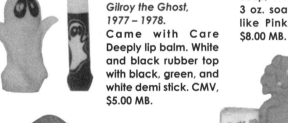

Terrible Tubbles Float-
ing Soap Dish and
Soap, 1977 – 1978.
Blue plastic dish with
3 oz. soap. CMV,
$7.00 MB.

Finger Puppet,
Huck L. Berry,
1977 – 1978.
Came with Care
Deeply lip balm.
Blue, yellow, and
white rubber top
with yellow and
white demi stick.
CMV, $5.00 MB.

Triceratops,
1977 – 1978.
8½ oz., green plas-
tic bottle. Came
with bubble bath
for children. CMV,
$3.00 MB.

Conair Hair Dryer,
1978 – 1979.
6 oz., off-white plastic.
Blue letters and cap. Held
Naturally Gentle sham-
poo. CMV, $4.00 MB.

Accusing Alligator, 1978 – 1979.
6 oz., green, yellow and tan plastic. Held bubble bath. CMV, $6.00 MB.

Heavy Hitter Decanter, 1978 – 1979.
4 oz., dark blue plastic. White letters. Held non-tear shampoo. CMV, $3.00 MB.

Outraged Octopus Toothbrush Holder, 1978 – 1979.
Purple and orange plastic toothbrush holder. Came with orange and white Avon toothbrushes. CMV, $2.00 MB.

Superman Bubble Bath, 1978 – 1979.
8 oz., blue, red, and gray plastic. Held bubble bath. Box came with two red and yellow plastic cutout capes. CMV $8.00 MB.

Batmobile, 1978 – 1979.
6 oz., blue and silver plastic with stick-on decals. Held bubble bath. CMV, $5.00 MB.

Lip-Pop Pomade, "Pepsi," 1978 – 1979.
Dark amber plastic. Gray cap. Looks like Pepsi Cola bottle. CMV, $3.00 MB.

Hang Ten Skateboard Decanter, 1978 – 1979.
5½ oz., yellow plastic with top stick-on decal. Held bubble bath for children. CMV, $3.00 MB.

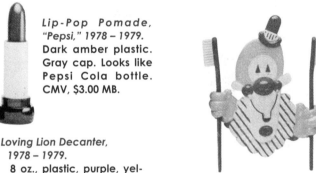

Loving Lion Decanter, 1978 – 1979.
8 oz., plastic, purple, yellow, pink, and orange. Held non-tear shampoo. CMV, $5.00 MB.

Toofie the Clown, 1978.
Orange, yellow, and white plastic toothbrush holder. Blue and pink toothbrushes. CMV, $2.00 MB.

Karrot Tan Decanter, 1978 – 1979.
4 oz., orange plastic with green leaf top. Held Bronze Glory tanning lotion. CMV, $4.00 BO. No box issued.

3 Ring Circus Children's Talc, 1978 – 1979.
5 oz., two center sections turn. CMV, $2.00 MB.

Pop-a-Duck Game, 1978.
6 oz., blue plastic with red-orange cap. Came with three green balls. Pink, orange, and yellow ducks and red-orange ball holder. Bottle held bubble bath. CMV, $4.00 MB.

Easter Dec-a-Doo for Children, 1978.
8 oz., plastic yellow base, pink top. Came with stick-on decals. This is different from 1968 – 1969 issue. Old one does not say "for children" on label. Held bubble bath. CMV, $3.00 MB.

Zany Zebra Hairbrush, 1978 – 1979.
White, black, pink, and green plastic. CMV, $2.00 MB.

Space Patroller Decanter, 1979 – 1980.
8 oz., gray plastic, black cap and stick-on decals. CMV, $3.00 MB.

Duster D. Duckling Fluff Puff, 1978 – 1982.
3½ oz., yellow plastic and fluff top. Held Delicate Daisies or Sweet Pickles perfumed talc. CMV, $3.00 MB.

Bunny Fluffpuff, 1979 – 1980.
3½ oz., yellow plastic with fluff tail and pink eyes and ears. Held children's talc. OSP, $6.00. CMV, $3.50 MB.

Tub Sub, 1978 – 1979.
6 oz., yellow plastic, 10" long. Held bubble bath. CMV, $3.00 MB.

Red Streak Car, 1979 – 1980.
7 oz., red plastic with blue and silver stick-on decals. Held bubble bath. OSP, $4.00. CMV, $3.00 MB.

Spiderman Toothbrush and Holder, 1979 – 1980.
Red and blue plastic. Yellow and green Avon toothbrushes. CMV, $3.00 MB.

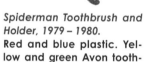

Bed of Nails Comb, 1978 – 1979.
5½" comb, tan, white, and red. CMV, $2.00 MB.

Most Valuable Gorilla, 1979 – 1980.
4 oz., orange and blue plastic stick-on front and back decals in any letter. Held bubble bath. CMV, $3.00 MB.

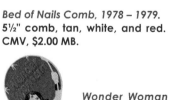

Wonder Woman Mirror, 1978 – 1979.
7½" long plastic mirror. CMV, $2.00 MB.

The Pink Panther Toothbrush Holder and Two Toothbrushes, 1979.
Pink plastic holder. Yellow and red toothbrushes. Blue and pink box. OSP, $6.00. CMV, $3.00 MB.

Willie Weatherman, 1979 – 1980.
6 oz., tan plastic, pink cap. Blue umbrella changes color with the weather. Held non-tear shampoo. CMV, $3.00 MB.

**Combsicle,
1979 – 1980.**
Popsicle box held brown and beige Avon comb. CMV, $1.00 MB.

Crayola Lip Gloss Set, 1980 – 1981.
Crayola box held three plastic crayon shaped Avon lip gloss tubes in chocolate, grape, and strawberry. CMV, $2.00 MB.

Tub Tug, 1980 – 1981.
5 oz., plastic. Came in yellow and green cap with non-tear shampoo, red and lavender cap with bubble bath, and blue and red cap with liquid cleanser. CMV, $1.00 each. No boxes.

Chocolate Chi-plick Compact, 1979 – 1980.
Tan and brown plastic, held lip gloss. CMV, $2.00 MB.

Tuggable Teddy Toothbrush Holder, 1980 – 1981.
Tan and blue plastic. Pink and green Avon toothbrushes. Orange ring on gold cord. CMV, $5.00 MB.

Power Drill, 1979 – 1980.
5 oz., yellow plastic drill with silver plastic drill cap. Held Wild Country after shave or Electric pre-shave. CMV, $4.00 MB.

Smiley Snail Tooth-brush Holder, 1980 – 1981.
Yellow and green plastic. Orange and blue Avon toothbrushes. CMV, $6.00 MB.

Clean-'em-up-Pump, 1981 – 1982.
8 oz., yellow plastic with white and yellow pump dispenser. Came with card of stick-on decals. Held liquid cleanser. CMV, $3.00 MB.

Imp the Chimp Bath Brush, 1980.
Brown plastic, yellow, black, and pink trim. 10" long. CMV, $4.00 MB.

I.M. Clean II "Robot," 1980 – 1981.
Blue plastic robot with pump dispenser. Came with card of stick-on decals. Held 8 oz. of liquid cleanser. CMV, $4.00 MB.

Ted E. Bear Baby Lotion Dispenser, 1981 – 1982.
10 oz., plastic, in choice of pink or blue bear. Came with matching pump dispenser. CMV, $2.00 MB.

Spongie the Clown, 1981.
6 oz. plastic bottle with green cap. Came with orange sponge for top. CMV, $3.00 MB.

Playful Pups Tooth-brush Holder, 1981 – 1982.
Blue and orange shoe, brown ears. Held green and pink Avon tooth-brushes. Dated 1981 on back. CMV, $3.00 MB.

Tweethouse Paper Cup Toothbrush Holder, 1982 – 1983.
White plastic cup holder with stick-on decals and two child-sized tooth-brushes. CMV, $4.00 MB.

Wabbit Car, 1983.
5 oz., blue plastic car and white rabbit cap. Choice of children's bubble bath or non-tear sham-poo. Came with sheet of stick-on decals to decorate. CMV, $6.00 MB.

Maria Makeover Bath Decanter, 1982.
6 oz., plastic face bottle and sheet of stick-on decals. Choice of non-tear shampoo or children's liquid cleanser. CMV, $2.00 MB.

Clean Flight Decanter, 1982.
6 oz., plastic, sea plane shaped. Choice of non-tear shampoo in yellow plastic with blue cap or liquid cleanser in or-ange with yellow cap. CMV, $3.00. No box issued.

E.T. Zipper Pull, 1984.
2", plastic. CMV, $1.00.

E.T. Flowers Figu-rine, 1984.
2½" high, hand-painted porce-lain. CMV, $5.00 MB.

E.T. and Elliott Decal Soap, 1983.
3 oz., blue bar with decal of E.T. on face. Back of bar says "I'll be right here." CMV, $5.00 MB.
E.T. Bath Decanter, 1983 – 1984.
7 oz., blue plastic with tan plastic head. Held bubble bath. CMV, $6.00 MB.
E.T. Mug, 1983 – 1984.
4½" high white porcelain mug with E.T. handle. CMV, $15.00 MB.

Christmas Toy Land Candy, 1984.
8¼" high tin can full of candy. CMV, $2.00 can only.

Bubba Lee Bunny Bath Buddies, 1982 – 1983.
6 oz., white plastic rabbit, yellow cap. Choice of bubble bath or non-tear shampoo. CMV, $5.00 MB.

Plush Lamb Bank, 1984.
8" long, 6" high. Fabric covered plastic bank. CMV, $8.00 MB.

E.T. and Gertie Decal Soap, 1984.
3 oz., pink bar. CMV, $6.00 MB.

On the Farm Bank, 1985.
Stick-on decals and packets of bubble bath inside. CMV, $3.00.

Sudsville Truck and Soap, 1986.
Box held yellow, blue, and red plastic dump truck and bar of yellow Sudsville soap. CMV, $7.00 MB.

Robot Bank, 1985.
Blue, yellow, and orange plastic bank. CMV, $3.00 MB.

Somersaults Products, 1985 – 1986.
Mini Dolls.
Miniature plastic toys — Zippy, Herby Derby, Charley Barley, Miss Pear, and Tallulah. CMV, $2.00 each, MB.
Tabina and Herby Derby.
2 oz., plastic cologne, green and yellow, and yellow and pink. CMV, $2.00 each.

Baby Bear Floating Decanter, 1987.
6 oz., yellow and blue plastic. Held shampoo. CMV, $4.00 MB.

Baby Elephant Pump, 1985.
8 oz., blue plastic, held baby lotion. CMV, $2.00 MB.

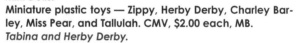

Tool Kit Wrench, 1986.
6½", green plastic. Held 3½ oz. non-tear shampoo. CMV, $2.00 MB.

Sun Sounds Tanning Lotion Decanter, 1987.
6 oz., blue plastic. CMV, $4.00 MB.

Tool Kit Screwdriver, 1986.
6¾", yellow plastic. Held 3½ oz. bubble bath. CMV, $2.00 MB.

Muppet Babies — Miss Piggy and Kermit, 1985.
4 oz. each, plastic, rubber finger puppet tops. Non-tear shampoo and bubble bath. CMV, $1.00 each, MB.

Fun in Space Soaps, 1986.
Box held yellow and blue soaps. CMV, $4.00 MB.

All-Star League "Baseball Bat," 1987.
9½" long, tan plastic bottle. Held shampoo. CMV, $2.00 MB.

Space Mission Decanter, 1988.
10¾" long spaceship in blue and yellow plastic. Held liquid soap and shampoo. CMV, $4.00 MB.

Tonka Truck and Soap Gift Set, 1993.
Yellow and black plastic and metal truck, 4½" long. Came with red soap. CMV, $5.00 MB, set.

Batman, 1993.
4 oz., plastic, held non-tear shampoo. Finger puppet. CMV, $3.00 MB.

Spotlight Mike Decanter, 1991.
9" long plastic microphone held 3 oz. of liquid cleanser. Blue and yellow plastic, red rope. CMV, $4.00 MB.

The Penguin, 1993.
4 oz., plastic, with finger puppet. Liquid cleanser. CMV, $3.00.

Mighty Morphin Power Rangers Finger Puppets, 1994.
4 oz. plastic bottles. Red, blue, or black Rangers. CMV, $2.00 each, MB.

Major League Mitt Decanter, 1993.
6 oz., plastic baseball glove. Blue cap. Non-tear shampoo. Card of 28 team stickers for glove. CMV, $6.00 MB.

Cat Woman, 1993.
4 oz., bubble bath, plastic. Finger puppet. CMV, $3.00.

Tweety Bath Mitt and Bubble Bath, 1994.
Yellow Tweety Bird mitt and Sylvester tube of bubble bath. CMV, $2.00 MB, set.

Barbie Phone Cologne, 2000.
2½ oz., pink plastic bottle. Came with white detachable antenna. CMV, $1.00 mint.

Children's Soaps

Warning! Keep all soaps out of sunlight as they fade quickly. All soaps must be mint and boxed for full value. Damaged soaps have no value.

Circus Soap Set, 1939 – 1941.
"5 Ring Circus" on box, held five figural soaps. This set is Avon's first figural soap set. Soaps are clown, elephant, monkey, seal, and horse. Very rare. CMV, $325.00 MB.

Bo Peep Soap, 1953 – 1954.
Blue and green box held three white sheep soaps. CMV, $75.00 MB.

Three Little Bears Soap Set, 1954.
Three brown bear soaps. CMV, $80.00 MB.

Best Friend Soap, 1956.
Blue and white box held blue dog soap. CMV, $60.00 MB.

Circus Wagon Soap Set, 1957 – 1958.
Pink, yellow, black, and white circus wagon box contained one blue elephant, one pink monkey, and one yellow lion soap. CMV, $75.00 MB.

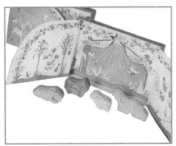

Away in the Manger Soap Set, 1955.
Box held four bars of pink, blue, white, and yellow soaps. Two different scenes. CMV, $80.00 MB, each set.

Santa's Helper Soaps, 1956.
Box held three green, yellow, and red soaps, Santa and two helpers. CMV, $120.00 MB.

"Old 99" Soap, 1958.
Yellow train engine soap. CMV, $65.00 MB.

Santa's Helper Soaps, 1955.
Box held green, red, and yellow soaps. Red Santa soap much larger than 1956 set. CMV, $110.00 MB.

Casey Jones, Jr., 1956 – 1957.
Red, white, and blue box held blue engine soap, yellow passenger car, and red caboose. CMV, $65.00 MB.

Texas Sheriff Soap, 1958.
Box held two blue pistol soaps and silver sheriff's badge. Box came with band around outside of box. OSP, $1.19. CMV, $65.00 MB.

Kiddie Kennel Soaps, 1955.
Blue and yellow box held blue, yellow, and pink dog soaps. CMV, $150.00 MB.

Fire Engine Soap, 1957.
Red box contained red fire truck soap. CMV, $70.00 MB.

Forward Pass! 1958.
7½ oz., brown football soap on a white rope. CMV, $45.00 MB.

Pool Paddlers Soap, 1959. Pond display box held green frog, yellow fish, and blue turtle soap. CMV, $45.00 MB.

Lil Folks Time Soap on a Rope, 1961 – 1962. Red box held yellow clock soap on a rope. CMV, $35.00 MB.

Sheriff's Badge Soap, 1962 – 1963. Box held yellow soap on a rope with embossed sheriff's badge. CMV, $35.00 MB.

High Score, 1960. Green net box held brown basketball soap on a rope. CMV, $15.00 soap only, mint. $30.00 MB.

A Hit! Soap on a Rope, 1961 – 1962. Box held white baseball soap on a rope. CMV, $30.00 MB.

Life Preserver Soap, 1963 – 1964. White life preserver soap on a rope. CMV, $35.00 MB.

Frilly Duck Soap, 1960. Box contained yellow and blue soap, 5¾ oz. CMV, $30.00 MB.

Lil Tom Turtle Soap, 1962 – 1963. Box held green turtle soap with white hat. CMV, $35.00 MB.

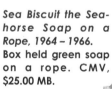

Sea Biscuit the Seahorse Soap on a Rope, 1964 – 1966. Box held green soap on a rope. CMV, $25.00 MB.

Avonlite Soap on a Rope, 1960 – 1961. Green bowling ball shaped soap in green box. Brochure says "Bowl 'em Over." Soap says "Avon Lite." CMV, $20.00 soap only, mint. $35.00 MB.

"Watch the Birdie" Soap, 1962 – 1964. White molded camera soap on a rope. CMV, $40.00 MB.

Packy the Elephant Soap, 1964 – 1965. Green box held pink elephant with white hat. CMV, $30.00 MB.

Hansel and Gretel Soap, 1965. Blue and pink soaps in a box. CMV, $35.00 MB.

Yo Yo Set, 1966 – 1967. Pink and red wood yo yo and pink soap. CMV, $6.00, yo yo only. $25.00 MB.

Bunny's Dream Soap on a Rope, 1967. Box held orange carrot soap on a green rope. CMV, $20.00 MB.

Little Shaver Soap, 1966 – 1967. Yellow shaver soap on a rope. CMV, $25.00 MB.

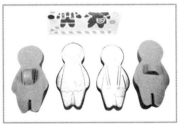

Gingerbread Soap Twins, 1965. Pink, white, and brown box held two blue plastic gingerbread cookie cutters with two yellow bars of gingerbread soap. CMV, $30.00.

Easter Quacker Soap on a Rope, 1968. Yellow soap. CMV, $18.00 MB.

Goldilocks Soap, 1966 – 1967. 5 oz., yellow soap. CMV, $25.00 MB.

Ruff, Tuff & Muff Soap Set, 1968 – 1969. Blue, pink, and yellow dog soaps. CMV, $12.00 MB.

Mr. Monkey Soap on a Rope, 1965. Brown monkey soap. CMV, $25.00 MB.

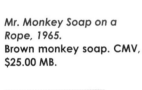

Speedy the Snail, 1966. Green snail soap on a rope. CMV, $30.00.

Sunny the Sunfish Soap, 1966. Yellow fish soap on a rope. CMV, $25.00 MB.

Light Bulb Soap on a Rope, 1967. Yellow soap on black, orange, and yellow rope. CMV, $25.00 MB.

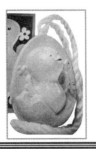

Chick-a-Dee Soap, 1966 – 1967. Yellow soap on a rope. CMV, $20.00 MB.

Tub Racers Soap, 1969. Green box held red, yellow, and green racer soaps. CMV, $15.00 MB.

Mighty Mitt Soap on a Rope, 1969 – 1972.
Brown soap. CMV, $15.00 MB.

First Down Soap, 1970 – 1971.
Box held brown 5 oz. football soap on a rope. This soap is different from 1965 version (see Children's Decanters and Toys section). Rope is on end of football. CMV, $10.00 MB.

Tub Racers, 1970 – 1972.
Three speedboat soaps in red, blue, and yellow. CMV, $10.00 MB.

Yankee Doodle Shower Soap, 1969 – 1970.
White drum shaped soap on a rope. CMV, $15.00 MB.

Peep a Boo Soap on a Rope, 1970.
Yellow chick soap on pink or white rope. CMV, $12.00 MB.

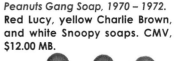

Modeling Soap, 1969 – 1970.
Pink 6 oz. soap in blue and pink box. CMV, $7.00 MB.

Peanuts Gang Soap, 1970 – 1972.
Red Lucy, yellow Charlie Brown, and white Snoopy soaps. CMV, $12.00 MB.

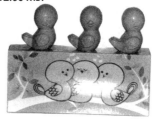

Easter Bonnet Soap on a Rope, 1970.
Yellow soap. CMV, $12.00 MB.

The Tweetsters Soaps, 1971.
Yellow box held three pink bird soaps. CMV, $12.00 MB.

The Mitten Kittens Soap, 1969 – 1970.
Pink, green, and yellow soaps. Blue box. CMV, $12.00 MB.

Tree Tots Soap, 1970 – 1972.
Red and green box held three squirrel soaps. CMV, $10.00 MB.

Scrub Tug Soap, 1971.
4" long plastic boat scrub brush held two oz. yellow boat soap. CMV, $1.00 brush only. $8.00 MB, brush and soap.

Aristocat Kittens Soap Trio, 1971.
Box held white, brown, and blue kitten soaps. CMV, $10.00 MB.

Percy Pelican Soap on a Rope, 1972 – 1973.
5 oz., yellow soap on white rope. CMV, $10.00 MB.

Snoopy's Pal Soap Dish and Soaps, 1973 – 1974.
4½" diameter red plastic dish says "Snoopy" on front with yellow bird. Came with two, 2 oz. white bone shaped soaps. CMV, $10.00 MB.

Sure Winner Shower Soap, 1972 – 1973.
White with blue cord. CMV, $8.00 MB.

Honey Lamb Soap on a Rope, 1971 – 1972.
5" high yellow soap on blue rope. CMV, $10.00 MB.

Hooty and Tooty Tugboat Soaps, 1973 – 1975.
2 oz., yellow and orange tugboat shaped soaps. CMV, $8.00 MB.

Blue Moo Soap on a Rope, 1972.
5 oz., blue cow soap on a rope. CMV, $10.00 MB.

Al E. Gator Soap on a Rope, 1971 – 1972.
5" high green soap on white rope. CMV, $10.00 MB.

Petunia Piglet Soap on a Rope, 1973 – 1974.
5 oz. pink soap on white rope. CMV, $10.00 MB.

Hydrojet Scrub Brush and Soap, 1972 – 1973.
Red plastic jet with yellow soap. CMV, $8.00 MB.

Three Nice Mice Soaps, 1971 – 1972.
Box held green, white, and pink mouse soaps. CMV, $10.00 MB.

Pig in a Tub Soap, 1973 – 1975.
3" long yellow scrub brush held 2 oz. pink pig soap. CMV, $6.00 MB. Reissued in 1979.

Sure Winner Soaps, 1973 – 1975.
Three snowmobile soaps in blue, red, and yellow. CMV, $7.00 MB.

Happy Hippos Nail Brush and Soap, 1973 – 1974.
3" long pink nail brush with yellow soap. CMV, $8.00 MB.

Hooper the Hound Soap Holder and Soap, 1974.
White and black plastic head with pink, green, and yellow hoops. Yellow soap. CMV, $8.00 MB.

M.C.P. Soap, 1977 – 1979. Tan color "Male Chauvinist Pig" soap. Came in Deep Woods scent. CMV, $8.00 MB.

Tubby Tigers Soap Set, 1974 – 1975.
Three orange soaps in orange and green box. CMV, $6.00 MB.

Gaylord Gator Scrub Brush and Soap, 1974 – 1975. Green plastic with white bristles. CMV, $8.00 MB.

Button Button Guest Soaps, 1977 – 1979. Cardboard spool container held five blue button shaped soaps. CMV, $8.00 MB.

Furry, Purry, and Scurry Soaps, 1978 – 1979.
Red box with white dots held three kitten shaped soaps in yellow, blue, and green. CMV, $6.00 MB.

Football Helmet Soap on a Rope, 1974 – 1975.
Yellow soap, white cord. CMV, $7.00 MB.

Good Habit Rabbit Scrub Brush and Soap, 1975.
Pink plastic with white bristles. CMV, $8.00 MB.

Tubbo the Hippo Soap Dish and Soap, 1978 – 1980.
Blue box held light green plastic hippo soap dish and 3 oz. pink embossed wrapped bar of hippo soap. CMV, $1.00 soap dish only. $1.50 soap only, wrapped. $6.00 MB.

Wilbur the Whale Soap on a Rope, 1974 – 1975.
5 oz., blue soap with white rope. CMV, $7.00 MB.

Gridiron Scrub Brush and Soap, 1976 – 1977.
Brown plastic with yellow soap. CMV, $8.00 MB.

Alka Seltzer Soaps, 1978 – 1979.
Blue, white, and red box held two white embossed bars. CMV, $7.00 MB.

Safe Combination Bank Soaps, 1978 – 1979.
Black and gold tin bank came with two yellow bars of soap embossed "Avon, 99.9 mint." Bottom of bank says "Made in England, exclusively for Avon." CMV, $10.00 MB.

Scribble Dee Doo Pencil Soaps, 1980 – 1981.
Three pencil shaped yellow soaps. CMV, $7.00 MB.

Orchard Fresh Guest Soaps, 1980 – 1981.
Choice of orange, lemon, or peach shaped soaps. Six bars in each box. CMV, $7.00 each.

Left: Bubble Blazer Soap, 1982 – 1983.
Box held 4 oz. yellow space gun bar. CMV, $5.00 MB.
Right: Party Line Soap on a Rope, 1982 – 1983.
Box held 5 oz. yellow telephone bar on white rope. CMV, $5.00 MB.
Bottom: Train Soap, 1982 – 1983.
5¾" long blue train soap breaks into three cars. Must be all together to be valuable. CMV, $5.00 MB.

Darling Ducklings Soap, 1983.
Box held three yellow duck soaps. CMV, $5.00 MB.

Storybook Soaps, 1984.
Book shaped soaps. Pinocchio, Hansel & Gretel, or Cinderella. CMV, $4.00 each, MB.

Animal Soaps, 1985.
Choice of elephant, hippo, or lion. CMV, $2.00 each, MB.

Easter Fun Bath Cubes, 1985.
Box held six Easter cubes. CMV, $3.00 MB.

Somersaults Soap and Mini Books, 1985.
Each box has different colored soaps. CMV, $3.00 each, MB.

Sweet Sea Soaps, 1986.
Different soaps, 2 oz. each. CMV, $2.00 each MB.

Sounds of Christmas Soaps, 1986.
Three different small bars. Drum, horn, or harp soap. CMV, $2.00 each, MB.

Bathtub Buggies Soap Set, 1986.
Box held blue, red, or yellow truck soaps. CMV, $4.00 MB.

Eggosaurs Soaps, 1986.
Yellow and blue shells held soaps. Came with 20-page miniature book. CMV, $5.00 MB.

Billy Rocket and Sky Blazers Cologne Gift Set, 1987.
Box held soap and 2 oz. cologne. CMV, $4.00 MB.

UR2B Clean Robot Soap, 1988.
Orange and lavender robot soaps. CMV, $3.00 each, MB.

Ducks on Parade, 1987.
Box held three small yellow duck soaps. CMV, $3.00 MB.

Soap Pets, 1987.
Ruffy the puppy in blue, Squeaky the mouse in lavender, and Fluffy the kitten in orange. CMV, $2.00 each, MB.

Tiny Teddy Bear Soaps, 1988.
Three yellow bear soaps. CMV, $2.00 MB.

Sea Sub and Crew Soaps, 1987.
Orange plastic boat held two small sea creature soaps. CMV, $6.00 MB.

Kitty Trio Soaps, 1987.
Three kitten soaps, 1 oz. each. CMV, $2.00 MB, set.

Mickey and Minnie Hollywood Soaps, 1989.
Mickey, blue, and Minnie, yellow. Box of two. CMV, $3.00 MB.

Bumble Babee Toy and Soap, 1987.
Bumblebee wind-up tub toy and matching soap. CMV, $5.00 MB.

Christmas Friends Ornament Soaps, 1988.
Red Santa, blue penguin, and green elf soaps. CMV, $2.00 each, MB.

Pumpkin Pals Soap Set, 1989.
Orange box held three black cat soaps. CMV, $3.00 MB.

Fish 'N Fun Finger Paint Soap, 1989.
Red, yellow, and blue fish soaps in matching plastic boxes. CMV, $6.00 MB, set.

Say Cheese Soap Set, 1990.
3 oz., pink mouse bar, snaps apart. CMV, $2.00 MB.

Arctic Antic Soaps, 1991.
1 oz. bars. Seal (green), penguin (red), or polar bear (blue). Boxed separately. CMV, $1.00 each, MB.

Baby Bunny Soaps,1989.
Three green bunny soaps. CMV, $2.50 MB.

Mickey and Friends Soaps, 1990.
Five different soaps. Mickey, Pluto, Minnie, Goofy, and Donald. 1 oz. each. CMV, $2.00 each, MB.

King for a Day Soap, 1991.
3 oz. lion bar marked "Dad is King." CMV, $2.50 MB.

Bonnie and Benny Buffle and Soap, 1990.
Plastic water squirters and 3 oz. bar of soap for each. CMV, $4.00 MB, each set.

Garfield Soap, 1990.
Orange cat soap. CMV, $2.50 MB.

Heart to Heart Soaps, 1991.
Pink, lavender, or peach heart shaped soaps. One to a box. CMV, $1.00 each, MB.

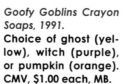

Goofy Goblins Crayon Soaps, 1991.
Choice of ghost (yellow), witch (purple), or pumpkin (orange). CMV, $1.00 each, MB.

Snoopy and Woodstock Soap, 1990.
White Snoopy and yellow Woodstock soaps. CMV, $2.00 MB.

Cottage Friends Soaps, 1991.
1 oz. bars. Bunny (lavender) or goose (yellow). CMV, $1.00 each, MB.

Ariel Soap Dish, 1991.
Red, white, and green, 6½" x 5" plastic soap dish. Sold separately. CMV, $6.00 MB.
Flounder Soap, 1991.
2 oz., yellow fish soap made to go with Ariel soap dish. Sold separately. CMV, $2.00 MB.

Garfield Soap Raft and Soap, 1992.
Inflatable Garfield soap dish. CMV, $7.00.
Garfield Soap, 1992.
Sold separately from raft. CMV, $2.00 MB.

Childhood Rhyme Soaps, 1991.
1 oz. bars. Mary Had a Little Lamb, Little Jack Horner, Cat and the Fiddle, Humpty Dumpty, and Little Boy Blue. CMV, $1.00 each, MB.

Suds of the Seasons Soaps, 1992.
1 oz. soap bars. Betty Bell (red), Timmy Twinkles (yellow), and Douglas Fir (green). CMV, $1.00 each, MB.

Sammy the Frog Float, 1991.
Green frog soap and green lily pad plastic floating base. CMV, $4.00 MB.

Three Bears Soap Set, 1992.
4" high, 5½" wide wicker sofa held three shades of brown bear soaps. CMV, $8.00 MB.

A Touch of Bubbly Soap, 1991.
3½ oz. champagne bottle shaped pink soap. CMV, $2.00 MB.

Songbird Soaps, 1993.
Pink, blue, or purple. Sold separately. CMV, $1.00 each, MB.

Jungle Love Soaps, 1992.
1 oz. each. Cupid Monkey, Cupid Lion, and Cupid Elephant. CMV, $2.00 each, MB.

Sea Striped Soaps, 1991.
Fish designed box held fish, starfish, and seahorse striped soaps. CMV, $2.00 MB.

Tiny Toon Cartoon Soaps, 1992.
Five different pop-up soap boxes, held 1 oz. soap bars in Buster Bunny, Babs Bunny, Plucky Duck, Hamton, and Dizzy David. CMV, $2.00 each, MB.

New Year's Greeting Soap, 1993.
1994 gold, 3 oz. soap. CMV, $2.00 MB.

Christmas Character Soaps, 1994.
1 oz. bars. Choice of Mrs. Claus (yellow), Rudolph (blue), or Santa (red). CMV, $1.00 each, MB.

Easter Pet Soaps, 1994.
Lamb (pink), duck (yellow), or rabbit (purple). 1 oz. bars. CMV, $1.00 each, MB.

Seven Dwarf Soaps, 1994.
Seven different 1 oz. soaps. CMV, $1.50 each, MB.

Christmas Characters Crayon Soaps, 1993.
1 oz., red Santa or green elf soaps. CMV, $1.00 each, MB.

Baby Saurus Soaps, 1993.
1 oz. bars, choice of Stegly (blue), Prosey (yellow), or Rexie (green). CMV, $1.00 each, MB.

Mickey and Minnie Mouse Soap Dishes and Soaps, 1995.
7" long, 6¼" wide plastic soap dishes, Mickey (blue), Minnie (pink). Mickey and Minnie shaped soaps sold separately. CMV, $1.50 each soap. $3.00 each dish.

Goblin Soaps, 1994.
1 oz. soaps in pumpkin, ghost, or cat. CMV, $1.00 each, MB.

Mighty Morphin Power Rangers, 1995.
1 oz. bars. Choice of red, yellow, pink, blue, and black. CMV, $1.00 each, MB.

Sea Friends Striped Soaps, 1995.
1 oz. bars. Frog, turtle, or crab. CMV, $1.50 each, MB.

Football Soaps on a Rope, 1995.
5 oz. bars in Triumph, Trailblazer, Wild Country, or Black Suede. CMV, $5.00 each, MB.

Mickey's Stuff for Kids Soaps, 1996.
2 oz. bars. Choice of Mickey Mouse (orange), Minnie Mouse (red), Donald Duck (yellow), or Goofy (green). CMV, $1.50 each, MB.

Izzy's Olympic Games Soaps, 1996.
2 oz. oval bars with Izzy. Choice of red, white, or blue soap. CMV. $1.50 each, MB.

Basketball Soap on a Rope, 1996.
5 oz. bar in Triumph (white bar, green rope), Wild Country (orange bar, blue rope) or Black Suede (yellow bar, black rope). CMV, $5.00 each, MB.

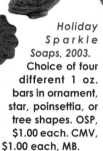

Muppet Treasure Island Soap on a Rope, 1996.
3 oz. bars. Pink bar is Miss Piggy, Light green bar is Kermit. CMV, $3.00 each, MB.

Holiday Sparkle Soaps, 2003.
Choice of four different 1 oz. bars in ornament, star, poinsettia, or tree shapes. OSP, $1.00 each. CMV, $1.00 each, MB.

Halloween Soaps, 2003.
Choice of four different 1-oz. soaps: cat, witch, short pumpkin, and tall pumpkin. OSP, $1.00 each. CMV, $1.00 each, MB.

Easter Soaps, 1996.
1 oz. bars each in choice of chick (yellow), bunny (red), or lamb (blue). CMV, $1.50 each, MB.

Snowman Bubble Bath, 2003.
Choice of four, 1-oz. bars with snowman embossed on soap. Choice of For Kids, fresh peach, soft pink, or vanilla cream. OSP, $1.00 each. CMV, $1.00 each, MB.

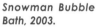

Bunny Bubble Bath Soap, 2003.
Choice of four different rabbit shaped 1-oz. bar soaps in soft pink, For Kids, vanilla cream, or fresh peach. OSP, $1.00 each. CMV, $1.00 each, MB.

Baseball Soap on a Rope, 1996.
Box held 5 oz. white baseball soap in choice of Triumph (red rope), Trailblazer (white rope), or Wild Country (blue rope). CMV, $5.00 each, MB.

Gingerbread Man Soaps, 2003.
Choice of four, 1-oz. bars in vanilla cream, soft pink, fresh peach, or For Kids. OSP, $1.00 each. CMV, $1.00 each, MB.

"Soap" Soap on a Rope, 2003.
5 oz. green soap on a white rope. OSP, $5.00. CMV, $5.00 MB.
"Kiss" Soap on a Rope, 2003.
5 oz. red soap on a white rope. OSP, $5.00. CMV, $5.00 MB.

Joyful Holidays "Bell" Soap, 2003.
Choice of red or green bell, 1 oz. bar. OSP, $1.00 each. CMV, $1.00 each, MB.

Holiday Ornament Soaps, 1997.
Three 1 oz. bars in choice of Santa (red), reindeer (green), or snowman (blue). CMV, $1.50 each, MB.

Fall Soaps, 2005.
Choice of mandarin or apple cranberry in 1-oz. bar. OSP, $1.00 each. CMV, $1.00 each, MB.

"Love" Heart Soaps, 2003 – 2004.
1 oz. bar in choice of pink or white. OSP, $1.00 each. CMV, $1.00 each, MB.

Holiday Angel Soaps, 2004.
Choice of four, 1-oz. angel soaps in soft pink, fresh peach, vanilla cream, or For Kids. OSP, $1.00 each. CMV, $1.00 each, MB.

Holiday Snowman Soaps, 2004.
Choice of three, 1-oz. snowman bars in cinnamon twist, candy cane, or apple cranberry. OSP, $1.00 each. CMV, $1.00 each, MB.

Candy Cane Soaps, 2005.
Choice of four, 1-oz. bars in vanilla cream, For Kids, soft pink, or fresh peach. OSP, $1.00 each. CMV, $1.00 each, MB.

Autumn Leaf Soaps, 2004.
Choice of green or orange leaf-shaped 1 oz. bar soaps. OSP, $1.00 each. CMV, $1.00 each, MB.

Chick Soaps, 2007.
Baby chicks coming out of shell soaps. 2⅜ oz. each in choice of blue, yellow, or pink. OSP, $1.99 each. CMV, $2.00 each, MB.

Soaps with Sponges

Sponges dry out, deteriorate, and crumble after about 20 or more years. These items will be very rare and must be in mint shape as they age for current market value (CMV).

Minnie the Moo Soap and Sponge, 1965 – 1966.
White foam cow with yellow ears and black eyes. Soap is in green wrapper. CMV, $14.00 MB.

Little Pro Soap, 1966.
White baseball soap and brown sponge. CMV, $14.00 MB.

Clarence the Sea Serpent, 1968 – 1969.
Orange and yellow sponge with bar of serpent soap in blue and yellow wrapper. CMV, $12.00 MB.

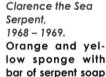
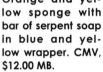

Spongaroo Soap and Sponge, 1966 – 1967.
Brown kangaroo sponge is 15" x 5¾". White kangaroo soap. CMV, $7.00 soap only, mint. $15.00 MB.

Nest Egg Soap and Sponge, 1967 – 1968.
Box held yellow nest sponge and pink soap. CMV, $12.00 MB.

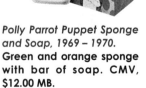

Polly Parrot Puppet Sponge and Soap, 1969 – 1970.
Green and orange sponge with bar of soap. CMV, $12.00 MB.

522

Charlie Brown Bath Mitt and Soap, 1969 – 1971. Red and white sponge with white bar of Snoopy embossed soap. CMV, $10.00 MB.

Soapy the Whale Bath Mitt and Soap, 1973 – 1974. 8½" long blue and red sponge mitt with blue soap. CMV, $7.00 MB.

Yakety Yak Taxi Soap and Sponge, 1978 – 1979. Box held yellow taxi and bar of wrapped Sweet Pickles soap. CMV, $7.00 MB.

Monkey Shines, 1969. Brown and pink sponge and bar of soap. CMV, $9.00 MB.

Left: Cedric Sea Serpent Sponge and Soap, 1973. 9½" long, green and pink sponge, white soap. CMV, $10.00 MB.
Right: Cedric Sea Serpent Sponge and Soap, 1974 – 1975. 9½" long, purple and pink sponge. CMV, $10.00 MB.

Misterjaw Bath Mitt and Soap, 1978. Blue sponge mitt, 9" long, with fish design bar of soap. CMV, $7.00 MB.

Bath Blossoms, 1969. Pink and yellow sponge with pink soap. CMV, $10.00 MB.

Bath Blossom Sponge and Soap, 1979 – 1980. Box held yellow, green and blue sponge and yellow soap. CMV, $6.00 MB.

Hubie the Hippo Soap and Sponge, 1970 – 1971. Turquoise and red sponge with hippo wrapped soap. CMV, $10.00 MB.

Good Habit Rabbit Bath Mitt and Soap, 1974. White and pink foam mitt with yellow carrot soap. CMV, $7.00 MB.

Worried Walrus Soap and Sponge, 1979 – 1980. Purple, green, and brown sponge. Came with wrapped bar of Sweet Pickles children's bath soap. CMV, $5.00 MB.

Little Leaguer Soap and Sponge, 1972. Tan sponge mitt and white baseball soap. Sponge is different from 1966 Little Pro soap and sponge. CMV, $10.00 MB.

Pink Panther Sponge Mitt and Soap, 1977 – 1980. Pink mitt, yellow eyes. Blue, green, and pink wrapped soap. CMV, $8.00 MB.

Fearless Fish Sponge and Soap, 1979 – 1980. Green fish sponge and Sweet Pickles wrapped soap with fish on a scooter. CMV, $4.00 MB.

Oscar Octopus and Soap, 1980 – 1981. Yellow and orange with blue and green trim sponge. Green, red, and purple rings, one bar of Sweet Pickles soap. CMV, $7.00 MB.

All Star Baseball Mitt and Soap, 1987. 7" orange sponge mitt and white baseball soap. No box. CMV, $5.00 MB.

Bath Time Basketball and Soap Set, 1989. Orange sponge basketball and purple slam dunk soap. CMV, $7.00 MB.

Spiderman Sponge and Soap, 1980. Blue and red sponge. Red wrapped soap. CMV, $6.00 MB.

Baby Kermit and Miss Piggy Sponge and Soap, 1986. 3½" high sponge with soap inside, doubles in size when wet. Kermit in green and Miss Piggy in red. CMV, $3.00 MB.

Cheery Chirpers Kitchen Soap and Sponge, 1990. Yellow chicken sponge, white chick soap. CMV, $4.00 MB.

Men's Soaps

Warning! Keep all soaps out of sunlight as they fade quickly. All soaps must be mint and boxed for full value. Damaged soaps have no value.

CPC Shaving Soap, 1908. White bar, embossed. Came in yellow box. CMV, $60.00.

Shaving Soap, 1936 – 1949. Two bars in maroon box, white soap. CMV, $42.50 MB.

Shaving Soap, 1949 – 1957. Two bars in green and red box. CMV, $32.50 MB.

Shaving Soap, 1930 – 1936. White bar. CMV, $35.00 MB.
Styptic Pencil, 1930. CMV, $10.00 MB.

Carriage Shower Soap, 1960 – 1962. Red, white, and black box contained 6 oz. cake of embossed stagecoach soap on red or white rope. CMV, $35.00 MB.

Oatmeal Soap, 1961 – 1963.
Two brown bars, two different boxes. "A spicy fragrance." CMV, $30.00 MB. $35.00 MB, deluxe box.

Bath Soap for Men, 1966 – 1967.
Two white soaps with red buttons, silver and white box. CMV, $25.00 MB.

On Duty 24 Soap, 1977 – 1984.
Deodorant soap. ÇMV, $1.00 each. Three different labels.

Most Valuable Soap Set, 1963 – 1964.
Yellow box held three yellow bars. CMV, $30.00 MB.

Shampoo Shower Soap for Men, 1972 – 1973.
5 oz. bar on red and black rope. Also came with white rope. Red and black box. CMV, $8.00 MB.

Royal Hearts Soap, 1978 – 1979.
King and queen box held two white bars with king and queen of hearts soaps. CMV, $7.00 MB.

Oatmeal Soap for Men Spicy, 1963 – 1964.
Embossed stagecoach on brown bar of soap. CMV, $10.00 in wrapping.

Suitably Gifted Soap, 1978 – 1979.
Blue box held blue bar that is shaped like a shirt and tie. CMV, $7.00 MB.

Buffalo Nickel 1913 Soap Dish and Soap, 1978 – 1979.
5" nickel plated buffalo nickel metal soap dish and light gray or off-white color soap. CMV, $10.00 MB.

Model 'A' 1928 Soap Set, 1975.
Two 3 oz. white bars of soap with dark and light blue wrapper and box. CMV, $8.00 MB.

Lonesome Pine Soap, 1966 – 1967.
Green and gold box held wood grain soap cut in half. CMV, $25.00 MB.

Golf Ball Soaps, 1975.
Three white soaps in yellow and green box. Spicy scented. CMV, $7.00 MB.

Barber Shop Duet Mustache Comb and Soap Set, 1978 – 1979.
Box held white bar of man's face soap and small brown plastic mustache comb. CMV, $6.00 MB, set.

Farmers' Almanac Thermometer and Soaps, 1979 – 1980.
Box held tin top with plastic bottom with two bars of Farmer's Almanac soap. Came with copy of Avon 1980 Farmers' Almanac. CMV, $12.00 MB, complete. CMV, $1.00 Farmers' Almanac only.

Ancient Mariner Box and Soap, 1982 – 1983.
Tin box with bar compass design soap. CMV, $6.00 MB.

Huddles Soap on a Rope and Cards, 1984.
Box held brown football marked "Huddles" and deck of NFL football team playing cards. CMV, $5.00 MB.

That's My Dad Decal Soaps, 1983.
Choice of three different decal soaps. "We love you dad," "You taught me all the important things, Dad," or "You're always there when I need you, Dad" (shown). CMV, $3.00 each, MB.

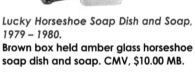

Lucky Horseshoe Soap Dish and Soap, 1979 – 1980.
Brown box held amber glass horseshoe soap dish and soap. CMV, $10.00 MB.

Men's Soaps, 1984.
Cool soap, Cordovan, Wild Country, or Musk for Men. CMV, $1.00 each.

Perpetual Calendar Container and Soap, 1979 – 1980.
Yellow box held Avon tin can calendar and white bar of soap. Bottom of can says "Made in England for Avon." CMV, $8.00 MB.

"Grandfathers and Grandmothers are Special" Soaps, 1983.
Metal can held choice of black or white grandfather or black or white grandmother. CMV, $6.00 each, MB.

Dad's Lucky Deal Decal Soap and Cards, 1984.
Bar of dog soap and deck of cards. CMV, $7.00 MB.

Weekend Soap on a Rope, 1979 – 1980.
Tan soap on green rope. CMV, $3.00 MB.

Musk for Men, 1983 – 1984.
Shower soap on a rope. CMV, $3.00 MB.

Dad Soap on a Rope, 1985.
Yellow bar. CMV, $4.00 MB.

Aures Soap on a Rope, 1986.
American Classic Soap on a Rope, 1987.
Both boxed, single bars on ropes. CMV, $2.00 each, MB.

Gentlemen's Quarter Gift Set, 1989.
Box held Black Suede soap and sponge. CMV, $7.00 MB.

Shower Soap on a Rope, 1992.
5 oz. bars, choice of Black Suede, Wild Country Musk, Wild Country, Everafter for Men, Cavalier, Musk for Men, Undeniable for Men, or Triumph. CMV, $2.00 each, MB.

Wilderness Box Soap, 1988.
Wood box, 3¼" wide with deer lid and soap. CMV, $6.00 MB.

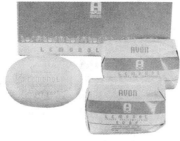

Sporting Duck Soap, 1990.
3 oz., brown duck bar. CMV, $2.00 MB.

Lemonol Soap, 1921 – 1933.
Box of 12 cakes. CMV, $100.00 MB.

Lemonol Toilet Soap, 1923 – 1931.
Box of three bars. CMV, $80.00 MB.

Lemonol Toilet Soap, 1936 – 1941.
Three yellow bars in turquoise and white box and wrapping. CMV, $40.00 MB. CMV, $60.00 box of 12 bars, MB. Add $3.00 per bar for CPC label, mint.

Facial Soap, 1945 – 1955.
Box held two bars. OSP, 79¢. CMV, $25.00 MB.

Lemonol Toilet Soap, 1931 – 1936.
Yellow soap wrapped in blue and silver paper. Came in box of three. CMV, $45.00 MB. CMV, $65.00 box of 12 bars MB.

Lemonol Soap, 1941 – 1958.
Yellow and green lemon box held three flat bars with round edges and flat bottoms. CMV, $35.00 MB.

Facial Soap, 1955 – 1961.
Turquoise box held two bars.
CMV, $20.00 MB.

Lemonol Soap, 1958 – 1966.
Yellow and green box held three
yellow bars with flat edges. Box
came lift-off (older) or flip-up.
CMV, $30.00 MB.

Hostess Bouquet Soap, 1959 – 1961.
Pink and yellow box held four bars.
CMV, $25.00 MB.

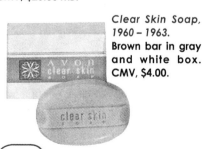

*Clear Skin Soap,
1960 – 1963.*
Brown bar in gray
and white box.
CMV, $4.00.

*Perfumed Soaps and Perfumed
Deodorant Soaps, 1961 – 1964.*
One bar each in Lemonol, Per-
sian Wood, Somewhere, Facial,
Floral, Royal Pink, Royal Jasmine,
Here's My Heart, Cotillion, To a
Wild Rose, Topaze, or Rose Gera-
nium. CMV, $4.00 each, mint.

Gift Bows Soap, 1962 – 1964.
Box held six bow tie soaps. CMV,
$30.00 MB.

*Soap Treasure,
1963.*
Gold and white
box held five bars
of perfumed soap
in choice of Lilac,
Lily of the Valley,
Floral, Lemonol, Cotillion, Here's My Heart, Rose
Geranium, To a Wild Rose, Royal Jasmine, Persian
Wood, Somewhere, Royal PIne, or Topaze. Came
with two different styles of soap as shown. CMV,
$25.00 MB each set.

*Perfumed Deodorant
Soap, 1963 – 1967.*
CMV, $4.00 mint.

*Hostess Soap Sampler,
1964 – 1965.*
Floral box held 12 cakes of soap.
CMV, $30.00 MB.

*Clear Skin,
1964 – 1969.*
Brown bar in gray
and white wrap-
per. CMV, $3.00.

*Lady Slippers Soaps,
1965 – 1966.*
Four shoe soaps in box.
CMV, $35.00 MB.

*Skin So Soft Soap,
1965 – 1974.*
3 oz. bar. CMV, $1.00
mint.

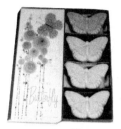

Butterfly Soap,
1966 – 1967.
Four bars in box. CMV,
$30.00 MB.

Bath Flowers Soap and Sponge,
1965 – 1966.
Pink and white floral box contained one bar of To a Wild Rose
soap and pink, green, and white
sponge. CMV, $12.00 MB.

Decorator Gift Soaps, 1969.
Pink box held three egg shaped
soaps in green, pink, and blue.
CMV, $12.00 MB.

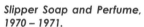

Bay Berry Soap, 1967.
Blue and gold box held
three wrapped bars in
plastic holder. CMV,
$5.00 each, soap only.
$25.00 MB, set.

Lemonol Soap, 1966 – 1967.
Blue and yellow box held six
2½" yellow bars. CMV, $30.00
MB.

Pine Cone Gift Soaps,
1970 – 1973.
Box contained blue, yellow,
and green pine scented
soaps. CMV, $10.00 MB.

Whipped Creams, 1968.
Green, blue, pink, and yellow
soaps. CMV, $15.00 MB.

Slipper Soap and Perfume,
1970 – 1971.
⅛ oz. bow tie perfume sits
in light pink slipper soap
in Cotillion, and dark pink
soap in Charisma. CMV,
$20.00 MB.

Cherub Soap Set,
1966 – 1967.
Blue box held two pink angel
soaps. CMV, $30.00 MB.

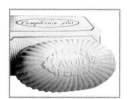

Partridge and Pear Soaps,
1968 – 1970.
Two green pears and white partridge soaps. CMV, $12.00 MB.

Complexion Bar,
1966 – 1970.
4 oz. bar. CMV, $4.00
MB.

Fruit Bouquet Soap,
1969.
Orange, lavender,
and green soaps.
CMV, $12.00 MB.

Spring Tulips Soap,
1970 – 1973.
Blue and pink box held
six green, white, and pink
soaps. CMV, $20.00 MB.

Sea Garden Perfumed Bath Soap,
1970 – 1973.
6 oz. blue bar with blue box.
CMV, $4.00 MB.

Hidden Treasure Soap,
1972 – 1975.
Two, 3 oz. turquoise soaps with
pearl colored and shaped ⅛
oz. bottle of perfume. Came
in Bird of Paradise only. CMV,
$12.00 MB.

Rich Moisture Bath Bar,
1972 – 1982.
Single 5 oz. bar, tur-
quoise and white wrap-
per. CMV, $1.00 mint.

Melon Ball Guest Soap,
1973.
1 oz. honeydew and
cantaloupe colored
balls inside canta-
loupe shaped plastic
container. CMV, $8.00
MB.

Grade Avon Hostess Soaps,
1971 – 1972.
Plastic carton held two blue
and two pink egg shaped
soaps. CMV, $8.00 MB.

Lacery Hostess Bath Soap,
1972 – 1973.
Cream colored with foil center
design. Box gold and pink. CMV,
$6.00 MB.

Soap Sav-
ers, 1973.
9 oz. total
of green
soaps in
spearmint fra-
grance. CMV, $10.00

Scented Soaps,
1971 – 1973.
3 oz. bars in match-
ing soap and wrap-
per. Mint, Pine Tar,
Almond, Camomile,
Papaya, or Avocado.
CMV, $4.00 MB.

Hostess Bouquet Guest
Soap, 1972 – 1973.
Three pink bars shaped
like flower bouquet tied
with green ribbon. Came
in pink and blue bouquet
box. CMV, $10.00 MB.

Cupcake Soap Set,
1972 – 1973.
Green, pink, and orange
soap. 2 oz. each. CMV,
$10.00 MB.

Fragrance and Frills Soap,
1972 – 1975.
Four lavender soaps in lavender plastic box. In center a ⅛
oz. bottle of Dazzling perfume
in Field Flowers or Bird of Paradise. CMV, $15.00 MB.

Soap for All Seasons,
1973.
1½ oz. each, four soaps,
yellow, green, blue, and
orange. CMV, $8.00 MB.

Recipe Treasures, 1974 – 1975.
Five orange scented soaps in yellow and orange decorative metal file box. CMV, $10.00 MB.

Bayberry Wreaths Gift Soaps, 1975.
Three Bayberry scented in Christmas box. CMV, $8.00 MB.

Tidings of Love Soaps, 1976.
Three pink soaps in pink and white box. CMV, $8.00 MB.

Country Kitchen Soap Dish and Soaps, 1974 – 1975.
Red plastic scooped dish contained five green apple fragrance soaps. CMV, $10.00 MB.

Angel Lace Soaps, 1975 – 1976.
Three blue soaps in blue and white box. CMV, $10.00 MB.

1876 Winter-scapes Hostess Soaps, 1976.
Two Currier & Ives scene soaps. Came in Special Occasion fragrance. CMV, $10.00 MB.

Partridge 'n Pear Hostess Soaps, 1974 – 1975.
Three yellow soaps in festive Christmas box. CMV, $10.00 MB.

Touch of Love Soaps, 1975.
Three white soaps in lavender box. Spring lavender fragrance. CMV, $8.00 MB.

Bouquet of Pansies Soaps, 1976 – 1977.
Blue box held two flower decorated Special Occasion white soaps. CMV, $8.00 MB.

Golden Beauties Hostess Soaps, 1974 – 1976.
2 oz. each, three cakes of yellow soap. CMV, $8.00 MB.

Pick a Berry Strawberry Soaps and Container, 1975 – 1976.
4½" high red plastic with six strawberry scented soaps. CMV, $10.00 MB.

Timeless Perfumed Soap, 1976 – 1978.
3 oz. bar. CMV, $1.00.

Little Choir Boys Hostess Soaps, 1976.
Box held three pink soaps. Came in light or dark pink. CMV, $8.00 MB.

Petit Fours Guest Soaps, 1975 – 1976.
Eight, 1 oz. soaps, three pink hearts, two yellow squares, and three rounds. Special Occasion fragrance. CMV, $10.00 MB.

Timeless Soap, 1975 – 1978.
Three cakes of amber soap in amber, gold, and yellow box. CMV, $7.00.

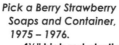

Tender Blossoms Guest Towels and Soaps, 1977 – 1978.
Came with 12 paper hand towels and three Special Occasion fragrance soaps. CMV, $7.00 MB.

Perfumed Soap Holiday Wrapping, 1977.
Came in Charisma and Touch of Roses in red poinsettia wrap; Sonnet and Field Flowers in green; and Moonwind and Bird of Paradise in blue. CMV, $3.00 each.

Treasure Basket Guest Soaps, 1978 – 1979.
Silver basket held two yellow and two pink tulip soaps. CMV, $5.00 MB.

Merry Elfkins Guest Soaps, 1977.
Box held three green soaps. CMV, $7.00 MB.

Candid Perfumed Soaps, 1977 – 1978.
Open end box, three cakes each. 3 oz. white bars. CMV, $5.00 MB.

Country Garden Soaps, 1978 – 1981.
Box held two Avon bar flower soaps with two different flower decals. CMV, $5.00 MB.

Winter Frolics Hostess Soaps, 1977 – 1978.
Came with two Festive fragrance scented soaps with long lasting decals. 3 oz. each. CMV, $8.00 MB.

Emprise Perfumed Soaps, 1977 – 1978.
Open end box held three beige color bars. CMV, $5.00 MB.

Christmas Carollers Soaps, 1978 – 1979.
Box held two turquoise carollers. CMV, $5.00 MB.

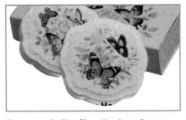

Summer Butterflies Hostess Soaps, 1977 – 1978.
Two scented soaps with long lasting decals. 3 oz. each. CMV, $7.00 MB.

Angel Fish Hostess Soaps, 1978.
Box held three blue fish soaps. CMV, $6.00 MB.

Beauty in Motion Ballet Picture and Soaps, 1978 – 1980.
White plastic box and lid held two blue picture decal bars of soap. CMV, $8.00 MB.

A Token of Love Hostess Soaps, 1978.
All three pieces are Special Occasion fragrance soaps. Light pink outside dark pink inside soap. CMV, $8.00 MB.

Perfumed Soap Christmas Wrap, 1979 – 1980.
Single fragrance bar in red Tempo or Ariane, bronze Candid, or blue Emprise or Unspoken. CMV, $2.00 MB.

Tapestry Hostess Soaps, 1981.
Box held two decorator bars. CMV, $6.00 MB.

Feelin' Fresh Soaps, 1978 – 1983.
Regular issue bar on left. CMV, $1.00. Introductory trial size bar on right, short issue. CMV, $2.00.

Bubbly Bear Soap-in-Soap, 1980 – 1981.
Blue box held small ribbon box of blue soap with small white bear soap inside. CMV, $7.00 MB.

Cream Soap, 1981 – 1983.
Pink, yellow, or blue wrapped bar. CMV, $1.00.

Ariane Perfumed Soaps, 1978.
Red box held three white soaps. CMV, $8.00 MB.

California Perfume Co. 1980 Anniversary Soaps, 1980 – 1981.
1980 CPC box held two Violet bars. CMV, $6.00 MB.

Hearts and Lace Glycerine Soap, 1981.
Pink flower wrapped bar. CMV, $1.00 mint.

Winter Glow Soap, 1981.
Green and white. CMV, $1.00.

Sweet Honesty Perfumed Soaps, 1978.
Three boxed cakes, 3 oz. each. CMV, $7.00 MB.

The Littlest Angels Hostess Soaps, 1980 – 1981.
Blue box held three blue angel soaps. CMV, $6.00 MB.

Fresh as Nature Soaps, 1982 – 1983.
Three different bars in Aloe Vera, Wheat Germ and Glycerine, or Witch Hazel and Lyme. CMV, $2.00 each, MB.

*Soft Musk Soap,
1982 – 1984.*
Single, 3 oz. bar.
CMV, $1.00 mint.

Floral Guest Soap, 1983.
Single, 1 oz. bar in box.
Different color soap for
each fragrance. Choice of
Roses Roses, Wild Jasmine,
or Hawaiian White Ginger.
CMV, $2.00 MB.

Floral Bath Cubes, 1984.
Box of six wrapped cubes. CMV,
$3.00 MB.

*Country Christmas Decal Soaps,
1982.*
Box held two bars. CMV, $5.00
MB.

*Christmas Wishes Decal
Soaps, 1983.*
Three different boxed
bars. Choice of Hap-
piness in pink, Togeth-
erness in green, or
Sharing in tan soap.
CMV, $2.00 each, MB.

Light Accent Soaps, 1984.
Single bar, choice of Tea
Garden, Willow, or Amber
Mist. CMV, $1.00 each.

Five Guest Soaps, 1983.
Flower design box held five small bars
in Timeless, Candid, Ariane, Tasha, Foxfire, Odyssey, or Soft Musk. CMV, $5.00
MB.

*Sweet Honesty
Soap, 1982 – 1983.*
Single bar. CMV,
$1.00.

Ultra Guest Soaps, 1984.
Silver box held choice of five small bars
in seven fragrances. CMV, $6.00 MB.
Water Lily Bath Cubes, 1985.
Blue box held six soap cubes. CMV,
$5.00 MB.

Floral Boxed Soaps, 1983.
Box had different flower design for
each fragrance. Four flowered bars.
Choice of Wild Jasmine (gold), Hawaiian White Ginger (white), Honeysuckle
(yellow), or Roses Roses (pink). CMV,
$4.00 MB.

*A Mother's Joy Soap Set,
1983.*
Blue box held two white
mother and child soaps.
CMV, $4.00 MB.

*Letter Perfect
Guest Soap,
1984.*
Single bar with
choice of per-
sonal letter on
soap. CMV,
$2.00 MB.

Five Guest Soaps, 1984.
Flowered box held five small bars in
choice of seven fragrances. CMV,
$6.00 MB.

Garden Fresh Soaps, 1985.
Box held three peach shaped soaps or box of six strawberry soaps. CMV, $5.00 each, MB.

California Perfume Co. Soaps, 1984.
Small bars, choice of Violet, Apple Blossom, or Lilac. CMV, $2.00 each, MB.

Spring Garden Glycerine Soaps, 1985.
White, pink, or yellow bars. CMV, $2.00 each, MB.

Valentine Soaps Set, 1986.
Pink box held three pink heart soaps. CMV, $4.00 MB.

Enchanted Land Soap Set, 1984.
Box held two white bars with fairy decals. CMV, $5.00 MB.

Peaceful Tidings Soap and Bath Cube Set, 1985.
Blue box held soap bar and two bath cubes. CMV, $5.00 MB.

Clearskin 2 Soap, 1984 – 1986.
Toccara Soap, 1981 – 1985.
Pearls & Lace Soap, 1984 – 1987.
All single bars. CMV, $1.00 each.

Colonial Accent Soap and Sachets, 1985.
Box held decorator bar soap and three packets of sachet. CMV, $5.00 MB.

Imari Luxury Perfumed Soaps, 1986.
Maroon and gold box held two bars. CMV, $4.00 MB.

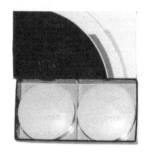

 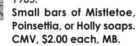

'Tis The Season Soaps, 1985.
Small bars of Mistletoe, Poinsettia, or Holly soaps. CMV, $2.00 each, MB.

Féraud Soap, 1985 – 1987.
5 oz. bar. Silver and black wrapper. CMV, $1.00.
Soft Musk Soap, 1982 – 1985.
CMV, $1.00.

Fifth Avenue Sculptured Soaps, 1986.
Black, white, and purple box held two lavender bars. CMV, $4.00 MB.

Tranquil Moments Soap, 1986.
Silk Taffeta Soap, 1986.
Single bars. CMV, $1.00 each.

Holiday Friends Soap, 1987.
Choice of Santa (red soap), teddy (green), or Mr. Snowman (white). CMV, $1.00 each, MB.

Jolly Reindeer Soap, 1987.
Box held 5" long soap that can break apart. Must be in one piece to be mint. CMV, $5.00 MB.

Gifts of the Sea Soap Set, 1988.
Box held four pink shell soaps. CMV, $4.00 MB.

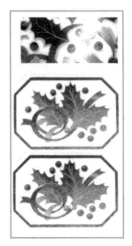

Christmas Berries Soap Set, 1988.
Holly box held two holly decal bars. CMV, $5.00 MB.

Friendship Garden Soaps, 1988.
Flower embossed bars in yellow, green, and violet. CMV, $2.00 each, MB.

Country Christmas Soaps, 1988.
Choice of green, pink, or yellow bars. CMV, $2.00 each, MB.

Citrus Scents Soap Set, 1989.
Box held three fruit slice bars. CMV, $4.00 MB.

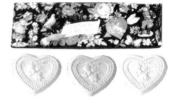

Scentimental Soaps, 1989.
Box held three pink heart bars. CMV, $4.00 MB.

Christmas Couples Miniature Soaps, 1989.
Choice of snowman, reindeer, or Santa Claus. CMV, $2.00 each, MB.

Peach Orchard Soap Set, 1989.
Three peach soaps in box. CMV, $3.00 MB.

Tender Love Soap Set, 1989.
**Box held two white swan soaps.
CMV, $4.00 MB.**

Pastel 'n Pretty Soaps, 1992.
**Box held three, 1 oz. ribbon-em-
bossed egg soaps. CMV, $4.00.**

*Dozen Roses for Mom
Soap Set, 1994.*
**Pink box held 12 rose
embossed soaps.
CMV, $6.00 MB, set.**

*Glistening Holiday Soaps,
1990.*
**1 oz. bars in angel, dove, or
bell. CMV, $2.00 each, MB.**

*Lahana Tropical Soaps,
1993.*
**Box held two blue flower
embossed soaps. CMV,
$3.00 MB.**

Floral Basket Soap Set, 1994.
**Box held three, 1 oz. basket
bars in pearlized pink, yellow,
and purple. Sold two times only.
CMV, $3.00 MB, set.**

Gem Soaps, 1990.
**Box held four gem-like bars. CMV,
$3.00 MB.**

*Christmas Classics Miniature
Soaps, 1993.*
**Box held three, 1 oz. bars in pearl-
ized colors of green, red, and
gold. CMV, $3.00 MB, set.**

*Elves at Play Soap,
1994.*
**Choice of elf on
sled, skates, or
jumping in tree.
White, red, or
green soaps. CMV,
$1.00 each, MB.**

Aspirin Soap, 1990.
**4 oz. white bar in-
scribed "ASPIRIN."
CMV, $2.00 MB.**

*Luxury Fragrance
Soaps, 1991.*
**Box held three 1
oz. bars in choice
of Imari, Splendour,
Everafter, or Beguil-
ing. CMV, $4.00
each set, MB.**

*Honey and Almond Soap Set,
1994.*
**Box held three bars, 2 oz.
each. CMV, $6.00 MB, set.**

*Angelic Splendor Soap
Set, 1994.*
**Box held eight white
cherub head soaps, 1 oz.
each. CMV, $7.00 MB.**

Hearts for You Soap Set, 1995.
Red box held five heart shaped soaps. CMV, $5.00 MB, set.

C'est Moi! Luxury Soaps, 1995.
Box held three white soaps. CMV, $15.00 MB, set.

Sweet Scent Soap, 1995.
Heart design box held choice of three heart shaped soaps embossed "True Love," "Sweet Heart," and "Hugs and Kisses." CMV, $1.00 each, MB.

Elegant Dove-Shaped Soap Set, 1995.
Box held two dove shaped soaps. CMV, $3.00 MB.

Sparkling Ornament Soaps, 1996.
1 oz. bars in choice of star (yellow), octagon (green), or teardrop (pinkish red). CMV, $1.00 each, MB.

Angel Soap Set, 1996.
Box held eight angel shaped white pearlized soaps. CMV, $8.00 set MB.

Cherub Soaps, 1997.
Three heart shaped soaps, ¾ oz. each. Choice of pink, cream, or lavender. CMV, $1.00 each, MB.

Angel Soaps, 1997 – 1999.
2 oz. angel bars. Choice of Vanilla Soft Musk, Odyssey, Night Magic Evening Musk, or Soft Musk. CMV, $1.00 each, MB.

Mother's Day Soap in a Soap, 1997.
Flower soap inside transparent outer soap. Choice of rose (pink), dahlia (blue), or sunflower (yellow). CMV, $1.00 each, MB.

Soap in a Soap, 1997.
3 oz. bars in choice of snowflake (blue), wreath (green), or cherub (red). CMV, $1.00 each, MB.

Floral Guest Soap Collection, 1999.
Box held three flower shaped white, blue, and pink bars. CMV, $6.00 MB.

Skin So Soft and Sensual Decorative Soap Set, 1999.
Box held three 1 oz. flower soaps. Two pink, one white. CMV, $4.00 MB.

Avon 2000 Edition Soap Set.
Silver box held four, 1 oz. bars. CMV, $5.00 MB.

Holiday Soaps Gift Set, 2007.
Red box held two green and two red soaps. CMV, $4.00 MB.

Soap Dishes and Soap Sets

Soaps must be mint for CMV. All soap containers are priced full. We will no longer picture soap sets in open straw baskets as there is no way to protect the soap and the straw will not hold up for a long period of time for future value.

Avon Soap Jar, 1965 – 1966.
Pink ribbon on clear glass jar and lid. Came with 12 cakes of soap. CMV, $6.00 jar only with ribbon and no soap. $16.00 jar and soap with mint ribbons. $25.00 MB.

Heavenly Soap Set, 1970.
White glass dish and two pink soaps. CMV, $14.00 MB.

Decorator Soap Dish and Soaps, 1971 – 1973.
7" long frosted glass dish on gold stand. Came with two pink soaps. CMV, $12.00 MB.

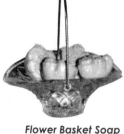

Flower Basket Soap Dish and Soap, 1972 – 1974.
Clear glass dish with gold handle. Came with five cakes of soap (two yellow, three pink), 1 oz. each. Hostess fragrance. CMV, $12.00 MB. Also came with double stamp on bottom, add $4.00.

Touch of Beauty, 1969 – 1970.
White milk glass hand held four small bars of pink soap. CMV, $15.00 MB.

Owl Soap Dish, 1971 – 1973.
5½" long white glass soap dish with two owl eyes in bottom of dish. Held two yellow bars of owl soap. CMV, $12.00 MB.

Dolphin Soap Dish and Hostess Soaps, 1970 – 1971.
Silver and aqua plastic soap dish held four blue soaps. CMV, $12.00 MB.

Gift of the Sea Soap Dish and Soaps, 1972 – 1973.
Iridescent white glass dish looks like a shell. Six cakes, 1 oz. each, pink soaps. Two each of three different shells. CMV, $10.00 MB.

Sittin' Kittens Soap Dish and Soaps, 1973 – 1975. White milk glass dish with three kitten soaps in gold, yellow, and orange. CMV, $10.00 MB.

Nutty Soap Dish and Soaps, 1974 – 1976. Plastic dish with two peanut scented soaps. CMV, $8.00 MB.

Bicentennial Plate and Soaps, 1975 – 1976. Clear glass plate with blue soaps embossed with the faces of George and Martha Washington on each. Some have Avon on bottom and some don't. CMV, $10.00 MB.

Nesting Hen Soap Dish and Soap, 1973. White milk glass hen with beige painted nest. Held four yellow egg soaps, 2 oz. each. CMV, $15.00 MB.

Lovebirds Soap Dish and Soaps, 1974. White milk glass dish with two, 4 oz. pink soaps. CMV, $10.00 MB.

Wings of Beauty Soap Dish and Soap, 1975 – 1976. White milk glass dish with two pink soaps. CMV, $10.00 MB.

Butter Dish and Hostess Soaps, 1973 – 1974. Clear glass with two yellow, 3 oz. butter soaps. CMV, $12.00 MB.

Beauty Buds Soap Dish and Soap, 1974 – 1976. 6" long, white milk glass with four yellow soaps. CMV, $10.00 MB.

Crystalucent Covered Butter Dish and Soap, 1975 – 1976. 7" long clear glass with two yellow soaps. CMV, $14.00 MB.

Love Nest Soap Dish and Soaps, 1973 – 1975. White dish with green plastic lining, held two aqua and one blue bird soaps. CMV, $8.00 MB.

Hostess Fancy Soap Dish and Soap, 1975 – 1976. 8" wide clear glass with five pink soaps. CMV, $10.00 MB.

Sunny Lemon Soap Dish and Soap, 1975 – 1976. 8½" long clear glass with three lemon scented yellow soaps. CMV, $9.00 MB.

Hostess Blossoms Flower Arranger Soap Dish and Soap, 1975 – 1976. 4½" high white milk glass, plastic top and light green soap. CMV, $10.00 MB.

"Heart & Diamond" Soap Dish and Soap, 1977. Fostoria clear glass soap dish. Came with red heart shaped Special Occasion fragrance soap. "Avon" on dish. CMV, $10.00 MB.

Mount Vernon Plate and Soaps, 1979 – 1980. 9" long blue glass plate. Has "Mount Vernon," George and Martha Washington on front. Came with two white George and Martha bars of soap. CMV, $11.00 MB.

Love Nest Soaps, 1978. Light green glass held three yellow bird soaps in Special Occasion fragrance. CMV, $10.00 MB.

Nature Bountiful Ceramic Plate and Soaps, 1976 – 1978. Wedgwood ceramic plate made in England, etched in 22K gold. Two soaps decorated with pears decals. "Avon" stamped on plate. CMV, $10.00 plate only. $20.00 MB.

Bird in Hand Soap Dish and Soaps, 1978 – 1980. 5½" long white glass hand soap dish with three small blue bird soaps. CMV, $8.00 MB.

Flowerfrost Collection Crescent Plate and Guest Soaps, 1979 – 1980. Frosted glass soap dish held three yellow flower soap bars. CMV, $14.00 MB.

Country Peaches Soap Jar and Soaps, 1977 – 1979. Replica of a nineteenth century mason jar. Held six yellow peach seed soaps. Blue glass jar with wire bail. "Avon" on bottom. CMV, $3.00 jar only. $10.00 MB.

Strawberry Porcelain Plate and Guest Soaps, 1978 – 1979. 7½" plate made in Brazil for Avon. Came with six red strawberry soaps. CMV, $8.00 plate only. $15.00 MB.

Fostoria Egg Soap Dish and Soap, 1977. Blue soap came in Spring Lilacs fragrance. Egg dish about 4½" long, clear glass. "Avon" on bottom. CMV, $5.00 dish only. $15.00 MB. First issue had "Mother's Day 1977" on bottom. CMV, $18.00 MB.

Flowerfrost Sherbet Glass and Soaps, 1979 – 1980. Frosted glass held six yellow Avon balls of soap. CMV, $11.00 MB.

Butterfly Fantasy Dishes and Soaps, 1979 – 1980. Two 4" porcelain dishes with butterfly designs. One pink butterfly soap. CMV, $12.00 MB.

Birds of Flight Ceramic Box and Soap, 1980 – 1981. Embossed ducks on lid and sides. Bar of duck soap inside. Made in Brazil. CMV, $23.00 MB.

Ultra Crystal Soap Dish and Soap, 1981 – 1982.
5" long clear glass soap dish and bar of cream colored soap. CMV, $10.00 MB.

Holiday Cachepot Soaps, 1985.
Metal can held five red apple soaps. CMV, $7.00 MB.

Shimmering Sea Soap Gift Set, 1990.
Seashell glass bowl held three pearlized seashell soaps. CMV, $10.00 MB.

Citrus Fresh Soaps, 1984.
Glass jar held five lemon soaps. CMV, $9.00 MB.

Sea Treasure Soaps, 1986.
Black and gold trim tin box held four pink seashell soaps. CMV, $6.00 MB.

Fostoria Heart Vase and Soaps, 1985.
5" high heart shaped vase with five pink heart soaps. CMV, $8.00 MB.

Gifts of the Sea Soaps and Basket, 1987.
6½" wide wicker basket held four pink seashell soaps. CMV, $6.00 MB.

Lahana Soap Dish Gift Set, 1992.
Box held 1⁷⁄₁₀ oz. cologne spray and two blue bars of flower design soaps in flower design ceramic dish. CMV, $6.00 MB.

Water Lily Soap Dish and Soaps, 1985.
Blue glass dish. Three white flower soaps. CMV, $8.00 MB.

Heart of Hearts Basket Soaps, 1988.
Red wicker basket held five 1 oz. red heart soaps. CMV, $8.00 MB.

Winter in Woodland Hills Soap Gift Set, 1992.
Etched glass bowl, 5⅝" wide, held pine scent potpourri and three 1 oz. pine cone soaps. CMV, $10.00 MB.

Love Cherub Soap Dish Set, 1996.
White ceramic dish is 4½" long and 4¼" high. Pink heart shaped soap. CMV, $8.00 MB, set.

Surroundings Fragrant Home Soap Set, 1998.
White bisque porcelain soap dish, 5½" long, 3¾" wide, 1¾" deep. Held three lavender scented glycerin soaps, 1 oz. each. CMV, $10.00 MB, set.

CPC Soaps

All soaps must be mint for CMV.

Savona Bouquet Soap, 1896.
Maroon box and wrapping. Two bars. OSP, 50¢. CMV, $110.00 MB.

Shaving Soap, 1905.
One bar of soap. OSP, 20¢. CMV, $70.00 in wrapper, mint.

Pure Imported Castile Soap, 1908.
5 oz. cake. First came out about 1893. OSP, 25¢. CMV, $60.00 MB.

Japan Toilet Soap, 1905.
Box of three cakes. OSP, 25¢. CMV, $110.00 MB.

Almond, Buttermilk, and Cucumber Soap, 1906.
Yellow, pink, and green box and wrapping held three bars soap. OSP, 40¢. CMV, $100.00 MB.

Starch Dressing Directions Sheet, 1911.
Came in box of Starch Dressing. Printed on both sides. CMV, $5.00 mint.

Almond Meal Toilet Soap, 1905.
Box of three cakes. OSP, 25¢. CMV, $110.00 MB.

Starch Dressing Sample, 1911.
1" size box held three samples. CMV, $60.00 MB.

Starch Dressing, 1911.
Paper box held 25 blue tablets. OSP, 25¢. CMV, $65.00 MB.

Almond Bouquet Toilet Soap, 1925.
Yellow, green, and pink wrapping around three bars of soap. Soap is embossed. OSP, 30¢. CMV, $90.00 MB.

Starch Dressing, 1925.
Twenty-five tablets in box. Each tablet is marked "CPC" and there was an instruction sheet in the box. OSP, 33¢. CMV, $60.00 MB.

A.B.C. Toilet Soap, 1915.
Six bars in yellow box with pink flowers on box. OSP, 40¢. CMV, $110.00 MB.

Genuine Imported Castile Soap, 1925.
One bar of soap. OSP, 33¢. CMV, $50.00 MB.

Peroxide Hard Water Toilet Soap, 1915.
Box of three cakes. OSP, 50¢. CMV, $95.00 MB.

Easy Cleaner, 1925.
Box of two, ½ lb. cakes. OSP, 33¢. CMV, $75.00 MB.

Savona Bouquet Toilet Soap Samples, 1929.
CMV, $15.00 each.

Vegetable Oil Soap, 1931 – 1936.
Individual bar, came in box of three bars. OSP, 45¢. CMV, $50.00 MB, set.

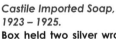

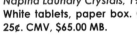

Naptha Laundry Crystals, 1915.
White tablets, paper box. OSP, 25¢. CMV, $65.00 MB.

Castile Imported Soap, 1923 – 1925.
Box held two silver wrapped bars. OSP, 60¢. CMV, $60.00 MB. Same box also came with one large bar. OSP, 33¢. CMV, $75.00 MB.

Naptha Laundry Crystals, 1925.
Two different box labels. One box has blue letters and one box has green letters. Thirteen white crystals in box, with instruction sheet. OSP, 33¢. CMV, $60.00 MB.

Castile Soap, 1931 – 1936.
Box held two silver wrapped bars. OSP, 60¢. CMV, $45.00 MB.

Savona Bouquet Toilet Soap, 1932 – 1936.
Box of six bars. OSP, 50¢. CMV, $70.00 MB.

Vegetable Oil Soap, 1936 – 1938.
Three light orange colored bars wrapped in turquoise and white paper and box. OSP, 46¢. CMV, $45.00 MB.

Castile Soap, 1936 – 1943.
Two white bars wrapped in silver paper and turquoise box. OSP, 62¢. CMV, $45.00 MB.

Savona Bouquet Soap Sample, 1936.
CMV, $15.00.

Savona Bouquet Toilet Soap, 1936 – 1943.
Turquoise and white box held six square bars. OSP, 72¢. 1936 – 1939 has CPC label on soap and box. CMV, $75.00 MB. 1940 – 1943 Avon label only on soap and box. CMV, $65.00 MB.

Dr. Zabriskie's Soaps

Cutaneous Soap, 1895.
One bar in box. OSP, 25¢. CMV, $85.00 MB.

Cutaneous Soap, 1931 – 1933.
Gray box held one bar. OSP, 31¢. CMV, $30.00 MB.

Cutaneous Soap, 1936 – 1956.
Green bar in turquoise box. OSP, 33¢. CMV, $25.00 MB. Add $5.00 for CPC label on box.

Soap, 1915.
Brown or green bar, embossed, came in blue box. OSP, 25¢. CMV, $60.00 MB.

Cutaneous Soap, 1933 – 1936.
Gray box held one bar. CPC and Avon on box. OSP, 33¢. CMV, $30.00 MB.

Cutaneous Soap, 1940 – 1947.
3 oz. green bar and box that says "Contains Ichthynat." OSP, 33¢. CMV, $25.00 MB.

Cutaneous Soap, 1920.
Green cake and box. OSP, 24¢. CMV, $50.00 MB.

Cutaneous Soap, 1956 – 1962.
Turquoise box held one green bar. OSP, 43¢. CMV, $20.00 MB.

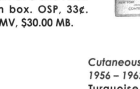

Mrs. Albee and Avon Lady Doll Awards

The Albees are the #1 collectibles in Avon collecting as of the publication of this book. Some collectors call them the Albees and some call them the Mrs. Albees. They are all the same. All are marked "Avon" and dated. See pages 11 and 12 for information on Mrs. Albee.

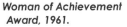

Woman of Achievement Award, 1961.
Painted ceramic figurine of 1886 sales lady. One given in each district for highest sales. Came with stained walnut base and gold plaque inscribed "Avon Woman of Achievement Award." Printed on bottom of figure, "Imported Expressly for Avon Products, Inc. Made in West Germany." CMV, $300.00.

Woman of Achievement Award, 1969.
White ceramic figure much the same as 1961 model. Base is tall and of white wood, with gold trim. Printed on bottom of figure, "Imported Expressly for Avon Products, Inc. Made in Western Germany, Dresden Art." Brass plaque on base (not shown) says "Presented to. . .for Outstanding Contribution to the Better Way." CMV, $275.00.

Albee Figurine Award, 1973.
Awarded to each representative in district with greatest total sales increase. Made by Hummel, numbered, and says "Made for Avon" on bottom. Figurine is 8" high, sits on white marble base with glass dome. CMV, $200.00.

Lladro Porcelain Lady, Division Manager Award, 1975.
12½" lady figurine made by Lladro in Spain. Came with detachable porcelain umbrella. Given to division managers only. Does not say Avon. Same figurine could also be purchased in fine stores. CMV not established.

First Lady Porcelain Figurine, 1976.
Blue, white, and pink porcelain made in Spain. Given to President's Club members only for outstanding sales at 90th Anniversary celebration. CMV, $75.00.

Mrs. Albee Award, England, 1978.
7" porcelain figurine made in England for top selling English Avon reps in 1978. Bottom is marked "Florence Albee." CMV, $400.00 MB.

Mrs. Albee Figurine Award #1, 1978.
First in series. Porcelain, 8½" high, in honor of the first Avon lady of 1886, Mrs. P.F.E. Albee. Given to top reps in sales in each district. Umbrella is also porcelain. CMV, $125.00 MB.

Mrs. Albee Figurine Award #2, 1979.
Second in the series. Hand painted porcelain figurine of the first Avon rep of 1886. Given to President's Club reps for outstanding sales. Colors are blue and pink. CMV, $100.00 MB.

Mrs. Albee Figurine Award #3, 1980.
Third in the Albee series. Given to President's Club reps only. CMV, $125.00 MB.

Mrs. Albee Figurine Award #4, 1981.
Fourth in the Albee series. Given to President's Club reps only. CMV, $65.00 MB.

Mrs. Albee Figurine Award #5, 1982.
Fifth in a series. Given to President's Club members for sales of $7,000 in one year. CMV, $50.00 MB.

Mrs. Albee Figurine Award #6, 1983. Sixth in Albee series. Purple dress lady given to all President's Club reps for top sales. CMV, $60.00 MB.

Mrs. Albee Figurine Award #10, 1987. Tenth in series. Porcelain figurine given to President's Club reps. Green dress. CMV, $60.00 MB.

Mrs. Albee Figurine Award #14, 1991. Fourteenth in series. Orange porcelain figurine. CMV, $100.00 MB.

Mrs. Albee Figurine Award #7, 1984. Seventh in series. Hand painted porcelain. Given to President's Club reps. CMV, $60.00 MB.

Mrs. Albee Figurine Award #11, 1988. Eleventh in series. Hand painted porcelain figurine, 11" high, with detachable umbrella. Lavender and white dress. CMV, $75.00 MB.

Mrs. Albee Figurine Award #15, 1992. Fifteenth in series. Blue and white dress lady sitting on striped love seat. Hand painted porcelain, 8" high, 6" wide. CMV, $100.00 MB.

Mrs. Albee Figurine Award #8, 1985. Eighth in series. Hand painted porcelain. CMV, $60.00 MB.

Mrs. Albee Figurine Award #12, 1989. Twelfth in series. Rose pink or maroon coat dress with detached cart. Given to Star President's Club Avon reps. CMV, $100.00 MB.

Mrs. Albee Figurine Award #16, 1993. Sixteenth in series. Peach and white dress and hat. Porcelain figurine. Blue door background. CMV, $100.00 MB.

Mrs. Albee Figurine Award #9, 1986. Ninth in series. Fine porcelain. Special design for Avon 100th Anniversary. CMV, $100.00 MB.

Mrs. Albee Figurine Award #13, 1990. Thirteenth in series. Porcelain figurine. Given for $8,500 in sales. CMV, $100.00 MB.

Mrs. Albee Figurine Award #17, 1994. Seventeenth in series. Porcelain figurine, 10" high. Pink dress, white jacket with black and white stripes. Given to top selling reps. CMV, $100.00 MB.

Mrs. Albee Figurine Award #18, 1995. Eighteenth in series. Porcelain figurine, white dress, green jacket. "Avon" on bottom. Given to all President's Club reps. CMV, $100.00 MB.

Mrs. Albee Figurine Award #22, 1999. Twenty-second in series. Hand painted porcelain figurine with gray, black, and red cape dress. Given to President's Club top selling reps. CMV, $100.00 MB.

Mrs. Albee Figurine Award #26, 2003. Twenty-sixth in series. Porcelain lady figurine with green dress and white trim and granny snowman. Given to reps for $10,000 in sales. CMV, $100.00 MB.

Mrs. Albee Figurine Award #19, 1996. Nineteenth in series. Given to reps for selling $8,700 or more in one year. Hand painted porcelain figurine is blue, white, and lavender dress, pink purse. CMV, $100.00 MB.

Mrs. Albee Figurine Award #23, 2000. Twenty-third in series. Hand painted porcelain figurine came with a stand-alone brown plastic grandfather clock. The clock is not marked Avon but must be with the Albee figurine to be complete. CMV, $100.00 MB.

Mrs. Albee Figurine Award #27, 2004. Twenty-seventh in series. Porcelain lady figurine. Given to Presidents' Club Avon reps for $10,100 in sales. CMV, $100.00 MB.

Mrs. Albee Figurine Award #20, 1997. Twentieth in series. Hand painted porcelain figurine with red dress and hat. Given to reps for $9,100 in sales. Dated 1997. CMV, $100.00 MB.

Mrs. Albee Figurine Award #24, 2001. Twenty-fourth in series. Porcelain lady figurine with lavender and white dress. Given to reps for $10,000 in sales. CMV, $100.00 MB.

Mrs. Albee Figurine Award #28, 2005. Twenty-eighth in series. Porcelain lady figurine and hat stand. Given to Presidents' Club reps for $10,100 in sales. CMV, $100.00 MB.

Mrs. Albee Figurine Award #21, 1998. Twenty-first in series. Fine hand painted porcelain figurine dated 1998. Blue and white dress. Given to reps for $9,400 in sales in one year. Birdbath on side. CMV, $100.00 MB.

Mrs. Albee Figurine Award #25, 2002. Twenty-fifth in series. Porcelain figurine with yellow dress. Hat box on left arm. Pink purse. Given to reps for $10,000 in sales. CMV, $100.00 MB.

Mrs. Albee Figurine Award #29, 2006. Twenty-ninth in series. Porcelain lady figurine with separate porcelain lamppost. Given to Presidents' Club Avon reps for $10,100 in sales. CMV, $100.00 MB.

1982   1983   1984   1985   1986   1987   1988   1989

1990   1993   1994   1995   1996   1997

1998   1999   2000   2001   2002   2003

2004   2005

Albee Miniature Figurine Awards, 1997 – 2008.
3" high porcelain miniature Albees to match the full size Albee for each year of Albee figurine awards. Avon did not issue an Albee mini in 1979 – 1981, 1991, or 1992. From 1982 to 1990 Avon only made the mini figurines without base or glass dome. From 1994 on each mini was issued with a decorative porcelain base and glass dome. CMV, $25.00 each mini with dome. CMV, $12.50 each Albee mini with no dome. For 1993 Albee, on lead crystal dish with mirror bottom, CMV, $35.00 MB.

Albee Team Leader Award, 1978.
Albee woven in silk and rayon. 5½" x 10". Gold frame, blue border. CMV, $45.00.

Albee Ring Award, 1982.
Gold plated sterling silver. Given to reps for meeting sales goals. CMV, $25.00 MB.

Small Treasures Albee Miniatures, 1982.
Pink box held miniature Albee figurines of numbers 2, 3, and 4 Albee awards. Given to Avon reps for fifth step sales goal. CMV, $125.00 MB, set.

Silver Tone Albee Award, 1985.
Four given in each district. Black base and came in red felt bag. CMV, $40.00.

Gold Tone Albee Award, 1985.
Gold tone Albee, two given in each district. Came in red felt bag and has black base. CMV, $50.00.

Albee Gold Ring Award, 1986.
14K gold ring. Albee lady on top of ring. We have no information on what this was given for but it is rare as this is the first one we have seen. CMV, $125.00.

Left and center: Mrs. Albee Figurine Award Factory Samples, 1988.
Unpainted white porcelain figurine on left and partly painted sample in center with different colors than regular issue. Not marked on bottom. Same size as regular 1988 Albee award. CMV, $300.00 each.

Right: Mrs. Albee Figurine Award Factory Sample, 1989.
Same as regular 1989 issue, only all white unpainted porcelain and buggy. Not marked on bottom. CMV, $300.00 mint.

Albee Framed Picture Award, 1986.
Picture of Albee ladies, 1978 to 1986. Only 100 given and each is numbered and signed by the artist. CMV, $50.00.

Albee Awards — Gold and Silver, 1986.
Same as 1985 Albees above, only bases have "Avon 100 1886 – 1986" to match the gold tone or silver tone. CMV, $50.00 MB, gold. $40.00 MB, silver.

Silver Tone Albee Award, 1987.
Only four given in each district. CMV, $60.00.

Gold Tone Albee Award, 1987.
Gold tone Albee, only two given in each district. Came with "PC 1987 Sales Excellence" plaque across base. CMV, $50.00.

Stained Glass Albee Award, 1988.
Blue glass, silver trim Albee given at President's Celebration. Only two given in each division. Not marked Avon — plain box. CMV, $45.00.

Mrs. Albee Avon 100 Award Mirror, 1986.
13" x 17" gold tone frame mirror. "AVON 1886 – 1986" embossed on mirror. Given to Avon managers at August conference and also given for sponsorship. CMV, $45.00.

Albee Awards, Gold and Silver, 1987 – 1988.
Gold tone, first in district in sales volume and sales increase. CMV, $50.00. Silver tone is second through fifth in sales volume and sales increase. CMV, $40.00.

Albee Lamp Award, 1988 – 1993.
29½" high lamp with blue and purple Mrs. Albee design on front. CMV, $135.00.
Left: Albee Plaque Award, 1988 – 1993.
10" high oval porcelain plaque on brass stand. Mrs. Albee design. CMV, $40.00.
Right: Albee Plate Award, 1988 – 1993.
9" porcelain Mrs. Albee plate. Brass stand. All awards are dated 1988 but were given out 1988 through 1993. CMV, $40.00.

Star Doll Award, 1989.
Only 12 dolls given in U.S. 17", porcelain face, hands, and feet. White satin dress, pink roses, blue ribbons. Given at Night of Avon Stars National Celebration. CMV, $450.00 in Avon box.

Mrs. Albee "Spring Magic Splendor" Award Plate, 1990.
7" porcelain plate. First in series of four. Given for $50.00 sales increase. CMV, $20.00 MB.

Mrs. Albee "Summer's Soft Whisper" Award Plate, 1990.
7" porcelain plate. Second in a series of four. Given for $50.00 sales increase. CMV, $20.00 MB.

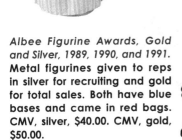

Albee Doll Award, 1988.
16" doll with porcelain face, hands, and legs. Dress is same as 1988 Albee Award figurine. Made by Effanbee. Not marked Avon. Two given in each division. CMV, $250.00 in Avon marked box.

Mrs. Albee "Autumn's Bright Blaze" Award Plate, 1990.
7" porcelain plate. Given to President's Club reps for top sales. Third in a series of four. CMV, $35.00 MB.

Mrs. Albee "Majesty of Winter" Award Plate, 1990.
7" porcelain plate. Fourth in a series of four. Given for top sales. CMV, $35.00 MB.

Albee Figurine Awards, Gold and Silver, 1989, 1990, and 1991.
Metal figurines given to reps in silver for recruiting and gold for total sales. Both have blue bases and came in red bags. CMV, silver, $40.00. CMV, gold, $50.00.

Albee Jewelry Box Award, 1989.
Wood box with Mrs. Albee etched in glass top. Not marked Avon. CMV, $25.00.

Albee Christmas Ornament, 1989.
Clear glass ornament with 1989 Albee etched on glass with "Avon 1989." Given to reps. CMV, $10.00 MB.

Albee Watch Award, 1990.
Gold tone watch with brown or white strap and picture of 1990 Albee on face. CMV, $25.00.

Albee Dome Awards, 1990s.

Left: large glass dome is 12" high. 8" wood base and felt lining. Fits most Albee award figurines. "Mrs. P.F.E. Albee" inscribed on top of dome. CMV, $75.00 dome and base only.

Center: Small Dome.

11" high and 5½" base. Inscribed "Mrs. P.F.E. Albee" on top of dome. CMV, $50.00 dome and base only.

Right: Large Dome.

12" high glass dome and wood base, made for full size Albee figurines only. Inscribed "Mrs. P.F.E. Albee" on top of dome. CMV, $75.00 dome and base only.

Honor Society Mrs. Albee Cup and Saucer Award, 1995.
Wood base with brass "1995 Honor Society" plaque. Blue, gold, and white cup and saucer. Given to reps for $16,200 in sales. CMV, $35.00 MB.

Honor Society Mrs. Albee Cup and Saucer Award, 1996.
White porcelain cup and saucer with flower design sits on wood base with dated 1996 brass plaque. Given to reps for sales of $16,200 in one year. CMV, $35.00 MB.

Honor Society Mrs. Albee Cup and Saucer Award, 1997.
White porcelain cup and saucer with red and gold trim. Sits on wood base and dated 1997 with brass plaque. Given to reps for $17,200 in sales in one year. CMV, $35.00 MB.

Mrs. Albee Gold and Silver Figurine Awards, 1991 – 1992.

Metal, gold tone statue on black plastic base. Plaque says "1992 District Award. #1 for Total Sales." CMV, $50.00 gold. Silver tone statue given for #2 in total sales. CMV, $40.00 silver.

Honor Society Mrs. Albee Cup and Saucer Award, 1998.
Blue and white porcelain cup and saucer sits on wood base with brass plaque dated 1998. Given to reps for $17,900 in sales in one year. CMV, $35.00 MB.

Honor Society Mrs. Albee Cup and Saucer Award, 1991.
1991 was the first year this award was given. Mrs Albee cup and saucer on wood base and brass plaque dated 1991 and 1992. Each year is different. CMV, $35.00 each, MB.

Honor Society Mrs. Albee Cup and Saucer Award, 1992.
This award was not given in 1993.

Honor Society Mrs. Albee Cup and Saucer Award, 1994.
Porcelain cup and saucer sits on wood base with brass plaque. CMV, $35.00 MB.

Honor Society Mrs. Albee Cup and Saucer Award, 1999 and 2000.
Porcelain Mrs. Albee design cups and saucers on wood bases with brass plaques with year and "Honor Society." 1999 on left and 2000 on right. CMV, $35.00 each, MB.

Honor Society Mrs. Albee Cup and Saucer Award, 2001.
Albee design porcelain cup and saucer sits on wood base. Brass plaque says "2001 Honor Society." CMV, $35.00 MB. *Honor Society Cup and Saucer Award not issued in 2002.*

Mrs. Albee Hutch Teapot Award, 1991.
9" high porcelain teapot with miniature Albee on top. Albee plates on front. Given for top sales in each state. Hard to find. CMV, $125.00.

Honor Society Mrs. Albee Cup and Saucer Award, 2003.
Albee design porcelain cup and saucer sits on wood base. Brass plaque says "2003 Honor Society." CMV, $35.00 MB.

Albee Figurine Music Box Award, 1991.
Porcelain figurine lady in white dress sitting next to table with small lamp and Christmas tree that lights up. Battery power turning base. Music box plays "Let It Snow." Plastic picture window background is 12" high from the base. Given to one representative in a drawing at each President's Celebration Meeting 1991. CMV, $350.00 MB.

Albee Picture Frame Award, 1992.
Gold frame, 3¼" x 4", has six Albee ladies in picture. "Through the Years" gift to President's Club reps. CMV, $15.00.

Honor Society Mrs. Albee Cup and Saucer Award, 2004.
Albee design porcelain cup and saucer on wood base with brass plaque with "2004 Honor Society." CMV, $35.00 MB.

Honor Society Mrs. Albee Cup and Saucer Award, 2005.
Albee design porcelain cup and saucer on wood base with brass plaque with "2005 Honor Society." CMV, $35.00 MB.

Mrs. Albee Throw Award, 1994 – 1995.
Blue first issue and pink second issue cotton throw given to reps at President's Club luncheon. CMV, $50.00 each, mint.

Mrs. Albee Throw Award, 1995 – 1996.
Teal green cotton throw. One to a district given to top rep in sales. CMV, $50.00 mint.

Honor Society Mrs. Albee Cup and Saucer Award, 2006.
Fine bone china cup and saucer. Given to Honor Society Avon reps for selling $20,200 in products. Sits on mahogany finish wood base. Brass plaque says "2006 Honor Society." CMV, $35.00 MB.

Mrs. Albee Birthday Gift Tin, 1992. Tin box with Mrs. Albee lady design. Came in box on right. Given to reps. CMV, $10.00 MB.

Albee Tribute Umbrella Award, 1995.
Hand painted Mrs. Albee umbrella. Wood handle says "Tribute 1995." One to a district given to reps. CMV, $85.00 mint.

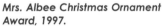

Albee Jewelry Box Award, 1996. Colorful cardboard box. CMV, $10.00 mint.

Mrs. Albee Christmas Ornament Award, 1997.

Four different Albee glass tree ornaments. Given to reps for sales increase. Each is dated 1980, 1978, 1979, 1997, given in that order. All were given in 1997. CMV, $20.00 each, MB. One given to Avon managers as demo. Box is marked "Manager's Demo." CMV, $25.00 MB.

Mrs. Albee Cookie Tin Award, 1997 – 1998. Brown tin can with Albee ladies on lid. Marked "P.C." on lid and "California Perfume Co." on ladies' bags. Came filled with cookies. CMV, $10.00 mint, empty.

Mrs. P.F.E. Albee Barbie Doll #2, 1998. Second and last in this series. Made by Mattel. 11½" tall vinyl doll has yellow beige dress trimmed in pink and white. Came in California Perfume decorated box. Sold only to Avon reps. CMV, $80.00 MB.

Mrs. Albee Bride Musical Figurine Award, 1998.

13½" high bisque porcelain bride figurine sits on white musical base. Will come with brass plaque of each winner on front of base. Given to reps for $800.00 to $1,000.00 total sales increase over four campaigns. This does not say Avon on the bottom, but it has Avon on the box. Base is 3" high, 9¼" wide. CMV, $250.00 MB.

Mrs. Albee Figurine Award, Factory Sample, 1997.

Porcelain figurine is same as regular 1997 issue except flowers in right arm are light orange with white flowers where regular issue has white flowers and dark orange. Sample hat has light and dark orange feathers where regular issue has one light orange feather and one dark orange feather. Sample figurine has plain white bottom with no markings. CMV, $200.00 mint.

Albee Mini Pewter Figurine Award, 1998.

Silvertone pewter figure stands 3" high. This could be a foreign mini Albee. President's Celebration Gift. CMV, $15.00.

Mrs. Albee Bronze Award, Australia, 1998. Bronze metal figurine, 9¾" high, sits on 4" wood base. Only 120 were made and given to top selling Avon reps in Australia in 1998. CMV, $250.00 MB.

Mrs. P.F.E. Albee Barbie Doll, 1997. First in a series of two Barbie dolls sold only to President's Club Avon reps. They could order only three dolls at $60.00 each. Vinyl doll stands 11½" tall and includes stand. She has a purple dress with ivory trim and purple hat. Came in nice California Perfume decorated box. Display box in English or French. CMV, $80.00 MB.

District Award Albee Trophies, 1998 – 1999. Green marble base with gold tone Mrs. Albee faced top. All look the same. Different plaques: Leadership, Recruiting, Sales, Sales Increase, Best New Performer, Customer Service Excellence, and Spirit of Avon. One gold tone top given in each district and four silver tone tops given in each district. CMV, $50.00 MB for each gold tone trophy. CMV, $35.00 MB for each silver tone trophy.

District Award Albee Trophies, 1999 – 2001.
2000 issue on left and 1999 issues on right. Marble base with gold or silver tone Mrs. Albee faced top. All look the same. Different plaques: Leadership, Recruiting, Sales, Sales Increase, Best New Performer, Customer Service Excellence, and Spirit of Avon. One gold tone top given in each district and four silver tone tops given in each district. CMV, $50.00 MB for each gold tone trophy. CMV, $35.00 MB for each silver tone trophy.

Albee Mini Curio Cabinet, 1999.
This white washed look cabinet was given as a door prize at the President's Club lunch. It held 12 mini Albee figurines which are not included. Says on decal at top, "California Perfume Co." Glass doors on cabinet. 18½" high, 20½" wide, 4¾" deep. CMV, $40.00.

Rose Circle Albee Plate Awards, 1999 – 2000.
1999 on left was first issue of this porcelain award plate series for sales of $34,500 in one year. 2000 plate on right second issue, to reps selling $35,500 in one year. Both porcelain plates feature the Mrs. Albee figurine of that year. CMV, $35.00 each, MB.

Rose Circle Albee Plate Award, 2001.
Porcelain plate with 2001 Albee lady on front. Plate inscribed "2001 Avon Rose Circle Award." Given to reps for $36,000 in sales. CMV, $35.00 MB.

Rose Circle Albee Plate Award, 2002.
Porcelain plate with 2002 Albee lady on front. Plate inscribed "2002 Avon Rose Circle Award" on front. Given to reps for $37,500 in sales. CMV, $35.00 MB.

Rose Circle Albee Plate Award, 2003.
Porcelain plate, gold trim. Front says "2003 Avon Rose Circle Award." Given to reps for $37,500 in sales. CMV, $35.00 MB.

Rose Circle Albee Plate Award, 2004.
Porcelain plate, gold trim. Given to Avon reps for $38,000 in sales. CMV, $35.00 MB.

Rose Circle Albee Plate Award, 2005.
Porcelain plate, gold trim. Given to Avon reps for $38,000 in sales. CMV, $35.00 MB.

Rose Circle Albee Plate Award, 2006.
Porcelain plate with 2006 Albee lady on front. Plate inscribed "2006 Avon Rose Circle Award." Given to Avon reps for $38,000 in sales. CMV, $35.00 MB.

Avon Representative Awards

What's Hot

Avon representative awards continue to be one of the hottest areas of Avon collecting. California Perfume Company products are the single best collectible, followed closely by Avon representative awards in the Avon collection.

Mrs. Albee or Albee figurine awards are the #1 best collectibles in Avon collecting. Other hot items include: all jewelry type awards that are marked Avon or have the Avon symbol on them; most all glass awards, figurines, clocks, watches, or ceramic items such as cups, dishes, and plates; anything with sterling silver or real gold in it. All of these must be marked "Avon" on the award. If it's not marked "Avon," we suggest you don't buy it. These are the main items most award collectors are looking for and would pay a fair price for.

What's Not Hot

Items not of real interest to collectors or items not very valuable include: plaques, picture frames or pictures, trophies, cloth items, clothes, bags, or anything that is too big or hard to display. In addition, paper items, purses, sets of silverware, display banners, guide books, and portfolios are not very desirable. Only things that are very old (1940s or older) of this type award will bring a fair price. Most collectors do not want these items as they don't display well. Many of thse items are not included in this book due to little collector interest. All of the above items should be bought with caution. Buy and collect only what you really love.

CPC Identification Pin, 1900.
Brass pin given to early day reps to show they worked for the CPC company. This is the first identification pin ever given by the CPC. CMV, $125.00.

CPC Identification Pin, 1910 – 1925.
Given to all representatives to identify them as official company representatives. Says "CPC 1886" on face. Also came with blue enamel center. CMV, $90.00 mint.

CPC Spoon, Sterling Silver, 1915.
Souvenir sold at the CPC exhibit at the Panama-Pacific International Exposition. Front reads "Palace of Liberal Arts — Panama-Pacific Exposition Tower of Jewels." Back of spoon reads "CPC 1915 Court of Four Seasons." CMV, $75.00 spoon only. $100.00 with card shown. Was also given to reps for selling 12 CPC talcum powders, one free for each 12 talcs.

CPC Sales Manager's Gift, 1909 – 1912.
4" x 4" size, pressed crystal glass jar with Rogers Silver Plate lid. Given to each rep for $50 in sales in December 1909 and 1912. The silver lid has an embossed floral design. CMV, $200.00 mint.

CPC Identification Honor Pin, 1910 – 1915.
Brass pin given to representatives for selling $250 in merchandise. CMV, $90.00 mint.

CPC Silverware, 1920 – 1930s.
Used in CPC factories for employee eating areas. CPC stamped on back of knife, fork, and spoons. CMV, $5.00 each piece.

Rose Perfume Lamp Award, 1926.
Pink rose colored frosted glass, rose shaped electric lamp with antique green metal base. Top of rose has a small indentation to put perfume to scent the air when lamp was burning. Lamp 4⅝" across, rose 5" high. Given to only eight reps for top sales. CMV, $200.00.

Top: CPC Avon Identification Pin, 1929 – 1938.
Given to all Reps to show they work for Avon and the CPC. Silver pin with blue enamel. "California Perfume Co., Inc., Avon" on face of pin. This pin is larger in size than the 1938 – 1945 I.D. pins. This pin came in two different ways. The "A" and "V" on Avon is close together on one and wide apart on the others. CMV, $45.00.
Bottom: Identification Honor Award Pin, 1929 – 1938.
Gold tone with dark blue enamel. Given to reps for $250 in sales. "CPC — AVON — HONOR" on face of pin. CMV, $55.00 mint.

Perfume Atomizer Award, 1927.
Peacock blue opaque crystal bottle with embossed gold top. Silk net over bulb. Given to six reps in each district for top sales of gift sets in December, 1927. CMV, $125.00 BO, mint. $165.00 MB.

Desk Valet — CPC Award, 1922.
Solid bronze. Marked "CPC 1922." Awarded to CPC reps. CMV, $100.00.

Mission Garden Perfume Award, 1923.
8" tall cut glass bottle with sterling silver trim, glass stopper. Given to reps for top sales. Very rare. CMV, $250.00 mint.

Gold Star Representative Medal — CPC, 1930 – 1931.
Highest honor given to representatives that achieved the goal of $1,000 in sales from January to January. If goal reached second year a second gold star is engraved, and so on. Made of gold. CMV, $275.00 MB.

Elephant Crystal Jar Award, 1928.
6" long and 4" high, wrinkled glass to look like skin. Came filled with Vernafleur Bath Salts. Glass top of elephant lifts off. Given to 36 reps for highest sales. This is considered the first decanter Avon ever issued. Very rare. CMV, $300.00 mint.

Fragrance Jar Award, 1924.
American Beauty fragrance jar, hand painted design in blue and gold. Pink and green flowers on lid. Pink ribbon. Given to reps for top sales. CMV, $350.00.

Plate Award, CPC, 1930s.
China plate, about 9", has two deer on face, gold trim. "CPC Avon" on back. No information. CMV, $100.00.

Gravy Boat Award, 1930s.
"CPC Avon" on bottom. Given to reps for sales award in 1930s. Blue and green flowers on both sides. Gold trim. CMV, $75.00.

President's Cup Award, 1932.
8½" tall, silver plate, gold lined. Given to only 20 reps in U.S. Engraved on side with winner's name, "from D.H. McConnell, President California Perfume Co., Inc., July 18, 1932." CMV, $300.00 mint.

50th Anniversary Spoon, 1936.
Gold spoon engraved "Compliments Mr. and Mrs. D. H. McConnell Anniversary 50." The gold on these spoons does not stay very well so many are found silver. CMV, $100.00 gold spoon in box, mint. CMV, $50.00 silver spoon only. CMV, $75.00 spoon with gold, mint.

Covered Dish Award, 1930s.
White ceramic bowl and lid. Gold trim with green and pink flowers. Bottom is stamped "CPCo. Avon" under glazing. Given to Avon reps for sales. CMV, $110.00 mint.

Cigarette Holder Award, 1934.
Made of solid ivory in velvet lined, custom made blue and gold box marked "Avon" inside lid. Green and silver center band. CMV, $75.00 MB.

Avon Brass Mold Stamp, 1936 – 1953.
2" brass mold stamp in reverse says "Avon Products Inc." Tulip A in center, "New York-Montreal." Rare. CMV, $150.00.

Face Powder Gold Key, 1936.
9½" long key is gold on one side with large tulip A and "Avon." Back side held silver face powder sample. Given to reps only. CMV, $25.00 mint as shown.

50th Anniversary Pin, 1936.
Red circle with gold feather. Given to every representative who made a house-to-house sales trip of her area. CMV, $40.00 mint.

Moose Award Plate, 1930s.
White ceramic plate with green edging trim with two moose in brown on face. Back of plate is marked "CPC Avon." CMV, $150.00 mint.

Star Representative Gold Medallion, 1931 – 1937.
10K gold filled medal. Given to representatives for selling $1,000 worth of Avon in any 12 month period. CMV, $150.00 medal only. $165.00 MB.

50th Anniversary Award Lamp, 1936.
Made only for Avon, "Lalique reproduction" lamp. 22" high, 19" wide shade. Frosted carved glass base. Pink ribbon on shade, clear beads around edge of shade. White painted base. Given only to 50 reps for top sales in nation. CMV, $300.00.

Star Representative Gold Medallion, 1937 – 1945. 10K gold filled medal, given to representatives for selling $1,000 worth of Avon in any 12 month period. CMV, $50.00, medallion only. $60.00 in black highest award box shown.

Identification Honor Pin and Case, Silver, 1938 – 1945. Silver with aqua enamel. Given to all representatives for identification. "Avon Products, Inc., Avon Honor" on face of pin. CMV, $30.00.

Identification Pin, Silver, 1938 – 1945. Silver with aqua enamel. Given to all representatives for identification. "Avon Products, Inc., Avon" on face of pin. CMV, $30.00 mint.

Honor Identification Pin, Gold, 1938 – 1945. Gold plated with aqua enamel Given for $250.00 in sales. "Avon Products, Inc., Avon Honor" on face of pin. CMV, $35.00 mint.

Service Award, 1938. Bronze medallion hangs from aqua colored bar with "Avon" in gold. Given to representatives for outstanding improvement in sales. CMV, $50.00 mint.

Silverware Award, 1938. Made only for Avon. Each piece marked on back "Simeon L. and George H. Rogers Co. Ltd. X-tra." Given for meeting sales goal during Avon's 50th Anniversary. Fifty-five piece set. CMV, $125.00 set in box, mint.

Employee Gift, 1939. Blue box with Avon's Suffern plant on box. Held Tulip Cotillion toilet water with tulip label and gold cap, and Cotillion powder sachet with CPC label. Rare. CMV, $125.00 MB.

Avon Pen Award, 1940s. Yellow and black plastic, "Avon" on clip. Fountain pen on one end, lead pencil on other end. No information. CMV, $40.00.

Betsy Ross Red Gift Set, 1941. Set given to employees of Avon's Suffern plant as anniversary campaign gift. Rare. Came with handwritten gift card. CMV, $100.00 MB.

Founder's Campaign Achievement Award Scarf, 1941. Blue and white folder held blue border, white, pink, and green silk scarf. Shows first CPC factory and first Avon lady with "The doorway to loveliness" marked under her. Given to reps in 1941. Very rare. CMV, $50.00 scarf only, mint. $75.00 in folder, mint.

Bowknot Award Pin, 1942. Gold pin with sequins, shaped like bow. Given to representatives for selling $100 to $150 in one campaign. CMV, $50.00 MB.

Victory Pin Award, 1942. Sterling silver wing pin with red, white, and blue center. Given to reps during Acres of Diamonds campaign, 1942, for getting new customers. CMV, $70.00, pin only. $80.00 MB.

Anniversary Album Awards Set, 1942.
Book type box opens to show two satin pillowettes with "56th Anniversary" on back of each. One is blue and one is pink. Given during anniversary campaign. CMV, $125.00.

Bow Pin Award, 1944.
Lapel pin is gold plated with center stone of synthetic aquamarine. Given to reps for selling over $300 in one campaign. CMV, $30.00, pin only. $45.00 MB.

Jeweled Pin, Pearl — Highest Honor Case, 1945 – 1961.
10K gold with black enamel background. Five Oriental pearls are set in the "A." Came in black highest award case shown. Given for sales of $1,000. CMV, $30.00 pin. $40.00 in case.

Identification Pin, 1945 – 1951.
Gold pin with black background. "A" has scroll design rather than jewels. Edges are plain, no writing. Given to representatives for $1,000 in sales. CMV, $20.00.

56th Anniversary Award, 1942.
Satin sachet pillow given to each rep who worked her territory for 56 hours during the anniversary campaign. Came two to a box, in blue and pink. CMV, $30.00 set, mint.

Award Pin, 1944 only.
Handmade sterling silver pin with roses and lilies, given to reps for selling $300 to $400 during Christmas campaign. CMV, $60.00 MB.

Jewel Pin Numeral Guards, 1945 – 1956.
Smooth gold numerals given for additional sales in multiples of $1,000 starting with No. 2. There was no No. 1. These are made to attach to the jewel "A" pin. Highest numeral known is

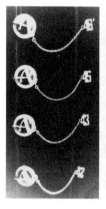

115. The higher the number, the more valuable. CMV, $8.00 on numbers 2 to 10. $12.00 on 11 to 20. $14.00 on 21 to 30. $18.00 on 31 to 40. $20.00 on 41 to 75. $25.00 each on 76 and up.

Manager's Award Pin, 1943.
Gold plated lapel pin with hand set stones, cost Avon $25 in 1943. Only two were given to the two top selling managers in the U.S. during loyalty campaign, March 2 – 22, 1943. CMV, $125.00.

58th Anniversary Gift Box, 1944
Held heart shaped sachet pillow. Given to all reps on Avon's 58th anniversary. CMV, $100.00 MB.

Glass Picture Frame Prize, 1943.
Etched glass frame held 8" x 10" picture. Given to reps for selling over $75 during a particular campaign. CMV, $150.00.

City Manager's Identification Pin and Pearl Guard, 1945 – 1961.
Given to all city managers. Pin has five pearls. Guard is set with 11 seed pearls. CMV, $75.00 mint.

Field Manager's Identification Pin and Guard, 1945 – 1961.
Same design as the jeweled pin but has no printing. The "M" guard is smooth gold. CMV, $55.00.

Jeweled Pin, Highest Honor, Pearl, 1945 – 1961.
10K gold with black enamel background, Oriental pearls are set in the "A." Given for sales of $1,000. CMV, $30.00.

Purse of Gold Award, 1948.
Cardboard tube contained eight samples of Golden Promise. Given to each representative sending in an order at the close of campaign 3. CMV, $30.00 in packages shown.

Medallion of Honor, 1945.
Made of solid gold, it is ⅞" long and 1⅜" wide. Woman on the front is raised. Back side is engraved with person's name and date. Came with award scroll. Medal can be worn on a ribbon or brooch. This medal was given to women only in 1945 during World War II, both military and civilian, for service to their country above and beyond the call of duty. Very few medals were given out. CMV, $50.00 scroll. $500.00 medal.

Avon Apron, 1948.
Aqua in color with white center. "Avon" in center and pictures of Avon products of 1948. Given to managers only for sales demo. CMV, $50.00 mint.

Manager's Gift Perfume, 1950.
½ oz. glass stopper bottle in plastic case. Given to managers to help introduce To A Wild Rose. Paper label on bottom reads "Perfume Avon Products, Inc., Distributor, New York, Montreal, Vol. ½ oz." Came with neck tassel. CMV, $250.00 mint in plastic case.

Manager's Introduction Book, 1945.
Blue cover, 28-page book, used by Avon managers to sign up new Avon reps. 11" x 14". Came with clear plastic cover. CMV, $35.00 mint.

President's Cup Award, 1949.
Sterling silver trophy engraved with top selling team in city and district in each division during President's Campaign during the late 1940s and early 1950s. Given to managers. CMV, $200.00 mint.

Silver Creamer Award, 1950s.
"Avon Wm. Rogers" on bottom. Silver-plate creamer. No information on this as Avon award. CMV, $35.00.

Conference Manager's Pin, 1946 – 1947.
On gold braided rope. Rare. CMV, $50.00 mint.

Pasadena Branch Dedication Booklet, 1947.
Gold spiralbound booklet given at opening of Pasadena Branch, Sept. 22 – 27, 1947. Front says "Avon Serves the Golden West." CMV, $25.00.

Ring the Bell Award, 1949.
Metal inscribed bell given to reps in 1949 for meeting their sales goals. CMV, $75.00.

Achievement Award, 1950. Pink and white with gold. Given for high sales during 64th anniversary celebration. This was celebrating new packaging and redesign of Cotillion. This matches packaging for this era. Approximately 10" x 14". CMV, $25.00.

Figure 8 Charm Bracelet, 1951. Sterling silver bracelet with two skates attached. Given to representatives for interviewing 120 Avon customers during the figure 8 campaign 3, 1951. Made only for Avon. CMV, $50.00.

Sugar and Creamer Award, 1952. Sterling silver base and glass tops. Given to Avon reps in 1952. White and silver striped box. Made by Fina. CMV, $55.00 MB, set.

Avon Calling Doorbell, 1950s. Used at Avon meetings. Has button on back to ring doorbell. CMV, $85.00 mint.

Clover Time Pin, 1951. Given to representatives for calling on 120 customers in one campaign. Made by Coro. Pin is outlined with imitation seed pearls and dotted with aquamarine stones for color. Does not say Avon. Came with certificate from Avon in Coro box. CMV, $40.00 MB.

Candy Dish Set Award, 1952. Sterling silver base by Fina. Glass screw-on tops. Given to Avon reps in 1952. Came in plain white box. CMV, $55.00.

64th Anniversary Scarf, 1950. Silk scarf was made only for Avon. Given to representatives for selling 64 pieces of Avon in campaign 9, 1950. Silk scarf has blue border, white center with sketches in turquoise and rose. Some words on scarf say "Long, long ago;" "A thing of beauty is a joy forever;" "The doorway to loveliness." CMV, $50.00.

Candlesticks Award, 1952. Sterling silver candlesticks, 2½" tall and 2¾" wide at the base. They were given to reps for calling on 120 customers during the 66th Avon anniversary campaign, 1952. Came in nice gift box. The candlesticks were not made just for Avon. Must be in box with Avon card as shown. CMV, $60.00 MB.

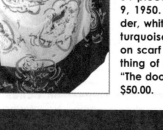
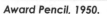

Award Pencil, 1950. Deluxe Eversharp, gold color. Given to reps for writing 50 or more orders in campaign 2, 1950. 5" long with "Avon Woman of Achievement" on pencil. CMV, $40.00 pencil only. $50.00 MB.

October 8 Award, 1951. 1 dram of Forever Spring perfume, smooth gold cap and bottle. Given to each representative for sending an order in campaign 12, 1951. CMV, $40.00 MB.

Nearness Manager's Pin, 1955. Gold shell pin with pearl. CMV, $35.00.

Star Guards, 1956 – 1961. Raised star on round gold metal pin. Given for each $5,000 in sales in any 12 month period. Four guards could be won, each had an additional diamond. Made to wear with the jeweled pin. CMV, $15.00 one diamond. Add $10.00 for each additional diamond.

Symphony Scarf, 1952. Blue background with pink rose and parts of letters in French. Pure silk. Purchased from store in New York and awarded for selling 36 products in the Prelude to Spring campaign. CMV, $30.00 mint.

Queen Elizabeth Cup and Saucer, 1953. Avon 67th Anniversary celebration coincided with Queen Elizabeth coronation. Awarded at a banquet for top organization. CMV, $80.00 mint.

Red Robin Pin, 1955. Sterling silver pin made by Cora Company. Does not say Avon on it. Given in pairs for getting 12 new customers. CMV, $30.00 MB.

Bud Vase Award, 1954. 8" tall sterling silver vase awarded to each rep in winning district during President's Campaign. CMV, $45.00.

President's Award Celebration Perfume, 1955. ½ oz. perfume, glass stopper. Given to the winning team members for top sales. CMV, $75.00 BO, mint. $100.00 MB.

Manager-Representative Introduction Book, 1952. Turquoise and silver booklet. Used by managers to train new Avon reps. CMV, $10.00.

President's Trophy, 1954 – 1956. 13⅝" high, sterling silver trophy was given to top selling city and district managers in each division during President's Campaign each year. Trophy sits on black base. CMV, $125.00.

Manager's Bracelet, 1956. Bracelet given to top selling city and district managers during President's Campaign 1956. CMV, $100.00 MB.

Award Bracelet, 1953. 1953 on back of sterling silver heart shaped charm. CMV, $40.00 MB.

Divisional Sales Campaign Award, 1954 – 1956. Only 20 black plaques with solid sterling silver rose were given each year to managers in top selling district in each of the 20 divisions in the U.S. CMV, $200.00.

Jeweled Pin, Diamond, 1956 – 1961. Same as pearl jeweled pin except has five diamonds instead of pearls. Came with black and gold star guard also containing five diamonds. This was the top award and was given after attaining the four diamond star guard. A minimum of $25,000 in sales were required for this award. CMV, $175.00 mint.

Crystal Salad Bowl Award, 1956.
7½" cut glass with silver plated edge. Came with serving fork and spoon and card from Avon. Given to reps during 70th anniversary celebration in 1956. Made by Fina. Not marked Avon. CMV, $55.00, complete.

Charm Bracelet, Silver, 1959.
Only two districts won in each branch. This was a test bracelet and very few were given for sales achievement. CMV, $200.00 mint with all six charms.

Money Clip, 1960.
10K, gold filled. Small 4A design on face and initials. Nothing on back. CMV, $75.00.

Anniversary Princess Bracelet, 1960.
Awarded for increased sales. Bracelet with diamond, emerald, ruby, or topaze. 14K gold. CMV, $260.00 each, MB.

Representative Award Bowl, 1956.
Sterling silver Paul Revere bowl was given to each rep in the top selling district in each division during President's Campaign, 1956. CMV, $45.00.

Golden Slipper Award, 1959.
All gold metal slipper with red stone in toe and clear plastic heel. ½ oz. glass stopper perfume bottle fits in slipper toe. No Avon name on shoe but has paper label on bottom of bottle saying "73rd Anniversary. Avon Products, Inc." Given to each representative in the winning group of each branch for top sales. CMV, $100.00 slipper and bottle with label. $150.00 MB.

Cotillion Perfume Award, 1957.
Black and gold box. Given to managers. Rare. CMV, $30.00 MB.

President's Trophy, 1959 – 1960.
Sterling silver trophy given to managers in top selling district in each division. Trophy is inscribed with winning team and year. CMV, $150.00.

4A Double Stickpin Award, 1960s – 1970s.
10K gold double 4A stickpin. We have no information on what it is. Please contact Collector Books if you know. Came in Avon box. CMV, $75.00 MB.

Silver Service Award Tray, 1957.
Silver tray, 13½" long. "Avon-Wm. Rogers" on bottom. Awarded to Avon ladies in anniversary campaign. CMV, $30.00.

Christmas Carol Candle Set, 1959.
Red velvet box with green lining held four red and white angel candles with blue eyes and blonde hair. Candles made by Gurley Novelty Co., label on bottom. Outside of box says "An Avon Christmas Carol." Given to Avon managers at Christmas 1959. CMV, $130.00 MB.

Golf League Charm, 1960.
1960 on back. Front has Avon League with 4A design and golfer. Solid brass. Given to Avon plant employees, Pasadena branch, for playing golf tournament. CMV, $40.00.

The Merry Moods of Christmas Ornament, 1960s.
Dark blue ornament for managers only. Other side says "Avon Presents" with 4A design. CMV, $35.00 mint.

Avon Sugar Bowl Club, 1960.
Awarded to sales ladies for getting new customers. CMV, $50.00.

Topaz Jewelry Awards, 1960.
Awarded for sales of Topaze products. 12K gold filled with imported topaz stones. CMV, $40.00 necklace only, $50.00 MB. CMV, $60.00 bracelet only, $70.00 MB. CMV, $30.00 earrings only, $40.00 MB.

Compote, 1960s.
Fostoria coin glass award. Must be in Avon box. Awarded to reps for sales. CMV, $45.00.

Avon Curtain, 1960s.
Used to decorate offices and Avon plant. CMV, $35.00.

Manager's Conference Corsage, 1960s.
Green and gold with red holly, has Avon 7 dollar bill attached. Bill says "United States of Avon." CMV, $22.00.

Manager's Diamond 4A Pin, 1961.
4A diamond pin with diamond crown guard. Given to managers reaching a special quota in 1961. CMV, $125.00.

Wall Plaque, 1960s.
Used at sales meetings. Blue and gold cardboard. CMV, $25.00.

Cake Plate, Fostoria Coin Glass Award, 1960s.
Fostoria glass cake plate awarded to reps for sales. Came in Avon box. Same piece was sold in local stores. Must be in Avon box as shown. CMV, $75.00 MB.

4A Wall Plaque, 1960s.
Used at sales meetings. Large size. CMV, $25.00.

Manager's Diamond Pin, 1961.
Gold 4A pin same as representative's, except has an "M" made of 11 diamonds. CMV, $100.00 MB.

Diamond 4A Pin, 1961 – 1976.
Larger than other 4A pins; set with diamond. Given for selling $3,000 at customer price in an 18 campaign period. In 1974 – 1976 you had to sell $4,500 in 13 campaigns. CMV, $35.00 MB.

Coin Glass, 1961 – 1972.
Must be in Avon boxes to be valuable. The same pieces were available in local stores with both 1886 and 1887 at low prices. Many pieces available at many different prices starting at $10 up to $100, in Avon box. First issue 1961.

Manager's Sales Meeting Notebook, 1961.
Campaigns 15,16,17, and 18 sales meeting plans. Inside front cover says "# so and so of a limited edition for the Management Staff Only." Cover is red satin 12" x 20", came in white box. "For you from Avon" on cover. CMV, $75.00 mint.

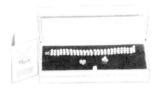

Bell Bracelet Award, 1961.
Silver bracelet and bell that rings. Avon not on bell. CMV, $30.00.

75th Anniversary Sales Champion Silver Tray, 1961.
Awarded to the top Avon district managers for best sales in campaigns 9 and 10, 1961. CMV, $40.00.

Key Pin Award, 1962.
Gold key, surprise gift for activity. CMV, $10.00.

Service Award Charm, 1962.
22K gold finish, slightly larger than a quarter, given to all representatives who sold 50 or more customers during campaign 6. CMV, $10.00.

Manager's Christmas Gift, 1961.
Pearl bracelet with small diamonds and matching earrings. Given to Avon managers at Christmas 1961. Does not say Avon. Made by Majestic. CMV, $300.00 MB.

Achievement Award, Silver Tray, 1961.
4A design in center of silver tray. CMV, $35.00.

Award Earrings, 1961.
Gold star design. Avon is not on them. CMV, $15.00 MB, pair.

Representative Gift, Cigarette Case, 1961.
Silver colored metal case. 4A design and "Christmas 1961" on lid. CMV, $47.50. Also given to managers in gold tone case. CMV, $70.00.

Dedicated to Service Award, 1962.
Engraved with "1886 – 1962," 4A design, gold tone. CMV, $10.00.

President's Award Silver Bowls, 1962.
Three sizes of silver bowls. 4A emblem and writing on outside. CMV (left to right), $27.50, $32.50, and $37.50.

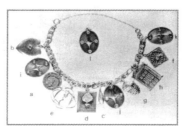

Manager's Charm Bracelet, 1963 – 1965.
One charm was given each quarter for three years, making a total of 12 charms possible. These were won by attaining certain sales increases which increased with each quarter, making the later charms very difficult to get. For this reason, charms past the eighth quarter are very hard to find. The bracelet charms are 10K gold. Only four bracelets were won with all 12 charms. A total of 6,191 individual charms were given to 1,445 managers. The last four charms are like the one pictured in the center of the bracelet. No. 9 has rubies, No. 10 has sapphires, No. 11, has emeralds, and No. 12 has diamonds. Each one had four stones. CMV, $45.00 first eight charms, plus bracelet. Nos. 9 and 10, $60.00 each. Nos. 11 and 12, $75.00 each. CMV, $800.00 all 12 charms, mint.

Money Clip, 1963.
10K gold filled. Back says "Pathways of Achievement 1963." 4A design on front and initials. CMV, $75.00 MB.

Sales Award Sachet, 1962.
Cream sachet in blue glass with blue, gold, and white lid. Gold metal stand. CMV, $12.00 jar only. $15.00 MB.

Perfume Creme Rollette, Christmas Gift, 1962.
⅓ oz., gold cap, 4A embossed bottle and box. Given to reps at Christmas 1962. Came in Here's My Heart, Persian Wood, To a Wild Rose, Topaze, Somewhere, or Cotillion. CMV, $12.00 in box shown.

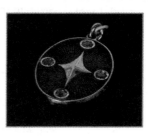

President's Award Perfume, 1963.
Clear glass with stopper, silver 4A tag and string. Given to national winners in each division for President's Campaign, 1963. Box is silver and white base with clear plastic lid. Bottom label on bottle says "Occur! Perfume Avon Products, Inc. N.Y., N.Y. contained 1 fl. oz." CMV, $200.00 BO. $250.00 MB with label and tag. Also came in ½ oz. size with gold neck 4A tag. 2 oz. size (same shape) given to top sales reps in U.S. Same CMV.

Sapphire 4A Pin or Ring, 1963 – 1976.
Set with a genuine sapphire. Awarded for reaching $2,000 in customer sales in a nine-campaign period. In 1974 – 1976 you had to sell $500 in 13 campaigns. CMV, $20.00 MB.

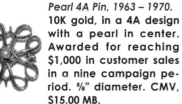

Pearl 4A Pin, 1963 – 1970.
10K gold, in a 4A design with a pearl in center. Awarded for reaching $1,000 in customer sales in a nine campaign period. ⅝" diameter. CMV, $15.00 MB.

1500 Pin, 1963.
Given to reps for $1,500 in sales in one campaign. CMV, $20.00.

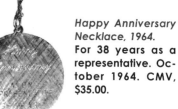

Christmas Gift Perfume, 1963. Given to Avon sales ladies for Christmas. The bottle at left is the same as the one sealed in the gold plastic container with green tassel and red ribbon. 4 – 10 oz. Christmas gift given to all representatives submitting an order in Dec. 1963. CMV, $40.00 complete. $15.00 BO.

Queen's Award Pin, 1964. Gold colored metal, 1¼" across. Given to each member of the winning team during the 78th anniversary for top sales. CMV, $20.00.

Lucky 7 Pin, 1964. Gold tone pin with simulated pearl in center. Given to each representative who sent in a certain size order. CMV, $10.00 pin only. $13.00 MB.

Happy Anniversary Necklace, 1964. For 38 years as a representative. October 1964. CMV, $35.00.

77th Anniversary Queen Award, 1963. Awarded to 10 reps in each district that had greatest dollar increase in sales. They were crowned queen and also received a Fostoria crystal serving dish with "Avon" 4A in bottom. Tiara not marked Avon. Came with "Avon Queen" certificate — two different certificates were given. Also came with "Avon Queen 1963" sash. 11¼" bowl. CMV, $50.00 bowl only. CMV, $50.00 tiara with certificate and ribbon. CMV, $100.00 MB, complete set.

Left: Silver Door Knocker Pin, 1964. Given to all managers in conjunction with the door knocker award program. CMV, $25.00 pin only. $30.00 MB.
Right: Gold Door Knocker Pin. 1964 – 1983.
Came on green or white cards. CMV, $2.00 pin only. CMV, $3.00 on card. Also came in blue box with white sleeve. Same CMV.

President's Day Large Bowl Award, 1964. 12¼" Oneida silver plate bowl. Center of bowl engraved with big 4A design and says "President's Day 1964 — Low Net." CMV, $45.00.
President's Day Small Bowl Award, 1964. 9⅛" Oneida bowl same as above. Center says "President's Day 1964 — Closest to Pin," 4A design. CMV, $40.00.

Silver Server Award, 1963. 12⁵⁄₁₆" x 2", given to the top four established reps in each district for sales improvement over the previous year. 4A design engraved in the bottom. Small 9" servers were given to three newer reps for highest sales and three for outstanding sales ability. CMV, $40.00, 9". $45.00, 12".

Bell Awards, 1964. Gold bell earrings. Christmas sales award. CMV, $20.00. Gold bell charm bracelet, Christmas sales award. CMV, $30.00.

Silver Server, 1964. 9" diameter. Same as 1963 server except no 12" bowls given and all are gold lined on the inside. CMV, $40.00.

78th Anniversary Fostoria Award Set, 1964.
Box marked "Avon Cosmetics" held Fostoria salt and pepper, cruet and glass tray. Given to reps. CMV, $45.00 in Avon box.

Rapture Pin, 1964.
Silver-gray in color. CMV, $7.00 pin only. $10.00 on Avon card pictured.

Distinguished Management Award Earrings, 1965 – 1968.
4A design clip-on earrings. CMV, $35.00 MB, pair.

Paul Gregory Plaque, 1964.
Silver plaque on black wood. Given to each manager in the winning division. CMV, $15.00.

Golden Circle Charm Bracelet Award, 1965.
22K gold finish double-link bracelet with safety chain and five gold charms. Each charm given for progressively higher sales. CMV, $7.00 each charm, plus bracelet $7.00. Came in an Avon box.

Avon Hawaiian Holiday Charm Award, 1965.
14K gold given to seven Avon managers in Hawaii in 1965. Each manager had his or her initials put on back. CMV, $150.00.

Silver Tray, 1965.
9⅞" x 1" given to each rep from the winning group in each branch during the General Manager's Campaign, engraved "Honor Award-General Manager's Campaign 1965." CMV, $35.00.

Avon Dunce Caps, 1964 – 1965.
Came in several different colors of plastic. Used at sales meetings. 4A design on top and bottom. CMV, $10.00 each.

Avon Queen Certificate, 1964 – 1965.
78th and 79th anniversary award certificates. One red and others blue border. Given to top selling reps only. CMV, $10.00 each.

Award Pin, 1965.
White plastic on blue background with silver or gold frame. CMV, $15.00 pin only. $25.00 in box.

Paul Gregory Plaque, 1965 – 1967.
Black and silver plaque given to winning division of Avon's Paul Gregory trophy. CMV, $20.00.

Division Champion Plaque, 1965. Given for highest sales during general manager's campaign 1965. CMV, $20.00.

Good Luck Bracelet, 1966. Gold double link bracelet with gold charm. "Good Luck" and four leaf clover on the front. Back is plain. Not marked Avon. CMV, $12.00 bracelet only. $15.00 MB.

National Champion Award, 1966. Glass bowl with 4A design on bottom. CMV, $50.00 MB.

Honor Award Cameo Perfume Glace Necklace, 1966. Blue and white set trimmed in gold. CMV, $12.00 necklace only. $17.50 MB.

Jewelry Box Award, 1965. White box has two lids, blue inside, 4A design and says "Bleding Corticelli" inside lid. Given to managers. CMV, $15.00 box only, mint.

Tour Guide Jacket Guards, 1966. Silver aluminum with 4A design. Used by Avon plant tour guides. CMV, $32.50.

Sounds of Seasons Music Box, 1966. Given to managers only. Box held green and gold Christmas tree pin, gold key, and bell. Came from Cartier in New York. CMV, $65.00 music box only. $85.00 MB, complete set.

Rapture Award Bowl, 1965. Fostoria glass bowl with Rapture doves etched in bottom. Given to each representatives in the winning district during the 79th anniversary campaign. CMV, $35.00 bowl only. $40.00 MB.

4A Men's Cufflinks, 1966. Silver links with 4A design. Given to plant and office employees only. CMV, $35.00 pair.

Division Manager's Trophy, 1966. Large pewter trophy given to winning manager in each division. CMV $80.00.

Door Knocker Earrings, 1966. Gold tone earrings. "Avon Calling" on them. CMV, $20.00 MB, pair.

Award Compact, 1966. Sterling silver compact. Engraved on back, "National Champion, President's Campaign, 1966." CMV, $17.00.

President's Campaign Compact Award, 1966. Sterling silver case, back marked "Branch Champions President's Campaign 1966." Came in white and gold Avon box in felt bag. CMV, $35.00 MB, in silver case.

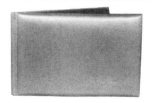

Picture Album Award, 1966.
White Avon box held large and small picture album and picture frame in brown and gold. Cover says "For you, from Avon." CMV, $45.00 MB.

Crown Performance Award, Earrings, 1966.
Gold with turquoise settings. Customer service award campaigns 14 – 18, 1966. Has green velvet box. CMV, $60.00 in box.
Crown Performance Award, Necklace, 1966.
Gold with turquoise setting and gold crown set in center, can also be worn as a pin. Has green velvet box. CMV, $50.00 MB.

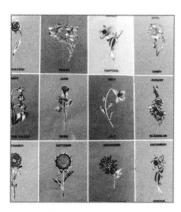

81st Anniversary Pins, 1967.
Sterling silver pins came in 12 different flowers. Representatives who met their personal prize goals for this anniversary campaign had their choice of one of these 12 flowers: Carnation, Violet, Daffodil, Daisy, Lily of the Valley, Rose, Lily, Gladiolus, Aster, Calendula. Chrysanthemum, or Jonquil. CMV, Rose, $15.00 pin only. $25.00 MB. Calendula, $30.00 pin only, $40.00 MB. All others, $20.00 each, pin only. $30.00 MB.

Distinguished Management Award, 1967.
Glass plate with 4A design on bottom. Came in white box lined in red velvet. CMV, $45.00 plate only. $55.00 MB.

President's Campaign Glace Award, 1967.
"Managers" is in script writing with white lined box. CMV, $18.50 compact only. $22.50 MB. "Representatives" is in block writing on President's Campaign with blue felt lined box. CMV, $10.00 glace only. $12.00 MB. Both came in Hawaiian White Ginger box.

Distinguished Management Award, 1967.
Sterling silver key chain with raised 4A design set in brushed finish area. Given to top manager in each division. CMV, $27.50 chain only. $35.00 MB.

Retirement Pin, 1967.
Gold disk with raised 4A design hanging from a golden bow. Given to retiring representatives with 10 years or more of service. CMV, $50.00.

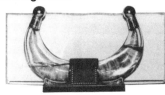

Western Choice (Steer Horns), "Managers," 1967.
Managers received the steer horns in a special box with "Avon" embossed all over the box. Was used to show at meetings on introduction of Steer Horns. Rare in this box. CMV, $45.00 MB as shown.

Manager's Diamond Ring, 1968.
¼K, art carved, 58 faceted diamond set in a gold 4A design mounting. Given to managers for achievement of sales goals for several quarters. CMV, $500.00 mint.

Anniversary Campaign Key Chain, 1968.
Silver charm and key chain. CMV, $15.00.

Shell Jewelry, 1968.
Given for recommending someone as a representative. For each name representatives could choose either the pin or earrings. For two or more names you got the set. CMV, $12.00 set.

Diary Clock, 1968.
Made by Seth Thomas. Gold, back opens and says "Avon Award." CMV, $40.00.

Anniversary Campaign Honor Award Key Chain, 1968.
White Avon box held gold and silver double key ring. Made by Swank. CMV, $15.00 MB.

Sweater Guard Award, 1968.
6" gold chain with 4A design clips on each end. Given as general manager's honor award to each representative of the winning team in each district. CMV, $25.00 guard only. $30.00 MB.

Cartier Crystal Bell Award, 1968.
Crystal bell in Cartier bag and box. Signed "Val Lambert." Is not marked Avon. Given to one rep per district for most recommendations. CMV, $65.00 MB.

Treble Clef Manager's Pin, 1968.
Gold in color. Awarded to managers. CMV, $15.00 pin only. $20.00 MB.

Field Operations Award, 1968.
Solid brass, Avon 4A emblem on front. "Field Operations Seminar" on back. Given to managers in Pasadena branch in Better Way program. CMV, $55.00.

Jewelry Box Award, 1968.
10" long, 5" wide brocade and brass music box. Red lined. Given to reps for top sales. Does not say Avon. CMV, $60.00 mint.

Anniversary Award Rose Pin, 1968.
Victory Luncheon, July 9, 1968. Gold rose pin with ruby stone in Avon box. CMV, $27.50 MB.

Avon Manager's Achievement Clock, 1968.
Box with 4A design and Avon outer sleeve. Clock set in top of brushed gold hourglass inscribed on bottom, "1968 Avon Manager's Achievement." CMV, $75.00 clock only, $100.00 MB with outer sleeve.

Rooster Award, 1968.
Rooster shaped, leather covered green glass bottom on wood base. Brass plaque says "Rooster Highest Percent Increase, 4A design and all 7 Avon branches." Given to district supervisor. CMV, $45.00.

Avon Attendance Charm, 1969 – 1970.
"1969 AD" on one round charm and 1970 heart shape "AD" on the other. Both charms and chain are gold tone. CMV, $17.00 each.

Money Clip Team Leader Award, 1969.
Green and white lined black and brass box held 12K gold filled money clip with solid 10K gold emblem with two small diamonds on top. Awarded to male team leaders. Rare. "Team Leader 1979" on back. CMV, $75.00 MB. Also given to male managers with "D.M." on back. CMV, $75.00 MB.

Avon's Spring Fever, 1968.
Green felt board with six tin painted flower pins. Managers gave a pin to each representative for recommending a new Avon representative. CMV, $25.00 complete card mint. $4.00 each pin.

Team Captain Pin, 1969 – 1970.
Torch pin says "TC-69-70." CMV, $20.00.

President's Court Charm, 1969.
22K gold finish charm. Given to all representatives of the team in each district. CMV, $10.00.

Charisma Jewelry Award, 1968.
Red and gold necklace, bracelet, and earrings. Given for meeting or exceeding a prize goal. CMV, $12.00 each, MB. $37.50 MB, set.

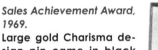

Sales Achievement Award, 1969.
Large gold Charisma design pin came in black Avon box. CMV, $20.00 MB.

Circle of Excellence Pin, 1969.
4A gold pin circled with pearls and diamonds in center. Managers only pin has a logo on back and can also be worn as a pendant. CMV, $200.00.

Money Clip, 1969.
Black and gold box held 10K gold filled 4A design on front with initials. Back says "Management Conference Atlanta, Georgia November 1969." CMV, $75.00 MB.

Tie Tac Award, 1969.
Small 10K gold tie tac given to Avon male executive with blue sapphire in center. Came in Avon box. CMV, $50.00 MB.

Division Manager's Award Clock, 1969.
Sterling silver Seth Thomas electric clock. 4" square face, bottom says, "Divisional Manager's Tribute 1969." CMV, $100.00 mint.

Charm Bracelet Award, 1969.
22K gold finish, double-link bracelet with safety chain and five charms. Each charm given for progressively higher sales. CMV, $5.00 each charm, plus bracelet.

Silver Award Bowl, 1969.
Silver plate bowl by Fina. Has 4A symbol and Avon in center of bowl. 2¾" high and 5" wide at top. Awarded to Avon reps. CMV, $20.00.

Division Manager's Tribute Pen, 1969.
Silver pen with 4A on clip. Came in blue flannel sleeve and white box. CMV, $35.00 MB.

Elusive Pink and Gold Scarf Award, 1969.
Given to Avon sales ladies on first Elusive sales campaign. White box has 4A design and signed by S.M. Kent, designer. CMV, $7.50 MB.

Avon Award Spoons, 1969.
Six silver plated demitasse spoons. Each engraved with a design signifying a different fragrance: Occur!, Rapture, Unforgettable, Régence, Brocade, and Charisma. Each spoon was given in this order for progressively higher sales. A seventh spoon was given to each rep in the winning district of each branch. It was engraved "1886 – 1969" and had a picture of the 1886 sales lady. CMV, $5.00 each spoon. $45.00 MB, set with sleeve. Seventh spoon, $12.50 in silver envelope.

Pen for Leadership Award, 1969.
Silver, black top with olive leaf on top. Garland Pen. Given to Avon reps. CMV, $15.00 MB.

Division Manager's Pen and Pencil Set Award, 1969.
Sterling silver pens. 4A emblem on pens. Came in blue brocade Cross pen box. Given to managers only. CMV, $20.00 each pen. $50.00 MB, set.

Circle of Excellence Charm Bracelet 1970s – 1980s.
10K gold bracelet and gold charms with diamonds and 4A design on each charm. Black and gold Avon box. Green inside. Given to managers only. You could win up to nine charms with the last charm having nine diamonds. CMV, $300.00 MB with one charm with one diamond. Add $50.00 per charm. This bracelet has (left to right) three, four, five, six, and the last charm has seven, diamonds with a CMV $500.00 total for this bracelet shown. Bracelet and all nine charms would have CMV, $700.00.

Circle of Excellence Passport Holders, 1969 – 1980.
Given each year. Each marked "Circle of Excellence." Given to top managers only for annual C of E trip. Different color each year. CMV, $10.00 each.

Christmas Cup, 1969.
White glass mug. "Avon" on bottom. Given to district managers for Christmas. CMV, $30.00.

Five-Year Service Award Key Ring, 1970s.
Sterling silver, 4A design on front, came in blue felt Tiffany bag and box. CMV, $25.00.

Five-Year Service Pin, 1970.
For Avon plant employees, not reps. Gold circle with 4A emblem and blue stone. CMV, $25.00 pin only. $30.00 MB.

15 Year Service Cufflinks, 1970s.
4A design on face and "Avon 15 years Loyal Service" on back with person's initials. Given to Avon male executives after 15 years service with Avon. Made of solid 10K gold. CMV, $300.00 pair mint. Also came 30 year service. Same cufflinks. Same CMV.

Door Knocker Tie Tac Award, 1970s.
10K gold. Given to male executives at Avon. CMV, $60.00.

25 Year Service Award Pin, 1970.
$1/10$ yellow, 10K gold 4A pin with "25" on it. Was for 25 years of service. Was never issued. Very rare. CMV, $100.00.

Circle of Excellence Pin, 1970s.
Brass, 4A design and "Celebration of Excellence." Given to managers only. CMV, $15.00.

1-2 Pin, 1970s.
Gold tone. CMV, $25.00.

Left: Clock, Field Operation Seminar, 1970.
Brass Relide seven jewel clock. CMV, $50.00.
Right: Clock, Summer Shape Up Award, 1970.
Brass Linder clock, top inscribed "Summer Shape Up Award." CMV, $75.00.

Loyal Service Award, 15 Years, 1970s.
Solid 10K gold. 4A emblem on front. "Avon 15 Years Loyal Service" on back. Given to employees of Avon. Came on 10K gold wrist chain. CMV, $150.00.

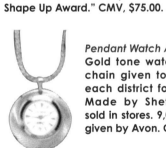

Pendant Watch Award, 1970.
Gold tone watch on neck chain given to six reps in each district for top sales. Made by Sheffield. Also sold in stores. 9,000 watches given by Avon. CMV, $20.00.

45th Anniversary Vase Award, 1970s.
9¾" high, 4" across. Atlantis engraved "45th Avon Anniversary." Given for 45 years of Avon service. CMV, $200.00.

4A Tie Clip Service Award, 1970s.
Gold tone with 4A design. Given to Avon employees. CMV, $25.00.

Key Chain Service Award, 10 Years, 1970s.
Gold tone key chain with blue stone in center of 4A design. Came in Avon white and green lined box. Given to managers. CMV, $15.00 MB.

Initial Glass Award, 1970.
Campaigns 12 and 13, 1970. Reps won the glasses and President's Club members won the goblet with initial of their choice for reaching sales goals in each campaign. The coasters were won by both for reaching sales goals both campaigns. CMV, $2.00 coasters set. $2.00 each glass. $3.00 each goblet.

Avon Beauty Advisor Pin, 1970s.
CMV, $15.00.

Give 'n Gain Prize, 1970.
10¾" high, 4" in diameter. A rose, butterfly, and ladybug are etched in glass. Given to Avon ladies as prize. This was also sold in stores to public. Came in plain box with "Avon" stamped on it. Made by Abilities. CMV, $20.00 MB.

Fostoria Coin Plate Award, 1970.
Does not say Avon. Must be in Avon box. CMV, $25.00 MB.

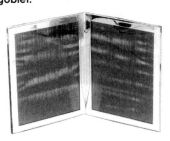

Retirement Picture Frame, 1970s – 1980s.
Sterling silver picture frame, 8" x 10". Given to managers for retirement. Not marked Avon. Came with letters from Avon. CMV, $75.00.

Circle of Excellence Mug, 1970s.
Pewter mug inscribed "Circle of Excellence Avon" on front. CMV, $25.00.

Circle of Excellence Steuben Vase Award, 1970.
9" high Steuben Vase, sits on black wood base. Brass name plate says "Circle of Excellence Repeat Member – 1970" plus name of winner. Came in Steuben felt bag and box. Given to top Circle of Excellence managers only. CMV, $500.00 MB. This vase alone sold in 1998 for $540.00.

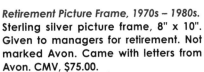

Left: Fostoria Coin Glass, Bud Vase Award, 1970s.
8" high in Avon box. CMV, $30.00 MB.
Right: Fostoria Coin Glass, Salt and Pepper Shaker Awards, 1970s.
Came with Avon literature. CMV, $15.00.

Fostoria Sugar and Creamer Set Award, 1970.
From Fostoria glass, box says "Avon Cosmetics." Given to reps for sales achievement. Design is from the Henry Ford Collection. CMV, $30.00 MB.

Shawnee Door Knocker in Lucite Award, 1970s.
Gold tone door knocker sealed in lucite. Has "Shawnee" in blue. CMV, $20.00.

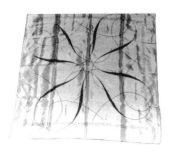

Silk Scarf Award, 1970.
Beige and brown silk scarf. 4A design. Given to Avon reps. CMV, $20.00.

Bird of Paradise Robe, 1970.
Blue terry cloth robe given to reps for selling 24 Bird of Paradise 3 oz. cologne mists in Campaign 19, 1970. Came in small, medium, and large sizes. Bird of Paradise on pocket. CMV, $35.00.

Circle of Excellence Ring, 1971.
Same design and style as pin, but it's a ring. CMV, $275.00 mint.

Avon Pens, 1970s.
Blue and silver "Diamond Quarter 1977." CMV, $2.00. Red pen says "Get Write to the Point – Sell Avon." CMV, $2.00.

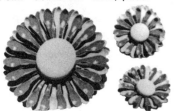

Hana Gasa Jewelry Awards, 1970.
Enameled pin and clip-on earrings are deep red and purple. Given when someone a representative recommended was appointed as a representative. CMV, $15.00 set.

Bird of Paradise Award Jewelry, 1970.
Gold pin, bracelet, and earrings with turquoise stones. CMV, $12.00 pin only. $20.00 MB, bracelet and earrings.

Employee's Gift, Key Chain, 1971.
Blue box with gray flannel bag held gold horseshoe with "Avon" on one side and "You're in Demand" on back side of charm. CMV, $20.00 MB.

Hana Gasa Umbrella, 1970.
Bamboo painted in Hana Gasa colors. Used at sales meetings at introduction of Hana Gasa. Came in Avon box. Very rare. CMV, $100.00 in box.

Golden Achievement Award, 1971 – 1976.
Bracelet and first charm awarded for $5,500 total sales in a six-month period. Each succeeding charm awarded for $5,500 within each subsequent six-month period. First charm — two joined 4A designs with green stone. Second charm — Avon Rose with red stone. Third charm — The First Lady with a genuine topaze. Fourth charm — The "World of Avon" set with a genuine aquamarine. Fifth charm — "The Door Knocker" with a genuine amethyst. Sixth charm — jeweled "A" with a genuine sapphire. Seventh charm — the "Key" with a genuine garnet. Eighth charm — Great Oak. CMV, $20.00 each charm. Charm No. 8, $30.00.

85th Anniversary Award Jewelry, 1971.
22K gold plated sterling silver neck-lace, ring, and earrings. Each shaped like a rose with a diamond in center. Necklace was for representatives not in the President's Club, and the ear-rings for the President's Club members only. Two diamond rings were given in each district by a drawing. One was given to a President's Club member, the other to a non-member. Ring also available in prize catalog for 2,400 points. CMV, $35.00 necklace, $40.00 MB. $80.00 ring, $85.00 MB. $35.00 ear-rings, $40.00 MB.

Antique Car Glasses, 1971.
Eight different glasses picturing Stanley Steamer, Silver Duesenberg, Gold Cadil-lac, Sterling Six, Electric Charger, Packard Roadster, Touring T, and Straight Eight. Sell-ing 10 Avon cars won a set of 4 glasses. Selling 15 Avon cars won a set of 8 glasses. CMV, $12.00 set of 4, $27.50 set of 8, MB.
Antique Car Pitcher, 1971.
Reps won this by having one person they rec-ommended a representative appointed. Also available in prize catalog for 1,400 points. Two different pitchers. Rare one has silver Duesen-berg and Stanley Steamer on it. CMV, $35.00 pitcher only, $40.00 MB. Most of them have Straight Eight and Packard Roadster decal on it. CMV, $25.00 pitcher only with decal. $30.00 MB.

Christmas Bells, Manager's Gift, 1971.
Red strap with five bells given to Avon managers at Christ-mas. Came with card with bells on it and "For you from Avon." Must have Avon card. CMV, $15.00 MB.

Christmas Gift Plate, 1971.
Sent to reps at Christ-mas. Clear glass with frosted First Avon Lady. CMV, $12.00 no box. $17.00 MB.

85th Anniversary Pins, 1971.
22K gold plated sterling silver pin with diamond. Small pin for representative not in Pres-ident's Club, representatives only. Given for meeting sales goal in Campaign 12, 1971. CMV, $15.00 small pin. $20.00 MB. $20.00 large pin only, $25.00 MB.

Renault Car Glass, 1971.
Some sets came with this Renault car in set. Rare. CMV, $15.00.

4A Quilt, 1971.
Reversible, ruffled edged, cotton filled comforter in gold, avocado, or blue. Given for having a person recommended as a rep-resentative appointed. CMV, $150.00 mint.
Not shown: 4A Quilt, 1969.
Pink quilt with white 4A design. CMV, $150.00 mint.

Moonwind Award Pin, 1971.
Sterling silver pin given to reps for meeting sales goals. CMV, $22.50.

Front Page Tumblers, 1971.
14 oz. tumblers with reps name printed on "front page" of glass. Given for having a person recom-mended as a rep ap-pointed. CMV, $25.00 MB, set of eight.

Top left: Moonwind Tray, 1971.
Blue glass tray trimmed in silver, emblem of Diana in center. Given for selling 10 Moonwind cologne mists during campaigns 18 and 19. CMV, $22.00 tray only. $25.00 MB.
Bottom left: Moonwind Jewelry Box, 1971.
Blue and silver. Emblem of Diana on top in silver. Given for selling 20 Moonwind cologne mists in Campaigns 18 and 19. CMV, $25.00 jewelry box only. $30.00 MB.
Right: Moonwind Robe, 1971.
Blue, zipper front with silvery trim. Zipper pull is emblem of Diana. Given to President's Club representatives for selling 35 Moonwind cologne mists. CMV, $30.00 robe only. $45.00 MB.

Mikasa China Set, 1972.
Candleholders and sugar/creamer set given for reaching first prize goal. CMV, $5.00 each, MB. Beverage server for reaching second goal, CMV, $10.00 MB. Eight cups and saucers for reaching third goal (to be won by President's Club members only), CMV, $4.00. For each cup and saucer set. These items must be in Avon boxes with card or *Outlook* as this set was not made just for Avon.

Manager Desk Set Award, 1972.
Has 4A emblem, marble base, 14K gold plated pen. Set made by Cross. CMV, $60.00 items only. $75.00 MB.

Circle of Excellence Key Chain, 1972.
Silver charm and chain with 4A design on one side and Mexico 1972. This was given by Mexico Avon branch to Circle of Excellence award-winning managers for the year 1971. Trip was made in 1972 for approximately 185 winning managers. CMV, $40.00 mint.

Christmas Gift Plate, 1972.
Sent to every rep at Christmas. Clear glass frosted rose. CMV, $10.00 no box. $15.00 MB.

Steak Knife and Carving Set, 1972.
Campaign 12, 1972. In Avon box. CMV, $20.00 each set, MB with sleeve.

People Who Like People Prize Program Awards, 1972.
Third level prize is a set of eight, 10 oz. crystal and silver glasses. Won by reps for meeting third level sales goals. Was not made only for Avon. CMV, $25.00 MB, set.

Traveling Trophy, 1972.
Gold 4A with first Avon lady over emblem on walnut base with engraved plate, "Team Honor Award." CMV, $20.00.

Avon Scarf, 1972.
All silk pink, orange, and white scarf with four big "a's" on it. "Avon" in corner. Made in Italy. Came in silver box. CMV, $12.00 mint.

Roses Roses Awards, 1972.
Hot Plate, 1972.
6" square, white Corning Ware with pink and green rose. Given for selling Mist of Roses cologne. CMV, $12.00 MB.
Goblet, 1972.
Gold trimmed goblet with bouquet of pink artificial roses. Came with card of congratulations. Given for selling Mist of Roses cologne. CMV, $15.00 MB.
Clock, 1972.
3" clock by Hamilton, four small roses on front. Given for selling Mist of Roses cologne. CMV, $18.00 MB.

Patchwork Canister Award, 1972.
Level three. Earned for selling cologne mists. White glass three-piece canister set with patchwork decals. CMV, $25.00 MB, set.

Patchwork Cooker Award, 1972.
Patchwork design. Level four. Earned for selling cologne mists. CMV, $30.00 cooker only. $35.00 MB.

Tour Guide Jacket Guards, 1973.
Gold metal with pressed flower in center of 4A. Used by Avon plant tour guides. CMV, $25.00.

Newark First Award Clock, 1973.
Alfry electric clock, black face, white painted over brass. Back side says "Newark First 1973" plus owner's initials. Given to district supervisors. CMV, $40.00.

Sonnet Awards, 1972.
All earned for selling cologne mist.
Vanity Tray.
10" white plastic, gold trim. CMV, $10.00.
Vanity Box.
White plastic, gold trim. CMV, $18.00 MB.
Three Panel Mirror.
White and gold. CMV, $24.00 MB.

Patchwork Refrigerator Award, 1972.
Level one. Earned by selling cologne mists. White plastic with orange, green, red, and yellow patchwork decals. CMV, $10.00 canisters only, set. $12.00 MB, set.

Ruby 4A Pin, 1973 – 1976.
10K gold with ruby in center. Awarded for $2,500 in customer sales in six-month period to become eligible for President's Club membership. CMV, $10.00.

Recommendation Gift Snack Set, 1973.
Fostoria lead crystal dish and bowl. Came in set of four each. Given to Avon reps for signing up new Avon ladies. CMV, $15.00 each setting. $60.00 for all eight pieces.

Patchwork Cookie Jar Award, 1972.
Level two. Earned for selling cologne mists. White glass with orange, green, red, and yellow. CMV, $15.00 jar only. $20.00 MB.

4A Key Ring Award, 1973 – 1975.
Gold lucite key ring in green or red lined box. CMV, $10.00 each, MB.

Christmas Gift Plate, 1973. Sent to reps who had been with company less than two years. Clear glass, frosted 4A. CMV, $10.00 no box. $15.00 MB.

China Bell Rep Gift, 1973. Christmas present to all reps that had been with Avon over two years. White china with pink roses. CMV, $10.00 MB.

Imperial Gardens Awards, 1973.
Earned for selling certain number of cologne mists for each level.
Level 1, Bud Vase.
White china with orange and gold trim. CMV, $8.00 MB.
Level 2, Tray.
White plastic with orange and gold trim. CMV, $10.00 tray only. $15.00 MB.
Level 3, Ginger Jar.
White china with orange and gold trim. CMV, $25.00 MB.

Desk Set, National G.M. Champion's Award, 1973. Marble base. CMV, $20.00.

Division Competition Award, 1973. Clear lucite paperweight given in Springdale branch. CMV, $10.00.

Imperial Garden Tea Set, 1973. White bone china with Imperial Garden design. Given to one representative in each district when her recommendation name was drawn at the Christmas party. CMV, $175.00 MB.

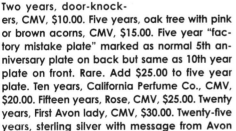

Representative's Award Plates, 1973 – 1979.
Awarded for years of service. First five, white with colored decals. Two years, door-knockers, CMV, $10.00. Five years, oak tree with pink or brown acorns, CMV, $15.00. Five year "factory mistake plate" marked as normal 5th anniversary plate on back but same as 10th year plate on front. Rare. Add $25.00 to five year plate. Ten years, California Perfume Co., CMV, $20.00. Fifteen years, Rose, CMV, $25.00. Twenty years, First Avon lady, CMV, $30.00. Twenty-five years, sterling silver with message from Avon president. CMV, $100.00. All prices are mint and boxed. CMV, $200.00 complete set, MB.

"Stick With It" Soap Holder, 1973. Rubber soap holder given to reps. Rare. CMV, $3.00.

Division Manager's Achievement Cufflinks Award, 1974. Same as awards pin, only cufflinks. Given to male division managers. CMV, $85.00 set, mint.

President's Celebration Clock Award, 1974.
Solid brass clock with "President's Celebration 1974" on face. Clock made by Relide, fifteen jewels. Given to Avon managers. Came in plain box and pink felt bag. CMV, $75.00 mint.

Tenderness Commemorative Plate, 1974.
9" diameter ceramic plate, pastel blue and greens. Awarded to reps for sending in orders for campaign 1, 2, and 3, 1974. Inscription on back in blue letters "Tenderness Commemorative Plate Special Edition, awarded to Reps. in January, 1974." Plate is made by Pontessa Ironstone of Spain. Award plate has "Pontessa" in blue letters. Plate also sold with no inscription on back. CMV, $22.00 MB, red letter plate only.

Manager's Achievement Award Pin and Charm Bracelet, 1974.
One given to top sales manager in each division. Brush sterling silver with blue sapphire in center of Avon door knocker. CMV, $70.00 each, pin and charm bracelet. $75.00 each, MB.

Recognition Award Pin, 1974.
About 1" size, gold tone. Given to branch employees, rare. CMV, $35.00.

President's Celebration Award, 1974.
14K gold necklace with three point diamond. Given to top 10 representatives in each of the 81 winning districts for outstanding sales during this President's Celebration. CMV, $60.00 MB.

Left: Pasadena Branch Wine Glass, 1974.
No. 1 in sales. 429 given. "1974 Avon Pasadena Branch" on glasses. CMV, $15.00.
Right: Circle of Excellence Glass, 1974.
Pasadena Branch No. 1 in sales, Circle of Excellence. Made by Fostoria, very thin glass. Only 30 given to managers. "C of E 1974" on side of glass. CMV, $25.00. Same glass also came in 1973 and 1975. Same CMV.

Christmas Gift Plate, 1974.
Sent to reps at Christmas. Clear glass with frosted door knocker. CMV, $8.00 no box. $12.00 MB.

Team Leader Pin, 1974.
Gold raised letters and trim. Given to team leaders. CMV, $4.00 pin only. $6.00 MB.

The President's Club Member's Watch, 1974.
Awarded to club members. Gold watch and hands with black strap. Box blue and white. CMV, $30.00 MB.

Spirit of '76 Crock Set Awards, 1974.
Left: Multipurpose pitcher, earned for $150 in sales. CMV, $7.00 MB.
Center: Bean pot casserole, earned for $200 in sales. CMV, $14.00 MB.
Right: Goodies jar, earned for $300 in sales. CMV, $18.00 MB.

88th Anniversary Award Bowl, 1974.
6" across, 3" high, silver plated, by Oneida. Paul Revere Silver. Given to top five sales reps in each district. CMV, $20.00. Same bowl given to top five President's Club sales reps and their award bowl says "President's Club" over 4A insignia. CMV, $20.00.

Christmas Ornaments Musical Gift Set, 1974.
Given to reps for getting new reps. Red and gold bell and green and gold ball. Both have music boxes inside. Made by Heinz Deichett, West Germany. Both came in red box as set. CMV, $30.00 each, no box. $75.00 MB, set.

President's Celebration Silver Chest, 1974.
Silver plated, red lined. Embossed rose on lid. CMV, $47.50 MB.

88th Anniversary Desk Set, 1974.
White marble base. Black pen. Turquoise and silver 4A says "Avon 88th Anniversary." Given to reps for selling $125 worth of Avon. CMV, $10.00 set. $15.00 MB.

Team Leader Bookmark, 1974.
Gold and red bookmark. For Avon reps use. CMV, $8.00.

Timeless Ultra Cologne Mist, President's Club, 1974.
2 oz. size, gold cap. First issued to Avon President's Club members only, had 4A design on bottom under label. Regular issue had "Avon" on bottom. Box also came with special card saying it was a collector's edition, fall 1974. CMV, $6.00 MB as shown.

Boca or Bust Manager's Key Chain, 1975.
Silver, 4A design, CMV, $15.00 MB.

Sunny Star Award Necklace, 1975.
Given to managers on introduction of Sunny Star necklace. This is the same one that was sold, only it has "Aug. 1975" engraved on it. It can easily be duplicated so a price above the cost from Avon should not be paid. Brass star and chain. CMV, $10.00 MB.

First Avon Lady Pendant Award, 1975.
Silver toned with scroll "A" design around glass insert. On the presentation card it starts "Congratulations! We're happy to present you with this exclusive award. Designed especially for you. It's symbolic of the personal service upon which Avon was founded and which has guided us throughout the years." CMV, $15.00 pendant only. $20.00 MB.

Top Sales Medallions, 1975.
Gold colored metal medallions. Avon lady carrying case. "Italy" at bottom of feet. No Avon on it. Given to Avon reps for top sales and touring Springdale plant. Two different designs, one star and one round. CMV, $17.00 each, medallion only. $22.50 each, MB.

Avon Sales Achievement Award Bracelet, 1975.
Given for sales. "Avon" on one side and "Sales achievement" on the other. Sterling. CMV, $15.00, bracelet only. $20.00 MB.

Team Leader Pin, 1975.
Gold with indented letters. Given to team leaders. CMV, $4.00 pin only. $6.00 MB.

Representative Christmas Gift, 1975.
Clear glass in blue box. Reproduction of Trailing Arbutus powder sachet. CMV, $10.00 MB.

Goblet, Circle of Excellence Award, 1975.
7½" high sterling silver goblet. Given to Circle of Excellence managers who went to Madrid, Spain, in 1975. Base says "Circle of Excellence, Madrid, 1975." CMV, $60.00.

Bird Plate Awards, 1975.
Campaign 10, 1975. Available to reps for meeting product goals; serving specified number of customers and meeting goals at suggested customer prices. Bluebird was lowest goal, yellow breasted chat second, and Baltimore oriole last. If total goals attained, rep received all three plates. CMV, $20.00 MB, bluebird. $20.00 MB, yellow breasted chat. $30.00 MB, Baltimore oriole.

Avon Lady Stemware Glasses Awards, 1975.
Campaign 20, 1975. Set of six, 10 oz. and six, 6 oz. glasses with first Avon Lady design. One set given to all reps in the winning district for top sales. CMV, $50.00 MB, set.

Osborne Cream Sherry Manager's Gift Set, 1975.
Wine cask on box lid. Box held two wine glasses with "Avon Espana 1975" painted in yellow, bottle of Osborne Cream Sherry with special label "Especially bottled for the 1974 members of the Circle of Excellence." This set was given to each manager on their Circle of Excellence trip to Madrid, Spain. Only 200 sets given out. CMV, $130.00 set, mint, full.

Division Sales Winner Tray Award, 1975.
17¾" long, 13" wide silver tray. Inscribed in center "Awarded to (name of manager) President's Program Best Wishes, David S. Mitchell." Given to top district managers in sales. Came in blue felt bag and white box. CMV, $150.00 MB in bag.

Wine Glass for Managers, 1975.
Yellow painted letters say "Avon Espana 1975." Came in 1975 Osborne cream sherry. Manager's gift set on trip to Spain. CMV, $37.50.

Pitcher and Bowl Recommendation Prize, 1975 – 1977.
Given for recommending someone, if appointed as a rep. Has "Avon" on bottom of both pieces. CMV, $50.00 set.

Gateway Appointment Goblet Award, 1975.
Poole silver plate. Inscribed on side. CMV, $20.00.

Outstanding Achievement Award, 1975.
Blue velvet on wood plaque, metal wreath with red, white, and blue ribbon with 4A pendant with green stone in center. CMV, $100.00.

Timeless Manager's Gift Set, 1975.
Gold box held perfume rollette, cologne mist, and creme perfume. Given to Avon managers only, at introduction of Timeless. CMV, $35.00 MB.

Charm, "A Day to Remember" Award, 1976.
Small gold tone charm marked "A Day to Remember – C21-76." Came in blue Avon box. CMV, $15.00 MB.

Letter Opener Manager Award, 1975.
Red and black box held wood handle letter opener. Brass Avon lady insignia and "K.C. No. 1, 1975" on hand. CMV, $20.00 MB.

"A" Pin Award, 1976 – 1978.
Given to reps for selling $1,500 in Avon in a 13 campaign period. Came in blue lined box, CMV, $5.00 MB. Red lined box, CMV, $4.00 MB.

President's Campaign Key Chain, 1976.
Chrome and white with red letters. Given to President's Club reps. CMV, $10.00.

Castanets Award, 1975.
Given to Circle of Excellence managers only, on trip to Spain. Came with Circle of Excellence orange award card as shown. CMV, $25.00 MB with card.

Sales Achievement Key Chain, 1976 – 1977.
Silver tone key chain. 4A emblem on front and back marked "Avon Sales Achievement Award C/23/76, C/9/77." In special "Sales Achievement Award" Avon box. CMV, $11.00 MB.

90th Anniversary Bicentennial Pendant Award, 1976.
Brass coin and chain given to reps for selling $285 worth of Avon in two campaigns. Front and back views shown. CMV, $15.00 MB.

Top Representative Pen Gift, 1975.
Brass and black design ballpoint pen. Small size. Came in red velvet lined, plastic display box and gold sleeve. Given for meeting sales goals. CMV, $5.00 pen only. $10.00 MB as shown.

Manager's Panelist Pin, 1976.
Gold tone name pin. Marked "Nat. District Manager Panelist." Given each year. CMV, $10.00.

Oak Tree Atlanta Branch Pendant, 1976.
Gray pewter on neck chain. CMV, $15.00.

#1 Pendant Award, 1976.
Given for top sales in Morton Grove Branch. Gold tone pendant. CMV, $15.00.

President's Celebration Award Clock, 1976.
Gold plastic and metal Westclock. Four red roses on face. Was not made only for Avon. CMV, $12.00.

Circle of Excellence Cup Award, 1976.
Polished pewter cup says "C of E 1976" engraved on side. Given to Circle managers only. CMV, $25.00.

Team Leader Mug Award, 1976.
White glass mug. CMV, $10.00.

Posset Pot Award, 1976.
9" high, stoneware. Bottom reads "Made in Brazil exclusively for Avon Products, Inc." CMV, $25.00.

Bicentennial Plates, 1976.
Blue and white. Given to reps that sent in order for campaigns 1, 2, and 3 totaling $100 or more. *Left:* Independence Hall. *Right:* Liberty Bell. Made in England. Have inscriptions on back. CMV, $20.00, Independence Hall. CMV, $30.00, Liberty Bell.

Wildflowers Award Plates, 1976 – 1978.
Each is 8¾". Southern wildflower plate for $195 in sales. Southern and Eastern given for $245 in sales, and Southern, Eastern, Northern, and Western flower plates for $330 in sales. Campaign 11, 1976. CMV, Southern, $10.00 MB. Eastern, $15.00 MB. All four plates, $60.00 MB, set. Northern and Western, $20.00 each, MB. These same plates were reissued by Geni Products, a division of Avon, in March, 1978, as awards to sales reps.

50 Year Service Plate, 1976.
Gold plated plate given to the late Mrs. Bessie O'Neal on July 27, 1976, by David Mitchell, president of Avon Products, for 50 continuous years as an Avon lady. A letter from Avon and Mr. Mitchell came with the plate. The plate is one of a kind and priceless. The plate is made by Dirilyte. No value established.

Heart Treasure Box Award, 1976.
Top sales teams in 252 winning districts won ceramic heart shaped box given in President's Celebration of 1976. Bottom says "Avon President's Celebration 1976." Made in Spain. CMV, $20.00 MB.

Highest Sales Award Bowl, 1976.
Silver plated fruit bowl was awarded to 10 different reps for highest sales in their category. Each bowl is engraved different from the other. The one is engraved with "4A" design. "Highest Percentage Increase Christmas 1976." CMV, $25.00, bowl only. $30.00 MB. Not awarded in all branches.

Avon Menu Scarf, 1976.
White silk scarf with "Circle of Excellence" dinner menu in L.A. Calif. 1976 printed in blue letters. CMV, $25.00.

April Showers Umbrella Gift, 1976.
Beige canvas, wood handle. "Avon" in blue letters. Given as recommendation prize. CMV, $27.50.

Circle of Excellence Letter Opener, 1976.
Given in Indiana only to Circle of Excellence reps. Only 25 were given. Brass plaque. Door knocker pin embedded in black plastic handle. CMV, $40.00.

Avon Christmas Card, 1976.
Green and gold Christmas card. Inside says "From your Avon Representative." Box of 75 cards given to Avon reps for recommendation of new Avon lady. CMV, $35.00 box of 75, mint. 50¢ each card, mint.

Frisbee — Gift to Reps, 1976.
White plastic with red letters. CMV, $6.00. White with red and green letters. CMV, $8.00.

Representative Christmas Card Gift, 1976.
White Avon embossed box held hand screened fold-out glass Christmas card given to all reps in 1976. CMV, $10.00 MB.

Candid Scarf Gift, 1976.
Silk scarf designed by S.M. Kent in Candid folder. Given to Avon President's Club members. CMV, $7.00.

15 Year Pen Set Award, 1976.
Two Cross 14K gold filled pens engraved "Avon 15 Years" and person's initials. Both pens are in gray felt bags and pink leather pen holder with gold. 4A pen with red ruby in center and gold rose embossed. CMV, $75.00 MB.

President's Campaign Bracelet Award, 1976.
Chrome chain and red letters on heart pendant. CMV, $10.00.

Heart Diamond "A" Pin, 1977.
14K gold heart shaped pin with 12 small diamonds. Can also be used as a pendant on chain. Came in gray felt box with white outer box. Only one given in each division for top rep. Rare. CMV, $400.00 mint.

Top 50 Pin Award, 1977.
Gold tone pin has "Top 50" and 4A design with red background. Given to top 50 reps in division for sales. CMV, $16.00.

TLC Necklace Award, 1977.
Given to team leaders. 14K gold. CMV, $25.00.

Sales Club Award, 1977.
$100,000 sales increase plaque. Atlanta branch. CMV, $15.00.

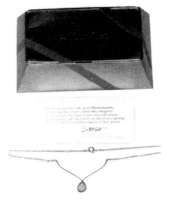

President's Celebration Diamond Ring Award, 1977.
14K gold ring with eight small diamonds in center. Given to managers in Pasadena branch for largest increase in sales. Only 20 rings given in this branch. Does not say Avon. CMV, $100.00.

Manager's Gift, Diamond Loop, 1977.
Diamond loop necklace given to managers in special gold bar type box, on introduction of Avon's new 14K gold filled jewelry. CMV, $40.00 MB as pictured.

Team Leader Watch, 1977.
Given to all Avon team leaders for Christmas 1977. Two different, left for women, or right for men. The cases are different and there is a difference in the size of the winding stem. Very few of the men's watches were given. CMV, $40.00 MB, women's. CMV, $100.00 MB, men's.
Not shown: Manager's Watch, 1977.
Same as team leader watch, only face says "Avon" in place of "Team Leader" and 4A symbol that rotates instead of Avon. Came in male and female size watches as above. CMV, $75.00 each, MB.

President's Celebration Star Award, 1977.
Sterling silver star and chain with small diamond made by Tiffany. Was given to winning district manager in division. CMV, $35.00.

Apple Stickpin, 1977.
Red apple with 4A design, "1977," and "P.C." for President's Club on green leaf. Pin is gold tone color. Given to winning team in each district for highest sales. CMV, $15.00.

Sales Achievement Award Pendant, 1977.
1" gold pendant with 18" chain. Says "1977 Avon Sales Achievement Award" and 4A design on other side. Came in white Avon box. Given to top 10% of sales reps in each division. CMV, $15.00 MB. Same pendant, slightly larger, came in blue box. CMV, $20.00 MB.

Outstanding Sales Management Clock Award, 1977.
Relide 15 jewel Swiss solid brass clock. Inscribed on top "In Recognition of Outstanding Sales Management — Third Quarter 1977." Given to No. 1 Avon manager in each division. CMV, $100.00.

Liberty Clock Award, 1977.
Given to managers for one million dollar sales increase. Gold tone clock by Bulova. Inside slide clock cover says "To a Million Dollar Baby (name of manager) Division $1,000,000.00 Sales Increase 1977." Came in Bulova Americana Collection. CMV, $75.00.

Hours for Excellence Clock Award, 1977.
Gold label on top of Bulova travel alarm. Does not say Avon. Given to reps. CMV, $15.00 MB.

First Division Glass Award, 1977.
Lead crystal champagne glass given to No. 1 division Avon managers. CMV, $30.00.

Team Achievement Award, 1977.
Goblet given in first and third quarters to top team in each district. Came in white embossed Avon box. CMV, $10.00 each quarter, MB.

Port O'Call Candy Dish and Bar, 1977.
China dish by Limoges, France, and bar of French candy given to managers for meeting appointment goal. Box has gold label "Meet me at the lamp post, Port O'Call Pasadena." CMV, $10.00 MB.

Prospect Coffee Jar and Cup Award, 1977.
Clear glass jar with green painted design on front says "1886-Avon 1977." Filled with coffee beans. CMV, $20.00 jar only. Coffee cup came with jar in white box as set. Has "Avon district manager 1977" on cup and other writings. Both given to Avon managers only. CMV, $10.00 cup only.

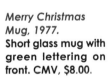

Merry Christmas Mug, 1977.
Short glass mug with green lettering on front. CMV, $8.00.

Currier & Ives Tea Set, 1977 – 1978.
Set consists of plate, teapot, sugar bowl, and creamer. "Avon Products, Inc." on bottom of each piece. Awarded to Avon reps for distinguished sales achievement in 1977. Plate — first step, CMV, $6.50. Sugar bowl and creamer — second step, CMV, $12.00. Teapot — third step, CMV, $17.50. Cup and saucer — fourth step. Saucer first issue marked "1977" on bottom, 1978 issue has no date, Add $2.00 each piece for 1977 date. CMV $35.00 set of four. Add $10.00 if writing on bottom is printed backwards for each piece.

Currier & Ives Collection Award, 1977 – 1978.
Made only for Avon and stamped on bottom. Given to Avon reps for meeting sales goals. First step — dinner bell, CMV, $6.50 MB. Second step — butter dish, CMV, $12.00 MB. Third step — water pitcher, 6½" high. CMV, $17.50 MB. Fourth step — cake plate, 9½" diam. CMV, $32.50 MB. Add $10.00 each piece for bottom writing printed backwards.

Decorator's Choice Pitcher and Bowl Prize, 1977.
Ceramic pitcher, 10" high, and bowl, 15¼" across. Made only for Avon. Given to reps for signing up one new Avon rep. CMV, $50.00.

President's Celebration Award Bowl, 1977.
Over 40,000 were given as awards. 6⅞" silver plated bowl given to Avon reps in two winning districts in each division for top sales. Inscription in center of bowl, "President's Celebration 1977"; on bottom of bowl, "Awarded exclusively to Avon Reps." F.B. Rogers. Came in white box as shown. Red silk rose also given at same time with name tag. CMV, $5.00 rose only with tag. CMV, $25.00 MB, bowl. Bowl did not come with rose.

Silver Server Award, 1977.
11¾" x 18¾" silver plated tray and cover. Marked "Avon Wm. Rogers" on bottom. No information on why it was given to reps. CMV, $45.00 mint.

Sales Excellence Award, 1977.
Paul Revere, Jostens Pewter 5" bowl, "C26-76-C9-77." Awarded to top sales reps. CMV, $20.00 MB.

El Camino Division Sugar and Creamer Set Award, 1977.
Silver plated creamer and sugar bowl. Tray is engraved "Top 10 Sales-El Camino Division Campaigns 10-22, 1977." Made by Sheridan. CMV, $35.00 set, mint.

91st Anniversary Coin Glass Award, 1977.
Footed compote on right won by reps for selling $270 in Campaigns 8 and 9, 1977. CMV, $7.00 MB. Centerpiece bowl and footed compote won for selling $540 in Campaigns 8 and 9, 1977. CMV, $12.00 MB, centerpiece bowl. A pair of candleholders won by President's Club members only with "P.C." embossed on bottom. This coin glass was made only for Avon, using Avon emblems in coins and "1886 – 1977" and the name "Avon." Came with card on each piece from Avon and in Avon box. CMV, $17.00 MB, candleholders. District managers received a full set of Coin glass with "D.M." embossed in center of each piece. CMV, $75.00 MB for complete "D.M." set.

Winter Recruiting Event Award Bowl, 1977.
8" International silver plate. Side inscribed with name, "Gateway Division Winner 1977 — Winter Recruiting Event." CMV, $20.00.

Ariane Necklace and Bouquet, 1977.
Wood basket and plastic flowers held sterling silver necklace with "August Conference 1977" on side. Given to Avon managers at August conference banquet. Necklace held sample vial of Ariane perfume. CMV, $65.00 mint.

Season's Greetings Avon Reps, 1977.
5½" high vase marked on bottom has 4A symbol. Given to all Avon reps at Christmas 1977 in special box. CMV, $10.00 MB.

President's Celebration Plaque, 1977.
Engraved wood plaque with Cape Cod water goblet. Given to team leaders with highest sales. CMV, $15.00 mint.

Million Dollar Select Group Award, 1977. **Plaque with bag of money on front from Sovereign Division. CMV, $75.00.**

President's Celebration Umbrella, 1977. **Marked "New York." Given to winning teams. CMV, $35.00.**

Currier & Ives Coasters, 1977. **Pack of six given to team leaders at Christmas. Also given to reps for recommendation prize. Marked "Avon." CMV, $5.00 pack of six.**

Top 10 Division Trophy, 1977. **4½" high, 4A design inside lucite top, on wood base, brass plaque. Given to top 10 sales reps in each division. Came in plain white box. CMV, $40.00.**

Inkwell and Pen Set Award, 1977. **Blue and gold display box held wood base with old glass inkwell and three feather quill pens and plastic bottle of ink. Avon card about pen set. Avon brass plaque on base. Given for recruiting new reps. CMV, $45.00 MB.**

Dollar "$" Sign Award, 1977. **Lucite "$" sign held chopped up money. Given to winning reps at 1977 Avon Forum in Texas. CMV, $35.00 mint.**

Polly Prospecting Bird Award, 1977. **Stuffed toy by Possum Trot. Tag has "Avon Products" on it. Given to Avon managers for recruiting new reps. Came with two large cards as shown. CMV, $25.00 with Avon tag. Add $1.00 each card. Came in Avon mailer tube with letter. CMV, $35.00 MB all.**

Candid Blazer and Tie, 1977. **Off-white blazer with "CA" on left pocket. Given to division managers only. Came in both male and female sizes. Tie is Candid color with "CA" on it. Very few of these blazers around. Modeled by Dwight Young. CMV, $75.00 blazer. $10.00 tie.**

Advertising Umbrella, 1977. **White Avon box held brown plastic handle umbrella. Has the names of Avon and magazines and TV shows Avon advertises on. Given to district managers. CMV, $30.00 MB.**

Tennis Official Button, 1977. **Red Futures circuit Avon official button. CMV, $5.00.**
Avon Futures Sponsor Button, 1980. **White with red letters. CMV, $5.00.**
Rose Parade Float Decorator Buttons. **1982 white, 1984 gold. CMV, $10.00 each.**
President's Day Corporate Medallion, 1983. **3" brass medallion with red, white, and blue ribbon. CMV, $20.00.**

Forum Money Pen Award, 1977.
Clear plastic pen full of chopped up money. CMV, $10.00.

Sales Excellence Award Cup, 1977.
6½" high pewter cup. "4A design, Avon Sales Excellence Award 1977" on side of cup. Given to top 2% of sales reps in each division. Same cup also in 1979, only dates are different. CMV, $15.00 MB.

Manager's Christmas Gift, Spoon, 1977.
Small silver spoon has Christmas tree and "Rejoice 1977" inscribed. Came in red and white felt boot bag. CMV, $15.00.

Emprise Purse Award, 1977.
Black satin purse with jewel snap. Has gold carrying chain inside. Purse does not say Avon on it. Given to reps for top sales of Emprise products. Came in clear plastic bag marked "Avon." Designed by S.M. Kent. CMV, $10.00 MB.

Left: President's Club Ring, Lady's, 1978.
Gold plated sterling 4A ring with red simulated ruby. Stone came in several different shades. Given to all female President's Club reps. CMV, $25.00 MB.
Right: Manager's 4A Ring, 1978.
Silver 4A ring with high grade ruby stone given to four managers in Atlanta branch for best planning. CMV price not established.

Heart Stickpin Award, 1978.
Sterling silver heart pin made by Tiffany and Co. with Avon products slip. Given to managers only, during President's Celebration. Does not say Avon. Must be in box with Tiffany and Co. Avon card. CMV, $15.00 MB.

Smoky Quartz Ring, Manager's, 1978.
Smoky quartz stone, 14K gold mounting marked "Avon." Given to managers in Campaign 26, 1978, for best activity event in Atlanta branch. CMV, $40.00.

Candid Sales Leader Trophy, 1977.
Wood base with brass plaque with bottle of Candid cologne mist glued in base. Given to one rep in each district who sold the most Candid cologne mists on its introduction. CMV, $12.50.

President's Club Ring for Men, 1978.
Gold plated sterling silver 4A ring with ruby stone. Given to male Avon reps for selling $6,000 worth of Avon in one year period. Came in plain blue velvet ring box. CMV, $100.00 MB.

Live-Love-Laugh Diamond Pin Award, 1978.
14K gold with two-point diamond. Given to Avon managers for reaching appointment goal for August conference. CMV, $30.00 MB.

Emprise Necklace Gift, 1977.
Gold double "e" necklace given to Avon team leaders to introduce the new fragrance. "T.L." on back side and it came in an Avon box. CMV, $10.00. District managers also got one marked "D.M." on back and in D.M. Avon box. CMV, $15.00 MB. Was also given to Division Managers. CMV, $15.00 MB. Emprise money clip for male reps. CMV, $15.00 MB.

Top 50 Pin Award, 1978.
Same as 1977 pin, only has red rose with green leaves. CMV, $12.50.

Key Chain District Manager Safe Driver Award, 1978.
Large brass key chain has "4A" on one side and "Avon District Manager Safe Driver Award 1978" on other side. Also came in white and green box. 4A on box lid. Also came with Avon card shown. CMV, $10.00 MB.

Smile Pendant Award, 1978.
Red and gold pendant, given to all Avon team leaders. Back side says "Avon, Team Leader, March 1978." CMV $10.00 MB. Also given to district managers with "D.M." on back. CMV, $15.00. Both came in red box with Avon sleeve. Smile pendant also given to division managers at conference. Back says "N.Y. March, 78, Avon." Red box came with plain white sleeve. CMV, $30.00 MB.

Valentine Heart Pendant Award, 1978.
14K gold heart. Does not say Avon. Only 2,500 were given to reps at sales meetings. Must have Campaign 3, 1978 brochure with heart to prove it's from Avon. CMV, $15.00 with brochure.

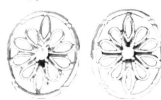

Earrings, Team Leader Christmas Gift, 1978.
10K solid gold with small diamond chip. Given to team leaders at Christmas, 1978. Came in Avon box. CMV, $40.00 MB.

"You're Precious to Us" Pendant, Manager's Gift, 1978.
14K gold, filled with real pearl and small diamond. Gold box says "You're Precious to Us" on lid. Given to Avon managers. Must be in box as described. Came with card signed by S.M. Kent. CMV, $50.00 MB.

Key Ring Five Year Service Award, 1978.
$\frac{1}{10}$ yellow, 10K gold, 4A symbol key ring given to Avon plant employees for five years of service. Started in 1978. CMV, $17.50 MB.

4A Blue Enamel Pin, 1978.
Gold tone and blue enamel pin. Came in Avon box. No information on what it's for. CMV, $12.00 MB.

International Running Circuit Medallion and Necklace, 1978 – 1982.
Silver tone medallion given to winners in each city in each age group for running in Avon races. Came in black and gold box. Rare. CMV, $125.00 MB.

Left: Clock 20 Year Award, 1978.
Small brass Tiffany and Co. quartz clock. Top engraved "Avon 20 Years" and winner's initials. Given to Avon managers for 20 years of service. CMV, $75.00.
Right: Clock August Conference Award, 1978.
Brass Relide 400 electronic clock. Given to managers for going to August conference in 1978, bottom engraved. CMV, $50.00.

Clock Speedway Division Award, 1978.
For outstanding sales. CMV, $35.00.

Field Support Pendant Award, 1978.
$1/20$ yellow, 12K gold filled. Back is dated "1978 Field Support Manager." Given to managers. CMV, $30.00.

Circle of Excellence Mug Award, 1978.
Avon "C. of E. District No. 1978" in red letters. Given to reps in winning districts. CMV, $10.00.

President's Celebration Tray Award, 1978.
12" silver plated tray marked "Awarded Exclusively to Avon Reps." on back side. Given to one winning team rep in each division. CMV, $35.00 MB.

Nat. District Manager Panelist Pin, 1978.
Gold tone. Given to managers. CMV, $10.00.

Achievement Award Mug, 1978.
"First Quarter 1978" on white ceramic mug, given to team getting most new Avon ladies to sign up. CMV, $10.00.

Perfume, Circle of Excellence, 1978.
1 oz. glass stopper bottle, made in France. Paper neck tag says "Made Exclusively For You. Circle of Excellence 1978." CMV, $100.00 mint.

Fostoria Lead Crystal Plate Awards, 1978.
Given for top sales. First four plates won by reps: Jeweled A, 1st rep., door knocker, great oak tree. CMV, $30.00 set of four or $7.00 each. President's Club reps and district managers could win first four plus four more: 4A Avon Key, World of Avon Globe, Avon Rose Last. President's Club set had "P.C." marked on rose plate and "D.M." marked on Jeweled A plate for manager's set. CMV, $100.00 D.M. set of eight. CMV, $75.00 P.C. set of eight.

Apple Paperweight Award, 1978.
Given to divisional managers for top sales. Clear crystal glass apple is engraved "You Made New York Smile," Avon, March 1978, on front side. CMV, $100.00.

"You Make Me Smile!" Glass Awards, 1978.
Set of six glasses made only for Avon, given to Avon reps for signing up a new Avon lady. CMV, $12.00 MB, set.

Million Dollar Increase Goblet, 1978.
Silver plated goblet given to all managers in top division for one million dollar increase in sales. CMV, $25.00.

Silver Flower Basket August Conference Award, 1978.
Sterling silver basket made by Cartier, handmade. "August Conference 1978" on top of handle. Yellow silk flowers, green leaves. Given to managers only. CMV, $100.00 mint.

Front: Cake Stand Award, 1978.
Given to top 50 reps in state. "Avon Division Top 50" inscribed in center. Silver plated. CMV, $25.00.

Back: Imperial Division Award Tray, 1979.
Silver plated, inscribed "Avon Imperial Division Top 50, 1979 #29." CMV, $25.00.

$1,000,000 Desk Set Award, 1978.
Wood base. Brass plaque. CMV, $50.00.

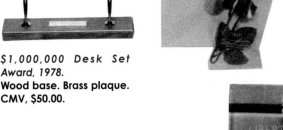

Oak Tree Paperweight Award, 1978.
Lucite case held oak tree coin with 4A design. "Atlanta #1 — 1978." CMV, $20.00.

Manager's Bud Vase Gift, 1978.
Same as Hudson Manor Bud Vase Gift, only says "August Conference 1978" on bottom instead of "Team Leader." CMV, $30.00 MB.

Right: Liberty Division Paperweight, 1978.
Clear lucite, has 4A design. "Liberty Division — Two Million Dollar Increase 1978." Given to top managers. CMV, $15.00.
Lower Left: Circle of Excellence Pins, 1979.
Small blue and gold tone pins say "C of E Winners 1979." Given to top managers. CMV, $10.00 each.

Ted. E. Bear Team Leader Gift, 1978.
Tan teddy bear with red shirt was given to all team leaders at end of year party, Nov. 1978. Fold-out teddy bear card was on each table at party. CMV, $4.00 card. $25.00 bear, mint.

Left: Tempo Manager's Gifts, 1978.
⅓ oz. splash cologne. Given to district sales managers at August conference, 1978. Came with red felt belt. CMV, $15.00 in bag.
Right: Tempo Spray Atomizer Gift, 1978.
Given to Avon reps for advanced orders of Tempo fragrance. Silver color container, red letters. "Tempo Fall 1978" printed on bottom of case. Came in beige velvet bag, red pull-string in special issue box. CMV, $10.00 MB.

International Women's Championship Marathon Award, Atlanta, 1978.
Same as above, only silver tone medallion with black background. CMV, $50.00.

Rep Christmas Gift Bowl, 1978.
Fostoria bowl with 4A design and 1978 on bottom. Given to all Avon reps for Christmas 1979. Box shown with red ribbon and gold tag and white and gold plastic bell given to managers. CMV, $10.00 MB, reps. CMV, $15.00 managers, with ribbon.

Hudson Manor Bud Vase Gift, 1978.
Avon silver plated bud vase and red rose in silver box. Bottom says "Team Leader, August 1978." Made in Italy. Same as regular issue, only regular issue does not say "Team Leader 1978" on bottom. CMV, $20.00.

Additions Award, 1978.
Black and clear plastic picture cube for recruiting new reps. CMV, $25.00 MB.

Avonopoly, 1978.
Game used by managers at Avon rep sales meeting, Campaign 12, 1978. Also came with Avon play money of 25 and 50 green notes. CMV, $12.00 set.

Dream Charm Manager's Necklace, 1979.
Gold tone necklace and three charms of orchid, butterfly, and seashell. Given to Avon managers at 1979 Dream Conference. Does not say Avon on charms. Came in maroon satin bag with pink tie string. CMV, $25.00 mint in bag.

Sales Mates Prizes, President's Club, 1978.
All are tan and beige in color, covered with "A" design. Umbrella, Beauty Showcase handbag, and jewelry demonstrator given to President's Club reps for selling $975 worth of Avon in Campaigns 4, 5, and 6, 1978. Umbrella, CMV, $20.00. Jewelry demo case, CMV, $7.00. Handbag, CMV, $7.00.

Music Box Team Award, 1978.
Red painted wood music box made in Japan only for Avon. Brass plate on lid says "You Made Avon Smile." Given to winning team for selling most lipsticks. CMV, $20.00.

Left: Spoon, President's Club Award, 1979.
Silver plated serving spoon marked "Avon President's Club 1979." Came in Avon box. CMV, $10.00 MB.
Right: Cake Server Award, 1978.
Silver plated serving spatula. "Avon 92nd Anniversary — President's Club 1978" on spoon. Given to all President's Club members. Special box and card. CMV, $10.00 MB.

President's Celebration "A" Pin Award, 1978.
White box held "A" sterling silver pin, given to President's Club reps only. CMV, $7.50 MB.

President's Celebration Diamond Heart Locket Award, 1979.
Given to top 20 reps in each district during President's Celebration. Inscribed on back, "President's Club 1979." CMV, $20.00 MB. Same given to district managers, only has "DM" inscribed on back also. CMV, $30.00 MB.

Acorn Stickpin Award, 1979.
Sterling silver acorn pin from Tiffany and Co., given to managers. Came with small card with great oak and Tiffany card for Avon products. CMV, $15.00 MB.

Dollar Increase Clock Award, 1978.
Dark amber lucite clock stand with pen set and 4A. CMV, $20.00.

Key Chain, "Thanks America" Award, 1979.
Team leader white box held silver tone heart key chain, "Thanks America for Making Us Number One." Back side says "Avon loves team leaders." CMV, $10.00 MB.

Christmas Gift, 1979.
Sterling silver gold-tone chain with 10K gold charm with two small diamonds. Came in black felt box. Back is marked "District managers 1979." CMV, $50.00. "Team Leaders 1979," CMV, $35.00.

Heart No. 1 Pendant Award, 1979.
14K gold heart with one small diamond given to one top rep in each division. In Avon blue velvet box. CMV, $90.00 MB.

Avon No. 1 Pin, Holland, 1979.
Gold tone pin given to Zone Avon managers in Holland. CMV, $50.00.

Perfect Attendance Pin, 1979 – 1982.
Gold tone pin given to Avon branch employee for perfect attendance at work for a one year period. Marked with each year record. CMV, $25.00.

Shell Sales Leader Award, 1979.
Sterling silver shell came in Tiffany felt bag and box. Given to managers. CMV, $125.00 MB.

C of E Winner's Pin, 1979.
Blue enamel on gold tone pin. CMV, $10.00.

#1 Diamond Heart Pendant Award, 1979.
Given to top manager for top sales. Seven diamonds on gold heart and chain. CMV, $50.00.

Eiffel Tower Manager's Pin, 1979.
Small gold tone tie tac type pin given to managers on Paris trip. Does not say Avon. In plain blue box. Pin is 1⅛" high. CMV, $15.00.

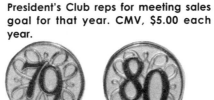

President's Club Ladies' Pins, 1979 – 1980.
Gold colored 4A pin — 79 in middle is first of an annual 4A year pin given to President's Club reps for meeting sales goal for that year. CMV, $5.00 each year.

Sales Achievement Award, 1979.
Solid bronze with oak tree on front with "District Manager Quarterly Sales Achievement Award — Avon" 4A symbol on back. Given to managers only. CMV, $50.00.

President's Club Men's Pin Award, 1979 – 1980.
Gold tone 4A design and "79" on one and "80" on the other. Given to all male President's Club members. Smaller than lady's pin. CMV, $15.00 each pin only. $20.00 each, MB.

Flag Pin Award, 1979.
Gold tone red, white, and blue enamel lapel pin. Given to Circle of Excellence winners on Paris trip. Came in red velvet Avon ring box. CMV, $25.00 MB.

Avon Pin, Division Manager, 1979.
Gold tone pin with red enamel filled heart shaped "O," given to division managers only. CMV, $15.00 MB, in red box.

Avon Pin, Reps, 1979.
Gold tone pin, same as above, only does not have red heart. CMV, $5.00 MB, in white box.

Not shown: Avon Pin, District Managers, 1979.
Same gold tone pin as reps above, only "DM" inscribed on back. CMV, $15.00 MB, in white box.

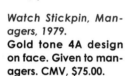

Color Up Watch Award, 1979.
Le Jour Time Co. watch in gold tone case, white strap. Back side says "For the most colorful time of your life." Came in white box, sleeve, and blue felt wrap. Given to reps for customers served. CMV, $25.00 MB.

Watch Stickpin, Managers, 1979.
Gold tone 4A design on face. Given to managers. CMV, $75.00.

Tasha Team Leader Cologne Award, 1979.
1⁴/₅ oz. spray cologne. Says "Team Leader 1979" in gold letters on front. Came in gold wrapped box with maroon color ribbon. CMV, $10.00 MB.
Not shown: Tasha "Go Ahead and Dream" Manager's Gift.
Same bottle as above, only "Go Ahead and Dream" in gold letters on face of bottle for managers at Christmas conference. CMV, $20.00 MB.

Sales Achievement Award, 1979.
Small gold tone trophy with wood base. Says "Avon Sales Achievement Award." CMV, $10.00.

Circle of Excellence Wine Glasses, 1979.
Given to managers. Glass embossed "C of E 1979." Came in set of two glasses. CMV, $25.00 each glass.

Top: **Springdale Founder's Club Coffee Cup Award, 1979.**
White glass cup given to all plant employees who had worked from 1965 to 1979. Red letters. CMV, $10.00.
Bottom: Color Up America Pen, 1979.
White, black, and silver pen on brown leather neck cord. Given to managers. CMV, $10.00.

Representative's Service Award Plates, 1979 – 1986.
Awarded for years of service. First issued in 1973 and some design changes in 1979. First five are white porcelain with decals. All are the same CMV as 1973 to 1979 plates, except the 25 year plate which is silver tone only and CMV, $40.00. CMV, $140.00 MB, complete set. 1979 – 1986 plates have pink rose borders.

Lenox China President's Club Bowl Award, 1979.
White box with gold trim and burgundy inside held 4A inscribed china bowl. Bottom inscribed "For Avon's Very Best," given to all President's Club members for 1980. Box has Avon outer sleeve. CMV, $30.00, bowl only. $40.00 MB.

Picture Frame, Dream Award, September Conference, 1979.
Ceramic picture frame. White, pink, and green flowers with white doves. Center is pink, says "Hold fast to your dreams, For if you do . . . Tomorrow you'll see More dreams can come true." CMV, $15.00.

Representative Christmas Gift, 1979.
Ceramic tile picture frame made in Japan. Box says "Happy Holidays Avon 1979." Given to all Avon reps at Christmas. CMV, $10.00 MB.

Left: President's Celebration Heart Award, 1979.
Lucite heart marked "You're our number one-Avon 1979 President's Celebration." Made in Taiwan. Came in white Avon box. CMV, $15.00 MB.
Right: Manager's Heart, "You're No. 1."
Clear lucite, has smaller hole on top and heart is about ½" smaller. Came in red velvet bag. This one was given to managers only. CMV, $20.00 mint in bag.

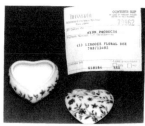

Limoges Floral Heart Box Award, 1979.
Small heart shaped ceramic box made by Limoges of France. Given to Avon managers. Must have Tiffany and Co. card as shown for Avon Products. Two different designs as shown. CMV, $25.00 with card.

Top Recruiter Pen Award, 1979.
Sterling silver pen set. Engraved "Top Recruiter May 1979." CMV, $100.00.

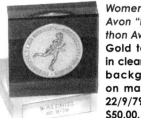

Women's International Avon "Running" Marathon Award, 1979.
Gold tone medallion in clear lucite with red background. Came on marble base with 22/9/79 plaque. CMV, $50.00.

Left: Manager's Flower Basket, 1979.
Basket of silk flowers with Avon tag given to managers. In Avon box. CMV, $15.00 MB with tag.
Right: Team Leader Flower Basket, 1979.
Same flower basket only different box and different tag given to team leaders. CMV, $10.00 MB.

Valentine Team Leader Gift, 1979.
3½" across, crystal heart shaped glass dish given to all team leaders for Valentine's Day. CMV, $12.50 MB.

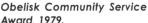

Obelisk Community Service Award, 1979.
8¼", clear lucite. One given to managers in each division. Has 4A design and message of Ralph Waldo Emerson in center. Came in two sizes — one is 2" shorter. CMV, $35.00 each.

Team Leader Plaque Award, 1979.
Given to team leaders in Circle of Excellence winning division. CMV, $30.00.

The Teddy Award, 1979.
Black base with plaque. Brown top and bear has red shirt with Avon in white. Given to one team leader for recommendation support in each district. CMV, $35.00 MB.

Teddy Bear Red Cookie Jar Award, 1979.
Tan and red ceramic bear cookie jar. Given to Team Leaders at Christmas. CMV, $50.00.

Teddy Bear Blue Cookie Jar Award, 1979.
Teddy bear, blue Avon shirt. Given to top team leaders at Christmas. CMV, $65.00.

Doorbell Door Knocker Award, 1979.
Redwood box with brass "Avon Calling" door knocker on front, doorbell on back side. Given to five managers in each division. CMV, $75.00.

You've helped us win like you always do, And along with our thanks comes a bear hug for you!

Teddy Bear Pen Award, 1979.
Cross chrome pen with small bear, marked "TL" for team leader. Avon bear sleeve fits over box. CMV $27.50 MB.

Left: Identification Pin, Australia, 1980.
Gold tone door knocker pin. CMV, $10.00.
Right: Avon Representative Stickpin, 1980.
Blue and gold. Says "Avon Representative." CMV, $20.00.

President's Club Pen Award, 1979.
Parker 75 silver and gold pen. Inscribed on side, "President's Club 1979." Came in blue felt Parker case. CMV, $20.00.

Door Knocker Ring Display Box Award, 1979.
Black ring box with gold tone door knocker on cover. Given to Avon managers. CMV, $30.00 mint.

President's Celebration Men's Award, Key Chain, 1980.
Sterling silver with oak tree on one side and inscribed on other. Given to men reps only for top sales. CMV, $100.00 MB.

Zany Radio, 1979.
Orange and pink Zany bottle shaped AM radio made in Hong Kong for Avon Products. Given to Avon customers in a drawing. Came in pink bag with certificate. CMV, $15.00 radio only. $20.00 mint in bag, complete. $25.00 MB.

Avon Small Teddy Bear Award, 1979.
About 6" high brown bear. Made in Korea, given to managers. CMV, $25.00.

President's Club Pin Award, 1980 – 1981.
Gold tone pin given to President's Club members only. Came in blue Avon box. Given in 1980 and 1981. CMV, $7.50 MB.

Sterling Clock Pen Award, 1979.
Sterling silver pen with digital clock and calendar inside. Inscribed "Number 1 in $ Inc.," plus name of division. Given to managers only. CMV, $50.00 MB.

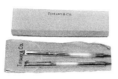

10 Year Service Awards, 1980.
Five different gifts. All of sterling silver. All marked with 4A design. Each came in Tiffany & Co. box. Given to Avon managers and all Avon employees for 10 years service. They had their choice of pen and pencil set with T clips, 3" purse mirror, cufflinks ⅞" diameter, Small 1¼" high silver flask that opens, or sterling silver chain, 23½" long. CMV, each item or set, $40.00 MB. Flask, $60.00. Pen set, $50.00 MB.

Acorn Necklace Award, 1980.
Sterling Silver acorn pendant and necklace. Came with great oak card and Tiffany & Co. Box in velvet pouch. Given to managers only. CMV, $40.00 MB with card.

15 Year Service Awards, 1980s.
All are marked "Avon" or have 4A design. Each came from Tiffany & Co. Given for 15 years of service at Avon. Choice of:
Sterling Silver Perpetual Calendar.
6" wide, 4¼" high. CMV, $50.00.
Crystal Decanter with Sterling Silver Tag.
11" high. CMV, $50.00.
Sterling Silver Salt and Pepper Set.
2¼" high. CMV, $50.00 set.
Sterling Silver Pin Box.
3" diameter. CMV, $50.00.

Shooting Star Pin, Manager's, 1980.
Gold tone pin in brown box with outer sleeve. Given to managers. CMV, $15.00 MB. Also came as tie tac for men. CMV, $25.00 MB.

Royal Ribbon Tac Pin Awards, 1980.
Sterling silver with yellow, red, white, or blue enamel. Given to managers for recruiting new reps. CMV, yellow, $5.00 MB. Red, $10.00 MB. White, $15.00 MB. Blue, $20.00 MB.

"C of E" Pin, 1980.
Small pin, says "C of E 1980." CMV, $10.00.

Cable Car Stickpin, 1980.
Gold tone, sterling silver cable car stickpin given to Avon managers on trip to San Francisco. Does not say Avon. CMV, $15.00.

Great Oak No. 1 Medallion Award, 1980.
Small medal, Avon oak tree on one side, "Pasadena No. 1 — 1980" 4A design on other side. CMV, $12.00.

President's Club, Men's Tie Tac, 1980 – 1981.
Small, gold tone 4A, — "81" on face. Given to male President's Club members. CMV, $15.00, tie tac only. $20.00 MB.

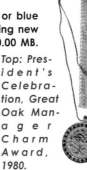

Top: President's Celebration, Great Oak Manager Charm Award, 1980.
Sterling silver cutout great oak tree charm. Came with oak tree card in Avon box. Given to top managers in each district. Also came in gold tone. CMV, $100.00 MB. One top manager in each division won a cutout silver oak charm with sapphire around edge. CMV, $150.00 MB. One top manager in each branch won same charm, only with rubies around edge. CMV, $200.00 MB. The top manager in the U.S. won same cutout oak charm with a diamond. Very rare. CMV not established.
Pendant, President's Celebration, 1980.
Sterling silver chain and pendant with 25 blue sapphires around edge. Oak tree in center. Back says "The President's Celebration 1980 Avon." Given to 250 top managers in U.S. one per division. CMV, $150.00.

Sales Leadership Award, 1980.
Gold tone and black face. Says "Outstanding Sales Leadership, 5th Qtr. 1979 – 80 Avon." Came with red velvet neck ribbon. CMV, $40.00.

Charm Bracelet Award, 1980.
Sterling silver charm and heart pendant. Both dated 1980 and "S.C." for Sales Coordinator and "TL" for Team Leader. Came in blue bag and blue Tiffany box, with white bow ribbon. CMV, $90.00, "SC," MB. CMV, $40.00, "TL," MB.

Rose Anniversary Pitcher Award, 1980.
9" tall, clear glass with engraved rose. Given to reps for selling $800 in Campaigns 14 and 15, 1980. CMV, $25.00 MB.

District Manager's Charm Bracelet, 1980.
Sterling silver chain and heart shaped charm says "DM 1980." Came in Tiffany & Co. box. Given to district managers at September conference. CMV, $75.00.

Five Year Heart Key Ring Award, 1980s.
In Tiffany box. Sterling silver. For five years of Avon service. CMV, $15.00.

Rose Anniversary Goblet Award, 1980.
6½" high with engraved rose. Set of four for selling $400 in Campaigns 14 and 15, 1980. CMV, $15.00 set of four.

President's Celebration Necklace, 1980.
Gold tone charm with great oak on one side and "The President's Celebration 1980" on other side. Given to top reps in each district. CMV, $10.00 MB. Same charm in silver tone given to top 10 winning district reps. CMV, $15.00 MB.

Running Circuit Avon Medal, 1980.
2¼" medal has red, white, and blue ribbon and medal that says "Avon International Running Circuit." Given to people who ran in Avon Running Circuit. CMV, $25.00.

20 Year Service Awards, 1980s.
Given for 20 years of service. All are marked "Avon" or have 4A emblem on it. All from Tiffany.
Choice of:
Sterling Silver Picture Frame.
9" high x 7" wide. CMV, $100.00.
Quartz Polished Brass Clock.
2½" square. CMV, $75.00.
Crystal Candlesticks — Tall.
9¼" high, 4⅛" wide base. CMV, $75.00 set.
Crystal Candlesticks — Short.
4½" high x 4⅛" wide bases. CMV, $75.00 set.

4A Stickpin Award, 1980.
1", 4A design in silver tone, gold outer trim. CMV, $10.00.

Customer Service Award Clock, 1980.
Brass Tiffany & Co. clock given to Avon managers. Engraved on top, "Avon Customer Service Award Conference 1980." Came in Tiffany box and felt bag. CMV, $75.00.

20 Year Service Awards, 1980s.
Given for 20 years of service. All are marked "Avon" or have 4A design. All came from Tiffany & Co.
Choice of: Crystal Pitcher.
5¾" high. CMV. $60.00.
Crystal Vase.
7½" wide. CMV. $60.00.
Crystal Tulip Wine Glasses.
Set of six, 8" high. CMV, $75.00 set.

Fashion History Glasses Award, 1980.
Set of six, 12 oz. glasses marked "1890s, 1920s, 1940s, 1950s, 1960s, and 1970s." Given as set to Avon reps for signing up new Avon reps. CMV, $20.00 set.

Precious Moments Rabbit Award, 1980.
Rabbit figurine, marked on bottom, "President's Club Luncheon 1980." Given to reps at President's Club Luncheon only. CMV, $20.00 MB.

Medal, 4A Pendant Award, 1980.
Silver tone and black 4A design, about 2½", on red, white, and blue neck ribbon. Given to managers only. Back says "You are a winner 1980" and name. CMV, $20.00.

Top: 20 Year Service Clock Award, 1980s.
7" wide x 4½" high Tiffany brass clock. "Avon" on top. Given for 30 years of service at Avon. CMV, $75.00.
Bottom: 30 Year Service Pearl Necklace Award, 1980s.
17" long cultured pearl necklace with 14K gold Avon marked clasp. Given for 30 years of service. Came in blue holder from Tiffany. CMV, $75.00 mint.

Precious Moments Award Set, 1980.
Set of three rabbit figurines given to reps for top sales. No. 1 is "Ready for an Avon day." CMV, $25.00. No. 2 is "My first call." CMV, $35.00. No. 3 is "Which shade do you prefer?" CMV, $60.00, each. CMV, $110.00 MB, set of three. Made in Japan, only for Avon.

Valentine Atomizer Award, 1980.
Small clear crystal bottle, chrome top and red squeeze bulb. Given to team leaders and district manager. "TL" or "DM" on bottom. CMV, $10.00, "TL" bottle MB. CMV, $20.00, "DM" bottle MB.

Precious Moments Christmas Mouse, 1980.
Given to Avon reps for signing up two new Avon reps. CMV, $55.00 MB.

Rose Anniversary Luncheon Plates Award, 1980.
Set of four clear glass 8" plates with engraved rose in center. Given to reps for selling $600 in Campaigns 14 and 15, 1980. CMV, $20.00 set of four plates.

20 Year Anniversary Plate, 1980s.
8½" porcelain plate. The first Avon representative on plate. Given for 20 years of service. First issued in 1987. CMV, $40.00 MB.

Limoges Floral Box Award, 1980.
Small white ceramic heart box with blue painted flowers. Given to managers. Does not say Avon. Must have Tiffany card for Avon Products. Was not made only for Avon. CMV, $25.00 MB with card.

Circle of Excellence Champagne Glasses, 1980.
"C of E 1980" embossed on glasses. Given to managers only, in sets of two glasses. CMV, $25.00 each glass.

Crystal Candleholders, 1980.
10" high, clear crystal. Given to reps for 30 years of continuous service. Base is inscribed "30th Avon Anniversary." CMV, $100.00 pair.

Great Scent Event Tray Award, 1980.
9½" x 17¾" gold tone mirror tray, given to 15 reps in each district for selling the most Ultra colognes. Does not say Avon on tray. Came with and must have Great Scent Event card from division manager. CMV, $20.00 with card.

Team Leader Jewelry Box, 1980.
Silver tone box with blue felt interior. Mirror inside tray says "Team Leader — President's Celebration 1980." CMV, $20.00 mint.

National District Sales Manager Panel Award, 1980.
Silver plated card case. Given to top managers only. Made by Reed & Barton. In box and blue bag. CMV, $50.00 MB.

Five Year Anniversary Plate, 1980s.
8½" porcelain plate, The great oak, for five years of service to Avon. First issued in 1987. CMV, $10.00 MB.

Team Leader Bell Award, 1980.
Fostoria bell inscribed, "Avon Team Leader Recruit a Thon 1980." Only one in each district given. CMV, $30.00.

15 Year Anniversary Plate, 1980s.
8½" porcelain plate. The Avon rose on plate. Given for 15 years of service. First issued in 1987. CMV, $30.00 MB.

Heart Porcelain Box Award, 1980.
Given to managers. Came in Tiffany & Co. box. Small porcelain heart box says "Bernardaud Limoges." Made in France. Does not say Avon. CMV, $25.00 in box with card.

Great Oak Lamp Award, 1980.
Electric light in wood base with solid hunk of clear glass with great oak engraved. Given to district managers at yearly conference. CMV, $75.00 mint.

Oak Tree Paperweight Award, 1980.
Clear lucite with silver tone 4A design and oak tree. "Pasadena No. 1 — 1980" inscribed inside. Given to managers. CMV, $25.00.

Circle of Excellence Crystal Vase, 1980.
Given to managers on trip to Spain. Box has "Avon Vase Soliflor." Was not made only for Avon. CMV, $40.00 in Avon box.

Doormat Awards, 1980s.
Red doormats, top one with white letters. Black rubber back. Bottom mat is 2" smaller and is red with black letters. CMV, $15.00 each.

Circle of Excellence Eight Year Pen Award, 1980.
Engraved sterling silver pen set. CMV, $125.00.

Paperweight, London, 1980.
Clear and red lucite. Avon Marathon. CMV, $35.00.

35th Anniversary Award, 1980s.
Silver plate pitcher engraved on front. Given to reps for 35 years service as an Avon rep. Came with Avon card. In Avon box from Tiffany & Co. Engraved on side of pitcher, "35th Avon Anniversary." CMV, $100.00 MB.

Sports Bag Awards, 1980s.
Avon Sports.
Silver and black bag. "Avon Sports" red patch on both sides. CMV, $30.00.
Avon Championships of Washington Tennis Racket Cover.
White, red trim. CMV, $25.00.
Girl Scout Avon Bag.
Silver and black bag. "Girl Scouts Leadership today and tomorrow" on back side. "Avon" on other. CMV, $30.00.
Avon Corporate President's Day, 1984.
Frisbee shaped blue and white bag unzips to make tote bag. CMV, $25.00.

Sales Leadership Award, 1980.
Large clear glass emerald diamond shaped paperweight. Engraved "Avon Sales Leadership Award Conference 1980." Tiffany & Co. on bottom. Came in "Tiffany box." Given to managers only. CMV, $100.00 MB.

President's Celebration Great Oak Plaque Award, 1980.
Scrimshaw great oak on white plastic center, wood frame. Came with Avon card also, with or without brass inscription plate on face. Given to managers only. CMV, $35.00.

Manager's Tambourine, 1970s.
Wood frame, skin marked "Avon." Made in China. CMV, $30.00.
License Plate Frame Award, 1980s.
White plastic, marked "Avon." CMV, $2.00.

Teddy Bear Candle Award, 1980.
Small plastic bear candleholder. Given to Avon team leaders. Neck tag says "From Avon with Love." Red candle. CMV, $15.00.

Award Bank, 1980.
Black and gold tin bank. Given to Avon managers in Springdale branch. Special hold label on front says "Fifth National Bank and Trust Co. Springdale Branch. Assets 367 Managers, R. Manning President." Bottom marked "Made in England for Avon." CMV, $30.00.

Tasha Umbrella, "I'm Number One!" 1980.
Tan silk umbrella given to reps on Flight to Fantasy Trip to Monte Carlo. CMV, $75.00.

Avon Tennis Umbrella, 1980.
Only 50 silver nylon with fine wood handle umbrellas were given to press and promoters of Avon tennis matches. Came in matching silver pouch. Rare. CMV, $125.00.

Avon Tennis Clothes Bag, 1980.
Red and white patch on silver and black nylon travel bag. Came in small carrying pouch. Given to players of Avon tennis matches. CMV, $50.00 rare.

Avon Tennis Wristbands, 1980.
Pair of white cotton wristbands used by players in Avon tennis matches. CMV, $4.00.
Avon Tennis Hand Towel, 1980.
White cotton, used by Avon tennis players. CMV, $10.00.

Umbrella and Bag Award, 1980.
Tan and brown Avon bag came with Avon umbrella. Given to reps for selling $425 of products in Campaigns 16 and 17, 1980. CMV, $18.00.

Top left: Frisbee, Avon, 1980.
White plastic, blue and red letters. CMV, $10.00.
Bottom right: Avon Cards Award, 1980.
Silver faced playing cards say "1980 – Avon New York — Las Vegas." Given to division managers at Las Vegas conference for Pasadena branch. CMV, $15.00 MB.

Tasha Awards, 1980.
Items such as this were won by reps on Avon trip to Monte Carlo. Monte Carlo scarf, CMV, $20.00.

McConnell Family Reunion Coasters, 1980.
Package of four white Fiesta Coasters. Center says "James McConnell Family Reunion 1980." Were given at first family reunion of David McConnell ancestors since 1948. Very rare. CMV, $50.00 mint.

Director's Chair Award, 1980.
White folding chair with green seat and back. Back says "You never looked so good." Given to reps for signing up new Avon reps. CMV, $30.00.

Radio Award, 1980.
Red and white plastic AM-FM Avon radio given one to each district manager to give at a drawing. Made by ISIS, in box. CMV, $60.00 MB.

Door Knocker Diamond Pin, 1981.
Gold with small diamond. Given to managers. Came in tan box. CMV, $40.00 MB.

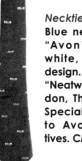

Necktie, 1980s.
Blue necktie with "Avon" in red, white, and blue design. Label says "Neatwear Tie London, The Club Tie Specialist." Given to Avon executives. CMV, $25.00.

Cup and Saucer, 1980s.
4A marked ceramic dinnerware used in Avon plant cafeterias. CMV, $3.00 each piece.

Avon Tennis Ballpoint Pen, 1980.
Gold tone pen says "Avon Tennis" and has tennis racket on side. Given to Avon tennis match players. Came in tan suede Avon tennis pouch. CMV, $20.00 mint.

Butterfly Pin Award, 1981.
Gold tone enameled stickpin given to reps. Does not say Avon. CMV, $5.00.

Unicorn Pin Award, 1981.
Brass unicorn lapel pin given to managers at August conference in 1981. Back inscribed "Conference 81." Avon box says "For Display Only — not for resale," CMV, $15.00 MB. Same pin given to team leaders, CMV with "TL" on back, $10.00. Pin also sold to public, only plain no marking on back, no CMV. Also came with "SC" on back, CMV, $20.00 MB.

Heat Thermometer Award, 1981.
Clear lucite, black letters and trim, given to managers in four test areas only. CMV, $25.00.

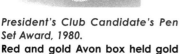

President's Club Candidate's Pen Set Award, 1980.
Red and gold Avon box held gold tone pen and pencil set. Inscribed on side of pens, "President's Club Candidate." CMV, $25.00 MB.

Don't Knock Me Door Knocker Necklace Award, 1981.
Gold tone door knocker with simulated diamond. Given to reps. Came in "Jo Anne Jewels" box. Made only for Avon. CMV, $15.00 MB.

Sell A Thon Tie Tac, 1981.
Red, white, and blue tie tac pin. Given to all reps at sales meeting. CMV, $2.00.

Telephone Tie Tac Award, 1981.
Gold tone telephone tie tac. Given to reps. CMV, $10.00.

President's Celebration Sales Achievement Medal, 1981.
Dated Dec. 11, 1981 on back side. Only one given to each branch. On red, white, and blue ribbon. CMV, $150.00.

Million Dollar Increase Award Clock, 1981.
Gold tone round Seth Thomas alarm clock. Given to managers for one million dollar increase in sales. Engraved on back side, "Our First Million $ Increase." CMV, $65.00.

Heat Clock Award, 1981.
Clear lucite, red face, "Avon" on front. CMV, $20.00.

Morton Grove 25 Year Pin, 1981.
Silver tone pin, not sterling. CMV, $8.00.

President's Club Man's Pocket Watch Award, 1981.
Gold tone Swiss made 17 jewel watch. Avon on face of watch, metal face cover. Given to male President's Club members. CMV, $100.00 MB.

Left: Woman's Watch, 1980.
Gold tone 17 jewel watch on chain. Back says "President's Club 81." CMV $30.00 MB.
Right: Man's Watch, 1980.
Gold tone pocket watch on chain given to male President's Club reps. Inscribed on back, "President's Club 1981." CMV, $100.00 MB. No face cover, CMV, $100.00 MB.

Great Oak Coin Award, 1981.
Sterling silver coin says "Kansas City #1 — 1981" with great oak tree. Given to managers, in Tiffany bag and box. CMV, $40.00.

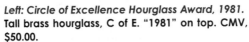

Left: Circle of Excellence Hourglass Award, 1981.
Tall brass hourglass, C of E. "1981" on top. CMV, $50.00.
Right: Avon 40th Anniversary Clock Award, 1981.
Hamilton Quartz clock, glass dome, Avon 40th name plate on base for 40 years of service. CMV, $100.00.

Pin, "Watch Us Grow" Award, 1981.
Green and white tie tac type pin. Says "Newark, Watch Us Grow." Given to managers. CMV, $5.00.

Circle of Excellence Medallion Award, 1981.
Gold tone, 4A design, 1981 on back. Red ribbon. CMV, $10.00.

Sell A Thon Clock Award, 1981.
Mirror clock. CMV, $20.00.

Rose Stickpin Award, 1981. Small sterling silver rose. No markings, in Tiffany & Co. turquoise box. Given to Avon reps for recruiting and sales goals. CMV, $20.00 MB.

Great American Sell A Thon Champagne Glass, 1981. Given to team leaders and managers, December 1981, on trip to Hawaii. CMV, $15.00.

Paperweight, Great Oak Award, 1981. Clear glass, "Avon, Kansas City #1-1981" etched on bottom. CMV, $50.00.

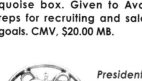

President's Club Pin Award, 1981. Gold tone pin with 81 in center of 4A design cut out. CMV, $5.00 MB.

Ultra Crystal Event Glass Award, 1981. Tiffany and Co. box held two engraved glasses. Given to reps who met sales goal by drawing for winner at sales meeting. CMV, $50.00 MB, set.

Currier & Ives Five-Piece Place Setting Award, 1981 – 1982. Each set has dinner plate, salad plate, cup and saucer, and soup bowl. Given to Avon reps for signing up one new Avon rep. CMV, $25.00 set of five pieces.

Not shown: Currier & Ives Five-Piece Place Setting Award, 1977 – 1981. Same set, only marked "1977 – 1981" on bottom of each piece in set. Only 300 sets got out from Newark branch. CMV, $100.00 MB, set with 1977 – 1981 bottom date.

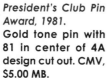

Tie Tac Men's President's Club Award, 1981– 1982. Gold tone 4A design tie tac given to men's President's Club. Came in Avon box with two different backs as shown. CMV, $20.00 MB.

Gold Panner Trophy, 1981. Metal gold panner. Plaque says "Sierra Division Achievement Break the Bank," 4A, 1981. Given to managers. CMV, $50.00.

Test Division Heart Pendant Award, 1981. Sterling silver and gold heart pendant and silver chain. Given to managers only, in Tiffany & Co. box. CMV, $150.00 MB.

Circle of Excellence Wine Award, 1981. Bottle of Abbey Chenin Blanc wine. Special black and gold label for Circle of Excellence. CMV, $40.00, unopened.

The Great American Sell A Thon Christmas Tree Award, 1981. Approximately 600 given out at President's Celebration in Hawaii. Has bottom Avon label and green and white gift box. CMV, $45.00.

Avon Loves Orders Heart Pin, 1981. CMV, $10.00.

Flower Basket Award, 1981.
Small white ceramic flower basket. CMV, $25.00.

Opportunity Unlimited Mug Award, 1981.
Brass mug inscribed on side. CMV, $20.00.

Opportunity Unlimited Glass Award, 1981.
Champagne glass inscribed on side. CMV, $10.00.

"Read! Listen! Follow Up!" Plaque, 1981.
4A design on sign. CMV, $10.00.

20 Year Silver Picture Frame Award, 1981.
Sterling silver picture frame from Tiffany & Co. given to Avon reps for 20 years of service. Bottom of frame engraved "Avon 20 Years," and the initial of person winning frame. Came in Tiffany felt bag. CMV, $100.00.

Jewelry Box (Male) Award, 1981.
Fine wood box made by Buxton given to male district managers or male team leaders. Brass label on front is only difference in both boxes. Same box could be bought in stores. Must have brass Avon name plate. District managers, CMV, $90.00. Team leaders, CMV, $75.00.

Pyramid Paperweight Award, 1981.
Clear lucite with gold 4A design on bottom and two sides on top. Given to district managers only. CMV, $50.00.

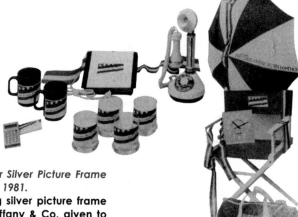

Teddy Bear Team Leader Gift, 1981.
White ceramic heart shaped box. Given to team leaders for 1981 year-end party. Could also be bought in Hallmark stores. Does not say Avon. CMV, $10.00 MB.

Monte Carlo Brass Box Award, 1981.
Brass box with burgundy velvet lining. Lid inscribed "Casino Monte Carlo." Given to Avon managers eligible to win a free trip to Monte Carlo. CMV, $40.00.

Great American Sell A Thon Awards, 1981.
Given to Avon reps for meeting top sales goals in Campaign 18, 1981. T-shirt: CMV, $5.00. Calculator: CMV, $20.00. Coffee mugs: set of two, CMV, $10.00. Drinking glasses: set of four, CMV, $12.00. Hot plate: CMV, $20.00. Telephone: antique, CMV, $75.00. Travel beach bag: CMV, $15.00. Clock: CMV, $35.00. Director's chair: CMV, $35.00. Umbrella: CMV, $25.00. Poncho in bag: CMV, $10.00. All are red, white, and blue decoration.

Umbrella Lipstick Award, 1981.
White nylon, black and red trim, red plastic handle. Given to team leaders. CMV, $25.00.

Cable Car Music Box Award, 1981.
Only 100 given to Circle of Excellence managers at San Francisco C of E meeting. Was not made for Avon. CMV, $35.00.

Toccara Necklace Award, 1981.
Toccara design on one side and "Avon Toccara 1981 K.C." on back. Sterling silver pendant and chain in Tiffany bag and box. Given to division managers. CMV, $100.00 MB.

Left: Bowling Avon Patches, 1981 – 1982.
Cloth patches from Baltimore and St. Louis Avon bowling tournaments. CMV, $20.00 each.
Right: Avon Tennis Championships Badges, 1981.
One red and one yellow badge. CMV, $20.00 each.

Team Leader and Manager's Christmas Gift, 1981.
Wood case jewelry music box with mirror inside says "Avon Team Leader 1981." CMV, $65.00. Same thing given to Avon managers, only says "Managers 1981." CMV, $85.00.

Rose Parade Jacket Awards, 1981 – 1983.
Avon Products issued 100 Rose Parade jackets in red to people working with Avon float in 1981 – 1983 parade, rare. Same inscription on front. CMV, $100.00 each.

"Feel Like a Star" Button, 1981.
3" blue and white button. CMV, $2.00.

Silver Circle Celebration Banquet Necklace Award, England, 1982.
Blue box held clear crystal pendant on sterling silver chain. Marked "Avon." Given to Silver Circle reps. CMV, $40.00 MB. Also shown with silver Circle Celebration Banquet menu. CMV, $5.00.

Team Leader Teddy Bear Award, 1982.
Sterling silver bear with movable arms and sterling silver chain. From Tiffany & Co. Approximately ½" high. Marked "T.L." on back of bear. CMV, $30.00 MB.

Avon's Best Pin Award, 1982.
Small brass pin says "Avon's Best, Morton Grove." With 4A design. Given to managers at Atlanta conference. CMV, $10.00.

President's Sales Challenge Award Watch, 1982.
Black face, Avon quartz and small diamond on 12 on face. Gold tone case. Black lizard strap. One top rep in each district won. Came in Avon gray felt case and outer sleeve. CMV, $100.00 MB and sleeve. Same watch, only gold face and no diamond and black lizard look leather strap in tan felt Avon case and outer sleeve. 20 given in each district to President's Club reps only. CMV, $30.00 MB and sleeve.

Left: Circle of Excellence Award Clock, 1982.
Clear lucite digital clock with engraved name of winning Avon manager. Is not marked Avon. CMV, $50.00.
Right: President's Club Card Case Award, 1982.
Silver plated card case in Tiffany box and felt bag. Engraved on case "President's Club" and 4A design. CMV, $20.00 MB.

Left: Men's President's Sales Challenge Watch Award, 1982.
Gold tone case and face marked "Avon." Black strap. Avon box. CMV, $100.00 MB.
Right: Winning is Beautiful Watch Award.
Lady's quartz watch. Avon on face and on box. CMV, $25.00 MB.

Top: Clock, "We're Hot!" Award, 1982.
White plastic Isis quartz battery clock. CMV, $75.00.
Bottom: Clock, "Avon," Award, 1982.
White plastic Isis electric clock. Face is red and marked "Avon." CMV, $75.00.
"Newark #1," Pendant Award, 1982.
Gold tone, ½" size pendant. Given to managers who got No. 1 in sales. Brown box. CMV, $15.00 MB.

Hop, Skip and Jump Medal Award, 1982.
Gold tone medal with 4A design on one side and "Hop, Skip and Jump Order Count Growth 1982" on back. Hangs on blue and yellow ribbon. CMV, $25.00.

Heart President's Sales Challenge Award, 1982.
Small clear crystal heart on gold tone ribbon pin. Maroon velvet Avon box and outer sleeve. CMV, $10.00 MB with sleeve.

Circle of Excellence Trinket Box, 1982.
Small leaded glass box with rose embossed on lid. Came with 4A brass coin. Back says "Roman Holiday C of E 1982." Only given to Pasadena branch managers. CMV, $35.00 box and coin.

Annie Pendant, Manager's, 1982.
14K gold-filled pendant and chain. Back marked "I love you" and marked "DM" on side. Given to district managers. Came in gray Avon box with special card from Avon. CMV, $60.00 MB.

 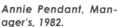

Collector's Corner Figurine Award, 1982.
Cherished Moments Collection mouse figurine. Given to 25 reps for top sales in Campaign 8, 1982, in each district. CMV, $25.00 MB.

Small Treasures Cherished Moments Miniature Awards, 1982.
Pink box held three miniature ceramic figurines. Given to reps for Step four sales goals. CMV, $15.00 MB, set.

Small Treasures Cabinet Award, 1982.
Small wood cabinet made in Brazil for small treasure figurines. CMV, $10.00.

Small Treasures, Fragrance Bottles, Miniature Awards, 1982.
Pink box held three miniature CPC reproductions with gold caps. Given to reps for step three of sales goals. CMV, $15.00 MB.

Small Treasures Currier & Ives Miniature Awards, 1982.
Pink box held miniature ceramic tea set. Given to reps for Step two of sales goal. Made in Japan. CMV, $15.00 MB, set.

Small Treasures Miniature Rose Award, 1982.
Pink box held small green leaf and pink ceramic rose. "The Avon Rose" on base, made in Taiwan. Given to reps for Step one of sales goal. CMV, $5.00 MB.

Ashtray, 1982.
Used at Avon plants. CMV, $2.50.

Currier & Ives Sugar and Creamer Award, 1982.
Set given to Avon reps for signing up one new Avon rep. CMV, $10.00 set.

Blazer Jackets, 1982 – 1983.
Blue blazer with 4A brass buttons and gold 4A insignia on jacket for reps. CMV, $75.00. Also made for managers with "M" in center of 4A insignia. CMV, $100.00.

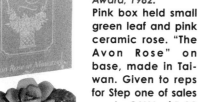

Subtle Reflections Heart Flower Vase and Flowers, 1982.
Small heart shaped lucite vase and silk flowers with Avon tag. Given to President's Club reps. Does not say Avon. CMV, $8.00.

Avon Tennis Paperweight, 1982.
Heavy sterling silver paperweight engraved "1982 Avon Tennis." Made by Tiffany & Co. CMV, $150.00.

A Special Thank You

$100,000 Trophy Award, 1982.
Glass dome held $100,000 of chopped up U.S. money. Says "$100,000" on dome. Wood base. Brass plaque with Avon 4A design given to one manager at Pasadena branch. CMV, $50.00.

Paperweight, San Francisco, 1982.
Small, clear lucite. Gold inner base. CMV, $30.00.

Parker Pen Award Set, 1982.
Two gold tone Parker pens. Says "Avon" on side. Given to managers. CMV, $35.00 MB.

President's Club Achievement Pin Awards, 1983, 1984, and 1985.
Brass pin with stones for sales increase. Four steps: one stone, two stones, three stones, four stones. 1983 — red stones; 1984 — pearl; 1985 — blue stones. CMV, $10.00 one stone. CMV, $15.00 two stones. CMV, $20.00 three stones. CMV, $25.00 four stones.

President's Sales Competition Jewelry Awards, 1983.
Three levels, all sterling silver, made by Tiffany.
Bracelet.
Given 10 to a district. CMV, $25.00 MB.
Pendant Necklace.
Given two to a district. CMV, $35.00 MB.
Lapel Pin.
Given to each rep in top sales group who met individual sales goals. CMV, $15.00 MB. Each came in Tiffany box with Avon card.

Golden Bell Collection Awards, 1983.
Four small brass bells given to managers for meeting sales goals for Campaigns 23, 24, and 25, 1983. First bell has 4A design on top. Second bell has acorn on top. Third bell has Avon door knocker. Fourth bell was given if all three bells were won in all three campaigns as a bonus. Fourth bell has a rose on top. CMV, first bell, $10.00 MB. Second bell, $10.00 MB. Third bell, $15.00 MB. Fourth bell, $20.00 MB. Add $5.00 to set if in plain boxes.

Group Sales Leader Pin Award, 1983.
Gold tone, 4A design. CMV, $8.00.

Great Oak Cufflinks Award, 1983.
Sterling silver, not marked Avon. Plain black box. Given to male division managers. CMV, $100.00.

G.S.L. #1 Pin, 1983.
Red pin. CMV, $10.00.

Going Avon Calling Award, 1982.
Yellow ceramic car with rabbit in pink, green base. Given to reps for recommendation prize. CMV, $50.00 MB.
Come Rain or Shine Award, 1983.
Ceramic Cherished Moments rabbit with screw-on ceramic umbrella. Given to reps for sales goals. First of three levels. CMV, $25.00 MB.

President's Sales Challenge Flower Award, 1983.
Glass and brass box held orchid. Label on top. Given to reps for trip to Hawaii. CMV, $45.00.

Sales Excellence Award, 1983.
Lead crystal glass box. Inscribed "Sales Excellence Award 1983 Avon President's Sales Competition." CMV, $50.00.

Clock Picture Frame Award, 1983.
Clear lucite, purple and red clock face. "Avon" on front. CMV, $25.00.

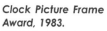

Representative of the Month Pin, 1983 – 1984.
Gold tone pin given to reps each month for meeting goals for the month. Two in each district. Passed on to new rep each month. CMV, $10.00.

Telephone, President's Club Award, 1983.
Red plastic touch tone, given to top sales reps only. Made by Webcor. Outer sleeve marked "Avon Calling." CMV, $25.00.

Townhouse Canister and Cookie Jar Set Awards, 1983.
Given to reps for meeting sales quota. First level, small, CMV, $10.00. Second level, CMV, $20.00. Third level, CMV, $30.00. Fourth level, cookie jar (right), CMV, $50.00. CMV, $90.00 entire set.

Group Sales Leader Identification Pin, 1984.
Gold tone stickpin came in red velvet box. Pin says "GSL — Avon." Came with outer sleeve with "Lang" all over it. CMV, $15.00 MB.

Rain Gear Umbrella Award, 1983.
Tan umbrella. Avon tags. CMV, $25.00.

President's Club Pin, Men's, 1984.
Brush gold tone stickpin or tie tac. Given to male reps for meeting sales goals. 4A design on each. First goal, one red ruby. CMV, $35.00. Two rubies, $50.00. Three rubies, $75.00. Four rubies, $100.00. All MB. In black velvet box. Maroon liner.

We Did It Together Tray, 1983.
7¼" x 12" silver plated server tray. Given to managers. CMV, $25.00.

Paperweight Award, 1983.
Square lucite with gold 4A center. Marked "The Answer is Avon." CMV, $20.00.

Paperweight Award Newark, 1983.
Small round lucite, with 1979 Susan B. Anthony dollar inside. CMV, $15.00.

Jewelry Box, President's Sales Competition Award, 1983.
Black lacquer music box made only for Avon. Bottom says "President's Sales Competition 1983." 8" x 4¾" size. Given for sales goals. Came with Avon card. CMV, $25.00.

World Sales Leader Ring Award, 1984.
14K gold ring, marked "Avon Division Sales Manager 1984" and globe of the world. Very rare. CMV, $300.00.

Trendsetter Pin Award, 1984.
Gold tone pin. CMV, $10.00.

President's Club Key Ring Award, 1984.
Gray box says "Avon Tribute 1984." Gold tone with Albee charm. CMV, $15.00.

Paperweight Award, Los Angeles, 1983.
Clear and red lucite, marked "Road to the Gold." CMV, $25.00.

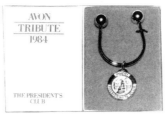

Rose Parade Avon Seat Cushion, 1984.
Reddish orange plastic, white letters. Only 150 made and given to people at Rose Bowl game 1984. CMV, $50.00.

Avon 5000 Pin, 1985.
Red, black, and gold pin says "Avon 5000." Given to reps for top sales. CMV, $15.00.

We Did It Together Award, 1985.
Two ceramic rabbit figurines in Cherished Moments collection. Given to reps. CMV, $25.00 MB.

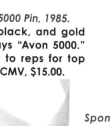

Sponsorship Medallion Award, 1985.
Gold tone pendant on white ribbon. CMV, $10.00.

Newark #1 Crystal Box Award, 1985 – 1986.
Lead crystal box with "Newark" with a heart, "1985 & 1986 #1" embossed on glass lid. Given to managers, in blue box. CMV, $25.00.

Gold Fever Award, 1985.
Small walnut plaque imprinted in wood says "Avon Gold Fever Additions Achievement September 1985" with winner's name on brass plaque. 1 oz. 999 fine pure gold "Avon Pasadena," 4A gold coin. Coin is loose but must be with plaque. CMV, $50.00 plus current value of 1 oz. of gold.

Honor Society Card Case Award, 1985.
Brass card case. CMV, $10.00.

Christmas Glasses and Tray Award, 1985.
Set of six, 12 oz. glasses with red and green Christmas tree design. CMV, $20.00 MB, set. Matching white ceramic two-tier serving tray with brass handle. CMV, $15.00 MB.

Royal Avon Pin, 1985.
Blue, white, and green enamel lapel pin. Given to managers. CMV, $10.00.

Thousandaire Club Pin, 1985.
Blue and white enamel. CMV with numbers up to four. CMV, $10.00 Add $5.00 for each number up to four.

I Love Avon Pin Award, 1985.
Gold tone, red heart. CMV, $5.00.

Peach Tree Pin, 1985.
CMV, $15.00.

Combourg Crystal Awards, 1985.
Each given to President's Club reps for sales goals. Crystal, made in France not just for Avon. CMV, decanter, $25.00. Set of six champagne glasses, $20.00. Set of six wine glasses, $20.00. Crystal and chrome ice bucket, $20.00.

Liberty Pin Award, 1985.
"Avon" on front. CMV, $5.00.

25 Year Service Plate Award, 1985 up.
8" sterling silver plate. Inscribed "In Grateful Appreciation of Twenty Five Years of Loyal Service to Avon Customers. James Preston — President Avon Division." CMV, $75.00 in Tiffany bag and box.

Radio Award, 1985.
White, plastic battery powered blue face. AM/FM in blue sleeve Avon box. Given to reps. CMV, $35.00 MB.

Honor Society Clock, 1986.
Small Lucite quartz clock given for selling $15,000 in Avon. CMV, $20.00.

Vision Award, 1985.
Clear lucite paperweight. Says "Avon Our Vision is Clear 1985." CMV, $15.00.

Sponsorship Pin, 1986.
Gold tone pin for sponsorship. CMV, $10.00.

Albee Avon 100 Pin, England, 1986.
Gold tone. Blue enamel. CMV, $65.00.

#1 Trendsetters Wall Tile Award, 1985.
White tile given at Morton Grove branch. CMV, $25.00.

Avon 100 Thousandaire Club Pin, 1986.
Red, white, and gold lapel pin. Came with numbers to hang below. Marked "1886 – 1986." CMV, $10.00 no numbers.

Avon 100 Thousandaire Club Pin, 1985.
Same pin only blue border design. CMV, $10.00.

Blue Heart Avon Award Pin, 1986.
Silver tone pin with blue heart stone. Given to reps in Newark branch for three orders. CMV, $10.00 MB.

Director Chair Award, 1985.
White fold-up chair, red canvas. Five given in each district. CMV, $35.00.

Avon 86 Rose Pin, 1986.
Gold tone rose, "Avon 86" lapel pin given to Avon reps. CMV, $5.00.

Thousandaire Club $5,000 Pin, 1986.
White and gold and red pin with "TC 1886 – 1986 $5,000" on face. CMV, $15.00.

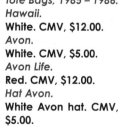

Tote Bags, 1985 – 1986.
Hawaii.
White. CMV, $12.00.
Avon.
White. CMV, $5.00.
Avon Life.
Red. CMV, $12.00.
Hat Avon.
White Avon hat. CMV, $5.00.

Thousandaire Club Pin, 1986.
White, gold, and red pin, "1886 –1986." CMV, $10.00.

Avon 100 Watch Award, 1986.
Black face quartz watch with "Avon 100" on face, brown leather grain strap. Given to managers in Newark branch. CMV, $65.00.

Avon 100 President's Club Pin, 1986.
Gold tone pin. Given to reps in black velvet Avon box. CMV, $15.00 MB.
Avon 100 Honor Society Pin, 1986 – 1987.
Same as President's Club, only came with "Honor Society" on bottom. CMV, $15.00.

Avon 100 Gold Pin Award, 1986.
14K gold. Small diamond. Given to division managers. CMV, $75.00.

Liberty Division Pin, 1986.
Blue and gold tone lapel pin. Statue of Liberty on face. Given to reps. CMV, $10.00.

Avon 100 Division Sales Medallions, 1986.
Gold tone, silver tone, and bronze tone medallions. Each say "PC-Avon 100." Given in each division, one gold, four silver and five bronze. CMV, $75.00 gold. CMV, $60.00 silver. CMV, $40.00 bronze.

Avon 100 Trendsetter Representative Pin, 1986.
Blue, white, and gold. CMV, $15.00.

Avon $1,000 Club Pin, 1986.
CMV, $10.00.

Avon 100 Award Pins, 1986.
Left: Newark branch manager's pin, 14K gold. Has hook on back to wear as necklace. Back says "Newark 1886 – 1986," 14K. CMV, $75.00 MB. Center: Newark branch. Gold tone. Larger in size. Very thin. CMV, $10.00. Right: Morton Grove pin. Thicker, gold tone. Design is different on all three. CMV, $10.00.

Paperweight, Christmas is for Children, 1986.
Avon — 1986 embossed on clear glass. Given to managers only at six places in U.S. CMV, $50.00.

Avon 100 Rose Key Chain Pendant, 1986.
Pink or gray Avon 100 box and sleeve has gold tone key chain and chain to use as necklace. Back says "Avon 1886 – 1986." Given to top 10 reps. CMV, $15.00.

Avon Rainbow Pin, 1986.
CMV, $15.00.

Arrow, Apple Pin, 1986.
Red apple, white cross stickpin. CMV, $15.00.

Avon 100 Mirror, 1986.
Red plastic holder and "Avon 100" printed on mirror. CMV, $2.00.

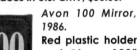

Avon 100 Matches, 1986.
Silver box. CMV, $1.00.

"Avon 100" Pill Box Award, 1986.
Small chrome box, "Avon 100" on lid. Given at President's Club luncheon. CMV, $10.00.

Miscellaneous Award Pins, 1986.
Avon 2000 Pin.
Black, white, and gold. CMV, $10.00.
Avon 100 Pin, Large.
"1886 – 1986," black, red, and gold. CMV, $10.00.
Avon Member Pin.
Blue, black, and gold. CMV, $10.00.

Avon Pin.
Black, red, and gold. CMV $10.00.
Avon 100 Pin.
Small, black, red, and gold. CMV, $10.00.
Avon 100 Pin.
Blue, white, and red. CMV, $10.00.
I Love Avon Pin.
Black, red, and gold. CMV, $10.00.

Avon 100 Award Pins, 1986.
Small gold tone on left with black letters. CMV, $7.00. Small silver tone with black letters. CMV, $7.00.

Avon 100 Champagne Award, 1986.
"1886 – 1986 Avon 100" label. Given to Honor Society reps. CMV, $25.00.

Avon 100 Glasses, 1986.
Set of four drinking glasses. Embossed "Avon 100." CMV, $15.00 set.

Avon 100 Binoculars Award, 1986.
7 x 35 power, black. Given to reps. Case says "Avon 100." CMV, $75.00.

Avon 100 Tote Bag Award, 1986.
White canvas bag trimmed in blue and red. Given to people on trip to New York for 100 year celebration. CMV, $25.00.

Avon 100 Coffee Cup Award, 1986.
Blue ceramic cup. "Avon 100 1886 – 1986" in gold letters. Given to representatives. CMV, $8.00.

Centennial Jewelry Case Award, 1986.
8¾" square brass box. Given to reps. CMV, $25.00.

Avon 100 Desk Caddy, 1986.
Clear plastic with "Avon 100 1886 – 1986" or caddy white pen and note paper. Given to managers. CMV, $15.00.

Avon 100 Albee Mirror, 1986.
13" x 17" gold tone frame mirror. "1886 – 1986" and first Avon rep embossed on mirror. Given to managers at August conference and also given for sponsorship. CMV, $45.00.

Avon 100 "Centennial Sales Leader" Ring Award, 1986.
Inscribed on 14K ring. Very rare. CMV, $300.00.

Avon 100 Coffee Mug, Pasadena, 1986.
White glass cup. "Avon 100" on front. CMV, $10.00.

Centennial Jewelry Collection Awards, 1986.
All gold tone and rhinestones. Given to reps. Pin, CMV, $10.00. Earrings, CMV, $15.00. Bracelet, CMV, $15.00. Necklace, CMV, $20.00.

Avon 100 Pasadena #1 Award, 1986.
Wood base, clear lucite Avon 100 plaque. CMV, $15.00.

Avon 100 Plate Award, 1986.
White porcelain plate. Back says "C26 — 1985 Limited Edition." Pasadena branch only. CMV, $25.00.

Avon 100 Manager's Compact Award, 1986.
Gold tone. Inscribed on back, "Avon Centennial 1986 Dist. Sales Managers Conference." CMV, $25.00.

Avon 100 Clock Award, 1986. Clear lucite clock. Black face and letters. Given to managers. CMV, $35.00.

Avon 100 Lemonade Set, 1986. White plastic pitcher and four plastic Avon 100 glasses. CMV, $20.00.

Spirit of Avon Award Plate, 1986. 7¼" clear glass plate. White lettering. One to a district. CMV, $35.00.

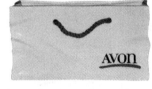

Ceramic Bag Award, 1986. White ceramic bag with red cord thru top. Given to reps. CMV, $20.00.

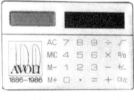

Avon 100 Calculator, 1986. Gold tone face, "Avon 1886 – 1986." Given to managers. CMV, $10.00.

Avon 100 Liberty Apron, 1986. Small red apron. White design from N.Y. Liberty Weekend. CMV, $25.00.

Ceramic Sack Award, 1986. White ceramic bag. Given to reps in U.S. and Canada. CMV, $20.00.

Avon 100 Bell, 1986. Clear glass bell, 5¾" high. "Avon 100" embossed. CMV, $25.00.

Avon 100 Ceramic Box, 1986. White porcelain. "Avon 100" on front and back. 4A on top in red. CMV, $35.00.

Telephone Honor Society Award, 1986. Red telephone given for $50,000 in sales. Engraved on top "PC Avon Honor Society." Came in Unisonic box. CMV, $75.00.

Centennial Arch Watch, 1986. Enameled arch stand with Avon face quartz pocket watch. Can be hung on chain around neck. Given to top 10 reps in each division for 100th anniversary. Came in Avon 100 pink box and white Avon sleeve. CMV, $60.00.

Jolly Santa Awards, 1986. All white and red ceramic.
Level 1: Candy jar, 7½" high. CMV, $10.00.
Level 2: Set of four Santa mugs. CMV, $15.00.
Level 3: Santa plate. CMV, $20.00.

Avon Telephone Award, 1986.
White phone, wall or desk mount. "Avon" in black letters, red slash. Given to reps. CMV, $25.00.

Devotee Treasure Box Award, 1986.
Brass and glass box, mirror bottom. Given to reps in black box. CMV, $25.00 MB.

Diamond Jubilee Paperweight Award, 1986.
Clear glass, marked "C-12-15-1986." In gray box with Diamond card. CMV, $30.00 MB.

Telephone Award, 1986.
Red wall mount or can sit on table. Says "Avon" in white letters. Given to reps. CMV, $20.00.

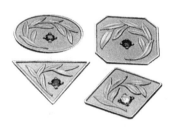

Sponsorship Lapel Pin, Men's Award, 1986 – 1988.
Gold filled pins given to male Avon reps for signing up new Avon reps.
1 Sapphire: CMV, $35.00 MB.
2 Ruby: CMV, $60.00 MB.
3 Emerald: CMV, $85.00 MB.
4 Diamond: CMV, $110.00 MB.

Avon Tennis Ball Key Chain Award, 1986.
Small yellow, red, and white tennis ball. CMV, $2.00.

White House Picture Frame Award, 1986.
100th year, signed by Ronald Reagan. CMV, $10.00.

Sponsorship Charm Awards, 1986 – 1988.
Gold filled charms with colored stones.
Step 1: Lapel Pin, CMV, $10.00.
Step 2: Sapphire, CMV, $25.00.
Step 3: Ruby, CMV, $50.00.
Step 4: Emerald, CMV, $75.00.
Step 5: Diamond, CMV, $100.00.

Fragrance 50 Club Fifth Avenue Bowl Award, 1986.
Clear glass bowl with blue lettering given to reps on intro of Fifth Avenue products. CMV, $20.00.

Glass Pen Set, 1986.
Beveled edge glass base with chrome and black pen. Says "AVON AVANT: DIVISION #1 USA 1986" CMV, $25.00.

Liberty Weekend Umbrella, 1986.
Red and white umbrella. Marked "Avon Liberty Weekend." Rare N.Y. Liberty Celebration. CMV, $150.00.

Hundred Year Manager's Watch Award, 1986.
Back says "1886 – 1986 Avon" gold tone band and case has three diamond type stones and says "Quartz." CMV, $100.00.

Circle of Excellence Pin, 1987.
Small pin, C of E 1987 4A design. CMV, $10.00.

Honor Society Goblet, 1987.
Clear glass with black 4A design. Given to top reps. CMV, $15.00.

Honor Society Pins, 1987.
"HS" on gold tone pin.
Level 1: has a ruby. CMV, $15.00.
Level 2: has a sapphire. CMV, $20.00.
Level 3: has a diamond. CMV, $25.00.
President's Club Pin, 1987.
Gold tone pin with "PC" on face.
Level 1: has a pearl. CMV, $10.00.
Level 2: has a topaz. CMV, $15.00.

10 Year Anniversary Plate, 1987.
8½" porcelain plate. "The California Perfume Co." for 10 years service to Avon. Four different plates issued starting in 1987. CMV, $15.00 MB.

Albee Key Chain, 1987.
Blue and gold tone. For sponsorship of new reps. CMV, $15.00.

Night Magic Pin, 1987.
CMV, $2.00.

C of E Imari Bowl, 1987.
Porcelain bowl given to Avon managers on 1987 Japan C of E trip. Not marked Avon. Must have C of E Avon card. CMV, $75.00 MB with card.

Gold Digger Pin, 1987.
Small gold tone pickax. Not marked Avon. Given for signing new Avon reps. CMV, $5.00.

Tribute Vase, 1987.
8" high clear glass vase. Embossed "Tribute 1987." Given to President's Club reps only. CMV, $10.00.

President's Club Silver Basket, 1987.
5½" high silver plated basket. Has "PC Avon President's Club" tag attached. Given only to President's Club reps only. CMV, $15.00.

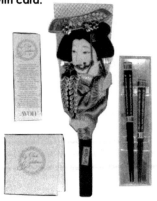

C of E Awards, 1987.
Left: Wood paddle, hand painted Yukata. Must have C of E Avon card. CMV, $20.00.
Right: C of E Chopsticks.
Set of two hand-painted chopsticks. Must have C of E Avon card. CMV, $5.00 MB.
Both items given to C of E Avon managers on 1987 Japan trip.

Avon Pin Award, 1987.
Gold tone Avon pin. CMV, $15.00.

President's Club Pin Award, 1987.
Gold tone with hanging rose. CMV, $25.00.

Great Oak Card Case Award, 1987.
Brass. CMV, $5.00.

Clock Avon Quartz Award, 1988. Clear lucite with red front clock, mirror back. CMV, $15.00.

President's Club Fruit Jars Award, 1988. Set of three glass jars marked "Avon President's Club" on side. CMV, $20.00 set.

PC Tribute Plate Award, 1988. 6" chrome plate marked "PC Tribute 1988." CMV, $5.00.

Triple Crown Necklace, 1988. 14K gold pendant with three crowns on it and chain. Given to managers. CMV, $40.00 MB.

President's Club Man's Tie Tac Award, 1988. Gold tone tie tac with small red stone. CMV, $15.00 MB.

President's Club Pin, 1988. Gold tone pin. "PC 88." Four levels.
No. 1: Pearl CMV, $10.00.
No. 2: Citron (topaz color), CMV, $15.00.
No. 3: Ruby, CMV, $20.00.
No. 4: Sapphire, CMV, $25.00.

Honor Society Award Pins, 1988 – 1989. Gold tone pins, "HS 88" or "HS 89." With:
Ruby: CMV, $20.00.
Sapphire: CMV, $25.00.
1 diamond: CMV, $30.00.
2 diamonds: CMV, $35.00.
3 diamonds: CMV, $40.00.

Circle of Excellence Pin, 1988. 4A, red and white or blue and white pin. CMV, $3.00.

Honor Society Key Chain Award, 1988. Gold tone key ring with "H-S" in red letters under clear Lucite. Given to top reps. Came in maroon box. CMV, $8.00.

Clock, Circle of Excellence Award, 1988. Gold and brass tone Seth Thomas clock. Has "1988 Circle of Excellence District" on face. Came in white box marked "Circle of Excellence." CMV, $125.00 MB.

Color Wheel Watch Award, 1988. Color Watch. "Avon" on back. Gray strap. Given for sales incentive. Came in plastic Avon box. CMV, $30.00 MB.

Sales Excellence Award, 1988. Wood plaque with brass Avon lady design, came with brass stand. "#1 Division" in gold. CMV, $100.00. Nos. 2 through 5 are silver tone. CMV, $75.00.

Ceramic Jar Award, 1988. Off-white ceramic jar with gold 4A on front. CMV, $15.00.

Whistle Key Chain Award, 1989. Brass whistle key chain says "Avon" in red letters. CMV, $6.00.

Avon Howard Miller Clock Award, 1989. Maroon case, brass "Avon" on front. CMV, $10.00.

President's Club Star Pin Awards, 1989 – 1990. Gold tone pin with gold star. CMV, $10.00. *Blue and white star charm.* CMV, $15.00. *Red star.* CMV, $15.00. *Green star.* CMV, $20.00. *Blue star.* CMV. $25.00. *White star.* CMV, $35.00. *Star charm with pearl.* CMV, $20.00. *Gold star in circle charm.* CMV, $15.00.

President's Club Pen, 1989. Bottom is black and gold with President's Club on side. CMV, $10.00.

Watch Incentive Award, 1989. Gold tone case. "Avon" on face. Made in China. Brown strap. CMV, $25.00.

Star Awards, 1989. *Left:* Small Tribute chrome picture frame. CMV, $3.00. *Star Paperweight.* *Center:* "Starr Tribute PC 89" on clear glass paperweight. CMV, $5.00. *Right: Sterling Star Pin.* Came in blue box. Sterling silver pin marked on back side "National Star Event 3/19/90." CMV, $75.00 MB.

PC Star Tribute Plate Award, 1989. 5" blue and silver porcelain plate. Marked "PC Star Tribute '89." CMV, $5.00.

Watch "PSST" Award, 1989. Quartz gold tone watch. "PSST" on face. Beige leather skin strap. CMV, $50.00.

Star, Best of Best Paperweight Award, 1989. Glass paperweight given to top manager in each division. One each given for best percent increase, best dollar increase, and best sales increase. CMV, $50.00 MB.

Stars System Pin, 1989. Silver tone star and blue inlay given for $4,500 in sales. CMV, $3.00 MB.

Townhouse Canister Award Set, 1989. Five ceramic canisters. Not marked Avon but lady on second canister has bag marked "Avon." CMV, $10.00 each. $25.00 for large one on right.

District Achievement Awards, 1989. Blue Lucite stand held one quarter oz. sterling silver Avon coin. Four Steps — Volume, Customers, Recruiting, and Sales Increase. CMV, $12.50 each. Also came in gold over silver "Best of the Best." CMV, $25.00.

Star Clock Award, 1989. 2¾" high clear lucite quartz clock says "Avon." CMV, $10.00.

Pen and Key Chain Set Award, 1989.
White pen and key chain. CMV, $3.00 MB, set.

Cinderella Additions Achievement Award, 1989.
Black plastic base with slipper shoe engraved on clear lucite top. CMV, $20.00.

Index Alarm Clock and Calculator Award, 1990.
Black case, red letters. CMV, $20.00.

Spirit of Avon Award Plate, 1990s.
8" glass plate, frosted trim. Given in "Star Tribute" sales program to top reps. CMV, $30.00.

Star Tribute Award Frame, 1990.
6¾" high, 5⅛" wide picture frame, gold ribbon and "PC" on frame. Given to top sales reps. CMV, $20.00.

Bud Vase Award, 1990 – 1991.
Silver plated with lead crystal ball at base. Given to reps for sales increase. Not marked Avon but box is. CMV, $5.00 MB.

Honor Society Pen Set Award, 1990.
Box held two black and gold tone pens with "Avon Honor Society" on side of each pen. CMV, $25.00 MB.

President's Club Pen Award, 1990.
Chrome pen with "PC" on it. CMV, $10.00.

Circle of Excellence Pen Set Award, 1990.
Gray box held three black quill pens with "C of E" on top of each pen. CMV, $35.00.

Acapulco Charm Bracelet Award, 1990.
Sterling silver sombrero charm. Marked "Avon" on back. CMV, $25.00 MB.

Signature Collection Avon Pin, 1990.
Gold tone pin for Avon reps. Has simulated diamonds and rubies. CMV, $8.00.

Excellence Rose Pin Award, 1990.
1" gold tone pin. Red enamel rose. "Excellence" on edge. Does not say Avon. CMV, $7.50.

Kiss Watch Award, 1990.
Gold tone watch, Avon and red lips on face. Given to reps. CMV, $50.00 MB.

Avon Calling America Phone Award, 1990.
Blue, white, and red telephone given to reps.
CMV, $40.00 MB.

Skin So Soft Radio Award, 1990.
Skin So Soft bottle is an AM/FM radio. Given to reps in 1990. CMV, $20.00 MB.

Rosebud Pin, 30 Years Service Award, 1990.
14K gold rose pin with diamond chip center. Given to Avon reps for 30 years of service. Made only for Avon. Not marked Avon. CMV, $100.00 MB.
Rosebud Earrings, 35 Years Service Award, 1990.
14K gold rose earrings with diamond chip. Given for 35 years of service. Does not say Avon. Made only for Avon. CMV, $125.00 MB.

Wheel of Fortune Clock, 1990.
Wall clock. White plastic with glass face, says "Avon." CMV, $25.00.

Sunglasses Award, 1990.
Sunglasses marked "Avon," came in red Avon case. Given for recruitment. CMV, $20.00.

Rising Star Pin Award, 1991.
Gold tone with three rhinestones and detachable silver tone star pin. Can be used as a lapel or tie pin. Given to reps for $4,500 in total sales. CMV, $5.00 MB.

Pearl Bracelet Watch Award, 1990.
Gold tone watch made in China. Pearl, face marked "Avon 1990." Given for top sales. CMV, $35.00.

Panda Bear Award, 1990.
9" tall panda bear with red Avon shirt given for recruitment. CMV, $20.00.

Las Vegas Avon Silver Coin Award, 1991.
Blue box held plastic encased pure silver 1 oz. coin marked "Las Vegas Avon 1991" on face; scales on back side. Must be in plastic case to be mint. CMV, $50.00 MB.

President's Club Heart Box Award, 1990.
White satin lining says "Avon PC 1990." Chrome heart box with gold ribbon on lid. CMV, $15.00.
President's Club Pen Award, 1990.
Black and gold Chromatic pen. Says "PC President's Club." CMV, $3.00.

National President's Trophy Award, 1990s.
Clear lucite trophy was given to top reps in the nation for "Sales," "Sales Increase," "Recruiting," and "Leadership." They were given each year and dated 1995 – 1996, 1996 – 1997, 1997 – 1998, and 1998 – 1999. CMV, $100.00 MB, each trophy for each year.

Star President's Club Pin Award, 1991.
Gold tone pin marked "PC." CMV, $10.00 MB.
Star Honor Society Pin Award, 1991.
Gold tone pin marked "HS." Issued for four different levels of sales: $16,000, $30,000, $50,000, and $75,000. CMV, $10.00, $15.00, $20.00, and $25.00 each, MB.

Top Hat Award, 1991.
3⅞" high, 5" x 5½" base, Black ceramic top hat. "Avon 1991" embossed on top. "You're the top. Tribute 1991" on black ribbon band around hat. Given for top sales. CMV, $15.00.

Crystal Star Trophy Award, 1991.
Fine crystal glass star given to top five national leaders in best "Total Sales," "Sales Increase," and "Recruiting." CMV, $250.00 each trophy, MB.

Star Trophy Branch Award, 1991.
Fine crystal glass trophy given to top reps in each branch for best in "Total Sales," "Sales Increase," and "Recruiting." CMV, $75.00 each trophy, MB.

Best New Performer Trophy Award, 1991.
Star Tribute lucite trophy given to top sales rep in each district. CMV, $50.00 MB.

"Through the Years" Jewelry Music Box Award, 1992.
Rare wood jewelry box. Given to President's Club reps. CMV, $75.00 mint.

President's Club Pin Award, 1993 – 1994.
Gold Tone "A" pin with "P.C." on it. For first year President's Club reps. CMV, $10.00 MB.

Honor Society Award Pin, 1993 – 1994.
Gold-tone "A" pin with "H.S." on it. Given to reps who had $16,000 in sales in 12 months. CMV, $15.00 MB.

Rose Circle Award Pin, 1993 – 1994.
Gold-tone "A" pin with "R.C." on it. Given to reps who had $30,000 in sales in 12 months. CMV, $20.00 MB.

David H. McConnell Club Award Pin, 1993 – 1994.
Gold-tone "A" pin with "D.M." on it. Given to reps for $50,000 in sales in 12 months. CMV, $25.00 MB.

President's Council Diamond Award Pin, 1993 – 1994.
14K gold "A" pin with small diamond on side. Given to reps for $75,000 in sales in 12 months. CMV, $60.00 MB.

President's Inner Circle Award Pin, 1993 – 1994.
14K gold square pin with cutout "A" and three small diamonds. Says "Inner Circle" on bottom. Given to reps for $200,000 in sales in 12 months. CMV, $125.00 MB.

Koala Bear, 1993.
10" stuffed koala with Avon logo t-shirt. Sold only to Avon reps. CMV, $10.00.

President's Club Holiday Plate Gift Set, 1994.
Avon box held four Arcoroc clear glass plates with sleigh ride and evergreen tree scene. CMV, $15.00 set MB.

Avon Honors Sales Award, 1994.
Lucite top with black base and mirror. Given to reps for top sales in district. CMV, $50.00.

Tree Ornament for Reps, 1994.
Metal Avon tree ornament. Given to Avon reps. CMV, $5.00.

President's Club Pin Award, 1995.
Gold tone pin with small stone marked "PC." Given to reps for $8,600 in sales. CMV, $10.00 MB.
Honor Society Pin Award, 1995.
Gold tone pin with blue stone and marked HS. Given to reps for $16,200 in sales. CMV, $15.00 MB.
Rose Circle Pin Award, 1995.
Gold tone pin with red stone marked "RC." Given to reps for $30,500 in sales. CMV, $20.00 MB.
David H. McConnell Club Pin Award, 1995.
Gold tone pin with "DHM" and small stone. Given to reps for $51,000 in sales. CMV, $25.00 MB.

President's Council Picture Album Award, 1995.
Silver plated cover says "New Orleans 95." Blue velvet book. CMV, $50.00 mint.

President's Club Vanity Box Award, 1995.
Silver plate top on glass box. "PC" on front and back sides. Given to reps. CMV, $50.00 MB.

Top: President's Recognition Sales Volume Award, 1995 – 1996.
Wood base, glass and brass or chrome award given to reps in each district for best sales volume increase. CMV, $50.00.
Bottom: President's Recognition Best New Performer Award.
Wood base and glass and brass or chrome award. Given to new President's Club reps in each district for highest total sales. CMV, $50.00.

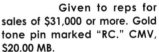

President's Club Pin Award, 1996 – 1997.
Gold tone pin marked "PC." Given to reps for sales of $8,700. CMV, $10.00 MB.
Honor Society Pin Award, 1996 – 1997.
Gold tone pin marked "HS." Given to reps for sales of $16,500. CMV, $15.00 MB.
Rose Circle Pin Award, 1996 – 1997.
Given to reps for sales of $31,000 or more. Gold tone pin marked "RC." CMV, $20.00 MB.
David H. McConnell Pin Award, 1996 – 1997.
Gold tone pin marked "DM," given to reps for sales of $52,000 or more. CMV, $25.00 MB.

President's Recognition Program Award, 1996 – 1997.
Glass and brass on marble base trophy given to top five reps in each district for "Top Sales," "Sales Increase," "Recruiting," and "Leadership." CMV, $50.00 each trophy, MB.

Representative Award Pins, 1998.
Each given to Avon reps for reaching higher level sales goals each year. Antique looking pins with blue cameo-like center stones.
President's Club Pin.
Marked "PC." CMV, $10.00 MB.
Honor Society Pin.
Marked "HS." CMV, $15.00 MB.
Rose Circle Pin.
Marked "RC." CMV, $20.00 MB.
D.H. McConnell Pin.
Marked "DHM." CMV, $25.00 MB.

Rep Award Pins, 1997.
President's Club Pin.
Marked "PC." CMV, $10.00 MB.
Honor Society Pin.
Marked "HS." CMV, $15.00 MB.
Rose Circle Pin.
Marked "RC." CMV, $20.00 MB.
D.H. McConnell Pin.
Marked "DHM." CMV, $25.00 MB. All are gold tone with lady's face in center.

Avon "Through The Years" Throw Award, 1998.
Large fabric throw with all the Avon and CPC logo's. Given to reps for recruiting five new Avon reps. CMV, $75.00 mint.

California Perfume Co. Hope Chest Award, 2000.
Wood hope chest marked "California Perfume Co." on front is 42" wide x 16" x 18". It had to be put together. Came in a box collapsed. CMV, $65.00 put together.

President's Recognition Program Trophy Award, 1997 – 1998.
Mrs. Albee etched in glass with brass and marble base. Five of each given in each district for "Top Sales," "Sales Increase," "Recruiting," and Leadership." CMV, $50.00 each trophy, MB.

President's Club Identification Pin, 1999.
Imitation pearl and gold tone pin. CMV, $10.00 MB.

California Perfume Co. Cookie Jar Award, 2000.
Large ceramic cookie jar. Says "California Perfume Co." on front. CMV, $45.00.

Customers Count Avon Pin Award, 1998.
Gold tone pin and simulated diamond given to all reps for a $50 order in first three sales periods of 1998. CMV, $5.00 MB.

President's Club Identification Pin Award, 2000.
Gold tone pocket watch style pin given to reps for $9,700 in sales in one year. Face says "Avon 2000 PC." CMV, $10.00 MB.

Mrs. Albee's Schoolhouse Cookie Jar Award, 2001.
Large ceramic cookie jar. Says "Mrs. Albee's Schoolhouse" on front. CMV, $45.00.

President's Celebration Candy Can Gift, 2001. Approximately 7" tall, metal can given to President's Club reps full of candy. CMV, $10.00 mint.

President's Club Achievement Charm Bracelet, 2003. Gold tone charm bracelet says "P.C. 2003," with colored stones. CMV, $15.00.

President's Club Achievement Locket Award, 2002. Gold tone locket with lavender and pink center. Says "P.C." inside. CMV, $15.00.

President's Recognition Program Awards, 2004, 2005, and 2006. Same trophy given over three years for "Top Sales," "Sales Increase," "Recruiting," and "Leadership." Silver tone. CMV, $25.00 each. Gold or brass tone, CMV, $35.00.

President's Recognition Achievement Jewelry, 2006. Given to President's Club Avon reps for sales of $10,100. Gold tone reversible pendant. Front side has pink crystal-like stone and rhinestones. Back side inscribed with highest level of achievement and year with rhinestones. Came with three-strand gold tone neck chain. CMV, $15.00 MB.

Mrs. Albee's House Cookie Jar Award, 2002. Large ceramic cookie jar. Front has sign that says "The Albees" and "Avon." CMV, $45.00.

President's Club Achievement Pendant Award, 2004. Silver plated pendant and chain, says "P.C." CMV, $15.00 MB.

Honor Society Clock Award, 2002. Brass tone and glass quartz clock. Plaque on base says, "Avon Honor Society 2002." Given for $20,000 in sales. CMV, $35.00 MB.

NAAC Bottles and Collectibles

These items (club bottles, plates, mirrors, convention bottles, bells, etc.) were sold only to members of NAAC (National Association of Avon Collectors) clubs. NAAC and club bottle offers were not affiliated with Avon Products, Inc.

What are they? Where did you get them? Club bottles were made for Avon Collector Clubs throughout the United States and Canada. These clubs are all members of the National Association of Avon Collectors (NAAC). Club bottles or plates were sold for a period of 60 days only and only the amount sold in that time were made. At the end of the sale period, the order was placed with the factory. Each bottle is numbered with the quantity made. All club bottles are hand painted porcelain of the finest quality.

All NAAC club and convention bottles and bells 1972 to 1986 were designed, created, and manufactured by Bud Hastin. Bud has created over 100 different hand-painted porcelain bottles and figurines. These include the bird and animal series cologne bottles of the early 1970s, and the Collector's Art dog, bird, and bull series distributed by McCormick Distilling Co. of Weston, Missouri. They have become very collectible over the years. All are very limited editions.

All annual NAAC national convention mirrors from 1995 forward have a CMV of $10.00 each. All are low issue.

First Annual NAAC Avon Club Bottle of First Avon Lady, 1972.

7" high, hand-painted porcelain bottle. Made for Avon club members only belonging to the National Association of Avon Collectors. First NAAC club bottle issued. Made in image of first CPC sales lady. Each bottle is numbered. Released in June 1972. Total issue was 2,870. Bottle made and issued by National Association of Avon Collectors. CMV, $200.00. There were 18 made with red hair and green purse. CMV, $600.00 for a redhead. No registration certificates were issued with the 1972 club bottle. Four bottles had blue lettering on them. All others had black letters. CMV, $700.00 blue letter bottom. 1972 factory sample of first lady sold by mistake. Same as above, only no lettering on bottom and neck is flush where cork fits top of bottle. No raised lip for cork as regular production was. Bottle has letter from Bud Hastin as one-of-a-kind sample. CMV, $500.00.

NAAC First Convention Mirror, 1972.
Only 300 made. Given at banquet. Some were made with pins instead of mirrors. These were dealers badges. CMV, $25.00 each.

Mid-America NAAC Convention Plate, 1972.
Clear glass with frosted lettering, 134 made for the first annual NAAC Convention in Kansas City, Kansas, June 1972. This plate was not made until 1975. CMV, $20.00.

Central Valley NAAC Convention Plate, 1973.
Clear glass, frosted lettering. 124 were made and sold for second annual NAAC convention at "Sacramento, Calif." This plate was not made until 1975. CMV, $20.00.

NAAC Convention Souvenir Badge, 1972.
Round, light blue background with first CPC lady in center. Has pin back. CMV, $10.00. Issued each year in a different color with the city and date from 1971 up to 2007.

Second NAAC McConnell Club Bottle, 1973.
Second annual club bottle issued by the NAAC clubs in honor of Mr. and Mrs. D. H. McConnell, founders of Avon. Registration certificate goes with the bottle. 5,604 bottles were sold and numbered. CMV, $50.00.

Convention Delegate's Ribbon, 1973.
Red ribbon with a red rosette was given to all delegates. Gold printing reads "Official Delegate National Association of Avon Clubs Convention Sacramento, California, June 22, 1973." Issued each year in a different color with the city and date from 1971 up to 2007. CMV, $8.00.

Not shown: Convention Board Member Ribbon, 1973.
Same as the delegate ribbon, only in blue instead of red. "Board Member" replaced the "Official Delegate" on the ribbon. CMV, $15.00.

Convention National Chairman Ribbon, 1973. Same as the delegate ribbon only in maroon instead of red. Only one of these ribbons was made. It is owned by Mr. Bud Hastin. No value established.

NAAC Convention Banquet Mirror, 1974.
Yellow and black, mirror on back. Convention held in Kansas City, Missouri, June 22, 1974. Given to each person attending the annual NAAC Avon convention banquet. CMV, $15.00.

Mid-America NAAC Convention Plate, 1974.
Crystal plate with frosted inscription made in honor of the Third NAAC Convention by Mid-America Club. 225 were made. CMV, $20.00.

NAAC CPC Factory Club Bottle, 1974.
Third annual club bottle issued by the NAAC clubs in honor of the first California Perfume Co. factory in 1886. Came with a registration card. 4,691 bottles were made. The mold was broken at the third annual NAAC convention, June 22, 1974, in Kansas City. CMV, $30.00.

Bud Hastin Club Bottle, 1974.
Issued by the Gold Coast Avon Club in honor of Bud Hastin for his contribution to the field of Avon collecting. First in an annual series. Only 2,340 bottles were made. Bottle is 8½" high, white pants, maroon coat, black turtleneck, black shoes. Few were made with white shirt. Rare. CMV, $25.00 black shirt. CMV, $75.00 white shirt.

Fourth Annual NAAC Club Bottle, 1975.
The modern day Avon lady is the 1975 club bottle from the NAAC. Blue hand-painted porcelain. Each bottle is numbered on bottom and came with registration card. 6,232 were made. CMV, $20.00. CMV, $50.00 club sample bottle.

NAAC Convention Plate, 1975.
Only 250 made for fourth annual NAAC Convention, Anaheim, Calif. CMV, $25.00.

NAAC Plate, 1974.
First in an annual series of plates. Clear crystal thumbprint plate with blue and red background. Only 790 plates were made. CMV, $20.00. Factory sample plate had decal instead of painted logo. CMV, $50.00.
Not shown: NAAC Board Member Plate, 1974. Same as regular issue only has "Board Member" on plate. CMV, $75.00.

Bud Hastin National Avon Club Bottle, 1974.
First issue club bottle by Bud Hastin Avon Club (later called Avon Times) is a three-piece Avon family scene. Three separate bottles showing the man, child and woman Avon collectors. 1,091 sets sold. Sold in sets only. CMV, $100.00.

NAAC Sample Plate, 1975.
Sample plate never issued to general public. 84 were made and sent to each Avon collector's club in NAAC, numbered on the back. CMV, $50.00.

Second Annual NAAC Plate, 1975.
General issue plate, Mr. and Mrs. McConnell, founders of Avon in center, gold 2" band around edge. CMV, $35.00 MB.

NAAC Board Member Plate, 1975.
2" wide, gold edge marked "Board member." Only seven were issued. This was a general issue plate. CMV, $100.00.

NAAC Board Member-Plate, 1975.
White plate with small gold edge marked "Board member." Only seven were made. This plate was never issued to the public. CMV, $100.00 MB.

NAAC Convention Banquet Mirror, 1975.
Blue and black, mirror on back. Convention held in Anaheim, Calif., June 21, 1975. CMV, $10.00. Given to each person attending the annual NAAC Avon convention banquet.

Worldwide Jo Olsen Avon Club Bottle, 1975.
Light blue dress, black hair. 1,102 bottles sold. Made in the image of Jo Olsen for her contribution to Avon collecting. CMV, $25.00.

Gold Coast Ron Price Club Bottle, 1975.
Green suit, brown hair, and brown shoes. Holding book "Testing 1-2-3." 1,096 bottles sold. Made in the image of Mr. Ron Price for his contribution to Avon collecting. Mr. Ron Price was a member of the board of directors of the NAAC. Mr. Price passed away in 1977. CMV, $25.00.

NAAC Convention Plates, 1975 – 1983.
Made by Mid-America Avon Club as the official NAAC convention souvenir plate each year. Very low issue on each. All are etched clear glass and signed by the artist. "1975 Orange County, CA"; "1977 Hollywood, FL"; "1978 Houston, TX"; "1979 St. Louis, MO"; "1980 Spokane, WA"; "1981 Long Beach, CA"; "1982 Las Vegas, NV"; "1983 Wilmington, DE." CMV, $20.00 each.

California Perfume Anniversary Keepsake Mold, 1975.
This is the actual steel mold Avon used to make the 1975 anniversary bottle. Mr. Art Goodwin from Avon Products, Inc., New York, presented this mold cut into five separate pieces to the National Association of Avon Clubs at the fourth annual NAAC convention banquet at Anaheim, Calif., June 19, 1975. The mold was auctioned off, bringing several hundreds of dollars on each piece. This is the first time an Avon mold has been destroyed and given to the general public. Very rare. CMV, $300.00 each.

The King II, "For Men," 1975.
Special label reads "Souvenir, June 19, 1975 NAAC Tour Monrovia Avon Plant." Given to each male taking the Avon plant tour at the NAAC Convention, Monrovia, California. Only 150 bottles have this label. CMV, $17.50.

Skip-a-Rope, "For Ladies," 1975.
Same special label given to all ladies on same tour as the King II. CMV, $17.50.

Blond Avon Lady, 1976. Of the 5,622 regular issue 1896 ladies, 120 had blond hair. Rare. CMV, $175.00.

NAAC Convention Banquet Mirror, 1976. Fifth annual Avon collector's convention mirror in white with blue letters. Held in Cincinnati, Ohio, June 25–27, 1976. Mirror on back. CMV, $10.00.

NAAC Avon Chessboard, 1975 – 1976. 21½" square plastic chessboard made for the Avon chess piece decanters. Silver and brown checkered top with black rim border and back. NAAC logo in center, silver over black. 105 were made for samples to each NAAC club with center gold logo over black. CMV, club sample with center gold logo. $200.00 MB. 1,500 are numbered and last 1,000 are not numbered on back. Regular issue silver logo with number, CMV, $100.00 MB. Black border, no number, CMV, $65.00 MB. Also came brown border with large black logo in center. CMV, $50.00 MB. Last one to be issued had brown border and small logos in center, brown back. CMV, $50.00.
Not shown: NAAC Board Member Chessboard.
Seven chessboards were made with white border. CMV, $300.00 each.

Bud Hastin Plate, 1976. Low issue porcelain plate of Bud Hastin issued by a NAAC club in 1976. CMV, $35.00.

Bud Hastin National Avon Club Bottle, 1976. Second issue. Hand-painted porcelain made in the image of Mr. Dale Robinson, past director of National Association of Avon Collectors. 1,000 bottles made and numbered. CMV, $30.00.

Fifth Annual NAAC Avon Club Bottle, 1976. In the image of the 1896 CPC Avon lady. Blue dress, black bag, and blue feather in hat. Black hair. 5,622 were made. Came with registration card and numbered on the bottom. CMV, $25.00.

Third Annual NAAC Five Year Avon Collector's Plate, 1976. 9⅜" porcelain plate showing the first four NAAC club bottles. 1,755 were made. OSP, $13.95. CMV, $35.00.

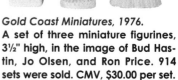

Gold Coast Miniatures, 1976. A set of three miniature figurines, 3½" high, in the image of Bud Hastin, Jo Olsen, and Ron Price. 914 sets were sold. CMV, $30.00 per set.

NAAC Convention Goblets, 1976 – 1983. Different color goblets sold each year at NAAC convention. First year, red, 1976, 276 made. CMV, $60.00. 1977, blue, 560 made. CMV, $30.00. 1978, smoke, 560 made. CMV, $20.00. 1979, clear, 576 made. CMV, $15.00. 1980, purple, 576 made. CMV, $15.00. 1978 – 1983, a special marked goblet given to each NAAC delegate. CMV, $25.00. Less than 100 delegate goblets made each year. Special marked goblets were made for each of the seven NAAC board members. CMV for board member goblet, $100.00 each year. 1981, 684 goblets made. CMV, $15.00. 1982, 700 made. CMV, $15.00. 1983, 322 made. CMV, $25.00. 1983 is the last year goblet was made.

Bicentennial Miniature Avon Lady Set No. 1, 1976.
Ten exact replicas in 3" high miniature figurines of the larger NAAC club bottles. Issued by the Bud Hastin National Avon Club (later called *Avon Times*). 1,775 sets were made and came with a numbered registration certificate. OSP, $60.00 for set of 10. CMV, $125.00 MB.

Queen City NAAC Convention Plate, 1976.
Clear glass with frosted letters. CMV, $20.00.

Anniversary Keepsake Mold Base, 1976.
Steel base of Avon anniversary keepsake mold given to National Association of Avon Collectors by Avon Products and auctioned off to Avon collectors. The numbers 17 and 5,215 were on bottom. CMV, $300.00.

Betsy Ross Mold, 1976.
Very rare steel mold given to Avon collectors at 1976 NAAC convention. Mold was cut into five pieces. Must have a letter from Avon Products stating it is one of a kind. CMV, $300.00 with letter.

NAAC Six Year Plate, 1977.
1886 Avon lady on plate. Made by Avon Products for the National Association of Avon Collectors. A beautiful china plate. Total of 5,000 were made with 1,500 gold rimmed, and numbered. CMV $35.00 MB. 3,500 were silver rimmed and not numbered. CMV, $30.00. Seven plates marked "Board member." CMV, $100.00 MB.

Betsy Ross NAAC Convention Souvenir, 1976.
Given by Avon Products to all collectors touring Avon plant in Springdale, Ohio, June 24, 1976. Special NAAC label on bottom. CMV, $17.50 with special label.

NAAC Club Bottle 1906 Avon Lady, 1977.
Sixth annual club bottle issued by the National Association of Avon Collectors. Made of porcelain and hand painted in the image of the 1906 Avon lady. She stands 7½" high with yellow dress, and brown hat, and carries the CPC Avon sales case of the period. Only 5,517 were made and sold. Came with NAAC registration certificate and is numbered on the bottom. CMV, $25.00 MB. 100 sample bottles were given to each NAAC Club and are the same, only they are numbered and marked "club sample" on bottom. CMV, $50.00 sample bottle.

NAAC Convention Banquet Mirror, 1977.
Sixth annual Avon collector's convention mirror in blue with yellow letters. Mirror on back. Hollywood, Florida, June, 1977. CMV, $10.00.

Avon Lady Miniature Set No. 2, 1977.
1,265 sets of 11 miniature Avon ladies of the 1886 – 1900 period. Issued by the Bud Hastin National Avon Club (later called *Avon Times*) in 1977. Set came in special display box. Each also came with numbered registration certificate. Sold only to Bud Hastin National Avon Club members. OSP, $60.00 set. CMV, $125.00 MB.

Clint Gold Coast Club Bottle, 1977.
7⅝" tall. Blue pants, shirt, jacket. Black shoes, brown hair. 1,264 made and numbered on the bottom. Came with registration card. Fourth annual club bottle. CMV, $25.00.

NAAC Convention Delegate Plate, 1977.
White china plate with the dates and places of six NAAC annual conventions. 85 total plates given to each NAAC club delegate attending the convention. CMV, $25.00. Seven board member plates were made the same, only marked "Board Member." CMV, $100.00.

NAAC Club Bottle, 1978.
Seventh annual club bottle made in the image of the 1916 CPC Avon lady. She stands 7½" high with a rust colored hat and coat. Brown hair. Only 5,022 were made. The bottle is numbered on the bottom and came with a registration certificate. Made of hand painted porcelain. CMV, $25.00. Club Sample was marked on bottom of 125 club bottles given to each club in the NAAC. Sample bottles are same as regular issue only marked club sample. CMV, $50.00.

Miniature Redhead Set, 1977.
965 sets of "Something Old — Something New" made. Issued by Bud Hastin National Avon Club with registration card. 3½" high. 1886 Avon lady on left has green purse and red hair. 1975 Avon lady on right has red hair and "Avon Colling" is misspelled on base of figurine. Sold as set only. CMV, $25.00 set.

NAAC Miniature McConnell and CPC Factory, 1978.
Miniature size figurines of the 1886 CPC factory and Mr. and Mrs. McConnell, the founders of Avon. Issued by the National Association of Avon Clubs. Only 1,200 sets were sold. Original set came with McConnell and factory. Factory was too large so a second smaller factory was issued. 1,200 small factories made. CMV, $35.00, set with one factory and McConnells. CMV, $55.00 with both factories.

NAAC Seven Year Plate, 1978.
Made by Avon Products for the National Association of Avon Collectors. A beautiful china plate with a decal of the 1906 Avon sales lady. Only 5,000 were made. 2,310 were gold rimmed plates. CMV, $35.00 MB. 2,690 are silver rimmed plates. CMV, $35.00 MB. Seven made for board members. CMV, $100.00 MB. Rare issue plate with backwards printing on back. CMV, $60.00 MB.

NAAC Club Bottle, 1926 Avon Lady, 1979.
Eighth annual club bottle. Purple and black. Brown hat and shoes. 4,749 were made and numbered on bottom. Came with certificate that says 4,725. Actual count is 4,749. CMV, $25.00. 150 club samples were issued to NAAC clubs. Bottom is marked "club sample." CMV, $50.00 club sample.

NAAC Plate 1896 Avon Lady, 1979.
Limited edition of 5,000. Made by Avon Products exclusively for the NAAC. Came with gold edge and numbered on back. CMV, $35.00 MB. Silver edge and no number, CMV, $25.00 MB. Sold only by NAAC clubs. Seven plates were made that were marked "board members." CMV, $100.00.

NAAC First Convention Bottle, 1980.
Sold only to NAAC club members. First in an annual series of NAAC convention bottles to commemorate the annual NAAC convention held in Spokane, Washington, in 1980. 7½" high, lavender dress of 1890s style. Hand painted porcelain. This bottle is the only one in the series that the cork is in the head, and 7½" size. All rest are 5½" size starting in 1981. The rest of the series will have a cork in the bottom to present a prettier bottle. Only 3,593 were made and sold. CMV, $25.00.

NAAC Convention Banquet Mirror, 1978.
Purple with mirror on back. Given to over 500 who attended the Avon collector's convention banquet in Houston, Texas, June 1978. CMV, $10.00.

NAAC Convention Banquet Mirror, 1979.
White and red, mirror on back. Given to over 500 people attending the annual Avon collector's convention banquet in St. Louis, Missouri, June 1979. CMV, $10.00.

Presidents, 1978.
A set of six, 3" high bust figurines of the first five presidents of the United States, plus Lincoln. Only 1,050 sets made. Hand painted porcelain and came with a numbered registration card. Issued by and sold only to members of the Bud Hastin National Avon Club, later called *Avon Times*. OSP, $40.00 for set of six. CMV, $85.00 MB.
Not shown: Presidents, All White, 1978.
Same set as painted presidents above, only all white porcelain. Only 150 sets made. OSP, $40.00. CMV, $125.00 MB.

NAAC Collectible Playing Cards, 1978.
CMV, $4.00.

St. Louis Blue Perfume, 1979.
Small glass bottle, white cap. Special perfume made and given by Mid-America Avon club and NAAC at convention in St. Louis, June 1979. 231 bottles with registration card and envelope. CMV, $20.00 mint. 120 bottles only given without envelope and card. CMV, $10.00 BO.

NAAC Club Bottle, 1936 Avon Lady, 1980.
Ninth annual club bottle. Purple dress, black bag. 7½" high. 4,479 were made and sold and numbered on the bottom as total sold. Did not come with certificate. Bottom cork. CMV, $25.00. Same bottle came with blue bag and marked "club sample" on bottom. 155 club samples were made and given to to NAAC clubs. CMV, $50.00 blue bag club sample.

Left: NAAC Fourth Convention Bell, 1980.
5½" high porcelain bell same as bottle, only dress colors reversed. Issued in 1984. Only 500 made by Bud Hastin. CMV, $25.00.
Right: NAAC First Convention Bottle Re-issue, 1982.
Same as 1980 bottle, only is 5½" high to match rest of series in size. Only 1,775 reissue bottles made. Reissued bottles sold in 1982. Cork in bottom. CMV, $25.00. 150 club sample bottles were made and marked in the bottom of the 5½" size. CMV, $50.00.

NAAC Plate, 1916 Avon Lady, 1980.
Limited edition of 4,000. Came with gold edge and number on the back. 2,060 made. CMV $35.00. Or silver edge, 1,940 made and no number, $35.00 MB. Made by Avon Products exclusively for the NAAC. Seven plates were also made marked "board member." CMV, $100.00.

NAAC Convention Banquet Mirror, 1980 – 1982.
Only 500 of each made for annual NAAC convention banquet. 1980 — Spokane, Washington; 1981 — Queen Mary, Long Beach, California; 1982 — Las Vegas, Nevada. CMV, $10.00 each.

Presidents Gold Set, 1980.
Set of six different U.S. presidents' busts, with antique brush gold finish. Only 250 sets made and issued by Bud Hastin Avon Club. OSP, $70.00 set. CMV, $100.00 MB, set.

NAAC Club Bottle, 1946 Avon Lady, 1981.
Tenth annual club bottle. Only 3,589 sold and made. Green dress, black bag, cork in bottom. CMV, $25.00. 140 sample club bottles made and marked "club sample" on bottom. CMV, $50.00.

NAAC Second Convention Bottle, 1981.
Long Beach, California, convention. 5½" high, hand painted porcelain bottle. Yellow and green dress of the 1800s style. Second in a series of 11 bottles of the 1800s style. Only 3,128 were made and sold to NAAC club members. CMV, $25.00.
Convention Club Sample, 1981.
140 club sample bottles were made for NAAC clubs. Each is marked "club sample" on bottom and numbered 140 edition. CMV, $50.00 club sample.
Fifth NAAC Convention Bell, 1981.
Same as bottle, only has green dress. 500 made and sold in 1984. CMV, $25.00.

NAAC Plate, 1926 Avon Lady, 1981.
Limited edition of 2,000. Gold rim. Marked on back. CMV, $35.00 MB.
Not shown: NAAC Board Member Plate, 1981.
Same plate as above, only back is marked "1981 board member sample." Only seven were made this way for NAAC board of directors. CMV, $100.00 MB.

NAAC Club Bottle, 1956 Avon Lady, 1982.
Eleventh annual club bottle for NAAC club members. 7½" high, red dress, bottom cork. Only 3,000 made and sold. CMV, $25.00. 150 club sample 1956 lady bottles made and marked on bottom. CMV, $50.00 for club sample.

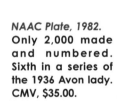

NAAC Plate, 1982.
Only 2,000 made and numbered. Sixth in a series of the 1936 Avon lady. CMV, $35.00.

Left: NAAC Third Convention Bottle, 1982.

Third in a series of 1800s style dress. Blue dress, pink bag and hat rim, blond hair. 5½" high, porcelain. Only 2,205 bottles were made and sold to NAAC. Convention was held in Las Vegas, Nevada. CMV, $25.00 mint. No club samples were made.

Right: NAAC Convention Bell, 1982. First issue, only 500 bells made in the same shape as the 1982 convention bottles. Only the dress colors are reversed. Pink dress and blue trim. You had to attend the eleventh annual NAAC convention in Las Vegas, June 22-27, 1982 to get a bell. CMV, $35.00.

NAAC Fourth Convention Bottle, 1983. 5½" high, bottom cork. Rust and brown color, hand painted porcelain. Fourth in a series of Avon ladies of the 1800s to commemorate the NAAC Avon collector's convention in Wilmington, Delaware, in June 1983. Only 1,875 made. Total number sold marked on bottom. CMV, $25.00. 150 club samples made and marked "club sample." One of 150 on bottom. CMV, $50.00.

NAAC Second Convention Bell, 1983. Same as 1983 convention bottle only dress colors are reversed and bottom is open as bell. Bottom label, only 500 made. CMV, $25.00. Bells created and sold by Bud Hastin.

NAAC Convention Banquet Mirror, 1983. Only 500 small mirrors for the twelfth annual Avon collector's convention in Wilmington, Delaware, 1983. CMV, $10.00.

NAAC Key Chain, 1983. Red and white with black pen insert. Given to Delaware convention attendees from Avon Products. Only 500 made. CMV, $5.00 each.

NAAC Club Bottle, Avon Representative, 1984. Thirteenth annual club bottle 7½" high, hand painted porcelain. Gray pant suit, pink blouse, red hair. Brown bag says "Avon." Bottom cork. Choice of a white or black representative. 1,133 white rep bottles were made. 1,070 black reps made. CMV, $25.00 each, MB.

NAAC Club Bottle, 1966 Avon Lady, 1983.

Twelfth annual club bottle. 7½" high, hand painted porcelain bottle made only for the National Association of Avon Collectors in the image of dress of the 1966 Avon lady. She wears a black and white striped dress. Blue bag. 2,350 made, bottom cork. CMV, $25.00. A new club bottle is issued each year to NAAC members only. 100 club samples made. CMV, $50.00.

NAAC Plate, 1983.
9" porcelain plate of the 1946 Avon lady. Only 1,125 made. Label on back. CMV, $35.00.

Not shown: NAAC Board Member Plate, 1983.
Same as regular issue, only back has special label marked "NAAC Board Member Sample." Only seven made with each board member's name on back. CMV, $100.00.

NAAC Plate, 1984.
Limited edition, 9" porcelain plate, 1956 Avon Lady. Eighth in series. CMV, $35.00.

NAAC Cup Plates, 1984 – 1986.
Sold at annual Avon convention. First issue 1984 in Kansas City. Light yellow glass. Second issue, 1985, Seattle, Washington. Green glass. Third issue 1986, Nashville, Tennessee. Red glass. All under 500 issued. CMV, $15.00 each.

NAAC Convention Mirror and Button, 1984 – 1985.
1984, yellow, Kansas City, Missouri, convention. 1985, green, Seattle, Washington, convention. Both less than 350 issued. CMV, $10.00 each mirror . CMV, $3.00 each button.

NAAC Sixth Convention Bottle and Bell, 1985.
Seattle, Washington, Avon convention. 5½" porcelain bottle. Pink dress with dark pink trim. 1,800 made. CMV, $25.00
Not shown: NAAC Convention Bell, 1985.
Is same as bottle, only dress color reversed. Only 500 bells made and sold by Bud Hastin. CMV, $25.00. Fifteen bells were painted same as convention bottle by mistake and came in bottle boxes. Some have no inside labels. Rare. CMV, $125.00.

NAAC Plate, 1985.
Ninth in series. 9" plate of 1966 Avon lady. Limited edition. CMV, $35.00.

NAAC Fifth Convention Bottle, 1984.
5½" high porcelain bottle, bottom cork. Brown dress, yellow and black umbrella. 1,650 made. Fifth in a series of 11 convention bottles to be sold through NAAC clubs of the Avon ladies of the 1890s for NAAC thirteenth annual convention in Kansas City, Missouri, June 1984. CMV, $25.00. 100 NAAC club samples made and marked "club sample" on bottom. One of 100. CMV, $50.00 club samples.
NAAC Third Convention Bell, 1984.
Same as 1984 NAAC convention bottle, only dress and umbrella colors reversed and bottom is open as bell. Bottom label. Only 500 made for Kansas City, NAAC convention. Bells created and sold by Bud Hastin. CMV, $25.00.

Convention Tray, 1984.
Glass tray given by Avon Products to NAAC convention. Marked "Avon Welcomes NAAC to Kansas City, Mo. Convention, June 19-24, 1984." CMV, $10.00.
Convention Card Holder, 1985.
Brass business card holder given by Avon Products to NAAC convention in Seattle, Washington, marked "Avon Welcomes NAAC Convention, July 1-7, 1985." CMV, $10.00.
NAAC Christmas Ornament, 1985.
First in series. Clear glass center, brass chain rim. Marked "NAAC 1985." CMV, $10.00.

NAAC Club Bottle, Mr. Avon, 1985.
7½" high porcelain bottle. Fourteenth and last in club bottle series. Only 1,800 made. CMV, $25.00 MB. 100 club sample bottles made. CMV, $50.00.

NAAC Seventh Convention Bottle and Bell, 1986.
5½" high porcelain bottle. Black dress, red hair on 100 club samples. CMV, $50.00. Regular issue has red dress, black trim. Only 1,800 made. CMV, $25.00.
NAAC Seventh Convention Bell, 1986.
Same as regular issue bottle, only bell with dress colors reversed. Only 500 made by Bud Hastin. CMV, $30.00.

NAAC Nashville Convention Mirror, 1986.
Only 400 made. Red button with white letter. Mirror back. Fifteenth annual. CMV, $10.00.

NAAC Chicago Convention Mirror, 1987.
400 made. White button, red letters, blue design. Given at sixteenth NAAC convention banquet. CMV, $10.00.

NAAC Convention Mirrors, 1988, 1989, and 1990.
1988 — San Diego, California.
1989 — Indianapolis, Indiana.
1990 — Canton, Ohio.
CMV, $10.00 each.

Left: NAAC Convention Bottle and Bell, 1987.
5½" high porcelain bottle. Eighth in series. 750 made for Chicago Avon collector convention. Hand painted porcelain, light blue, dark blue trim. CMV, $25.00.
Right: Convention Bell.
Same, only dress color reversed. Only 300 made. CMV, $30.00.

NAAC Convention Bottle and Bell, San Diego, California, 1988.
5½" high, porcelain, brown and tan dress. 800 made with brown trim on hat. CMV, $18.00.
100 Club Samples.
Made with blue trim on hat. CMV, $25.00.
400 Bells.
Made with dress color reversed. CMV, $22.00.

NAAC Convention Mirror, 1994.
"Rochester, N.Y., June 19-26, 1994. 23rd Annual Avon Collector Convention" on front, mirror on back. Less than 300 made. CMV, $10.00.

NAAC Rose Bowl Plate, 1987.
9" porcelain plate. First in a series of Avon floats in the annual Rose Bowl parade. Less than 2,000 made. No NAAC plate was made in 1986. CMV, $35.00.

NAAC Mrs. Albee Commemorative Bottle and Bell, 1988.
1,200 made of porcelain, 5½" high. Black handbag. CMV, $18.00.
100 Club Samples.
Made with brown handbag. CMV, $35.00.
Not shown: Bells.
400 were made with dress color reversed. CMV, $22.00.

NAAC Convention Bottle and Bell, Indianapolis, 1988.
5½" high, all are yellow dress with green trim. Indianapolis Avon convention, 700 made of each. Brown hair, yellow fan. CMV, $18.00.
Convention Bell.
Reverse color dress, with green fan. 400 made. CMV, $22.00.
100 Club Samples.
Made with red fan. CMV, $35.00.
100 Convention Delegate Bottles.
Made with blond hair. CMV, $35.00.

Best Places to Sell or Buy Avon Collectibles

If you are looking for the best place to buy or sell Avon collectibles, I can only recommend two avenues that get results, both of which are on the internet.

If you are a CPC (California Perfume Company) collector, go to www.californiaperfumecompany.net. This great website is for CPC collectors. Rusty Mills is the man to go to for CPCs. E-mail rusty at revrlmills@embarqmail.net

The largest internet auction site for Avon collectibles is www.ebay.com. Go to the Avon collectibles section.

If you have a large collection and you don't have time or want to mess with selling it, contact your tax advisor for information on donating it to a charity and deduct the gift on your income tax. You will need this *Avon Collector's Encyclopedia* to verify the current market value, make a complete list, and get a receipt from the charity you give it to. Remember, you must first ask your tax advisor for your own personal situation.

If you want to join a local Avon club near you or start a local Avon club, contact Connie Clark, president of the National Association of Avon Collectors (NAAC) at P.O. Box 7006, Kansas City, MO 64113. Send a "SASE" for an answer. This is a non-profit organization.

Tips on Buying and Selling Avon Collectibles

I get a lot of calls from people who have been given an Avon collection after a friend or relative has died and passed it on. The best advice I can give you is that collectors accumulate a collection one piece at a time and seldom buy a large collection because they already have most of what someone has to sell. If they do buy a large collection all at one time, they pay a fraction of the collector book price. To get the best price, you have to sell each item one at a time. This is true with any collectible, not just Avon. Most big collections sell for $1.00 per item straight across the board when sold all at one time, and sometimes even less. Then that person has to invest his or her time and money in marketing the collection to get the best price possible.

When you advertise a collection for sale, you must put prices you want. If you say "make me a offer." Most people will not waste their time with you. The lower the price, the faster you will sell it. This is common sense that goes with anything you are selling. The only time you should ask for offers is if you have very old California Perfume items that are rare and have a high book value. Only the rare items will bring top dollar. Most Avon from the late 1960s forward is not rare.

How important are boxes? Most collections do not show boxes, but when you buy and sell them, the boxes are very important to ship them safely. Without the original box, they often get broken in shipping unless you use a lot of packing. As Avon items get old, 1950s or older, the boxes become more valuable. Look in the CPC section for box prices. The older they get, the higher the price for the box.

Sometimes donating a large collection to charity and deducting it from your income taxes at the end of the year is the best way to get the best price and benefit if you are in a hurry and don't have the time to sell a collection one item at a time. I am told by other collectors that you can deduct the full value that our latest edition of the *Avon Collector's Encyclopedia* lists for current market value when you donate the collection to charity. You need to make a complete list and price each item and get it signed by the charity to which you donate it. You need to keep the latest copy of this book to prove prices in case of a tax audit. Do not do this until you check with your tax advisor.

Avon items do not always go up in value. They fluctuate with the market just like everything else in life. When the economy is good, collectibles sell well. When the economy is bad, you have to wait longer to sell your items and usually at a lower price, just like in the house market.

Avon jewelry does not have much of a market in the Avon collecting world. Most people just do not want to collect Avon jewelry because too much was made of each piece. Avon Products is the largest producer of costume jewelry in the world. Sell all the jewelry at a garage sale. You should sell most of it just as jewelry, not as an Avon collectible. You know how women love jewelry at garage sales. Jewelry is made to wear, not collect. For those who want more info on Avon jewelry, there is a small book for $30, *Avon Collectible Fashion Jewelry and Awards*, at www.amazon.com.

Avon Products, Inc. made very few new collectibles in the late 1990s and 2000s, and still makes very few today. Most do not have "Avon" marked on the product. If it does not say Avon on the product, we advise you not buy it for an Avon collection, as most collectors will not buy it later from you. It has to be marked "Avon" on the product itself before it will appear in the *Avon Collector's Encyclopedia*.

Bud Hastin
P.O. Box 11004
Ft. Lauderdale, FL 33339
Phone: 954-566-0691
e-mail: budhastin@hotmail.com

H

I

J

K

P

Y

Z

Awards Index

Bud Hastin's 18th Edition
Avon Collector's Encyclopedia™
Order Form

All books will be sent fourth class mail. Allow up to three (3) weeks for delivery. Money Orders, your order is filled immediately. Personal Checks, order is held untill the check has cleared your bank. All Avon book orders of 10 or more are shipped in boxes of 10 books. All orders over 10 are shipped in two or more boxes.

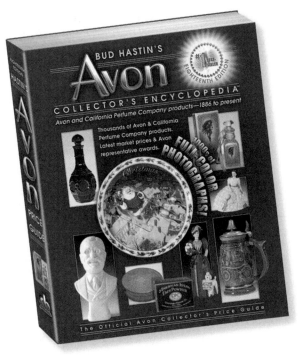

U.S.A.		Canada	
1 Book	$29.95	1 Book	$29.95
S&H	$3.00	S & H	$7.00
Total Price $32.95		Total Price $36.95	

U.S. Funds - Money Orders only from Canada.
Credit cards are *not* accepted.
Make all checks for Avon books payable to
Bud Hastin.

Books	Cost
2-3	$31.95 each Post Paid
4-6	$25.50 each Post Paid
7-9	$24.00 each Post Paid
10 & up	$21.50 each Post Paid

Bud Hastin will sign all books ordered directly from him.

Please Send Me_____18th Edition Avon books. I have enclosed Money Order_____

Personal Check_____Area Code/Phone number_____

Please Print (NAME)_____

(ADDRESS) _____

(CITY) _____(STATE)_____(ZIP)_____

Send orders to: **Bud Hastin**
P.O. Box 11004
Ft. Lauderdale, FL 33339
Call 954-566-0691
e-mail: budhastin@hotmail.com

more great TITLES from collector books